#42 Robertson Branch Library
1719 S. Robertson Boulevard
Los Angeles, CA 90035

FEB 2 2 2006

WITHDRAWN

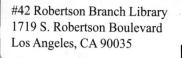

W9-BFP-297

CANCÚN, COZUMEL, YUCATÁN PENINSULA

Where to Stay and Eat
for All Budgets

Must-See Sights
and Local Secrets

Ratings You Can Trust

972.6T
F6535
2006

Fodor's Travel Publications   New York, Toronto, London, Sydney, Auckland
www.fodors.com

166619107

FODOR'S CANCÚN, COZUMEL, YUCATÁN PENINSULA 2006
Editor: Sarah Gold

Editorial Production: Tom Holton
Editorial Contributors: Robin Goldstein, Jeanine Kitchel, Shelagh McNally, Maribeth Mellin, Jane Onstott
Maps: David Lindroth *cartographer;* Bob Blake and Rebecca Baer, *map editors.* Additional cartography provided by Henry Colomb, Mark Stroud, and Ali Baird, Moon Street Cartography.
Design: Fabrizio La Rocca *creative director;* Guido Caroti, Chie Ushio, Tina Malaney, Brian Ponto
Photography: Melanie Marin, *senior picture editor*
Cover Photo (Coastline at Tulum, Yucatán Peninsula): Robin Hill, Index Stock Imagery
Cover Design: Moon Sun Kim
Production/Manufacturing: Robert B. Shields

COPYRIGHT
Copyright © 2006 by Fodors LLC

Fodor's is a registered trademark of Random House, Inc.

All rights reserved under International and Pan-American Copyright Conventions. Published in the United States by Fodor's Travel Publications, a unit of Fodors LLC, a subsidiary of Random House, Inc., and simultaneously in Canada by Random House of Canada Limited, Toronto. Distributed by Random House, Inc., New York.

No maps, illustrations, or other portions of this book may be reproduced in any form without written permission from the publisher.

ISBN 1–4000–1546–4

ISSN 1051–6336

SPECIAL SALES
This book is available for special discounts for bulk purchases for sales promotions or premiums. Special editions, including personalized covers, excerpts of existing books, and corporate imprints, can be created in large quantities for special needs. For more information, write to Special Markets/ Premium Sales, 1745 Broadway, MD 6-2, New York, New York 10019, or e-mail specialmarkets@ randomhouse.com.

AN IMPORTANT TIP & AN INVITATION
Although all prices, opening times, and other details in this book are based on information supplied to us at press time, changes occur all the time in the travel world, and Fodor's cannot accept responsibility for facts that become outdated or for inadvertent errors or omissions. So **always confirm information when it matters,** especially if you're making a detour to visit a specific place. Your experiences—positive and negative—matter to us. If we have missed or misstated something, **please write to us.** We follow up on all suggestions. Contact the Cancún editor at editors@fodors. com or c/o Fodor's at 1745 Broadway, New York, New York 10019.

PRINTED IN THE UNITED STATES OF AMERICA

10 9 8 7 6 5 4 3 2 1

Be a Fodor's Correspondent

Your opinion matters. It matters to us. It matters to your fellow Fodor's travelers, too. And we'd like to hear it. In fact, we *need* to hear it.

When you share your experiences and opinions, you become an active member of the Fodor's community. That means we'll not only use your feedback to make our books better, but we'll publish your names and comments whenever possible. Throughout our guides, look for "Word of Mouth," excerpts of your unvarnished feedback.

Here's how you can help improve Fodor's for all of us.

Tell us when we're right. We rely on local writers to give you an insider's perspective. But our writers and staff editors—who are the best in the business—depend on you. Your positive feedback is a vote to renew our recommendations for the next edition.

Tell us when we're wrong. We're proud that we update most of our guides every year. But we're not perfect. Things change. Hotels cut services. Museums change hours. Charming cafés lose charm. If our writer didn't quite capture the essence of a place, tell us how you'd do it differently. If any of our descriptions are inaccurate or inadequate, we'll incorporate your changes in the next edition and will correct factual errors at fodors.com *immediately.*

Tell us what to include. You probably have had fantastic travel experiences that aren't yet in Fodor's. Why not share them with a community of like-minded travelers? Maybe you chanced upon a beach or bistro or B&B that you don't want to keep to yourself. Tell us why we should include it. And share your discoveries and experiences with everyone directly at fodors.com. Your input may lead us to add a new listing or highlight a place we cover with a "Highly Recommended" star or with our highest rating, "Fodor's Choice."

Give us your opinion instantly at our feedback center at www.fodors.com/feedback. You may also e-mail editors@fodors.com with the subject line "Cancún Editor." Or send your nominations, comments, and complaints by mail to Cancún Editor, Fodor's, 1745 Broadway, New York, NY 10019.

You and travelers like you are the heart of the Fodor's community. Make our community richer by sharing your experiences. Be a Fodor's correspondent.

¡Buen Viaje!

Tim Jarrell, Publisher

CONTENTS

WHAT'S WHERE

CANCÚN	Although not exactly a jewel, Cancún is certainly the rhinestone of the Caribbean coast. This 30-years-young city is Mexico's most popular destination. And why not? The 7-shaped barrier island is blessed on both sides by soft white sands. Cancún's beachfront high-rises offer loads of creature comforts and nonstop water sports; hotels inland are more reasonably priced and let you enjoy a more authentic Mexican experience. Overall, though, Cancún is more the domain of sun worshippers and party animals—old and young, straight and gay—than culture hounds. Those who want to learn about history can visit nearby Maya ruins and centuries-old cities that are everything that Cancún is not.
ISLA MUJERES	A 30-minute jaunt across the water from Cancún, five-mile-long Isla Mujeres is light-years away in temperament. Day-trippers come for lunch and wind up falling in love with the place: it's more laid-back, less crowded, and cheaper than almost anywhere on the mainland. Hotels and restaurants have popped up along the best beaches, but staff members are native Isleños, the seafood is fresh-caught, and the water is shallow and turquoise blue. A steady increase in visitors has raised the tourist-kitsch factor—but natural, easy pleasures still reign.
COZUMEL	Mellower than Cancún and hipper than Isla Mujeres, Cozumel lies 12 mi (19 km) east of Playa del Carmen. The island is hugely popular with two separate groups of visitors, the first being scuba divers. Ever since Jacques Cousteau first made Cozumel's interconnected series of coral reefs (known collectively as the Maya Reef) famous in the 1970s, divers and snorkelers have flocked here. Aboveground, however, the island plays host to a much different crowd: cruise-ship passengers. Six giant ships per day currently ferry day-trippers to Cozumel, and during prime visiting hours the downtown area is choked. To avoid the crowds, you can horseback ride along the island's windward side in search of crumbled monuments to the goddess Ixchel, fish at Isla de la Pasión, or wander off the town's main drag to hobnob with residents. Or, you can always slip underwater.

THE CARIBBEAN COAST	
	The dazzling white sands and glittering blue-green waters of the Riviera Maya beckon to sun worshippers and spa goers as well as snorkelers, divers, and bird-watchers. Although sugary beaches are the principal draw here, the seaside ruins of Tulum, jungle-clad pyramids at Cobá, and several other Maya sites are all nearby. This swatch of coast between Cancún and Tulum is popular with developers; jungle lodges and campgrounds now coexist with extravagant spa resorts. The town of Playa del Carmen is almost as big as Cancún, although it has a more authentic Mexican feel. Nature lovers can head farther south, to the pristine beaches of the Costa Maya or to the Reserva de la Biosfera Sian Ka'an, with more than a million acres of wild coastline and jungle.
MÉRIDA, CHICHÉN ITZÁ & YUCATÁN STATE	
	The capital city of Yucatán State is the cultural hub of the entire peninsula. Bustling with traffic and swelteringly hot for much of the year, Mérida's restaurants, hotels, shops, and museums still bring visitors back year after year. Weekends, when downtown streets are closed to cars and free shows are held on the main square, are especially magical. Outside of Mérida, villages offer charming shops and restaurants, and the chance to see modern Maya at work and play. Shell-strewn beaches line the remote north coast, and clouds of pink flamingos converge on protected wetlands. The state's major claim to fame, however, is its spectacular Maya ruins, including Chichén Itzá and Uxmal.
CAMPECHE	
	Mellow and almost completely unvisted by tourists, Campeche is a world unto itself. Campeche City's historic district, filled with colonial buildings, gardens, museums, and shops, is a lovely place to stroll; remnants of the walls and ramparts that once protected the city from pirates lend romance. The rest of the state is traversed by two-lane highways, which lead to Maya villages where three-wheeled bike-taxis rule the road and women dress in embroidered *huipiles*. Far to the south, along the Guatemalan border, the Reserva de la Biosfera Calakmul is home to thousands of birds, butterlies, and plants—but only hosts about a dozen visitors a day.

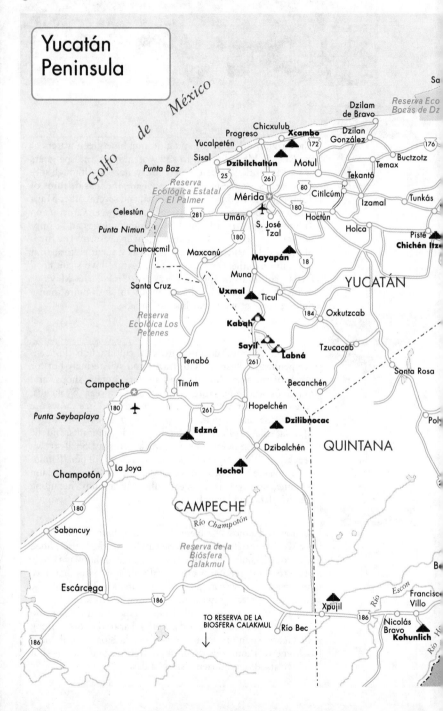

Yucatán Peninsula

Golfo de México

Sa

Reserva Eco Bocás de Dz

Dzilam de Bravo

Chicxulub   **Xcambo**   Dzilan González   176

Progreso   172

Yucalpetén

Sisal   **Dzibilchaltún**   Motul   Buctzotz

Punta Baz   25   261   Tekantó   Temax

Reserva Ecológica Estatal El Palmer   **Mérida**   80   Citilcúm   Tunkás

Celestún   180   Izamal

Punta Nimun   Umán   S. José Tzal   Hoctún   Holca   Pisté   **Chichén Itzá**

Chuncucmil   Maxcanú   180   **Mayapán**   18   **YUCATÁN**

Santa Cruz   Muna   **Uxmal**   Ticul   184   Oxkutzcab

Reserva Ecológica Los Petenes   **Kabah**   **Sayil**   **Labná**   Tzucacab

Tenabó   261   Santa Rosa

Campeche   Tinúm   Becanchén   Pol

Punta Seybaplaya   180   261   Hopelchén   **Dzilibnocac**

Edzná   Dzibalchén   **QUINTANA**

Champotón   La Joya   **Hochol**

CAMPECHE   Río Champotón   Be

Sabancuy   Reserva de la Biósfera Calakmul

Escárcega   186   Escon   Francisc Villo

Xpujil   Nicolás Bravo

TO RESERVA DE LA BIOSFERA CALAKMUL   Río Bec   186   **Kohunlich**

186

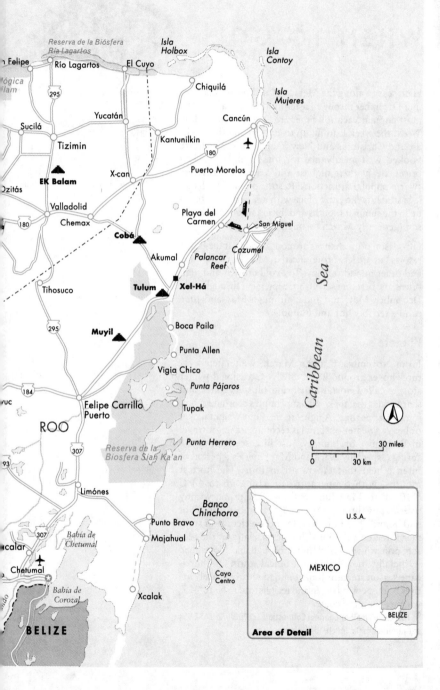

n Felipe
Reserva de la Biósfera
Ría Lagartos
Isla
Holbox
Isla
Contoy
Río Lagartos
El Cuyo
ógica
lam
(295)
Chiquilá
Isla
Mujeres
Sucilá
Yucatán
Cancún
Tizimin
Kantunilkin
(180)
EK Balam
X-can
Puerto Morelos
zitás
Valladolid
Chemax
(180)
Playa del
Carmen
San Miguel
Cobá
Cozumel
Akumal
Palancar
Reef
Tihosuco
Tulum
Xel-Há
Sea
Muyil
Boca Paila
(295)
Punta Allen
Vigia Chico
(184)
Punta Pájaros
uc
ROO
Felipe Carrillo
Puerto
Tupak
(307)
Punta Herrero
0   30 miles
Reserva de la
Biosfera Sian Ka'an
0   30 km
Caribbean
93
Limónes
Banco
Chinchorro
(307)
Punta Bravo
Bahía de
calar
Chetumal
Majahual
U.S.A.
Chetumal
Cayo
Centro
MEXICO
Bahía de
Corozal
Xcalak
ndo
BELIZE
BELIZE
Area of Detail

WHEN TO GO

High season along the Mexican Caribbean runs from mid-December through Easter (or the week after). The most popular vacation times are *Semana Santa* (Holy Week, the week leading up to Easter) and the weeks around Christmas and New Year's. Most hotels are booked well in advance for these holidays, when prices are at their highest and armies of travelers swarm popular attractions. Resorts popular with college students (i.e., any place with a beach) tend to fill up in the summer months and during spring-break season (generally March through April).

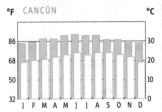

Off-season price changes are considerable at the beach resorts but are less pronounced in Mérida, Campeche, and other inland regions. To avoid crowds and high prices, the best times to go are September through early December, May, and June, although May and June can be terribly hot and humid.

Climate

From November through March, winter temperatures hover around 27°C (80°F). Occasional winter storms called *nortes* can bring blustery skies and sharp winds that make air temperatures drop and swimming unappealing. A light- to medium-weight jacket or heavy sweater or shawl is recommended for travel in December or January, just in case. During the spring (especially April and May) there's a period of intense heat that tapers off in June. The hottest months, with temperatures reaching up to 43°C (110°F), are May, June, and July. The primary rainy season, July through the end of September, also is hot and humid. The rains that farmers welcome in summer threaten occasional hurricanes later in the season, primarily mid-September through mid-November. (Officially, the Caribbean tropical storm and hurricane season starts in June, but bad weather rarely arrives before September.) Inland regions tend to be 10°–15° warmer than the coast.

Forecasts Weather Channel Connection ☎ 900/932–8437, 95¢ per minute from a Touch-Tone phone.

ABOUT THIS BOOK

Our Ratings

Sometimes you find terrific travel experiences and sometimes they just find you. But usually the burden is on you to select the right combination of experiences. That's where our ratings come in.

As travelers we've all discovered a place so wonderful that its worthiness is obvious. And sometimes that place is so experiential that superlatives don't do it justice: you just have to be there to know. These sights, properties, and experiences get our highest rating, **Fodor's Choice**, indicated by orange stars throughout this book.

Black stars highlight sights and properties we deem **Highly Recommended**, places that our writers, editors, and readers praise again and again for consistency and excellence.

By default, there's another category: any place we include in this book is by definition worth your time, unless we say otherwise. And we will.

Disagree with any of our choices? Care to nominate a place or suggest that we rate one more highly? Visit our feedback center at www. fodors.com/feedback.

Budget Well

Hotel and restaurant price categories from ¢ to $$$$ are defined in the opening pages of each chapter. For attractions, we always give standard adult admission fees; reductions are usually available for children, students, and senior citizens. Want to pay with plastic? **AE, D, DC, MC, V** following restaurant and hotel listings indicate if American Express, Discover, Diners Club, MasterCard, and Visa are accepted.

Restaurants

Unless we state otherwise, restaurants are open for lunch and dinner daily. We mention dress only when there's a specific requirement and reservations only when they're essential or not accepted—it's always best to book ahead.

Hotels

Hotels have private bath, phone, TV, and air-conditioning and operate on the European Plan (a.k.a. EP, meaning without meals), unless we specify that they use the Continental Plan (CP, with a Continental breakfast), Breakfast Plan (BP, with a full breakfast), or Modified American Plan (MAP, with breakfast and dinner) or are all-inclusive (including all meals and most activities). We always

list facilities but not whether you'll be charged an extra fee to use them, so when pricing accommodations, find out what's included.

Many Listings

★	Fodor's Choice
★	Highly recommended
⊠	Physical address
✦	Directions
⌖	Mailing address
☎	Telephone
🖷	Fax
⊕	On the Web
✉	E-mail
☞	Admission fee
☉	Open/closed times
►	Start of walk/itinerary
Ⓜ	Metro stations
⊟	Credit cards

Hotels & Restaurants

🏨	Hotel
🛏	Number of rooms
⚲	Facilities
¶◎¶	Meal plans
✕	Restaurant
⌂	Reservations
🏛	Dress code
⚲	Smoking
₪	BYOB
✕🏨	Hotel with restaurant that warrants a visit

Outdoors

🏌	Golf
⛺	Camping

Other

☺	Family-friendly
⊞	Contact information
⇨	See also
⊠	Branch address
☞	Take note

IF YOU LIKE...

... Spas

There are more than 20 spa resorts scattered throughout the Yucatán peninsula, most of them along the coast. Here, decadent body treatments are offered in luxurious seaside settings. Some incorporate indigenous healing techniques into their services, using *temazcal* (an ancient sweat-lodge ritual), and plant extracts in aromatherapy facials. Others feature seawater and marine algae in mineral-rich thalassotherapy treatments; still others go the high-tech route with cutting-edge flotarium tanks and guided Pilates sessions. You won't have any trouble getting your pampering fix here—especially in the areas around Playa del Carmen and the rest of the Riviera Maya—-but you'll likely pay top dollar for it.

Spas here that get the most consistent raves include Punta Tanchacté's **Paraiso de la Bonita Resort and Thalasso,** where you can soak away stress in specially built saltwater pools; **Maroma** in Punta Maroma, with its relaxing, womblike flotation tanks; and **Ikal del Mar,** in Punta Bete, where you can follow up your Maya massage with a sumptuous Yucatecan meal. **Spa del Mar,** at Cancún's Le Meridien hotel, is justifiably famous for its seaweed hydrotherapy; and at the **Hotel El Rey del Caribe Spa,** also in Cancún, it's hard to imagine a sweeter way to end the day than a honey massage.

... Diving & Snorkeling

The turquoise waters of the Mexican Caribbean coast are strewn with stunning coral reefs, underwater canyons and sunken shipwrecks—all of them teeming with marine life. The visibility can reach 100 feet, so even on the surface, you'll be amazed by what you can see.

Made famous decades ago by Jacques Cousteau, Cozumel is still considered one of the world's premier diving destinations. The **Maya Reef,** just off the western coast, stretches some 32 km (20 mi)—and more than 100 dive operators on the island offer deep dives, drift dives, wall dives, night dives, wreck dives, and dives focusing on ecology and underwater photography.

Farther south, the town of Tankah is known for its **Gorgonian Gardens,** a profusion of soft corals and sponges that's created an underwater Eden. Near the border of Belize, Mexico's largest coral atoll, **Banco Chinchorro,** is a graveyard of vessels that have foundered on the corals over the centuries. Experienced divers won't want to miss Isla Contoy's **Cave of the Sleeping Sharks.** Here, at 150 feet, you can see the otherwise dangerous creatures "dozing" in a state of relaxed nonaggression.

The freshwater *cenotes* (sinkholes) that punctuate Quintana Roo, Yucatán, and Campeche states are also favorites with divers and snorkelers. Many of these are private and secluded even though they lie right off the highways; others are so popular that they've become tourist destinations. At **Hidden Worlds Cenote Park** (on the highway between Xel-ha and Tankah), for example, you can float through cavernous sinkholes filled with otherworldly stalactites, stalagmites, and rock formations.

. . . Maya Ruins

The ruins of ancient Maya cities are magical; and they're scattered all across the Yucatán. Although Chichén Itzá, featuring the enormous and oft-photographed El Castillo pyramid, is the most famous of the region's sites, Uxmal is the most graceful. Here, the perfectly proportioned buildings of the Cuadrángulo de las Monjas (Nun's Quadrangle) make a beautiful "canvas" for facades carved with snakes and the fierce visages of Maya gods. At the more easterly Ek Balam, workers on makeshift scafolding brush away centuries of accumulated grime from huge monster masks that protect the mausoleum of a Maya king. On the amazing friezes, winged figures dressed in full royal regalia gaze down.

At Cobá, the impressive temples and palaces—including a 79-foot-high pyramid—are surrounded by thick jungle, and only sparsely visited by tourists. In contrast, nearby Tulum is the peninsula's most-visited archaeological site. Although the ruins here aren't as architecturally arresting, their location—on a cliff top overlooking the blue-green Caribbean—makes it unique among major Maya sites.

Farther afield, in Campeche state, the elaborate stone mural of Balamkú is hidden deep within another temple, sheltered from the elements for more than a millennium. Thousands of structures lie buried under the profuse greenery of Mexico's largest eco-corridor at the Reserva de la Biosfera Calakmul, where songbirds trill and curious monkeys hang from the trees. These and other intriguing cities have been extensively excavated for your viewing pleasure, and throughout the peninsula, too-symmetrical "hills" hide mysterious mounds that only future generations will be priviledged to explore.

. . . Exotic Cuisine

Pickled onions tinged a luminous pink, blackened habañero chiles floating seductively in vinaigrette, lemonade spiked with the fresh green plant called *chaya*. Yucatecan cuisine is different from that of any other region in Mexico. In recent years, traditional dishes made here with local fruits, chilis, and spices have also embraced the influence of immigrants from such places as Lebanon, France, Cuba, and New Orleans. The results are deliciously sublime.

Among the best-known regional specialties are *cochinito pibíl* and *pollo pibíl* (pork or chicken pit-baked in banana leaves). Both are done beautifully at Hacienda Teya, an elegant restaurant outside Mérida that was once a henequen hacienda. The *poc chuc* (marinated pork served with pickled onions and a plateful of other condiments) is delicious at El Príncipe Tutul-Xiu, an off-the-beaten-path and very authentic restaurant in the ancient Yucatán town of Maní. *Papadzules*—hard-boiled eggs rolled inside tortillas and drenched in a sauce of pumpkin seed and fried tomatoes—are a specialty at Labná, in Cancún's El Centro district.

In Campeche, a signature dish is *pan de cazón,* a casserole of shredded shark meat layered with tortillas, black beans, and tomato sauce; the best place to order it is La Pigua, in Campeche City. The dish known as *tixin-xic* (fish marinated in sour orange juice and chiles and cooked over an open flame) is the dish of choice at Isla Mujeres' Playa Lancheros Restaurant.

Some of the Yucatán's tastiest treats come in liquid form. *Xtabentún,* a thick liqueur of fermented honey and anise, can be sipped at room temperature, poured over ice, or mixed with a splash of sparkling water.

GREAT ITINERARIES

CANCÚN & DAY-TRIPS

Cancún is the place where you'll likely start your visit, and if sunbathing, water sports, and partying are what you're after, you won't need to set foot outside the Zona Hotelera (or even your resort). If you're staying for a week or so, though, you should definitely check out some of the attractions that are easy day-tripping distance from Cancún: nature parks, Maya ruins, and some of the world's best snorkeling and diving are all just a short drive or boat trip away.

Days 1 & 2: Arrival/Cancún

After arriving at your hotel, spend your first day or two doing what comes naturally: lounging at the hotel pool, playing in the waves, parasailing, and going out for dinner and drinks. If you start to feel restless your second day, you can head to the Museo de Arte Popular, catch an evening performance at El Embarcadero, or take a ride into El Centro (Cancún city) and browse the shops and open-air markets along Avenida Tulum.

Day 3: Cozumel or Isla Mujeres

Spend the day visiting one of the islands off Mexico's Caribbean coast. If beachcombing and a laid-back meal of fresh seafood under a palapa sounds like your bag, take a ferry from Puerto Juárez and head for Isla Mujeres; once you're there, chill on Playa Norte, or rent a moped and hit one of the beach clubs on the southeastern coast (stopping at the Tortugranja turtle farm along the way). If you like underwater sealife, drive or take a bus south from Cancún to Puerto Morelos, where you can catch a boat over to Cozumel. There are over a hundred scuba and snorkeling outfits on the island, all of which run trips out to the spectacular Maya Reef.

Day 4: Playa Del Carmen/Xcaret

In the morning, grab your bathing suit and a towel, take a taxi to the Xcaret bus station near Playa Caracol, and grab a 9:45 AM bus to this magical nature park. You can easily spend an entire day here snorkeling through underwater caves, visiting the butterfly pavilion, sea turtle nursery, and reef aquarium, and (if you reserve a spot early) bonding with dolphins. Alternatively, get up early and take a rental car south along Carretera 307 toward Playa del Carmen, about an hour and a half away. Once you arrive, head to Avenida 5 along the waterfront, where you can choose from dozens of places to lunch (if you want to splurge, try the ceviche or the namesake specialty at Blue Lobster). Then spend the afternoon either wandering among the shops and cafés and watching the street performers, or else jump in the car and head 10 minutes south of town to Xcaret.

Days 5 & 6: Tulum/Cobá

If you have the time, it's worth spending a day at each of these beautiful Maya ruin sites near Playa del Carmen; each is entirely different from the other. Cobá, which is about a half-hour's drive west from Playa, is a little-visited but spectacular ancient city that's completely surrounded by jungle; you can climb atop a 79-foot-high temple, explore pyramids and ball courts, all while listening to the calls of exotic birds and howler monkeys in the trees. Tulum, as the only major Maya site built right on the water, has less stunning architecture, but a dazzling location overlooking the Caribbean. After picking through the ruins, you can take a path down from the cliffs and laze for a while on the fabulous beach below.

Be warned, though; since Tulum is just a 45-minute drive south from Playa, it's the Yucatán's most popular Maya site. You won't have much privacy here.

YUCATÁN & THE MAYA INTERIOR

If you have more than a week to spend on the peninsula, you're in luck. You'll have time to visit some of the most beautiful—and famous—ruin sites in the country, and explore some authentically Mexican inland communities that feel worlds away from the touristy coast.

For days 1–6, follow the itinerary outlined above in **Cancún & Day-trips.**

Day 7: Valladolid & Chichén Itzá

Get up early, check out of your hotel, and make the drive inland along Carretera 180 toward the world-renowned Chichén Itzá ruins. Stop en route for a late breakfast or early lunch in Valladolid, about 2½ hours hours from Cancún; one of the best places to go is the casual eatery at Cenote Zaci, where you can also swim in the lovely jade-green sinkhole. Continue another half hour to Chichén Itzá and check into one of the area hotels (the Hacienda Chichén is a terrific choice). Then spend the afternoon exploring the site before it closes at 5 PM. Climb El Castillo; check out the former marketplace, steam bath, observatory, and temples honoring formidable Maya gods. Chill for an hour or two before the light-and-sound show, then turn in after dinner at your hotel.

Days 8 & 9: West To Mérida

Have a substantial breakfast at your hotel before checking out. Then either take an easterly detour for an on-the-hour tour at the limestone caverns of Grutas de Balancanchén, or head immediately west on Carretera 180 for the hour-long drive to Mérida. After checking into a hotel in the city (Villa Mercedes is an especially delightful choice), wander the zócalo and surrounding streets, take a horse-drawn carriage to Parque Centenario or to see the mansions along Paseo de Montejo, and then have a drink and a meal before returning to your hotel for the evening. Spend the next day shopping, visiting museums, and enjoying Mérida's vibrant city scene.

Day 10: Uxmal & The Ruta Puuc

Wake up early and drive south to the gorgeous ruins at Uxmal. You'll want to spend two to three hours exploring the site, including the mysterious, 125-foot-high Pyramid of the Magician. Afterward, you can return to Mérida, stopping first for lunch at Cana Nah near the ruins. Or, if you're spending the night in Uxmal, you'll have time after lunch to either to lounge by your hotel's pool or to tour some or all of the Ruta Puuc sites—Kabah, Labná, Sayil, and the Grutas de Loltún. The first three are Maya ruins, the latter, a fascinating underground system of caves that once hid Mayas from invading Spaniards.

Days 11 & 12: East To Cancún/ Departure

The drive from Mérida or Uxmal back to Cancún will take you some five or six hours on Carretera 180, so if you're flying out of Cancún airport the same day, get an early

GREAT ITINERARIES

start. Otherwise, if you can afford to take your time, stop at the lovely town of Izamal on the way back; you can take a horse-drawn carriage tour of artisans' shops, visit the stately cathedral, or climb to the top of crumbling Kinich Kakmó pyramid. Arrive in Cancún in the afternoon, take a last swim on the sugar-sand beach before dinner, and get a good night's sleep at your hotel before your departure the next day.

TIPS

❶ Since both the hotel/spa and restaurant at the JW Marriott have received a Fodor's Choice designation, you might splurge for this fabulous accommodation in the center of Cancún's Hotel Zone. You can also choose to stay in more rustic, reasonably priced lodgings in the downtown area—such as the charming El Rey del Caribe.

❷ If possible, try to arrange Days 8 and 9, in Mérida, during a weekend. Saturday evening and all day Sunday the city offers free concerts and folk-dancing; in squares near the main plaza vendors sell crafts and homemade snacks, and the streets are closed to cars.

❸ Despite this full itinerary, take every opportunity to rest—or at least get out of the sun—during the heat of the day between noon and 3 PM.

❹ Driving is the best way to see the peninsula, especially if your time is limited. However, there's nothing on this itinerary that can't be accessed by either bus or taxi.

WINTER	
December	**Fiesta de la Concepción Inmaculada** (Feast of the Immaculate Conception) is observed for six days in the villages across the Yucatán, with processions, dances, fireworks, and bullfights culminating on the feast day itself, December 8. **Fiesta de la Virgen de Guadalupe** (Festival of the Virgin of Guadalupe) is celebrated throughout Mexico on December 12. The **Procesión Acuática** highlights festivities at the fishing village of Celestún, west of Mérida. **Navidad** (Christmas) is celebrated throughout the Yucatán. Among the many events are *posadas,* during which families gather to eat and sing, and lively parades with colorful floats and brass bands, culminating December 24, on **Nochebuena** (Holy Night).
January	**El Día de los Reyes** (Three Kings' Day/Feast of the Epiphany), January 6, is the day children receive gifts brought by the three kings (instead of Santa Claus). El Día de los Reyes coincides with Mérida's **Founding Day**. Traditional gift-giving is combined with parades and fireworks. On **El Día de San Antonio Abad** (St. Anthony the Abbot Day), January 17, animals are taken to churches to be blessed.
February–March	**Carnival** festivities take place the week before Lent, with parades, floats, outdoor dancing, music, and fireworks; they're especially spirited in Mérida, Cozumel, Isla Mujeres, Campeche, and Chetumal.
SPRING	
March–April	Parades are held on Benito Juárez's Birthday, **Aniversario de Benito Juárez,** March 21, to honor the national hero. On the **equinoxes** (March 20 or 21 and September 22 or 23), shadows on the steps of the temple at Chichén Itzá create the image of a snake. **Semana Santa** is the most important holiday in Mexico. Reenactments of the Passion, family parties and meals, and religious services are held during this week leading up to Easter Sunday.
April	The **Sol a Sol International Regatta,** launched from St. Petersburg, Florida, in late April, brings a party atmosphere to its destination, Isla Mujeres, along with music and regional dance exhibitions. The **International Billfish Tournament** takes place in Cozumel in late April.
May	Many businesses are closed on Labor Day, **Día del Trabajo** (May 1), as nearly everyone gets the day off. Celebrated throughout Mexico by masons and construction workers, the **Fiesta de la Santa Cruz,** or Holy Cross Day (May 3), is feted by the population at large in Celestún, Yucatán and Hopelchén, Campeche, with cockfights, dances, and fireworks. **Cinco de Mayo,** May 5, is the Mexican national hol-

ON THE CALENDAR

	iday commemorating Mexico's defeat of the French army at Puebla in 1862. *El Día de la Madre* (Mother's Day), May 10, honors mothers with the usual flowers, kisses, and visits. Since 1991, the *Cancún Jazz Festival,* held the last weekend in May, has featured such top musicians as Wynton Marsalis and Gato Barbieri.
SUMMER	
August	*Founder's Day,* August 17, celebrates the founding of Isla Mujeres with six days of races, folk dances, music, and regional cuisine.
FALL	
September	*Fiesta de San Román* attracts thousands of devout Catholics to Campeche to view the procession carrying the Black Christ of San Román—the city's best-loved saint—through the streets. The two-week celebration culminates on September 28. *Vaquerías* (traditional cattle-branding parties) attract cowboy (and cowgirl) types to rural towns for bullfights, fireworks, and music throughout September. *Día de Independencia* (Independence Day) is celebrated throughout Mexico with fireworks and parties beginning 11 PM September 15, and continuing on the 16th. *Fiesta de Cristo de las Ampollas* (Feast of the Christ of the Blisters) is an important religious event that takes September 17–27, with daily mass and processions during which people dress in typical clothing; dances, bullfights, and fireworks take place in Ticul and other small villages.
October	Ten days of festivities and a solemn parade marks the *Fiesta del Cristo de Sitilpech,* during which the Christ image of Sitilpech village is carried to Izamal. The biggest dances (with fireworks) are toward the culmination of the festivities on October 28.
October & November	*Día del Muertos* (Day of the Dead), called Hanal Pixan in Mayan, is a joyful holiday during which graves are refurbished and symbolic meals are prepared to lure the spirits of family members back to earth for the day. Deceased children are associated with All Saints Day, November 1, while adults are feted on All Souls Day, November 2. Traditional tamales are pit roasted—the earth and corn symbolizing the marriage of life and death. In Mérida, altars erected in the main square show the traditional offerings of bread, tamales, sweets, and other food and drink.
November– December	Eight days of festivities mark the *Fiesta de la Inmaculada Concepción,* honoring Isla Mujeres' patron saint, the Virgin of the Immaculate Conception. After a solemn procession, a series of festivities culminates in a big party and dance on December 8. This festival is also celebrated in Champotón, Campeche.

SMART TRAVEL TIPS

Finding out about your destination before you leave home means you won't squander time organizing everyday minutiae once you've arrived. You'll be more streetwise when you hit the ground as well, better prepared to explore the aspects of Cancún, Cozumel, and the Yucatán Peninsula that drew you here in the first place. The organizations in this section can provide information to supplement this guide; contact them for up-to-the-minute details, and consult the A to Z sections in each chapter for facts on the various topics as they relate to the different regions. Happy landings!

ADDRESSES

The Mexican method of naming streets can be exasperatingly arbitrary, so **be patient when searching for addresses.** Streets in the centers of many colonial cities are laid out in a grid surrounding the *zócalo* (main square) and often have different names on opposite sides of the square. Other streets simply acquire a new name after a certain number of blocks or when they cross a certain street. Numbered streets are sometimes designated *norte* (north), *sur* (south), *oriente* (east), or *poniente* (west) on either side of a central avenue.

Blocks are often labeled numerically, according to distance from a chosen starting point, as in "la Calle de Pachuca," "2a Calle de Pachuca," and so on. Many Mexican addresses have "s/n" for *sin número* (no number) after the street name. This is common in small towns where there aren't many buildings on a block.

Addresses all over Mexico are written with the street name first, followed by the street number (or "s/n"). A five-digit *código postal* (postal code) precedes, rather than follows, the name of the city: *Hacienda Paraíso, Calle Allende 211, 68000 Oaxaca.* Apdo. (*apartado*) means box; Apdo. Postal, or A. P., means post-office box number.

In many cities, most addresses include their *colonia* (neighborhood), which is abbreviated as Col. Other abbreviations used in addresses include: Sm (*Super Manzana*, meaning block or square); Av. (*avenida*, or avenue); Calz. (*calzada*, or road); Fracc.

(*fraccionamiento,* or housing estate); and Int. (interior).

Mexican states have postal abbreviations of two or more letters. To send mail to the regions of Mexico covered in this book, you can use the following: Campeche: Camp.; Quintana Roo: Q. Roo; Yucatán: Yuc.

AIR TRAVEL

There are direct flights to Cancún from hub airports such as New York, Houston, Dallas, Miami, Chicago, Los Angeles, Charlotte, or Atlanta. From other cities, you must generally change planes. Some flights go to Mexico City, where you must pass through customs before transferring to a domestic flight to Cancún. This applies to air travel from the United States, Canada, the United Kingdom, Australia, and New Zealand. Be sure to have all your documents in order for entry into the States, otherwise you may be turned back.

BOOKING

When you book, look for nonstop flights and remember that even "direct" flights sometimes make stops. Try to avoid connecting flights, which require a change of plane. Two airlines may operate a connecting flight jointly, so ask whether your airline operates every segment of the trip; you may find that the carrier you prefer flies you only part of the way. To find more booking tips and to check prices and make online flight reservations, log on to www.fodors.com.

CARRIERS

You can reach the Yucatán either by U.S., Mexican, or regional carriers. The most convenient flight from the United States is a nonstop one on a domestic or Mexican airline. Booking a carrier with stopovers adds several hours to your travel time. Flying within the Yucatán, although not cost efficient, saves you precious time if you are on a tight schedule. A flight from Cancún to Mérida, for example, can cost as much as one from Mexico City to Cancún. Select your hub city for exploring before making your reservation from abroad.

Since all the major airlines listed here fly to Cancún, and often have the cheapest and most frequent flights there, it's worthwhile to consider it as a jumping-off point even if

you don't plan on visiting the city. Aeroméxico, American, Continental, and Mexicana also fly to Cozumel. Aeroméxico, Delta, and Mexicana fly to Mérida. Aviacsa also connects many major U.S. cities with Cancún, Mérida, and Chetumal via their hubs in Monterrey and Mexico City.

Within the Yucatán, Aerocaribe serves Cancún, Cozumel, Mérida, Chichén Itzá, Palenque, Chetumal, and Playa del Carmen. Flight service from the new Kuau airport near Pisté connects to Palenque, Cancún, and Cozumel. Aeroméxico flies to Campeche and Ciudad del Carmen from Mexico City. Aviacsa serves Cancún, Chetumal, and Mérida.

🛪 Major Airlines Aeroméxico ☎ 800/237-6639. American ☎ 800/433-7300. Continental ☎ 800/231-0856. Delta ☎ 800/221-1212. Mexicana ☎ 800/531-7921. Northwest ☎ 800/447-4747. US Airways ☎ 800/428-4322.

🛪 Within the Yucatán Aerocaribe ☎ 998/884-2000, 55/5448-3000 Ext. 4013 in Mexico City. Aeroméxico ☎ 800/021-4010, 55/5133-4010 in Mexico City. Aviacsa ☎ 01800/006-2200 toll-free in Mexico. Mexicana ☎ 01800/509-8960 toll-free in Mexico, 55/5448-1050 in Mexico City.

CHECK-IN & BOARDING

Always **find out your carrier's check-in policy.** Plan to arrive at the airport about 2 hours before your scheduled departure time for domestic flights and 2½ to 3 hours before international flights. You may need to arrive earlier if you're flying from one of the busier airports or during peak air-traffic times.

There are three departure terminals at Cancún airport. If you are flying to Mexico City to catch a connecting flight you will be leaving from the Domestic Departures Terminal. This is at the east end of the main terminal (also known as the International Departures Terminal). Regular flights leave from the main terminal. Charter flights leave from a separate terminal, ½ km (¼ mi) west of the main terminal. In peak season lines can be long and slow-moving; plan accordingly. Be sure to ask your airline about your check-in location and departure terminal. To avoid delays at airport-security checkpoints, try not to wear any metal. Jewelry, belt and other buckles, steel-toe shoes, barrettes, and underwire bras are among the items that can set off detectors.

Assuming that not everyone with a ticket will show up, airlines routinely overbook planes. When everyone does, airlines ask for volunteers to give up their seats. In return, these volunteers usually get a several-hundred-dollar flight voucher, which can be used toward the purchase of another ticket, and are rebooked at no further charge on the next flight out. If there are not enough volunteers, the airline must choose who will be denied boarding. The first to get bumped are passengers who checked in late and those flying on discounted tickets, so get to the gate and check in as early as possible, especially during peak periods.

Always **bring a government-issued photo ID** to the airport; even when it's not required, a passport is best.

CUTTING COSTS

The least-expensive airfares to Cancún are priced for round-trip travel and must usually be purchased in advance. Some airlines also have a 30-day restriction for discount tickets. After 30 days the price goes up. Airlines generally allow you to change your return date for a fee; most low-fare tickets, however, are nonrefundable. It's smart to call a number of airlines and check the Internet; when you are quoted a good price, book it on the spot—the same fare may not be available the next day, or even the next hour. Always check different routings and look into using alternate airports. Also, price off-peak flights, which may be significantly less expensive than others.

Consolidators are another good source. They buy tickets for scheduled flights at reduced rates from the airlines, then sell them at prices that beat the best fare available directly from the airlines. Sometimes you can even get your money back if you need to return the ticket. Carefully read the fine print detailing penalties for changes and cancellations, purchase the ticket with a credit card, and confirm your consolidator reservation with the airline.

When you fly as a courier, you trade your checked-luggage space for a ticket deeply subsidized by a courier service. There are restrictions on when you can book and how long you can stay. Some courier companies list with membership organizations, such as the Air Courier Association and the International Association of Air Travel Couriers; these require you to become a member before you can book a flight. Most courier traffic to Mexico goes to Mexico City, where you can catch a cheap domestic flight into Cancún.

⊡ Consolidators AirlineConsolidator.com ☎ 888/468-5385 ⊕ www.airlineconsolidator.com; for international tickets. **Best Fares** ☎ 800/576-8255 or 800/576-1600 ⊕ www.bestfares.com; $59.90 annual membership. **Cheap Tickets** ☎ 800/377-1000 or 888/922-8849 ⊕ www.cheaptickets.com. **Expedia** ☎ 800/397-3342 or 404/728-8787 ⊕ www.expedia. com. **Hotwire** ☎ 866/468-9473 or 920/330-9418 ⊕ www.hotwire.com. **Now Voyager Travel** ✉ 45 W. 21st St., 5th fl., New York, NY 10010 ☎ 212/459-1616 ⊕ www.nowvoyagertravel.com. **Onetravel.com** ⊕ www.onetravel.com. **Orbitz** ☎ 888/656-4546 ⊕ www.orbitz.com. **Priceline.com** ⊕ www.priceline.com. **Travelocity** ☎ 888/709-5983 in the U.S., 877/282-2925 in Canada, 0870/111-7060 in the U.K. ⊕ www.travelocity.com.

⊡ Courier Resources Air Courier Association/Cheaptrips.com ☎ 800/461-8856 ⊕ www. aircourier.org or www.cheaptrips.com; $20 annual membership. **International Association of Air Travel Couriers** ☎ 308/632-3273 ⊕ www.courier. org; $45 annual membership.

ENJOYING THE FLIGHT

State your seat preference when purchasing your ticket, and then repeat it when you confirm and when you check in. For more legroom, you can request one of the few emergency-aisle seats at check-in, if you are capable of lifting at least 50 pounds—a Federal Aviation Administration requirement of passengers in these seats. Seats behind a bulkhead also offer more legroom, but they don't have under-seat storage. Don't sit in the row in front of the emergency aisle or in front of a bulkhead, where seats may not recline.

Ask the airline whether a snack or meal is served on the flight. If you have dietary concerns, request special meals when booking. These can be vegetarian, low-cholesterol, or kosher, for example. It's a good idea to pack some healthful snacks and a small (plastic) bottle of water in your carry-on bag. On long flights, try to maintain a normal routine, to help fight jet lag. At night, get some sleep. By day, eat light meals, drink water (not alcohol), and **move around the cabin** to stretch your legs. For additional jet-lag tips consult *Fodor's FYI: Travel Fit & Healthy* (available at bookstores everywhere).

All flights to and within Mexico are no-smoking.

Most of the larger U.S. airlines no longer offer meals on flights to the Yucatán Peninsula. The flights are considered short-haul flights because there is a stopover at a hub airport (where you can purchase your own overpriced meals). The snacks provided on such flights are measly at best, so you may want to **bring food on board** with you. Aeroméxico and Mexicana both provide full meals.

FLYING TIMES

Cancún is 3½ hours from New York and Chicago, 4½ hours from Los Angeles, 3 hours from Dallas, 11¾ hours from London, and 18 hours from Sydney. Add another 1–4 hours if you change planes at one of the hub airports. Flights to Cozumel and Mérida are comparable in length, but are more likely to have a change along the way.

HOW TO COMPLAIN

If your baggage goes astray or your flight goes awry, complain right away. Most carriers require that you **file a claim immediately.** The Aviation Consumer Protection Division of the Department of Transportation publishes *Fly-Rights,* which discusses airlines and consumer issues and is available online. You can also find articles and information on mytravelrights.com, the Web site of the nonprofit Consumer Travel Rights Center.

🛈 Airline Complaints **Aviation Consumer Protection Division** ⊠ U.S. Department of Transportation, C-75, Room 4107, 400 7th St. SW, Washington, DC 20590 ☎ 202/366-2220 ⊕ airconsumer.ost.dot.gov. **Federal Aviation Administration Consumer Hot-**

line ⊠ for inquiries: FAA, 800 Independence Ave. SW, Washington, DC 20591 ☎ 800/322-7873 ⊕ www.faa.gov.

RECONFIRMING

Check the status of your flight before you leave for the airport. You can do this on your carrier's Web site, by linking to a flight-status checker (many Web booking services offer these), or by calling your carrier or travel agent. Always confirm international flights at least 72 hours ahead of the scheduled departure time. Charter flights, especially those leaving from Cancún, are notorious for last-minute changes. Be sure to ask for an updated telephone number from your charter company before you leave so you can call to check for any changes in flight departures. Most recommend you call within 48 hours. This check-in also applies for the regular airlines, although their departure times are more regular. Their changes are usually due to weather conditions rather than seat sales.

AIRPORTS

Cancún Aeropuerto Internacional (CUN) and Cozumel Aeropuerto Internacional (CZM) are the area's major gateways. The inland Hector José Vavarrette Muñoz Airport (MID), in Mérida, is smaller but closest to the major Maya ruins. Campeche, Chetumal, and Playa del Carmen have even smaller airports served primarily by domestic carriers. The ruins at Palenque and Chichén Itzá also have airstrips that handle small planes.

Airfares to Cancún are generally cheaper than fares to Mérida and Cozumel. All three airports are no more than 20 minutes from downtown. Car rentals are a bit less expensive in Mérida than in Cancún and Cozumel, but not enough to warrant a four-hour drive to Cancún if it's your hub.
🛈 Airport Information **Cancún Aeropuerto Internacional** ☎ 998/886-0341. **Cozumel Aeropuerto Internacional** ☎ 987/872-0485. **Hector José Vavarrette Muñoz Airport** ☎ 999/946-1340.

DUTY-FREE SHOPPING

Cancún and Cozumel are duty-free shopping zones with more variety and better prices than the duty-free shops at the airports.

BOAT & FERRY TRAVEL

The Yucatán is served by a number of ferries and boats. Most popular are the efficient speedboats that run between Playa del Carmen and Cozumel or from Puerto Juárez, Punta Sam, and Isla Mujeres. Smaller and slower boat carriers are also available in many places.

FARES & SCHEDULES

Most carriers follow schedules, with the exception of boats going to the smaller, less-visited islands. However, departure times can vary with the weather and the number of passengers.

For specific fares and schedules, *see* Boat & Ferry Travel *in* the A to Z section in each chapter.

BUS TRAVEL

The Mexican bus network is extensive and also the best means of getting around, since passenger trains have just about become obsolete. Service is frequent and tickets can be purchased on the spot (except during holidays and on long weekends, when advance purchase is crucial). Bring something to eat on long trips in case you don't like the restaurant where the bus stops; **bring toilet tissue**; and **wear a sweater,** as the air-conditioning is often set on high. Most buses play videos or television continually until midnight, so if you are bothered by noise **bring earplugs.** Smoking is prohibited on a growing number of Mexican buses, though the rule is occasionally ignored.

CLASSES

Buses range from comfortable, fast, air-conditioned coaches with bathrooms, televisions, and complimentary beverages (*especial,* deluxe, and first-class) to dilapidated "vintage" buses (second-class), which stop at every village along the way and pick up anyone who flags them from the highway. On the more rural routes passengers will include chickens, pigs, or baby goats. A second-class bus ride can be interesting if you're not in a hurry and want to see the sights and experience the local culture. The fare is usually at least 20% cheaper. For comfort's sake alone, travelers planning a long-distance haul are advised

to buy first-class or especial tickets. Several truly first-class bus companies offer service connecting Mexico's major cities. ADO (Autobuses del Oriente) is the Yucatán's principal first-class bus company.

FARES & SCHEDULES

Bus travel in the Yucatán, as throughout Mexico, is inexpensive by U.S. standards, with rates averaging $2–$6 per hour depending on the level of luxury (or lack of it). Schedules are posted at bus stations; the bus leaves more or less around the listed time. Often, if all the seats have been sold, the bus will leave early. Check with the driver.

RESERVATIONS

Most bus tickets, including first-class or especial and second-class, can be reserved in advance in person at ticket offices. ADO allows you to reserve tickets 48 hours in advance over the Internet. ADO and ADO GL (deluxe service) travel to Cancún, Chiapas, Oaxaca, Tampico, Veracruz, Villahermosa, and Yucatán from Mexico City.

🚍 Bus Information **ADO** ☎ 55/5133-2424, 01800/ 702-8000 toll-free in Mexico ⊕ www.adogl.com. mx/home.asp.

BUSINESS HOURS

In well-traveled places such as Cancún, Isla Mujeres, Playa del Carmen, Mérida, and Cozumel, businesses generally are open during posted hours. In more off-the-beaten-path areas, neighbors can tell you when the owner will return.

BANKS & OFFICES

Banks are open weekdays 9–5. Some banks open on Saturday morning. Most banks will exchange money only until noon. Most businesses are open weekdays 9–2 and 4–7.

GAS STATIONS

Most gas stations are open 24 hours. However, in the remote areas, some gas stations close from midnight until 6 AM.

MUSEUMS & SIGHTS

Most museums throughout Mexico are closed on Monday and open 8–5 the rest of the week. But it's best to call ahead or ask at your hotel. Hours of sights and attractions in this book are denoted by a clock icon, ☉.

PHARMACIES

The larger pharmacies in Cancún and Cozumel are usually open daily 8 AM–10 PM, and each of the big cities has at least one 24-hour pharmacy. Ask at your hotel if you need to find the all-night place. Smaller pharmacies are often closed on Sunday.

SHOPS

Stores in the tourist areas such as Cancún and Cozumel are usually open 10–9 Monday through Saturday and on Sunday afternoon. Shops in more traditional areas, such as Campeche and Mérida, close weekdays between 1 PM and 4 PM, opening again in the evening. They are generally closed Sunday.

CAMERAS & PHOTOGRAPHY

Mexico, with its majestic landscapes, ruins, and varied cityscapes, is a photographer's dream. Mexicans seem amenable to having picture-taking visitors in their midst, but you should always **ask permission before taking pictures in churches or of individuals.** They may ask you for a *propina*, or tip, in which case a few pesos is customary. (Note that most indigenous peoples don't ever want to be photographed; taking pictures is also forbidden in some churches.) Also, **don't snap pictures of military or high-security installations** anywhere in the country. It's forbidden.

To avoid the blurriness caused by shaky hands, get a mini-tripod—they're available in sizes as small as 6 inches. (Although cameras are permitted at archaeological sites, many of them strictly prohibit the use of tripods.) Buy a small beanbag to support your camera on uneven surfaces. If you plan to take photos on some of the country's many beaches, bring a skylight (81B or 81C) or polarizing filter to minimize haze and light problems. If you're visiting forested areas, bring high-speed film or a digital camera to compensate for low light under the tree canopy and invest in a telephoto lens to photograph wildlife; standard zoom lenses in the 35–88 range won't capture enough detail.

Casual photographers should **consider using inexpensive disposable cameras** to reduce the risks inherent in traveling with sophisticated equipment. One-use cameras with panoramic or underwater functions are also nice supplements to a standard camera and its gear.

The *Kodak Guide to Shooting Great Travel Pictures* (available at bookstores everywhere) is loaded with tips.

🖪 Photo Help **Kodak Information Center** ☎ 800/242-2424 ⊕ www.kodak.com.

EQUIPMENT PRECAUTIONS

Don't pack film or equipment in checked luggage, where it is much more susceptible to damage. X-ray machines used to view checked luggage are extremely powerful and therefore are likely to ruin your film. Try to ask for hand inspection of film, and keep videotapes and computer disks away from metal detectors. Carry an extra supply of batteries, and be prepared to turn on your camera, camcorder, or laptop to prove to airport security personnel that the device is real.

Humidity and heat are problems for cameras in this region. Always **keep your camera, film, tape, and computer disks out of the sun.** Try to **keep sand out of your camera.** You may want to invest in a special filter to protect your lens from sand. After a trip to the beach be sure to clean your lens, since salt air can leave a film on the lens and grains of sand may scratch it. Keep a special cleansing solution and cloth for this purpose. Also, as petty crime can be a problem, **keep a close eye on your gear.**

FILM & DEVELOPING

Film is widely available in Cancún, Cozumel, Playa del Carmen, Campeche City, and Mérida, and all have one-hour photo development places. (Check to see that all the negatives were developed into pictures; sometimes a few are missed.) Prices are a bit more expensive than those in the United States. Fuji and Kodak are the most popular brands with prices for a roll of 36-exposure color print film starting at about $5. The more sophisticated brands of film, such as Advantix, will be available at American outlet stores such as

Wal-Mart and Costco. These stores also offer bulk packages of film.

VIDEOS

The local standard for videotape in Mexico is the same as in the United States. All videos are NTSC (National Television Standards Committee). Prices are a bit more expensive than those in the United States. American outlet stores like Wal-Mart and Costco will have more variety and lower prices. Be careful buying DVDs while in Mexico. Most have been programmed for use only in Latin America and will not play on your machine back home.

CAR RENTAL

An economy car with no air-conditioning, manual transmission, and unlimited mileage begins at $40 a day or about $200 a week in Cancún; in Mérida, rates are about $40 a day or $230 a week; and in Campeche, $30 a day or $200 a week. Count on about $10 a day more with air-conditioning and automatic transmission. This does not include tax, which is 10% in Cancún and on the Caribbean coast and 15% elsewhere. If you reserve online before your departure you can save up to 50% and often get upgraded.

🚗 **Alamo** ☎ 800/522-9696 ⊕ www.alamo.com. **Avis** ☎ 800/331-1084 in the U.S., 800/879-2847 in Canada, 0870/606-0100 in the U.K., 02/9353-9000 in Australia, 09/526-2847 in New Zealand ⊕ www. avis.com. **Budget** ☎ 800/527-0700 in the U.S., 0870/156-5656 in the U.K. ⊕ www.budget.com. **Dollar** ☎ 800/800-6000 in the U.S., 0124/622-0111 in the U.K., where it's affiliated with Sixt, 02/9223-1444 in Australia ⊕ www.dollar.com. **Hertz** ☎ 800/654-3001 in the U.S., 800/263-0600 in Canada, 0870/844-8844 in the U.K., 02/9669-2444 in Australia, 09/256-8690 in New Zealand ⊕ www. hertz.com. **National Car Rental** ☎ 800/227-7368 in the U.S., 0870/600-6666 in the U.K. ⊕ www. nationalcar.com.

CUTTING COSTS

For a good deal, book through a travel agent who will shop around. Also, price local car-rental companies—whose prices may be lower still, although their service and maintenance may not be as good as those of major rental agencies—and research rates on the Internet. Remember to ask about required deposits, cancellation penalties, and drop-off charges if you're planning to pick up the car in one city and leave it in another. If you're traveling during a holiday period, also make sure that a confirmed reservation guarantees you a car.

Do look into wholesalers, companies that do not own fleets but rent in bulk from those that do and often offer better rates than traditional car-rental operations. Prices are best during off-peak periods. Rentals booked through wholesalers often must be paid for before you leave home.

🚗 Local Agencies **Buster Renta Car** ☎ 998/849-7221. **Econorent** ☎ 998/887-6487. **Executive** ☎ 998/886-0065 (airport) or 998/884-2699 (downtown) in Cancún, 999/946-1387 (airport) or 999/920-3732 (downtown) in Mérida ⊕ www.executive.com. mx. **Localiza** ☎ 998/884-9197 or 998/887-3109 in Cancún ⊕ www.localizarentacar.com.

🚗 Wholesaler **Auto Europe** ☎ 800/223-5555 or 207/842-2000 ⊕ www.autoeurope.com.

INSURANCE

When driving a rented car you are generally responsible for any damage to or loss of the vehicle. You also may be liable for any property damage or personal injury that you may cause while driving. Before you rent, see what coverage you already have under the terms of your personal auto-insurance policy and credit cards.

Regardless of any coverage afforded to you by your credit-card company, you must **obtain Mexican auto-liability insurance.** This is usually sold by car-rental agencies and included in the cost of the car. Be sure that you have been provided with proof of such insurance; if you drive without it, you are not only liable for damages, but you're also breaking the law. If you are in a car accident and you don't have insurance, you may be placed in jail until you are proven innocent. If anyone is injured you will remain in jail until you make retribution to all injured parties and their families—which will likely cost you thousands of dollars. Mexican laws favor nationals.

REQUIREMENTS & RESTRICTIONS

In Mexico the minimum driving age is 18, but most rental-car agencies require you to be between 21 and 25. Your own driver's license is acceptable, but an international driver's license is a good idea. It's available from the U.S. and Canadian automobile associations, and, in the United Kingdom, from the Automobile Association or Royal Automobile Club.

SURCHARGES

Before you pick up a car in one city and leave it in another, ask about drop-off charges or one-way service fees, which can be substantial. Note, too, that some rental agencies charge extra if you return the car before the time specified in your contract. To avoid a hefty refueling fee, fill the tank just before you turn in the car, but be aware that gas stations near the rental outlet may overcharge. It's almost never a deal to buy the tank of gas that's in the car when you rent it; the understanding is that you'll return it empty, but some fuel usually remains.

CAR TRAVEL

Though convenient, cars are not a necessity in this part of Mexico. Cancún offers excellent bus and taxi service; Isla Mujeres is too small to make a car practical. Cars are not needed in Playa del Carmen because the downtown area is quite small and the main street is blocked off to vehicles. You will need a car in Cozumel only if you wish to explore the eastern side of the island. Cars are actually a burden in Mérida and Campeche City because of the narrow cobbled streets and the lack of parking spaces. Driving is the easiest way to explore other areas of the region, especially those off the beaten track. But even then a car is not absolutely necessary, as there is good bus service.

Before setting out on any car trip, **check your vehicle's fuel, oil, fluids, tires, and lights.** Gas stations and mechanics can be hard to find, especially in more remote areas. Consult a map and have your route in mind as you drive. Be aware that Mexican drivers often think nothing of tailgating, speeding, and weaving in and out of traffic. **Drive defensively** and keep your cool. When stopped for traffic or at a red light, always **leave sufficient room between your car and the one ahead** so you can maneuver to safety if necessary.

EMERGENCY SERVICES

The Mexican Tourism Ministry operates a fleet of some 350 pickup trucks, known as Angeles Verdes, or the Green Angels, to render assistance to motorists on the major highways. You can call the Green Angels directly or call the Ministry of Tourism's hotline and they will dispatch them. The bilingual drivers provide mechanical help, first aid, radio-telephone communication, basic supplies and small parts, towing, and tourist information. Services are free, and spare parts, fuel, and lubricants are provided at cost. Tips are always appreciated.

The Green Angels patrol fixed sections of the major highways twice daily 8 AM to dusk, later on holiday weekends. If your car breaks down, **pull as far as possible off the road,** lift the hood, hail a passing vehicle, and ask the driver to **notify the patrol.** Most bus and truck drivers will be quite helpful. Do not accept rides from strangers. If you witness an accident, do not stop to help but instead find the nearest official.

🚗 Angeles Verdes ☎ 800/903–9200 Ministry of Tourism hotline, 55/5250–8221.

GASOLINE

Pemex, Mexico's government-owned petroleum monopoly, franchises all gas stations, so prices throughout the Yucatán are the same. Prices tend to be about 30% higher than those in the United States. Gas is always sold in liters and you must pay in cash since none of the Pemex stations accept foreign credit cards. Premium unleaded gas is called *super*; regular unleaded gas is *magna sin*. At some of the older gas stations you may find leaded fuel called *nova*. Avoid using this gas; it's very hard on your engine. Fuel quality is generally lower than in the United States and Europe.

There are no self-service stations in Mexico. When you have your tank filled, **ask for a specific amount in pesos** to avoid being overcharged. Check to make sure that the attendant has set the meter back to zero and that the price is shown. Watch the attendant check the oil as well—to make sure you actually need it—and watch while he pours it into your car.

Never pay before the gas is pumped, even if the attendant asks you to. Always **tip your attendant** a few pesos. Finally, keep your gas tank full, because gas stations are not plentiful in this area. If you run out of gas in a small village and there's no gas station for miles, ask if there's a store that sells gas from containers.

PARKING

Always **park your car in a parking lot,** or at least in a populated area. Tip the parking attendant or security guard a few dollars and ask him to look after your car. **Never park your car overnight on the street.** Never leave anything of value in an unattended car. There is usually a parking attendant available who will watch your car for a few pesos.

ROAD CONDITIONS

The road system in the Yucatán Peninsula is extensive and generally in good repair. Carretera 307 parallels most of the Caribbean coast from Punta Sam, north of Cancún, to Tulum; here it turns inward for a stretch before returning to the coast at Chetumal and the Belize border. Carretera 180 runs west from Cancún to Valladolid, Chichén Itzá, and Mérida, then turns southwest to Campeche, Isla del Carmen, and on to Villahermosa. From Mérida, the winding, more scenic Carretera 261 also leads to some of the more off-the-beaten-track archaeological sites on the way south to Campeche and Francisco Escárcega, where it joins Carretera 186 going east to Chetumal. These highways are two-lane roads. Carretera 295 (from the north coast to Valladolid and Felipe Carrillo Puerto) is also a good two-lane road.

The *autopista,* or *carretera de cuota,* a four-lane toll highway between Cancún and Mérida, was completed in 1993. It runs roughly parallel to Carretera 180 and cuts driving time between Cancún and Mérida—otherwise about 4½ hours—by about 1 hour. Tolls between Mérida and Cancún total about $24, and the stretches between highway exits are long. Be careful when driving on this road, as it retains the heat from the sun and can make your tires blow if they have low pressure or worn threads.

Many secondary roads are in bad condition—unpaved, unmarked, and full of potholes. If you must take one of these roads, the best course is to **allow plenty of daylight hours and never travel at night.** Slow down when approaching towns and villages—which you are forced to do by the *topes* (speed bumps)—because small children and animals are everywhere. Children selling oranges, candy, or other food will almost certainly approach your car.

ROAD MAPS

Maps published by Pemex are available in bookstores and papelerías, but gas stations don't sell them. The best guide is Guía Roji.

RULES OF THE ROAD

There are two absolutely essential points to remember about driving in Mexico. First and foremost is to **carry Mexican auto insurance.** If you injure anyone in an accident, you could well be jailed—whether it was your fault or not—unless you have insurance. Second, **if you enter Mexico with a car, you must leave with it.** In recent years, the high rate of U.S. vehicles being sold illegally in Mexico has caused the Mexican government to enact stringent regulations for bringing a car into the country. You must be in your foreign vehicle at all times when it is driven. You cannot lend it to another person. Do not, under any circumstances, let a national drive your car. It is illegal for Mexicans to drive foreign cars and if they are caught by the police your car will be impounded by customs and you will be given a very stiff fine to pay. Newer models of vans, SUVs, and pickup trucks can be impossible to get back once impounded.

You must cross the border with the following documents: title or registration for your vehicle; a birth certificate or passport; a credit card (AE, DC, MC, or V); a valid driver's license with a photo. The title holder, driver, and credit-card owner must be one and the same—that is, if your spouse's name is on the title of the car and yours isn't, you cannot be the one to bring the car into the country. For financed, leased, rental, or company cars, you must **bring a notarized letter of permission** from the bank, lien holder, rental agency, or company. When you submit your paperwork at the border and pay the $27 charge on your credit card, you'll receive a car permit and a sticker to put on your vehicle, all valid for up to six months. You may go back and forth across the border during this six-month period, as long as you check with immigration and bring all your permit paperwork with you. If you are planning to stay and keep your car in Mexico for longer than six months, however, you will have to get a new permit before the original one expires.

One way to minimize hassle when you cross the border with a car is to **have your paperwork done in advance** at a branch of Sanborn's Mexican Insurance; look in the Yellow Pages for an office in almost every town on the U.S.–Mexico border. You'll still have to go through some of the procedures at the border, but all your paperwork will be in order, and Sanborn's express window will ensure that you get through relatively quickly. There's a $10 charge for this service on top of the $10 per day and up for auto insurance. The fact that you drove in with a car is stamped on your tourist card, which you must give to immigration authorities at departure. If an emergency arises and you must fly home, there are complicated customs procedures to face.

When you sign up for Mexican car insurance, you should receive a booklet on Mexican rules of the road. It really is a good idea to read it to avoid breaking laws that differ from those of your country. If an oncoming vehicle flicks its lights at you in daytime, slow down: it could mean trouble ahead. When approaching a narrow bridge, the first vehicle to flash its lights has right of way. One-way streets are common. One-way traffic is indicated by an arrow; two-way, by a double-pointed arrow. Other road signs follow the widespread system of international symbols.

Mileage and speed limits are given in kilometers: 100 kph and 80 kph (62 mph and 50 mph, respectively) are the most common maximums. A few of the toll roads allow 110 kph (68 mph). In cities and small towns, observe the posted speed limits, which can be as low as 20 kph (12 mph). Seat belts are required by law throughout Mexico.

SAFETY ON THE ROAD

Never drive at night in remote and rural areas. While there are few *banditos* on the roads here, there are large potholes, free-roaming animals, cars with no working lights, road-hogging trucks, and difficulty in getting assistance. If you must travel at night, use the toll roads whenever possible; although costly, they're much safer.

Some of the biggest hassles on the road might be from police who pull you over for supposedly breaking the law, or for being a good prospect for a scam. Remember to **be polite**—displays of anger will only make matters worse—and be aware that a police officer might be pulling you over for something you didn't do. Although efforts are being made to fight corruption, it's still a fact of life in Mexico, and the $5 it costs to get your license back is definitely supplementary income for the officer who pulled you over with no intention of taking you down to police headquarters.

If you're stopped for speeding, the officer is supposed to take your license and hold it until you pay the fine at the local police station. But the officer will always prefer a *mordida* (small bribe) to wasting his time at the station. If you decide to dispute a charge that seems preposterous, do so with a smile, and tell the officer that you would like to talk to the police captain when you get to the station. The officer usually will let you go rather than go to the station. However, if you're in a hurry, you may choose to negotiate a payment.

Although pedestrians have the right of way by law, Mexican drivers tend to disregard it. And more often than not, if a driver hits a pedestrian, he'll drive away as fast as he can without stopping, to avoid jail. Many Mexican drivers don't carry auto insurance, so you'll have to shoulder your own medical expenses.

CHILDREN IN CANCÚN

If they enjoy travel in general, your children will do well throughout the Yucatán.

Note that Mexico has one of the strictest policies about children entering the country. All children, including infants, must have proof of citizenship (a birth certificate) for travel to Mexico. All children up to age 18 traveling with a single parent must also have a notarized letter from the other parent stating that the child has his or her permission to leave their home country. If the other parent is deceased or the child has only one legal parent, a notarized statement saying so must be obtained as proof. In addition, parents must now fill out a tourist card for each child over the age of 10 traveling with them.

If you are renting a car, don't forget to **arrange for a car seat** when you reserve. For general advice about traveling with children, consult *Fodor's FYI: Travel with Your Baby* (available in bookstores everywhere).

BABYSITTING

Most hotels offer babysitting services, especially if there is a kids' club at the hotel. The sitters will be professionally trained nannies who speak English. Rates range from $20 to $30 per hour.

🅵 Agency **Cancún Baby Sitting Services,** c/o Veronica C. Flores ✉ Torres Cancún 15, Sm 28 ☎ 998/880-9098 ⊕ www.cancun-baby-sitting-services.com.

FLYING

If your children are two or older, ask about children's airfares. As a general rule, infants under two not occupying a seat fly at greatly reduced fares or even for free. But if you want to guarantee a seat for an infant, you have to pay full fare. Consider flying during off-peak days and times; most airlines will grant an infant a seat without a ticket if there are available seats. When booking, confirm carry-on allowances if you're traveling with infants. In general, for babies charged 10% to 50% of the adult fare you are allowed one carry-on bag and a collapsible stroller; if the flight is full, the stroller may have to be checked or you may be limited to less.

Experts agree that it's a good idea to use safety seats aloft for children weighing less than 40 pounds. Airlines set their own policies: if you use a safety seat, U.S. carriers usually require that the child be ticketed, even if he or she is young enough to ride free, because the seats must be strapped into regular seats. And even if you pay the full adult fare for the seat, it may be worth it, especially on longer trips. Do **check your airline's policy about using safety seats during takeoff and landing.** Safety seats are not allowed everywhere in the plane, so get your seat assignments as early as possible.

When reserving, request children's meals or a freestanding bassinet (not available at all airlines) if you need them. But note that bulkhead seats, where you must sit to use the bassinet, may lack an overhead bin or storage space on the floor.

FOOD

The more populated areas, such as Cancún, Mérida, Campeche City, Cozumel, and Playa del Carmen, have U.S. fast-food outlets, and most restaurants that serve tourists have a special children's menu with the usual chicken fingers, hot dogs, and spaghetti. Yucatecan cuisine also has plenty of dishes suited for children's taste buds. It's common for parents to share a plate with their children, so no one will look twice if you order one meal with two plates.

LODGING

Most hotels in the Yucatán Peninsula allow children under 12 to stay in their parents' room at no extra charge, but others charge for them as extra adults; be sure to **find out the cutoff age for children's discounts.** Most of the chain hotels offer services that make it easier to travel with children. These include connecting family rooms, wading pools and playgrounds, and kids' clubs with special activities and outings. Check with your hotel before booking to see if the price includes the services you're interested in.

🅵 Best Choices **Fiesta Americana Mérida** ✉ Av. Colón 451, at Paseo Montejo, 97000 Mérida ☎ 800/343-7821 or 999/942-1111 ⊕ www.fiestaamericana.com. **Gran Caribe Real Club** ✉ Blvd. Kukulcán, Km 5.5, 77500 Cancún ☎ 998/881-7300 ⊕ www.real.com.mx. **Occidental Caribbean Village** ✉ Blvd. Kukulcán, Km 13.5, Zona Hotelera, 77500 Cancún, Quintana Roo ☎ 800/225-2258 ⊕ www.occidentalhotels.com.

PRECAUTIONS

Since children are particularly prone to diarrhea, be especially careful with their food and beverages. Peel all fruits, cook vegetables, and stay away from ice unless it comes from a reliable source. Ice cream from vendors should also be avoided. Infants and young children may be bothered by the heat and sun; make sure they drink plenty of fluids, wear sunscreen, and stay out of the sun at midday (⇨ Health).

SIGHTS & ATTRACTIONS

The larger tourist areas have plenty of activities for children, including museums, zoos, aquariums, and theme parks. Places that are especially appealing to children are indicated by a rubber-duckie icon (⊙) in the margin.

SUPPLIES & EQUIPMENT

Fresh milk is hard to find—most of the milk here is reconstituted and sold in cartons. Most other necessities, including *pañales desechables* (disposable diapers) and *fórmula infantil* (infant formula), can be found in almost every small town.

COMPUTERS ON THE ROAD

If you are traveling with your laptop, watch it carefully. The biggest danger, aside from theft, is the constantly fluctuating electricity, which will eventually damage your hard drive. Invest in a Mexican surge protector (available at most electronics stores for about $45) that can handle the frequent brownouts and fluctuations in voltage. The surge protectors you use at home probably won't give you much protection. It's best to leave repairs until you are back home.

CONSUMER PROTECTION

Whether you're shopping for gifts or purchasing travel services, **pay with a major credit card** whenever possible, so you can cancel payment or get reimbursed if there's a problem (and you can provide documentation). If you're doing business with a particular company for the first time, contact your local Better Business Bureau and the attorney general's offices in your state and (for U.S. businesses) the company's home state as well. Have any complaints been filed? Finally, if you're buying a package or tour, always **consider travel insurance** that includes default coverage (⇨ Insurance).

The Mexican consumer protection agency, the Procuraduría Federal de Consumidor (PROFECO), also helps foreigners. However, the complaint process with PROFECO is cumbersome and can take up to several months to resolve.

🖪 BBBs **Council of Better Business Bureaus** ✉ 4200 Wilson Blvd., Suite 800, Arlington, VA 22203 ☎ 703/276-0100 ⊕ www.bbb.org. **Procuraduría Federal de Consumidor (PROFECO)** ☎ 998/884-2634 in Cancún, 55/5547-1084 in Mexico City.

CRUISE TRAVEL

Cozumel and Playa del Carmen have become increasingly popular ports for Caribbean cruises. The last few years have seen many changes in the cruise business. Several companies have merged and several more are suffering financial difficulties. Due to heavy traffic, Cozumel and Playa del Carmen have limited the amount of traffic coming into their ports. Carnival and Cunard leave from Galveston, New Orleans, and Miami while Norwegian departs from Houston, New Orleans, Miami, and Charleston, SC. Holland America, Cunard, Carnival, Princess, Royal Caribbean, and Celebrity Cruises dock at Cozumel.

To learn how to plan, choose, and book a cruise-ship voyage, consult *Fodor's FYI: Plan & Enjoy Your Cruise* (available in bookstores everywhere).

🖪 Cruise Lines **Carnival Cruise Lines** ☎ 800/304-2319 ⊕ www.cruise-carnival.net. **Cunard** ☎ 800/728-6273 ⊕ www.cunard.com. **Norwegian** ☎ 800/327-7030 ⊕ www.ncl.com. **Princess** ☎ 800/774-6237 ⊕ www.princess.com. **Royal Caribbean International** ☎ 800/398-9819 ⊕ www.royalcaribbean.com.

DISCOUNT CRUISES

Usually, the best deals on cruise bookings can be found by consulting a cruise-only travel agency.

🖪 **National Association of Cruise Oriented Agencies (NACOA)** ✉ 3191 Coral Way, Suite 622, Miami, FL 33145 ☎ 305/663-5626 ⊕ www.nacoaonline.com.

CUSTOMS & DUTIES

When shopping abroad, keep receipts for all purchases. Upon reentering the country, **be ready to show customs officials what you've bought.** Pack purchases together in an easily accessible place. If you think a duty is incorrect, appeal the assessment. If you object to the way your clearance was handled, note the inspector's badge number. In either case, first ask to see a supervisor. If the problem isn't resolved, write to the appropriate authorities, beginning with the port director at your point of entry.

IN AUSTRALIA

Australian residents who are 18 or older may bring home A$400 worth of souvenirs and gifts (including jewelry), 250 cigarettes or 250 grams of cigars or other tobacco products, and 1,125 ml of alcohol (including wine, beer, and spirits). Residents under 18 may bring back A$200 worth of goods. Members of the same family traveling together may pool their allowances. Prohibited items include meat products. Seeds, plants, and fruits need to be declared upon arrival.

🅵 **Australian Customs Service** 🖅 Regional Director, Box 8, Sydney, NSW 2001 ☎ 02/9213-2000 or 1300/363263, 02/9364-7222 or 1800/020-504 quarantine-inquiry line ⊕ www.customs.gov.au.

IN CANADA

Canadian residents who have been out of Canada for at least seven days may bring in C$750 worth of goods duty-free. If you've been away fewer than seven days but more than 48 hours, the duty-free allowance drops to C$200. If your trip lasts 24 to 48 hours, the allowance is C$50. You may not pool allowances with family members. Goods claimed under the C$750 exemption may follow you by mail; those claimed under the lesser exemptions must accompany you. Alcohol and tobacco products may be included in the seven-day and 48-hour exemptions but not in the 24-hour exemption. If you meet the age requirements of the province or territory through which you reenter Canada, you may bring in, duty-free, 1.5 liters of wine *or* 1.14 liters (40 imperial ounces) of liquor *or* 24 12-ounce cans or bottles of

beer or ale. Also, if you meet the local age requirement for tobacco products, you may bring in, duty-free, 200 cigarettes and 50 cigars. Check ahead of time with the Canada Customs and Revenue Agency or the Department of Agriculture for policies regarding meat products, seeds, plants, and fruits.

You may send an unlimited number of gifts (only one gift per recipient, however) worth up to C$60 each duty-free to Canada. Label the package UNSOLICITED GIFT—VALUE UNDER $60. Alcohol and tobacco are excluded.

🅵 **Canada Customs and Revenue Agency** ✉ 2265 St. Laurent Blvd., Ottawa, Ontario K1G 4K3 ☎ 800/461-9999, 204/983-3500, or 506/636-5064 ⊕ www.ccra.gc.ca.

IN MEXICO

Upon entering Mexico, you'll be given a baggage declaration form and asked to itemize what you're bringing into the country. You are allowed to bring in 3 liters of spirits or wine for personal use; 400 cigarettes, 25 cigars, or 200 grams of tobacco; a reasonable amount of perfume for personal use; one movie camera and one regular camera and 12 rolls of film for each; and gift items not to exceed a total of $300. If driving across the U.S. border, gift items must not exceed $50. You aren't allowed to bring firearms, meat, vegetables, plants, fruit, or flowers into the country. You can bring in one of each of the following items without paying taxes: a cell phone, a beeper, a radio or tape recorder, a musical instrument, a laptop computer, and a portable copier or printer. Compact discs are limited to 20 and DVDs to five.

Mexico also allows you to bring one cat, one dog, or up to four canaries into the country if you have two things: (1) a pet health certificate signed by a registered veterinarian in the United States and issued not more than 72 hours before the animal enters Mexico; and (2) a pet vaccination certificate showing that the animal has been treated for rabies, hepatitis, pip, and leptospirosis. Aduana Mexico (Mexican Customs) has a striking and informative Web site, though everything is in Spanish.

Aduana Mexico ⊕ www.aduanas.sat.gob.mx. **Mexican Consulate** ✉ 2401 W. 6th St., Los Angeles, CA 90057 ☎ 231/351-6800 ⊕ www.consulmex-la.com ✉ 27 E. 39th St., New York, NY 10016 ☎ 212/217-6400 ⊕ www.consulmexny.org.

IN NEW ZEALAND

All homeward-bound residents may bring back NZ$700 worth of souvenirs and gifts; passengers may not pool their allowances, and children can claim only the concession on goods intended for their own use. For those 17 or older, the duty-free allowance also includes 4.5 liters of wine or beer; one 1,125-ml bottle of spirits; and either 200 cigarettes, 250 grams of tobacco, 50 cigars, *or* a combination of the three up to 250 grams. Meat products, seeds, plants, and fruits must be declared upon arrival to the Agricultural Services Department.

New Zealand Customs ✉ Head office: The Customhouse, 17-21 Whitmore St., Box 2218, Wellington ☎ 0800/428-786 or 09/300-5399 ⊕ www.customs.govt.nz.

IN THE U.K.

From countries outside the European Union, including Mexico, you may bring home, duty-free, 200 cigarettes or 50 cigars; 1 liter of spirits or 2 liters of fortified or sparkling wine or liqueurs; 2 liters of still table wine; 60 ml of perfume; 250 ml of toilet water; plus £145 worth of other goods, including gifts and souvenirs. Prohibited items include meat products, seeds, plants, and fruits.

HM Customs and Excise ✉ Portcullis House, 21 Cowbridge Rd. E, Cardiff CF11 9SS ☎ 0845/010-9000 or 0208/929-0152, 0208/929-6731 or 0208/910-3602 complaints ⊕ www.hmce.gov.uk.

IN THE U.S.

U.S. residents who have been out of the country for at least 48 hours may bring home, for personal use, $800 worth of foreign goods duty-free, as long as they haven't used the $800 allowance or any part of it in the past 30 days. This exemption may include 1 liter of alcohol (for travelers 21 and older), 200 cigarettes, and 100 non-Cuban cigars. Family members from the same household who are traveling together may pool their $800 personal exemptions. For fewer than 48 hours, the duty-free allowance drops to $200, which may include 50 cigarettes, 10 non-Cuban cigars, and 150 ml of alcohol (or 150 ml of perfume containing alcohol). The $200 allowance cannot be combined with other individuals' exemptions, and if you exceed it, the full value of all the goods will be taxed. Antiques, which the U.S. Bureau of Customs and Border Protection defines as objects more than 100 years old, enter duty-free, as do original works of art done entirely by hand, including paintings, drawings, and sculptures. This doesn't apply to folk art or handicrafts, which are in general dutiable.

You may also send packages home duty-free, with a limit of one parcel per addressee per day (except alcohol or tobacco products or perfume worth more than $5). You can mail up to $200 worth of goods for personal use; label the package PERSONAL USE and attach a list of its contents and their retail value. If the package contains your used personal belongings, mark it AMERICAN GOODS RETURNED to avoid paying duties. You may send up to $100 worth of goods as a gift; mark the package UNSOLICITED GIFT. Mailed items do not affect your duty-free allowance on your return.

To avoid paying duty on foreign-made high-ticket items you already own and will take on your trip, register them with customs before you leave the country. Consider filing a Certificate of Registration for laptops, cameras, watches, and other digital devices identified with serial numbers or other permanent markings; you can keep the certificate for other trips. Otherwise, bring a sales receipt or insurance form to show that you owned the item before you left the United States.

U.S. Bureau of Customs and Border Protection ✉ for inquiries and equipment registration: 1300 Pennsylvania Ave. NW, Washington, DC 20229 ⊕ www.customs.gov ☎ 877/287-8667 or 202/354-1000 ✉ for complaints: Customer Satisfaction Unit, 1300 Pennsylvania Ave. NW, Room 5.5D, Washington, DC 20229.

DISABILITIES & ACCESSIBILITY

For people with disabilities, traveling in the Yucatán can be both challenging and rewarding. Travelers with mobility impairments used to venturing out on their own should not be surprised if locals try to prevent them from doing things. This is mainly out of concern; most Mexican families take complete care of relatives who use wheelchairs, so the general public is not accustomed to such independence. Additionally, very few places in the Yucatán have handrails, let alone special facilities and means of access. Although some of the newer hotels are accessible to wheelchairs, not even Cancún offers wheelchair-accessible transportation. Knowing how to ask for assistance is extremely important. If you are not fluent in Spanish, be sure to take along a pocket dictionary. Travelers with vision impairments who have no knowledge of Spanish probably need a translator; people with hearing impairments who are comfortable using body language usually get along very well.

LODGING
Le Meridien, and the Occidental Caribbean Village in Cancún, the Presidente InterContinental Cozumel, and the Fiesta Americana Mérida are the only truly wheelchair-accessible hotels in the region. Individual arrangements must be made with other hotels.

🗹 Best Choices **Fiesta Americana Mérida** ✉ Av. Colón 451, at Paseo Montejo, 97000 Mérida, Yucatán ☎ 800/343-7821 or 999/942-1111 ⊕ www.fiestaamericana.com. **Le Meridien** ✉ Retorno Del Rey, Km. 14, 77500 Cancún, Quintana Roo ☎ 800/543-4300 or 998/881-2200 ⊕ www.meridienCancún.com.mx. **Occidental Caribbean Village** ✉ Blvd. Kukulcán, Km 13.5, Zona Hotelera, 77500 Cancún, Quintana Roo ☎ 800/225-2258 or 998/848-8000 ⊕ www.occidentalhotels.com. **Presidente InterContinental Cozumel** ✉ Carretera Chankanaab, Km 6.5, 77600 Cozumel, Quintana Roo ☎ 800/327-0200 or 987/872-0322 ⊕ www.interconti.com.

RESERVATIONS
When discussing accessibility with an operator or reservations agent, ask hard questions. Are there any stairs, inside *or* out? Are there grab bars next to the toilet *and* in the shower/tub? How wide is the doorway to the room? To the bathroom? For the most extensive facilities meeting

the latest legal specifications, opt for newer accommodations. If you reserve through a toll-free number, consider also calling the hotel's local number to confirm the information from the central reservations office. Get confirmation in writing when you can.

SIGHTS & ATTRACTIONS
Few beaches, ruins, and sites around the Yucatán are accessible for people who use wheelchairs. The most accessible museums are found in Mérida (although there are stairs and no ramp) and in Cancún. Xcaret is wheelchair accessible; special transport is available but must be arranged in advance.

🗹 **Xcaret Guest Services** ✉ Blvd. Kukulcán, Km 2.5, Zona Hotelera, Cancún ☎ 998/883-3144 ⊕ www.xcaret.com ✍ info@grupoxcaret.com.

TRANSPORTATION
There isn't any special transportation for travelers who use wheelchairs. Public buses are simply out of the question, there are no special buses, and some taxi drivers are not comfortable helping travelers with disabilities. Have your hotel arrange for a cab.

🗹 Complaints **Aviation Consumer Protection Division** (⇨ Air Travel) for airline-related problems. **Departmental Office of Civil Rights** ✉ for general inquiries, U.S. Department of Transportation, S-30, 400 7th St. SW, Room 10215, Washington, DC 20590 ☎ 202/366-4648 ⊕ www.dot.gov/ost/docr/index.htm. **Disability Rights Section** ✉ NYAV, U.S. Department of Justice, Civil Rights Division, 950 Pennsylvania Ave. NW, Washington, DC 20530 ☎ 800/514-0301, 800/514-0383 TTY, 202/514-0383 TTY, 202/514-0301 ADA information line ⊕ www.ada.gov. **U.S. Department of Transportation Hotline** ☎ 800/778-4838 or 800/455-9880 TTY for disability-related air-travel problems.

TRAVEL AGENCIES
In the United States, the Americans with Disabilities Act requires that travel firms serve the needs of all travelers. Some agencies specialize in working with people with disabilities.

🗹 Travelers with Mobility Problems **Access Adventures/B. Roberts Travel** ✉ 206 Chestnut Ridge Rd., Scottsville, NY 14624 ☎ 585/889-9096 ⊕ www.brobertstravel.com, run by a former physical-rehabilitation counselor. **CareVacations** ✉ No. 5, 5110-50 Ave., Leduc, Alberta, Canada T9E 6V4 ☎ 877/478-7827 or 780/986-6404 ⊕ www. carevacations.com, for group tours and cruise vacations. **Flying Wheels Travel** ✉ 143 W. Bridge St., Box 382, Owatonna, MN 55060 ☎ 507/451-5005 ⊕ www.flyingwheelstravel.com.

🖪 Travelers with Developmental Disabilities **New Directions** ✉ 5276 Hollister Ave., Suite 207, Santa Barbara, CA 93111 ☎ 888/967-2841 or 805/967-2841 ⊕ www.newdirectionstravel.com.

DISCOUNTS & DEALS

The best discounts you will find in Cancún are those offered on the various coupons handed out—often by welcoming committees at airports. These coupons offer discounts on restaurants, gifts, and entrance fees to local attractions.

Be a smart shopper and compare all your options before making decisions. A plane ticket bought with a promotional coupon from travel clubs, coupon books, and direct-mail offers or purchased on the Internet may not be cheaper than the least-expensive fare from a discount ticket agency. And always keep in mind that what you get is just as important as what you save.

DISCOUNT RESERVATIONS

To save money, look into discount reservations services with Web sites and toll-free numbers, which use their buying power to get a better price on hotels, airline tickets (⇨ Air Travel), even car rentals. When booking a room, always **call the hotel's local toll-free number** (if one is available) rather than the central reservations number—you'll often get a better price. Always ask about special packages or corporate rates.

When shopping for the best deal on hotels and car rentals, look for guaranteed exchange rates, which protect you against a falling dollar. With your rate locked in, you won't pay more, even if the price goes up in the local currency.

🖪 Hotel Rooms **Accommodations Express** ☎ 800/444-7666 or 800/277-1064 ⊕ www. accommodationsexpress.com. **Hotels.com** ☎ 800/ 246-8357 ⊕ www.hotels.com. **Quikbook** ☎ 800/

789-9887 ⊕ www.quikbook.com. **Steigenberger Reservation Service** ☎ 800/223-5652 ⊕ www.srs-worldhotels.com. **Turbotrip.com** ☎ 800/473-7829 ⊕ www.turbotrip.com.

PACKAGE DEALS

Don't confuse packages and guided tours. When you buy a package, you travel on your own, just as though you had planned the trip yourself. Fly/drive packages, which combine airfare and car rental, are often a good deal. In cities, ask the local visitor's bureau about hotel packages that include tickets to major museum exhibits or other special events.

EATING & DRINKING

The restaurants we list are the cream of the crop in each price category. Properties indicated by a ✕🏠 are lodging establishments whose restaurant warrants a special trip.

MEALS & SPECIALTIES

Desayuno can be either a breakfast sweet roll and coffee or milk or a full breakfast of an egg dish such as *huevos a la mexicana* (scrambled eggs with chopped tomato, onion, and chilies), *huevos rancheros* (fried eggs on a tortilla covered with salsa), or *huevos con jamón* (scrambled eggs with ham), plus juice and tortillas. Lunch is called *comida* or *almuerzo* and is the biggest meal of the day. Traditional businesses close down between 2 PM and 4 PM for this meal. It usually includes soup, a main dish, and dessert. Regional specialties include *pan de cazón* (baby shark shredded and layered with tortillas, black beans and tomato sauce), in Campeche; *pollo pibíl* (chicken baked in banana leaves), in Mérida; and *tikinchic* (fish in a sour-orange sauce), on the coast. Restaurants in tourist areas also serve American-style food such as hamburgers, pizza, and pasta. The lighter evening meal is called *cena*.

MEALTIMES

Most restaurants are open daily for lunch and dinner during high season (December–April), but hours tend to be more erratic during the rest of the year. It's always a good idea to **phone ahead.**

Unless otherwise noted, the restaurants listed in this guide are open daily for lunch and dinner.

PAYING

Most small restaurants do not accept credit cards. Larger restaurants and those catering to tourists take credit cards, but their prices reflect the fee placed on all credit-card transactions.

RESERVATIONS & DRESS

Reservations are always a good idea; we mention them only when they're essential or not accepted. Book as far ahead as you can, and reconfirm as soon as you arrive. (Large parties should always call ahead to check the reservations policy.) We mention dress only when men are required to wear a jacket or a jacket and tie.

WINE, BEER & SPIRITS

Almost all restaurants in the region serve beer and some also offer wine. Larger restaurants have beer, wine, and spirits. The Mexican wine industry is relatively small, but notable producers include L.A. Cetto, Bodegas de Santo Tomás, Domecq, and Monte Xanic; as well as offering Mexican vintages, restaurants may offer Chilean, Spanish, Italian, and French wines at reasonable prices. You pay more for imported liquor such as vodka, brandy, and whiskey; tequila and rum are less expensive. Take the opportunity to try some of the higher-end small-batch tequila—it's a completely different experience from what you might be used to. Some small lunch places called *loncherias* don't sell alcohol, but you can bring your own as long as you are discreet. Almost all corner stores sell beer and tequila; grocery stores carry all brands of beer, wine, and spirits. Liquor stores are rare and usually carry specialty items. You must be 18 to buy liquor, but this rule is often overlooked.

ECOTOURISM

Ecoturismo is fast becoming a buzzword in the Mexican tourism industry, even though not all operators and establishments employ practices that are good for the environment. For example, in the Riviera Maya, an area south of Cancún, hotel developments greatly threaten the ecosys-tem, including the region's coral reefs. Nevertheless, President Vicente Fox has pledged to support more ecotourism projects, and recent national conferences have focused on this theme. For more information about ecotourism in the Yucatán region, check out **www.gocancun.com/ ecoturism.asp.**

DOLPHIN ENCOUNTERS

One of the most heavily advertised activities in Cancún is swimming with dolphins. The water parks offering such "dolphin encounters" often bill the experience as "educational" and "enchanting," and every year, thousands of tourists who understandably love dolphins pay top dollar to participate in the activity. Many environmental and anti-cruelty organizations, however, including the Humane Society of the United States, Greenpeace, WDCS (Whale and Dolphin Conservation Society), and CSI (Cetacean Society International), have spoken out against such dolphin encounters. One contention these organizations make is that several water parks have broken international laws regulating the procurement of dolphins from restricted areas; another is that the confined conditions at such parks have put dolphins' health at risk. Some of the animals are kept in overcrowded pens and suffer from stress-related diseases; others have died from illnesses that may have come from human contact; some have even behaved aggressively toward the tourists swimming with them.

These organizations believe that keeping any dolphins in captivity is wrong, and have been pressuring the water parks to adhere to international regulations and treat their dolphins with better care. Until conditions improve, however, you may wish to visit dolphins at a facility like Xcaret, which has a track record of handling its animals humanely—or applying the current $100-plus fee for this activity toward a snorkeling or whale-watching trip, where you can see marine life in its natural state.

🇫 Cetacean Society International ⊕ http://csi-whalesalive.org. **Greenpeace** ⊕ www.greenpeace.org. **Humane Society of the United States**

⊕ www.hsus.org. **Whale and Dolphin Conservation Society** ⊕ www.wdcs.org.

ELECTRICITY

Electrical converters are not necessary because Mexico operates on the 60-cycle, 120-volt system; however, many outlets have not been updated to accommodate three-prong and polarized plugs (those with one larger prong), so **bring an adapter.**

EMBASSIES

🇦🇺 Australia **Australian Embassy** ✉ Calle Rubén Darío 55, Col. Polanco, 11580 Mexico City ☎ 55/5531-5225 ⊕ www.mexico.embassy.gov.au.

🇨🇦 Canada **Canadian Embassy** ✉ Calle Schiller 529, Col. Polanco, 11580 Mexico City ☎ 55/5724-7900 ⊕ www.dfait-maeci.gc.ca/mexico-city/menu-en.asp.

🇲🇽 Mexico **Australia** ✉ 14 Perth Ave., Yarralumla ACT 2600 ☎ 02/6273-3963 or 02/6273-3905 🖶 02/6273-1190 ⊕ www.embassyofmexicoinaustralia.org. **Canada** ✉ 45 O'Connor St., Suite 1000, Ottawa K1P 3M6 ☎ 513/233-8988 🖶 613/235-9123 ⊕ www.embamexcan.com. **New Zealand** ✉ 111 Customhouse Quay, Level 8, Wellington ☎ 644/472-0555 🖶 644/496-3559 ⊕ www.mexico.org.nz. **United Kingdom** ✉ 16 St. George St., Hanover Sq., London W1S 1LX ☎ 44/20-7499-8586 ⊕ www.embamex.co.uk. **United States** ✉ 1911 Pennsylvania Ave, Washington, D.C. 20006 ☎ 202/728-1600 🖶 202/234-4498 ⊕ www.embassyofmexico.org.

🇳🇿 New Zealand **New Zealand Embassy** ✉ Jaime Balmes No. 8, 4th fl., Colonia Los Morales, Col. Polanco, 11510 Mexico City ☎ 55/5283-9460.

🇬🇧 United Kingdom **British Embassy** ✉ Av. Río Lerma 71, Col. Cuauhtémoc, 06500 Mexico City ☎ 55/5242-8500 ⊕ www.embajadabritanica.com.mx.

🇺🇸 United States **U.S. Embassy** ✉ Paseo de la Reforma 305, Col. Cuauhtémoc, 06500 Mexico City ☎ 55/5080-2000 ⊕ www.usembassy-mexico.gov/emenu.html.

EMERGENCIES

It's helpful, albeit daunting, to know ahead of time that you're not protected by the laws of your native land once you're on Mexican soil. However, if you get into a scrape with the law, you can call the Citizens' Emergency Center in the United States. In Mexico, you can also call INFOTUR, the 24-hour English-speaking hotline of the Mexico Ministry of Tourism (Sectur). The hotline can provide immediate assistance as well as general, nonemergency guidance. **In an emergency, call ☎ 060 from any phone.**

📞 **Air Ambulance Network** ☎ 800/327-1966 or 95800/010-0027 ⊕ www.airambulancenetwork.com. **Angeles Verdes** (emergency roadside assistance in Mexico City) ☎ 55/5250-8221 or 55/5520-8555. **Citizens' Emergency Center** ☎ 202/647-5226 weekdays 8:15 AM-10 PM EST and Sat. 9 AM-3 PM, 202/647-4512 after hrs and Sun. **Global Life Flight** ☎ 01800/305-9400 toll-free in Mexico, 888/554-9729 in the U.S., 877/817-6843 in Canada ⊕ www.globallifeflight.com. **INFOTUR** ☎ 800/482-9832 in the U.S., 01800/903-9200 toll-free in Mexico ⊕ www.sectur.gob.mx.

ETIQUETTE & BEHAVIOR

In the United States, being direct, efficient, and succinct are highly valued traits. In Mexico, where communication tends to be more diplomatic and subtle, this style is often perceived as rude and aggressive. People will be far less helpful if you lose your temper or complain loudly, as such behavior is considered impolite. Remember that things move at a much slower rate here. There is rarely a stigma attached to being late. Try to accept this pace gracefully. Learning basic phrases such as *por favor* (please) and *gracias* (thank you) in Spanish will make a big difference.

BUSINESS ETIQUETTE

Business etiquette is much more formal and traditional in Mexico than in the United States. Personal relationships always come first, so developing rapport and trust is essential. A handshake is an appropriate greeting, along with a friendly inquiry about family members. With established clients, do not be surprised if you are welcomed with a kiss on the check or full hug with a pat on the back. Mexicans love business cards—be sure to present yours in any business situation. Without a business card you may have trouble being taken seriously. In public always be respectful of colleagues and keep confrontations private. Meetings may or may not start on time, so be patient with delays. When invited to dinner at the home of a customer or business associate, it's not necessary to bring a gift.

GAY & LESBIAN TRAVEL

Gender roles in Mexico are rigidly defined, especially in rural areas. Openly gay couples are a rare sight, and two people of the same gender may have trouble getting a *cama matrimonial* (double bed) at hotels. All travelers, regardless of sexual orientation, should be extra cautious when frequenting gay-friendly venues, as police sometimes violently crash these clubs, and there's little recourse or sympathy available to victims. The companies below can help answer your questions about safety and travel to the Yucatán.

🏳 Gay- & Lesbian-Friendly Travel Agencies **Different Roads Travel** ⊠ 8383 Wilshire Blvd., Suite 520, Beverly Hills, CA 90211 ☎ 800/429–8747 Ext. 14 or 323/651–5557 Ext. 14 ✍ lgernert@tzell.com. **Kennedy Travel** ⊠ 130 W. 42nd St., Suite 401, New York, NY 10036 ☎ 800/237–7433 or 212/840–8659 ⊕ www.kennedytravel.com. **Now, Voyager** ⊠ 4406 18th St., San Francisco, CA 94114 ☎ 800/255–6951 or 415/626–1169 ⊕ www.nowvoyager.com. **Skylink Travel and Tour** ⊠ 1455 N. Dutton Ave., Suite A, Santa Rosa, CA 95401 ☎ 800/225–5759 or 707/546–9888; serving lesbian travelers.

GUIDEBOOKS

Plan well and you won't be sorry. Guidebooks are excellent tools—and you can take them with you. You may want to check out color-photo-illustrated *Fodor's Exploring Mexico,* which is thorough on culture and history. It's available at online retailers and bookstores everywhere.

HEALTH

Medical clinics in all the main tourist areas have English-speaking personnel. Many of the doctors in Cancún have studied in Miami and speak English fluently. You will pay much higher prices than average for the services of English-speaking doctors or for clinics catering to tourists. Campeche and the more rural areas have few doctors who speak English.

DIVERS' ALERT

Do not fly within 24 hours of scuba diving.

FOOD & DRINK

In Mexico the major health risk, known as *turista,* or traveler's diarrhea, is caused by eating contaminated fruit or vegetables or drinking contaminated water. So **watch what you eat.** Stay away from ice, uncooked food, and unpasteurized milk and milk products, and **drink only bottled water** or water that has been boiled for at least 10 minutes, even when you're brushing your teeth. When ordering at a restaurant, be sure to ask for *agua mineral* (mineral water) or *agua purificada* (purified water). Mild cases of turista may respond to Imodium (known generically as loperamide or Lomotil) or Pepto-Bismol (not as strong), both of which you can buy over the counter; keep in mind, though, that these drugs can complicate more serious illnesses. Drink plenty of bottled water or tea; chamomile tea (*te de manzanilla*) is a good folk remedy and it's readily available in restaurants throughout Mexico. In severe cases, rehydrate yourself with Gatorade or a salt-sugar solution (½ teaspoon salt and 4 tablespoons sugar per quart of water). If your fever and diarrhea last longer than three days, see a doctor— you may have picked up a parasite that requires prescription medication.

When ordering cold drinks at untouristed establishments, **skip the ice:** *sin hielo.* (You can usually identify ice made commercially from purified water by its uniform shape and the hole in the center.) Hotels with water-purification systems will post signs to that effect in the rooms; even then, be wary. As a general rule, don't eat any raw vegetables that haven't been, or can't be, peeled (e.g., lettuce and raw chili peppers). Ask for your plate *sin ensalada* (without the salad). Some people choose to bend these rules at the most touristy establishments in cities like Cancún and Cozumel, where the risks are relatively less, though still present. When eating food that's sold on the street or in very simple *taquerías,* be sure to avoid the usual garnishes like cilantro, onions, chili peppers, and salsas: they're delicious but dangerous. It's also a good idea to pass up ceviche, raw fish cured in lemon juice—a favorite appetizer, especially at seaside resorts. The Mexican Department of Health warns that marinating in lemon juice does not constitute the "cooking" that would make the shellfish safe to eat. Also, be wary of hamburgers sold from street stands, because you can never be certain what meat they are made with.

MEDICAL PLANS

No one plans to get sick while traveling, but it happens, so consider signing up with a medical-assistance company. Members get doctor referrals, emergency evacuation or repatriation, hotlines for medical consultation, cash for emergencies, and other assistance.

Medical Assistance Companies International SOS Assistance ⊕ www.internationalsos.com ✉ **United States** ⊠ 8 Neshaminy Interplex, Suite 207, Trevose, PA 19053 ☎ 800/523-8930 or 215/244-1500, 215/245-4707 for emergencies ✉ **United Kingdom** ⊠ Landmark House, Hammersmith Bridge Rd., 6th fl., London W6 9DP ☎ 020/8762-8000, 020/8762-8008 for emergencies ✉ **Singapore** ⊠ 331 N. Bridge Rd., 17-00, Odeon Towers, Singapore 188720 ☎ 6338-7800, 6338-7800 for emergencies.

OVER-THE-COUNTER REMEDIES

Farmacias (pharmacies) are the most convenient place for such common medicines as *aspirina* (aspirin) or *jarabe para la tos* (cough syrup). You'll be able to find many U.S. brands (e.g., Tylenol, Pepto-Bismol, etc.), especially at American chain outlets such as Wal-Mart. There are pharmacies in all small towns and on practically every corner in larger cities.

PESTS & OTHER HAZARDS

It's best to be cautious and go indoors at dusk (called the "mosquito hour" by locals). An excellent brand of *repelente de insectos* (insect repellent) called Autan is readily available; do not use it on children under age two. If you want to bring a mosquito repellent from home, make sure it has at least 10% DEET or it won't be effective. If you're hiking in the jungle, wear repellent and long pants and sleeves; if you're camping in the jungle use a mosquito net and invest in a package of mosquito coils (sold in most stores). Another local flying pest is the *tabaño,* a type of deer fly, which resembles a common household fly with yellow stripes. Some people swell up after being bitten, but taking an antihistamine can help. Some people may also react to ant bites. Watch out

for the small red ants, in particular, as their bites can be quite irritating. Scorpions also live in the region; their sting is similar to a bee sting. They are not poisonous but can cause strong reactions in small children. Those who are allergic to bee stings should go to the hospital. Again, antihistamines help. Clean all cuts carefully, as the rate of infection is much higher here. The Yucatán has many poisonous snakes; in particular, the coral snake, easily identified by its black and red markings, should be avoided at all costs, since its bite is fatal. If you are planning any jungle hikes, be sure to wear hard-sole shoes and stay on the path. For more remote areas hire a guide and make sure there is an antivenin kit accompanying you on the trip.

Other hazards to travelers in Mexico are sunburn and heat exhaustion. The sun is strong here; it takes fewer than 20 minutes to get a serious sunburn. Avoid the sun between 11 AM and 3 PM all year round. Wear a hat and use sunscreen. You should **drink more fluid than you do at home**—Mexico is probably hotter than what you're used to and you will perspire more. Rest in the afternoons and stay out of the sun to avoid heat exhaustion. The first signs of dehydration and heat exhaustion are dizziness, extreme irritability, and fatigue.

SHOTS & MEDICATIONS

According to the U.S. government's National Centers for Disease Control and Prevention (CDC) there is a limited risk of malaria and dengue fever in certain rural areas of the Yucatán Peninsula, especially the states of Campeche and Quintana Roo. Travelers in mostly urban or easily accessible areas need not worry. However, if you plan to visit remote regions or stay for more than six weeks, **check with the CDC's International Travelers' Health Hotline.** In areas where mosquito-borne diseases like malaria and dengue are prevalent, use mosquito nets, wear clothing that covers the body, apply repellent containing DEET, and use spray for flying insects in living and sleeping areas. You might **consider taking antimalarial pills,** but the side effects are quite strong and the current strain of

Mexican malaria can be cured with the right medication. There is no vaccine to combat dengue, although the strain found in Quintana Roo is not life-threatening.

🖪 Health Warnings **National Centers for Disease Control and Prevention (CDC)** ✉ National Center for Infectious Diseases, Division of Quarantine, Travelers' Health, 1600 Clifton Rd. NE, Atlanta, GA 30333 ☎ 877/394-8747 international travelers' health hotline, 404/498-1600 Division of Quarantine, 800/311-3435 other inquiries ⊕ www.cdc.gov/travel.

HOLIDAYS

The lively celebration of holidays in Mexico interrupts most daily business, including banks, government offices, and many shops and services, so plan your trip accordingly: New Year's Day; February 5, Constitution Day; May 5, Anniversary of the Battle of Puebla; September 1, the State of the Union Address; September 16, Independence Day; October 12, Day of the Race; November 1, Day of the Dead; November 20, Revolution Day; December 12, Feast of Our Lady of Guadalupe; and Christmas Day.

Banks and government offices close during Holy Week (the Sunday before Easter until Easter Sunday), especially the Thursday and Friday before Easter Sunday. Some private offices close from Christmas to New Year's Day; government offices usually have reduced hours and staff.

INSURANCE

The most useful travel-insurance plan is a comprehensive policy that includes coverage for trip cancellation and interruption, default, trip delay, and medical expenses (with a waiver for preexisting conditions).

Without insurance you'll lose all or most of your money if you cancel your trip, regardless of the reason. Default insurance covers you if your tour operator, airline, or cruise line goes out of business. Trip-delay covers expenses that arise because of bad weather or mechanical delays. Study the fine print when comparing policies.

If you're traveling internationally, a key component of travel insurance is coverage for medical bills incurred if you get sick on the road. Such expenses aren't generally covered by Medicare or private policies.

U.K. residents can buy a travel-insurance policy valid for most vacations taken during the year in which it's purchased (but check preexisting-condition coverage). British and Australian citizens need extra medical coverage when traveling overseas.

Always **buy travel policies directly from the insurance company;** if you buy them from a cruise line, airline, or tour operator that goes out of business you probably won't be covered for the agency or operator's default, a major risk. Before making any purchase, review your existing health and home-owner's policies to find what they cover away from home.

🖪 Travel Insurers In the United States: **Access America** ✉ 6600 W. Broad St., Richmond, VA 23230 ☎ 800/284-8300 ⊕ www.accessamerica. com. **Travel Guard International** ✉ 1145 Clark St., Stevens Point, WI 54481 ☎ 800/826-1300 or 715/345-0505 ⊕ www.travelguard.com.

🖪 In Australia: **Insurance Council of Australia** ✉ Insurance Enquiries and Complaints, Level 3, 56 Pitt St., Sydney, NSW 2000 ☎ 1300/363683 or 02/9251-4456 ⊕ www.iecltd.com.au.

🖪 In Canada: **RBC Insurance** ✉ 6880 Financial Dr., Mississauga, Ontario L5N 7Y5 ☎ 800/565-3129 ⊕ www.rbcinsurance.com.

🖪 In New Zealand: **Insurance Council of New Zealand** ✉ 111-115 Customhouse Quay, Level 7, Box 474, Wellington ☎ 04/472-5230 ⊕ www.icnz.org. nz.

🖪 In the United Kingdom: **Association of British Insurers** ✉ 51 Gresham St., London EC2V 7HQ ☎ 020/7600-3333 ⊕ www.abi.org.uk.

LANGUAGE

Spanish is the official language, although Indian languages are spoken by approximately 7% of the population and some of those people speak no Spanish at all. Basic English is widely understood by most people employed in tourism, less so in the less-developed areas. At the very least, shopkeepers will know the numbers for bargaining purposes. As in most other foreign countries, knowing the mother tongue has a way of opening doors, so **learn some Spanish words and phrases.** Mexicans welcome even the most halting attempts to use the language.

Castilian Spanish, the kind spoken in Spain, is different from Latin American

Spanish not only in pronunciation and grammar but also in vocabulary. If you've been schooled in Castilian grammar, you'll find that Mexican Spanish ignores the *vosotros* form of the second person plural, using the more formal *ustedes* in its place. As for pronunciation, the lisped Castilian "c" or "z" is dismissed in Mexico as a sign of affectation. The most obvious differences are in vocabulary: Mexican Spanish has thousands of indigenous words and uses *¿mande?* instead of *¿cómo?* (what?). Also, be aware that words or phrases that are harmless or everyday in one country can offend in another. Unless you are lucky enough to be briefed on these nuances by a native coach, the only way to learn is by trial and error. Most Mexicans are very forgiving of errors and will appreciate your efforts.

LANGUAGE-STUDY PROGRAMS

There is a recommended Spanish-language study center in Playa del Carmen, the Playalingua del Caribe. Students can stay at the center while they learn or lodge with a local family.

🏠 Program **Playalingua del Caribe** ✉ Calle 20 Norte between Avs. 5A and 10A, 77710 Playa del Carmen ☎ 984/873-3876 ⊕ www.playalingua.com.

LANGUAGES FOR TRAVELERS

A phrase book and language-tape set can help you get started. *Fodor's Spanish for Travelers* (available at bookstores everywhere) is excellent.

LODGING

The price and quality of accommodations in Mexico vary from superluxurious, international-class hotels and all-inclusive resorts to modest budget properties, seedy places with shared bathrooms, *casas de huéspedes* (guesthouses), youth hostels, and *cabañas* (beach huts). You may find appealing bargains while you're on the road, but if your comfort threshold is high, look for an English-speaking staff, guaranteed dollar rates, and toll-free reservation numbers.

The lodgings we list are the cream of the crop in each price category. Properties are assigned price categories based on the range from their least-expensive standard double room at high season (excluding holidays) to the most expensive. We always list the facilities that are available—but we don't specify whether they cost extra; when pricing accommodations, **always ask what's included and what costs extra.** Lodgings are denoted in the text with a house icon, 🏠 ; establishments with restaurants that warrant a special trip have ✕🏠 .

Assume that hotels operate on the **European Plan** (EP, with no meals) unless we specify that they use either the **Continental Plan** (CP, with a Continental breakfast), the **Modified American Plan** (MAP, with breakfast and dinner), the **Full American Plan** (FAP, with all meals included), or **all-inclusive** (AI, including all meals and most activities).

APARTMENT & VILLA RENTALS

If you want a home base that's roomy enough for a family and comes with cooking facilities, **consider a furnished rental.** These can save you money, especially if you're traveling with a group. Home-exchange directories sometimes list rentals as well as exchanges.

Local rental agencies can be found in Isla Mujeres, Cozumel, and Playa del Carmen. They specialize in renting out apartments, condos, villas, and private homes.

🏠 International Agents **At Home Abroad** ✉ 405 E. 56th St., Suite 6H, New York, NY 10022 ☎ 212/421-9165 ⊕ www.athomeabroadinc.com. **Hideaways International** ✉ 767 Islington St., Portsmouth, NH 03801 ☎ 800/843-4433 or 603/430-4433 ⊕ www.hideaways.com; annual membership $145. **Vacation Home Rentals Worldwide** ✉ 235 Kensington Ave., Norwood, NJ 07648 ☎ 800/633-3284 or 201/767-9393 ⊕ www.vhrww.com. **Villanet** ✉ 1251 N.W. 116th St., Seattle, WA 98177 ☎ 800/964-1891 or 206/417-3444 ⊕ www.rentavilla.com. **Villas and Apartments Abroad** ✉ 370 Lexington Ave., Suite 1401, New York, NY 10017 ☎ 800/433-3020 or 212/897-5045 ⊕ www.ideal-villas.com. **Villas International** ✉ 4340 Redwood Hwy., Suite D309, San Rafael, CA 94903 ☎ 800/221-2260 or 415/499-9490 ⊕ www.villasintl.com.

🏠 Local Agents **Akumal Villas** ✉ Carretera 307, Km 104, 77600 Akumal, Quintana Roo ☎ 984/875-9088 ⊕ www.akumal-villas.com. **Caribbean Realty**

✉ Centro Commercial Marina, 77750 Puerto Aventuras ☎ 984/873-5098 ⊕ www.caribbean-realty. com. **Cozumel Vacation Villas** ✉ 3300 Airport Rd., Boulder, CO 80301 ☎ 800/224-5551 or 303/442-7644 🖷 303/442-0380 ⊕ www.cozumel-villas.com.

Lost Oasis Property Rentals ✉ 77400 Isla Mujeres, Quintana Roo ☎ 998/877-0951 ⊕ www.lostoasis. net/. **Playa Beach Rentals** ✉ Retorno Copan Lote 71, 77710 Playa del Carmen, Quintana Roo 🖷🖷 984/873-2952 ⊕ www.playabeachrentals.com.

Turquoise Waters ✉ AKA Liza Piorkowski, 77500 Puerto Morelos, Quintana Roo ☎ 877/215-0052 or 998/874-4794 ⊕ www.turquoisewater.com.

BED-AND-BREAKFASTS

B&Bs are relatively new to Mexico and consequently there are only a handful found throughout the Yucatán peninsula. The establishments listed in this guide are closer to small hotels that offer breakfast.

CAMPING

There are no official campgrounds in the Yucatán. Since all beachfront is federal property, you can legally camp on the beach. However, there are no services and this can be a dangerous practice, especially for women traveling alone. Those wishing to sleep out on the beach in safety and comfort should contact Kai Luum II. Las Ruinas Camp Grounds in Playa del Carmen have palapas, tents, and RV spaces.

🚩 **Kai Luum II** ✉ La Posada del Capitán Lafitte, off Carretera 307 at Km 62, 77400, Quintana Roo reservations: **Turquoise Reef Group** ⌕ Box 2664, Evergreen, CO 81439 ☎ 800/538-6802 ⊕ www.turqreef. com. **Las Ruinas Camp Grounds** ✉ Calle 2 and Av. 5 Norte, 77400 Playa del Carmen, Quintana Roo ☎ 984/873-0405.

HOME EXCHANGES

If you would like to exchange your home for someone else's, **join a home-exchange organization,** which will send you its updated listings of available exchanges for a year and will include your own listing in at least one of them. It's up to you to make specific arrangements.

🚩 Exchange Clubs **HomeLink International** ⌕ Box 47747, Tampa, FL 33647 ☎ 800/638-3841 or 813/975-9825 ⊕ www.homelink.org; $110 yearly for a listing, online access, and catalog; $70 without

catalog. **Intervac U.S.** ✉ 30 Corte San Fernando, Tiburon, CA 94920 ☎ 800/756-4663 ⊕ www. intervacus.com; $105 yearly for a listing, online access, and a catalog; $50 without catalog.

HOSTELS

No matter what your age, you can save on lodging costs by staying at hostels. In some 4,500 locations in more than 70 countries around the world, Hostelling International (HI), the umbrella group for a number of national youth-hostel associations, offers single-sex, dorm-style beds and, at many hostels, rooms for couples and family accommodations. Membership in any HI national hostel association, open to travelers of all ages, allows you to stay in HI-affiliated hostels at member rates; one-year membership is about $28 for adults (C$35 for a two-year minimum membership in Canada, £13.50 in the United Kingdom, A$52 in Australia, and NZ$40 in New Zealand); hostels charge about $10–$30 per night. Members have priority if the hostel is full; they're also eligible for discounts around the world, even on rail and bus travel in some countries.

🚩 Organizations **Hostelling International–Canada** ✉ 205 Catherine St., Suite 400, Ottawa, Ontario K2P 1C3 ☎ 800/663-5777 or 613/237-7884 ⊕ www.hihostels.ca.**Hostelling International–USA** ✉ 8401 Colesville Rd., Suite 600, Silver Spring, MD 20910 ☎ 301/495-1240 ⊕ www.hiayh.org. **YHA Australia** ✉ 422 Kent St., Sydney, NSW 2001 ☎ 02/9261-1111 ⊕ www.yha.com.au.**YHA England and Wales** ✉ Trevelyan House, Dimple Rd., Matlock, Derbyshire DE4 3YH U.K. ☎ 0870/870-8808, 0870/770-8868, or 0162/959-2700 ⊕ www.yha.org.uk. **YHA New Zealand** ✉ Level 1, Moorhouse City 166 Moorhouse Ave., Box 436, Christchurch ☎ 0800/278-299 or 03/379-9970 ⊕ www.yha.org.nz.

HOTELS

Hotel rates are subject to the 10%–15% value-added tax, in addition to a 2% hotel tax. Service charges and meals generally aren't included in the hotel rates.

The Mexican government categorizes hotels, based on qualitative evaluations, into *gran turismo* (superdeluxe, or five-star-plus, properties, of which there are only about 30 nationwide); five-star down to one-star; and economy class. Keep in mind that many hotels that might otherwise be rated higher have opted for a lower category to avoid higher interest rates on loans and financing.

High- versus low-season rates can vary significantly. In the off-season, Cancún hotels can cost one-third to one-half what they cost during peak season. Keep in mind, however, that this is also the time that many hotels undergo necessary repairs or renovations.

Hotels in this guide have private bathrooms with showers, unless stated otherwise; bathtubs aren't common in inexpensive hotels and properties in smaller towns.

RESERVING A ROOM

Reservations are easy to make in this region over the Internet. If you call hotels in the larger urban areas, there will be someone who speaks English. In more remote regions you will have to make your reservations in Spanish.

Local Contacts Cancún Hotel/Motel Association ☒ Plaza San Angel, Av. Acanceh, Sm 15, 77500 ☎ 998/884–9347. Cozumel Island Hotel Association ☒ Calle 2 Norte 15A, 77600 ☎ 987/872–3132. **Hotels Tulum** ⊕ www.hotelstulum.com.

Toll-Free Numbers Best Western ☎ 800/528–1234 ⊕ www.bestwestern.com. **Choice** ☎ 800/424–6423 ⊕ www.choicehotels.com. **Days Inn** ☎ 800/325–2525 ⊕ www.daysinn.com. **Doubletree Hotels** ☎ 800/222–8733 ⊕ www.doubletree.com. **Four Seasons** ☎ 800/332–3442 ⊕ www.fourseasons.com. **Hilton** ☎ 800/445–8667 ⊕ www.hilton.com. **Holiday Inn** ☎ 800/465–4329 ⊕ www.sixcontinentshotels.com. **Hyatt Hotels & Resorts** ☎ 800/233–1234 ⊕ www.hyatt.com. **Inter-Continental** ☎ 800/327–0200 ⊕ www.intercontinental.com. **Le Meridien** ☎ 800/543–4300 ⊕ www.lemeridien-hotels.com. **Marriott** ☎ 800/228–9290 ⊕ www.marriott.com. **Nikko Hotels International** ☎ 800/645–5687 ⊕ www.nikkohotels.com. **Omni** ☎ 800/843–6664 ⊕ www.omnihotels.com. **Radisson** ☎ 800/333–3333 ⊕ www.radisson.com. **Ritz-Carlton** ☎ 800/241–3333 ⊕ www.ritzcarlton.com. **Sheraton** ☎ 800/325–3535 ⊕ www.starwood.com/sheraton. **Westin Hotels & Resorts** ☎ 800/228–3000 ⊕ www.starwood.com/westin. **Wyndham Ho-**

tels & Resorts ☎ 800/822–4200 ⊕ www.wyndham.com.

MAIL & SHIPPING

Mail can be sent from your hotel or the local post office. Be forewarned, however, that mail service to, within, and from Mexico is notoriously slow and can take anywhere from 10 days to 12 weeks. **Never send anything of value to or from Mexico via the mail,** including cash, checks, or credit-card numbers.

POSTAL RATES

It costs 10.50 pesos (about 95¢) to send a postcard or letter weighing under 20 grams to the United States or Canada; it's 13 ($1.17) to Europe and 14.50 ($1.30) to Australia.

RECEIVING MAIL

To receive mail in Mexico, you can have it sent to your hotel or use *poste restante* at the post office. In the latter case, the address must include the words "a/c Lista de Correos" (general delivery), followed by the city, state, postal code, and country. To use this service, you must first register with the post office at which you wish to receive your mail. Mail is held for 10 days, and a list of recipients is posted daily. Postal codes for the main Yucatán destinations are as follows: Cancún, 77500; Isla Mujeres, 77400; Cozumel, 77600; Campeche, 24000; Mérida, 97000. Keep in mind that the postal service in Mexico is very slow; it can take up to 12 weeks for mail to arrive.

Holders of American Express cards or traveler's checks can have mail sent to them in care of the local American Express office. For a list of offices worldwide, write for the *Traveler's Companion* from American Express.

American Express ✉ Box 678, Canal Street Station, New York, NY 10013 ⊕ www.americanexpress.com.

SHIPPING PARCELS

Hotel concierges can recommend international carriers, such as DHL, Estafeta, or Federal Express, which give your package a tracking number and ensure its arrival back home.

Despite the promises, *overnight* courier service is rare in Mexico. It's not the fault of the courier service, which may indeed have the package there overnight. Delays occur at customs. Depending on the time of year, all courier packages are opened and inspected. This can slow everything down. You can expect one- to three-day service in Cancún and two- to four-day service elsewhere. **Never send cash through the courier services.**

🗺 Major Services AeroMexpress ☎ 998/886-0123. DHL ☎ 998/887-1906 🌐 www.dhl.com. Estafeta ☎ 998/887-4003 🌐 www.estafeta.com. Federal Express ☎ 998/887-4003 🌐 www.federalexpress.com.

MONEY MATTERS

Prices in this book are quoted most often in U.S. dollars. We would prefer to list costs in pesos, but because the value of the currency fluctuates considerably, what costs 90 pesos today might cost 120 pesos in six months.

If you travel only by air or package tour, stay at international hotel-chain properties, and eat at tourist restaurants, you might not find Mexico such a bargain. If you want a closer look at the country and aren't wedded to standard creature comforts, you can spend as little as $35 a day on room, board, and local transportation. Speaking Spanish is also helpful in bargaining situations and when asking for dining recommendations.

Cancún is one of the most expensive destinations in Mexico. Cozumel is on par with Cancún, and Isla Mujeres in turn is slightly less expensive than Cozumel. You're likely to get the best value for your money in Mérida and the other Yucatán cities less frequented by visitors, like Campeche. For obvious reasons, if you stay at international chain hotels and eat at restaurants designed with tourists in mind (especially hotel restaurants), you may not find the Yucatán such a bargain.

Peak-season sample costs: cup of coffee, 10 pesos–20 pesos; bottle of beer, 20 pesos–50 pesos; plate of tacos with trimmings, 25 pesos–100 pesos; grilled fish platter at a tourist restaurant, 75

pesos–300 pesos; 2-km (1-mi) taxi ride, 20–50 pesos.

Prices throughout this guide are given for adults. Substantially reduced fees are almost always available for children, students, and senior citizens. For information on taxes, *see* Taxes.

ATMS

ATMs (*cajeros automáticos*) are becoming more commonplace. Cirrus and Plus are the most frequently found networks. Before you leave home, **ask what the transaction fee will be** for withdrawing money in Mexico. (It can be up to $5 a pop.)

Many Mexican ATMs cannot accept PINs (personal identification numbers) with more than four digits; if yours is longer, **ask your bank about changing your PIN (*número de clave*) before you leave home,** and keep in mind that processing such a change often takes a few weeks. If your PIN is fine yet your transaction still can't be completed—a regular occurrence—chances are that the computer lines are busy or that the machine has run out of money or is being serviced.

For cash advances, plan to use Visa or MasterCard, as many Mexican ATMs don't accept American Express. Some may not accept foreign credit cards for cash advances or may impose a cap of $300 per transaction. The ATMs at Banamex, one of the oldest nationwide banks, tend to be the most reliable. Bancomer is another bank with many ATM locations, but they usually provide only cash advances. The newer Serfín banks have reliable ATMs that accept credit cards as well as Plus and Cirrus cards. *See also* Safety, on avoiding ATM robberies.

CREDIT CARDS

Credit cards are accepted in most tourist areas. Smaller, less expensive restaurants and shops, however, tend to take only cash. In general, credit cards aren't accepted in small towns and villages, except in hotels. Diners Club is usually accepted only in major chains; the most widely accepted cards are MasterCard and Visa. When shopping, you can usually get better prices if you **pay with cash.**

At the same time, when traveling internationally you'll **receive wholesale exchange rates** when you make purchases with credit cards. These exchange rates are usually better than those that banks give you for changing money. In Mexico the decision to pay cash or use a credit card might depend on whether the establishment in which you are making a purchase finds bargaining for prices acceptable. To avoid fraud, it's wise to **make sure that "pesos" is clearly marked on all credit-card receipts.**

Before you leave for Mexico, be sure to **find out the lost-card telephone numbers** of your credit card issuer banks that work in Mexico (toll-free numbers often don't). **Carry these numbers separately from your wallet** so you'll have them if you need to call to report lost or stolen cards.

Throughout this guide, the following abbreviations are used: **AE**, American Express; **D**, Discover; **DC**, Diners Club; **MC**, MasterCard; and **V**, Visa.

🔲 Reporting Lost Cards **American Express** ☎ 55/5326-2522 ⊕ www.americanexpress.com. **Diners Club** ☎ 52/5258-3320 ⊕ www.dinersclub.com. **Discover** ☎ 801/902-3100 (U.S. number). **MasterCard** ☎ 55/5480-8000 ⊕ www.mastercard.com. **Visa** ☎ 410/581-9994 (U.S. number, call collect) ⊕ www.visa.com.

CURRENCY

At this writing, the peso was still "floating" after the devaluation enacted by the Zedillo administration in late 1994. Although exchange rates have been as favorable as 11.1 pesos to US$1, 8.9 pesos to C$1, 21.1 pesos to £1, 8.7 pesos to A$1, and 8.0 pesos to NZ$1, the market and prices continue to adjust. Check with your bank or the financial pages of your local newspaper for current exchange rates. For quick, rough estimates of how much something costs in U.S. dollar terms, divide prices given in pesos by 10. For example, 50 pesos would be just under $5.

Mexican currency comes in denominations of 10-, 20-, 50-, 100-, 200-, 500-, and 1,000-peso bills. Coins come in denominations of 1, 5, 10, and 20 pesos and 5, 10, 20, and 50 centavos. Many of the coins

and bills are very similar, so check carefully.

U.S. dollar bills (but not coins) are widely accepted in border towns and in many parts of the Yucatán, particularly in Cancún and Cozumel, where you'll often find prices in shops quoted in dollars. However, you'll get your change in pesos. Many tourist shops and market vendors as well as virtually all hotel service personnel also accept dollars. Wherever you are, though, watch out for bad exchange rates—you'll generally do better paying in pesos.

CURRENCY EXCHANGE

For the most favorable rates, **change money through banks.** Although ATM transaction fees may be higher abroad than at home, ATM rates are excellent because they're based on wholesale rates offered only by major banks. You won't do as well at exchange booths in airports or rail and bus stations, in hotels, in restaurants, or in stores. To avoid lines at airport exchange booths, get a bit of local currency before you leave home.

Most banks only change money on weekdays until noon (though they stay open until 5), while *casas de cambio* (private exchange offices) generally stay open until 6 or 9 and often operate on weekends. Bring your photo ID or passport when you exchange money. Bank rates are regulated by the federal government and are therefore invariable, while casas de cambio have slightly more variable rates. Exchange houses in the airports and in areas with heavy tourist traffic tend to have the worst rates, often considerably lower than the banks. Some hotels also exchange money, but for providing you with this convenience they help themselves to a bigger commission than banks.

When changing money, count your bills before leaving the bank, and don't accept any partially torn, ink-marked, or taped-together bills; they will not be accepted anywhere. Also, many shop and restaurant owners are unable to make change for large bills. Enough of these encounters may compel you to request *billetes chicos* (small bills) when you exchange money.

? Exchange Services **International Currency Express** ✉ 427 N. Camden Dr., Suite F, Beverly Hills, CA 90210 ☎ 888/278-6628 orders ⊕ www. foreignmoney.com. **Thomas Cook International Money Services** ☎ 800/287-7362 orders and retail locations ⊕ www.us.thomascook.com.

TRAVELER'S CHECKS

When travelling abroad meant having to move around with large wads of cash, traveler's checks were a godsend, because lost checks could be replaced, usually within 24 hours. But nowadays, credit cards and ATM cards have all but eliminated the need for traveler's checks, and as a result, fewer establishments accept them in Mexico. If you want to carry traveler's checks as a last line of defense, however, be sure to buy them from American Express, or at a bank. You must always show a photo ID when cashing traveler's checks.

PACKING

Pack light, because you may want to save space for purchases: the Yucatán is filled with bargains on clothing, leather goods, jewelry, pottery, and other crafts.

Bring lightweight clothes, sundresses, bathing suits, sun hats or visors, and cover-ups for the Caribbean beach towns, but also pack a jacket or sweater to wear in the chilly, air-conditioned restaurants, or to tide you over during a rainstorm or an unusual cool spell. For trips to rural areas or Mérida, where dress is typically more conservative and shorts are considered inappropriate, women may want to pack one longer skirt. If you plan to visit any ruins, **bring comfortable walking shoes** with rubber soles. Lightweight rain gear is a good idea during the rainy season. Cancún is the dressiest spot on the peninsula, but even fancy restaurants don't require men to wear jackets.

Pack sunscreen, sunglasses, and umbrellas for the Yucatán. Other handy items—especially if you are traveling on your own or camping—include toilet paper, facial tissues, a plastic water bottle, and a flashlight (for occasional power outages or use at campsites). Snorkelers should consider bringing their own equipment unless traveling light is a priority; shoes with rubber soles for rocky underwater surfaces are also advised.

In your carry-on luggage, pack an extra pair of eyeglasses or contact lenses and enough of any medication you take to last a few days longer than the entire trip. You may also ask your doctor to write a spare prescription using the drug's generic name, as brand names may vary from country to country. In luggage to be checked, **never pack prescription drugs, valuables, or undeveloped film.** And don't forget to carry with you the addresses of offices that handle refunds of lost traveler's checks. Check *Fodor's How to Pack* (available at online retailers and bookstores everywhere) for more tips.

To avoid customs and security delays, carry medications in their original packaging. Don't pack any sharp objects in your carry-on luggage, including knives of any size or material, scissors, and corkscrews, or anything else that might arouse suspicion.

To avoid having your checked luggage chosen for hand inspection, don't cram bags full. The U.S. Transportation Security Administration suggests packing shoes on top and placing personal items you don't want touched in clear plastic bags.

CHECKING LUGGAGE

You're allowed to carry aboard one bag and one personal article, such as a purse or a laptop computer. Make sure what you carry on fits under your seat or in the overhead bin. Get to the gate early, so you can board as soon as possible, before the overhead bins fill up.

Baggage allowances vary by carrier, destination, and ticket class. On international flights, you're usually allowed to check two bags weighing up to 70 pounds (32 kilograms) each, although a few airlines allow checked bags of up to 88 pounds (40 kilograms) in first class. Some international carriers don't allow more than 66 pounds (30 kilograms) per bag in business class and 44 pounds (20 kilograms) in economy. On domestic flights, the limit is usually 50 to 70 pounds (23 to 32 kilograms) per bag. In general, carry-on bags shouldn't exceed 40 pounds (18 kilograms). Most airlines won't accept bags that weigh more than 100 pounds (45 kilograms) on domestic or international flights. Check baggage restrictions with your carrier before you pack.

Airline liability for baggage is limited to $2,500 per person on flights within the United States. On international flights it amounts to $9.07 per pound or $20 per kilogram for checked baggage (roughly $640 per 70-pound bag), with a maximum of $634.90 per piece, and $400 per passenger for unchecked baggage. You can buy additional coverage at check-in for about $10 per $1,000 of coverage, but it often excludes a rather extensive list of items, shown on your airline ticket.

Before departure, itemize your bags' contents and their worth, and label the bags with your name, address, and phone number. (If you use your home address, cover it so potential thieves can't see it readily.) Include a label inside each bag and **pack a copy of your itinerary.** At check-in, make sure each bag is correctly tagged with the destination airport's three-letter code. Because some checked bags will be opened for hand inspection, the U.S. Transportation Security Administration recommends that you leave luggage unlocked or use the plastic locks offered at check-in. TSA screeners place an inspection notice inside searched bags, which are resealed with a special lock.

If your bag has been searched and contents are missing or damaged, file a claim with the TSA Consumer Response Center as soon as possible. If your bags arrive damaged or fail to arrive at all, file a written report with the airline before leaving the airport.

🔝 Complaints **U.S. Transportation Security Administration Consumer Response Center** ☎ 866/289-9673 ⊕ www.tsa.gov.

PASSPORTS & VISAS

When traveling internationally, carry your passport even if you don't need one (it's always the best form of ID) and **make two photocopies of the data page** (one for someone at home and another for you, carried separately from your

passport). If you lose your passport, promptly call the nearest embassy or consulate and the local police.

U.S. passport applications for children under age 14 require consent from both parents or legal guardians; both parents must appear together to sign the application. If only one parent appears, he or she must submit a written statement from the other parent authorizing passport issuance for the child. A parent with sole authority must present evidence of it when applying; acceptable documentation includes the child's certified birth certificate listing only the applying parent, a court order specifically permitting this parent's travel with the child, or a death certificate for the non-applying parent. Application forms and instructions are available on the Web site of the U.S. State Department's Bureau of Consular Affairs (⊕ www.travel.state.gov).

ENTERING MEXICO

For stays of up to 180 days, Americans must prove citizenship through either a valid passport, certified copy of a birth certificate, or voter-registration card (the last two must be accompanied by a government-issue photo ID). Minors traveling with one parent need notarized permission from the absent parent. For stays of more than 180 days, all U.S. citizens, even infants, need a valid passport to enter Mexico. Minors also need parental permission.

Canadians need only proof of citizenship to enter Mexico for stays of up to six months. U.K. citizens need only a valid passport to enter Mexico for stays of up to three months.

Mexico has instituted a visitor fee of about $20 (not to be confused with the VAT taxes or with the airport departure tax) that applies to all visitors—except those entering by sea at Mexican ports who stay less than 72 hours, and those entering by land who do not stray past the 26-km–30-km (16-mi–18-mi) checkpoint into the country's interior. For visitors arriving by air, the fee, which covers visits of more than 72 hours and up to 30 days, is usually tacked on to the airline ticket price. You must pay the fee each time you extend your 30-day tourist visa. The fee is usually automatically added into the cost of your plane ticket.

You get the standard tourist visas on the plane without even asking for them. They're also available through travel agents and Mexican consulates and at the border if you're entering by land. The visas can be granted for up to 180 days, but this is at the discretion of the Mexican immigration officials. Although many officials will balk if you request more than 90 days, be sure to ask for extra time if you think you'll need it; going to a Mexican immigration office to renew a visa can easily take a whole day.

PASSPORT OFFICES

The best time to apply for a passport or to renew is in fall and winter. Before any trip, check your passport's expiration date, and, if necessary, renew it as soon as possible.

🇦🇺 Australian Citizens **Passports Australia** ☎ 131-232 ⊕ www.passports.gov.au.

🇨🇦 Canadian Citizens **Passport Office** ✉ to mail in applications: 200 Promenade du Portage, Hull, Québec]8X 4B7 ☎ 800/567-6868 or 819/994-3500 ⊕ www.ppt.gc.ca.

🇳🇿 New Zealand Citizens **New Zealand Passports Office** ☎ 0800/225-050 or 04/474-8100 ⊕ www. passports.govt.nz.

🇬🇧 U.K. Citizens **U.K. Passport Service** ☎ 0870/ 521-0410 ⊕ www.passport.gov.uk.

🇺🇸 U.S. Citizens **National Passport Information Center** ☎ 888/362-8668 or 888/498-3648 TTY [calls are $5.50 each], 900/225-5674 or 900/225-7778 TTY [calls are 55¢ per min for automated service, $1.50 per min for operator service] ⊕ www. travel.state.gov.

RESTROOMS

Expect to find clean flushing toilets, toilet tissue, soap, and running water at public restrooms in the major tourist destinations and at tourist attractions. Although many markets, bus and train stations, and the like have public facilities, you may have to pay a couple of pesos for the privilege of using a dirty toilet that lacks a seat, toilet paper (keep tissues with you at all times), and possibly even running water. You're better off popping into a restaurant, buying a little something, and using its rest-

room, which will probably be simple but clean and adequately equipped.

SAFETY

The Yucatán remains one of the safest areas in Mexico. But even in resort areas like Cancún and Cozumel, you should use common sense. Make use of hotel safes when available, and carry your own baggage whenever possible unless you are checking into a hotel. Leave expensive jewelry at home, since it often entices thieves and will mark you as a *turista* who can afford to be overcharged.

When traveling with all your money, be sure to keep an eye on your belongings at all times and distribute your cash and any valuables between different bags and items of clothing. Do not reach for your money stash in public. If you carry a purse, choose one with a zipper and a thick strap that you can drape across your body; adjust the length so that the purse sits in front of you at or above hip level.

There have been reports of travelers being victimized after imbibing drinks that have been drugged in Cancún nightclubs. Never drink alone with strangers. Avoid driving on desolate streets, and don't travel at night, pick up hitchhikers, or hitchhike yourself. Use luxury buses (rather than second- or third-class vehicles), which take the safer toll roads. It's best to take only registered hotel taxis or have a hotel concierge call a *sitio* (stationed cab). If you plan on hiking in remote areas, leave an itinerary with your hotel and hire a local guide to help you. Several of the more deserted beaches in the Playa del Carmen area are not safe and should be avoided by single women.

Use ATMs during the day and in big, enclosed commercial areas. Avoid the glass-enclosed street variety of banks where you may be more vulnerable to thieves who force you to withdraw money for them. This can't be stressed strongly enough.

Bear in mind that reporting a crime to the police is often a frustrating experience unless you speak excellent Spanish and have a great deal of patience. If you're victimized, contact your local consular agent or the consular section of your country's embassy in Mexico City.

WOMEN IN THE YUCATÁN PENINSULA

A woman traveling alone will be the subject of much curiosity, since traditional Mexican women do not venture out unless accompanied by family members or friends. Violent crimes against women are rare here, but you should still be cautious. Part of the machismo culture is being flirtatious and showing off in front of *compadres,* and lone women are likely to be subjected to catcalls, although this is less true in the Yucatán than in other parts of Mexico.

Although annoying, it is essentially harmless. The best way to get rid of unwanted attention is to simply ignore the advances. Avoid direct eye contact with men on the streets—it invites further acquaintance. It's best not to enter into a discussion with harassers, even if you speak Spanish. When the suitor is persistent say "no" to whatever is said, walk briskly, and leave immediately for a safe place, such as a nearby store. Dressing conservatively may help; clothing that seems innocuous to you, such as brief tops or Bermuda shorts, may be inappropriate in more conservative rural areas. Never go topless on the beach unless it is a recognized nude beach with lots of other people and **never** alone on a beach—no matter how deserted it appears to be. Mexicans, in general, do not sunbathe nude, and men may misinterpret your doing so as an invitation.

SENIOR-CITIZEN TRAVEL

There are no established senior-citizen discounts in Cancún, so ask for any hotel or travel discounts before leaving home.

To qualify for age-related discounts, mention your senior-citizen status up front when booking hotel reservations (not when checking out) and before you're seated in restaurants (not when paying the bill). Be sure to have identification on hand. When renting a car, ask about promotional car-rental discounts, which can be cheaper than senior-citizen rates.

🎓 Educational Programs Elderhostel ⊠ 11 Ave. de Lafayette, Boston, MA 02111-1746 ☎ 877/426- 8056, 877/426-2167 TTY, 978/323-4141 international callers ⊕ www.elderhostel.org. **Interhostel** ⊠ University of New Hampshire, 6 Garrison Ave., Durham, NH 03824 ☎ 800/733-9753 or 603/862-1147 ⊕ www.learn.unh.edu.

SHOPPING

You often get better prices by paying with cash (pesos or dollars) or traveler's checks because Mexican merchants frequently tack the 3%–6% credit-card company commission on to your bill. If you can do without plastic, you may even get the 12% sales tax lopped off.

If you are just window-shopping, use the phrase "*Sólo estoy mirando, gracias*" (*solo ess-toy* mee-*ran*-do, *gras*-yas; I'm just looking, thank you). This will ease the high-pressure sales pitch that you invariably get in most stores.

Most prices are fixed in shops, but bargaining is expected at markets. Start by offering half the price, and let the haggling begin. Keep in mind, though, that many small-town residents earn their livelihoods from the tourist trade; rarely are the prices in such places outrageous. Shopping around is a good idea, particularly in crafts markets where things can be very competitive. Just be sure to examine merchandise closely: some "authentic" items—particularly jewelry—might be poor imitations. And don't plan to use your ceramic plates, bowls, and cups for anything other than decoration—most items have high levels of lead in them.

KEY DESTINATIONS

Cozumel is famous for its jewelry, and there are many good deals to be found on diamonds and other precious gemstones. For authentic arts and crafts, you must journey inland to Mérida and Campeche. To buy hammocks, shoes, and pottery directly from artisans go to the tiny village of Ticul, one hour south of Mérida. Perhaps the richest source of crafts and the least-visited area is La Ruta de los Artesanos in Campeche along Carretera 180. Here you will find villages filled with beautiful crafts: Calkiní, famed for its lovely pottery; Nunkiní, known for its beautiful woven mats and rugs; Pomuch, with its famous bakery; and Becal, where the renowned Panama hats are woven by locals.

SMART SOUVENIRS

T-shirts and other commonplace souvenirs abound in the area. But there are also some unique gifts to be found. This area is well-known for its vanilla. There is also a special variety of bees on the peninsula that produces Yucatecan honey—a rich, aromatic honey that is much sought after. Supermarkets and outdoor markets carry a variety of brands, which are priced considerably lower than in the United States.

The Yucatecan hammock is considered the finest in the world and comes in a variety of sizes, color, and materials. You can find the best hammocks from street vendors or at the municipal markets. Prices start from $25 and go up to $100. A hand-embroidered *huipile* (the traditional dress of Maya women) or a *guayabera* shirt both make lovely souvenirs. Prices depend on the material and amount of embroidery done. The simplest dresses and shirts start at $25 and can go as high as $100. You can also pick up handwoven shawls for under $30.

Mexico is also famous for its amber. Most of the "amber" sold by street merchants is plastic, but there are several fine amber shops to be found in Playa del Carmen. Prices depend on the size of the amber.

WATCH OUT

If you pay with a credit card, watch that your card goes through the machine only once. If there's an error and a new slip needs to be done make sure the original is destroyed before your eyes. Another favorite scam is to ask you to wait while the clerk runs next door to use their phone or verify your number. Often they are making extra copies. Don't let your card leave the store without you.

Items made from tortoiseshell (or any sea turtle products) and black coral aren't allowed into the United States. Neither are birds or wildlife curios such as stuffed iguanas or parrots. Cowboys boots, hats, and sandals made from the leather of endangered species such as crocodiles will also be taken from you at customs. Both

the U.S. and Mexican governments also have strict laws and guidelines about the import/export of antiquities. The same applies to paintings by such Mexican masters as Diego Rivera and Frida Kahlo, which, like antiquities, are defined as part of the national patrimony.

Although Cuban cigars are readily available, American visitors will have to enjoy them while in Mexico. However, Mexico has been producing some fine alternatives to Cuban cigars. If you're bringing any Mexican cigars back to the States, make sure they have the correct Mexican seals on both the individual cigars and on the box. Otherwise they may be confiscated.

SIGHTSEEING GUIDES

In the states of Quintana Roo and the Yucatán most of the tour guides found outside the more popular ruins are not official guides. Some are professionals, but others make it up as they go along (which can be highly entertaining). Official guides will be wearing a name tag and identification issued by INAH, Instituto Nacional de Antropología e Historia (National Institute of Anthropology and History). These guides are excellent and can teach you about the architecture and history of the ruins. At the smaller ruins, guides are usually part of the research or maintenance teams and can give you an excellent tour.

All guides in Campeche have been trained by the state and are very knowledgeable. They must be booked through the Campeche tourist office. Costs vary. At the smaller sites usually a $5 tip will suffice. At the larger ruins the fees can run as high as $30. Those charging more are scam artists. The larger ruins have the more aggressive guides. Turn them down with a very firm *No, gracias,* and if they persist, lose them at the entrance gate.

STUDENTS IN THE YUCATÁN PENINSULA

Unless you are enrolled in a local school (and therefore considered a resident), there aren't many established discounts for students. Cancún offers deals for spring breakers on hotels, meals, and drinks but this is only for a few weeks in spring.

🔳 IDs & Services STA Travel ✉ 10 Downing St., New York, NY 10014 ☎ 800/777-0112 24-hr service center, 212/627-3111 ⊕ www.sta.com. **Travel Cuts** ✉ 187 College St., Toronto, Ontario M5T 1P7 Canada ☎ 800/592-2887 in the U.S., 416/979-2406 or 866/246-9762 in Canada ⊕ www.travelcuts.com.

TAXES

AIRPORT TAXES

An air-departure tax of $18—not to be confused with the fee for your tourist visa—or the peso equivalent must be paid at the airport for international flights from Mexico. For domestic flights the departure tax is around $10. It's important that you save a little cash for this transaction, as traveler's checks and credit cards are not accepted, but U.S. dollars are. However, many travel agencies and airlines automatically add this cost to the ticket price.

HOTELS

Hotels in the state of Quintana Roo charge a 12% tax, which is a combined 10% Value Added Tax with the 2% hotel tax; in Yucatán and Campeche, expect a 17% tax since the VAT is 15% in these states.

VALUE-ADDED TAX (VAT)

Mexico has a value-added tax (VAT), or IVA (*impuesto de valor agregado*), of 15% (10% along the Cancún–Chetumal corridor). Many establishments already include the IVA in the quoted price. Occasionally (and illegally) it may be waived for cash purchases.

TELEPHONES

AREA & COUNTRY CODES

The country code for Mexico is 52. When calling a Mexico number from abroad, dial the country code and then all of the numbers listed for the entry.

DIRECTORY & OPERATOR ASSISTANCE

Directory assistance is 040 nationwide. For international assistance, dial 00 first for an international operator and most likely you'll get one who speaks English; tell the operator in what city, state, and country you require directory assistance, and he or she will connect you.

INTERNATIONAL CALLS

To make an international call, dial 00 before the country code, area code, and number. The country code for the United States and Canada is 1, the United Kingdom 44, Australia 61, New Zealand 64, and South Africa 27.

LOCAL & LONG-DISTANCE CALLS

The cheapest and most dependable method for making local or long-distance calls is to buy a prepaid phone card and dial direct (*see* Phone Cards). Another option is to find a *caseta de larga distancia,* a telephone service usually operated out of a store such as a papelería, pharmacy, restaurant, or other small business; look for the phone symbol on the door. Casetas may cost more to use than pay phones, but you have a better chance of immediate success. To make a direct long-distance call, tell the person on duty the number you'd like to call, and she or he will give you a rate and dial for you. Rates seem to vary widely, so shop around. Sometimes you can make collect calls from casetas, and sometimes you cannot, depending on the individual operator and possibly your degree of visible desperation. Casetas will generally charge 50¢–$1.50 to place a collect call (some charge by the minute); it's usually better to call *por cobrar* (collect) from a pay phone.

LONG-DISTANCE SERVICES

AT&T, MCI, and Sprint access codes make calling long-distance relatively convenient, but you may find the local access number blocked in many hotel rooms. First ask the hotel operator to connect you. If the hotel operator balks, ask for an international operator, or dial the international operator yourself. One way to improve your odds of getting connected to your long-distance carrier is to travel with more than one company's calling card (a hotel may block Sprint, for example, but not MCI). If all else fails, call from a pay phone.

🔳 Access Codes AT&T Direct ☎ 01800/288-2872 or 01800/462-4240 both toll-free in Mexico. **MCI World-Phone** ☎ 95800/674-7000. **Sprint** ☎ 01800/234-0000 or 01800/877-8000 both toll-free in Mexico.

PHONE CARDS

In most parts of the country, pay phones accept prepaid cards, called Ladatel cards, sold in 30-, 50- or 100-peso denominations at newsstands or pharmacies. Many pay phones accept only these cards; coin-only pay phones are usually broken. Still other phones have two unmarked slots, one for a Ladatel (a Spanish acronym for "long-distance direct dialing") card and the other for a credit card. These are only for Mexican bank cards, but some accept Visa or MasterCard. Mexican pay phones do not accept U.S. phone cards.

To use a Ladatel card, simply insert it in the appropriate slot, dial 001 (for calls to the States) or 01 (for calls in Mexico) and the area code and number you're trying to reach. Local calls may also be placed with the card. Credit is deleted from the card as you use it, and your balance is displayed on a small screen on the phone.

TOLL-FREE NUMBERS

Toll-free numbers in Mexico start with an 800 prefix. To reach them, you need to dial 01 before the number. In this guide, Mexico-only toll-free numbers appear as follows: 01800/123–4567. Some toll-free numbers use 95 instead of 01 to connect. The 800 numbers listed simply 800/123–4567 are United States numbers and generally work north of the border only.

TIME

Mexico has two time zones. The west coast and middle states are on Pacific Standard Time. The rest of the country is on Central Standard Time, which is one hour behind Pacific Time.

TIPPING

When tipping in Mexico, remember that the minimum wage is the equivalent of $3 a day and that most workers in the tourism industry live barely above the poverty line. There are also Mexicans who think in dollars and know, for example, that in the United States porters are tipped about $2 a bag. Many of them expect the peso equivalent from foreigners and may complain if they feel they deserve more—you must decide.

What follows are some guidelines. Natu-

rally, larger tips are always welcome: porters and bellhops, 10 pesos per bag at airports and moderate and inexpensive hotels and 20 pesos per person per bag at expensive hotels; maids, 10 pesos per night (all hotels); waiters, 10%–15% of the bill, depending on service, and less in simpler restaurants (anywhere you are, make sure a service charge hasn't already been added, a practice that's particularly common in resorts); bartenders, 10%–15% of the bill, depending on service (and, perhaps, on how many drinks you've had); taxi drivers, 5–10 pesos is nice, but only if the driver helps you with your bags as tipping cabbies isn't necessary; tour guides and drivers, at least 50 pesos per half day; gas-station attendants, 3–5 pesos unless they check the oil, tires, and so on, in which case tip more; parking attendants, 5–10 pesos, even if it's for valet parking at a theater or restaurant that charges for the service.

TOURS & PACKAGES

Because everything is prearranged on a prepackaged tour or independent vacation, you spend less time planning—and often get it all at a good price.

BOOKING WITH AN AGENT

Travel agents are excellent resources. But it's a good idea to collect brochures from several agencies, as some agents' suggestions may be influenced by relationships with tour and package firms that reward them for volume sales. If you have a special interest, find an agent with expertise in that area; the American Society of Travel Agents (ASTA; ⇨ Travel Agencies) has a database of specialists worldwide. You can log on to the group's Web site to find an ASTA travel agent in your neighborhood.

Make sure your travel agent knows the accommodations and other services of the place being recommended. Ask about the hotel's location, room size, beds, and whether it has a pool, room service, or programs for children, if you care about these. Has your agent been there in person or sent others whom you can contact?

Do some homework on your own, too: local tourism boards can provide information about lesser-known and small-niche operators, some of which may sell only direct.

BUYER BEWARE

Each year consumers are stranded or lose their money when tour operators—even large ones with excellent reputations—go out of business. So check out the operator. Ask several travel agents about its reputation, and try to **book with a company that has a consumer-protection program.** (Look for information in the company's brochure.) In the United States, members of the National Tour Association and the United States Tour Operators Association are required to set aside funds to cover payments and travel arrangements in the event that the company defaults. It's also a good idea to choose a company that participates in the American Society of Travel Agents' Tour Operator Program; ASTA will act as mediator in any disputes between you and your tour operator.

Remember that the more your package or tour includes, the better you can predict the ultimate cost of your vacation. Make sure you know exactly what is covered, and beware of hidden costs. Are taxes, tips, and transfers included? Entertainment and excursions? These can add up.

🗎 Tour-Operator Recommendations **American Society of Travel Agents** (⇨ Travel Agencies). **National Tour Association (NTA)** ✉ 546 E. Main St., Lexington, KY 40508 ☎ 800/682-8886 or 859/226-4444 ⊕ www.ntaonline.com. **United States Tour Operators Association (USTOA)** ✉ 275 Madison Ave., Suite 2014, New York, NY 10016 ☎ 212/599-6599 ⊕ www.ustoa.com.

THEME TRIPS

🗎 Adventure **TrekAmerica** ✍ Box 189, Rockaway, NJ 07866 ☎ 800/221-0596 or 973/983-1144 ⊕ www.trekamerica.com.
🗎 Art & Archaeology **Far Horizons Archaeological & Cultural Trips** ✍ Box 2546, San Anselmo, CA 87199-1900 ☎ 800/552-4575 or 415/842-4800 ⊕ www.farhorizons.com. **Maya Sites** ☎ 877/620-8715 or 719/256-5186 ⊕ www.mayasites.com. **The Mayan Traveler** ✉ 5 Grogan's Park, Suite 102, The Woodlands, TX 77380 ☎ 800/451-8017 or 281/367-3386 🖷 281/298-2335 ⊕ www.themayantraveler.com.
🗎 Bicycling **Aventuras Tropicales de Sian** ✉ 37 S. Clearwater Rd., Grand Marais, MN 55604 ☎ 218/

388-9455 ⊕ www.boreal.org/yucatan. **Backroads** ✉ 801 Cedar St., Berkeley, CA 94710-1800 ☎ 800/462-2848 or 510/527-1555 ⊕ www.backroads.com.
🗎 Ecotourism **Ecoturismo Yucatán** ✉ Calle 3 No. 235, between Calles 32A and 34, Col. Pensiones, 97219 Mérida ☎ 999/925-2772 or 999/925-2187 ⊕ www.ecoyuc.com. **Emerald Planet** ✉ 2602 Timberwood Dr. No. 16, Fort Collins, CO 80528 ☎ 888/883-0736 or 970/204-4484 ⊕ www.emeraldplanet.com.
🗎 Fishing **Costa de Cocos** ✉ 2 km [1 mi] outside of Xcalak, Quintana Roo ⊕ www.costadecocos.com. **Fishing International** ✉ 1825 4th St., Santa Rosa, CA 95404 ☎ 800/950-4242 or 707/542-4242 🖷 707/526-3474 ⊕ www.fishinginternational.com.

TRAVEL AGENCIES

A good travel agent puts your needs first. Look for an agency that has been in business at least five years, emphasizes customer service, and has someone on staff who specializes in your destination. In addition, **make sure the agency belongs to a professional trade organization.** The American Society of Travel Agents (ASTA)—the largest and most influential in the field with more than 20,000 members in some 140 countries—maintains and enforces a strict code of ethics and will step in to help mediate any agent-client disputes involving ASTA members if necessary. ASTA (whose motto is "Without a travel agent, you're on your own") also maintains a Web site that includes a directory of agents. (If a travel agency is also acting as your tour operator, *see* Buyer Beware *in* Tours & Packages.)

🗎 Local Agent Referrals **American Society of Travel Agents (ASTA)** ✉ 1101 King St., Suite 200, Alexandria, VA 22314 ☎ 800/965-2782 24-hr hotline, 703/739-2782 ⊕ www.astanet.com. **Association of British Travel Agents** ✉ 68-71 Newman St., London W1T 3AH ☎ 020/7637-2444 ⊕ www.abta.com. **Association of Canadian Travel Agencies** ✉ 130 Albert St., Suite 1705, Ottawa, Ontario K1P 5G4 ☎ 613/237-3657 ⊕ www.acta.ca. **Australian Federation of Travel Agents** ✉ 309 Pitt St., Level 3, Sydney, NSW 2000 ☎ 02/9264-3299 ⊕ www.afta.com.au. **Travel Agents' Association of New Zealand** ✉ Tourism and Travel House, Level 5, 79 Boulcott St., Box 1888, Wellington 6001 ☎ 04/499-0104 ⊕ www.taanz.org.nz.

VISITOR INFORMATION

Learn more about foreign destinations by checking government-issued travel advisories and country information. For a broader picture, consider information from more than one country.

Mexico Tourism Board Canada ✉ 1 Pl. Ville Marie, Suite 1931, Montréal, Québec H3B 2C3 ☎ 800/446-3942 (44-MEXICO) ✉ 2 Bloor St. W, Suite 1801, Toronto, Ontario M4W 3E2 ☎ 800/446-3942 ✉ 999 W. Hastings St., Suite 1110, Vancouver, British Columbia V6C 2W2 ☎ 800/446-3942.

United Kingdom ✉ Wakefield House, 41 Trinity Sq., London EC3N 4DJ ☎ 020/7488-9392.

United States ☎ 800/446-3942 (44-MEXICO) ⊕ www.visitmexico.com ✉ 21 E. 63rd St., 3rd fl., New York, NY 10021 ☎ 800/446-3942 ✉ 300 N. Michigan Ave., 4th fl., Chicago, IL 60601 ☎ 800/446-3942 ✉ 2401 W. 6th St., 5th fl., Los Angeles, CA 90057 ☎ 800/446-3942 ✉ 4507 San Jacinto, Suite 308, Houston, TX 77004 ☎ 800/446-3942 ✉ 5975 Sunset Dr., Suite 305, South Miami, FL 33143 ☎ 800/446-3942.

Government Advisories Australian Department of Foreign Affairs and Trade ☎ 02/6261-1299 Consular Travel Advice Faxback Service ⊕ www.dfat.gov.au.

Consular Affairs Bureau of Canada ☎ 800/267-6788 or 613/944-6788 ⊕ www.voyage.gc.ca. **New Zealand Ministry of Foreign Affairs and Trade** ☎ 04/439-8000 ⊕ www.mft.govt.nz.

U.K. Foreign and Commonwealth Office ✉ Travel Advice Unit, Consular Division, Old Admiralty Bldg., London SW1A 2PA ☎ 020/7008-0232 or 020/7008-0233 ⊕ www.fco.gov.uk/travel. **U.S. Department of State** ✉ Overseas Citizens Services Office, Room 4811, 2201 C St. NW, Washington, DC 20520 ☎ 888/407-4747, 202/647-5225 interactive hotline ⊕ www.travel.state.gov; enclose a cover letter with your request and a business-size SASE.

WEB SITES

Do check out the World Wide Web when planning your trip. You'll find everything from weather forecasts to virtual tours of famous cities. Be sure to visit Fodors.com (⊕ www.fodors.com), a complete travel-planning site. You can research prices and book plane tickets, hotel rooms, rental cars, vacation packages, and more. In addition, you can post your pressing questions in the Travel Talk section. Other planning tools include a currency converter and weather reports, and there are loads of links to travel resources.

The official web site for Mexico tourism is ⊕ www.visitmexico.com; it has information on tourist attractions and activities, and an overview of Mexican history and culture. If you would like to get a feel for the country's political climate, check out the president's site at ⊕ www.presidencia.gob.mx; he also has a site for children at ⊕ www.elbalero.gob.mx. For more information specifically on the Yucatán Peninsula, try ⊕ www.yucatantoday.com, or www.locogringo.com; these are two comprehensive sites with information on nightlife, hotel listings, archaeological sites, area history, and other useful information for travelers.

Cancún

Beach of Hotel Camino Real (Zona Hotelera), Cancún

WORD OF MOUTH

"One of the highlights of our last stay in Cancún was after hearing some live music during lunch in [El Centro], we wandered in the direction of the music and came upon a children's festival with thousands of attendees. There was music and dancing and art and food, and we were the only non-locals there. It was an experience neither we, nor my husband's 72-year-old mother, will ever forget."

—Diana

AROUND CANCÚN

Sunbathing on the Zona Hotelera

Getting Oriented

Cancún is a great place to experience 21st-century Mexico. The main attractions for most travelers to Cancún lie along the Zona Hotelera—a 22½-km (14-mi) barrier island shaped roughly like the numeral 7. Off the eastern side is the Caribbean; to the west is a system of lagoons, the largest being Laguna Nichupté. Downtown Cancún—El Centro—is 4 km (2½mi) west of the Zona Hotelera on the mainland.

TOP 5
Reasons to Go

1. Dancing the night away to salsa, maria-chi, reggae, jazz, or hip-hop at one of the Zona Hotelera's many nightclubs.

2. Watching the parade of gorgeous suntans on the white sands of Playa Langosta.

3. Getting wild on the water: renting a Jet-ski, windsurfer, or kayak and skimming across Laguna Nichupté.

Nightlife in the Zona Hotelera

4. Browsing for Mexican crafts at the colorful stalls of Mercado Veintiocho.

5. Indulging in local flavor with dishes like *poc chuc* and drinks like tamarind margaritas.

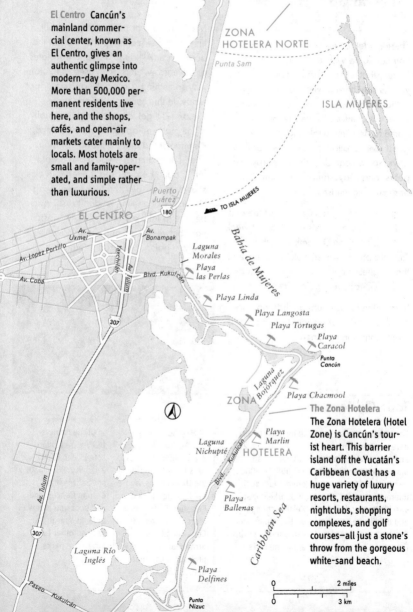

The Zona Hotelera Norte A separate northern strip called Punta Sam, north of Puerto Juárez, is sometimes referred to as the Zona Hotelera Norte (Northern Hotel Zone). This area is quieter than the main Zona, but there are some smaller hotels, marinas, and restaurants.

El Centro Cancún's mainland commercial center, known as El Centro, gives an authentic glimpse into modern-day Mexico. More than 500,000 permanent residents live here, and the shops, cafés, and open-air markets cater mainly to locals. Most hotels are small and family-operated, and simple rather than luxurious.

ZONA HOTELERA NORTE

Punta Sam

ISLA MUJERES

Puerto Juárez

EL CENTRO   180

Av. Uxmal

Av. Bonampak

Av. López Portillo

Yaxchilán

Av. Tulum

Av. Cobá

307

TO ISLA MUJERES

Bahía de Mujeres

Laguna Morales

Playa las Perlas

Blvd. Kukulcán

Playa Linda

Playa Langosta

Playa Tortugas

Playa Caracol

Punta Cancún

Laguna Bojórquez

ZONA

Playa Chacmool

The Zona Hotelera

The Zona Hotelera (Hotel Zone) is Cancún's tourist heart. This barrier island off the Yucatán's Caribbean Coast has a huge variety of luxury resorts, restaurants, nightclubs, shopping complexes, and golf courses—all just a stone's throw from the gorgeous white-sand beach.

Playa Marlin

Laguna Nichupté

HOTELERA

Blvd. Kukulcán

Av. Tulum

Playa Ballenas

Caribbean Sea

307

Laguna Río Inglés

Playa Delfines

Paseo Kukulcán

Punta Nizuc

0   2 miles

0   3 km

CANCÚN PLANNER

When to Go, How Long to Stay

There's a lot to see and do in Cancún—if you can force yourself away from the beach, that is. Understandably, many visitors stay here a week, or even longer, without ever leaving the silky sands and seductive comforts of their resorts. If you're game to do some exploring, though, it's a good idea to allow an extra two or three days, so you can day-trip to nearby eco-parks, and Maya ruins like Tulum, Cobá, or even Chichén Itzá.

High season for Cancún starts at the end of November and lasts until the first week in April. Between December 15th and January 5th, however, hotel prices are at their highest—and may rise as much as 30%–50% above regular rates.

If you plan to visit during Christmas, spring break or Easter, you should book at least three months in advance.

On Mexico Time

Mexicans are far more relaxed about time than their counterparts north of the border are. Although *mañana* translates as "tomorrow," it is often used to explain why something is not getting done or not ready. In this context, *mañana* means, "Relax—it'll get taken care of eventually." If you make an appointment in Mexico, it's understood that it's for half an hour later. For example, if you make a date for 9, don't be surprised if everyone else shows up at 9:30. The trick to enjoying life on Mexican time is: don't rush. And be sure to take advantage of the siesta hour between 1 PM and 4 PM. How else are you going to stay up late dancing?

Boulevard Kukulcán

Tour Options

The companies listed here can book tours and also arrange for plane tickets and hotel reservations. For more information about specific tour options and details, *see* "Tour Options" *in* Cancún Essentials.

■ **Intermar Caribe**
(✉ Av. Tulum 225, at Calle Jabali, Sm 20 ☎ 998/881-0000) offers tours such as snorkeling at Xel-ha, shopping on Isla Mujeres or exploring the ruins at Chichén Itzá.

■ **Mayaland Tours**
(✉ Av. Robalo 30, Sm 3 ☎ 998/987-2450) runs tours to Mérida, the Uxmal ruins, and the flamingo park at Celestún. Self-guided tours to Tulum and Cobá can also be arranged; the agency provides a car, maps, and an itinerary.

■ **Olympus Tours**
(✉ Av. Yaxchilán, Lote 13, Sm 17, Mza 2 ☎ 998/881-9030) specializes in tours around Cancún and can book you reservations to Xcaret, Xel-ha, and other local adventure parks.

Booking Your Hotel Online

A growing number of Cancún hotels are now encouraging people to make their reservations online. Some allow you to book rooms right on their own Web sites, but even hotels without their own sites usually offer reservations via online booking agencies, such as www.docancun.com, www.cancuntoday.net, and www.travel-center.com. Since hotels customarily work with several different agencies, it's a good idea to shop around online for the best rates before booking with one of them.

Besides being convenient, booking online can often get you a 10%–20% discount on room rates. The down side, though, is that there are occasional breakdowns in communication between booking agencies and hotels. You may arrive at your hotel to discover that your Spanish-speaking front desk clerk has no record of your Internet reservation or has reserved a room that's different from the one you specified. To prevent such mishaps from ruining your vacation, be sure to print out copies of all your Internet transactions, including receipts and confirmations, and bring them with you.

Need More Information?

The **Cancún Visitors and Convention Bureau Visitor** (CVB, ✉ Blvd. Kukulcán, Km 9, Zona Hotelera ☎ 998/884–6531 ⊕ www.cancun.info) has lots of information about area accommodations, restaurants, and attractions.

The **Cancún Travel Agency Assocation** (AMAV, ✉ Blvd. Kukulcán, Km. 9, Cancún Convention Center, Zona Hotelera ☎ 998/887–1670) can refer you to local travel agents who'll help plan your visit to Cancún.

How's the Weather?

The sun shines an average of 253 days a year in Cancún. The months between December and April have nearly perfect weather; temperatures hover at around 84°F during the day and 64°F at night. May through September are much hotter and more humid; the temperatures can reach upwards of 97°F.

The rainy season starts mid-September and lasts until mid-November—which means afternoon downpours that can last anywhere from 30 minutes to two hours. The streets of El Centro often get flooded during these storms, and traffic can grind to a halt. During these months there are also occasional tropical storms, with high winds and rain that may last for days.

Dining & Lodging Prices

WHAT IT COSTS in Dollars

	$$$$	$$$	$$	$	¢
Restaurants	over $25	$15–$25	$10–$15	$5–$10	under $5
Hotels	over $250	$150–$250	$75–$150	$50–$75	under $50

Restaurant prices are per person, for a main course at dinner, excluding tax and tip. Hotel prices are for a standard double room in high season, based on the European Plan (EP) and excluding service and 12% tax (which includes 10% Value Added Tax plus 2% hospitality tax).

EXPLORING CANCÚN

Cancún is a great place to experience 21st-century Mexico. There isn't much that's "quaint" or "historical" in this distinctively modern city; the people living here have eagerly embraced all the accoutrements of urban middle-class life—cell phones, cable TV—that are found all over the Western world. Most locals live on the mainland, in the part of the city known an El Centro—but many of them work in the much more posh Zona Hotelera, the barrier island where Cancún's most popular resorts are located.

Boulevard Kukulcán is the main drag in the Zona Hotelera, and because the island is so narrow—less than 1 km (½ mi) wide—you can see both the Caribbean and the lagoons from either side of it. Regularly placed kilometer markers alongside Boulevard Kukulcán indicate where you are. The first marker (Km 1) is near downtown on the mainland; Km 20 lies at the south end of the Zone at Punta Nizuc. The area in between consists entirely of hotels, restaurants, shopping complexes, marinas, and time-share condominiums. It's not the sort of place you can get to know by walking, although there is a bicycle-walking path that starts downtown at the beginning of the Zona Hotelera and continues through to Punta Nizuc. The beginning of the path parallels a grassy strip of Boulevard Kukulcán decorated with reproductions of ancient Mexican art, including the Aztec calendar stone, a giant Olmec head, the Atlantids of Tula, and a Maya Chacmool (reclining rain god).

South of Punta Cancún, Boulevard Kukulcán becomes a busy road, difficult to cross on foot. It's also punctuated by steeply inclined driveways that turn into the hotels, most of which are set at least 100 yards from the road. The lagoon side of the boulevard consists of scrubby stretches of land alternating with marinas, shopping centers, and restaurants. ■ TIP➜➜ Because there are so few sights, there are no orientation tours of Cancún: just do the local bus circuit to get a feel for the island's layout.

When you first visit El Centro, the downtown layout might not be self-evident. It is not based on a grid but rather on a circular pattern. The whole city is divided into districts called Super Manzanas (abbreviated Sm in this book), each with its own central square or park. The main streets curve around the manzanas, and the smaller neighborhood streets curl around the parks in horseshoe shapes. Avenida Tulum is the main street—actually a four-lane road with two northbound and two southbound lanes. The inner north and south lanes, separated by a meridian of grass, are the express lanes. Along the express lanes, smaller roads lead to the outer lanes, where local shops and services are. ⚠ This setup makes for some amazing traffic snarls, and it can be quite dangerous crossing at the side roads. Instead, cross at the speed bumps placed along the express lanes that act as pedestrian walkways.

Avenidas Bonampak and Yaxchilán are the other two major north–south streets that parallel Tulum. The three major east–west streets are Avenidas Cobá, Uxmal, and Chichén. They are marked along Tulum by huge traffic circles, each set with a piece of sculpture.

Numbers in the text correspond to numbers in the margin and on the Cancún map.

A Good Tour

Cancún's scenery consists mostly of beautiful beaches and crystal-clear waters, but there are also a few intriguing historical sites tucked away among the modern hotels. In addition to the attractions listed below, two modest vestiges of the ancient Maya civilization are worth a visit, but only for dedicated archaeology buffs. Neither is identified by name. On the 12th hole of Pok-Ta-Pok golf course (Boulevard Kukulcán, Km 6.5)—the name means "ball game" in Maya—stands a ruin consisting of two platforms and the remains of other ancient buildings. And the ruin of a tiny Maya shrine is cleverly incorporated into the architecture of the Hotel Camino Real, on the beach at Punta Cancún.

You don't need a car in Cancún, but if you've rented one to make extended trips, start in the Zona Hotelera at **Ruinas del Rey** ❶ ▶. Drive north to **Yamil Lu'um** ❷, and then stop in at the **Cancún Convention Center** ❸, with its anthropology and history museum, before heading farther north to the **Museo de Arte Popular** ❹, in El Embarcadero marina, and finally turning west to reach **El Centro** ❺.

What to See

❸ **Cancún Convention Center.** This strikingly modern venue for cultural events is the jumping-off point for a 1-km (½-mi) string of shopping malls that extends west to the Presidente InterContinental Cancún. The **Instituto Nacional de Antropología e Historia** (National Institute of Anthropology and History; ☎ 998/883–0305), a small, ground-floor museum, traces Maya culture with a fascinating collection of 1,000- to 1,500-year-old artifacts from throughout Quintana Roo. Admission to the museum is about $3; it's open Tuesday–Sunday 9–7. Guided tours are available in English, French, German, and Spanish. ⊠ *Blvd. Kukulcán, Km 9, Zona Hotelera* ☎ *998/884–6531.*

❺ **El Centro.** The downtown area is a combination of markets and malls that offer a glimpse of Mexico's emerging urban lifestyle. Avenida Tulum, the main street, is marked by a huge sculpture of shells and starfish in the middle of a traffic circle. The sculpture, one of Cancún's icons, is particularly dramatic at night when the lights are turned on. It's also home to many restaurants and shops as well as Mercado Veintiocho (Market 28)—an enormous crafts market just off Avenidas Yaxchilán and Sunyaxchén. Bargains can also be found along Avenida Yaxchilán as well as in the smaller shopping centers.

★ ❹ **Museo de Arte Popular.** The enormous, entrancing Folk Art Museum is on the second floor of El Embarcadero marina. Original works by the country's finest artisans are arranged in fascinating tableaux here; plan to spend a couple of hours if you can, and be sure to visit the museum's shop. Other marina complex attractions include two restaurants, a rotating scenic tower, the Teatro Cancún, and ticket booths for the Xcaret nature park south of Playa del Carmen, and the El Garrafón snorkeling park on Isla Mujeres. ⊠ *Blvd. Kukulcán, Km 4, Zona Hotelera* ☎ *998/ 849–4848* ☜ *$10* ☉ *Daily 9* AM–9 PM.

Cancún

Bahía de Mujeres

TO PUNTA SAM

Puerta Juárez

TO ISLA MUJERES

180

EL CENTRO

Av. Uxmal

Av. Bonampak

Av. Lopez Portillo

Yaxchilán

Av. Tulum

Blvd.

5

Kukulcán

Laguna Morales

Playa las Perlas

Playa Linda

Av. Cobá

307

4

Playa Langosta

Playa Tortugas

Play Carace

3

Punt Cancú

Laguna Bojórquez

Playa Chacmool

ZONA

2

Playa Marlin

HOTELERA

Av. Tulum

Laguna Nichupté

Blvd. Kukulcán

Playa Ballenas

Caribbean Sea

307

1

Laguna Río Inglés

Playa Delfines

Punta Nizuc

Paseo Kukulcán

TO TULUM

0   2 miles

0   3 km

KEY

Ferry

Start of driv

1

🏔️ ⚑ ❶ **Ruinas del Rey.** Large signs on the Zona Hotelera's lagoon side, roughly opposite Playa Delfines, point out the small Ruins of the King. First entered into Western chronicles in a 16th-century travelogue, then sighted in 1842 by American explorer John Lloyd Stephens and his draftsman, Frederick Catherwood, the ruins were finally explored by archaeologists in 1910, though excavations didn't begin until 1954. In 1975 archaeologists, along with the Mexican government, began restoration work.

Dating from the 3rd to 2nd century BC, del Rey is notable for having two main plazas bounded by two streets—most other Maya cities contain only one plaza. The pyramid here is topped by a platform, and inside its vault are paintings on stucco. Skeletons interred both at the apex and at the base indicate that the site may have been a royal burial ground. Originally named Kin Ich Ahau Bonil, Maya for "king of the solar countenance," the site was linked to astronomical practices in the ancient Maya culture. If you don't have time to visit the major sites, this one will give you an idea of what the ancient cities were like. ✉ *Blvd. Kukulcán, Km 17, Zona Hotelera* ☎ *998/883–0305* 💲 *$3* ⊙ *Daily 8–5.*

🏔️ ❷ **Yamil Lu'um.** A small sign at Sheraton Cancún Resort directs you to a dirt path leading to this site, which is on Cancún's highest point (the name Yamil Lu'um means "hilly land"). Although it comprises two structures—one probably a temple, the other probably a lighthouse—this is the smallest of Cancún's ruins. Discovered in 1842 by John Lloyd Stephens, the ruins date from the late 13th or early 14th century. ✉ *Blvd. Kukulcán, Km 12, Zona Hotelera* ☎ *No phone* 💲 *Free.*

BEACHES

Cancún Island is one long continuous beach. By law the entire coast of Mexico is federal property and open to the public. In reality, security guards discourage locals from using the beaches outside hotels. Some all-inclusives distribute neon wristbands to guests; those without a wristband aren't actually prohibited from being on the beach—just from entering or exiting via the hotel. Everyone is welcome to walk along the beach, as long as you get on or off from one of the public points. Although these points are often miles apart, one way around the situation is to find a hotel open to the public, go into the lobby bar for a drink or snack, and afterward go for a swim along the beach. All of the beaches can also be reached by public transportation; just let the driver know where you are headed.

Most hotel beaches have lifeguards, but, as with all ocean swimming, use common sense—even the calmest-looking waters can have currents and riptides. Overall, the beaches on the windward stretch of the island—those facing the Bahía de Mujeres—are best for swimming; farther out, the undertow can be tricky. ⚠ *Don't swim when the red or black danger flags fly; yellow flags indicate that you should proceed with caution, and green or blue flags mean the waters are calm.*

🕐 **Playa las Perlas** is the first beach on the drive heading east from El Centro along Boulevard Kukulcán. It's a relatively small beach on the pro-

Cancún's History

THE FIRST KNOWN SETTLERS OF THE AREA, the Maya, arrived in what is now Cancún centuries ago, and their ancestors remain in the area to this day. During the golden age of the Maya civilization (also referred to as the Classic Period), when other areas on the peninsula were developing trade routes and building enormous temples and pyramids, this part of the coast remained sparsely populated. Consequently Cancún never developed into a major Maya center; although exacavations have been done at the El Rey ruins (located in what is now the Zona Hotelera), the Maya communities that lived here around AD 1200 simply used this area for burial sites. Even the name given to the area was not inspiring: In Maya, Cancún means *nest of snakes*.

When Spanish conquistadores began to arrive in the early 1500s, much of the Maya culture was already in decline. Over the next three centuries, the Spanish largely ignored coastal areas like Cancún—which consisted mainly of low-lying scrub, mangroves, and swarms of mosquitoes—and focused on settling inland where there was more economic promise.

Although it received a few refugees from the War of the Castes, which engulfed the entire region in the mid-1800s, Cancún remained more or less undeveloped until the middle of the 20th century. By the 1950s, Acapulco had become the number-one tourist attraction in the country—and given the Mexican government its first taste of tourism dollars. When Acapulco's star began to fade in the late '60s, the government hired a market research company to determine the perfect location for developing Mexico's next big tourist destination—and the company picked Cancún.

In April 1971, Mexico's President, Luis Echeverria Alvarez, authorized the Ministry of Foreign Relations to buy the island and surrounding region. With a $22 million development loan from the World Bank and the Inter-American Development Bank, the transformation of Cancún began. At the time there were just 120 residents in the area, most of whom worked at a coconut plantation; by 1979, Cancún had become a resort of 40,000, attracting over two million tourists a year. And that was only the beginning: today, more than 500,000 people live in Cancún, and the city has become the most lucrative source of tourist income in Mexico.

tected waters of the Bahía de Mujeres, and is popular with locals. There aren't many public facilities here, and most of the water-sports activities are available only to those staying at the nearby resorts such as Club las Perlas or the Blue Bay Getaway. At Km 4 on Boulevard Kukulcán, **Playa Linda** is where the ocean meets the fresh water of Laguna Nichupté to create the Nichupté Channel. There's lots of boat activity along the channel, and the ferry to Isla Mujeres leaves from the adjoining Embarcadero marina, so the area isn't safe for swimming—although it's a great place to people-watch. Small, placid **Playa Langosta**, which starts at Boulevard Kukulcán's Km 4, has calm waters that make it an excellent place for a swim, although it has no public facilities. It's usually filled with tourists and vacationing spring-breakers since it's close to many of the large all-inclusive hotels. Its safe waters and gentle waves make it a popular beach with families as well. **Playa Tortugas,** the last "real" beach along the east–west stretch of the Zona Hotelera, has lots of hotels with lots of sand in between. There are restaurants, changing areas, and restrooms at either end of the beach (it stretches between about Km 6 and Km 8 on Boulevard Kukulcán). The swimming is excellent, and many people come here to sail, snorkel, kayak, paraglide, and use Wave Runners.

Playa Caracol, the outermost beach in the Zona Hotelera, is a beach only in name. The whole area has been eaten up by development—in particular the monstrous Xcaret bus station and office complex. This beach is also hindered by the rocks that jut out from the water marking the beginning of Punta Cancún, where Boulevard Kukulcán turns south. There are several hotels along this beach and a few sports rental outfits, but almost no one uses this beach for swimming. Heading down from Punta Cancún onto the long, southerly stretch of the island, **Playa Chacmool** is the first beach on the Caribbean's open waters. It's close to several shopping centers and the party zone, so there are plenty of restaurants nearby. The shallow clear water makes it tempting to walk far out into the ocean, but be careful—there's a strong current and undertow. **Playa Marlin,** at Km 13 along Boulevard Kukulcán, is in the heart of the Zona Hotelera and accessible via area resorts (access is easiest at Occidental Caribbean Village). It's a seductive beach with turquoise waters and silky sands, but like most beaches facing the Caribbean, the waves are strong and the currents are dangerous. There aren't any public facilities.

Playa Ballenas starts off with some rather large rocks at about Km 14 on Boulevard Kukulcán, but it widens shortly afterward and extends down for another breathtaking—and sandy—3 km (5 mi). The wind here is strong, making the surf rough, and several hotels have put up ropes and buoys to help swimmers make their way safely in and out of the water. Access is via one of the hotels, such as Le Meridien or JW Marriott. **Playa Delfines** is the final beach, at Km 20 where Boulevard Kukulcán curves into a hill. There's an incredible lookout over the ocean; on a clear day you can see at least four shades of blue in the water, though swimming is treacherous unless one of the green flags is posted. Though this beach is starting to become popular with the gay and surfing crowds, there are usually few people here—so if you like solitary sunbathing, this is the place for you. South of the El Rey ruins (which are across the street from the water) the beach becomes very narrow and rocky, disappearing altogether by the time you reach the Westin Regina.

WHERE TO EAT

Cancún attracts chefs—as well as visitors—from around the globe, so the area has choices to suit just about every palate (from Provençal cuisine to traditional Mexican and American diner fare). Both the Zona Hotelera and El Centro have plenty of great places to eat. Menus at the more upscale spots change on a regular basis, usually every three to six months, so expect to be pleasantly surprised.

While there are some pitfalls—restaurants that line Avenida Tulum are often noisy and crowded; gas fumes make it hard to enjoy alfresco meals; and Zona Hotelera chefs often cater to what they assume is a visitor preference for bland food—one key to eating well is to find the local haunts, most of which are in El Centro. The restaurants in the Parque de las Palapas, just off Avenida Tulum, serve expertly prepared Mexican food. Farther into the city center, you can find fresh seafood and traditional fare at dozens of small, reasonably priced restaurants in the Mercado Veintiocho (Market 28).

Dress is casual in Cancún, but many restaurants do not allow bare feet, short shorts, bathing suits, or no shirt. At upscale restaurants, pants, skirts, or dresses are favored over shorts at dinnertime. Unless otherwise stated, restaurants serve lunch and dinner daily. Large breakfast and brunch buffets are among the most popular meals in the Zona Hotelera. With prices ranging from $3 to $15 per person, they are a good value—if you eat on the late side, you won't need to eat again until dinner. They are especially pleasant at palapa restaurants on the beach.

The success or failure of many restaurants is dependent on how Cancún is doing as a whole. The city is currently undergoing a great deal of development, with properties being sold and major renovations being planned. Some of the restaurants listed here may have changed names, or menus, by the time you visit.

Prices

	WHAT IT COSTS In Dollars				
	$$$$	$$$	$$	$	¢
AT DINNER	over $25	$15–$25	$10–$15	$5–$10	under $5

Per person, for a main course at dinner, excluding tax and tip.

Zona Hotelera

Contemporary

$$$$ ✕ **Club Grill.** The dining room here is romantic and quietly elegant—with rich wood, fresh flowers, crisp linens, and courtyard views—and the classic dishes have a distinctly Mexican flavor. The menu changes every six months, but might include starters like coconut-infused scallops and lobster cream soup, or main

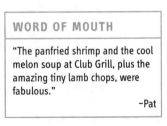

WORD OF MOUTH

"The panfried shrimp and the cool melon soup at Club Grill, plus the amazing tiny lamb chops, were fabulous."

–Pat

courses like chipotle-roasted duck or seared sea bass with artichoke ravioli. The tasting menu offers a small selection of all the courses paired with wines and followed by wickedly delicious desserts. ⊠ *Ritz-Carlton Cancún, Blvd. Kukulcán, Km 14 (Retorno del Rey 36), Zona Hotelera* ☎ *998/881–0808* ▤ *AE, MC, V* ☾ *No lunch.*

$$$–$$$$ ✕ **Le Basilic.** The dishes here—created by French chef Henri Charvet—are as sophisticated as the oak-and-marble dining room where they're served. The squid with sweet garlic or the terrine of lobster makes the perfect opener to your meal; the oven-roasted robalo fish stuffed with lime and perfumed with fresh thyme is also supremely satisfying. Reservations are recommended. ⊠ *Fiesta Americana Grand Coral Beach, Blvd. Kukulcán, Km 9.5, Lote 6, Zona Hotelera* ☎ *998/881–3200 Ext. 3380* ⊟ *AE, MC, V.*

$$$–$$$$
Fodor'sChoice
★
✕ **Laguna Grill.** Intricate tile work adorns this restaurant's floors and walls, and a natural stream divides the open-air dining room, which overlooks the lagoon. Chef Alex Rudin's menu changes often, but is consistently imaginative: choices might include Thai duck satay or panko-crusted softshell crabs as starters, or entrées like lobster-and-truffle lasagna or sesame-blackened ahi tuna. On Fridays and Saturdays, the prime rib special is a showstopper. The wine menu is excellent, too. ⊠ *Blvd. Kukulcán, Km 15.6, Zona Hotelera* ☎ *998/885–0267* ⊟ *AE, MC, V.*

Italian

$$$–$$$$ ✕ **La Madonna.** This dramatic-looking restaurant is a great place to enjoy a selection of martinis and cigars, as well as Italian food "with a creative Swiss twist." You can enjoy classics like lasagna, fettuccine with shrimp and sun-dried tomatoes, glazed beef fillet au gratin, and three-cheese ravioli alongside large Greek caryatid-style statues, and a mas-

> **WORD OF MOUTH**
>
> "We stumbled onto La Madonna by a stroke of luck about two years ago. What an exceptional evening! The atmosphere, service, martini bar, and food were memorable."
> –Andy Bouchard

sive reproduction of the Mona Lisa. The Panama Jack martini (a classic martini with a splash of rum) is a tad expensive but worth it. ⊠ *La Isla Shopping Village, Blvd. Kukulcán, Km 12.5, Zona Hotelera* ☎ *998/883–4837* ⌕ *Reservations essential* ⊟ *AE, D, MC, V.*

$$–$$$$ ✕ **Casa Rolandi.** The secret to this restaurant's success is its creative handling of Swiss and northern Italian cuisine. Be sure to try the *carpaccio di pesce* (thin slices of fresh raw fish), the homemade lasagna, or the *saltimbocca alla romana* (veal scaloppine sautéed with Parma ham). Appetizers are also tempting: there's puff bread from a wood-burning oven, and a huge salad and antipasto bar. The beautiful dining room and attentive service might make you want to stay for hours. ⊠ *Plaza Caracol, Blvd. Kukulcán, Km 8.5, Zona Hotelera* ☎ *998/883–2557* ⊟ *AE, D, MC, V.*

$$–$$$$
Fodor'sChoice
★
✕ **Gustino Italian Beachside Grill.** From the moment you walk down the dramatic staircase to enter this restaurant, you'll know you're in for a memorable dining experience. The dining room has sleek leather furniture, artistic lighting, and views of the wine cellar and open-air kitchen—where chef Richard Sylvester works his magic. The *ostriche alla provenzale* (black-shelled mussels in a spicy tomato sauce) appetizer is a standout, as are the salmon-stuffed ravioli and seafood risotto entrées. The service here is impeccable; the violin music adds a dash

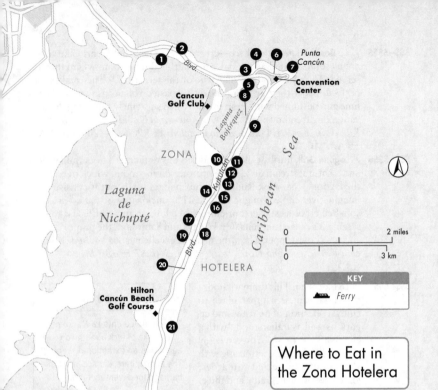

Where to Eat in
the Zona Hotelera

of romance. Reservations are recommended. ⊠ *JW Marriott Resort, Blvd. Kukulcán, Km 14.5, Zona Hotelera* ☎ *998/848–9600 Ext. 6649* ▭ *AE, MC, V* ⊗ *No lunch.*

$–$$$ ✕ **Cenacola.** Reliably good pizza and pasta have made this casual restaurant a favorite with locals, as well as visitors. Though it's located inside a mall, the dining room is pleasant, and has a garden patio looking out onto the street. The green salads here are fresh, and the ravioli and lasagna are rich and tasty. ⊠ *Kukulcán Plaza, Blvd. Kukulcán, Km 13, Zona Hotelera* ☎ *998/885-3603* ▭ *AE, MC, V.*

$–$$$ ✕ **La Dolce Vita.** This grand dame of Cancún restaurants delivers on the promise of its name (which means "the sweet life" in Italian). Whether you dine indoors or on the terrace overlooking the lagoon, the candlelit tables adorned with fine linen and china, soft music, and discreet waiters will make you feel you've arrived. The Italian fare includes Bolognese-style lasagna, green taglierini with lobster medallions, and veal ravioli in wild mushroom sauce; the wine list is also excellent.

> **WORD OF MOUTH**
>
> "We loved this romantic Italian restaurant, La Dolce Vita. Our table overlooked the lagoon . . . BEAU-TIFUL! The waiter was knowledgeable and the food was *delicioso*!
> –Leah

Be patient when waiting for your order, though—good food takes time. ⊠ *Blvd. Kukulcán, Km 14.5, Zona Hotelera* ☎ *998/885–0150* ▭ *AE, D, MC, V.*

Japanese

$$$–$$$$ ✕ **Mitachi.** The moonlight on the water, the sounds of the surf, the superbly attentive staff, and the artwork by Japanese ceramist Mineo Mizumo all help to make this restaurant feel like a sanctuary. The setting is the star attraction here but there are also some good menu choices, like the crisp yellowtail snapper and the Caribbean seafood hot pot. ⊠ *Hilton Cancún, Blvd. Kukulcán, Km 17 (Retorno Lacandones), Zona Hotelera* ☎ *998/881–8000* ▭ *AE, D, MC, V.*

$–$$$ ✕ **Mikado.** Sit around the *teppanyaki* tables and watch the utensils fly as the showmen chefs here prepare steaks, seafood, and vegetables. The menu includes Thai as well as Japanese specialties. The sushi, tempura, grilled salmon, and beef teriyaki are feasts fit for a shogun. ⊠ *Marriott Casa Magna, Blvd. Kukulcán, Km 14.5, Zona Hotelera* ☎ *998/881–2000* ▭ *DC, MC, V* ⊗ *No lunch.*

Mexican

$$–$$$$ ✕ **La Joya.** The dramatic interior of this restaurant has three levels of stained-glass windows, a fountain, artwork, and beautiful furniture from central Mexico. The food is traditional but creative; one especially popular dish is the beef medallions marinated in red wine. The lobster quesadilla is also wonderful, as is the salmon fillet with vegetable tamales. ⊠ *Fiesta Americana Grand Coral Beach, Blvd. Kukulcán, Km 9.5* ☎ *998/881–3200 before 5 PM Ext. 3380, after 5 PM Ext. 4200* ▭ *DC, MC, V.*

$$–$$$ ✕ **La Destileria.** Be prepared to have your perceptions of tequila changed forever. In what looks like an old-time Mexican hacienda, you can sam-

ple from a list of 100 varieties—in shots or superb margaritas—and also visit an on-site tequila museum and store. The traditional Mexican menu focuses on wonderfully fresh fish and seafood; highlights include the *aguascaliente* soup (a creamy concoction with zucchini flowers) and the Veracruz-style fresh fish. Be sure to leave room for the caramel crepes—they're a traditional Mexican dessert. ⊠ *Blvd. Kukulcán, Km 12.65 (across from Plaza Kukulcán), Zona Hotelera* ☎ *998/885–1086 or 998/885–1087* ☐ *AE, MC, V.*

$$–$$$ ✕ **Maria Bonita.** This is one of the best places in the Hotel Zone to get authentic Mexican cuisine—so be adventurous! Traditional fare like chicken almond mole (with chocolate, almonds, and chilies) is fabulous here—and if you're unsure about what to order, the menu explains the different chilies used in many of the dishes. The glass-enclosed patio with its water view is a great place to linger over tequila—

> ### WORD OF MOUTH
>
> "Make sure you're in a party mood before you come to Maria Bonita."
> –Frank

or to try the tamarind margaritas. ⊠ *Dreams Cancún Resort & Spa, Punta Cancún, Blvd. Kukulcán, Km 9, Zona Hotelera* ☎ *998/848–7082* ☐ *AE, D, MC, V* ☺ *No lunch.*

$–$$$ ✕ **La Casa de las Margaritas.** With folk art and traditional textiles adorning every inch of space, this restaurant is a festive (though not exactly tranquil) place to enjoy a Mexican meal. Appetizers include yummy pork tamales and a poblano-pepper cream soup; for a main course, you can try tequila chicken, beef fajitas, or mango shrimp. The rich *tres leche* (three milk) cake makes a fine finish. ⊠ *La Isla Shopping Village, Blvd. Kukulcán, Km 12.5, Zona Hotelera* ☎ *998/883–3222* ☐ *MC, V.*

$–$$$ ✕ **Hacienda el Mortero.** The main draw at this eatery is the setting: it's a replica of a 17th-century traditional hacienda, complete with courtyard fountain, flowering garden, and even a strolling mariachi band. Although there's nothing outstanding on the traditional Mexican menu, the tortilla soup is delicious and the chicken fajitas and rib-eye steaks are decent. Fish lovers may also like the *pescado Veracruzana*, fresh grouper prepared Veracruz-style with olives, garlic, and fresh tomatoes. This is a popular restaurant for large groups, so be warned: it can get boisterous. ⊠ *NH Krystal Cancún, Blvd. Kukulcán, Km 9, Zona Hotelera* ☎ *998/848–9800* ☐ *AE, MC, V.*

$–$$$ ✕ **Isabella's.** Popular with an older crowd, this restaurant is part of the Royal Bandstand entertainment center at the Royal Sands Resort. Beveled glass doors, fresh flowers, polished wood, comfortable high-backed chairs and European oil paintings create a warm and intimate setting here. Menu highlights include the goat cheese and mango salad, Tampico chicken breast, rack of lamb and pork tenderloin. After dinner, you can hit the club next door for live music and dancing. ⊠ *Royal Sands Resort, Blvd. Kukulcán, Km 13.5, Zona Hotelera* ☎ *998/881–2220* ☐ *AE, MC, V* ☺ *No lunch.*

Seafood

$$–$$$$ ✕ **Plantation House.** You can't beat the romantic location overlooking the lagoon of this restaurant done up to resemble an elegant plantation home. Walk down the steps into the lobby and you are actually over the water. The menu focuses on lobster and seafood done in a variety of ways. Dishes are named after Caribbean islands such as St. Lucia— a medley of sea scallops in a garlic-chili vinaigrette. Dress code in effect. ⊠ *Blvd. Kukulcán, Km 10.5 Zona Hotelera* ☎ *998/883–1455 or 998/883–1433* ⊟ *AE, MC, V.*

$–$$$$ ✕ **Lorito Joe's.** This restaurant has a lovely terrace overlooking the Laguna Nichupté and surrounding mangroves. The crab-and-lobster all-you-can-eat buffet (displayed on two giant oyster shells) is a great deal, especially for families; other menu items here, however, tend to be overpriced. ⊠ *Blvd. Kukulcán, Km 14.5, Zona Hotelera* ☎ *998/885–1536* ⊟ *AE, MC, V.*

$–$$$ ✕ **Mocambo.** This tiny, excellent beachside eatery is a perfect place for a relaxed lunch or dinner. Sit outside on the deck or inside—both overlook the Langosta pier and beach—and enjoy black pasta with garlic shrimp or a freshly grilled catch of the day. The Wednesday all-you-can-eat special, which costs $14 and includes beer, is the best bargain in the Hotel Zone. ⊠ *Blvd. Kukulcán, Km 4, beside the Scenic tower, Zona Hotelera* ☎ *998/883–0398* ⊟ *No credit cards.*

Steak

$$–$$$$ ✕ **Porterhouse Grill.** The wooden floors and elegantly set tables at this eatery evoke a New York–style steak house. After choosing your steak from a display case, you can watch as it's prepared in the open-grill kitchen. If you're not tempted by the pan-seared filet mignon or the cowboy rib eye, try the sautéed fish in a Creole pecan sauce. The wine list is superb here, as are the martinis; you can also top off your dinner with a cigar from the excellent collection. ⊠ *Blvd. Kukulcán, Km 12, Zona Hotelera* ☎ *998/848–8390* ⊟ *MC, V.*

$–$$$ ✕ **Rio Churrascaria Steak House.** It's easy to overlook this Brazilian restaurant because of its generic, unimpressive exterior—but make no mistake, it's the best steak restaurant in the Zona Hotelera. The waiters here walk among the tables carrying different mouthwatering meats that have been slow-cooked over charcoal on skewers (beside Angus beef, there are also cuts of pork, chicken, and sausages). Simply point at what you'd like; the waiters slice it directly onto your plate. There are some good seafood starters, including the oyster cocktail and king crab salad—but if you're not a true carnivore, you probably won't be happy here. ⊠ *Blvd. Kukulcán, Km 3.5, Zona Hotelera* ☎ *998/849–9040* ⊟ *AE, MC, V.*

El Centro

Cafés

$–$$ ✕ **Roots.** Locals and tourists mingle here to enjoy fusion jazz and flamenco music (piped-in during the day, but live at night). The performances are the main attraction, but there's also an eclectic, international menu of salads, soups, sandwiches, and pastas offered. The tables nearest the window are the best place to tuck into your Chinese chicken or German sausage, since the air tends to get smoky closer to the stage. ⊠ *Av. Tulipanes 26, Sm 22* ☎ *998/884–2437* ⊟ *D, MC, V* ☉ *Closed Sun. No lunch.*

¢–$ ✕ **La Pasteleteria-Crepería.** This small café and bakery has cheerful green-and-white booths, where you can sample terrific soups and crepes (the turkey-breast crepe makes a perfect lunch), as well as a variety of sumptuous pastries baked on site. There's a small gourmet shop selling hard-to-find items like speciality vinegars and oils, too. ⊠ *Av. Cobá 7, Sm 25* ☎ *998/884–3420* ▭ *AE, V.*

¢–$ ✕ **Ty-Coz.** Tucked behind the Comercial Mexicana grocery store and across from the bus station on Avenida Tulum, this restaurant serves excellent Continental breakfasts with croissants and freshly brewed coffee. Lunches are a combination of sandwiches and salads served on freshly baked baguettes. Pictures of the Brittany region of France adorn the walls of the bright dining room. ⊠ *Av. Tulum, Sm 2* ☎ *No phone* ▭ *No credit cards.*

Caribbean

$–$$$ ✕ **La Habichuela.** Elegant yet cozy, the much-loved Green Bean has a dining area full of Maya sculptures and local trees and flowers. Don't miss the famous *crema de habichuela* (a rich, cream-based seafood soup) or the *cocobichuela* (lobster and shrimp in a light curry sauce served inside

> **WORD OF MOUTH**
>
> "You cannot say you have visited Cancún unless you eat at La Habichuela."
>
> –Jim

a coconut). Finish off your meal with Xtabentun, a Maya liqueur made with honey and anise. ⊠ *Av. Margaritas 25, Sm 22* ☎ *998/884–3158* ▭ *AE, MC, V.*

Chinese

¢–$$ ✕ **Hong Kong.** If you're missing your favorite take-out Chinese food, then head over to Hong Kong. You can order from the take-out counter or sit in the cozy restaurant filled with plants. It serves the usual egg rolls, fried rice, sweet-and-sour chicken, and garlic spareribs—and a morning breakfast buffet that's a terrific bargain. The food may not be particularly inspired, but it's fresh and reasonably priced. ⊠ *Av. Cobá 97, Sm 21* ☎ *998/892–3456* ▭ *D, MC, V.*

Eclectic

$–$$ ✕ **Mesón del Vecindario.** This sweet little restaurant, tucked away from the street, resembles a Swiss A-frame house. The menu has all kinds of cheese and beef fondues along with terrific salads, fresh pasta, and baked goods. Breakfasts are hearty and economical, and very popular with locals. ⊠ *Av. Uxmal 23, Sm 3* ☎ *998/884–8900* ▭ *AE, MC, V* ⊗ *Closed Sun.*

Italian

$$–$$$$ ✕ **Locanda Paolo.** Flowers and artwork lend warmth to this sophisticated restaurant, and the staff is attentive without being fussy. The southern Italian cuisine—which includes black pasta with calamari, steamed lobster in garlic sauce, and grilled dorado (mahimahi)—is inventive and delicious. ⊠ *Av. Bonampak 145, between Avs. Uxmal and Cobá, Sm 3* ☎ *998/887–2627* ▭ *AE, D, DC, MC, V.*

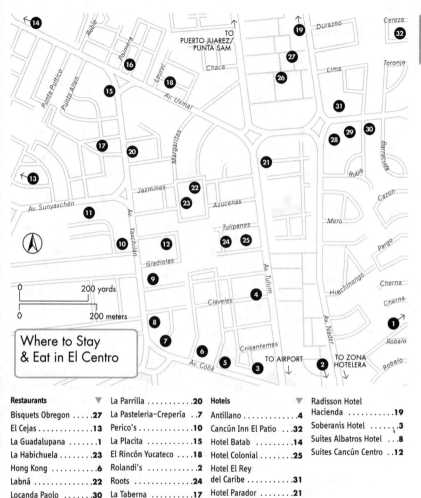

Where to Stay
& Eat in El Centro

Restaurants ▼
Bisquets Obregon **27**
El Cejas **13**
La Guadalupana **1**
La Habichuela **23**
Hong Kong **6**
Labná **22**
Locanda Paolo **30**
Mesón del
Vecindario **28**
100% Natural **11**

La Parrilla **20**
La Pasteleria-Crepería . . **7**
Perico's **10**
La Placita **15**
El Rincón Yucateco **18**
Rolandi's **2**
Roots **24**
La Taberna **17**
El Tacolote **5**
Ty-Coz **26**
Yamamoto **29**

Hotels ▼
Antillano **4**
Cancún Inn El Patio . . **32**
Hotel Batab **14**
Hotel Colonial **25**
Hotel El Rey
del Caribe **31**
Hotel Parador **21**
Maria de Lourdes **9**
Mexico Hostels **16**

Radisson Hotel
Hacienda **19**
Soberanis Hotel . . . . . , .**3**
Suites Albatros Hotel . . .**8**
Suites Cancún Centro . . **12**

Japanese

$–$$$ ✕ **Yamamoto.** The sushi here is some of the best in the area, althought there's also a menu of traditional Japanese dishes (like beef teriyaki and tempura) for those who prefer their food cooked. The dining room is tranquil, with Japanese art and bamboo accents—but you can also call for delivery to your hotel room. ⊠ *Av. Uxmal 31, Sm 3* ☎ *998/887–3366, 998/860–0269 for delivery service* ▭ *AE, MC, V.*

Mexican

$$–$$$$ ✕ **La Parrilla.** With its palapa-style roof, flamboyant live mariachi music, and energetic waiters, this place is a Cancún classic. The menu isn't fancy, but it offers good, basic Mexican food. Two reliably tasty choices are the mixed grill (chicken, steak, shrimp) and the grilled Tampiqueña-style steak; for accompaniment, you can choose from a wide selection of tequilas. ⊠ *Av. Yaxchilán 51, Sm 22* ☎ *998/884–8193* ▭ *AE, D, MC, V.*

★ **$–$$$** ✕ **Labná.** Yucatecan cuisine reaches new and exotic heights at this Maya-themed restaurant, with fabulous dishes prepared by chef Carlos Hannon. The *papadzules*—tortillas stuffed with eggs and covered with pumpkin sauce—are a delicious starter; for an entrée, try the savory *papadzules* (tortillas stuffed with eggs in pumpkin sauce), *poc chuc*, tender pork loin in a sour-orange sauce, or *Longaniza de Valladolid,* traditional sausage from the village of Valladolid. Finish off your meal with some *guayaba* (guava) mousse and Xtabentun-infused Maya coffee. ⊠ *Av. Margaritas 29, Sm 22* ☎ *998/885–3158* ▭ *AE, D, MC, V.*

$–$$$ ✕ **Perico's.** Okay—it's a tourist trap. But it's really fun. Bar stools here are topped with saddles, and waiters dressed as *zapatas* (revolutionaries) serve flaming drinks and desserts while mariachi and marimba bands play (loudly). Every so often everyone jumps up to join the conga line; your reward for galloping through the restaurant and nearby streets is a free shot of tequila. The Mexican menu is passable but the real reason to come is the nonstop party. ⊠ *Av. Yaxchilán 61, Sm 25* ☎ *998/884–3152* ▭ *AE, MC, V.*

$–$$ ✕ **La Guadalupana.** This lively cantina serves up steak, fajitas, tacos, and other traditional Mexican dishes to an appreciative crowd. It's decorated with art and photos of famous bullfighters—very appropriate since it's right next to Cancún's bullring. ⊠ *Av. Bonampak (Plaza de Toros), Sm 4* ☎ *998/887–0660* ▭ *MC, V.*

¢–$$ ✕ **El Tacolote.** A great place to stop for lunch, this popular *taqueria* (taco stand) sells delicious fajitas, grilled kebabs, and all kinds of tacos. The salsa, which comes free with every meal, is fresh and *muy picante* (very hot). ⊠ *Av. Cobá 19, Sm 22* ☎ *998/887–3045* ▭ *MC, V.*

¢–$ ✕ **Bisquets Obregon.** With its cheery lunch counter and two levels of tables, this cafeteria-style spot is *the* place to have breakfast downtown. Begin your day early (food is served starting at 7 AM) with hearty Mexican classics like huevos rancheros (eggs sunny-side up on tortillas, covered with tomato salsa). The *cafe con leche* (coffee with hot milk) is also delicious—and just watching the waiters pour it is impressive. ⊠ *Av. Náder 9, Sm 2* ☎ *998/887–6876* ▭ *MC, V.*

¢–$ ✕ **La Placita.** The menu is simple but tasty at this colorfully decorated, casual taqueria. The mixed grill of chicken breast, steak, and pork chops is a standout, as are the glorious barbequed ribs and the tequila shrimp. A cold beer makes a perfect accompaniment. ⊠ *Av. Yaxchilán 12, Sm 22* ☏ *998/884–0407* ⊟ *No credit cards.*

¢–$ ✕ **El Rincón Yucateco.** It's so small here that the tables spill out onto the street—but that makes it a great place to people-watch. The traditional Yucatecan dishes here are outstanding; the *panuchos* (puffed corn tortillas stuffed with black beans and topped with barbecued pork), and the *sopa de lima* (shredded chicken in a tangy broth of chicken stock and lime juice) should not be missed. ⊠ *Av. Uxmal 35, Sm 22* ☏ *No phone* ⊟ *No credit cards.*

¢–$ ✕ **La Taberna.** This is a local cyber-bar where you can surf the Web, check your e-mail and enjoy great bar food like hamburgers, sandwiches, and nachos. The full screen TV showing a variety of sports, pool tables and card games are a big draw with locals. Lunch specials off the menu are a good bargain and there is an extensive beer and cocktail menu for you to enjoy the afternoon and evening happy hour. ⊠ *Av. Yaxchilán 23-A, Sm 22* ☏ *998/887–5423* ⊟ *No credit cards.*

Pizza

¢–$$ ✕ **Rolandi's.** A Cancún landmark for over 15 years, Rolandi's continues to draw crowds with its scrumptious wood-fired pizzas. There are 15 varieties to choose from—if you can't make up your mind, try the delicious one made with Roquefort cheese. Homemade pasta dishes are also very good. Anything on the menu can be delivered to your hotel (a nice option if the staff is having a cranky night). ⊠ *Av. Cobá 12, Sm 3* ☏ *998/884–4047* ⊟ *MC, V.*

Seafood

$–$$$ ✕ **El Cejas.** The seafood is fresh at this open-air eatery and the clientele is lively—often joining in song with the musicians who stroll among the tables. If you've had a wild night, try the *vuelva la vida*, or "return to life" (conch, oysters, shrimp, octopus, calamari, and fish with a hot tomato sauce). The ceviche and hot, spicy shrimp soup are both good as well, though the quality can be inconsistent. ⊠ *Mercado Veintiocho, Av. Sunyaxchén, Sm 26* ☏ *998/887–1080* ⊟ *No credit cards.*

> **WORD OF MOUTH**
>
> "El Cejas is tricky to find but do yourself a favor and find it. The packed house of locals will clue you in on the quality and value. Start off with a cold bottle of Sol cerveza. Follow-up with an appetizer of ceviche to experience manna. Finish with an entrée of whole-grilled snapper to complete your dining experience. You'll be back."   –Vince

Vegetarian

¢–$ ✕ **100% Natural.** Looking for something light and healthy? Head to one of these cheery open-air restaurants, where you'll be surrounded by plants and modern Maya sculptures. The menus emphasize soups, veggie salads, fresh fruit drinks, and other nonmeat items, though egg dishes, sandwiches, grilled chicken and fish, and Mexican and Italian specialties are also available. ⊠ *El Centro: Av. Sunyaxchén 62, Sm 25* ☏ *998/884–0724* ⊟ *D, MC, V.* ⊠ *Zona Hotelera: Kukulcán Shopping Plaza, Blvd. Kukulcán, Km 13.5* ☏ *998/885–2904.*

WHERE TO STAY

You might find it bewildering to choose among Cancún's many hotels, not least because brochures and Web sites make them sound—and look—almost exactly alike. For luxury and amenities, the Zona Hotelera is the place to stay. Boulevard Kukulcán, the district's main thoroughfare, is artfully landscaped with palm trees, sculpted bushes, waterfalls, and tiered pools. The hotels pride themselves on delivering endless opportunities for fun; most have water sports, golf, tennis, kids' clubs, fitness centers, spas, shopping, entertainment, dining, and tours and excursions (along with warm attentive Mexican service). None of this comes cheaply, however; hotels here are expensive. In the modest Centro, local color outweighs facilities. The hotels here are more basic and much less expensive than those in the Zona.

Recently, Cancún has been experiencing a wave of new development, and as a result many of the hotels have been renovating, going up for sale, and changing hands. As a result, you may find that some properties listed in this guide are slightly different when you visit than they were when the original reviews were written. Some may even have different names.

Prices

Many hotels have all-inclusive packages, as well as theme-night parties complete with food, beverages, activities, and games. Mexican, Italian, and Caribbean themes seem to be the most popular. Take note, however, that the larger the all-inclusive resort, the blander the food. (It's difficult to provide inventive fare when serving hundreds of people.) For more memorable dining, you may need to leave the grounds. Expect high prices for food and drink in most hotels. Many of the more exclusive hotels are starting to enforce a "no outside food or drink" policy—so be discreet when bringing outside food or drinks into your room, or they may be confiscated.

Many of the larger and more popular all-inclusives will no longer guarantee an ocean-view room when you book your reservation. If this is crucial to your stay, then check that all rooms have ocean views at your chosen hotel, or book only at places that will guarantee a view. Be sure to bring your confirmation information with you to prove you paid for an ocean-view room. Also be careful with towel charges since many of the resorts have started charging up to $25 for towels not returned. Be sure your returns are duly noted by the pool staff.

WHAT IT COSTS In Dollars				
$$$$	$$$	$$	$	¢
FOR 2 PEOPLE over $250	$150–$250	$75–$150	$50–$75	under $50

All prices are for a standard double room in high season, based on the European Plan (EP) and excluding service and 12% tax (10% Value Added Tax plus 2% hospitality tax).

Isla Blanca/Punta Sam

The area north of Cancún is slowly being developed into an alternative hotel zone, known informally as Zona Hotelera Norte. This is an ideal area for a tranquil beach vacation, since the shops, restaurants, and nightlife of Cancún are about 45 minutes away by cab.

$–$$ ▦ **Hacienda Punta Sam.** Surrounded by trees, and set on a private beach just minutes away from the Puerto Juárez docks, this hotel feels far away from the bustle of the Zona Hotelera. The rooms here are spacious, with palapa-roofed decks or terraces, large windows, and king-size or double beds. There's a freshwater swimming pool and a game room, and the garden and beach are both gorgeous. Since this place is popular with Europeans, topless sunbathing is permitted. Children are also welcome. An all-inclusive rate (including three meals per day with two dining rooms to choose from) is available. You must book online. ⊠ *Carr. Puerto Juárez–Punta Sam, Km 3.5, 77500 Punta Sam* ☎ *998/887–9330* 🖷 *998/884–0520* ⊕ *www.travel-center.com/hoteles/hoteles.asp?Hotel=0074* ➶ *35 rooms* ♨ *2 restaurants, 2 pools, beach, private dock, game room, laundry service, car rental; no room TVs, no room phones* ⊟ *AE, MC, V* ⦿ *AI, EP.*

Zona Hotelera

★ **$$$$** ▦ **Fiesta Americana Grand Aqua.** Opened in December 2004, this five-star hotel with its sleek, modern architecture epitomizes understated elegance. Rooms are chic and clean-lined, with every amenity imaginable—including flat-screen TVs, Molton Brown toiletries, and a pillow menu. While all rooms have balconies and most are spacious, not all have ocean views—the less expensive rooms overlook the garden. Yoga and Pilates classes, as well as *temezcal* (Maya-style sweat lodge) and beauty treatments, are offered at the spa. The on-site restaurants serve fare ranging from Mediterranean seafood to deli sandwiches. ⊠ *Blvd. Kukulcán, Km 12.5, Zona Hotelera* ☎ *998/881–7633* 🖷 *998/881–7635* ⊕ *www.fiestaamericana.com* ➶ *335 rooms, 36 suites* ♨ *4 restaurants, cable TV with DVDs, in-room data ports, 2 bars, 8 pools, hot tubs, business services, meeting rooms, beauty salon, spa, fitness center, shops, 2 tennis courts, children's programs (ages 4–12)* ⊟ *AE, D, DC, MC, V.*

★ **$$$$** ▦ **Fiesta Americana Grand Coral Beach.** If luxury's your bag, you'll feel right at home at this distinctive salmon-colored hotel. The vast lobby has stained-glass skylights, sculptures, plants, and mahogany furniture; guest rooms have marble floors, small sitting rooms, and balconies overlooking the Bahía de Mujeres. The beach here is small, but there's a 660-foot pool surrounded by a lush exotic flower garden. Exceptional dining is only steps away at the hotel's restaurant, Le Basilic. ⊠ *Blvd. Kukulcán, Km 9.5, Zona*

> **WORD OF MOUTH**
>
> "The Fiesta Americana Grand Coral Beach has the best beach location in Cancún. The ocean is calm and perfect for swimming. And the pools are fantastic with swim-up bars."
>
> –Sangeet

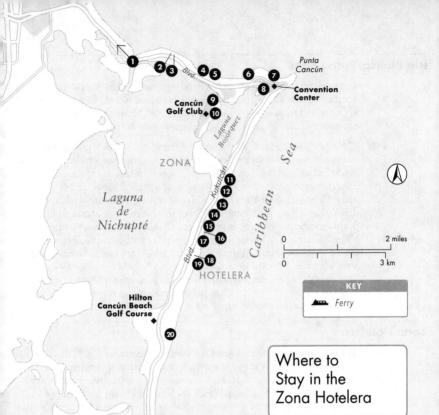

Where to
Stay in the
Zona Hotelera

Hotelera ☎ *998/881–3200 or 800/343–7821* 📠 *998/881–3273* ⊕ *www. fiestaamericana.com* 🛏 *542 rooms, 60 suites* ⚐ *5 restaurants, cable TV with video games, pool, health club, hair salon, spa, beach, 5 bars, babysitting, children's programs (ages 4–12), Internet, business services, car rental, free parking* ⊟ *AE, D, DC, MC, V.*

$$$$ ☒ **Golden Crown Paradise Spa.** Romantic rooms at this all-inclusive, adults-only resort have private Jacuzzis, and are warmly decorated with sunset colors, flower arrangements, and rich wood furniture. Small sitting areas open up onto balconies with ocean or lagoon views. The beach here is small, but there's a comfortable pool area with two tiers of deck chairs and palapas. The spa offers massages and facials and the restaurants are bright and airy. This hotel provides great luxury at a reasonable price. ☒ *Blvd. Kukulcán, Km 14.5 (Retorno Sn. Miguelito Lt. 37), Zona Hotelera* ☎ *998/885–0909* 📠 *998/885–1919* ⊕ *www. crownparadise.com* 🛏 *214 rooms* ⚐ *4 restaurants, cable TV, miniature golf, tennis courts, pools, spa, beach, billiards, 4 bars, Internet, car rental, travel services, free parking; no kids* ⊟ *AE, D, DC, MC, V* ⍾⊙⍾ *AI.*

$$$$ ☒ **JW Marriott Cancún Resort & Spa.**

Fodor'sChoice
★

This is the best hotel for luxury Cancún style and service. Plush is the name of the game at this towering beach resort, where manicured lawns are dotted with fountains and pools, and large vaulted windows let sunlight stream into a lobby decorated with marble, rich carpets and beau-

WORD OF MOUTH

"What sets the JW Marriott apart is the incredible service and attitude of the staff. You are literally treated like royalty."

–Mariah

tiful flower arrangements. All rooms have ocean views and are elegantly decorated with blond wood and cream-colored leather. The palatial marble bathrooms have spalike, spray-jet showers. For more pampering, you can visit the spa for massages and facials. Afterwards you can also relax by the 20-foot dive pool with its artificial reef. In the evening you can dine at the delicious Gustino Italian Beachside Grill. ☒ *Blvd. Kukulcán, Km 14.5, Zona Hotelera* ☎ *998/848–9600 or 800/228–9290* 📠 *998/848–9601* ⊕ *www.marriott.com* 🛏 *448 rooms, 36 suites* ⚐ *3 restaurants, cable TV with video games, 2 tennis courts, 2 pools, hot tub, gym, hair salon, spa, beach, dock, 3 bars, 2 shops, children's programs (ages 4–12), Internet, meeting rooms, travel services* ⊟ *AE, DC, MC, V.*

★ **$$$$** ☒ **Le Meridien.** High on a hill, this refined yet relaxed hotel is an artful blend of art deco and Maya styles; there's lots of wood, glass, and mirrors. Rooms have spectacular ocean views. The many thoughtful details—like having different-temperatured water in each of the

WORD OF MOUTH

"The pool is reason enough for staying at Le Meridien—it is beautiful."

–Sheree McClure

swimming pools—make a stay here truly special. The Spa del Mar is the best in the Zona Hotelera, with the latest European treatments (including seaweed hydrotherapy) and an outdoor hot tub and waterfall.

The Aioli restaurant serves fabulous French food. ⊠ *Blvd. Kukulcán, Km 14 (Retorno del Rey, Lote 37), Zona Hotelera* ☎ 998/881–2200 or 800/543–4300 🖷 998/881–2201 ⊕ *www.meridiencancun.com.mx/main.html* ⇲ *187 rooms, 26 suites* ♻ *3 restaurants, cable TV with video games, 2 tennis courts, 3 pools, gym, health club, hot tub, spa, beach, 2 bars, shops, children's programs (ages 4–12)* ⊟ *AE, MC, V.*

$$$$ 🏨 **Ritz-Carlton Cancún.** Although outfitted with sumptuous carpets, beautiful antiques, and elegant oil paintings, this hotel's style is so European that you may forget you're in Mexico! Rooms are done in understated shades of teal, beige, and rose with wall-to-wall carpeting, large balconies overlooking the Caribbean, and marble bathrooms with separate tubs and showers. For families with small children, special rooms with cribs and changing tables are available. The service can be chilly.

> **WORD OF MOUTH**
>
> "Service at the Ritz-Carlton was excellent—available when you wanted [it], but not pushy when you wanted to relax."
>
> –JR

⊠ *Blvd. Kukulcán, Km 14 (Retorno del Rey 36), Zona Hotelera* ☎ 998/881–0808 or 800/241–3333 🖷 998/881–0815 ⊕ *www.ritzcarlton.com* ⇲ *365 rooms, 40 suites* ♻ *3 restaurants, 3 tennis courts, pro shop, 2 pools, health club, hot tub, spa, beach, 2 bars, shops* ⊟ *AE, D, DC, MC, V.*

$$$ 🏨 **Fiesta Americana Condesa.** This hotel is easily recognized by the 118-foot-tall palapa that covers its lobby. Despite the rustic roof, the rest of the architecture here is extravagant, with marble pillars, stained-glass awnings, and swimming pools joined by arched bridges. The three seven-story towers overlook an inner courtyard with hanging vines and fountains. Standard rooms share balconies with ocean views; suites have hot tubs on their terraces. You may want to avoid the time-share salespeople who now haunt the property—and you may also want to pass on the all-inclusive option, which doesn't include (among other things) morning coffee. ⊠ *Blvd. Kukulcán, Km 16.5, Zona Hotelera* ☎ 998/881–4200 🖷 998/885–4262 ⊕ *www.fiestaamericana.com* ⇲ *476 rooms, 25 suites* ♻ *4 restaurants, some kitchenettes, cable TV with video games, 3 tennis courts, 3 pools, gym, spa, beach, 3 bars, children's programs (ages 3–12), travel services* ⊟ *AE, MC, V* ℐ◎ℐ *AI, EP.*

$$$ 🏨 **Flamingo Cancún Resort & Plaza.** Just across the street from the Flamingo Plaza, this modest hotel is a great bargain. The brightly decorated rooms all have king-size beds; half have ocean views. Above the rather tiny beach is a wonderfully expansive (45-foot-long) courtyard pool with a swim-up bar (especially popular during spring break season). Though the food here is good, you may wish to forgo the all-inclusive plan since you're within walking distance of many restaurants. Several handicapped-accessible rooms are available upon request. The staff is delightful here. ⊠ *Boulevard Kukulcán, Km 11.5, Zona Hotelera* ☎ 998/883–1544 🖷 998/883–1029 ⊕ *www.flamingocancun.com* ⇲ *208 rooms, 13 junior suites* ♻ *2 restaurants, cable TV, 3 pools, gym, 2 bars, billiards, free parking* ⊟ *AE, MC, V* ℐ◎ℐ *AI, EP.*

$$$ ⛨ **Gran Meliá Cancún.** This enormous beachfront hotel has been built to resemble a modernist Maya temple; the lobby's atrium, which is filled with plants, even has a pyramid-shaped roof skylight. The rooms, however, aren't as impressive as the architecture or the magnificent pool. The furnishings are nothing special, although the balconies and terraces (many of which have ocean views) are quite private. This is a good thing, given that the rest of the property—with its convention center and six meeting halls—isn't exactly intimate. Golfers will enjoy the 9-hole course. ✉ *Blvd. Kukulcán, Km 16, Zona Hotelera* ☎ *998/881–1100* 📠 *998/881– 1740* ⊕ *www.solmelia.com* 🛏 *636 rooms, 64 suites* ♨ *5 restaurants, cable TV with video games, 9-hole golf course, tennis court, 2 pools, health club, spa, beach, paddle tennis, volleyball, 3 bars, shops, babysitting, convention center, car rental, travel services* ⊟ *AE, DC, MC, V.*

$$$ ⛨ **Hilton Cancún Beach & Golf Resort.** This older hotel's magnificent championship 18-hole, par-72 course makes it popular with the golf crowd. Some guest rooms are rather small, but all have private views of either the ocean or the lagoon. The best ones are the oceanfront villas of the Beach Club, which are a bit more expensive than regular rooms but have more privacy. The landscaping incorporates a series of lavish, interconnected swimming pools that wind through palm-dotted lawns, ending at the beach (which, unfortunately, is a bit rocky). Great Japanese fare is available on-site at the romantic seaside restaurant, Mitachi. ✉ *Blvd. Kukulcán, Km 17 (Retorno Lacandones), Zona Hotelera* ☎ *998/881–8000 or 800/445–8667* 📠 *998/881–8080* ⊕ *www.hilton. com* 🛏 *426 rooms, 4 suites* ♨ *2 restaurants, cable TV with video games, 18-hole golf course, 2 tennis courts, 7 pools, fitness classes, gym, hair salon, hot tubs, sauna, beach, 3 bars, lobby lounge, shops, children's programs (ages 4–12), car rental* ⊟ *AE, DC, MC, V* ⊙ *CP.*

$$$ ⛨ **Marriott Casa Magna.** The sister property to the JW Marriott, this hotel has sweeping grounds that lead up to an eclectically designed six-story hotel. The lobby has large windows and crystal chandeliers; rooms have tile floors, soft rugs, and ocean views, and most have balconies. Three restaurants overlook the pool area and the ocean; check out Mikado, the Japanese steak house, whose chefs perform dazzling table-side displays. Sports fans can visit the Champion Sports Bar next door. ✉ *Blvd. Kukulcán, Km 14.5, Zona Hotelera* ☎ *998/881–2000 or 888/236–2427* 📠 *998/ 881–2085* ⊕ *www.marriott.com* 🛏 *414 rooms, 36 suites* ♨ *3 restaurants, cable TV with video games, 2 tennis courts, health club, hair salon, hot tubs, sauna, beach, dock, bar, shops* ⊟ *AE, DC, MC, V.*

$$$ ⛨ **Occidental Caribbean Village.** Popular with both spring breakers and families, this all-inclusive beachfront resort has terrific amenities. All rooms in the three-tower compound have ocean views, double beds, and small sitting areas done up in sunset colors. The superb beach offers snorkeling and deep-sea fishing, and there are two large pools. If you stay here you are also allowed to visit the other Allegro resorts in Cancún, Playa del Carmen, and Cozumel, as part of a "Stay at One, Play at Four" promotion. The hotel has three rooms specially equipped for people with disabilities. ✉ *Blvd. Kukulcán, Km 13.5, Zona Hotelera* ☎ *998/848–8000, 01800/ 645–1179 toll-free in Mexico* 📠 *998/885–8002* ⊕ *www.occidentalhotels. com* 🛏 *300 rooms* ♨ *4 restaurants, snack bars, cable TV, 2 tennis courts,*

pool, gym, beach, dive shop, snorkeling, windsurfing, 3 bars, shops, children's programs (ages 4–12) ☰ *AE, DC, MC, V* ⦿ *AI.*

$$$ ⊞ **Riu Palace Las Americas.** A colossal nine-story property at the north end of the Zona, the Palace is visually stunning. The lobby has a lovely stained-glass ceiling, and the rooms—which are all junior suites—have mahogany furniture, and spacious sitting areas that lead to ocean-view balconies. There are two major drawbacks: the beach is almost non-existent, and you must make restaurant reservations by 7 AM for food that's mediocre at best. Fortunately there's an exchange program, which allows you access the hotel's sister properties, the Riu Cancún (next door) and Riu Caribe (five minutes away), where the beaches and food are much better. ⊠ *Blvd. Kukulcán, Km 8.5, Zona Hotelera* ☎ *998/891–4300 or 888/666–8816* ⦿ *www.riu.com* ⇨ *368 junior suites* ⚐ *6 restaurants, cable TV, 2 pools, spa, sauna, gym, hot tub, 5 bars, dance club, theater, playground, meeting rooms* ☰ *AE, MC, V* ⦿ *AI.*

$$$ ⊞ **Villas Tacul.** These villas—originally built for visiting dignitaries—are surrounded by well-trimmed lawns and landscaped gardens that lead to the beach. Each has a kitchen, between two and five bedrooms, tile floors, colonial-style furniture, wagon-wheel chandeliers, and tinwork mirrors. Less expensive rooms without kitchens are also available, although they're set far from the beach and close to noisy Boulevard Kukulcán. ⊠ *Blvd. Kukulcán, Km 5.5, Zona Hotelera* ☎ *998/883–0000* 🖷 *998/849–7070* ⦿ *www.villastacul.com.mx* ⇨ *23 villas, 79 rooms* ⚐ *Restaurant, kitchens, cable TV, 2 tennis courts, pool, beach, basketball, bar* ☰ *AE, D, MC, V.*

$$$ ⊞ **Westin Regina Resort Cancún.** On the southern end of the Zona Hotelera, this hotel is quite secluded—which means you'll get privacy, but you'll also have to drive to get to shops and restaurants. Rooms here have cozy beds dressed in soft white linens, oak tables and chairs, and pale walls offsetting brightly tiled

> **WORD OF MOUTH**
>
> "The Westin is great if you want to avoid the sometimes crazy party-around-the-clock atmosphere of Cancún."
>
> –Calvin

floors. The ocean beach has been eroded away by years of tropical storms, but the one on the Laguna Nichupté side is very pleasant. Although advertised as a family hotel, the kids will get bored here very quickly. ⊠ *Blvd. Kukulcán, Km 20, Zona Hotelera* ☎ *998/848–7400 or 888/625–5144* 🖷 *998/891–4462* ⦿ *www.starwood.com/westin* ⇨ *278 rooms, 15 suites* ⚐ *4 restaurants, cable TV with video games, 2 tennis courts, 5 pools, gym, health club, hot tubs, beach, 3 bars, children's programs (ages 4–12)* ☰ *AE, MC, V.*

$$–$$$ ⊞ **Gran Costa Real.** Resembling an oversized Mediterranean villa, this resort is both luxurious and affordable. The rooms are medium-size, but elegantly decorated, and most have ocean-view balconies. The larger junior suites have small kitchenettes. The pool has shallow-water shelves to put lounge chairs on, so you can sunbathe while dangling your toes in the water. The beach is tiny, but though it can get crowded, it's spotless, and has small huts for shade. Four rooms are specially equipped for wheelchairs. The all-inclusive plan is optional and the food is decent. ⊠ *Blvd.*

Kukulcán, Km 4, Zona Hotelera ☎ *998/881–7300* 🖷 *998/881–7399* ⊕ *www.realresorts.com.mx* 💲 *218 rooms, 108 junior suites ⚖ 3 restaurants, cable TV with DVD players, pool, spa, gym, 2 bars, car rental, gift shop, children's programs (ages 4–12)* ▭ *AE, MC, V* ⭐ *AI, EP.*

$$–$$$ 🖼 **Presidente InterContinental Cancún.** This landmark hotel is located on the silky sands of Playa Tortugas, one of the best and safest beaches in Cancún. The rest of the property is pretty impressive, too. The interiors are filled with local touches like Talavera pottery, and the larger-than-average guest rooms have wicker furniture and area rugs on stone floors. Most don't have balconies, but those on the first floor have patios and outdoor hot tubs. Suites have contemporary furnishings, in-room VCRs and DVD players, and spacious verandas. The pool has a waterfall in the shape of a Maya pyramid, and of course, the beach is divinely peaceful despite the annoying new "beach club" fees. ✉ *Blvd. Kukulcán, Km 7.5, Zona Hotelera* ☎ *998/848–8700 or 888/567–8725* 🖷 *998/ 883–2602* ⊕ *www.ichotelsgroup.com* 💲 *299 rooms, 6 suites ⚖ 2 restaurants, cable TV with video games, some in-room VCRs, tennis court, 2 pools, gym, hair salon, hot tubs, beach, bar, shops* ▭ *AE, MC, V.*

$$ 🖼 **Best Western Cancún Clipper Club.** A good choice for families, this economy hotel is set alongside the lagoon. Rooms are done up in bright tropical colors with rattan furniture with water views; there are also suites with fully equipped kitchens, living rooms, and pull-out couches. Although there's no beach, there's a pretty pool with a large deck, which is set amid lush gardens, and a children's playground. The beaches, shops, and restaurants are within walking distance. ✉ *Blvd. Kukulcán, Km 9, Zona Hotelera* ☎ *998/891–5999* 🖷 *998/ 891–5989* ⊕ *www.clipper.com. mx* 💲 *72 rooms ⚖ Restaurant, cable TV, pool, tennis court, fitness center, beauty salon, playground, laundry facilities* ▭ *AE, MC, V.*

$$ 🖼 **Holiday Inn Express.** Within walking distance of the Cancún Golf Club, this hotel was built to resemble a Mexican hacienda—but with a pool instead of a courtyard at its center. Rooms have either patios or small balconies that overlook the pool and deck. All rooms are bright in blues and reds; furnishings are modern. Although not luxurious, it's perfect for families in which Dad wants to golf, Mom wants to shop, and the kids want to hit the beach. A free shuttle runs to the shops and beaches, which are five minutes away; taxis are inexpensive alternatives. ✉ *Paseo Pok-Ta-Pok, Zona Hotelera* ☎ *998/883–2200* 🖷 *998/883–2532* ⊕ *www. ichotelsgroup.com/h/d/ex/hd/cnnex* 💲 *119 rooms ⚖ Restaurant, cable TV, pool* ▭ *AE, MC, V* ⭐ *BP.*

$$ 🖼 **Tucan Cun Beach Resort Villas.** The architecture at this all-inclusive resort isn't exactly inspiring (more like squat and bulky); nor is color scheme particularly restful (there's lots of loud red). But, it does offer reasonably priced, super-clean rooms with large balconies overlooking the ocean or lagoon. The main pool is almost as large as the hotel and the beach is superb. Food and drink are simply mediocre. Since it's close to all the shops, this is a good resort for families with older children. The "villas" are a bit of a misnomer, since all the rooms here are identical but ocean-view rooms are more expensive than the corner rooms. ✉ *Blvd. Kukulcán, Km 13.5, Lote 24, Zona Hotelera* ☎ *998/885–0814* 🖷 *998/ 885–0615* 💲 *265 rooms, 55 villas ⚖ 4 restaurants, cable TV, tennis* *court, 3 pools, exercise room, 4 bars, recreation room, travel services* ⊟ *AE, MC, V* ⏍ *AI.*

¢–$$ 🏨 **Suites Sina.** These economical suites are in front of Laguna Nichupté and close to the Pok-Ta-Pok golf course. Each unit has comfortable furniture, a kitchenette, a dining-living room with a sofa bed, a balcony or a terrace, and double beds. Outside is a central pool and garden. The cleaning staff can drag their feet here—although they'll get to your room eventually. ⊠ *Club de Golf, Calle Quetzal 33, Zona Hotelera* ☎ *998/883–1017 or 877/666–9837* 🖷 *998/883–2459* ⊕ *www. cancunsinasuites.com.mx/* ⤶ *33 suites* ⚲ *Kitchenettes, cable TV, pool* ⊟ *AE, MC, V.*

El Centro

$$ 🏨 **Antillano.** This small, well-kept hotel has a cozy lobby bar and a decent-size pool. Each of its rooms has wood furniture, one or two double beds, a sink area separate from the bath, and tile floors. The quietest rooms face the pool—avoid the noisier ones overlooking Avenida Tulum. ⊠ *Av. Tulum and Calle Claveles, Sm 21* ☎ *998/884–1532* 🖷 *998/ 884–1878* ⊕ *www.hotelantillano.com* ⤶ *48 rooms* ⚲ *Cable TV, pool, bar, shops, babysitting* ⊟ *AE, D, MC, V.*

$$ 🏨 **Radisson Hotel Hacienda.** Rooms in this pink, hacienda-style building are on the generic side but do have pleasant Mexican accents like wall prints and flower arrangements. The rooms overlook a large pool surrounded by tropical plants. The gym has state-of-the-art equipment and the business center offers e-mail access. The daily breakfast buffet is popular with locals, and there's a shuttle to the beach. This place is a great bargain. ⊠ *Av. Náder 1, Sm 2* ☎ *998/887–4455 or 888/201–1718* 🖷 *998/ 884–7954* ⊕ *www.radisson.com* ⤶ *248 rooms* ⚲ *2 restaurants, cable TV, tennis court, pool, gym, hair salon, 2 bars, nightclub, laundry facilities, business services, car rental, travel services* ⊟ *AE, DC, MC, V.*

$ 🏨 **Hotel Batab.** Located in the heart of downtown where all the Mexicans live and shop, this budget hotel offers clean and comfortable rooms. The decor is minimal: two double beds, one table, two chairs, and the TV. The bathrooms are a decent size and there is plenty of hot water. The white lobby has plants scattered around and is bright and cheerful, just like the staff. Buses to the Hotel Zone are just outside the door. This is a chance to see the real Cancún, practice your Spanish and meet the locals. ⊠ *Av. Chichen Itza No. 52, Sm 23* ☎ *998/884–3822* 🖷 *998/884–3821* ⊕ *www.hotelbatab.com* ⤶ *68 rooms* ⚲ *Restaurant, laundry, Internet, travel services* ⊟ *MC, V.*

$ 🏨 **Hotel El Rey del Caribe.** Thanks to the use of solar energy, a water-recycling system, and composting toilets, this unique hotel has very little impact on the environment—and its luxuriant garden blocks the heat and noise of downtown. Hammocks hang poolside, and wrought-iron tables and chairs dot the grounds. Rooms are small but pleasant, and there's even a spa where you can book honey massages or Reiki treatments. El Centro's shops and restaurants are within walking distance. ⊠ *Avs. Uxmal and Náder, Sm 2* ☎ *998/884–2028* 🖷 *998/884–9857* ⊕ *www.reycaribe.com* ⤶ *25 rooms* ⚲ *Kitchenettes, cable TV, pool, hot tub* ⊟ *MC, V.*

FodorśChoice ★

1

$ ⊞ **Maria de Lourdes.** A great pool, clean and basic rooms, and bargain prices are the draw at this downtown hotel. Rooms overlooking the street are noisy, but they're brighter and airier than those facing the hallways. This hotel gets many repeat customers who tend to hang out by the pool playing cards. Downtown shops and restaurants are minutes away. ⊠ *Av. Yaxchilán 80, Sm 22* ☎ *998/884–4744* 🖷 *998/884–1242* ⊕ *www. hotelmariadelourdes.com* 🛏 *57 rooms* ♿ *Restaurant, cable TV, pool, bar, parking (fee)* ⊟ No credit cards.

¢–$ ⊞ **Cancún Inn El Patio.** This charming, traditional-looking residence has been converted into a European-style guesthouse. The entrance leads off a busy street into a central patio, landscaped with trees, flowers, and a lovely tiled fountain; inside, there's a comfy sitting area with a game room and library. Upstairs, large, airy rooms have Spanish-style furniture and Mexican photos and ceramics. Downtown attractions are a short cab or bus ride away. This hotel is an excellent hotel for women traveling alone; the owners will make sure you are safe and comfortable. ⊠ *Av. Bonampak 51, Sm 2* ☎ *998/884–3500* 🖷 *998/884–3540* ⊕ *www. cancun-suites.com* 🛏 *18 rooms* ♿ *Cable TV, recreation room; no smoking* ⊟ *MC, V.*

¢–$ ⊞ **Hotel Parador.** Rooms at this centrally located hotel line two narrow hallways, which lead to a pool, garden, and palapa bar. Rooms are spare but functional; the bathrooms are large and the showers hot. You can walk to nightlife hot spots in minutes, and the bus to the Zona Hotelera stops right outside. ⊠ *Av. Tulum 26, Sm 5* ☎ *998/884–1310* 🖷 *998/ 884–9712* 🛏 *66 rooms* ♿ *Restaurant, cable TV, pool, bar* ⊟ *MC, V.*

¢–$ ⊞ **Suites Cancún Centro.** You can rent suites or rooms by the day, week, or month at this quiet hotel. Though it abuts the lively Parque de las Palapas, the property manages to maintain a tranquil atmosphere, with lovely and private rooms that open onto a courtyard and a midsize pool. Tiled bathrooms are small but pleasant, and there are king-size as well as single beds. Suites have fully equipped kitchenettes along with sitting and dining areas. Some rooms only have fans, so be sure to ask when you make reservations. ⊠ *Calle Alcatraces 32, Sm 22* ☎ *998/884– 2301* 🖷 *998/884–7270* 🛏 *30 suites* ♿ *Kitchenettes, cable TV; no a/c in some rooms* ⊟ *MC, V.*

¢ ⊞ **Hotel Colonial.** A charming fountain and garden are at the center of this hotel's colonial-style buildings. Rooms are simple but comfortable, each with a double bed, dresser, and bathroom. What it lacks in luxury it makes up for in value and location; you are five minutes away from all the downtown concerts, clubs, restaurants, shops, and attractions. ⊠ *Av. Tulipanes 22, Sm 21* ☎☎ *998/884–1535* 🛏 *46 rooms* ♿ *Restaurant, cable TV, free parking* ⊟ *D, MC, V.*

¢ ⊞ **Mexico Hostels.** The cheapest place to stay in Cancún, this clean but cramped hostel is four blocks from the main bus terminal. Some rooms are lined with bunk beds and share baths; others are more private. There are lockers to secure your belongings, and access to a full kitchen, a lounge area, laundry facilities, and the Internet on-site. Those who want to sleep outdoors can share a space with 20 others under a palapa roof. The hostel is open 24 hours. ⊠ *Calle Palmera 30 (off Av. Uxmal), Sm 23* ☎ *998/887–0191 or 212/699–3825 Ext. 7860* 🖷 *425/962–8028*

⊕ *www.hostels.com/en/availability.php/HostelNumber.880* ⤳ *64 beds* ⚭ *Café, lounge, laundry facilities, Internet; no a/c* ⊟ *No credit cards* ❘⊙❘ *CP.*

¢ 🔲 **Soberanis Hotel.** The rooms here are an excellent bargain: they're clean and uncluttered, with modern furniture and white tile floors. There's also a hostel section, with four bunks to a room and lockers. The neighboring cybercafé has great breakfasts, along with a travel agency and bulletin board where other travelers have posted information. Downtown banks, shops, and restaurants are within walking distance. ⊠ *Av. Cobá, Sm 22* ☎☎ *998/884–4564* ⊕ *www.soberanis.com.mx* ⤳ *78 rooms* ⚭ *Restaurant, room service, some cable TV, Internet, meeting room, free parking* ⊟ *MC, V* ❘⊙❘ *CP.*

¢ 🔲 **Suites Albatros Hotel.** This charming budget hotel offers pleasant and clean but spartan rooms, with double beds, private baths, and small kitchenettes that look out onto a pretty tropical garden. The bus to the beach stops just outside the door, and downtown shops and restaurants are a 10-minute walk away. ⊠ *Av. Yaxchilán 154, Sm 20* ☎☎ *998/884–2242* ⊕ *www.cancun.net/links/small_properties/suitesalbatros/* ⤳ *9 rooms* ⚭ *Kitchenettes, BBQs, garden; no room TVs, no room phones* ⊟ *No credit cards.*

SPORTS & THE OUTDOORS

Boating & Sailing

There are lots of ways to get your adrenaline going on the waters of Cancún. You can arrange to go parasailing (about $35 for eight minutes), waterskiing ($70 per hour), or jet skiing ($70 per hour, or $60 for Wave Runners). Paddleboats, kayaks, catamarans, and banana boats are readily available, too.

☾ **Aqua Fun** (⊠ Blvd. Kukulcán, Km 16.5, Zona Hotelera ☎ 998/885–2930) maintains a large fleet of water toys such as Wave Runners, Jet Skis, speedboats, kayaks, and Windsurfers. **AquaWorld** (⊠ Blvd. Kukulcán, Km 15.2, Zona Hotelera ☎ 998/848–8300 ⊕ www.aquaworld.com.mx) rents boats and water toys and offers parasailing and tours aboard a submarine. **El Embarcadero** (⊠ Blvd. Kukulcán, Km 4, Zona Hotelera ☎ 998/849–4848), the marina complex at Playa Linda, is the departure point for ferries to Isla Mujeres and several tour boats.

Marina Asterix (⊠ Blvd. Kukulcán, Km 4.5, Zona Hotelera ☎ 998/883–4847) gives tours to Isla Contoy and Isla Mujeres, and snorkeling trips.

Marina Manglar (⊠ Blvd. Kukulcán, Km 20, Zona Hotelera ☎ 998/885–1808) offers a Jet Ski jungle tour.

Bullfighting

☾ The Cancún **bullring** (⊠ Blvd. Kukulcán and Av. Bonampak, Sm 4 ☎ 998/884–8372 or 998/884–8248), a block south of the Pemex gas station, hosts year-round bullfights. A matador, *charros* (Mexican cowboys), a mariachi band, and flamenco dancers entertain during the hour preceding the bullfight (from 2:30 PM). Tickets cost about $40. Fights are held Wednesday at 3:30.

Continued on page 40

NIGHTLIFE

Señor Frogs

We're not here to judge: we know that when you come to Cancún, you come to party. Sure, if you want fine dining and dancing under the stars, you'll find it here. But if your tastes run more toward bikini contests, all-night chug-a-thons or cross-dressing Cher impersonators, rest assured: Cancún delivers.

DINNER CRUISES

ZONA HOTELERA

Sunset boat cruises that include dinner, drinks, music and sometimes dancing are very popular in Cancún—especially for couples looking for a romantic evening, and visitors who'd rather avoid the carnival atmosphere of Cancún's clubs and discos.

The **Capitán Hook** (✉ El Embarcadero, Blvd. Kukulcán, Km 4.5 ☎ 998/849–4451 or 998/849–4452), lets you watch a pirate show aboard a replica of an 18th-century Spanish galleon, then enjoy a lobster dinner as the ship cruises around at sunset. When it's dark the boat lights up, the bar opens, and the music gets turned on for dancing under the stars.

Caribbean Carnival Tours (✉ Playa Tortuga/Fat Tuesday Marina, Kukulcán Km 6.5 ☎ 998/881-0000) start off on a large two-level catamaran at sunset. There's an open bar for the sail across to Isla Mujeres; once you reach shore you'll join in a moonlight calypso cookout and a full dinner buffet followed by a Caribbean carnival show.

Columbus Lobster Dinner Cruises (✉ Royal Mayan Yacht Club & Marina, Blvd. Kukulcán, Km 16.5 ☎ 998/849–4748) offers tranquil, couples-only cruises on a 62-foot galleon. A fresh lobster dinner is served while the sun sets over Laguna Nichupté; afterward, the boat continues to cruise so you can stargaze.

Spinning at *La Boom*

DISCOS

Cancún wouldn't be Cancún without its glittering discos, which generally start jumping around 10:30. A few places open earlier, around 9, but make no mistake—the later it gets, the crazier it gets.

ZONA HOTELERA

La Boom (⊠ Blvd. Kukulcán, Km 3.5 ☎ 998/849–7588) is always the last place to close; it has a video bar with a light show and weekly events such as dance contests. If you're a good-looking gal you might want to enter the Bikini Contest—the winner gets a $1,500 prize. There are Hot Male Body contests, too, but if you're a guy you won't make any money (although you will get your ego stroked).

The **Bull Dog Night Club** (⊠ Krystal Cancún hotel, Blvd. Kukulcán, Km 9, Lote 9 ☎ 998/848–9800) has an all-you-can-drink bar, the latest dance music, and an impressive laser-light show. The stage here is large, and some very well-known rock bands, including Guns n' Roses and Radiohead, have played on it. Another, somewhat bawdier draw here is the private hot tub, where you can have "the Jacuzzi bikini girls" scrub your back. Naturally, this place is popular with spring-breakers.

The wild, wild **Coco Bongo** (⊠ Blvd. Kukulcán, Km 9.5, across the street from Dady'O ☎998/883–5061) has no chairs, but there are plenty of tables that everyone dances on. There's also a popular floor show billed as "Las Vegas meets Hollywood," featuring celebrity impersonators; and an amazing gravity-defying aerial acrobatic show with an accompanying 12-piece orchestra. After the shows the techno gets turned up to full volume and everyone gets up to get down.

Dady'O (⊠ Blvd. Kukulcán, Km 9.5 ☎ 998/883–3333) has been around for a while but is still very "in" with the younger set. A giant screen projects music videos above the always-packed dance floor, while laser lights whirl across the crowd. During spring break, the place gets even livelier during the Hawaiian Bikini contests. Next door to Dady'O,

Dady Rock (✉Blvd. Kukulcán, Km 9.5 ☎ 998/883–3333) draws a high-energy crowd that likes entertainment along with dinner. Live bands usually start off the action—but when the karaoke singers take over, the real fun begins. On Tuesday nights, there are regular Hot Legs contests; Wet Body contests are on Thursdays and the Hot Male contests on Sunday. Winners take home $1,000 in cash.

Bikini Contest *at La Boom*

Fat Tuesday (✉ Blvd. Kukulcán, Km 6.5 ☎ 998/849–7199), with its large daiquiri bar and live and piped-in disco music, is another place to dance the night away.

Glazz (✉ La Isla Shopping Village, Blvd. Kukulcán, Km 12.5 ☎ 998/883–1881) is an upscale restaurant and club with a large dance floor, where all kinds of music are played. The crowd tends to be more mature (and much better dressed) here. The menu is ghastly and pretentious, but the dancing and cocktails are terrific.

LIVE MUSIC

ZONA HOTELERA

Azucar (✉ Hotel Camino Real, Blvd. Kukulcán, Km 9 ☎ 998/883–0100) showcases the very best Latin American bands. Go just to watch the locals dance (the beautiful people tend to turn up here really late). Proper dress is required—no jeans or sneakers.

The **Blue Bayou Jazz Club** (✉Blvd. Kukulcán, Km 10.5 ☎ 998/883–0044), the lobby bar in the Hyatt Cancún Caribe, has nightly jazz.

Tragar Bar (✉ Laguna Grill, Blvd. Kukulcán, Km 15.6 ☎ 998/885–0267) in the Laguna Grill has a DJ after 10 PM on weekends; if you show up early, you can sample some terrific cocktails at the plush aquarium bar.

The **Royal Bandstand** (✉ Blvd. Kukulcán, Km 13.5 Royal Sands Hotel ☎ 998/848–8220) is the place for ballroom dancing. Its terrific live band plays golden oldies, romantic favorites, and the latest hits. There's a dinner menu, too, if you get hungry.

EL CENTRO

Mambo Café (✉ Av. Tulum, Plaza las Americas, 2nd fl., Sm 4 ☎ 998/887–7894), which opens its doors after 10 PM, plays hot salsa music so you can practice your moves with the locals.

The classy **Roots Bar** (✉ Av. Tulipanes 26, near Parque de las Palapas, Sm 22 ☎ 998/884–2437) is the place to go for jazz, fusion, flamenco, and blues.

Sabor Latino (✉ Plaza Hong Kong, Loc 31, Sm 20 ☎ 998/884–5329) has a live salsa band and lots of locals to show you new dance moves. Wednesday is Ladies Night, when Chippendales dancers perform in bow ties and not much else. To mingle with locals and hear great music for free, head to the ♥ **Parque de las Palapas** (✉ Bordered by Avs. Tulum, Yaxchilán, Uxmal, and Cobá, Sm 22) in El Centro. Every Friday night at 7:30 there's live music that ranges from jazz to salsa to Caribbean; lots of locals show up to dance. On Sunday afternoons, the Cancún Municipal Orchestra plays.

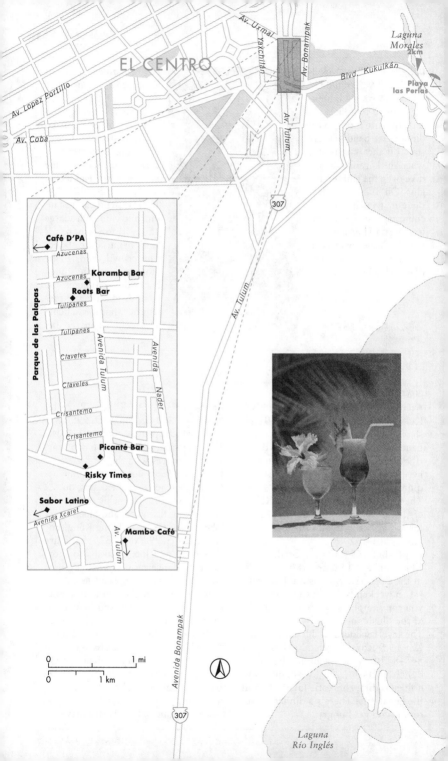

EL CENTRO

Laguna
Morales
2km

Playa
las Perlas

Av. Uxmal

Av. Bonampak

Blvd. Kukulkán

Av. López Portillo

Av. Cobá

Yaxchilán

Av. Tulum

307

Av. Tulum

Café D'PA

Azucenas

Azucenas

Karamba Bar

Roots Bar

Tulipanes

Parque de las Palapas

Tulipanes

Avenida Tulum

Avenida Nader

Claveles

Claveles

Crisantemo

Crisantemo

Picanté Bar

Risky Times

Sabor Latino

Avenida Xcaret

Mambo Café

Av. Tulum

Avenida Bonampak

307

Laguna
Río Inglés

0   1 mi

0   1 km

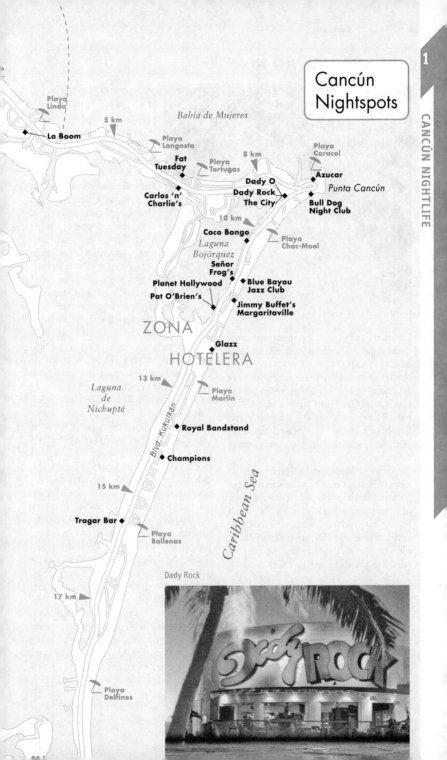

Cancún Nightspots

Bahía de Mujeres

Playa Linda

5 km

◆ **La Boom**

Playa Langosta

Fat Tuesday

Playa Tortugas

8 km

Carlos 'n' Charlie's

Dady O

Dady Rock

The City

Playa Caracol

◆ **Azucar**

Punta Cancún

Bull Dog Night Club

10 km

Coco Bongo

Laguna Bojórquez

Playa Chac-Mool

Señor Frog's

Planet Hollywood

◆ **Blue Bayou Jazz Club**

Pat O'Brien's

Jimmy Buffet's Margaritaville

ZONA

◆ **Glazz**

HOTELERA

Laguna de Nichupté

13 km

Playa Marlin

Blvd. Kukulkán

◆ **Royal Bandstand**

◆ **Champions**

15 km

Tragar Bar ◆

Playa Ballenas

Caribbean Sea

17 km

Playa Delfines

Dady Rock

GAY AND LESBIAN NIGHTSPOTS

Drag performers at *Karamba Bar*

Cancún has become a popular destination for gay and lesbian travelers, and lots of gay-friendly clubs have sprung up in the area as a result. These nightspots get especially busy in mid-May, when the International Gay Festival takes place. This celebration includes a welcome party, Caribbean cruise, beach- and bar-hopping, and sightseeing tours to area attractions.

While most Mexicans will treat gay visitors with respect, many are still uncomfortable with open public displays of affection. Discretion is advised. You won't see any open advertisements for the clubs listed below and all of them have fairly discreet entrances. Very few women attend the gay clubs with strip shows.

EL CENTRO

Cafe D' PA (⊠ Parque de Palapas, Mza. 16, Sm 22 ☎ 998/884–7615 or 998/887–8944) is a cheerful bar and restaurant offering a menu of specialty crepes; since it opens at lunchtime, it's a popular place to gather before the city's other gay bars and nightclubs open their doors. If dancing till the wee hours is your bag, **Glow Dance Club** (⊠ Av. Tulipanes 33, Sm

22 ☎ 998/827-0724) is the place for you. The DJs here play a range of up-tempo disco and techno, which keeps the terrace dance floor packed. The doors don't close until 5 AM.

Karamba Bar (⊠ Av. Tulum 11 at Calle Azucenas, Sm 5 ☎ No phone ⊕ www.karambabar.com) is a large open-air disco and club that's known for its stage performers. A variety of drag shows with the usual lip-synching and dancing celebrity impersonators are put on every Wednesday and Thursday. On Friday night the Go-Go Boys of Cancún entertain, and strip shows are on Saturday and Sunday. The bar opens at 10:30 and the party goes on until dawn. There's no cover charge.

Picante Bar (⊠ Plaza Gallerias, Av. Tulum 20, Sm 5 ☎ No phone ⊕ www.picantebar.com), the oldest gay bar in Cancún, has been operating for 14 years. (It survived several raids and closures during less lenient times in the '90s.) The drag shows here tend to reflect local culture; for instance, during Carnival there is a special holiday beauty pageant followed by the crowning of "the Queen." The owner, "Mother Picante," emcees the floor show that includes Las Vegas-type dance revues, singers, and strippers. Doors open at 9 and close at 5 AM, and there's no cover. .

Risky Times (⊠ Avs. Tulum and Cobá, Sm 4 ☎ 998/884–7503) has a famously rowdy after-hours scene that doesn't get started until 12 AM but usually lasts until dawn. Be careful here; the crowd can be a bit rough.

RESTAURANT PARTY CENTERS

The following restaurants all serve decent food—but the real attractions are the nightly parties they host, often with live music, and often lasting till dawn.

ZONA HOTELERA

At **Carlos n' Charlie's** (⊠ Blvd. Kukulcán, Km 5.5 ☎ 998/849-4053), the waiters will occasionally abandon their posts to rush up on stage and start singing or dancing along with live bands. It's not unusual for them to roust everyone from their seats to join in a conga line before going back to serving food.

Champions (⊠ Marriott Casa Magna hotel, Blvd. Kukulcán, Km 14.5 ☎ 998/881-2000 Ext. 6341) has a giant sports screen with 40 monitors, a live DJ, pool tables, cold beer, and dancing until the wee hours.

The City (⊠ Blvd. Kukulcán, Km 9.5 ☎ 998/ 848-8380) is a giant party complex with a daytime water park; at night, there's a cavernous dance floor with stadium seating and several large bars selling overpriced drinks. Dancing and live shows are the main draw. This is by far the loudest club in the Zona Hotelera, so don't be surprised if you go home with a ringing in your ears.

You can enjoy a cheeseburger in paradise, along with music and drinks, at **Jimmy Buffett's Margaritaville** (⊠ Plaza Flamingo, Blvd. Kukulcán, Km 11.5 ☎ 998/885-2375). Of course, you'll especially like this place if you're a "parrothead" (a Jimmy Buffett fan).

Pat O'Brien's (⊠ Blvd. Kukulcán, Km 11.5 ☎ 998/883–0832) brings the New Orleans party scene to the Zona with live rock bands and its famous cocktails balanced on the heads of waiters as they dance through the crowd. The really experienced waiters can balance up to four margaritas or strawberry daiquiris at once! It's always Mardi Gras here, so the place is decorated with lots of balloons, banners and those infamous beads given out to brave patrons.

Planet Hollywood (⊠ Plaza Flamingo, Blvd. Kukulcán, Km 11.5 ☎ 998/883–0921) has a very loud but popular disco with live music until 2 AM. The dance floor is warmed up nightly by a laser light show; then the bands start up and the dancing begins. This place is popular with the young crowd—both college students and vacationing professionals.

Señor Frog's (⊠ Blvd. Kukulcán, Km 12.5 ☎ 998/883–1092) is known for its over-the-top drinks; foot-long funnel glasses are filled with margaritas, daiquiris or beer, and you can take them home as souvenirs once you've chugged them dry. Needless to say, spring-breakers adore this place and often stagger back night after night.

Cancun's Zona Hotelera at dawn

Fishing

Some 500 species—including sailfish, wahoo, bluefin, marlin, barracuda, and red snapper—live in the waters off Cancún. You can charter deep-sea fishing boats starting at about $350 for four hours, $450 for six hours, and $550 for eight hours. Rates generally include a captain and first mate, gear, bait, and beverages.

Marina Barracuda (⊠ Blvd. Kukulcán, Km 14.1, Zona Hotelera ☎ 998/885–3444), which has one of Cancún's largest fishing fleets, offers deep-sea and fly-fishing. **Marina Punta del Este** (⊠ Blvd. Kukulcán, Km 10.3, Zona Hotelera ☎ 998/883–1210) is right next to the convention center. **Marina del Rey** (⊠ Blvd. Kukulcán, Km 15.5, Zona Hotelera ☎ 998/885–0263) offers boat tours and has a small market and a souvenir shop. **Mundo Marino** (⊠ Blvd. Kukulcán, Km 5.5, Zona Hotelera ☎ 998/849–7257) is the marina closest to downtown and specializes in deep-sea fishing.

Golf

Cancún's main golf course is at **Club de Golf Cancún** (⊠ Blvd. Kukulcán between Km 6 and Km 7, Zona Hotelera ☎ 998/883–1230 ⊕ www.cancungolfclub.com). The club has fine views of both sea and lagoon; its 18 holes were designed by Robert Trent Jones Sr. The club also has a practice green, a swimming pool, tennis courts, and a restaurant. The greens fees start at $100 and include your cart; club rentals are $26, shoes $16. The 13-hole executive course (par 53) at the **Gran Meliá Cancún** (⊠ Blvd. Kukulcán, Km 12, Zona Hotelera ☎ 998/885–1160) forms a semicircle around the property and shares its beautiful ocean views. The greens fee is about $40. There is an 18-hole championship golf course at the **Hilton Cancún Beach & Golf Resort** (⊠ Blvd. Kukulcán, Km 17, Zona Hotelera ☎ 998/881–8016); greens fees are $120 ($85 for hotel guests), carts are included, and club rentals run from $30 to $40.

🕭 If you're looking for a less strenuous golf game, **Mini Golf Palace** (⊠ Cancún Palace, Blvd. Kukulcán, Km 14.5, Zona Hotelera ☎ 998/881–3600 Ext. 6655) has a complete 36-hole minigolf course around pyramids, waterfalls, and a river on the grounds of the Cancún Palace.

Snorkeling & Scuba Diving

The snorkeling is best at Punta Nizuc, Punta Cancún, and Playa Tortugas, although you should be careful of the strong currents at Tortugas. You can rent gear for about $10 per day from many of the scuba-diving places as well as at many hotels.

Scuba diving is popular in Cancún, though it's not as spectacular as in Cozumel. Look for a scuba company that will give you lots of personal attention: smaller companies are often better at this than larger ones. Regardless, ask to meet the dive master, and check the equipment and certifications thoroughly. ⚠ A few words of caution about one-hour courses that many resorts offer for free: such courses *do not* prepare you to dive in the open ocean—only in shallow water where you can easily surface without danger. If you've caught the scuba bug and want to take deep or boat dives, prepare yourself properly by investing in a full certification course.

Wet, Wild Water Sports

CLOSE UP

1

CANCÚN IS ONE OF THE WATER-SPORTS CAPITALS OF THE WORLD, and, with the Caribbean on one side of the island and the still waters of Laguna Nichupté on the other, it's no wonder. The most popular activities are snorkeling and diving along the coral reef just off the coast, where schools of colorful tropical fish and other marine creatures live. If you want to view the mysterious underwater world but don't want to get your feet wet, a glass-bottom boat or "submarine" is the ticket. You can also fish, sail, jet ski, parasail, or windsurf. If you prefer your water chlorinated, lots of hotels also have gorgeous pools—many featuring waterfalls, Jacuzzis, and swim-up bars serving drinks with umbrellas. Several hotels offer organized games of water polo and volleyball as well as introductory scuba courses in their pools.

Since the beaches along the Zona Hotelera can have a strong undertow, you should always respect the flags posted in the area. A black flag means you simply can't swim at all. A red flag means you can swim but only with extreme caution. Yellow means approach with caution, while green means water conditions are safe. You are almost never going to see the green flag—even when the water is calm—so swim cautiously, and don't assume you're immune to riptides because you're on vacation. At least one tourist drowns per season after ignoring the flags.

Unfortunately Laguna Nichupté has become polluted from illegal dumping of sewage and at times can have a strong smell. In 1993 the city began conducting a clean-up campaign that included handing out fines to offenders, so the quality of the water is slowly improving. There is very little wildlife to see in the lagoon so most advertised jungle tours are glorified jet-ski romps where you get to drive around fast and make a lot of noise but not see many animals.

While the coral reef in this area is not as spectacular as farther south, there is still plenty to see with over 500 species of sea life in the waters. If you are lucky you may see angelfish, parrot fish, blue tang, and the occasional moray eel. But the corals in this area are extremely fragile and currently endangered. To be a good world citizen follow the six golden rules for snorkeling or scuba diving:

1. Don't throw any garbage into the sea as the marine life will assume it's food, an often lethal mistake.

2. Never stand on the coral.

3. Secure all cameras and gear onto your body so you don't drop anything onto the fragile reef.

4. Never take anything from the sea.

5. Don't feed any of the marine animals.

6. Avoid sunblock or tanning lotion just before you visit the reef.

🕒 **Barracuda Marina** (✉ Blvd. Kukulcán, Km 14, Zona Hotelera ☎ 998/885–3444) has a two-hour Wave Runner jungle tour through the mangroves, which ends with snorkeling at the Punta Nizuc coral reef. The fee (which starts at $35) includes snorkeling equipment, life jackets, and refreshments. **Scuba Cancún** (✉ Blvd. Kukulcán, Km 5, Zona Hotelera ☎ 998/849–7508) specializes in diving trips and offers NAUI, CMAS, and PADI instruction. It's operated by Luis Hurtado, who has more than 35 years of experience. A two-tank dive starts at $64. **Solo Buceo** (✉ Blvd. Kukulcán, Km 9.5, Zona Hotelera ☎ 998/883–3979) charges $60 for two-tank dives and has NAUI, SSI, and PADI instruction. The outfit goes to Cozumel, Akumal, and Isla Mujeres. Extended trips are available from $130.

SHOPPING

The *centros comerciales* (malls) in Cancún are fully air-conditioned and as well kept as similar establishments in the United States or Canada. Like their northerly counterparts, they also sell just about everything: designer clothing, beachwear, sportswear, jewelry, music, video games, household items, shoes, and books. Some even have the same terrible mall food that is standard north of the border. Prices are fixed in shops. They're also generally—but not always—higher than in the markets, where bargaining for better prices is a possibility.

There are many duty-free stores that sell designer goods at reduced prices—sometimes as much as 30% or 40% below retail. Although prices for handicrafts are higher here than in other cities and the selection is limited, you can find handwoven textiles, leather goods, and handcrafted silver jewelry.

> **AVOID TORTOISESHELL**
>
> Refrain from buying anything made from tortoiseshell. The turtles from which it comes are an endangered species, and it's illegal to bring tortoiseshell products into the United States and several other countries. Also be aware that there are some restrictions regarding black coral. You must purchase it from a recognized dealer.

Shopping hours are generally weekdays 10–1 and 4–7, although more stores are increasingly staying open throughout the day rather than closing for siesta. Many shops keep Saturday-morning hours, and some are now open on Sunday until 1. Centros comerciales tend to be open weekdays 9 AM or 10 AM to 8 PM or 9 PM.

Districts, Markets & Malls

Zona Hotelera

There is only one open-air market in the Zona Hotelera. **Coral Negro** (✉ Blvd. Kukulcán, Km 9, Zona Hotelera), next to the convention center, is a collection of about 50 stalls selling crafts. It's open daily until late evening. Everything here is overpriced, but bargaining does work.

Forum-by-the-Sea (✉ Blvd. Kukulcán, Km 9.5, Zona Hotelera ☎ 998/883–4428) is a three-level entertainment and shopping plaza in the Zona. There's a large selection of brand-name restaurants here, and chain shops like Paloma, Wayan, and Sunglass Island, all in a circuslike atmosphere.

The glittering, ultratrendy, and ultraexpensive **La Isla Shopping Village** (⊠ Blvd. Kukulcán, Km 12.5, Zona Hotelera ☎ 998/883–5025) is on the Laguna Nichupté under a giant canopy. A series of canals and small bridges is designed to give the place a Venetian look. In addition to shops, the mall has a marina, an aquarium, a disco, restaurants, and movie theaters. You won't find any bargains here, but it's a fun place to window-shop.

The largest and most contemporary of the malls, **Plaza Caracol** (⊠ Blvd. Kukulcán, Km 8.5, Zona Hotelera ☎ 998/883–4760) is north of the convention center. It houses about 200 shops and boutiques, including two pharmacies, art galleries, a currency exchange, and folk art and jewelry shops, as well as a café and restaurants. Boutiques include Benetton, Bally, Gucci, and Ralph Lauren, with prices lower than those of their U.S. counterparts. You can rest your feet upstairs at the café, where there are often afternoon concerts, or have a meal at one of the fine restaurants.

Plaza la Fiesta (⊠ Blvd. Kukulcán, Km 9, Zona Hotelera ☎ 998/883–2116) has 20,000 square feet of showroom space, and over 100,000 different products for sale. This is probably the widest selection of Mexican goods in the hotel zone, and includes leather goods, silver and gold jewelry, handicrafts, souvenirs, and swimwear. There are some good bargains here.

Plaza Flamingo (⊠ Blvd. Kukulcán, Km 11.5, across from the Hotel Flamingo Resort & Plaza, Zona Hotelera ☎ 998/883–2945) is a small plaza beautifully decorated with marble. Inside are a few designer emporiums, duty-free shops, an exchange booth, sportswear shops, restaurants, and boutiques selling Mexican handicrafts.

Plaza Kukulcán (⊠ Blvd. Kukulcán, Km 13, Zona Hotelera ☎ 998/885–2304) is a seemingly endless mall, with around 80 shops, six restaurants, a liquor store, and a video arcade. The plaza is also notable for the many cultural events and shows that take place in the main public area. For two years the plaza has been undergoing massive renovations that should be completed in early 2006.

Leading off Plaza Caracol is the oldest and most varied commercial center in the Zona, **Plaza Mayafair** (⊠ Blvd. Kukulcán, Km 8.5, Zona Hotelera ☎ 998/883–2801). Mayafair has a large open-air center filled with shops, bars, and restaurants. An adjacent indoor shopping mall is decorated to resemble a rain forest, complete with replicas of Maya stelae.

El Centro

There are lots of interesting shops downtown along Avenida Tulum (between Avenidas Cobá and Uxmal). **Fama** (⊠ Av. Tulum 105, Sm 21 ☎ 998/884–6586) is a department store that sells clothing, English books and magazines, sports gear, toiletries, liquor, and *latería* (crafts made of tin). The oldest and largest of Cancún's crafts markets is **Ki Huic** (⊠ Av. Tulum 17, between Bancomer and Bital banks, Sm 3 ☎ 998/884–3347).

It is open daily 9 AM–10 PM and houses about 100 vendors. **Mercado Veintiocho** (Market 28), just off Avenidas Yaxchilán and Sunyaxchén, is a popular souvenir market filled with shops selling many of the same items found in the Zona Hotelera but at half the price. **Ultrafemme** (✉ Av. Tulum 111, at Calle Claveles, Sm 21 ☎ 998/885–1402) is a popular downtown store that carries duty-free perfume, cosmetics, and jewelry. It also has branches in the Zona Hotelera at Plaza Caracol, Plaza Flamingo, Plaza Kukulcán, and La Isla Shopping Village.

Plaza las Americas (✉ Av. Tulum, Sm 4 and Sm 9 ☎ 998/887–3863) is the largest shopping center in downtown Cancún. Its 50-plus stores, three restaurants, eight movie theaters, video arcade, fast-food outlets, and five large department stores will—for better, for worse—make you feel right at home.

Plaza Bonita (✉ Av. Tulum 260, Sm 7 ☎ 998/884–6812) is a small outdoor plaza next door to Mercado Veintiocho (Market 28). It has many wonderful specialty shops carrying Mexican goods and crafts.

Plaza Cancún 2000 (✉ Av. Tulum 42, Sm 7 ☎ 998/884–9988) is a local shopping mall popular with locals. There are some great bargains to be found here on shoes, clothes, and cosmetics.

Plaza Hong Kong (✉ Avs. Xcaret and Labná, Lote 6, Sm 35 ☎ 998/884–66315) has an eclectic assortments of shops and boutiques. A few sell Chinese goods like chopsticks, rice, noodles, and soy sauce.

Specialty Shops

Galleries

The Attic (✉ La Isla Shopping Village, Blvd. Kukulcán, Km 12.5, Zona Hotelera ☎ 998/883–5466), found in Las Margaritas restaurant, specializes in gold and silver jewelry from Taxco, as well as traditional Mexican art. Serious collectors visit **Casa de Cultura** (✉ Prolongación Av. Yaxchilán, Sm 25 ☎ 998/884–8364) for regular art shows featuring Mexican artists. The **Huichol Collection** (✉ Forum-by-the-Sea, Blvd. Kukulcán, Km 9.5, Zona Hotelera ☎ 998/883–5856) sells handcrafted beadwork and embroidery made by the Huichol Indians of the West Coast. You can also watch a visiting tribe member doing this amazing work. The **Iguana Wana** (restaurant ✉ Plaza Caracol, Blvd. Kukulcán, Km 8.5, Zona Hotelera ☎ 998/883–0829) displays a small collection of art for sale. **Sergio Bustamante** (✉ Plaza Kukulcán, Blvd. Kukulcán, Km 13, Zona Hotelera ☎ 998/885–2206) is a Mexican artist who's well-known for his whimsical ceramic, papier-mâché, and gold sculptures.

Grocery Stores

The few grocery stores in the Zona Hotelera tend to be expensive. It's better to shop for groceries downtown. **Chedraui** (✉ Av. Tulum, Sm 21 ✉ Plaza las Americas, Av. Tulum, Sm 4 and Sm 9 ☎ 998/887–2111 for both locations) is a popular department store with two central locations. **Mega Comercial Mexicana** (✉ Avs. Tulum and Uxmal, Sm 2 ☎ 998/884–4524 ✉ Avs. Kabah and Mayapan, Sm 21 ☎ 998/880–9164) is one of the major Mexican grocery store chains, with three locations. The most convenient is at Avenidas Tulum and Uxmal, across from the bus station; its largest store is farther north on Avenida Kabah, which is open 24 hours.

If you are a member in the States, you can visit **Costco** (⊠ Avs. Kabah and Yaxchilán, Sm 21 ☎ 998/881–0250). **Sam's Club** (⊠ Av. Cobá, Lote 2, Sm 21 ☎ 998/881–0200) has plenty of bargains on groceries and souvenirs. Most locals shop at **San Francisco de Asís** (⊠ Av. Tulum 18, Sm 3 ⊠ Mercado Veintiocho, Avs. Yaxchilán and Sunyaxchén, Sm 26 ☎ 998/884–1155 for both locations) for its many bargains on food and other items. **Wal-Mart** (⊠ Av. Cobá, Lote 2, Sm 21 ☎ 998/884–1383) is a popular shopping spot.

CANCÚN ESSENTIALS

Transportation

BY AIR

AIRPORT   The Aeropuerto Internacional Cancún is 16 km (9 mi) southwest of the heart of Cancún and 10 km (6 mi) from the Zona Hotelera's southernmost point.

🛈 **Aeropuerto Internacional Cancún** ⊠ Carretera Cancún–Puerto Morelos/Carretera 307, Km 9.5 ☎ 998/886-0183

CARRIERS   Aeroméxico flies nonstop to Cancún from New York, Atlanta, and Miami, with limited service from Los Angeles. Most flights from Los Angeles transfer in Mexico City. American Airlines has limited nonstop service from Chicago, New York, Dallas, and Miami to Cancún; most flights, however, stop over in Dallas or Miami. Continental only has daily direct service from Houston. Mexicana has nonstop flights from Los Angeles and Miami. United Airways has direct flights from Miami, Denver, and Washington.

From Cancún, Mexicana subsidiaries Aerocaribe and Aerocozumel fly to Cozumel, the ruins at Chichén Itzá, Mérida, and other Mexican cities.

🛈 **Aerocaribe and Aerocozumel** ☎ 998/884-2000. **Aeroméxico** ☎ 998/287-1860 or 998/886-0003. **American** ☎ 800/904-6000 or 998/883-4461. **Continental** ☎ 800/900-5000 or 998/886-0169. **Mexicana** ☎ 998/881-2333 or 998/881-9042. **United Airways** ☎ 800/003-0777.

AIRPORT   To get to or from the airport, you can take taxis or *colectivos* (vans);
TRANSFERS   although buses are allowed into the airport, they will only take you as far as the bus station downtown (where you will have to transfer to a public bus to get to the Zona Hotelera). There's a well-marked counter just outside of the main international arrival terminal where you can buy bus tickets. There is also a second counter at the airport exit selling colectivo and taxi tickets; prices range from $15 to $75, depending on the destination and driver. Don't hesitate to barter with the cab drivers. The colectivos have fixed prices and usually wait until they are full before leaving the airport. Tickets start at $9. They drive to the far end of the Zona Hotelera and drop off passengers along the way back to the mainland; it's slow but cheaper than a cab, which can charge any-

where from $32 up to $75. Getting back to the airport for your departure is less expensive; taxi fares range from about $15 to $22. Hotels post current rates. Be sure to agree on a price before getting into a cab.

BY BOAT & FERRY

There are several places to catch ferries from Cancún to Isla Mujeres. Some ferries carry vehicles and passengers between Cancún's Punta Sam and Isla's dock; others carry passengers from Puerto Juárez. Transportes Maritimos Magaña runs its boats *Miss Valentina* and *Caribbean Lady* every half hour with the final ferry at 10:30 PM. A one-way ticket costs $3.50.

Ferries traveling directly from the Zona Hotelera run on more limited schedules. Ferries leave the Embarcadero dock for Isla Mujeres at 9:15, 10:30, 11:30, 1:30, and 4:15 daily. At Playa Tortugas, they leave for Isla at 9:15, 11:30, 1:45, and 3:45 daily. Ferries from Playa Caracol leave Cancún for Isla at 9, 11, 1, and 3 daily. Round-trip fares at all three departure points start at $16 per person.

Embarcadero dock ferries ✉ Blvd. Kukulcán, Km 4. **Playa Caracol ferries** ✉ Blvd. Kukulcán, Km 9. **Playa Tortugas ferries** ✉ Blvd. Kukulcán, Km 7.5. **Transportes Maritimos Magaña** ☎ 998/877-0065.

BY BUS

The City of Cancún contracts bus services out to two competing companies. The result is frequent, reliable public buses running between the Zona Hotelera and El Centro from 6 AM to midnight; the cost is 75¢. There are designated stops—look for blue signs with white buses in the middle along Boulevard Kukulcán in the Hotel Zone and along Tulum Avenue downtown. Take Ruta 8 (Route 8) to reach Puerto Juárez and Punta Sam for the ferries to Isla Mujeres. Take Ruta 1 (Route 1) to and from the Zona Hotelera. Ruta 1 buses will drop you off anywhere along Avenida Tulum, and you can catch a connecting bus into El Centro. Try to have the correct change and be careful of drivers trying to shortchange you. Also, hold on to the tiny piece of paper the driver gives you. It's your receipt, and bus company officers sometimes board buses and ask for all receipts. To get off the bus, walk to the rear and press the red button on the pole by the back door. If the bus is crowded and you can't make it to the back door, call out to the driver, *La proxima parada, por favor*—The next stop, please.

Autocar and Publicar, in conjunction with the Cancún tourist board, has published an excellent pocket guide called "TheMAP" that shows all the bus routes to points of interest in Cancún and surrounding area. The map is free and is easiest to find at the airport. Some of the mid-range hotels carry copies and if you are lucky you may find one on a bus.

First- and second-class buses arrive at the downtown bus terminal (terminal de autobuses) from all over Mexico. Check the schedule, either at the terminal or online, for departure times for Tulum, Chetumal, Cobá, Valladolid, Chichén Itzá, and Mérida. Schedules may change at the last minute but the prices will stay the same.

Autobuses del Oriente, or ADO, is one of the oldest buslines in Mexico and offers regular bus service to Puerto Morelos and Playa del Carmen every hour from 5:00 AM until noon, and every 20 minutes from noon until midnight. Playa Express/Mayab Bus Lines have express buses that leave every 20 minutes for Puerto Morelos and Playa del Carmen. To go further south you must transfer at Playa del Carmen. Riviera Autobuses have first and second class buses leaving for destinations along the Riviera Maya every hour.

🚌 **Autobuses del Oriente (ADO)** ☎ 998/884-5542. **Playa Express/Mayab Bus Lines** ☎ 998/887-4455. **Riviera Autobuses** ☎ 998/884-4352. **Terminal de Autobuses** ✉ Avs. Tulum and Uxmal, Sm 23 ☎ 998/887-1149 ⊕ www.ticketbus.com.mx.

BY CAR

⚠ Driving in Cancún isn't for the faint of heart. Traffic moves at a breakneck speed; adding to the danger are the many one-way streets, *glorietas* (traffic circles), sporadically working traffic lights, ill-placed *topes* (speed bumps), numerous pedestrians, and large potholes. Be sure to observe speed limits as traffic police are vigilant and eager to give out tickets. As well as being risky, car travel is expensive, since it often necessitates tips for valet parking, gasoline, and costly rental rates.

Although driving in Cancún isn't recommended, exploring the surrounding areas on the peninsula by car is. The roads are excellent within a 100-km (62-mi) radius. Carretera 180 runs from Matamoros at the Texas border through Campeche, Mérida, Valladolid, and into Cancún. The trip from Texas can take up to three days. Carretera 307 runs south from Cancún through Puerto Morelos, Tulum, and Chetumal, then into Belize. Carretera 307 has several Pemex gas stations between Cancún and Playa del Carmen. For the most part, though, the only gas stations are near major cities and towns, so keep your tank full. When approaching any community, watch out for the speed bumps—hitting them at top speed can ruin your transmission and tires.

CAR RENTAL   Most rental cars in Cancún are standard-shift subcompacts and jeeps; air-conditioned cars with automatic transmissions should be reserved in advance (though bear in mind that some smaller car-rental places have only standards). The larger chain agencies (see Car Rental *in* Smart Travel Tips A to Z for contact information) tend to have the newer and more expensive cars; local companies can have much lower prices. Rates start at $20–$35 per day for manuals and between $55 to $75 for automatics. Better prices can sometime be found on the Internet—but if you book online, be sure to bring a copy of your rental agreement with you to Cancún. If you'd rather not book a rental yourself, the Car Rental Association can help you arrange one.

🚗 Local Agencies & Contacts **Buster Renta Car** ✉ Plaza Nautilus Kukulcán, Km 3.5, Zona Hotelera ☎ 998/849-7221. **Caribetur Rent a Car** ✉ Plaza Terramar, Blvd. Kukulcán, Km 8.5 ☎ 998/883-1071. **Car Rental Association** ✉ Calle La Costa 28, Sm 2 ☎ 998/863-1071. **Econorent** ✉ Avs. Bonampak and Cobá, Sm 4 ☎ 998/887-6487. **Mónaco Rent a Car** ✉ Av. Yaxchilán 65, Lote 5, Sm 25 ☎ 998/884-6540. **Vip Top Rent a Car** ✉ Av. Luis Donaldo Colosio, Km 344, Col. Alfredo V. Bonfil, Fracc. Bonfil 2000 ☎ 998/886-2391.

BY MOPED

⚠ Riding a moped in Cancún is extremely dangerous, and you may risk serious injury by using one in either the Zona or El Centro. If you have never ridden a moped or a motorcycle before, *this is not the place to learn.* Mopeds rent for about $25 a day; you are required to leave a credit-card voucher for security. You should receive a crash helmet, which by law you must wear. Read the fine print on your contract; companies will hold you liable for all repairs or replacement in case of an accident and will not offer any insurance to protect you.

BY TAXI

Taxi rides within the Zona Hotelera cost $6–$10; between the Zona Hotelera and El Centro, they run $8 and up; and to the ferries at Punta Sam or Puerto Juárez, fares are $15–$20 or more. Prices depend on distance, your negotiating skills, and whether you pick up the taxi in front of a hotel or save a few dollars by going onto the avenue to hail one yourself (look for green city cabs). Most hotels list rates at the door; confirm the price with your driver *before* you set out. Some drivers ask for such outrageously high fares it's not worth trying to bargain with them. Just let them go and flag down another cab. If you lose something in a taxi or have questions or a complaint, call the Sindicato de Taxistas. Don't be disappointed if your lost item stays lost; most locals assume that something lost means it doesn't have to be returned.

🔟 **Sindicato de Taxistas** ☎ 998/871-0298.

Contacts & Resources

BANKS & EXCHANGE SERVICES

Banks are generally open weekdays 9 to 5; money-exchange desks have hours from 9 to 1:30. Automatic teller machines (ATMs) usually dispense Mexican money; some newer ones also dispense dollars. ATMs at the smaller banks are often out of order, and if your personal identification number has more than four digits, your card may not work. Also, don't delay in taking your card out of the machine. ATMs are quick to eat them up, and it takes a visit to the bank and a number of forms to get them back. If your transactions require a teller, arrive at the bank early to avoid long lines. Banamex and Bital both have El Centro and Zona Hotelera offices and can exchange or wire money.

🔟 **Banamex** Downtown ✉ Av. Tulum 19, next to City Hall, Sm 1 ☎998/884-6403 ✉ Plaza Terramar, Blvd. Kukulcán, Km 37, Zona Hotelera ☎ 998/883-3100. **Bital** ✉ Av. Tulum 15, Sm 4 ☎998/884-1433 ✉ Plaza Caracol, Blvd. Kukulcán, Km 8.5, Zona Hotelera ☎998/ 883-4652.

EMERGENCIES

For general emergencies throughout the Cancun area, dial **060.**

🔟 Emergency Services **Fire Department** ☎ 998/884-1202. **Hotel Zone Police** ☎ 998/ 885-0569 **Municipal Police** ☎ 998/884-1913. **State Police** ☎ 998/884-1171. **Immigration Office** ☎ 998/884-1749. **Red Cross** ✉ Avs. Xcaret and Labná, Sm 21 ☎ 998/884-1616. **Green Angels (for highway breakdowns)** ☎ 998/884-2950.

🔟 Hospitals **Hospital Amat (emergency hospital)** ✉ Av. Náder 13, Sm 3 ☎ 998/887-4422. **Hospital Americano** ✉ Retorno Viento 15, Sm 4 ☎ 998/884-6133. **Hospital Amerimed Cancún** ✉ Ave. Tulum Sur 260, Sm 7 ☎ 998/881-3400, 998/881-3434 for emergencies. **Hospiten** ⊠ Avda. Bonampak, Lote 7, Sm 10 ☎ 998/881-3700. **Total Assist** ⊠ Claveles 5 , Sm 22 ☎ 998/884-8022.

🔲 **Pharmacies Farmacia Cancún** ⊠ Av. Tulum 17, Sm 22 ☎ 998/884-1283. **Farmacia Extra** ⊠ Plaza Caracol, Blvd. Kukulcán, Km 8.5, Zona Hotelera ☎ 998/883-2827. **Farmacia Walmart (24 hrs)** ⊠ Av. Cobá, Lote 2, Sm 21 ☎ 998/884-1383 Ext. 140. **Paris** ⊠ Av. Yaxchilán 32, Sm 3 ☎ 998/884-3005. **Roxanna's** ⊠ Plaza Flamingo, Blvd. Kukulcán, Km 11.5, Zona Hotelera ☎ 998/885-1351.

INTERNET, MAIL & SHIPPING

The *correos* (post office) is open weekdays 8–5 and Saturday 9–1; there's also a Western Union office in the building and a courier service. Postal service to and from Mexico is extremely slow. Avoid sending or receiving parcels—and never send checks or money through the mail. Invariably they are stolen. Your best bet is to use a courier service such as DHL or Federal Express.

Most hotels offer Internet service but at exorbitant rates. Some go as high as $25 per hour. Most of the Internet cafés in the Zona Hotelera charge by the minute and have computers that take at least 10 minutes to boot up. Compu Copy, in the Zona Hotelera, is open daily 9–9. Downtown, the Internet Café is open Monday–Saturday 11–10, and Infonet is open daily 10 AM–11 PM. Rates at all three start at $2 per hour. Head to El Centro if you need to send more than one e-mail.

🔲 **Cybercafés Compu Copy** ⊠ Plaza Kukulcán, Blvd. Kukulcán, Km 13, Zona Hotelera ☎ 998/885-0055. **Infonet** ⊠ Plaza las Americas, Av. Tulum, Sm 4 and Sm 9 ☎ 998/887-9130. **Internet Café** ⊠ Av. Tulum 10 behind Comercial Mexicana, across from the bus station, Sm 2 ☎ 998/887-3168. **Sycom Internet** ⊠ Av. Náder 45, Sm 2 ☎ 998/887-5675.

🔲 **Mail & Shipping Airborne Express** ⊠ Calle Liebre 15, Sm 20 ☎ 998/849-0959. **Correos (Post Office)** ⊠ Avs. Sunyaxchén and Xel-Há, Sm 26 ☎ 998/884-1418. **DHL** ⊠ Av. Tulum 200, Sm 26 ☎ 998/887-1813. **Federal Express** ⊠ Av. Tulum 9, Sm 22 ☎ 998/887-3279. **Mail Boxes Etc.** ⊠ Av. Xpuhil 3, behind Mercado 28, Sm 27 ☎ 998/887-4918.

MEDIA

You can pick up many helpful publications at the airport, malls, tourist kiosks, and many hotels. Indeed, you can't avoid having them shoved into your hands. Most are stuffed with discount coupons offering some savings. The best of the bunch is *Cancún Tips,* a free pocket-size guide to hotels, restaurants, shopping, and recreation. Although it's loaded with advertising and coupons, the booklet, published twice a year in English and Spanish, has some useful information. The accompanying *Cancún Tips Magazine* has informative articles about local attractions. The *Mapa Pocket Guide* is handy for its Zona Hotelera map and some local contact information. Since the folks who own the parks of Xcaret, Xel-Há, El Embarcadero, and Garrafón publish this guide, they often leave out information on any competitors while heavily promoting their own interests. *Map@migo* has an excellent map of the Zona Hotelera as well as El Centro. It's a handy brochure filled with numbers and coupons to restaurants. Along the same lines in a smaller, booklet format, *Passport Cancún* also has helpful numbers and information along with more coupons.

Tour Options

BOAT TOURS   Day cruises to Isla Mujeres generally include snorkeling, a trip to the center of town, and lunch. Blue Waters Adventures runs daily cruises through Laguna Nichupté and to Isla in a glass-bottomed boat. Kolumbus Tours offers tours to Isla Mujers and Isla Contoy on replica boats of the *Pinta,* the *Niña,* and the Spanish galleon *Cosario.* Two Much Fun-N-A Boat runs sailing and snorkeling trips to Isla in the mornings and evenings.

🚩 **Blue Waters Adventures** ⊠ Playa Tortuga/Fat Tuesday Marina, Blvd. Kukulcán, Km 6.5, Zona Hotelera ☎ 998/889–4444 ⊕ www.bluewateradventures.com.mx. **Kolumbus Tours** ⊠ Punta Conoco 36, Punta Sam ☎ 998/884–1598 ⊕ www.kolumbustours.com. **Two Much Fun-N-A Boat** ⊠ Las Jaibas Marina, Punta Sam ☎ 998/105–5667 ⊕ www. twomuchfun-n-aboat.com.

áThe 500,000-acre Reserva Ecológica El Edén, 48 km (30 mi) northwest of Cancún, is in the area known as Yalahau. The reserve was established by one of Mexico's leading naturalists, Arturo Gómez-Pompa, and his nephew, Marco Lazcano-Barrero, and is dedicated to research and conservation. It offers excursions for people interested in exploring wetlands, mangrove swamps, sand dunes, savannas, and tropical forests. Activities include bird-watching, animal-tracking, stargazing, and archaeology. Rates start at $75 per person for a full-day visit. If you're not into roughing it, these trips aren't for you.

Eco Colors runs adventure tours to the wildlife reserves at Isla Holbox and Sian Ka'an, El Eden, and to remote Maya ruin sites. The company also offers bird-watching, kayaking, camping, and biking excursions around the peninsula. Prices start at $48 for day trips, $336 for 3-day trips and $780 for 7-day trips. MayaSites Travel Services offers educational eco-tours for families to a variety of Maya ruins—including trips to Chichén Itzá during the spring equinox.

🚩 **Eco Colors** ⊠ Calle Camarón 32, Sm 27 ☎ 998/884–9580 ⊕ www.ecotravelmexico. com. **MayaSites Travel Services** ⊠ 1217 Truman Avenue SE, Albuquerque, NM 87108 ☎ 877/620–8715 ⊕ www.mayasites.com. **Reserva Ecológica El Edén** ☎ 998/880– 5032 ⊕ http://maya.ucr.edu/pril/el_eden/Home.html.

SUBMARINE   Aquaworld's Sub See Explorer is a "floating submarine"—a glass-bot-
TOURS   tomed boat that submerges halfway into the water. On a 1-hour cruise ($40) you can experience the beauty of Cancún's reef and watch the exotic fish while staying dry. Tours leave on the hour daily 9–3 PM, and include refreshments.

If you like the idea of scuba diving but don't have time to get certified, check out B.O.B. (Breathing Observation Bubble) Cancún. Instead of using scuba gear, you can sit on a machine resembling an underwater motor scooter, and steer your way through the reef while wearing a pressurized helmet that lets you breathe normally. It's safe and requires minimal exertion. The 2½-hour tour through the Bahía de Mujeres costs $75 per person and includes a video of your adventure. Tours leave at 9, 11:30, 2, and 4.

🚩 **AquaWorld's Sub See Explorer** ⊠ Blvd. Kukulcán, Km 15.1, Zona Hotelera ☎ 998/ 883–8300. **B.O.B. (Breathing Observation Bubble) Cancún** ⊠ Playa Langosta, Blvd. Kukulcán, Km 4, Zona Hotelera ☎ 998/892–4106 ⊕ www.cancunbob.com.

Isla Mujeres

Playa Norte, Isla Mujeres

WORD OF MOUTH

"We have stayed at Isla Mujeres and loved it. It's very laid-back yet only a 20-minute ferry ride from the hustle and bustle of Cancún. The beach and the restaurants are really outstanding. Also, you're close enough to the mainland to do some of the excursions to the Maya ruins."

—Lisa

AROUND ISLA MUJERES

Getting Oriented

Sleepy, unassuming, and magical, Isla Mujeres has resisted change in an otherwise quickly developing region. Just 8 km (5 mi) long and 1 km (½ mi) wide, its landscapes include flat sandy beaches in the north and steep rocky bluffs to the south. Swimming or snorkeling, exploring the remnants of the island's past, drinking cold beer and eating fresh seafood, and lazing under thatched *palapas* are the liveliest activities here.

TOP 5 Reasons to Go

1. Getting away from the crowd. Although Isla is just 5 mi across the bay from Cancun, the peace and quiet make it seem like another universe.

2. Exploring the southeastern coast, where craggy cliffs meet the blue Caribbean, by bumping along in a golf cart.

3. Eating fresh grilled seafood under a beach-front palapa at Playa Norte.

4. Scuba diving the underwater caverns off Isla to see "sleeping" sharks.

5. Taking a boat trip to Isla Contoy, where more than 70 species of birds make their home.

Snorkeling at Isla Mujeres

Playa Norte   Playa Norte

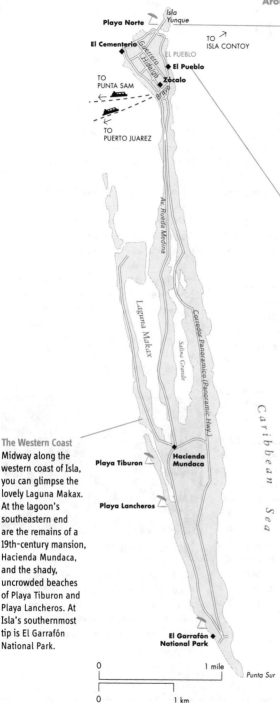

Playa Norte With its waist-deep turquoise waters and wide soft sands, Playa Norte is the most northerly and most beautiful beach on Isla. Most of the island's resorts and hotels are located here; El Pueblo and the historic El Cementerio are just a short walk away.

El Pueblo Directly in front of the ferry piers, El Pueblo is Isla's only town. It extends the full width of the northern end and is sandwiched between sand and sea to the south, west, and northeast. The *zócalo* (main square) here is the hub of Isleño life.

The Western Coast Midway along the western coast of Isla, you can glimpse the lovely Laguna Makax. At the lagoon's southeastern end are the remains of a 19th-century mansion, Hacienda Mundaca, and the shady, uncrowded beaches of Playa Tiburon and Playa Lancheros. At Isla's southernmost tip is El Garrafón National Park.

El Garrafón National Park

Map labels:

Isla Yunque
Playa Norte
El Cementerio
EL PUEBLO
El Pueblo
Zócalo
TO ISLA CONTOY
TO PUNTA SAM
TO PUERTO JUAREZ
Guerrero Hidalgo
Bravo
Av. Rueda Medina
Laguna Makax
Salina Grande
Corredor Panoramico (Panoramic Hwy.)
Caribbean Sea
Playa Tiburon
Hacienda Mundaca
Playa Lancheros
El Garrafón National Park
Punta Sur

0   1 mile
0   1 km

ISLA MUJERES PLANNER

Getting There & Getting Around

The only way to get to Isla is by ferry from Puerto Juárez on the mainland, just north of Cancún. The boat rides are quick—usually making the journey to Isla in 30 minutes or less. Be sure to buy your ferry ticket on board the boat; the people you see selling them on the docks aren't official ticket sellers and will charge you more.

There's no reason to bring a car to Isla, and there aren't any car-rental agencies on the island. If you want to drive once you're there, grab a taxi—they're cheap, and they line up near the ferry port around the clock. Since the island's so small, though, bikes, mopeds, and golf carts are the most popular ways to get around. Just be sure to watch out for the ubiquitous speed bumps (or *topes*), and the occasionally reckless local drivers.

Mopeds are extremely popular, and the daily or hourly rates vary depending on the moped's make and age. Many moped places also rent bikes. Just remember that it's hot, so keep hydrated and limit your mileage. And don't even think about night rides: few roads have streetlights. Golf carts (which rent for as little as $40 a day) are a lot of fun, especially if you have kids. In fact, carts have become so popular that taxis have started to feel pinched—all the more reason to establish cab fares before setting off.

Behaving Yourself

Since Isla is still primarily a sleepy fishing community, life here moves slowly. You'll find most *isleños* are laid-back and friendly, especially if you make the effort to speak a few words of Spanish. Still, Isla residents are protective of their peaceful island sanctuary, and so their attitudes about risqué behavior (like public drunkenness and topless sunbathing) are conservative. The Virgin Mary is an important icon on the island, so it's considered respectful to cover yourself up before visiting any of the churches. Spring-breakers are not welcome here, so if you want to want to party and drink into the wee hours of the morning, Cancún is the better choice for you.

Need More Information?

The **Isla Mujeres tourist office** (✉ Av. Rueda Medina 130 ☎ 998/877–0307 ⊕ www.isla-mujeres.com.mx) is open weekdays 8–8 and weekends 8–noon, and has lots of general information about the island.

Staying Awhile

If you want to rent a home or apartment on the island, there are several Internet-based rental agencies that can help you. www.islabeckons.com, for example, lists fully equipped apartments and houses for rent (and also handles reservations for hotel rooms). www.morningsinmexico.com offers smaller and less expensive properties. Most rental homes have fully equipped kitchens, bathrooms, and bedrooms. You can opt for a house downtown or a more secluded one on the eastern coast.

Island Dining

Perhaps it's the fresh air and sunlight that whet the appetite, making Isla's simple meals so delicious. There's plenty of fish and shellfish, including grilled lobster. There are also pleasant variations on pasta, pizza, steak, and sandwiches. Sweet fruits, fresh coffee, and baked goods make breakfast a treat. Like island life, meals don't need to be complicated.

Dining & Lodging Prices

WHAT IT COSTS in Dollars

	$$$$	$$$	$$	$	¢
Restaurants	over $25	$15–$25	$10–$15	$5–$10	under $5
Hotels	over $250	$150–$250	$75–$150	$50–$75	under $50

Restaurant prices are per person, for a main course at dinner, excluding tax and tip. Hotel prices are for a standard double room in high season, based on the European Plan (EP) and excluding service and 12% tax (which includes 10% Value Added Tax plus 2% hospitality tax).

How's the Weather?

Isla enjoys its best weather between November and May, when temperatures usually hover around 80°F.

June, July, and August are the hottest and most humid months, when temperatures routinely top 95°F.

The rainy hurricane season lasts from late September until mid-November, bringing frequent downpours in the afternoons, as well as the occasional hairy tropical storm.

Save the Dates

Sol a Sol Regatta: late April. Founder's Day: Aug. 17. Day of the Dead celebrations: Oct. 31–Nov. 2. Immaculate Conception Feast: Dec. 1–8. Book well in advance, and come if you can.

EXPLORING ISLA MUJERES

The minute you step off the boat, you'll get a sense of how small Isla is. The sights and properties on the island are strung along the coasts; there's not much to the interior except the two saltwater marshes, Salina Chica and Salina Grande, where Maya inhabitants harvested salt centuries ago. The main road

HEAD TO TAIL
To get your bearings, try thinking of Isla Mujeres as a long, narrow fish, the head being the south-eastern tip, the northwest prong the tail.

is Avenida Rueda Medina, which runs the length of the island; southeast of a village known as El Colonia, it turns into Carretera El Garrafón. Smaller street names and other address details don't really matter much here.

Numbers in the text correspond to numbers in the margin and on the Isla Mujeres map.

A Good Tour

You can walk to Isla's historic **Cementerio** ❶ ▶ by going northwest from the ferry piers on Avenida López Mateos. Then head southeast (by car or other vehicle) along Avenida Rueda Medina past the piers to reach the Mexican naval base, where you can see flag ceremonies at sunrise and sunset. Just don't take any pictures—it's illegal to photograph military sites in Mexico. Continue southeast; 2½ km (1½ mi) out of town is **Laguna Makax** ❷, on the right. Two smaller salt water marshes, Salina Chica and Salina Grande run parallel to the lagoon.

At the lagoon's southeast end, a dirt road on the left leads to the remains of the **Hacienda Mundaca** ❸. About a block west, where Avenida Rueda Medina splits, is a statue of Ramon Bravo, Isla's first environmentalist, who passed away in 1998 but who remains a hero to many islanders. If you turn right (northwest) and follow the road for about ½ km (¼ mi), you'll reach Playa Tiburon, and the Tortugranja (turtle farm). If you turn left (southwest), you'll see Playa Lancheros almost immediately. Both are good swimming beaches.

Continue southeast past Playa Lancheros to **El Garrafón National Park** ❹. Slightly more than ½ km (¼ mi) farther along the same road, on the windward side of the tip of Isla Mujeres, is the site of a small Maya ruin, once a temple dedicated to Ixchel, the Santuario Maya a la Diosa Ixchel. Although little remains here, the ocean and bay views are still worth the stop—but you must pay to see them and get past the kitschy Caribbean village and bizarre sculpture park first. Follow the paved eastern perimeter road northwest back into town. Known as either the Corredor Panorámico (Panoramic Highway) or Carretera Perimetral al Garrafón (Garrafón Perimeter Highway), this is a scenic drive with a few pull-off areas along the way. ⚠ This side of the island is quite windy, with strong currents and a rocky shore, so swimming is not recommended. The road curves back into Avenida Rueda Medina near the naval base.

CLOSE UP

The Hot Stuff: Tequila and Chile Peppers

TEQUILA IS THE NATIONAL DRINK OF MEXICO, and chances are you will be offered a glass sooner or later. There are hundreds of tequilas available, ranging from the super-smooth to the pretty harsh varieties. To be considered authentic, tequila must come from the state of Jalisco and have a seal of certification. There are basically three types, all of which are made from the blue agave plant. Blanco (white) or plata (silver) tequila is fresh from the still and retains most of the flavor of the agave plant. Sometimes a caramel coloring is added to this tequila and then it is known as joven (young). Reposado (rested) is tequila that has been aged in a white oak cask anywhere between two months and a year. It has a mellow flavor and pale color. Añejo (aged) tequila has been aged in an oak cask for between one and four years. The aging process allows it to take on an amber color and a smooth taste. Muy añejo (very aged) refers to tequila aged between three to five years.

Liquor made from any other kind of agave plant is known as mezcal. It, too, comes in varying degrees of smoothness.

Most Mexicans prefer to sip añejo tequila in a brandy snifter so the aroma can be savored. Blanco and reposado are usually served with sangrita, which is a mix of tomato and orange juice with salt and lime. All tequilas should be enjoyed at room temperature and are always sipped, even when put into the small shot glasses known as cabalitos. Most of the places offering all-you-can-drink menus will be serving joven—which can leave you with a wicked hangover. Reposado is the favored tequila in margaritas because it is somewhat smooth, but many places do use joven combined with a premixed lime juice and lots of salt and crushed ice to mask the harshness. Again, drinking these can make you feel a little rough the morning after. An authentic margarita will have minimal ice, freshly squeezed lime juice, and just a hint of salt around the rim that should be tasted with each sip to enhance the flavor of the drink.

Before tasting anything with chiles be sure to ask ¿Es muy picante? (Is it very hot?) The mildest chiles are the pimiento green or red peppers. Next up in the heat scale are poblano chiles, which are mildly spicy. The serrano chile is used in many restaurant's salsas, and can be very hot. But slender, green jalapeño chiles, often used in sauces, are even hotter. Another hot chile is the chipotle, which has a smoky flavor—but which still packs less of a punch than the habanero chile, used in many Yucatecan dishes. The deadliest of all is the rubio (white) chile—most gringos simply can't handle it.

Since a chile's heat comes not from the actual pepper itself, but from the oil of the seeds inside, when your mouth is on fire it's best to eat a piece of bread or tortilla to soak up the oil. Salt also helps. Vast quantities of beer or tequila will only spread the flame—although after a while, you may not care or notice.

2

What to See

▶ ❶ **El Cementerio.** Isla's unnamed cemetery, with its century-old gravestones, is on Avenida López Mateos, the road that runs parallel to Playa Norte. Many of the tombstones are covered with carved angels and flowers; the most elaborate and beautiful mark the graves of children. Hidden among them is the tomb of the notorious Fermín Mundaca. This

TIMING

Although it's possible to explore Isla in one day, if you take your time, rent a moped or golf cart, and spend a couple of days, you'll be able to soak up more of the nuances of island life.

19th-century slave trader—who's often billed more glamorously as a pirate—carved his own skull-and-crossbones gravestone with the ominous epitaph: AS YOU ARE, I ONCE WAS; AS I AM, SO SHALL YOU BE. Mundaca's grave is empty, however; his remains lie in Mérida, where he died. The monument is tough to find—ask a local to point out the unidentified marker.

❹ **El Garrafón National Park.** Despite participation in the much publicized "Garrafón Reef Restoration Program," much of the coral reef at this national marine park remains dead (the result of hurricane damage, as well as damage from boats and too many careless tourists). There are still some colorful fish to be seen here, but many of them will only come near if bribed with food. Although there's no longer much for snorkelers here, the park does have kayaks and ocean playground equipment (such as platforms to dive from), as well as a three-floor facility with restaurants, bathrooms, and gift shops. Be prepared to spend big money here; the basic entry fee doesn't include snorkel gear, lockers, or food, all of which are pricey. (The Beach Club Garrafón de Castilla next door is a much cheaper alternative; the snorkeling is at least equal to that available in the park. The club is open to everyone and the entrance fee is $2. You can take a taxi from town.)

The park also has the **Santuario Maya a la Diosa Ixchel,** the sad vestiges of a Maya temple once dedicated to the goddess Ixchel. Unsuccessful attempts to restore it were made after Hurricane Gilbert greatly damaged the site in 1988. A lovely walkway around the area remains, but the natural arch beneath the ruin has been blasted open and "repaired" with concrete badly disguised as rocks. The views here are spectacular, though: you can look to the open ocean on one side and the Bahía de Mujeres (Bay of Women) on the other. On the way to the temple there is a cutesy re-creation of a Caribbean village selling overpriced jewelry and souvenirs. Just before you reach the ruins you will pass the sculpture park with its abstract blobs of iron painted in garish colors. Inside the village is an old lighthouse, which you can enter for free. Climb to the top for an incredible view to the south; the vista in the other direction is marred by a tower from a defunct amusement ride (Ixchel would not be pleased). The ruin, which is open daily 9 to 5:30, is at the point where the road turns northeast into the Corredor Panorámico. To visit just the ruins and sculpture park the admission is

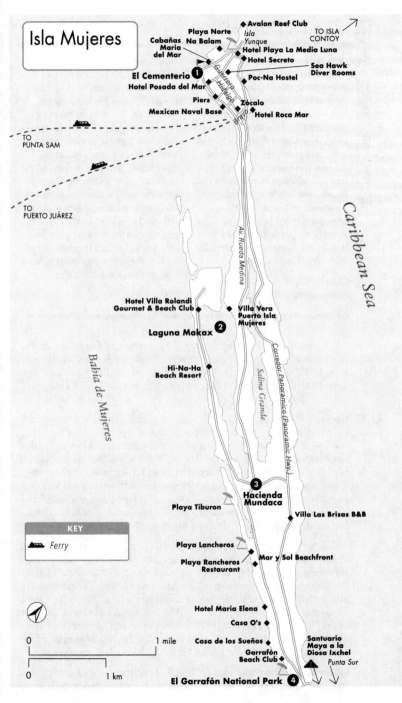

Isla Mujeres

TO ISLA CONTOY

Avalon Reef Club

Isla Yunque

Playa Norte

Cabañas Maria del Mar

Na Balam

Hotel Playa La Media Luna

Hotel Secreto

Sea Hawk Diver Rooms

El Cementerio ❶

Poc-Na Hostel

Hotel Posada del Mar

Piers

Zócalo

Mexican Naval Base

Hotel Roca Mar

TO PUNTA SAM

TO PUERTO JUÁREZ

Caribbean Sea

Av. Rueda Medina

Hotel Villa Rolandi Gourmet & Beach Club

Villa Vera Puerto Isla Mujeres

Laguna Makax ❷

Corredor Panoramico (Panoramic Hwy.)

Hi-Na-Ha Beach Resort

Salina Grande

Bahía de Mujeres

Hacienda Mundaca ❸

Playa Tiburon

Villa Las Brisas B&B

KEY

🛥 *Ferry*

Playa Lancheros

Playa Rancheros Restaurant

Mar y Sol Beachfront

Hotel Maria Elena

Casa O's

0 _____ 1 mile

Casa de los Sueños

Santuario Maya a la Diosa Ixchel

0 _____ 1 km

Garrafón Beach Club

Punta Sur

El Garrafón National Park ❹

Who Was Ixchel?

IXCHEL (ee-shell) IS A PRINCIPAL FIGURE IN THE PANTHEON OF MAYA GODS. Originally married to the earth god Voltan, Ixchel fell in love with the moon good Itzamna, considered the founder of the Maya because he taught them how to read, write, and grow corn. When Ixchel became his consort, she gave birth to four powerful sons known as the Bacabs, who continue to hold up the sky in each of the four directions. Sometimes called Lady Rainbow, Ixchel is the goddess of childbirth, fertility, and healing. She controls the tides and all water on earth.

Often portrayed as a wise crone, she is seen wearing a skirt decorated with crossbones and a crown of serpents while carrying a jug of water. The crossbones are a symbol of her role as the giver of new life and keeper of dead souls. The serpents represent her wisdom and power to rejuvenate. The water jug alludes to her dual role as both a benign and destructive deity. Although she gives mankind the continual gift of water—the most essential element of life—according to Maya myth, Ixchel also sent floods to cleanse the earth of wicked men who had stopped thanking the gods. She is said to give special protection to those making the sacred pilgrimage to her sites on Cozumel and Isla Mujeres.

$3. Admission to the village is free. ⊠ *Carretera El Garrafón, 2½ km (1½ mi) southeast of Playa Lancheros* ☎ *998/884–9420 in Cancún, 998/877–1100 to the park* ⊕ *www.garrafon.com* ⊠ *Basic entrance fee: $16. Tours from Cancun: $29–$59. Tours from Isla: $44* ☉ *Daily 8:30 AM–6:30 PM.*

Hacienda Mundaca. A dirt drive and stone archway mark the entrance to what's left of a mansion constructed by 19th-century slave trader–turned–pirate Fermín Mundaca de Marechaja. When the British navy began cracking down on slavers, Mundaca settled on the island. He fell in love with a local beauty nicknamed La Trigueña (The Brunette). To woo her, Mundaca built a sprawling estate with verdant gardens. Apparently unimpressed, La Trigueña instead married a young islander—and legend has it that Mundaca went slowly mad waiting for her to change her mind. He ended up dying in a brothel in Mérida.

The actual hacienda has vanished. All that remain are a rusted cannon and a ruined stone archway with a triangular pediment carved with the following inscription: HUERTA DE LA HACIENDA DE VISTA ALEGRE MDCC-CLXXVI (Orchard of the Happy View Hacienda 1876). The gardens are also suffering from neglect, and the animals in a small on-site zoo seem as tired as the rest of the property. Mundaca would, however, approve of the cover charge; it's piracy. ⊠ *East of Av. Rueda Medina (take main road southeast from town to S-curve at end of Laguna Makax and turn left onto dirt road)* ☎ *No phone* ⊠ *$2.50* ☉ *Daily 9 AM–dusk.*

Iglesia de Concepion Inmaculada (Church of the Immaculate Conception). In 1890 local fishermen landed at a deserted colonial settlement known

Isla's History

CLOSE UP

THE NAME ISLA MUJERES MEANS "ISLAND OF WOMEN," although no one knows who dubbed it that. Many believe it was the ancient Maya, who were said to use the island as a religious center for worshipping Ixchel, the Maya goddess of rainbows, the moon, and the sea, and the guardian of fertility and childbirth. Another popular legend has it that the Spanish conquistador Hernández de Córdoba named the island when he landed here in 1517 and found hundreds of female-shaped clay idols dedicated to Ixchel and her daughters. Others say the name dates later, from the 17th century, when visiting pirates stashed their women on Isla before heading out to rob the high seas. (Legend has it that both Henry Morgan and Jean Lafitte buried treasure on Isla, although no one has ever found any pirate's gold.)

It wasn't until after 1821, when Mexico became independent, that people really began to settle on Isla. In 1847, refugees from the War of the Castes fled to the island and built its first official village of Dolores—which was welcomed into the newly created territory of Quintana Roo in 1850. By 1858, a slave trader–turned–pirate named Fermín Mundaca de Marechaja began building an estate on Isla, which took up 40% of the island. By the end of the century the population had risen to 651, and residents had begun to establish trade—mostly by supplying fish to the owners of chicle and coconut plantations on the mainland coast. In 1949 the Mexican Navy built a base on Isla's northwestern coast; around this time, the island also caught the eye of some wealthy Mexican sportsmen, who began using it as a vacation spot.

Tourism flourished on Isla during the later half of the 20th century, party due to the island's most famous resident, Ramón Bravo (1927–98). A diver, cinematographer, ecologist, and colleague of Jacques Cousteau, Bravo was the first underwater photographer to explore the area. He discovered the now-famous Cave of the Sleeping Sharks, and produced dozens of underwater documentaries for American, European, and Mexican television. Bravo's efforts to maintain the ecology on Isla has helped keep development here to a minimum. Even today, Bravo remains a hero to many *isleños* (ees-*lay*-nyos); his statue can be found beside Hacienda Mundaca where Avenida Rueda changes into the Carretera El Garrafón, and there is a museum named after him on nearby Isla Contoy.

---

as Ecab, where they found three identical statues of the Virgin Mary, each carved from wood with porcelain face and hands. No one knows for certain where the statues originated, but it is widely believed they're gifts from the conquistadores during a visit in 1770. One statue went to the city of Izamal, Yucatán, and another was sent to Kantunikin, Quintana Roo. The third remained on the island. It was housed in a small wooden chapel while this church was being built; legend has it that the chapel burst into flames when the statue was removed. Some islanders still believe the statue walks on the water around the island from dusk until dawn, looking for her sisters. You can pay your respects daily from

Isla's Salt Mines

The ancient salt mines whose remains still exist in Isla's interior were created during the Postclassic period of Maya history, which lasted roughly between the years 1000 and 1500 AD. Salt was an important commodity for the Maya; they used it not only for preserving and flavoring food, but for creating battle armor. Since the Maya had no metal, they soaked cotton cloth in salt until it formed a hard coating.

Today, the shallow marshes where salt was long ago harvested bear modern names: Salina Chica (small salt mine) and Salina Grande (large salt mine). Unfortunately there is little to see at the salt mines today. They are simply shallow marshes with murky water and quite a few mosquitoes at dusk. Since both the island's main roads (Avenida Rueda Medina and the Corredor Panorámico) pass by them, however, you can have a look at them on your way to visiting other parts of Isla.

10 AM until 11:30 AM and then from 7 PM until 9 PM. ✉ *Avs. Morelos and Bravo, south side of zócalo.*

❷ **Laguna Makax.** Pirates are said to have anchored their ships in this lagoon while waiting to ambush hapless vessels crossing the Spanish Main (the geographical area in which Spanish treasure ships trafficked). These days the lagoon houses a local shipyard and provides a safe harbor for boats during hurricane season. It's off Avenida Rueda Medina about 2½ km (1½ mi) south of town, about two block south of the naval base and some *salinas* (salt marshes).

El Malecón. To enjoy the drama of Isla's eastern shore while soaking up some rays, stroll along this mile-long boardwalk. It's the beginning of a long-term improvement project and will eventually encircle the island. Currently, it runs from Half Moon Bay to El Colonia, with several benches and look-out points. You can visit El Monumento de Tortugas (Turtle Monument) along the way.

☾ **Tortugranja** (Turtle Farm). After a dispute with the landowner that forced the temporary closing of this scientific station, the turtle farm has been reopened. It's now being run by the Mexican government and private funders who continue conservation efforts on behalf of the endangered sea turtle. You can see rescued turtle hatchlings in three large pools or watch the larger turtles in the sea pens. There is also a small museum with an excellent display about turtles and the ecosystem. ✉ *Take Av. Rueda Medina south of town; about a block southeast of Hacienda Mundaca, take the right fork (the smaller road that loops back north called Sac Bajo); the entrance is about ½ km (¼ mi) farther, on the left* ☎ *998/877–0595* ✆ *$3* ☉ *Daily 9–5.*

BEACHES

Playa Norte is easy to find: simply head north on any of the north–south streets in town until you hit this superb beach. The turquoise sea is as

2

calm as a lake here, and you can wade out for 40 yards in waist-deep water. According to isleños, Hurricane Gilbert's only good deed in 1988 was to widen this and other leeward-side beaches by blowing sand over from Cancún. Enjoy a drink and a snack at one of the area's palapa bars; Buho's is especially popular with locals and tourists who gather to chat, eat fresh seafood, drink cold beer, and watch the sunset. Lounge chairs and hammocks at Sergios are free for customers but to relax in front of Maria del Maria in a lounge chair will cost you $3. Na Balam charges a whopping $10 for one chair and umbrella. Tarzan Water Sports rents out snorkeling gear, Jet Skis, floats, and sailboards. Seafriends offers snorkeling classes and kayaks.

There are two beaches between Laguna Makax and El Garrafón National Park. **Playa Lancheros** is a popular spot with an open-air restaurant where locals gather to eat freshly grilled fish. The beach has grittier sand than Playa Norte, but more palm trees. The calm water makes it the perfect spot for children to swim—although it's best if they stay close to shore, since the ocean floor drops off steeply. The souvenir stands here are fairly low-key and run by local families. There is a small pen with domesticated and quite harmless *tiburones gatos*— nurse sharks. (These sharks are much friendlier than the *tintoreras*, or blue sharks, which live in the open seas, have seven rows of teeth, and weigh up to 1,100 lbs.) You can swim with them or get your picture taken for $1. **Playa Tiburon,** like Playa Lancheros, is on the west coast facing Bahía de Mujeres, and so its waters are also exceptionally calm. It's a more developed beach with a large, popular seafood restaurant (through which you actually enter the beach). There are several souvenir stands selling the usual T-shirts as well as handmade seashell jewelry. On certain days there are women who will braid your hair or give you a temporary henna tattoo. This beach also has two sea pens with the sleepy and relatively tame nurse sharks. You can have a low-key and very safe swim with these sharks—and get your picture taken doing so—for $2.

> ### NOT ALL BEACHES ARE FOR SWIMMING!
>
> While the beaches on the eastern side of the island (often referred to as the Caribeside) are quite beautiful, they are not safe for swimming because of the dangerous undertows, several drownings have occurred at these beaches. Another gorgeous but dangerous beach is found northeast, just kitty-corner to Playa Norte. Playa Media Luna (Half Moon beach) is very tempting, but the strong currents make it treacherous for swimmers.

WHERE TO EAT

Dining on Isla is a casual affair. Restaurants tend to serve simple meals: seafood, pizza, salads, and Mexican dishes, mostly prepared by local cooks. Fresh ingredients and hospitable waiters make up for the island's lack of elaborate menus and master chefs. It's cash only in most of the restaurants.

Locals often eat their main meal during siesta hours, between 1 and 4, and then have a light dinner in the evening. Unless otherwise stated, restaurants are open daily for lunch and dinner. Some restaurants open late and close early Sunday; others are closed Monday. Most restaurants welcome children and will cater to their tastes.

Though informal, most indoor restaurants do require that you wear a shirt and shoes when dining. Some outdoor terrace and palapa restaurants also request that you wear shoes and some sort of cover-up over your bathing suit.

It's customary in Mexico for the waiter NOT to bring you the bill until you ask for it (*"la cuenta, por favor"*). Always check your bill to make sure you didn't get charged for something you didn't order, and to make sure the addition is correct. The "tax" on the bill is often a service charge—kind of a guaranteed tip.

Prices

		WHAT IT COSTS In Dollars			
	$$$$	**$$$**	**$$**	**$**	**¢**
AT DINNER	over $25	$15–$25	$10–$15	$5–$10	under $5

Per person, for a main course at dinner, excluding tax and tip.

El Pueblo

$–$$$ ✕ **Picus Cocktelería.** Kick off your shoes and settle back with a cold beer
Fodor'sChoice   at this charming beachside restaurant right near the ferry docks. You
★   can watch the fishing boats come and go while you wait for some of the freshest seafood on the island. The grilled fish and grilled lobster with garlic butter are both magnificent here, as are the shrimp fajitas—but the real showstopper is the mixed seafood ceviche, which might include conch, shrimp, abalone, fish, or octopus. ⊠ *Av. Rueda Medina, 1 block northwest of ferry docks* ☎ *No phone* ▭ *No credit cards.*

$–$$$ ✕ **Sunset Grill.** The perfect place for a sunset dinner, this spot has beachside tables where you can sip cocktails and a covered dining terrace where large picture windows overlook the sea. The evening menu has a wide range of Mexican and Italian-American dishes, including coconut shrimp, fresh pasta, and fried snapper; soft music and candlelight add to the romantic ambience. There's also a lunch menu with Mexican favorites like tacos and quesadillas, and an excellent breakfast buffet. ⊠ *Av. Rueda Medina, North End, Condominios Nautibeach, Playa Norte* ☎ *998/877–0785* ▭ *MC, V.*

$–$$$ ✕ **Zazil Ha.** At this beachside restaurant, you can dine downstairs under big, shady palms or upstairs under a palapa roof. The menu offers innovative vegetarian fare—like salads with avocado and grapefruit, or coconut, mango, and mint vinaigrette—as well as traditional Mexican dishes. The chicken with cilantro sauce is especially good. ⊠ *Na Balam hotel, Calle Zazil-Ha 118* ☎ *998/877–0279* ▭ *AE, MC, V.*

$–$$ ✕ **Bamboo.** This casual restaurant with its bright tablecloths and bamboo-covered walls has two different chefs. In the morning, the first cooks up hearty breakfasts of omelets and hash browns with freshly brewed coffee. Later in the day, however, the second chef switches to Asian-fusion-style lunches and dinners, including a knockout shrimp tempura, vegetable stir-fry, and chicken satay in a spicy peanut sauce. On some evenings, there's live salsa or Caribbean music, and the place fills with locals. ⊠ *Plaza Los Almendros No. 4* ☎ *998/877–1355* ▤ *No credit cards.*

$–$$ ✕ **Fayne's.** The vibe at this brightly painted spot is hip and energetic. Best known for its terrific cocktails (don't miss the mango margaritas), this funky restaurant serves good island fare such as Tex-Mex sandwiches, garlic shrimp, calamari stuffed with spinach, and grilled snapper. The well-stocked bar has a colorful aquarium underneath, and the original artwork on the walls is for sale. ⊠ *Av. Hidalgo 12A, between Avs. Mateos and Guerrero* ☎ *No phone* ▤ *No credit cards.*

$–$$ ✕ **Jax Bar & Grill/Jax Upstairs Lounge.** The downstairs of this palapa-roofed hot spot is a lively sports bar, which serves up huge, thick, perfectly grilled burgers along with cold beer. The satellite TV is always turned to ESPN, and there's usually a game of pool or darts in progress. Upstairs is more elegant; you can enjoy the softly lit bar and piped-in smooth jazz while watching the sunset over fresh grilled seafood. ⊠ *Av. Adolfo Mateos 42* ☎ *998/887—1218* ▤ *MC, V.*

$ ✕ **Los Amigos.** This authentic isleño eatery really lives up to its name; once you've settled at one of the street-side tables, the staff treats you like an old friend. Though it used to be known mainly for its superb pizza, the menu has grown to include excellent fish, meat, pasta, and vegetarian dishes as well. The Steak Roquefort and garlic shrimp are sure bets—and be sure to try the rich chocolate cake or flambéed crepes. ⊠ *Av. Hidalgo between Avs. Matamoros and Abasolo* ☎ *No phone* ▤ *No credit cards.*

¢–$ ✕ **Angelo.** Named for its Italian expat chef, this small, charming bistro is done up with crisp linens, soft lighting, and a wood-fired oven. You may have trouble choosing just which pizza or pasta from the delicious-sounding menu, but you can't go wrong with the classic tomato and basil pizza, the pasta Gorgonzola, or the seafood-stuffed ravioli. ⊠ *Plaza Los Almendros No. 6* ☎ *998/877–1273* ▤ *No credit cards.*

¢–$ ✕ **Café Cito.** This cheery, seashell-decorated café was one of Isla's first cafés—and it's still one of the best places to breakfast on the island. The menu includes fresh waffles, fruit-filled crepes, and egg dishes, as well as great cappuccino and espresso; lunch specials are also available daily. After your meal, be sure to head to the Soñadores del Sol shop next door; the proprietor gives great tarot readings. ⊠ *Avs. Juárez and Matamoros* ☎ *998/877–0438* ▤ *No credit cards.*

★ ¢–$ ✕ **La Cazuela M&J.** Next door to the Hotel Roca Ma, this restaurant is perched right at the ocean's edge (if it gets too breezy for you outside, you can seek refuge in the sunny dining room). The breakfast menu, considered by many locals to be the best on the island, includes fresh-squeezed juices, fruit, crepes, and egg dishes—including the heavenly La Cazuela, somewhere between an omelet and a soufflé. Grilled chicken with homemade barbecue sauce and thick juicy hamburgers are on the lunch menu. ⊠ *Calle Nicolas Bravo, Zona Maritima* ☎ *998/877–0101* ▤ *No credit cards* ☉ *Closed Mon. No dinner.*

¢–$ ✕ **Don Chepo.** Mexican grill cuisine (tacos, fajitas, and steak) is the draw at this lively restaurant resembling a small hacienda. Inside the focal point is the large and well-stocked bar where you can chat with other visitors or enjoy the (sometimes live) mariachi music. Tables outside are perfect for watching all the downtown action on Hidalgo Street. The *arrachera,* a fine cut of beef steak grilled to perfection and served with rice, salad, baked potato, warm tortillas, and beans, is a reliably excellent choice. ✉ *Avs. Hidalgo and Francisco Madero* ☎ *No phone* ▭ *MC, V.*

¢–$ ✕ **Fredy's Restaurant & Bar.** This friendly, family-run restaurant specializes in simple fish, seafood, and traditional Mexican dishes like fajitas and tacos. There ain't much in the way of decor here—unless you call plastic chairs and tables decor—but the staff is wonderfully friendly, the food is fresh, and the beer is cold. The tasty daily specials are a bargain and attract both locals and visitors. Be sure to check out the two-for-one drink specials offered in the evenings. ✉ *Av. Hidalgo just below Av. Mateos* ☎ *998/810–1691* ▭ *No credit cards.*

¢–$ ✕ **Mañana Restaurant & Bookstore.** It's hard to miss this bright orange restaurant with a yellow sun stretching its rays over the front door. But you won't want to miss the great breakfasts here, with their yummy egg dishes, fresh baguettes, and Italian coffee. Salads, homemade burgers (meat or vegetarian), and fresh fruit shakes are served at lunch and dinnertime. If you're in a hurry, you can grab a quick snack at the outdoor counter with its palapa roof—but since Cosmic Cosas bookstore is also located here you may want to lounge on the couch and read after your meal. ✉ *Av. Guerrero 17* ☎ *998/877–0555* ▭ *No credit cards* ☾ *No dinner.*

¢–$ ✕ **Sergio's Playa Sol.** Delicious chicken nachos, guacamole, and fish kabobs are on the menu at this great Playa Norte beach bar. You can easily spend the whole day here and stay for the sunset; there are free hammocks, beach chairs, and umbrellas for customers. ✉ *North end of Playa Norte* ☎ *998/705–3250* ▭ *No credit cards.*

¢–$ ✕ **Taquería.** For delicious Yucatecan specialties—*salbutes* (fried corn tortillas smothered in chicken and salsa), *panuchos* (fried corn tortillas with chicken, refried beans, and shredded turkey *tortas* (sandwiches), or tamales—check out this hole-in-the-wall eatery. The two sisters who do the cooking don't speak much English but manage to communicate with their foreign customers using the international language of gestures. ✉ *Av. Juárez, 1 block south of cemetery* ☎ *No phone* ▭ *No credit cards.*

¢–$ ✕ **Tonyo's.** Equipped with the standard Isla decor (plastic chairs and tables), this tiny hole-in-the-wall pizzeria is run by enthusiatic locals who welcome you like family. The pepperoni pizza with roasted habañero and olive oil sauce is to die for. The soups, salads, and garlic bread are also memorable. ✉ *Rue Hidalgo 2 (south end of street)* ☎ *No phone* ▭ *No credit cards.*

¢ ✕ **Los Aluxes Cafe.** The perfect spot for an early-morning or late-night cappuccino (it opens at 6:30 AM and closes at 10 PM), this place also has terrific desserts and baked goods. The New York Cheesecake and Triple Fudge Turtle Brownies are especially decadent. There's also a great selection of exotic teas, and the local art and jewelry on display are for sale. The prices here are *cheap.* ✉ *Av. Matamoros 87* ☎ *998/877–1317* ▭ *No credit cards.*

2

¢ ✕ **Aquí Estoy.** It may be small, with only a few stools to sit on—but what pizza! The thick-crusted pies here are smothered with cheese and spicy tomato sauce, along with choices like grilled vegetables, pepperoni, and mushrooms. Everything is fresh and prepared on the spot. For dessert, try a slice of apple pie. A great place for a quick snack on your way to the beach! ✉ *Av. Matamoros 85* ☎ *No phone* ▭ *No credit cards.*

Elsewhere on the Island

$$–$$$$ ✕ **Casa O's.** This restaurant is more expensive than others downtown—
FodorsChoice   and worth every penny. The magic starts at the footpath, which leads
★   over a small stream before entering the three-tiered circular dining room overlooking the bay. As you watch the sun set, you can choose your fish—salmon, Chilean bass, tuna, snapper, or grouper—and have the chef prepare it to your individual taste; or you can pick out a fresh lobster from the on-site pond. Be sure to save room for the incredible key lime pie—it's the house speciality. The restaurant is named for its waiters—all of whose names end in the letter "o." ✉ *Carretera El Garrafón s/n* ☎ *998/888–0170* ▭ *MC, V.*

★ $$–$$$$ ✕ **Casa Rolandi.** This hotel restaurant is casually sophisticated, with an open-air dining room leading out to a deck that overlooks the water. Tables are done up with beautiful linens, china, and cutlery. The northern Italian menu here includes the wonderful carpaccio *di tonno alla Giorgio* (thin slices of tuna with extra-virgin olive oil and lime juice), along with excellent pastas—even the simplest dishes such as angel hair pasta in tomato sauce are delicious. For something different, try

> ### WORD OF MOUTH
>
> "Roaming around the markets and malls, getting hungrier and hungrier, we came upon Rolandi's. The menu looked acceptable and the dinner turned out to be a delightful experience. Superb and friendly service. The fresh pasta made the lasagna and ravioli better than average. The puff bread was fantastic."   –Paul

the saffron risotto or the *costoletto d'agnello al forno* (lamb chops with a thyme infusion). The sunset views are spectacular. ✉ *Hotel Villa Rolandi Gourmet & Beach Club, Fracc. Laguna Mar Makax, Sm 7* ☎ *998/877–0100* ▭ *AE, D, MC, V.*

$–$$$ ✕ **Playa Lancheros Restaurant.** One of Isla's best and most authentic
FodorsChoice   restaurants, this eatery is worth taking a short taxi ride for. It's located
★   right on the beach (the fish doesn't come any fresher than this), and its menu fuses traditional Mexican and regional cuisine. The house speciality is the Yucatecan *tikinchic* (fish marinated in a sour-orange sauce and chili paste then cooked in a banana leaf over an open flame)—and there are also delicious tacos and grilled fish, fresh guacamole, and salsa. The food may take a while to arrive, so bring your swimsuit, order a beer, and take a dip while you wait. On Sundays there is music, dancing, and the occasional shark wrestler. ✉ *Playa Lancheros where Avenida Rueda Medina splits into Sac Bajo and Carretera El Garrafón* ☎ *998/877–0340* ▭ *No credit cards.*

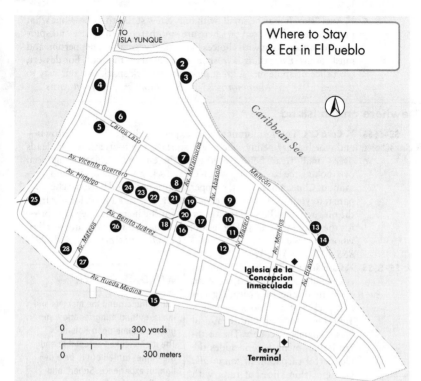

Where to Stay & Eat in El Pueblo

Restaurants	▼
Los Aluxes Cafe	**20**
Los Amigos	**17**
Angelo	**23**
Aquí Estoy	**21**
Bamboo	**22**
Café Cito	**18**
La Cazuela M&J	**13**
Don Chepo	**12**
Fayne's	**19**
Fredy's Restaurant & Bar	**24**
Jax Bar & Grill	**28**
Mañana Restaurant & Bookstore	**8**
Picus Cockteleria	**15**
Sergio's Playa Sol	**1**
Sunset Grill	**25**
Taquería	**26**
Tonyo's	**11**
Zazil Ha	**4**

Hotels	▼
Los Arcos	**16**
Cabañas María del Mar	**5**
Hotel Belmar	**12**
Hotel Carmelina	**10**
Hotel Frances Arlene	**9**
Hotel Playa la Media Luna	**2**
Hotel Posada del Mar	**27**
Hotel Roca Mar	**14**
Hotel Secreto	**3**
Na Balam	**4**
Poc-Ná	**7**
Sea Hawk Diver Rooms	**6**
Urban Hostel	**19**

WHERE TO STAY

Isla hotels focus on providing a relaxed, tranquil beach vacation. Many have simple rooms, usually with ceiling fans, and some have air-conditioning, but few have TVs or phones. Generally, modest budget hotels can be found in town, while the more expensive resorts are around Punta Norte or the peninsula

WORD OF MOUTH

"As long as you stay on the north end of the island, everything you need is in walking distance: restaurants, shops, moped/golf cart rental places."   –dazzle

near the lagoon. Local travel agents can provide information about luxury condos and residential homes for rent—an excellent option if you're planning a long stay.

Many of the smaller Isla hotels don't accept credit cards and some add a 10% surcharge to use one. Isla has also been tightening up its cancellation policy, so check with your hotel about surcharges for changing reservations. ■ TIP→→ Before paying, always ask to see your room to make sure everything is working—especially at the smaller hotels.

A growing number of Isla hotels are now encouraging people to make their reservations online. Some allow you to book rooms right on their own Web sites, but even hotels without their own sites usually offer reservations via online booking agencies, such as **www.docancun.com** and **www. lostoasis.net.** You may see these agency Web sites listed in some of the hotel reviews below—but since hotels customarily work with several different agencies, it's a good idea to shop around online for the best rates before booking with one of them.

Booking online is certainly convenient, and can often get you a 10%–20% discount on room rates. The bad news, though, is that there may be an occasional breakdown in communication between a booking agency and a hotel. You may arrive at the hotel to discover that your Spanish-speaking front desk clerk has no record of your Internet reservation, or has reserved a room that's different from the one you specified. If you arrive during the day there should be time to sort out the problem. But late at night, the hotel may ask you to pay for your room before sorting out your reservation the following day. ■ TIP→→ If you do end up booking online, be sure to print out copies of all your Internet transactions, including receipts and confirmations, and bring them with you.

Prices

WHAT IT COSTS In Dollars				
$$$$	**$$$**	**$$**	**$**	**¢**
FOR 2 PEOPLE over $250	$150–$250	$75–$150	$50–$75	under $50

All prices are for a standard double room in high season, based on the European Plan (EP) and excluding service and 12% tax (10% Value Added Tax plus 2% hospitality tax).

El Pueblo

$$$ Hotel Secreto. It's beautiful. It's famous. It's très, très chic. But if you're looking for a warm, inviting atmosphere, this may not be the place for you. Although the sense of reserve makes it perfect for honeymoon couples who want to be alone, singles may find it too quiet, and children are not appreciated here. Rooms have floor-to-ceiling windows, veiled king-size four-poster beds, and balconies overlooking Half Moon Bay. Mexican artwork looks bold against the predominantly white color

WORD OF MOUTH

"I would choose Secreto in a second. We *loved* this place. The rooms are bright and clean, and we really enjoyed the CD players in the rooms. Nice to play some soft music and sit on the decks gazing at the most beautiful "secret" cove. It's also just a very short walk to the best beaches and restaurants."
–Ally

scheme, and a small, intimate dining room sits alongside a small oceanside pool. This place isn't much of a secret anymore, so you'll need to make reservations far in advance. ⊠ *Sección Rocas, Lote 11, Half Moon Bay* ☎ *998/877–1039* 🖷 *998/877–1048* ⊕ *www.hotelsecreto. com* 🖙 *9 rooms* ⚘ *Restaurant, cable TV, pool, bar* ⊟ *AE, MC, V* ¶◎¶ *CP.*

$$$
Fodor'sChoice
★
Na Balam. Tranquil, and quietly elegant without being pretentious, this hotel is a true sanctuary. Each guest room in the main building has a thatched palapa roof, Mexican folk art, a large private bathroom, an eating area, and a spacious balcony or patio facing the ocean. The beach here is private, with its own bar serving snacks and drinks. Across the street are eight more spacious rooms surrounding a pool, a garden, and a meditation room where yoga classes are held. ⊠ *Calle Zacil-Ha*

WORD OF MOUTH

"I found Na Balam to be a treat. The staff was very friendly and helpful. Showers are nice: roomy and hot with good water pressure." –drjmcb

118 ☎ *998/877–0279* 🖷 *998/877– 0446* ⊕ *www.nabalam.com* 🖙 *31 rooms* ⚘ *Restaurant, pool, beach, bar; no room phones, no room TVs* ⊟ *AE, MC, V.*

$$–$$$ Hotel Playa la Media Luna. This breezy palapa-roofed bed-and-breakfast lies along Half Moon Beach, just south of Playa Norte. Guest rooms here are done in bright Mexican colors, with king-size beds and balconies or terraces that look out over pool and the ocean beyond. A Continental breakfast is served in a sunny dining room. The hotel also offers small, clean, but spartan "Roca" rooms with no view, for $60 per night. ⊠ *Sección Rocas, Punta Norte, Lote 9/10* ☎ *998/877–0759* 🖷 *998/ 877–1124* ⊕ *www.playamedialuna.com* 🖙 *18 rooms* ⚘ *Dining room, cable TV, pool, beach, massage* ⊟ *AE, MC, V* ¶◎¶ *CP.*

$$ Cabañas María del Mar. One of Playa Norte's first hotels, this property includes a hodgepodge of buildings that reflects the way it's expanded over the years. Rooms in the "Castle section" have white, minimalist decor and are the brightest but face the street. Thatch-roofed cabanas by the pool are private but dark, while the beachfront rooms in the three-story "Tower section" have little privacy due to poor soundproofing and lots of guest traffic. Locals flock to the restaurant-bar, Buho's, for drinks and moderately priced meals. The hotel also rents mopeds and golf carts. The staff here is a funny mix of friendly alongside hostile. ⊠ *Av. Arq. Carlos Lazo 1* ☎ *998/877–0179* 🖷 *998/877–0213* ⊕ *www.cabanasdelmar. com* ⤶ *24 tower rooms, 31 cabana rooms, 18 castle rooms* ♿ *Restaurant, refrigerators, 2 pools, beach, video game room* 🍴 *MC, V* 🍽 *CP.*

\$\$ 🏨 **Hotel Roca Mar.** You can smell, hear, and see the ocean from the simply furnished, blue-and-white guest rooms at this hotel; it's located right on the eastern malecón (boardwalk). Since it's tucked away at the southern end of the town square, there isn't much to distract you from the ocean—except at Carnival, when the music can get loud. The freshwater pool and courtyard—filled with plants, birds, and benches—overlook the ocean, too. ⊠ *Calle Nicolas Bravo and Zona Maritima* ☎☎ *998/877–0101* ⊕ *www.mjmnet.net/HotelRocaMar/home.htm* ⤶ *31 rooms* ♿ *Restaurant, fans, pool, beach, snorkeling; no a/c in some rooms, no room phones, no room TVs* 🍴 *No credit cards.*

\$\$ 🏨 **Sea Hawk Divers Rooms.** Catering largely to divers, this hotel is half a block from Playa Norte. Lovely rooms, above the first-floor dive shop, have king-size beds, hammocks, brightly tiled bathrooms, wooden furnishings, and huge private balconies that face either the ocean or the garden patio. There's also a studio suite, which has a full kitchenette and large outdoor deck perfect for breakfasts. The third floor terrace, open to all, is a great place to watch the sunset. Diving and deep-sea fishing trips are offered at the shop. This hotel encourages online booking. ⊠ *Calle Carlos Lazo, just before Buho's restaurant* ☎ *998/877–0296* ⊕ *www.mjmnet.net/seahawkdivers/rooms.htm* ⤶ *4 rooms, 1 studio suite* ♿ *Fans, one kitchenette, dive shop, fishing; no room TVs, no room phones* 🍴 *MC, V.*

\$–\$\$ 🏨 **Hotel Posada del Mar.** There are two types of accommodation here: bungalow rooms, which face the pool, and the stone archways and gardens that surround it; and remodeled rooms in the main buildings, which have patios or balconies and face the beach. The hotel is within walking distance of downtown restaurants and shops. Hot water can be erratic. ⊠ *Av. Rueda Medina 15A* ☎ *998/877–0044* 🖷 *998/877–0266* ⊕ *www.posadadelmar.com* ⤶ *42 rooms* ♿ *Restaurant, bar, pool, fans, cable TV* 🍴 *AE, MC, V.*

★ **\$** 🏨 **Los Arcos** Located in the heart of the downtown area, this hotel is a terrific value. The comfortable suites are all cheerfully (if sparsely) decorated with Mexican-style furnishings; each has a small kitchenette with a microwave and fridge, a fully tiled bathroom with great water pressure, a small sitting area, and a king-size bed. The balconies are large and sunny with lounge chairs; some have a view of the street, while those at the back of the building are more private. The pleasant and helpful staff is an added bonus. This hotel encourages online booking. ⊠ *Av. Hidalgo 58, between Abasolo and Matamoros* ☎☎ *998/877–1343* ⊕ *www.vtoursonline.com/losarcos/* ⤶ *12 rooms* ♿ *Kitchenettes, fans, in-room safes, cable TV; no room phones* 🍴 *MC, V.*

¢–\$ 🏨 **Hotel Belmar.** Rooms at this small, hacienda-style hotel are cozy and cheerfully decorated with flowers, plants, and Mexican artwork. The beds are large and the showers have good water pressure. Front rooms have terraces that open up onto the main street where you can watch all the downtown action; back rooms are quieter. You can get pizza delivered to your room from Rolandi's restaurant, which is just downstairs. ⊠ *Av. Hidalgo Norte 110, between Avs. Madero and Abasolo* ☎ *998/877–0430* 🖶 *998/977–0429* ⊕ *www.rolandi.com* 📞 *12 rooms* ⚛ *Room service, fans, cable TV, laundry service* ⊟ *MC, V.*

¢–$ 🔲 **Hotel Frances Arlene.** This small hotel is a perennial favorite with visitors. The Magaña family takes great care to maintain the property—signs everywhere remind you to save electricity and keep noise to a minimum. Rooms surround a pleasant courtyard and are outfitted with double beds, bamboo furniture, and refrigerators. Some have kitchenettes. Playa Norte is a few blocks north; downtown is a block away. This is one of the few Isla hotels that accommodates wheelchairs. ⊠ *Av. Guerrero 7* 🖶 *998/877–0310* ⊕ *www.francisarlene.com/welcome.html* 📞 *11 rooms* ⚛ *Fans, some kitchenettes, refrigerators; no a/c in some rooms* ⊟ *MC, V.*

> **WORD OF MOUTH**
>
> "The Francis Arlene is a great deal with spacious rooms, A/C, refrigerators, etc. A full-service hotel. I plan to go back." –Janet

¢ 🔲 **Hotel Carmelina.** This family hotel's clean, comfortable lodgings have a simple charm. Bright blue and purple doors lead to a cheerful courtyard; inside, the rooms are minimally furnished, but have comfortable beds; the bathrooms have plenty of hot water; and everything is spotless. Balconies face out onto the downtown streets—the third-floor rooms have excellent views of both Playa Norte and downtown. This place is child-friendly. ⊠ *Avs. Juárez and Francisco Madero* ☎ *998/877–0006* 📞 *25 rooms* ⚛ *Fans; no room phones, no room TVs, no a/c in some rooms* ⊟ *No credit cards.*

¢ 🔲 **Poc-Ná.** This co-ed youth hostel is one of El Pueblo's best deals. There are dormitories with fans, and private rooms with air-conditioning; there are also a camping area and an outdoor sand garden with hammocks that's great for socializing. To promote the community spirit, the hostel hosts movie nights, board and card games, and regular parties. It's within walking distance of Playa Norte and all the downtown shops, restaurants, and bars. Book your room online to guarantee your room. ⊠ *Av. Matamoros 15* ☎ *998/877–0090 or 998/877–0059* ⊕ *www.hostels.com/en/availability.php/HostelNumber.2230l* 📞 *14 beds* ⚛ *Restaurant, bar, Internet, laundry service; no a/c in some rooms, no room phones, no room TVs* ⊟ *No credit cards.*

¢ 🔲 **Urban Hostel.** Isla's newest hostel has three private rooms and seven nonsmoking dormitories, and shared bathrooms that are large and clean. The beds are comfortable, and there's a living room, fully equipped kitchen, and laundry facilities for all to use. There are also a bar and a natural juice bar on the balcony. Coffee and water are free all day. Book online to get a bed since it fills up quickly. ⊠ *Av. Matamoros 9* 🖶 *998/877–1573* ⊕ *www.hostels.com/en/availability.php/HostelNumber.7116* 📞 *3 private rooms, 7 dorms* ⚛ *Dining room, bar, laundry facilities; no room TVs, no room phones* ⊟ *No credit cards.*

Elsewhere on the Island

$$$$ ☐ **La Casa de los Sueños.** What started out as a B&B is now a high-end spa and meditation center with New-Age aspirations. Rooms are named after celestial elements like Sun, Moon, Harmony, Peace, and Love and are decorated with unique crafts and artwork from all over Mexico. A large interior courtyard leads to a sunken, open-air lounge area done in sunset colors; this, in turn, extends to a terrace with a cliff-side swimming pool overlooking the ocean. Spa treatments include massages, body wraps, and facials using herbs and essential oils. What might ruin your inner balance are the restaurant prices. Bookings for this hotel must be done online. ⊠ *Carretera El Garrafón, Fracc. Turqueza, Lotes 9A and 9B* ☎ *998/877–0651 or 800/505–0252* 🖷 *998/877–0708* ⊕ *www. casadelossuenosresort.com* ⤶ *9 rooms* ♧ *Dining room, fans, pool, exercise equipment, spa, beach, dock, snorkeling, boating, bicycles; no room phones, no room TVs, no kids, no smoking* ☱ *AE, MC, V.*

$$$$ ☐ **Hotel Villa Rolandi Gourmet & Beach Club.** A private yacht delivers you from Cancún's Embarcadero Marina to this property. Each of its elegant, brightly colored suites has an ocean view, a king-size bed, and a sitting area that leads to a balcony with a heated whirlpool bath. Showers have *six* adjustable heads and can be converted into saunas. Both the Casa Rolandi restaurant and the garden pool overlook the Bahía de Mujeres; a path leads down to an intimate beach. The pool and beach can get crowded at times. For the best view ask for a second- or third-floor room. ⊠ *Fracc. Laguna Mar SM. 7 Mza. 75, Lotes 15 and 16, Carretera Sac-Bajo* ☎ *998/877–0700 or 998/877–0500* 🖷 *998/877–0100* ⊕ *www.villarolandi.com* ⤶ *20 suites* ♧ *Restaurant, in-room hot tubs, cable TV, pool, gym, spa, beach, dock, boating, no-smoking rooms; no kids under 13* ☱ *AE, MC, V* ⧖ *MAP.*

$$$–$$$$ ☐ **Villa Vera Puerto Isla Mujeres.** Yachties love this hideaway, which is located at Isla's main yacht club. Rooms are awash in rose and blue and have cozy seating areas. The large pool, which has a fountain and swim-up bar, is surrounded by a garden and lawn. Paths lead to the dock and the lagoon, where a shuttle boat ferries you to a beach club that faces Cancún. Families are warmly welcomed. This hotel offers a discount when you book online. ⊠ *Puerto de Abrigo, Laguna Makax* ☎ *998/287–3340 or 800/508–7923* 🖷 *998/287–3346* ⊕ *www.docancun.com/Hotels-Isla-Mujeres/villa-vera-puerto-isla-mujeres.htm* ⤶ *17 suites, 4 villas* ♧ *Restaurant, in-room hot tubs, some kitchenettes, cable TV, in-room VCRs, 3 pools, beach, marina* ☱ *AE, MC, V* ⧖ *CP.*

$$$ ☐ **Villa Las Brisas B&B.** It can be difficult to get reservations at this romantic hideaway tucked away on the eastern coast—you must book online, and it sometimes takes a few days for the proprietors to confirm by e-mail—but most agree it's worth the wait. All rooms here have fantastic sea views and are equipped with king-size beds, hammocks, conch-head showers, ceiling fans, and refrigerators. A restaurant and a small pool are on-site. It's a bit of a jaunt to downtown, but the hotel can arrange for a taxi or a golf-cart rental for you. This hotel gets lots of wind so be prepared for some sand in your bed! ⊠ *Carretera Perimetral al Garrafón* ☎ *998/888–0342* ⊕ *www.villalasbrisas.com* ⤶ *6*

*rooms △ Restaurant, fans, refrigerators, pool, laundry service; no a/c
in some rooms, no room phones, no room TVs, no kids under 16
⊟ MC, V* ⍉ *CP.*

$ 🏨 **Hotel & Beach Club Garrafón de Castilla.** The snorkeling at this small
family-owned hotel is better than what you're likely to experience at El
Garrafón National Park next door (the reef is less crowded, and so it's
healthier, with more fish). Rooms have double beds and balconies overlooking the water; some have refrigerators. Decorations are minimal, but
the overall effect is bright, cheery, and comfortable. *⊠ Carretera Punta
Sur, Km 6* ☎ *998/877–0107* 📠 *998/877–0508* ⊕ *www.isla-mujeres.
net/castilla/home.htm* ⇆ *14 rooms △ Snack bar, minibars, some refrigerators, beach, dive shop, snorkeling; no room phones, no room TVs*
⊟ *MC, V.*

¢ 🏨 **Hotel Maria Elena.** The bright, cheery pink rooms have single or double beds at this budget hotel near El Garrafón National Park. They're
small, but all of them have balconies with ocean views over the Bahía
de Mujeres. Back stairs lead down to a small snack bar selling cold beer,
and a large heated pool. There is also a nice beach good for swimming.
The prices drop the longer you stay. *⊠ Carretera El Garrafón, Km 5.5*
📠 *998/888–0471* ⊕ *www.mexcon.net/hmariaelena.htm* ⇆ *28 rooms
△ Snack bar, fans, pool, beach; no room phones* ⊟ *No credit cards.*

¢ 🏨 **Mar y Sol Beachfront.** Tucked away at the south end of the island, these
rustic beachfront apartments have double beds, basic bathrooms and
kitchenettes, small dining areas. The upstairs units have palapa-shaded
balconies; the ones downstairs open right onto the beach. Swimming
can be iffy on this part of the island because of the sometimes heavy
seaweed, but Playa Lancheros is five minutes away and town a five-minute
cab ride. Since this property has no phone, you must book your room
online. *⊠ Carretera El Garrafón, Km 4.5, near Playa Lancheros* ☎ *No
phone* ⊕ *www.morningsinmexico.com/marysol.htm* ⇆ *4 rooms △ Kitchenettes, fans, beach; no room phones, no room TVs* ⊟ *MC, V accepted
with online bookings.*

NIGHTLIFE & THE ARTS

Nightlife

Isla has developed a healthy nightlife with a variety of clubs from which
to choose. **La Adelita** (⊠ Av. Hidalgo Norte 12A ☎ No phone) is a popular spot for enjoying reggae, salsa, and Caribbean music while trying
out a variety of tequila and cigars. **Buho's** (⊠ Cabañas María del Mar,
Av. Arq. Carlos Lazo 1 ☎ 998/877–1479) remains the favorite restaurant on Playa Norte for a relaxing sunset drink—although the drinks
have started to become overpriced. **Jax Bar & Grill** (⊠ Av. Adolfo Mateos 42, near the lighthouse ☎ 998/887–1218) has live music, cold
beer, good bar food, and satellite TV that's always turned to ESPN.

You can dance the night away with the locals at **Nitrox** (⊠ Av. Matamoros 87 ☎ 998/887–0568). Wednesday night is salsa night and the
weekend is a blend of disco, techno, and house. It's open from 9 PM until
3 AM. **Bar OM** (⊠ Lote 19, Mza. 15 Calle Matamoros ☎ 998/820–
4876) is an eclectic lounge bar offering wine, organic teas, and self-serve

In Search of the Dead

EL DÍA DE LOS MUERTOS (the Day of the Dead) is often billed as "Mexican Halloween," but it's much more than that. The festival, which takes place October 31 through November 2, is a hybrid of pre-Hispanic and Christian beliefs that honors the cyclical nature of life and death. Local celebrations are as varied as they are dynamic, often laced with warm tributes and dark humor.

To honor departed loved ones at this time of year, families and friends create *ofrendas*, altars adorned with photos, flowers, candles, liquor, and other items whose colors, smells, and potent nostalgia are meant to lure their spirits back for a family reunion. The favorite foods of the deceased are also included, prepared extra spicy so that the souls can absorb the essence of these offerings. Although the ofrendas and the colorful *calaveritas* (skeletons made from sugar that are a treat for Mexican children) are common everywhere, the holiday is observed in so many ways that a definition of it depends entirely on what part of Mexico you visit.

In a sandy Isla Mujeres cemetery, Marta, a middle-age woman wearing a tidy pantsuit and stylish sunglasses, rests on a fanciful tomb in the late-afternoon sun. "She is my sister," Marta says, motioning toward the teal-and-blue tomb. "I painted this today." She exudes no melancholy; rather she's smiling, happy to be spending the day with her sibling.

Nearby, Juan puts the final touches—vases made from shells he's collected—on his father's colorful tomb. A glass box holds a red candle and a statue of the Virgin Mary, her outstretched arms pressing against the glass as if trying to escape the flame. "This is all for him," Juan says, motioning to his masterpiece, "because he is a good man."

—David Downing

draft-beer taps at each table. **La Peña** (⊠ Calle Nicolas Bravo, Zona Maritima ☎ 998/845–7384), just across from the downtown main square, has a lovely terrace bar that serves a variety of sinful cocktails, and a DJ who sets the mood with techno, salsa, reggae, and dance music. **Sergio's Playa Sol** (⊠ Playa Norte ☎ 998/705–3250) is another popular beach bar, where you can enjoy the sunset while sipping a cold beer. The bar at **El Sombrero de Gomar** (⊠ Av. Hidalgo 5 ☎ 998/877–0627) is well-stocked with beer and tequila, and its central location makes it a perfect spot for people-watching. The service, though, tends to be hit-or-miss and the food should be avoided.

The Arts

Isleños celebrate many religious holidays and festivals in El Pueblo's zócalo, usually with live entertainment. Carnival, held annually in February, is spectacular fun. Other popular events include the springtime regattas and fishing tournaments. Founder's Day, August 17, marks the island's official founding by the Mexican government. Isla's cemetery is among the best places to mark the Día de los Muertos (Day of the Dead) on

November 1. Families decorate the graves of loved ones with marigolds and their favorite objects from life, then hold all-night vigils to commemorate their lost loved ones.

Casa de la Cultura (✉ Av. Guerrero ☎ 998/877–0639) has art, drama, yoga, and folkloric-dance classes year-round. It's open Monday–Saturday 9–1 and 4–8.

SPORTS & THE OUTDOORS

Boating
Puerto Isla Mujeres (✉ Puerto de Abrigo, Laguna Makax ☎ 998/877–0330 ⊕ www.puertoislamujeres.com) is a full-service marina for vessels up to 170 feet. Services include mooring, a fuel station, a 150-ton lift, customs assistance, hookups, 24-hour security, laundry and cleaning services, and boatyard services. If you prefer to sleep on land, the Villa Vera Puerto Isla Mujeres resort is steps away from the docks. The shallow waters of Playa Norte make it a pleasant place to kayak. You can rent kayaks—as well as sailboats and paddleboats starting at $20 for the day—from **Tarzan Water Sports** located in the middle of Playa Norte.

Fishing
Captain Anthony Mendillo Jr. (✉ Av. Arq. Carlos Lazo 1 ☎ 998/877–0213) provides specialized fishing trips aboard his 29-foot vessel, the *Keen M.* **Sea Hawk Divers** (✉ Av. Arq. Carlos Lazo ☎ 998/877–0296) runs fishing trips—for barracuda, snapper, and smaller fish—that start at $200 for a half day. **Sociedad Cooperativa Turística** (the fishermen's co-operative) (✉ Av. Rueda Medina at Contoy Pier ☎ No phone) rents boats for a maximum of four hours and six people ($120). An island tour with lunch (minimum six people) costs $20 per person. Native resident **Captain Tony Garcia** (✉ Calle Matamoros 7A ☎ 998/877–0229) offers tours on his boat the *Guadalupana.* He charges $40 per person for trips to Isla Contoy; his rates for snorkeling depend on the number of people and length of time.

Snorkeling & Scuba Diving
DIVING SAFETY Although diving is extremely safe on Isla, accidents can still happen. You may want to consider buying dive-accident insurance from the **Divers Alert Network (DAN)** (✉ The Peter B. Bennett Center, 6 West Colony Pl., Durham, NC 27705-5588 ☎ 800/446–2671 ⊕ www.diversalertnetwork. org/insurance/). DAN insurance covers dive accidents and injuries. Their emergency hotline can help you find the best local doctors, hyperbaric chambers, and medical services to assist you. They can also arrange for airlifts.

DIVE SITES Most area dive spots are also described in detail in *Dive Mexico* magazine, which is available in many local shops. The coral reefs at El Garrafón National Park have suffered tremendously because of human negligence, boats dropping their anchors (now an outlawed practice), and the effects of Hurricane Gilbert in 1988. Some good snorkeling can be had near Playa Norte on the north end.

CLOSE UP

Shhh . . . Don't Wake the Sharks

THE UNDERWATER CAVERNS off Isla Mujeres attract a dangerous species of shark—though nobody knows exactly why. Stranger still, once the sharks swim into the caves they enter a state of relaxed nonaggression seen nowhere else. Naturalists have two explanations, both involving the composition of the water inside the caves—it contains more oxygen, more carbon dioxide, and less salt. According to the first theory, the decreased salinity causes the parasites that plague sharks to loosen their grip, allowing the remora fish (the sharks' personal vacuum cleaner) to eat the parasites more easily. Perhaps the sharks relax in order to facilitate the cleaning, or maybe their deep state of relaxation is a side effect of having been scrubbed clean.

Another theory is that the caves' combination of fresh- and saltwater may produce euphoria, similar to the effect scuba divers experience on extremely deep dives. Whatever the sharks experience while "sleeping" in the caves, they pay a heavy price for it: a swimming shark breathes automatically and without effort (water is forced through the gills as the shark swims), but a stationary shark must laboriously pump water to continue breathing. If you dive in the Cave of the Sleeping Sharks, be cautious: many are reef sharks, the species responsible for the largest number of attacks on humans. Dive with a reliable guide and be on your best diving behavior.

Isla is a good place for learning to dive, since the snorkeling is close to shore. Offshore, there are excellent diving and snorkeling at Xlaches (pronounced *ees*-lah-chayss) reef, due north on the way to Isla Contoy. One of Contoy's most alluring dives is the **Cave of the Sleeping Sharks,** east of the northern tip. The cave was discovered by an island fisherman, Carlos Gracía Castilla, and extensively explored by Ramón Bravo, a local diver, cinematographer, and Mexico's foremost expert on sharks. The cave is a fascinating 150-foot dive for experienced divers only.

At 30 feet to 40 feet deep and 3,300 feet off the southwestern coast, the coral reef known as **Los Manchones** is a good dive site. During the summer of 1994, an ecology group hoping to divert divers and snorkelers from El Garrafón commissioned the creation of a 1-ton, 9¾-foot bronze cross, which was sunk here. Named the Cruz de la Bahía (Cross of the Bay), it's a tribute to everyone who has died at sea. Another option is the Barco L-55 and C-58 dive, which takes in sunken World War II boats just 20 minutes off the coast of Isla.

DIVE SHOPS   You can find out more about the various dive shops on Isla by visiting the island's new dive Web site: **www.isladiveguide.com.** Most of the shops offer a variety of dive packages with rates depending on the time of day, the reef visited and the number of tanks. The PADI-affiliated **Coral Scuba Dive Center** (⊠ Av. Matamoros 13A ☎ 998/877–0763 ⊕ www. coralscubadivecenter.com) has a variety of dive packages. Fees start at

$29 for 1-tank dives and go up to $59 for 2-tank adventure and ship-wreck dives. Snorkeling trips tare also available.

Mundaca Divers (⊠ Av. Francisco Madero 10 ☎ 998/877–0607 ⊕ www.mundacadivers.com) has a good reputation with professional divers and employs a PADI instructor. Beginner 2-tank reef dives cost $40, while dives to the Cave of Sleeping Sharks or various shipwrecks are $60–$80. Special 4-reef dive packages start at $75.

Sea Hawk Divers (⊠ Av. Arq. Carlos Lazo ☎ 998/877–0296 ⊕ www.mjmnet.net/seahawkdivers/home.htm) runs reef dives from $45 (for 1 tank) to $60 (for 2 tanks). Special excursions to the more exotic ship-wrecks cost between $75–$95. The PADI courses taught here are highly regarded. For nondivers there are snorkel trips.

Cruise Divers (⊠ Avs. Rueda Medina and Matamoros ☎ 998/877–1190) offers 2-tank dives starting at $49 and a dive resort course (a quickie learn-to-scuba course that doesn't allow you to dive in the open sea) for $69. The dive resort course is a good introduction course for beginners.

SHOPPING

Aside from seashell art and jewelry, Isla produces few local crafts. The streets are filled with souvenir shops selling T-shirts, garish ceramics, and seashells glued onto a variety of objects. But amidst all the junk, you may find good Mexican folk art, hammocks, textiles, and silver jewelry. Most stores are small family operations that don't take credit cards, but everyone gladly accepts American dollars. Stores that do take credit cards sometimes tack on a fee to offset the commission they must pay. Hours are generally Monday–Saturday 10–1 and 4–7, although many stores stay open during siesta hours (1–4).

Books
Cosmic Cosas (⊠ Av. Guerrero 17 ☎ 998/877–0555) is the island's only English-language bookstore and is found in **Mañana Restaurant & Bookstore.** This friendly shop offers two-for-one-trades (no Harlequin romances) and rents out board games. You can have something to eat and then settle in on the couch for some reading.

Crafts
Artesanías Arcoiris (⊠ Avs. Hidalgo and Juárez ☎ No phone) has Mexican blankets and other handicrafts. Staffers here also braid hair. Many local artists display their works at the public **Artesanías Market** (⊠ Avs. Matamoros and Arq. Carlos Lazo ☎ No phone), where you can find plenty of bargains. For custom-made clothing, visit **Hortensia**; hers is the last stall on the left after you come through the market entrance. You can choose from bright Mexican fabrics and then pick a pattern for a skirt, shirt, shorts, or a dress; Hortensia will sew it up for you within a day or two. You can also buy off-the-rack designs.

Look for Mexican ceramics and onyx jewelry at **Artesanías Lupita** (⊠ Av. Hidalgo 13 ☎ No phone). **Casa del Arte Mexicano** (⊠ Av. Hidalgo 16 ☎ No phone) has a large selection of Mexican handicrafts, including ceramics and silver jewelry. **De Corazón** boutique (⊠ Av. Abasolo between Avs. Hidalgo and Guerrero ☎ 998/877–1211) has a wide variety of jewelry, T-shirts, and personal care products. **Gladys Galdamez** (⊠ Av. Hidalgo 14 ☎ 998/877–0320) carries Isla-designed and -manufactured clothing and accessories for both men and women, as well as bags and jewelry.

Grocery Stores

For fresh produce, the **Mercado Municipal** (Municipal market; ⊠ Av. Guerrero Norte near the post office ☎ No phone) is your best bet. It's open daily until noon. **Mirtita Grocery** (⊠ Av. Juárez 6 at Av. Bravo ☎ No phone) is a good place to find American products like Kraft Dinners, Cheerios, and Ritz Crackers. **Super Express** (⊠Av. Morelos 3, in the plaza ☎998/877–0127), Isla's main grocery store, is well-stocked with all the basics.

Jewelry

Jewelry on Isla ranges from tasteful creations to junk. Bargains are available, but beware of street vendors—most of their wares, especially the amber, are fake. **Gold and Silver Jewelry** (⊠ Av. Hidalgo 58 ☎ No phone) specializes in precious stones such as sapphires, tanzanite, and amber in a variety of settings. **Joyeria Maritz** (⊠ Av. Hidalgo between Avs. Morelos and Francisco Madero ☎☎ 998/877–0526) sells jewelry from Taxco (Mexico's silver capital) and crafts from Oaxaca at reasonable prices. **Van Cleef & Arpels** (⊠ Avs. Juárez and Morelos ☎ 998/877–0331) stocks rings, bracelets, necklaces, and earrings with precious stones set in 18K gold. Many of the designs are innovative; prices are often lower than in the United States. You can also check out the Van Cleef sister store, **The Silver Factory** (⊠ Avs. Juárez and Morelos ☎ 998/877–0331), which has a variety of designer pieces at reduced prices.

SIDE TRIP TO ISLA CONTOY

Some 30 km (19 mi) north of Isla Mujeres, Isla Contoy (Isle of Birds) is a national wildlife park and bird sanctuary. Just 6 km (4 mi) long and less than 1 km (about ½ mi) wide, the island is a protected area—the number of visitors is carefully regulated in order to safeguard the flora and fauna. Isla Contoy has become a favorite among bird-watchers, snorkelers, and nature lovers who come to enjoy its unspoiled beauty.

More than 70 bird species—including gulls, pelicans, petrels, cormorants, cranes, ducks, flamingos, herons, doves, quail, spoonbills, and hawks—fly this way in late fall, some to nest and breed. Although the number of species is diminishing—partly as a result of human traffic, partly from the effects of Hurricane Gilbert—Isla Contoy remains a treat for bird-watchers.

The island is rich in sea life as well. Snorkelers will see brilliant coral and fish. Manta rays, which average about 5 feet across, are visible in the shallow waters. Surrounding the island are large numbers of shrimp, mackerel, barracuda, flying fish, and trumpet fish. In December, lobsters pass through in great (though diminishing) numbers, on their southerly migration route.

Sand dunes inland from the east coast rise as high as 70 feet above sea level. Black rocks and coral reefs fringe the island's east coast, which drops off abruptly 15 feet into the sea. The west coast is fringed with sand, shrubs, and coconut palms. At the north and the south ends, you find nothing but trees and small pools of water.

The island is officially open to visitors daily from 9 to 5:30; overnight stays aren't allowed. Other than the birds and the dozen or so park rangers who live here, the island's only residents are iguanas, lizards, turtles, hermit crabs, and boa constrictors. You can read more about the Isla Contoy by visiting a new Web site devoted to the island: www.islacontoy.org.

Two different tour operators, **Sociedad Cooperativa Isla Mujeres** (✉ Contoy Pier, Av. Rueda Medina ☎ 998/877–0500) and **La Isleña** (✉ Avs. Morelos and Juárez, ½ block from pier ☎ 998/877–0578), offer daily boat trips from Isla to Isla Contoy, leaving from Contoy Pier at Rueda Medina (located right by the ferries) at 8:30 AM and returning at 4 PM. Groups are a minimum of 6 and a maximum of 12 people.

Captain Ricardo Gaitan, a local Isla Contoy expert, also provides an excellent tour for large groups (6 to 12 people) aboard his 36-foot boat *Estrella del Norte* (✉ Contoy Pier, Av. Rueda Medina ☎ 998/877–1363).

Contoy Express Tours (✉ Av. Rueda Medina between Avs. Matamoros and Abasolo ☎ 998/877–1367) offers daily tours aboard the 40-foot *Caribbean Express* sailboat. Groups are from 6 to 15 people.

The trip to Isla Contoy takes about 45 minutes, depending on the weather and the boat; the cost is between $38 and $50. The standard tour begins with a fruit breakfast on the boat and a stopover at Xlaches reef on the way to Isla Contoy for snorkeling (gear is included). As you sail, your crew trolls for the lunch it will cook on the beach—you may be in for anything from barracuda to snapper (beer and soda are also included). While the catch is being barbecued, you have time to explore the island, snorkel, check out the small museum and biological station, or just laze under a palapa.

Everyone landing on Isla Contoy must purchase a $5 authorization ticket; the price is usually included in the cost of a guided tour. Check with your tour operator to make sure that you'll actually land on the island; many larger companies simply cruise past. The best tours leave directly from Isla Mujeres; these operators know the area and therefore are more committed to protecting Isla Contoy. Tours that leave from Cancún can charge up to three times as much for the same service.

WHAT TO SEE ON ISLA CONTOY

Once on shore, visit the outdoor museum, which has a small display of animals along with photographs of the island. Climb the nearby tower for a bird's-eye view. Remember to obey all rules in order to protect the island: it's a privilege to be allowed here. Government officials may someday stop all landings on Isla Contoy in order to protect its fragile environment.

ISLA MUJERES ESSENTIALS

Transportation

BY AIR

Isla's only airport is for private planes and military aircraft, so the closest you'll get to the island by plane is the Aeropuerto Internacional Cancún. Three companies can pick you up at the Cancún airport in an air-conditioned van and deliver you to the ferry docks at Puerto Juárez: AGI Tours, Best Day, and Cancún Valet.

If you aren't in a rush, you may also consider booking a *colectivo* at the airport. These 12-passenger white vans are the cheapest transportation option. You won't leave until the van is full, but that usually doesn't take long. The downside is that vans drop off passengers in Cancún's Zona Hotelera before heading over to Puerto Juárez. The entire trip takes about 45 minutes. You can also opt to get off in the Zona Hotelera and take the fast Isla ferry that leaves from the docks at Playa Caracol. Look for the sign for the Xcaret nature park just across from the Plaza Caracol Shopping Mall—the ferry to Isla is right beside the Xcaret store. Colectivos usually congregate just outside the international terminal at the airport. The cost of the trip is $9 per person, one-way.

🛈 **Aeropuerto Internacional Cancún** ✉ Carretera Cancún–Puerto Morelos/Carretera Hwy. 307, Km 9.5 ☎ 998/886-0028. **AGI Tours** ☎ 998/887-6967 ⊕ ww.agitours.com. **Best Day** ☎ 998/881-7206 or 998/881-7202 ⊕ www.bestday.com/Transfers/. **Cancun Valet** ☎ 998/892-4014 or 888/479-9095 ⊕ www.cancunvalet.com.

BY BOAT & FERRY

Isla ferries are actually speedboats that run between the main dock on the island and Puerto Juárez on the mainland. The *Miss Valentina* and the *Caribbean Lady* are small air-conditioned cruisers able to make the crossing in just under 20 minutes, depending on weather. A one-way ticket costs $3.50 and the boats leave daily, every 30 minutes from 6:30 AM to 8:30 PM, with a late ferry at 11:30 PM for those returning from partying in Cancún. You can also choose to take a slower, open-air ferry; its trips take about 45 minutes, but the fare is cheap: tickets are $1.60 per person. Slow ferries run from 5 AM until 6 PM.

Since all official tickets are sold on the ferries by young girls easily identified by their uniforms and money belts, you shouldn't buy your ticket from anyone on the dock. Ticket sellers will accept American dollars, but your change will be given in Mexican pesos.

Always check the times posted at the dock. Schedules are subject to change, depending on the season and weather. Boats will wait until there are enough passengers to make the crossing worthwhile, but this delay never lasts long. Both docks have porters who will carry your luggage and load it on the boat for a tip. (They're easy to spot; they're the ones wearing T-shirts with the English slogan "Will carry bags for tips.") One dollar per person for 1–3 bags is the usual gratuity. To avoid long lines with Cancún day-trippers, catch the early-morning ferry or the ferry after 5 PM. The docks get busy from 11 AM until 3 PM.

More expensive fast ferries to Isla's main dock also leave from El Embarcadero marina complex, and from the Xcaret office complex at Playa Caracol just across from Plaza Caracol Shopping Mall. Both are in the Cancún's Zona Hotelera. The cost is between $10 and $15 round-trip, and the voyage takes about 30 minutes.

Although it's not necessary to have a car on Isla, there is a car ferry that travels between the island and Punta Sam, a dock north of Puerto Juárez. The ride takes about 45 minutes, and the fare is $1.50 per person and about $18–$26 per vehicle, depending on the size of your car. The ferry runs five times a day and docks just a few steps from the main dock on Isla. The first ferry leaves at 8 AM and the last one at 8 PM.

🛈El Embarcadero fast ferries ☎998/883-3448. Isla ferries from Puerto Juárez ☎998/877-0065.

BY CAR

There aren't any car-rental agencies on Isla, and there's little reason to bring a car here. Taxis are inexpensive, and bikes, mopeds, and golf carts are much better ways to get around.

BY MOPED, BIKE & GOLF CART

■ TIP→→ Mopeds are the most popular mode of transportation on Isla. Since local drivers aren't always considerate of moped-riding tourists, though, it's best to rent one only if you're experienced at piloting one. Most rental places charge $22–$27 a day, or $5.50–$11 per hour, depending on the moped's make and age. One of the most reliable rental outfits is Rentadora Ma José; rentals start at $10 per hour or $25 per day.

You can also rent bicycles on Isla, but keep in mind that it's hot here and the roads have plenty of speed bumps. Don't ride at night; many roads don't have streetlights, so drivers have a hard time seeing you. David's Bike Rental rents bikes starting at $6 per day for beaters and $12 per day for fancy three-speeds. You can negotiate for a better deal if you want a weekly rental.

■ TIP→→ Golf carts are another fun way to get around the island, especially with kids. Ciro's Motorent has an excellent choice of new new flatbed golf carts. They rent from $35 for 24 hours. P'pe's Rentadora also has a large fleet of carts (rental prices start at $40 for 24 hours) and of mopeds (rental prices start at $25 per day).

Regardless of what you're riding in or on, watch out for the *topes* (speed bumps) that are everywhere on Isla; El Pueblo also has lots of one-way streets, so pay attention to the signs. Avenida Benito Juárez runs south to north; Avenida Madero and Avenida Matamoros run east to west, and Avenida Abasolo runs west to east.

Although motorists are generally accommodating, be prepared to move to the side of the road to let vehicles pass. Whether walking or driving, exercise caution when traveling through the streets—Isleños like to drive their mopeds at breakneck speeds, and sometimes even ignore the one-way signs!

🛈Ciro's Motorent ✉Av. Guerrero Norte 1 and Av. Matamoros ☎998/877-0578. David's Bike Rental ✉Across from the Pemex station, Rueda Medina ☎No phone. P'pe's

Rentadora ✉ Av. Hidalgo 19 ☎ 998/877-0019. **Rentadora Ma José** ✉ Francisco y Madero No. 25 ☎ 998/877-0130.

BY TAXI

Taxis line up by the ferry dock around the clock. Fares run $2 to $3 from the ferry to hotels along Playa Norte. A taxi to the south end of the island should be about $5.50. You can also hire a taxi for an island tour for about $16.50 an hour. Always establish the price before getting into the cab. If it seems too high, decline the ride; you'll always be able to find another. If you think you've been overcharged or mistreated, contact the taxi office.

◪ **Taxi office** ☎ 998/877-0066.

Contacts & Resources

BANKS & EXCHANGE SERVICES

Bital, the island's only bank, is open weekdays 8:30–6 and Saturday 9–2. Its ATM often runs out of cash or has a long line, especially on Sunday, so plan accordingly. Bital exchanges currency Monday–Saturday 10–noon. You can also exchange money at several currency exchanges; all are open weekdays 8:30–7 and Saturday 9–2 and most are located within two blocks of the bank.

◪ **Bital** ✉ Av. Rueda Medina 3 ☎ 998/877-0005. **Cunex Money Exchange** ✉ Av. Francisco Madero 12A and Av. Hidalgo ☎ 998/877-0474. **Dollar Bill** ✉ Av. Hidalgo No.14 ☎ No phone. **Monex Exchange** ✉ Av. Morelos 9, Lote 4 ☎ No phone.

EMERGENCIES

For general emergencies throughout Isla, dial 060.

◪ **Centro de Salud** (Health Center) ✉ Avenida Guerrero de Salud, on the plaza ☎ 998/877-0017. **Farmacia Isla Mujeres** ✉ Av. Juárez 8 ☎ 998/877-0178. **Hyperbaric Chamber/Naval Hopsital of Isla** ✉ Carretera El Garrafón, Km 1 ☎ 998/872-0001. **Diver's Alert Network (DAN)** ☎ EmergencyDive Accident Hotline 919/684-4326 accepts collect calls. **Police** ☎ 998/877-0458. **Port Captain** ☎ 998/877-0095. **Red Cross Clinic** ✉ Colonia La Gloria, south side of island ☎ 998/877-0280. **Tourist/Immigration Department** ✉ Av. Rueda Medina ☎ 998/877-0307.

INTERNET, MAIL & SHIPPING

The *correos* (post office) is open weekdays 8–7 and Saturday 9–1. You can have mail sent to "Lista de Correos, Isla Mujeres, Quintana Roo, Mexico"; the post office will hold it for 10 days, but note that it can take up to 12 weeks to arrive. There aren't any courier services on the island; for Federal Express or DHL, you have to go to Cancún.

Internet service is available in downtown stores, hotels, and offices. The average price is 15 pesos per hour. Cafe Internet and DigaMe have the fastest computers.

◪ Cybercafés **Cafe Internet Isla Mujeres.com** ✉ Av. Francisco Madero 17 ☎ 998/877-0461. **Digit Centre** ✉ Av. Juárez between Avs. Mateos and Matamoros ☎ 998/877-2025. **DigaMe** ✉ Av. Guerrero 6, between Avs. Matamoros and Abasolo ☎ 1/608/467-4202; this cybercafé also rents out mobile phones for $5 per day and voice mail services for $2 per day.

Mail Services **Correos** Avs. Guerrero and Lopez Mateos, 1/2 block from the market, ☎ 998/887-0085.

MEDIA

Islander is a small monthly publication (free) with maps, phone numbers, a history of the island, and other useful information. It publishes sporadically, but you should be able to pick up a copy at the tourist office.

TOUR OPTIONS

Caribbean Realty & Travel Enterprises offers several different tours of Isla and the surrounding region. The agents there can also help you with long-term rentals and real estate. La Isleña Tours offers several tours to Isla Contoy at $42 per person, including snorkeling trips. Fishing excursions are also offered for a maximum of four hours and four people ($120) or for a maximum of eight hours and four people. Viajes Prisma is a small agency with good rates for a variety of local day trips, including snorkeling and visits to Maya ruins along the Riviera Maya.

🄵 **Caribbean Realty & Travel Enterprises** ✉ Calle Abasolo 6 ☎ 998/877-1371 or 998/877-1372 ⊕ www.caribbeanrealtytravel.com. **La Isleña Tours** ✉ Av. Morelos, one block up from the ferry docks ☎ 998/877-0578 ⊕ www.isla-mujeres.net/islenatours/index.htm. **Viajes Prisma** ✉ Av. Rueda Medina 9C ☎ 998/877-0938.

Cozumel

Reef near San Miguel de Cozumel

WORD OF MOUTH

"On Cozumel, at San Gervasio, a relatively small site compared to others, [ancient] people had an underground cave system where they went to get out of the sun and heat. You can actually go into it and imagine them sitting in the cool passageways."

—Diana

Sealife on the Maya Reef

Getting Oriented

A 490-square-km (189-square-mi) island 19 km (12 mi) east of the Yucatán peninsula, Cozumel is mostly flat, with an interior covered by parched scrub, low jungle, and marshy lagoons. White beaches with calm waters line the island's leeward (western) side, which is fringed by a spectacular reef system; the windward (eastern) side, facing the Caribbean Sea, has rocky strands and powerful surf.

TOP 5
Reasons to Go

1. Scuba diving the world-famous 20-mi Maya Reef, where a technicolor profusion of fish coral, and other underwater creatures reside.

2. Swinging lazily in a *hamaca* at Mr. Sancho's, Nachi Cocom, or any of the other western beach clubs.

3. Watching beribboned traditional dancers at the annual Feria del Cedral festival.

4. Joining the locals at the Plaza Central in San Miguel on Sunday nights for music and dancing.

5. Riding a jeep along the wild, undeveloped eastern coast, and picnicking at secluded beaches.

Snorkeling off Cozumel

The Northwest Coast Broad beaches, and the island's first golf course, lie at the northwest tip of Cozumel. Close to town, the sand gives way to limestone shelves jutting over the water; hotels that don't have big beaches provide ladders down to excellent snorkeling spots, where parrot fish crunch on coral.

San Miguel Cozumel's only town, where cruise ships loom from the piers and endless souvenir shops line the streets, still retains some of the flavor of a Mexican village. On weekend nights, musical groups and food vendors gather in the main square, attracting a lively crowd.

The Southwestern Beaches Proximity to Cozumel's best reefs makes the beaches south of San Miguel a home base for divers. Accordingly, a parade of hotels, beach clubs, commercial piers, and dive shops lines the shore here.

The Windward Coast The rough surf of the Caribbean pounds against the limestone shore here, creating pocket-size beaches perfect for solitary sunbathing. The water can be rough, though, so pay attention to the tides, currents, and sudden drop-offs in the ocean floor.

The Southern Nature Parks Cozumel's natural treasures are protected both above and below the sea. At Parque Punta Sur, mangrove lagoons and beaches shelter nesting sea turtles. Parque Chankanaab, one of Mexico's first marine parks, is superb for snorkeling. Parque Marino Nacional Arrecifes de Cozumel encompasses the coral reefs along the southwest edge of the island.

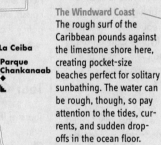

Punta Molas

THE NORTHWEST COAST

3

Isla de Pasión

Punta Norte

Cozumel Country Club

Playa Santa Pilar

Playa San Juan

Airport

Plaza Central

Av. Benito Juárez

Playa Los Cocos

SAN MIGUEL

Av. Rafael Melgar

La Ceiba
Parque Chankanaab

THE WINDWARD COAST

Playa de San Martín

Playa Corona
Playa San Clemente
Playa San Francisco

Playa Sol

El Cedral

Punta Francesca

Parque Punta Sur

Playa Paradíso

Playa del Palancar

Laguna Colombia

Laguna Chunchacaab

MAYA REEF

0   6 mile

0   4 km

COZUMEL PLANNER

Getting There & Getting Around

Cozumel is perfect for a week-long vacation—though some visitors wind up hanging around for months. As well as diving, snorkeling, and sunbathing, which are the main activities here, you can explore town, and take day trips to nearby ruins or eco-parks.

Hotel rooms should be booked up to a year in advance for the Christmas, Easter, and Carnival seasons. Room rates are highest around the winter holidays. Flights to Cozumel increase during the winter months, especially from Dallas, Charlotte, and other hub cities. Fares for direct flights tend to be high year-round; you may save considerable bucks by flying to Cancún and taking a regional flight (though the schedule changes frequently). The cheapest alternative is to fly into Cancún and take the bus to Playa del Carmen and ferry to Cozumel. It's a bit tedious, but only costs about $16.

The island isn't known for its public transportation. Bus service is basically limited to San Miguel. Mopeds are popular, but accidents involving them are frequent. Rental cars are a good option, though you should stick to paved routes (see Easy Riding, *right*). Taxis may well be the best choice. They wait outside all the hotels, and you can hail them on the street. Rates are fixed and reasonable, and tipping isn't necessary. Note that drivers quote prices in dollars or pesos, and the peso rate may be cheaper. Regardless of which currency is used, be sure you're clear about the fare from the get-go.

Easy Riding

A vehicle comes in handy on Cozumel, but driving can be deceptively tricky. Locals rely on rickety bicycles and mopeds to get around, often piled high with relatives and friends. Though they're adept at weaving around faster, bigger vehicles, you'll need to keep careful watch to make sure you don't hit them. This is especially important on roads around the cruise ship piers and on major cross streets in San Miguel. Separate lanes for scooters on the busy southwest coast reduce the hazards somewhat.

Another driving tip to keep in mind: though it's tempting to drive on Cozumel's dirt roads (which lead to uncrowded beaches and the wild northeastearn coast), most car-rental companies have a policy that voids your insurance once you leave the paved roadway.

Tour Options

Tours of the island's sights, including the San Gervasio ruins, El Cedral, Parque Chankanaab, and the Museo de la Isla de Cozumel, cost about $50 a person and can be arranged through travel agencies. **Fiesta Holidays** (✉ Calle 11 Sur 598, between Avs. 25 and 30 ☎ 987/872–0923), which has representatives in many hotels, sells several tours. Another option is to take a private tour of the island via taxi, which costs about $70 for the day.

Booking Your Hotel Online

A growing number of Cozumel hotels are now encouraging people to make their reservations online. Some allow you to book rooms right on their own Web sites, but even hotels without their own sites usually offer reservations via online booking agencies, such as www.cozumel-hotels.net, www.comeetocozumel.com, or cozumel-mx.com. Since hotels customarily work with several different agencies, it's a good idea to shop around online for the best rates before booking with one of them.

Besides being convenient, booking online can often get you a 10%–20% discount on room rates. The downside, though, is that there are occasional breakdowns in communication between booking agencies and hotels. You may arrive at your hotel to discover that your Spanish-speaking front desk clerk has no record of your Internet reservation or has reserved a room that's different from the one you specified. To prevent such mishaps from ruining your vacation, be sure to print out copies of all your Internet transactions, including receipts and confirmations, and bring them with you.

How's the Weather?

Weather conditions are more extreme here than you might expect on a tropical island. *Nortes*—winds from the north—blow through in December, churning the sea and making air and water temperatures drop. If you visit during this time, bring a shawl or jacket for the chilly 65° evenings. Summers, on the other hand, can be beastly hot and humid. The windward side is calmer in winter than the leeward side, and the interior is warmer than the coast.

Need More Information?

The Web site www.cozumelmycozumel.com, edited by full-time residents of the island, has insider tips on activities, sights, and places to stay and eat. There's a bulletin board, too, where you can post questions.

Olmec head,
Chankanaab Natural Park

Dining & Lodging Prices

WHAT IT COSTS in Dollars

	$$$$	$$$	$$	$	¢
Restaurants	over $25	$15–$25	$10–$15	$5–$10	under $5
Hotels	over $250	$150–$250	$75–$150	$50–$75	under $50

Restaurant prices are per person, for a main course at dinner, excluding tax and tip. Hotel prices are for a standard double room in high season, based on the European Plan (EP) and excluding service and 12% tax (which includes 10% Value Added Tax plus 2% hospitality tax).

EXPLORING COZUMEL

It's all about the water here—the shimmering, clear-as-glass aquamarine sea that makes you want to kick off your shoes, slip on your fins, and dive right in. Once you come up for air, though, you'll find that Mexico's largest Caribbean island is pretty fun to explore on land, too. Cozumel is 53 km (33 mi) long and 15 km (9 mi) wide, and its paved roads (with the exception of the one to Punta Molas) are excellent. The dirt roads, however, are another story; they're too deeply rutted for most rental cars, and in the rainy season, flash flooding makes them even tougher to navigate.

Cozumel's main road is Avenida Rafael E. Melgar, which runs along the island's western shore. South of San Miguel, the road is known as Carretera Chankanaab or Carretera Sur; it runs past hotels, shops, and the international cruise-ship terminals. South of town, the road splits into two parallel lanes, with the right lane reserved for slower motor-scooter and bicycle traffic. After Parque Chankanaab, the road passes several excellent beaches and a cluster of resorts. At Cozumel's southernmost point, the road turns northeast; beyond that point, it's known simply as "the coastal road." North of San Miguel, Avenida Rafael E. Melgar becomes Carretera Norte along the North Hotel Zone and ends near the Cozumel Country Club.

Alongside Avenida Rafael E. Melgar in San Miguel is the 14-km (9-mi) walkway called the *malecón*. The sidewalk by the water is relatively uncrowded; the other side, packed with shops and restaurants, gets clogged with crowds when cruise ships are in port. Avenida Juárez, Cozumel's other major road, stretches east from the pier for 16 km (10 mi), dividing town and island into north and south.

San Miguel is laid out in a grid. *Avenidas* are roads that run north or south; they're numbered in increments of five. A road that starts out as an "avenida norte" turns into an "avenida sur" when it crosses Avenida Juárez. *Calles* are streets that run east–west; those north of Avenida Juárez have even numbers (Calle 2 Norte, Calle 4 Norte) while those south have odd numbers (Calle 1 Sur, Calle 3 Sur).

Plaza Central, or *la plaza*, the heart of San Miguel, is directly across from the docks. Residents congregate here in the evenings, especially on weekends, when free concerts begin at 8. Shops and restaurants abound in the square. Heading inland (east) takes you away from the tourist zone and toward the residential sections. The heaviest commercial dis-

COZUMEL'S LANDSCAPES

Outside its developed areas, Cozumel consists of sandy or rocky beaches, quiet coves, palm groves, lagoons, swamps, scrubby jungle, and a few low hills (the highest elevation is 45 feet). Brilliantly feathered tropical birds, lizards, armadillos, coatimundi (raccoon-like mammals), deer, and small foxes populate the undergrowth and mangroves. Several minor Maya ruins dot the island's eastern coast, including El Caracol, which was an ancient lighthouse.

trict is concentrated between Calle 10 Norte and Calle 11 Sur to beyond Avenida Pedro Joaquin Coldwell.

Numbers in the text correspond to numbers in the margin and on the Cozumel map.

A Good Tour

Head south from **San Miguel** ① ➤ to **Parque Chankanaab** ②. Continue past the park to reach the beach clubs. A red arch on the left marks the turnoff to reach the village of **El Cedral** ③.

Back on the coast road, continue south until you reach the turnoff for Playa del Palancar, where the famous reef lies offshore. Continue to the island's southernmost tip to reach **Parque Punta Sur** ④. The park encompasses Laguna Colombia and Laguna Chunchacaab as well as an ancient Maya lighthouse, El Caracol, and the modern lighthouse, Faro de Celarain. Leave your car at the gate and use the public buses or bicycles to enter the park.

At Punta Sur the road swings north, passing several beaches and small restaurants. At Punta Este, the coast road intersects with Avenida Juárez, which crosses the island to the opposite coast. Follow this road back to San Miguel.

North of Punta Morena, an inaccessible dirt road runs along the rest of the windward coast to **Punta Molas**. The area includes several marvelously deserted beaches, including Ixpal Barco, Los Cocos, Hanan Reef, and Ixlapak. Beyond them is **Castillo Real** ⑤, a small Maya site. Farther north are a few other minor ruins, including a lighthouse, **Punta Molas Faro** ⑥, at the island's northern tip.

Take Avenida Juárez from Punta Este to the well-marked turnoff for the ruins of **San Gervasio** ⑦. Turn right and follow this well-maintained road for 7 km (4½ mi) to reach the ruins. To return to San Miguel, go back to Avenida Juárez and keep driving west.

What to See

⑤ **Castillo Real.** A Maya site on the coast near the island's northern end, the "royal castle" includes a lookout tower, the base of a pyramid, and a temple with two chambers capped by a false arch. The waters here harbor several shipwrecks, and it's a fine spot for snorkeling because there are few visitors to disturb the fish. Note, however, that you can't get here by rental car; plan to explore the area on a guided tour.

③ **El Cedral.** Spanish explorers discovered this site, once the hub of Maya life on Cozumel, in 1518. Later, it became the island's first official city, founded in 1847. Today it's a farming community with small well-tended houses and gardens. Conquistadores tore down much of the Maya temple and, during World War II, the U.S. Army Corps of Engineers destroyed the rest to make way for the island's first airport. All that remains of the Maya ruins is one small structure with an arch. Nearby is a green-and-white cinder-block church, decorated inside with crosses shrouded in embroidered lace; legend has it that Mexico's first Mass was held here. Each May there's a fair here with dancing and bullfights.

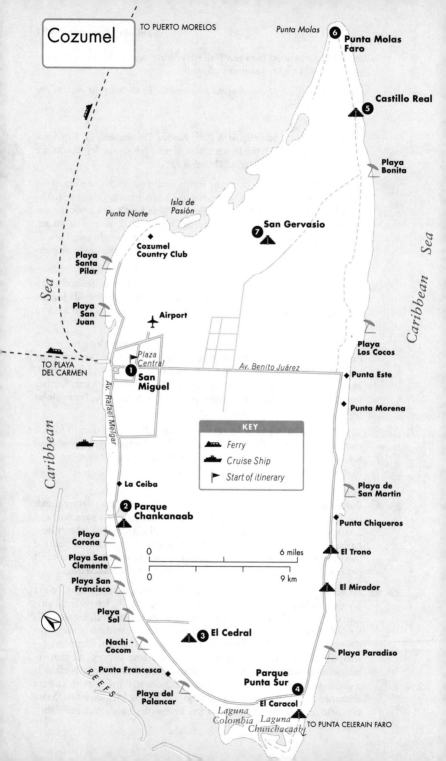

Cozumel

TO PUERTO MORELOS

Punta Molas

6 Punta Molas Faro

5 Castillo Real

Playa Bonita

Isla de Pasión

Punta Norte

7 San Gervasio

Cozumel Country Club

Playa Santa Pilar

Playa San Juan

Airport

Playa Los Cocos

Sea

Caribbean Sea

Plaza Central

TO PLAYA DEL CARMEN

1 San Miguel

Av. Benito Juárez

Punta Este

Punta Morena

Caribbean

Av. Rafael Melgar

KEY

⛴ *Ferry*

🚢 *Cruise Ship*

⚐ *Start of itinerary*

La Ceiba

Playa de San Martin

2 Parque Chankanaab

Punta Chiqueros

Playa Corona

El Trono

Playa San Clemente

0   6 miles

Playa San Francisco

0   9 km

El Mirador

Playa Sol

Nachi - Cocom

3 El Cedral

Punta Francesca

Playa Paradiso

R E E F S

Playa del Palancar

Parque Punta Sur

4 El Caracol

Laguna Colombia

Laguna Chunchacaab

TO PUNTA CELERAIN FARO

More small ruins are hidden in the surrounding jungle, but you need a guide to find them. Check with horseback riding companies for specialized tours. ⊠ *Turn at Km 17.5 off Carretera Sur or Av. Rafael E. Melgar, then drive 3 km (2 mi) inland to the site* ☎ *No phone* 🖃 *Free* ☉ *Daily dawn–dusk.*

Isla de Pasión (Passion Island). This tiny island in Abrigo Bay, east of Punta Norte, is part of a state reserve. It's difficult to reach, but it has secluded beaches and good bird-watching, and fishing is permitted. There are no facilities. To arrange a visit, contact **Island Adventures** (⊠ Calle 11 between Avs. 15 and 20 ☎ 987/872–5858).

★ ☾ **Museo de la Isla de Cozumel.** Cozumel's island museum is housed on two floors of a former hotel. As part of an $800,000 renovation project in 2004–2005, the museum's facade and exhibit spaces were remodeled. Displays on natural history, with exhibits on the island's origins, endangered species, topography, and coral reef ecology were updated, and new exhibits on the pre-Columbian and colonial periods were added. The photos of the island's transformation over the 20th and 21st centuries are especially fascinating, as is the exhibit of a typical Maya home. Guided tours are available, and the museum now has a ramp, elevator, and restroom for wheelchair access. ⊠ *Av. Rafael E. Melgar, between Calles 4 and 6 Norte* ☎ *987/872–1434* 🖃 *$3* ☉ *Daily 9–5.*

need a break? On the terrace off the second floor of the Museo de la Isla de Cozumel, the **Restaurante del Museo** (☎ 987/872–0838) serves breakfast and lunch from 7 to 2. The Mexican fare is enhanced by a great waterfront view, and the café is as popular with locals as tourists.

★ ⛰ ☾ ❷ **Parque Chankanaab.** A short drive from San Miguel, Chankanaab (which means "small sea") is a national park with a saltwater lagoon, an archaeological park, and a botanical garden. Established in 1980, it's among Mexico's oldest marine parks.

Scattered throughout the archaeological park are reproductions of a Maya village, and of Olmec, Toltec, Aztec, and Maya stone carvings. The botanical garden has more than 350 plant species. You can enjoy a cool walk through pathways leading to the lagoon, where 60-odd species of marine life make their home.

> **WORD OF MOUTH**
>
> "Parque Chankanaab has great family snorkeling! We loved the fact that our 9 year old son could snorkel safely and enjoy fabulous underwater scenery. We also appreciated that all the prices charged in the park were extremely reasonable."   –darcy

Swimming is no longer allowed in the lagoon; the area's ecosystem has become quite fragile since the collapse of the underwater tunnels that linked the lagoon to the sea. But you can swim, scuba dive, or snorkel at the beach. Sea Trek and Snuba programs allow nondivers to spend time underwater while linked up to an above-water oxygen system (there's an extra charge for this activity). There's plenty to see under the sea: a sunken ship, crusty old cannons and anchors, a statue of Chac-

CLOSE UP

Cozumel's History

COZUMEL'S NAME IS BELIEVED to have come from the Maya "Ah-Cuzamil-Peten" ("land of the swallows"). For the Maya, who lived here intermittently between about AD 600 and 1200, the island was a center for trade and navigation, but it was also a sacred place. Pilgrims from all over Mesoamerica came to honor Ixchel, the goddess of fertility, childbirth, the moon, and rainbows. Viewed as the mother of all other gods, Ixchel was often depicted with swallows at her feet. Maya women, who were expected to visit Ixchel's site at least once during their lives, made the dangerous journey from the mainland by canoe. Cozumel's main exports were salt and honey; at the time, both were considered more valuable than gold.

In 1518 Spanish explorer Juan de Grijalva arrived on Cozumel, looking for slaves. His tales of treasure inspired Hernán Cortés, Mexico's most famous Spanish explorer, to visit the island the following year. There he met Geronimo de Aguilar and Gonzales Guerrero, Spanish men who had been shipwrecked on Cozumel years earlier. Initially enslaved by the Maya, the two were later accepted into their community. When Cortés and his company landed, Aguilar reportedly jumped into the ocean and swam to the ship, while Guerrero refused to leave his Maya wife and children. Aguilar joined forces with Cortés, helping set up a military base on the island and using his knowledge of the Maya to defeat them. Guerrero died defending his adopted people; the Maya still consider him a hero. By 1570, most Maya islanders had been massacred by Spaniards or killed by disease. By 1600 the island was abandoned.

In the 17th and 18th centuries, pirates found Cozumel to be the perfect hideout. Two notorious buccaneers, Jean Laffite and Henry Morgan, favored the island's safe harbors and hid their treasures in the Maya's catacombs and tunnels. By 1843, Cozumel had again been abandoned. Five years later, 20 families fleeing Mexico's brutal War of the Castes resettled the island; their descendants still live on Cozumel.

By the early 20th century, the island began capitalizing on its abundant supply of *zapote* (sapodilla) trees, which produce chicle, prized by the chewing-gum industry (think Chiclets). Shipping routes began to include Cozumel, whose deep harbors made it a perfect stop for large vessels. Jungle forays in search of chicle led to the discovery of ruins; soon archaeologists began visiting the island as well. Meanwhile, Cozumel's importance as a seaport diminished as air travel grew, and demand for chicle dropped off with the invention of synthetic chewing gum.

For decades Cozumel was another backwater where locals fished, hunted alligators and iguanas, and worked on coconut plantations to produce *copra*, the dried kernels from which coconut oil is extracted. Cozumeleños subsisted largely on seafood, still a staple of local economy. During World War II, the U.S. Army built an airstrip and maintained a submarine base here, accidentally destroying some Maya ruins. Then, in the 1960s, the underwater explorer Jacques Cousteau helped make Cozumel a vacation spot by featuring its incredible reefs on his television show. Today Cozumel is among the world's most popular diving locations.

3

mool (the Maya messenger god), and a sculpture of the Virgen del Mar (Virgin of the Sea). Hordes of brilliantly colored fish swim around the coral reef. To preserve the ecosystem, park rules forbid touching the reef or feeding the fish.

Close to the beach are four dive shops, two restaurants, three gift shops, a snack stand, and dressing rooms with lockers and showers. There's also a sea-lion enclosure and an aviary. A small but worthwhile museum nearby offers exhibits on coral, shells, and the park's history as well as some sculptures. Arrive early—the park fills up fast, particularly when the cruise ships dock. ⊠ *Carretera Sur, Km 9* ☎ *987/872–2940* ⊡ *$10* ⊙ *Daily 7–5.*

☾ ❹ **Parque Punta Sur.** This 247-acre national preserve at Cozumel's southernmost tip is a protected habitat for numerous birds and animals, including crocodiles, flamingos, egrets, and herons. Cars aren't allowed, so you'll need to use park transportation (rented bicycles or public buses) to get around here. From observation towers you can spot crocodiles and birds in **Laguna Colombia** or **Laguna Chunchacaab.** Or visit the ancient Maya lighthouse, **El Caracol,** constructed to whistle when the wind blows in a certain direction. At the park's (and the island's) southernmost point is the **Faro de Celarain,** a lighthouse that is now a museum of navigation. Climb the 134 steps to the top; it's a steamy effort, but the views are incredible. Beaches here are wide and deserted, and there's great snorkeling offshore. Snorkeling equipment is available for rent, as are kayaks. The park also has an excellent restaurant (it's prohibited to bring food and drinks to the park), an information center, a small souvenir shop, and restrooms. Without a rental car, expect to pay about $40 for a round-trip taxi ride from San Miguel. ⊠ *Southernmost point in Punta Sur Park and the coastal Rd.* ☎ *987/872–2940 or 987/872–8462* ⊡ *$10* ⊙ *Daily 9–5.*

★ ❻ **Punta Molas Faro** (Molas Point Lighthouse). The lighthouse, at Cozumel's northernmost point, is an excellent destination for exploring the island's wild side. The jagged shoreline and open sea offer magnificent views, making it well worth the cost of a guided tour. Even tour Jeeps and dune buggies may not be able to make it all the way to the lighthouse if storms have completely destroyed the road, but the scenery is still awesome. Most tours include stops at Maya sites and plenty of time for snorkeling at Hanan Reef about a 10-minute swim off the coast.

When booking a tour, ask about the size of the group. Some companies work with the cruise ships and lead large groups on limited schedules. If you're taking young children along you may want to think twice before booking a Jeep tour, as the bumps along the road could bounce the kids right out of the vehicle.

The enthusiastic guides at **Aventuras Naturales** (☎ 987/872–1628, 858/ 366–4632 in the U.S. ⊕ www.aventurasnaturalascozumel.com) offer five-hour Jungle Jeep tours that include a stop at Castillo Real to explore the ruins, snorkeling, and then lunch on a beach strewn with seashells. Prices start at $85 per person. For $89, **Dune Buggy Tours** (☎ 987/872–0788) will take you on a wild buggy ride (you can drive yourself if you

The Quieter Cozumel

BLAZING-WHITE CRUISE SHIPS parade in and out of Cozumel as if competing in a big-time regatta. Rare is the day there isn't a white behemoth looming on the horizon. Typically, hundreds of day-trippers wander along the waterfront, packing franchise jewelry and souvenir shops and drinking in tourist-trap bars. Precious few explore the beaches and streets favored by locals.

Travelers staying in Cozumel's one-of-a-kind hotels experience a totally different island. They quickly learn to stick close to the beach and pool when more than two ships are in port (some days the island gets six). If you're lucky enough to stay overnight, consider these strategies for avoiding the crowds.

1. Time your excursions. Go into San Miguel for early breakfast and errands, then stay out of town for the rest of the day. Wander back after you hear the ships blast their departure warnings (around 5 PM or 6 PM).

2. Dive in. Hide from the hordes by slipping underwater. But be sure to choose a small dive operation that travels to less popular reefs.

3. Drive on the wild side. Rent a car and cruise the windward coast, still free of rampant construction. You can picnic and sunbathe on private beaches hidden by limestone outcroppings. Use caution when swimming; the surf can be rough.

4. Frequent the "other" downtown. The majority of Cozumel's residents live and shop far from San Miguel's waterfront. Avenidas 15, 20, and 25 are packed with taco stands, stationery stores (or *papelerías*), farmacias, and neighborhood markets. Driving here is a nightmare. Park on a quieter side street and explore the shops and neighborhoods to glimpse a whole different side of Cozumel.

like), with stops at the ruins and reef and a lunch on the beach. **Wild Tours** (☎ 987/872–56747 or 800/202–4990 ⊕ www.wild-tours.com) offers all-terrain-vehicle excursions for $70 per person. The company picks you up at the cruise ship piers or your hotel; the tour includes a stop at a restaurant on the windward side.

🔺 ❼ **San Gervasio.** Surrounded by a forest, these temples comprise Cozumel's largest remaining Maya and Toltec site. San Gervasio was once the island's capital and ceremonial center, dedicated to the fertility goddess Ixchel. The Classic- and Postclassic-style buildings were continuously occupied from AD 300 to 1500. Typical architectural features include limestone plazas and arches atop stepped platforms, as well as stelae and bas-reliefs. Be sure to see the "Las Manitas" temple with red handprints all over its altar. Plaques clearly describe each structure in Maya, Spanish, and English. At the entrance there are crafts shops and a snack bar. ⊠ *From San Miguel, take the cross-island road (follow signs to the airport) east to San Gervasio access road; turn left and follow road for 7 km (4½ mi)* ⌑ *$5.50* ☉ *Daily 8–5.*

★ ❶ **San Miguel.** Wait until the cruise ships sail toward the horizon before visiting San Miguel, then stroll along the malecón and take in the ocean breeze. Cozumel's only town feels more traditional the farther you walk away from the water; the waterfront has been taken over by large shops selling jewelry, imported rugs, leather boots, and souvenirs to cruise-ship passengers. Head inland to the pedestrian streets around the plaza, where family-owned restaurants and shops cater to locals and savvy travelers.

3

BEACHES

Cozumel's beaches vary from sandy treeless stretches to isolated coves to rocky shores. Most of the development on the island is on the leeward (western) side, where the coast is relatively sheltered by the mainland. Beach clubs have sprung up on the southwest coast; a few charge admission despite the fact that Mexican beaches are public property. However, admission is usually free, as long as you buy food and drinks. Beware of tour buses in club parking lots—they indicate that hordes of cruise-ship passengers have taken over the facilities. Clubs offer typical tourist fare: souvenir shops, *palapa* (thatch-roofed) restaurants, kayaks, and cold beer. A cab ride from San Miguel to most of the beach clubs costs about $15 each way. Reaching beaches on the windward (eastern) side is more difficult, but the solitude is worth the effort.

Leeward Beaches

Wide sandy beaches washed with shallow waters are typical at the far north and south ends of Cozumel's west coast. The topography changes between the two, with small sandy coves interspersed with limestone outcroppings. ■ TIP→→ Generally, the best snorkeling is located wherever piers or rocky shorelines provide a haven for sergeant majors and angelfish. The southwest beaches have the best access to good shore diving.

Playa Santa Pilar runs along the northern hotel strip and ends at Punta Norte. Long stretches of pure white sand and shallow water encourage long leisurely swims. The privacy diminishes as you swim south past hotels and condos. **Playa San Juan,** south of Playa Santa Pilar, has a rocky shore with no easy ocean access. It's usually crowded with guests from nearby hotels. The wind can be strong here, which makes it popular with windsurfers. **Playa Azul,** beside the hotel of the same name, is among the north coast's few easily accessed beaches. It has a small restaurant and is packed with families on weekends. There's a small gate just north of the hotel for public access.

A small parking lot on the side of Carretera Sur just south of town marks the entrance to **Playa Caletita.** A few palapas are up for grabs, and the small restaurant has restrooms and beach chairs. There's nothing fancy about **Dzul Ha;** though it has a small pool, snorkeling gear rentals and a bar where you can get guacamole, chips, and beer, it's very low-key here, and there's no cover charge. Climbing in and out of the water on ladders and slippery steps is a small price to pay for the relative solitude.

Uvas (✉ Carretera Sur Km 8.5 ☎ 987/872–3539) is the one beach club/restaurant/nightclub on Cozumel with a sexy, South-Beach-style attitude. White couches and day beds around the pool and beach let you lounge like a pasha, and all the amenities you could wish for are here: lockers, restrooms with showers, a dive shop, and a shop that rents see-through kayaks for paddling. At night candles illuminate the pool and beach and Uvas becomes a hip restaurant and club. Though there's no cover charge, you're expected to buy food and drink when you're here. During the day, guests sit around in their bathing suits nibbling on fajitas and fish kebabs; at night, people dress up a little to feast on steak, shrimp and crab. Dinner and tapas are served until midnight. **Playa Corona,** on the old road to Chankanaab parallel to Careterra Sur, is a rocky beach that shares the park's access to the Yucab reef. Snorkeling equipment is available for rent, and the restaurant here serves conch and shrimp ceviche. The beach is best for experienced snorkelers who can handle the water dashing upon the rocks.

If it weren't for the pretentious stone arch at the entrance, **Playa San Francisco** would look much like it did a decade ago. The inviting 5-km (3-mi) stretch of sandy beach which extends along Carretera Sur, south of Parque Chankanaab at about Km 10, is among the longest and finest on Cozumel. Encompassing beaches known as Playa Maya and Santa Rosa, it's typically packed with cruise-ship passengers in high season. On Sunday locals flock here to eat fresh fish and hear live music. Amenities include two outdoor restaurants, a bar, dressing rooms, gift shops, volleyball nets, beach chairs, and water-sports equipment rentals. Divers use this beach as a jumping-off point for the San Francisco reef and Santa Rosa wall. However, the abundance of turtle grass in the water makes this a less-than-ideal spot for swimming.

☾ The club at **Paradise Beach** (✉ Carretera Sur, Km 14.5 ☎ 987/871–9010 ⊕ http://paradise-beach-cozumel.net) has cushy lounge chairs and charges a flat $5 fee for full-day use of kayaks, snorkel gear, a trampoline, and a climbing wall that looks like an iceberg in the water. Food prices are high (few beach burgers are worth $9.50). The beach club is open until 11 PM for those who can't bear to stay out of the water until bedtime.

★ ☾ There's no charge to enter **Mr. Sancho's Beach Club** (✉ Carretera Sur, Km 15 ☎ 987/876–1629 ⊕ www.mrsanchos.com), but there's always a party going on: scores of holidaymakers come here to swim, snorkel, and drink buzz-inducing concoctions out of pineapples. Seemingly every water toy known to man is here; kids shriek happily as they hang onto banana boats dragged behind speedboats. Guides lead horseback and ATV rides into the jungle and along the beach, and the restaurant holds a lively, informative tequila seminar at lunchtime. Grab a swing seat at the beach bar and sip a mango margarita, settle into the 30-person hot tub, or nap through a massage. Showers and lockers are available, and souvenirs aplenty are for sale. Mr. Sancho's is one of the few Cozumel beaches whose lifeguard tower sometimes actually houses a lifeguard.

Usually one of the calmer beach clubs, **Nachi-Cocom** (✉ Carretera Sur, Km 16.5 ☎ 987/872–0555 ⊕ www.cozumelnachicocom.net) has a wide, uncluttered, and shallow beach, a freshwater pool, lounge chairs, a dive shop, a restaurant, and a beach bar. It gets around charging an admission by having a food-or-beer minimum of $10 per adult and $5 per child. South of the resorts lies the mostly ignored (and therefore serene) ★ **Playa Palancar** (⊠ Carretera Sur ☎ 987/878–5238). The deeply rutted and potholed road to the beach is a sure sign you've left tourist hell. Offshore is the famous Palancar Reef, easily accessed by the on-site dive shop. There's also a water-sports center, a bar-café, and a long beach with hammocks hanging under coconut palms. The aroma of grilled fish with garlic butter is tantalizing. Playa del Palancar keeps prices low and rarely feels crowded.

Windward Beaches

The east coast of Cozumel presents a splendid succession of mostly deserted rocky coves and narrow powdery beaches poised dramatically against the turquoise Caribbean. ⚠ Swimming can be treacherous here if you go out too far—in some parts, a deadly undertow can sweep you out to sea in minutes. But the beaches are perfect for solitary sunbathing. Several casual restaurants dot the coastline here; all close after sunset.

Punta Chiqueros, a half-moon-shaped cove sheltered by an offshore reef, is the first popular swimming area as you drive north on the coastal road (it's about 12 km [8 mi] north of Parque Punta Sur). Part of a longer beach that some locals call Playa Bonita, it has fine sand, clear water, and moderate waves. This is a great place to swim, watch the sunset, and eat fresh fish at the restaurant, also called Playa Bonita. Not quite 5 km (3 mi) north of Punta Chiqueros, a long stretch of beach begins along the Chen Río Reef. Turtles come to lay their eggs on the section known as **Playa de San Martín** (although some locals call it Chen Río, after the reef). During full moons in May and June, the beach is sometimes blocked by soldiers or ecologists to prevent the poaching of the turtle eggs. Directly in front of the reef is a small bay with clear waters and surf that's relatively mild, thanks to a protective rock formation. This is a particularly good spot for swimming when the water is calm. A restaurant, also called Chen Río, serves cold drinks and decent seafood.

About 1 km (½ mi) to the north of Playa San Martín, the island road turns hilly, providing panoramic ocean views. Coconuts, a hilltop restaurant, offers additional lookout spots as well as good food. The adjacent Ventanas al Mar hotel is the only hotel on the windward coast and attracts locals and travelers who enjoy solitude. Locals picnic on the long beach directly north of the hotel. When the water's calm, there's good snorkeling around the rocks beneath the hotel. Surfers and boogie-boarders have adopted **Punta Morena,** a short drive north of Ventanas al Mar, as their official hangout. The pounding surf creates great waves, and the local restaurant serves typical surfer food (hamburgers, hot dogs, and french fries). Vendors sell hammocks by the side of the road. The owners allow camping here. The beach at **Punta Este** has been nicknamed Mezcalitos, after the much-loved restaurant here. The Mezcalito Café serves seafood and beer and can get pretty rowdy. Punta Este is a typical windward beach—great for beachcombing but unsuitable for swimming.

A sandy road beside Mezcalitos leads to Punta Molas and a scattering of Maya ruins on private property. When the cruise piers are busy, tour groups on ATVs parade down the road, interspersed with other groups in four-wheel-drive vehicles. Don't even think about taking a moped or standard rental vehicle down this road. Your chances of getting stuck in a sand drift or plowing into a rock are excellent, and rescues are unpredictable. A small Navy base is the only permanent settlement on the road for now, though some of the scrub jungle is divided into housing lots. Beachcombers find sea glass, bottles, seedpods and other treasures on the wild windswept beaches, which are sometimes horrifically littered with trash from the open sea.

WHERE TO EAT

Dining options on Cozumel reflect the island's nature: breezy and relaxed with few pretensions (casual dress and no reservations are the rule here). Most restaurants emphasize fresh ingredients, simple presentation, and amiable service. Nearly every menu includes seafood; for a regional touch, go for *pescado tixin-xic* (fish spiced with achiote and baked in banana leaves). Only a few tourist-area restaurants serve regional Yucatecan cuisine, though nearly all carry standard Mexican fare like tacos, enchiladas, and huevos rancheros. Budget meals are harder and harder to find, especially near the waterfront. The best dining experiences are usually in small, family-owned restaurants that seem to have been here forever.

Many restaurants accept credit cards; café-type places generally don't. Tip: Don't follow cab drivers' dining suggestions; they're often paid to recommend restaurants.

Prices

WHAT IT COSTS In Dollars				
$$$$	**$$$**	**$$**	**$**	**¢**
AT DINNER over $25	$15–$25	$10–$15	$5–$10	under $5

Per person, for a main course at dinner, excluding tax and tip.

Zona Hotelera Norte

$$–$$$$ ✕ **La Cabaña del Pescador Lobster House.** You'll walk a gangplank to enter this palapa restaurant, where seashells and nets hang from the walls. Yes, it's kitschy, but worth it if you're craving lobster, even though it may be frozen. There's really no menu here—just crustaceans sold by weight (at market prices). You pay for the lobster; veggies and rice are included in the price. Another local favorite is La Cabaña's sister establishment, the less expensive Guacamayo King Crab House next door. ⊠ *Carretera Costera Norte, Km 4, across from Playa Azul Golf and Beach Resort* ☎ *987/872–0795* ▭ *AE, MC, V* ☯ *No lunch.*

Zona Hotelera Sur

$$$–$$$$ ✕ **Alfredo.** The Presidente InterContinental's elegant Italian restaurant, until recently called Arrecife, has been renamed for the "Emperor of Fet-

Island Dining

CLOSE UP

THE AROMAS OF SIZZLING SHRIMP, grilled chicken and steak, spicy sauces, and crisp pizza fill the air of San Miguel in the evening. Waiters deliver platters of enchiladas, tacos, and fajitas to sidewalk tables along pedestrian walkways, where strollers eye others' dinners while deciding where to stop for a meal. At rooftop restaurants, groups gather over Cajun and Italian feasts; along the shoreline, lobster and the catch of the day are the delicacies of choice. There's no shortage of dining choices on Cozumel, where entrepreneurs from Louisiana, Texas, Switzerland, and Italy have decided to make a go of their dreams. Foods familiar to American taste buds abound. In fact, in can be hard to find authentic regional cuisine. Yucatecan dishes such as *cochinita pibíl* (pork with achiote spice), *queso relleno* (Gouda cheese stuffed with ground meat), and *sopa de lima* (lime soup) rarely appear on tourist-oriented menus, but

are served at small family-owned eateries in San Miguel. Look for groups of local families gathered at wobbly tables in tiny cafés to find authentic Mexican cooking. Even the finest chefs tend to emphasize natural flavors and simple preparations rather than fancy sauces and experimental cuisine. Trends aren't important here. There are places where you can wear your finest sundress or silky Hawaiian shirt and dine by candlelight, for sure. But clean shorts and shirts with buttons are considered dress-up clothing suitable for most establishments. At the finer restaurants, guitarists or trios play soft ballads while customers savor lobster salad, filet mignon, and chocolate mousse. But the most popular dining spots are combination restaurant-bars in the Carlos 'n Charlie's style, where diners fuel up on barbecued ribs and burgers before burning those calories away on the dance floor.

tuccine." Though the ambience certainly doesn't jibe with Cozumel's character—an accordionist wanders among the tables singing "O Sole Mio" and other laments—the candlelit dining room is romantic, and the pasta dishes and flavorful breads are satisfying (and tastier than the fish and meat dishes). Reservations are recommended. ⊠ *Carretera Chankanaab, Km 6.5* ☎ *987/872–0322* ⊟ *AE, D, DC, MC, V* ⊘ *No lunch.*

★ $–$$ ✕ **Coconuts.** The T-shirts and bikinis hanging from the palapa roof at this windward-side hangout are a good indication of its party-time atmosphere. Jimmy Buffett tunes play in the background here, while lively crowds down *cervezas* (beers). The scene is more peaceful if you choose a palapa-shaded table on the rocks overlooking the water. The calamari and garlic shrimp are good enough to write home about. Assign a designated driver and hit the road home before dark (remember, there are no streetlights). ⊠ *East-coast road near the junction with Av. Benito Juárez* ☎ *No phone* ⊟ *No credit cards* ⊘ *No dinner.*

¢–$ ✕ **Playa Bonita.** Locals gather on Sunday afternoons at this casual beach café. The water is usually calm here, and families alternate between swimming and lingering over long lunches of ceviche and fried fish. Weekdays are quieter; this is a good place to spend the day if you want access to food, drinks, and showers, but aren't into the rowdy beach-club scene. ⊠ *East-coast Rd.* ☎ *987/872–4868* ▤ *No credit cards* ☺ *No dinner.*

San Miguel

$$–$$$$ ✕ **Pepe's Grill.** This nautical-themed eatery has model boats, ship's wheels, and weather vanes covering the walls—appropriate since its popular with the cruise-ship crowds. The upstairs dining room's tall windows allow for fantastic sunset views; the chateaubriand, T-bone steaks, and prime rib are all done to perfection. Long waits for a table aren't uncommon here. ⊠ *Av. Rafael E. Melgar and Calle Adolfo Rosado Salas* ☎ *987/ 872–0213* ⌕ *Reservations not accepted* ▤ *AE, MC, V* ☺ *No lunch.*

$$$ ✕ **Mesa 17.** Owners Glenn and Trish Terrell describe the menu at their sophisticated restaurant as "world cuisine"—and they're right on the mark. Shrimp-and-lobster spring rolls here come with a tangy mango dipping sauce; thin slices of yucca form a puffy crust on the fish of the day; guava glazes the beef tenderloin; and the pork loin is stuffed with prosciutto and blue cheese. The homemade *cajeta* ice cream with warm carmelized apple tart is a divine dessert combination. Soft jazz plays in the dining room, where golden walls seem to glow in candlelight. ⊠ *Calle 17 and Av. 25 Sur* ☎ *987/878–4928* ▤ *No credit cards* ☺ *Closed Sun. and Mon.*

$$–$$$ ✕ **La Veranda.** Romantic and intimate, this wooden Caribbean house has comfortable rattan furniture, soft lighting, and a terrace that's perfect for evening cocktails (it's also a popular wedding venue). You can start with goat-cheese-stuffed poblano chiles or Roquefort quesadillas, then move on to shrimp curry or jerk chicken. The menu changes as the chef experiments with new dishes, which are sometimes overambitious. ⊠ *Calle 4 Norte 140, between Avs. 5 and 10 Norte* ☎ *987/872–4132* ▤ *MC, V.*

$–$$$ ✕ **Casa Mission.** Part private home and part restaurant, this estate evokes a country hacienda in mainland Mexico. The on-site botanical garden has mango and papaya trees, and a small zoo with caged birds and a pet lion (kept out of view). The setting, with tables lining the veranda, outshines the food. Stalwart fans rave about huge platters of fajitas and grilled fish. It's out of the way, so you'll need to take a cab. ⊠ *Av. Juárez and Calle 55A* ☎ *987/872–3248* ▤ *AE, MC, V* ☺ *No lunch.*

$–$$$ ✕ **La Choza.** Purely Mexican in design and cuisine, this family-owned restaurant is a favorite for mole *rojo* (with cinnamon and chilies) and *cochinita pibíl* (marinated pork baked in banana leaves). Leave room for the chilled chocolate pie or the equally intriguing avocado pie. ⊠ *Calle Adolfo Rosado Salas 198, at Av. 10* ☎ *987/872–0958* ▤ *AE, MC, V.*

$–$$$ ✕ **French Quarter.** Bodacious portions of home-style gumbo, jambalaya, and crawfish étouffée are the draws here, and owner Mike Slaughter makes sure everyone gets happily stuffed to the gills. You can dine outside on the cool rooftop terrace or inside among colorful murals. The bar stocks imported beer and wine at reasonable prices. ⊠ *Av. 5 Sur, between Calles Adolfo Rosado Salas and 3* ☎ *987/872–6321* ▤ *AE, MC, V* ☺ *No lunch.*

★ **$–$$$** ✕ **Guido's.** Chef Ivonne Villiger works wonders with fresh fish—if the wahoo with spinach is on the menu, don't miss it. But Guido's is best

3

known for its pizzas baked in a wood-burning oven, which makes sections of the indoor dining room rather warm. Sit in the pleasantly overgrown courtyard instead, and order a pitcher of sangria to go with the puffy garlic bread. ⊠ *Av. Rafael E. Melgar 23, between Calles 6 and 8 Norte* ☎ 987/872–0946 ▤ *AE, D, MC, V* ⊗ *Closed Sun.*

> **WORD OF MOUTH**
>
> "Definitely find a seat in Guido's courtyard, where fans and shade from the beautiful flowering vines will help keep you cool. Don't miss the garlic bread!!"   –Lisa

$–$$ ✕ **Plaza Leza.** The outdoor tables here are a wonderful place to linger; you can watch the crowds in the square while savoring Mexican dishes like *poc chuc* (tender pork loin in a sour-orange sauce), enchiladas, and lime soup. Breakfast is available here as well. For more privacy, there's also a somewhat secluded, cozy inner patio. ⊠ *Calle 1 Sur, south side of Plaza Central* ☎ 987/872–1041 ▤ *MC, V.*

$–$$ ✕ **San Miguel Cafe.** Cozumeleños far outnumber visitors at this sunny coffeeshop, where baskets of fresh *pan dulce*—Mexican pastries—are placed on every table at breakfast (you'll be charged for what you eat). Sunday mornings are particularly pleasant, with grown-ups enjoying platters of savory huevos rancheros and kids devouring pancakes. An inexpensive, multicourse *comida corrida* (meal of the day) is served from 1–5 every day; the kitchen is open until 11 every night but Sunday. ⊠ *Ave 15 No. 301, between Calles 2 and 4* ☎ 987/872–3467 ▤ *MC, V* ⊗ *No dinner Sun.*

$–$$ ✕ **Las Tortugas.** "Delicious seafood at accessible prices" is the motto at this simple eatery. The menu consists primarily of fish, lobster, and conch caught by local fishermen, and changes according to what's available. Fajitas and other traditional Mexican dishes are also options. Don't look for Las Tortugas on Avenida 10—that location closed several years ago. ⊠ *Av. Pedro Joaquin Coldwell (also called Av. 30) and Calle 19 Sur* ☎ 987/872–1242 ▤ *MC, V* ⊗ *Closed Mon.*

$ ✕ **La Perlita.** The ceviche and whole fried fish are as fresh as can be at this neighborhood seafood market and restaurant. Lunch is the main meal and the crowd is largely made up of families and local workers on break. Take a taxi—it's far from downtown and hard to find. ⊠ *Av. 65 Norte 49, between Calles 8 and 10* ☎ 987/ 872–3452 ▤ *MC, V* ⊗ *No dinner.*

> **WORD OF MOUTH**
>
> "Casa Denis is a GREAT little local restaurant—the first on the island. The Mayan food is excellent, the margaritas generous, and the waiters . . . are humorous and efficient."   –Todd

★ **¢–$** ✕ **Casa Denis.** This little yellow house near the plaza has been satisfying cravings for Yucatecan *pollo pibil* (spiced chicken baked in banana leaves) and other local favorites since 1945. *Tortas* (sandwiches) and tacos are a real bargain, and you'll start to feel like a local if you spend an hour at one of the outdoor tables, watching shoppers dash about while you relax. ⊠ *Calle 1 Sur 132, between Avs. 5 and 10* ☎ 987/872–0067 ▤ *No credit cards.*

¢–$ ✕ **Cocos Cozumel.** Start the day with a bountiful breakfast at this cheery café, where the coffee is strong, the muffins enormous, and the egg dishes

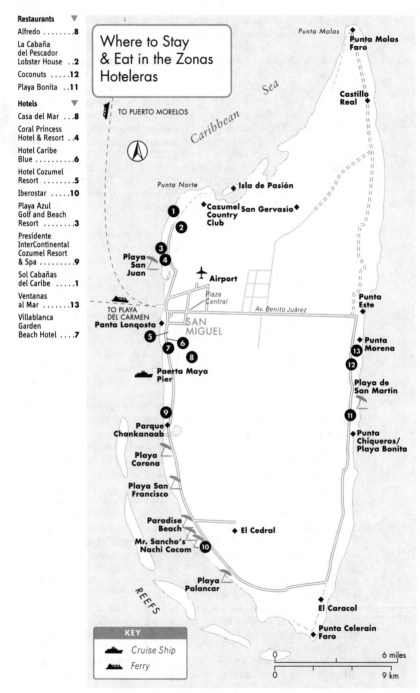

Where to Stay
& Eat in the Zonas
Hoteleras

perfectly prepared. If you've come early enough to beat the heat, sit at a table under the front awning and watch the town come to life. The restaurant is open 6 AM–noon. ⊠ *Av. 5 Sur 180* ☎ *987/872–0241* ♨ *Reservations not accepted* ⊟ *No credit cards* ☉ *Closed Mon. and Sept. and Oct. No dinner.*

¢–$ ✕ **El Foco.** Locals fuel up before and after partying at this traditional *taquería* (it's open until midnight, or until the last customer leaves). The soft tacos stuffed with pork, chorizo, cheese, or beef are cheap and filling; the graffiti on the walls, and the late-night revelers, provide the entertainment. ⊠ *Av. 5 Sur 13B, between Calles Adolfo Rosado Salas and 3 Sur* ☎ *987/872–5980* ⊟ *No credit cards.*

¢–$ ✕ **Garden of Eatin'.** If you think you can't bear another taco, the healthful sandwiches and salads at this cheery, green-and-yellow café are a nice change. All ingredients are washed in purified water; you can "build" your own salad or sandwich from a long list of veggies, meats, and cheeses. The eggplant, goat cheese, and pine nut sandwich is especially yummy, as is the smoked salmon with avocado. ⊠ *Calle Adolfo Rosado Sala, between Avs. Rafael E. Melgar and 5 Sur* ☎ *987/878–4020* ⊟ *No credit cards* ☉ *Closed Sun.*

☾ ¢–$ ✕ **Jeanie's Waffles & Raul's Tacos.** Craving familiar flavors? If you're from the United States you'll be thrilled with Jeanie's fluffy waffles, perfect grilled cheese sandwiches, and frothy root beer floats. Tables in the dining room look out to the sea; sidewalk tables have a view of traffic and travelers walking to and from town. The waffles are fresh, light, and available in more variations than you can imagine. Jeanie's husband Raul takes over in the evening with a menu of seafood, pastas, and burgers. ⊠ *Av. Rafael E. Melgar and Calle 11* ☎ *987/878–4647* ⊟ *No credit cards.*

¢–$ ✕ **Rock 'n Java Caribbean Café.** The extensive breakfast menu here includes delicious whole-wheat French toast and cheese crepes. For lunch or dinner consider the vegetarian tacos or linguine with clam sauce, or choose from more than a dozen salads. There are also scrumptious pies, cakes, and pastries baked here daily. You can enjoy your healthful meal or sinful snack while sitting on the wrought-iron studio chairs or in a comfy booth. ⊠ *Av. Rafael E. Melgar 602-6* ☎ *987/872–4405* ⊟ *No credit cards.*

¢–$ ✕ **El Turix.** Off the tourist track near Corpus Christi church and park, this simple place is worth the five-minute cab ride from downtown San Miguel. Here, you'll get the chance to experience true Yucatecan cuisine, like pollo pibíl or the poc chuc, served up by Rafael and Maruca Ponce, the amiable owners. There are also daily specials, and paella is available on request (call 24 hours ahead). ⊠ *Calle 17 between Avs. 20 and 25* ☎ *987/872–5234* ⊟ *No credit cards* ☉ *Closed Oct. No lunch.*

WHERE TO STAY

Small, one-of-a-kind hotels have long been the norm in Cozumel. Glamour and glitz are non-existent—you won't find lavish resorts with Bulgari toiletries and Frette linens here. Instead, the emphasis is on relaxed comfort and reasonable rates (though prices are rising). Most of Cozumel's hotels are on the leeward (west) and south sides of the island, though there is one peaceful hideaway on the windward (east) side. The larger

resorts are north and south of San Miguel; the less expensive places are in town. Divers and snorkelers tend to congregate at the southern properties, while swimmers and families prefer the hotels to the north, where smooth white-sand beaches face calm, shallow water.

Prices

	WHAT IT COSTS In Dollars			
	$$$$	**$$$**	**$$**	**$**	**¢**
FOR 2 PEOPLE	over $250	$150–$250	$75–$150	$50–$75	under $50

All prices are for a standard double room in high season, based on the European Plan (EP) and excluding service and 12% tax (10% Value Added Tax plus 2% hospitality tax).

Zona Hotelera Norte

★ **$$$** 🏨 **Playa Azul Golf and Beach Resort.** The bright airy rooms of this boutique hotel face the ocean or gardens and have mirrored niches, wicker furnishings, and sun-filled terraces. Master suites have hot tubs. Small palapas shade lounge chairs on the beach, and you can arrange snorkeling and diving trips at the hotel's own dock. The Palma Azul restaurant serves Continental meals, and all rooms have coffeemakers. Golf fees are included in the room rate; some guests hit the course daily. ⊠ *Carretera Costera Norte, Km 4* ☎ *987/872–0043* 🖷 *987/872–0110* ⊕ *www.playa-azul.com* ⇆ *34 rooms, 16 suites* 🍴 *Restaurant, room service, in-room safes, some in-room hot tubs, minibars, pool, beach, dive shop, dock, snorkeling, billiards, 2 bars, laundry service, car rental, free parking* ▭ *AE, MC, V.*

$$–$$$ 🏨 **Coral Princess Hotel & Resort.** Great snorkeling off the rocky shoreline makes this a north coast standout. Princess Villas each have two bedrooms, two bathrooms, a kitchen, and a terrace; Coral Villas have one bedroom, a kitchen-dining area, and a terrace. These large rooms are often taken by time-share owners, though there's no pressure to attend a sales demo. Room service will deliver a

WORD OF MOUTH

"The Coral Princess is a beautiful hotel for moderate budget couples. This hotel has a great oceanside view. The knowledge of the staff, especially at the bar and the front desk, made our vacation!"
–Eugene Tate

reasonably priced 5-gallon jug of purified water, a great money saver for extended stays. Except for 61 studios, all rooms overlook the ocean. ⊠ *Carretera Costera Norte, Km 2.5* ☎ *987/872–3200 or 800/253–2702* 🖷 *987/872–2800* ⊕ *www.coralprincess.com* ⇆ *100 rooms, 37 villas, 2 penthouses* 🍴 *Restaurant, snack bar, room service, in-room safes, some kitchens, refrigerators, cable TV, 2 pools, gym, dive shop, dock, snorkeling, volleyball, bar, laundry service, car rental, free parking* ▭ *AE, DC, MC, V.*

$–$$ 🏨 **Sol Cabañas del Caribe.** Some Cozumel visitors return again and again to the freshly painted cabañas at this refurbished old-timer. Granted, they're so close together your neighbors can see your messy room, but it's the kind of place where everybody knows your name anyway. Rooms in the low-rise hotel building overlooking the beach are a bit more private. There's a small pool and narrow beach, and snorkeling is particularly good under the restaurant deck, thanks to the many diners who've long fed the fish. The only TV is in the lobby—but who needs CNN when you've got a hammock by the sea? ⊠ *Carretera Costera Norte Km 5.1* ☎ *987/ 872–0411 or 888/341–5993* 🖷 *987/872–1599* ⊕ *www.solmelia.com* ⇆ *39 rooms, 9 cabanas* 🍴 *Restaurant, refrigerators, pool, wading pool, beach, snorkeling, laundry service, free parking* ▭ *AE, MC, V.*

Zona Hotelera Sur

$$$$ 🏨 **Iberostar.** Jungle greenery surrounds this all-inclusive resort at Cozumel's southernmost point. Rooms are small but pleasant; each has wrought-iron details, one king-size or two queen-size beds, and a terrace or patio with hammocks. There isn't much privacy—pathways through the resort wind around the rooms—but this is the most enjoyable all-inclusive on the south coast. Although the resort closed temporarily to repair hurricane damage, it plans to reopen in November of 2005. ⊠ *Carretera Chankanaab, Km 17, past El Cedral turnoff* ☎ *987/ 872–9900 or 888/923–2722* 🖷 *987/872–9909* ⊕ *www.iberostar.com*

♨ *300 rooms* ᗜ *3 restaurants, in-room safes, 2 tennis courts, 2 pools, health club, hot tub, spa, beach, dive shop, dock, windsurfing, boating, bicycles, 3 bars, theater, children's programs (ages 4–12), car rental, free parking* ▤ *AE, D, MC, V* ▯◯▯ *AI.*

☺ $$$$ ▦ **Presidente InterContinental Cozumel**
Fodor'sChoice Resort & Spa. Comfortable elegance
★ and serenity are hallmarks at the divine Presidente. It's the fanciest hotel on Cozumel, without being pretentious or glitzy. Bellmen greet guests like old friends, waiters quickly learn diners' preferences, and housekeep-

> **WORD OF MOUTH**
>
> "Just got back from 4 nights at the Presidente . . . and have no plans to EVER stay anywhere else on the island."   –Stacy

ers leave towels rolled into animal shapes on the beds. Rooms, all refurbished in 2004, are stylish and contemporary, with white cedar furnishings, coffeemakers, and private terraces or balconies. Snorkeling along the beach is excellent, and the Maya-influenced Serenity Spa is open to nonguests, who may also use the hotel's facilities for a $40 day-use fee. This property is all about quiet luxury; if you're looking for a swim-up bar, volleyball in the pool, and loud music, stay elsewhere. ✉ *Carretera Chankanaab, Km 6.5* ☎ *987/872–9500 or 800/327–0200* 🖷 *987/872–2928* ⊕ *www.interconti.com* ♨ *253 rooms, 7 suites* ᗜ *2 restaurants, snack bar, room service, in-room safes, minibars, 2 tennis courts, pool, gym, spa, hot tub, beach, dive shop, dock, snorkeling, 3 bars, shops, children's programs (ages 4–12), laundry service, concierge, Internet, business services, meeting rooms, car rental, free parking, no-smoking rooms* ▤ *AE, DC, MC, V.*

$$$ ▦ **Hotel Cozumel Resort.** Dolphins from Chankanaab take refuge during storms in the enormous pool at this all-inclusive hotel. On sunny days in high season families and revelers surround the pool; activity directors enliven the crowd with games and loud music. The scene is quieter at the beach club, accessed via a tunnel that looks like an underground aquarium. The hotel has undergone several names, owners and remodeling efforts over the years, and is currently one of the best deals around. The large rooms are reminiscent of a moderate chain hotel, with cool tile floors, comfy beds, bathtub-shower combos, and plenty of closet and drawer space. Stick with the Mexican specialties in the main restaurant; snacks by the pool and beach are mediocre. ✉ *Carretera Sur Km. 1.7* ☎ *987/872–2900 or 877/454-4355* 🖷 *987/872–2154* ⊕ *www. hotelcozumel.us* ♨ *178 rooms* ᗜ *2 restaurants, snack bar, room service, in-room safes, cable TV, 3 pools, wading pool, gym, beach, dive shop, snorkeling, billiards, bar, shop, laundry service, Internet, car rental, free parking* ▤ *MC, V* ▯◯▯ *AI.*

$$ ▦ **Casa del Mar.** Rooms vary considerably at this three-story hotel catering to divers. Some are decorated with Mexican artwork and have large TVs and coffeemakers; balconies facing the sun are best as rooms tend to be dark. Only a few have bathtubs. The bi-level cabanas, which sleep three or four, are a good deal. As well as an in-house dive shop, the property also has dive gear-storage areas. The beach is across the street, and hotel guests get discounts at Nachi Cocom Beach Club on the south coast. Food at the restaurant is only adequate. ✉ *Carretera Sur, Km 4* ☎ *987/872–*

1900 or 888/577–2758 🖷 *987/872–1855* ⊕ *www.casadelmarcozumel.com* ➷ *98 rooms, 8 cabanas* ⚖ *Restaurant, some fans, pool, hot tub, dive shop, 2 bars, laundry service, meeting room, car rental, some free parking* ⊟ *AE, D, MC, V.*

WORD OF MOUTH

"Casa del Mar is a little gem of a resort. One of the best 'Happy Hour' spots on the island, with live music and domestic drinks—not just beer. By the end of our stay, we knew all of the staff and they knew us. A home away from home . . ."   –Crissy

$$ 🖼 **Villablanca Garden Beach Hotel.** The architecture of this hotel is striking—from the white Moorish building facade to the archways separating the living and sleeping areas of some guest rooms. All rooms have sunken bathtubs; some include refrigerators and private terraces. The hotel's beach club, which is across the street from the main building, has a dive shop. Guests tend to return annually, often with dive groups. There's not much happening at night, since divers tend to turn in early. ⊠ *Carretera Chankanaab, Km 3* ☎ *987/872–0730 or 888/790–5264* 🖷 *987/872–0865* ⊕ *www.villablanca.net* ➷ *2 rooms, 25 suites, 1 penthouse, 3 villas* ⚖ *Restaurant, fans, some kitchens, some refrigerators, tennis court, pool, beach, dock, bicycles, laundry service, some free parking* ⊟ *AE, D, MC, V.*

$ 🖼 **Hotel Caribe Blue.** Refurbished in 2004, these inexpensive rooms are just right for wet, sandy divers who need to stash a lot of damp gear, take a powerful hot shower, and rush back to the beach. The aptly named hotel sits beside the sea on a limestone shelf, just a short walk from town. The owners also run the adjacent Blue Angel dive shop. Lazing here in a beachside hammock after a perfect morning dive is the quintessential Cozumel experience. ⊠ *Carretera Sur, Km. 2.2* ☎ *987/872–0188* 🖷 *987/872–1631* ⊕ *www.caribeblu.net* ➷ *20 rooms* ⚖ *Restaurant, in-room safes, some refrigerators, pool, beach, dive shop, snorkeling, laundry service* ⊟ *MC, V.*

San Miguel

$$ 🖼 **Casa Mexicana.** The dramatic staircase leading up to the windswept lobby and well-designed guests rooms make this place distinctive. The rooms, decorated in subtle blues and yellows, are equipped with irons and ironing boards, hair dryers, and Internet access. Some face the ocean and the traffic noise on Avenida Rafael E. Melgar; others overlook the pool and terrace. The price includes a full buffet breakfast. Two sister properties, Hotel Bahía and Suites Colonial, offer equally comfortable but less expensive suites with kitchenettes (the Bahía has some ocean views; the Colonial is near the square). You can contact all three hotels using the central reservation number. ⊠ *Av. Rafael E. Melgar Sur 457, between Calles 5 and 7* ☎ *987/872–0209 or 877/228–6747* 🖷 *987/872–1387* ⊕ *www.casamexicanacozumel.com* ➷ *90 rooms* ⚖ *In-room safes, minibars, in-room data ports, pool, gym, laundry service, concierge, business services, car rental* ⊟ *AE, D, MC, V* ⦿ *BP.*

$$ 🖼 **Hacienda San Miguel.** Continental breakfast is delivered to your room at this small gem where two-story buildings surround a lush courtyard.

Rooms on the second story get far more air and light than those at ground level, but all have extra touches like coffeemakers, purified water, hand-carved furnishings, and only-sometimes-dingy bathrobes. The plaza is five blocks south and the closest beach a 10-minute walk north. Guests get discounts at the affiliated Mr. Sancho's Beach Club. You can use the office phone, but won't be able to hook up your laptop. ⊠ *Calle 10 Norte 500, at Av. 5* ☎ *987/872–1986* 🖷 *987/872–7043* ⊕ *www.haciendasanmiguel. com* 🛏 *7 studios, 3 junior suites, 1 master suite* ◊ *In-room safes, kitchenettes, car rental; no room phones* 🖃 *MC, V* ¶◎¶ *CP.*

$$ 🏨 **Vista del Mar.** A total makeover in 2004 transformed a formerly run-down hotel into a cozy inn that could charge far higher rates if it were on the beach. The soft beige, brown, and white walls are decorated with shells and beach stones; mosquito nets drape over the beds at night. Room 405 has a spot-on view of the sea, letting you know just how many cruise ships are docked in town. Making your way through the sometimes rude and annoying crowds in front of the hotel can be a hassle. On the other hand, it's rather amusing to watch the sweating shoppers from a deck chair beside the hot tub overlooking a shopping arcade. Metal hurricane shutters on the street facing windows help cut the noise but make rooms dark as night. ⊠ *Av. Rafael E. Melgar 45, between Calles 5 and 7* ☎ *987/872–0545 or 888/309–9988* 🖷 *987/872–7036* ⊕ *www. hotelvistadelmar.com* 🛏 *20 rooms* ◊ *In-room safes, refrigerators, cable TV, pool, outdoor hot tub, shops, laundry service* 🖃 *MC, V* ¶◎¶ *CP.*

$ 🏨 **Hotel Flamingo.** You get a lot for your pesos at this stellar, almost-budget hotel, including a rooftop sundeck with water view and a courtyard with barbecue and group dining facilities (bring your own catch of the day). Three blocks from the ferry in the heart of downtown, the hotel has a beach club at Playa Azul. Large rooms are done in bright colors with wrought-iron furnishings. Those in front have balconies but can be noisy. Dive packages are available. ⊠ *Calle 6 Norte 81, near the Cozumel Museum* ☎ *987/872–1264 or 800/806–1601* ⊕ *www.hotelflamingo.com* 🛏 *16 rooms, 1 penthouse* ◊ *Fans, Internet* 🖃 *AE, D, MC, V.*

¢ 🏨 **Hotel Pepita.** Despite being more than 50 years old, the Pepita is one of the best budget hotels on the island. The blue-and-white facade is painted frequently, as are the rooms. Wooden shutters cover screened windows that keep out the bugs (who thrive happily among the courtyard's many plants and shrubs). Cable TV, refrigerators, and air-conditioning are surprising pluses for such low rates. Shelves in the lobby are stacked

WORD OF MOUTH

"I stay at Hotel Pepita often and believe it is an unmatched value in Cozumel. The rooms are clean, well maintained with air and cable TV (rare in this price range) and the staff is friendly and hospitable. Excellent choice!"
        —Robert

high with novels in several languages, and German and Dutch are as common as Spanish and English during conversations over free coffee around the long wooden table in the courtyard. There's no pool or kitchen facilities, but plenty of small markets and cafés in the neighborhood. ⊠ *Av. 15 Sur 120* ☎🖷 *987/872–0098* 🛏 *20 rooms* ◊ *Fans, refrigerators, cable TV* 🖃 *No credit cards.*

¢ ⊞ **Palma Dorada Inn.** This family-owned budget inn gives guests as many amenities as they care to purchase. The best rooms come with air-conditioners and fully equipped kitchenettes. The least expensive have fans and three single beds. Jugs of purified water sit in the hallways, and you can use the communal microwave and request an iron or hair dryer. The waterfront is a half block away, and restaurants and bars abound in the neighborhood, but the nearest swimming beach is a 15-minute walk south. ⊠ *Calle Adolfo Rosado Salas 44* ☎ *987/872–0330* 🖨 *987/ 872–0248* ⟳ *14 rooms, 3 suites* ⚭ *Some fans; no a/c in some rooms, no TV in some rooms* ☰ *MC, V.*

¢ ⊞ **Safari Inn.** Above the Aqua Safari dive shop on the waterfront, this small hotel has comfy beds, powerful hot-water showers, air-conditioning, and the camaraderie of fellow scuba fanatics. The owner also operates Condumel, a small, comfortable condo complex that's perfect for setting up house for one night, a week, or longer. Rates are reasonable and the setting is peaceful, with excellent snorkeling. ⊠ *Av. Rafael E. Melgar and Calle 5* ☎ *987/872–0101* 🖨 *987/872–0661* ⊕ *www. aquasafari.com* ⟳ *12 rooms* ⚭ *Dive shop, snorkeling* ☰ *MC, V.*

Windward Side

★ $$ ⊞ **Ventanas al Mar.** The lights of San Miguel are but a distant glow on the horizon when you look west from the only hotel on the windward coast. Turn east, though, and you can watch shooting stars flash through the nighttime sky over the foaming sea. Escape is complete at this small, eco-friendly inn that runs on solar power; there are no phones, no computer hookups. The rooms are commodious and comfortable, and have microwaves, refrigerators, and coffeemakers. Full breakfast is served in the open-air lobby, and meals are available at Coconuts, next door, until dusk. Sea turtles nest on the long beach beside the hotel in summer, and tropical fish and anemones gather by the rocky point in front of the rooms. ⊠ *East-coast road north of Coconuts* ☎ *No phone* 🖨 *No fax* ⊕ *www. cozumel-hotels.net/ventanas-al-mar/* ⟳ *14 rooms* ⚭ *Fans, kitchenettes, microwaves, refrigerators, beach, snorkeling, free parking; no room TVs* ☰ *No credit cards* ⧖ *BP.*

NIGHTLIFE & THE ARTS

Discos and trendy clubs are not Cozumel's scene. In fact, some visitors complain that the town seems to shut down completely by midnight. Perhaps it's the emphasis on sun and scuba diving that sends everyone to bed early. (It's hard to be a night owl when your dive boat leaves first thing in the morning.) In fact, the cruise ship passengers mobbing the bars seem to party more than those staying on the island. Sometimes, the rowdiest action takes place in the afternoon, when revelers pull out the stops before reboarding their ships back to the mainland.

Bars

Sports fans come to bet on their favorite teams, watch the games, and catch the ESPN news at **All Sports** (⊠ Av. 5 Norte and Calle 2 ☎ 987/ 869–2246). **Carlos 'n Charlie's, El Shrimp Bucket, and Señor Frog's** (⊠ Av.

CLOSE UP

A Ceremonial Dance

WOMEN REGALLY DRESSED in embroidered, lace-trimmed dresses and men in their best guayabera shirts carry festooned trays on their heads during the Baile de las Cabezas de Cochino (dance of the pig's head) at the Fería del Cedral. The trays are festooned with trailing ribbons, *papeles picados* (paper cutouts), piles of bread, and, in some cases, the head of a barbecued pig.

The pig is a sacrificial offering to God, who supposedly saved the founders of this tiny Cozumel settlement. According to legend, the tradition began during the 19th-century War of the Castes, when Yucatán's Maya rose up against their oppressors. The enslaved Maya killed most of the mestizos in the mainland village of Sabán. Casimiro Cardenas, a wealthy young man, survived while clutching a small wooden cross. He promised he would establish an annual religious festival once he found a new home.

Today the original religious vigils and novenas blend into the more secular fair, which runs from April 27 to May 3. Festivities include horse races, bullfights, and amusement park rides, and stands selling hot dogs, corn on the cob, and cold beer. Celebrations peak during the ritualistic dance, which is usually held on the final day.

The music begins with a solemn cadence as families enter the stage, surrounding one member bearing a multi-tiered tray. The procession proceeds in a solemn circle as the participants proudly display their costumes and offerings. Gradually, the beat quickens and the dancing begins. Grabbing the ends of ribbons trailing from the trays, children, parents, and grandparents twirl in ever-faster circles until the scene becomes a whirling blend of grinning, sweaty faces and bright colors.

Rafael E. Melgar at Punta Langosta ☎ 987/872–0191) are all members of the Carlos Anderson chain of rowdy restaurant-bars that attract lively crowds. The *Animal House* ambience includes loud rock music and a liberated, anything-goes dancing scene that's especially attractive to the cruising set.

Drink too many martinis at **Cielo Lounge Bar** (⌧ Av. 15 between Calles 2 and 4 ☎ 987/872–3467) and you might feel like you're floating in an aquarium, what with the narrow room's blue lighting and tinted glass bar. The lounge is behind San Miguel Cafe and serves as a late-night hangout for locals watching music videos on a big screen (Luis Miguel is a hit) or belting out boleros during impromptu karaoke sessions. The restaurant is open until 11:30 every night but Sunday, and the lounge is open until 2 AM on Friday and Saturday. Lively, rowdy **Fat Tuesdays** (⌧ Av. Juárez between Av. Rafael E. Melgar and Calle 3 Sur ☎ 987/872–5130) draws crowds day and night for frozen daiquiris, ice-cold beers, and blaring rock.

Stylish and blissfully free of pounding bass, **Uvas** (⊠ Carretera Sur Km 8.5 ☎ 987/872–3539) is geared toward well (if skimpily) dressed grown-ups ordering crab quesadillas and fried calamari with curry as they listen to lounge tunes. Dinner and tapas are served until midnight. Live music and local celebrations are common. Most events are open to the public.

Discos

Cozumel's oldest disco, **Neptune Dance Club** (⊠ Av. Rafael E. Melgar and Av. 11 ☎ 987/872–1537), is the island's classiest night spot, with a dazzling light-and-laser show. **Viva Mexico** (⊠ Av. Rafael E. Melgar ☎ 987/ 872–0799) has a DJ who spins Latin and American dance music until the wee hours. There's also an extensive snack menu.

Live Music

Sunday evenings 8–10, locals head for the zócalo to hear mariachis and island musicians playing tropical tunes. The band at the **Hard Rock Cafe** (⊠ Av. Rafael E. Melgar between Av. Juárez and Calle 2, 2nd fl. ☎ 987/ 872–5273) often rocks until near dawn. Air-conditioning is a major plus.

★ For sophisticated jazz, smart cocktails, and great cigars, check out the **Havana Club** (⊠ Av. Rafael E. Melgar between Calles 6 and 8, 2nd fl. ☎ 987/872–2098). Beware of ordering imported liquors such as vodka and scotch; drink prices are very high. The food isn't the draw at **Joe's Lobster House** (⊠ Av. Rafael E. Melgar, across from the ferry pier ☎ 987/ 872–3275), but the reggae and salsa bring in the crowds nightly, from 10:30 until dawn.

Movies

Locals say the best thing to happen in years is the opening of **Cineopolis** (⊠ Av. Rafael E. Melgar ☎ 987/869–0799). The modern, multi-screen theater shows current hit films in Spanish and English and has afternoon matinees and nightly shows.

SPORTS & THE OUTDOORS

Most people come to Cozumel for the water sports—especially scuba diving, snorkeling, and fishing. Services and equipment rentals are available throughout the island, especially through major hotels and water-sports centers at the beach clubs. If you're curious about what's underneath Cozumel's waters, but don't like getting wet, **Atlantis Submarine** (⊠ Carretera Sur, Km 4, across from Hotel Casa del Mar ☎ 987/ 872–5671 ⊕ www.goatlantis.com) runs 1½-hour submarine rides that explore the Chankanaab Reef and surrounding area; tickets for the tours are $79 for adults and $45 for children. Claustrophobes may not be able to handle the sardine-can conditions.

Bicycling

Biking is great on Cozumel when winds are calm and humidity low—although these conditions are the exception rather than the norm (except during the colder winter months). Traffic is another concern, and

Continued on page 120

COZUMEL DIVING & SNORKELING

First comes the giant step, a leap from a dry boat into the warm Caribbean Sea. Then the slow descent to white sand framed by rippling brain coral and waving purple sea fans. If you lean back, you can look up toward the sea's surface. The water off Cozumel is so clear you can see puffy white clouds in the sky even when you're submerged at 20 feet.

With more than 30 charted reefs whose depths average 50–80 feet and water temperatures around 24°C–27°C (75°F–80°F) during peak diving season (June–August, when hotel rates are co-incidentally at their lowest), Cozumel is far and away *the* place to dive in Mexico. More than 60,000 divers come here each year.

Because of the diversity of coral formations and the dramatic underwater peaks and valleys, divers consider Cozumel's Palancar Reef (promoters now call it the Maya Reef) to be one of the top five in the world. Sea turtles headed to the beach to lay their eggs swim beside divers in May and June. Fifteen-pound lobsters wave their antennae from beneath coral ledges; they've been protected in Cozumel's National Marine Park for so long they've lost all fear of humans. Long green moray eels still appear rather menacing as they bare their fangs at curious onlookers, and snaggle-toothed barracuda look ominous as they swim by. But all in all, diving off Cozumel is relaxing, rewarding, and so addictive you simply can't do it just once.

Snorkelers have nearly as much fun as divers in Cozumel's calm waters. There's good snorkeling off nearly every hotel beach snorkel gear. All you need is a pair of fins, a mask, a snorkel, and a sense of curiosity.

SCUBA DIVING

The water is so warm and clear—around 80 degrees with near-100-foot visibility most of the year—that diving feels nearly effortless. There's no way anyone can do all the deep dives, drift dives, shore dives, wall dives, and night dives in one trip, never mind the theme dives focusing on ecology, archaeology, sunken ships, and photography.

Many hotels and dive shops offer introductory classes in a swimming pool. Most include a beach or boat dive. Resort courses cost about $50–$60. Many dive shops also offer full open-water certification classes, which take at least four days of intensive classroom study and pool practice. Basic certification courses cost about $350, while advanced certification courses cost as much as $700. You can also do your classroom study at home, then make your training and test dives on Cozumel.

DIVING SAFELY There are more than 100 dive shops in Cozumel, so look for high safety standards and documented credentials. The best places offer small groups and individual attention. Next to your equipment, your dive master is the most important consideration for your adventure. Make sure he or she has PADI or NAUI certification (or FMAS, the Mexican equivalent). Be sure to bring your own certification card; all reputable shops require customers to show them before diving. If you forget, you may be able to call the agency that certified you and have the card number faxed to the shop.

Keep in mind that much of the reef off Cozumel is a protected National Marine Park. Boats aren't allowed to anchor in certain areas, and you shouldn't touch the coral or take any "souvenirs" from the reefs when you dive there. It's best to swim at least 3 feet above the reef—not just because coral can sting or cut

you, but also because it's easily damaged and grows very slowly; it has taken 2,000 years to reach its present size.

There's a reputable recompression chamber at the **Buceo Médico Mexicano** (✉ Calle 5 Sur 21B ☎ 987/872–1430 24-hr hotline). The **Cozumel Recompression Chamber** (✉ San Miguel Clinic, Calle 6 between Avs. 5 and 10 ☎ 987/872–3070) is also a fully equipped recompression center. These chambers, which aim for a 35-minute response time from reef to chamber, treat decompression sickness, commonly known as "the bends," which occurs when you surface too quickly and nitrogen bubbles form in the bloodstream. Recompression chambers are also used to treat nitrogen narcosis, collapsed lungs, and overexposure to the cold.

You may also want to consider buying dive-accident insurance from the U.S.-based **Divers Alert Network (DAN)** (☎ 800/446–2671 ⊕ www.diversalertnetwork.org) before embarking on your dive vacation. DAN insurance covers dive accidents and injuries, and their emergency hotline can help you find the best local doctors, hyperbaric chambers and medical services to assist you. They can also arrange for airlifts.

DIVE SITES

Cozumel's reefs stretch for 32 km (20 mi), beginning at the international pier and continuing to Punta Celarain at the island's southernmost tip. Following is a rundown of Cozumel's main dive destinations.

Chankanaab Reef. This inviting reef lies south of Parque Chankanaab, about 350 yards offshore. Large underground caves are filled with striped grunt, snapper, sergeant majors, and butterfly fish. At 55 feet, there's another large coral formation that's often filled with crabs, lobster, barrel sponges, and angelfish. If you drift a bit farther south, you can see the Balones de Chankanaab, balloon-shaped coral heads at 70 feet. This is an excellent dive site for beginners.

Colombia Reef. Several miles off Palancar, the reef reaches 82–98 feet and is best suited for experienced divers. Its underwater structures are as varied as those of Palancar Reef, with large canyons and ravines to explore. Clustered near the overhangs are large groupers, jacks, rays, and an occasional sea turtle.

Felipe Xicotencatl (C-53 Wreck). Sunk in 2000 specifically for scuba divers, this 154-foot-long minesweeper is located on a sandy bottom about 80 feet deep near Tormentos and Chankanaab. Created as an artificial reef to decrease some of the traffic on the natural reefs, the ship is open so divers can explore the interior and is gradually attracting schools of fish.

Maracaibo Reef. Considered one of the most difficult reefs, Maracaibo is a thrilling dive with strong currents and intriguing old coral formations. Although there are shallow areas, only advanced divers who can cope with the current should attempt Maracaibo.

Palancar Reef. About 2 km (1 mi) offshore, Palancar (sometimes called the Maya Reef) is actually a series of varying coral formations with about 40 dive locations. It's filled with winding canyons, deep ravines, narrow crevices and archways, tunnels, and caves. Black and red coral and huge elephant-ear and barrel sponges are among the attractions. At the section called Horseshoe, a series of coral heads form a natural horseshoe shape. This is one of the most popular sites for dive boats and can become crowded.

Paraíso Reef. About 330 feet offshore, running parallel to the international cruise-ship pier, this reef averages 30–50 feet. It's a perfect spot to dive before you head for deeper drop-offs such as La Ceiba and Villa Blanca. There are impressive formations of star and brain coral as well as sea fans, sponges, sea eels, and yellow rays. It's wonderful for night diving.

Paseo El Cedral. Running parallel to Santa Rosa reef, this flat reef has gardenlike valleys full of fish, including angelfish, grunt, and snapper. At depths of 35–55 feet, you can also spot rays.

San Francisco Reef. Considered Cozumel's shallowest wall dive (35–50 feet), this 1-km (½-mi) reef runs parallel to Playa San Francisco and has many varieties of reef fish. You'll need to take a dive boat to get here.

Santa Rosa Wall. North of Palancar, Santa Rosa is renowned among experienced divers for deep dives and drift dives; at 50 feet there's an abrupt yet sensational drop-off to enormous coral overhangs. The strong current drags you along the tunnels and caves, where there are huge sponges, angelfish, groupers, and rays— and sometime even a shark or two.

Tormentos Reef. The abundance of sea fans, sponges, sea cucumbers, arrow crabs, green eels, groupers, and other marine life—against a terrifically colorful backdrop—makes this a perfect spot for underwater photography. This variegated reef has a maximum depth of around 70 feet.

Yucab Reef. South of Tormentos Reef, this relatively shallow reef is close to shore, making it an ideal spot for beginners. About 400 feet long and 55 feet deep, it's teeming with queen angelfish and sea whip swimming around the large coral heads. The one drawback is the strong current, which can reach 2 or 3 knots.

Caribbean Sea

10m

5m

Isla de
Pasión

Punta Norte

15 ft

✈ **Airport**

TO PLAYA
DEL CARMEN

30 ft

Av. Benito Juárez

Punta Langosta

San Miguel

Paraíso Reef

Queen Angelfish

Chankanaab Reef
Felipe Xicotencatl (C-53 Wreck)
Tormentos Reef
Yucab Reef

Rock beauty

San Francisco Reef

Santa Rosa Wall

Paseo El Cedral

Laguna
Colombia

Laguna
Chunchacaab

Palancar Reef

Colombia Reef

Punta Sur

KEY TO DIVE SITES

Beginner

Advanced

Punta Celarain

0

6 miles

0

9 km

Maracaibo Reef

30 ft

50 ft

DIVE SHOPS & OPERATORS

It's important to choose a dive shop that suits your expectations. Beginners are best off with the more established, conservative shops that limit the depth and time you spend underwater. Experienced divers may be impatient with this approach, and are better suited to shops that offer smaller group dives and more challenging dive sites. More and more shops are merging these days, so don't be surprised if the outfit you dive with one year has been absorbed by another the following year. Recommending a shop is dicey. The ones listed below are well-established and are recommended by experienced Cozumel divers.

WHAT IT COSTS	
Regulator & BC	$15
Underwater camera	$35
Video camera	$75
Pro videos of your dive	$160
Two-tank boat trips	$70–$100
Specialty dives	$70–$100
One-tank afternoon dives	$30–$35
Night dives	$30–$35
Marine park fee	$2

■ TIP →→Dive shops handle more than 1,000 divers per day; many run "cattle boats" packed with lots of divers and gear. It's worth the extra money to go out with a smaller group on a fast boat, especially if you're experienced.

Because dive shops tend to be competitive, it's well worth your while to shop around. Many hotels have their own on-dive shops in town. **ANOAAT** (Aquatic Sports Operators Association; ☎ 987/872–5955) has listings of affiliated dive operations. Before signing on, ask experienced divers about the place, check credentials, and look over the boats and equipment.

Aqua Safari (✉ Av. Rafael E. Melgar 429, between Calles 5 and 7 Sur ☎ 987/872–0101) is among the island's oldest and most professional shops. Owner Bill Horn has long been involved in efforts to protect the reefs and stays on top of local environmental issues. The shop provides PADI certification, classes on night diving, deep diving and other interests, and individualized dives.

Sergio Sandoval of **Aquatic Sports and Scuba Cozumel** (✉ Calle 21 Sur and Av. 20 Sur ☎ 987/872–0640) gets rave reviews from his clients, many of them guests at the Flamingo Hotel. His boats carry only 6–8 divers so the trips are extremely personalized.

Blue Angel (✉ Carretera Sur Km. 2.3 ☎ 987/872–11631) offers combo dive and snorkel trips so families who don't all scuba can still stick together. Along with dive trips to local reefs, they have summer trips to swim with the whale sharks that migrate to the shores of Isla Holbox, north of Cancún. Though you

can do the trip in a very long day, it's best to chose the overnight option.

Long located at the La Ceiba hotel, **Del Mar Aquatics** (⊠ Casa Del Mar Hotel Carretera Sur, Km 4 ☎ 987/872–5949) has merged with Dive Palancar (another established dive shop) and moved to the Casa Del Mar Hotel. The location is ideal for shore and night dives.

Dive Cozumel-Yellow Rose (⊠ Calle Adolfo Rosado Salas 85, between Avs. Rafael E. Melgar and 5 Sur ☎ 987/872–4567) specializes in cave diving for highly experienced divers, along with regular open-water dives. Classes in cavern and other technical diving specialties are also available. Tours are made on a customized 48-foot boat, for a maximum of 12 people.

Eagle Ray Divers (⊠ La Caleta Marina, near the Presidente InterContinental hotel ☎ 987/872–5735) offers snorkeling trips (the three-reef snorkeling trip gives nondivers a chance to explore beyond the shore) and dive instruction. As befits their name, the company keeps track of the eagle rays that appear off Cozumel from December to February and runs trips for advanced divers to walls where the rays congregate. Beginners can also see rays around some of the reefs.

Grouper

Pepe Scuba (⊠ Carretera Costera Norte, Km 2.5 ☎ 987/872–6740) operates out of the Coral Princess Hotel and offers boat dives and several options for resort divers. They also have dive packages available for people staying at the hotel. **Proscuba** (⊠ Calle 3 Norte 299, between Avs. 15 and 20 ☎ 987/872–5994) is a small family-run operation offering personalized service.

Dive magazines regularly rate **Scuba Du** (⊠ at the Presidente InterContinental hotel ☎ 987/872–9505) among the best dive shops in the Caribbean. Along with the requisite Cozumel dives, the company offers an advanced divers' trip searching for eagle rays and a wreck dive to a minesweeper sunk in 2000.

SNORKELING

Snorkeling equipment is available at nearly all hotels and beach clubs as well as at Parque Chankanaab, Playa San Francisco, and Parque Punta Sur. Gear rents for less than $10 a day. Snorkeling tours run about $60 and take in the shallow reefs off Palancar, Chankanaab, Colombia, and Yucab.

☾ **Cozumel Sailing** (⊠ Carretera Norte at the marina ☎ 987/869–2312) offers sailing tours with open bar, lunch, snorkeling, and beach time for $65. Sunset cruises aboard the trimaran *El Tucan* are also available; they include unlimited drinks and live entertainment and cost about $25. They also offer boat rentals.

Fury Catamarans (⊠ Carretera Sur beside Casa del Mar hotel ☎ 987/872–5145) runs snorkeling tours from its 45-foot catamarans. Rates begin at about $58 per day and include equipment, a guide, soft drinks, beer, and margaritas and a beach party with lunch.

it takes the skill of a Manhattan bike messenger to negotiate busy streets. But for serious cyclists nothing beats pedaling the island's circumference. **Isla Bicicleta** (⊠ Ave. 10 Sur at Calle 1 ☎ 987/878–4919 ⊕ www.cozumelbikes.com) rents mountain and road bikes for $13 a day, along with helmets and ever-essential locks. Bike tours start at $65 per person.

Fishing

The waters off Cozumel swarm with more than 230 species of fish, making this one of the world's best deep-sea fishing destinations. During billfish migration season, from late April through June, blue marlin, white marlin, and sailfish are plentiful, and world-record catches aren't uncommon.

Deep-sea fishing for tuna, barracuda, wahoo, and dorado is good year-round. You can go bottom-fishing for grouper, yellowtail, and snapper on the shallow sand flats at the island's north end and fly-fish for bonefish, tarpon, snook, grouper, and small sharks in the same area. Regulations forbid commercial fishing, sportfishing, spear fishing, and collecting marine life in certain areas around Cozumel. It's illegal to kill certain species within marine reserves, including billfish, so be prepared to return some prize catches to the sea.

Charters

You can charter high-speed fishing boats for about $420 per half-day or $600 per day (with a maximum of six people). Your hotel can help arrange daily charters—some offer special deals, with boats leaving from their own docks. **Albatros Deep Sea Fishing** (☎ 987/872–7904 or 888/333–4643) offers full-day rates that include boat and crew, tackle and bait, and lunch with beer and soda. All equipment and tackle, lunch with beer, and the boat and crew are also included in **Marathon Fishing & Leisure Charters'** full-day rates (☎ 987/872–1986). **3 Hermanos** (☎ 987/872–6417 or 987/876–8931) specializes in deep-sea and fly-fishing trips. Their rates for a half-day deep-sea fishing trip start at $350. They also offer scuba diving trips.

Golf

The **Cozumel Country Club** (⊠ Carretera Costera Norte, Km 5.8 ☎ 987/872–9570 ⊕ www.cozumelcountryclub.com.mx) has an 18-hole championship golf course. The gorgeous fairways amid mangroves and a lagoon are the work of the Nicklaus Design Group. The greens fee is $149, which includes a golf cart. Many hotels offer golf packages here.

☾ If you're not a fan of miniature golf, the challenging **Cozumel Mini-Golf** (⊠ Calle 1 Sur 20 ☎ 987/872–6570) might convert you. The jungle-themed course has banana trees, birds, two fountains, and a waterfall. You can choose your music from a selection of more than 800 CDs and order your drinks via walkie-talkie; they'll be delivered as you try for that hole in one. Admission is $7 for adults, $5 for kids; it's open Monday–Saturday 10 AM–11 PM and Sunday 5 PM–11 PM.

Horseback Riding

Aventuras Naturales (⊠ Av. 35 No. 1081 ☎ 987/872–1628 or 858/366–4632 ⊕ www.aventurasnaturalascozumel.com) runs a two-hour guided horseback tour through the jungle to El Cedral. Prices start at $30. Groups are small and the guides fun and informative. **Rancho Buenavista** (⊠ Av. Rafael E. Melgar and Calle 11 Sur ☎ 987/872–1537) provides four-hour rides through the jungle starting at $65 per person.

Kayaking

Located at Uvas beach club, **Clear Kayak** (⊠ Carretera Sur Km 8.5 ☎ 987/872–3539) runs what's called "dry snorkeling" tours in see-through kayaks (imagine what the fish must be thinking). Paddling around with water seeming to flow past your toes is great fun, and there's time for real snorkeling as well. Tours, which cost $49 for adults and $32 for children, include snorkel gear, buffet lunch, and round-trip transportation from your hotel.

SHOPPING

Cozumel's main souvenir shopping area is downtown along Avenida Rafael E. Melgar and on some side streets around the plaza. There are also clusters of shops at Plaza del Sol (east side of the main plaza) and Vista del Mar (Av. Rafael E. Melgar 45). Malls at the cruise-ship piers aim to please passengers seeking jewelry, perfume, sportswear, and low-end souvenirs at high-end prices.

Most downtown shops accept U.S. dollars; many goods are priced in dollars. To get better prices, pay with cash or traveler's checks—some shops tack a hefty surcharge on credit-card purchases. Shops, restaurants, and streets are always crowded between 10 AM and 2 PM, but get calmer in the evening. Traditionally, stores are open from 9 to 1 (except Sunday) and 5 to 9, but those nearest the pier tend to stay open all day, particularly during high season. Most shops are closed Sunday morning.

⚠ When you shop in Cozumel, be sure you don't buy anything made with black coral. Not only is it overpriced—it's also an endangered species, and you may be barred from bringing it to the United States and other countries.

Markets

★ ☺ There's a **crafts market** (⊠ Calle 1 Sur behind the plaza) in town, which sells a respectable assortment of Mexican wares. It's the best place to practice your bartering skills while shopping for blankets, T-shirts, hammocks, and pottery. For fresh produce try the **Mercado Municipal** (⊠ Calle Adolfo Rosadao Salas between Avs. 20 and 25 Sur ☎ No phone), open Monday–Saturday 8–5.

Shopping Malls

Forum Shops (⊠ Av. Rafael E. Melgar and Calle 10 Norte ☎ 987/869–1687) is a flashy marble-and-glass mall with jewels glistening in glass cases and an overabundance of eager salesclerks. Diamonds International and Tanzanite International have shops in the Forum and all over Avenida Rafael E. Melgar, as does Roger's Boots, a leather store. There's a Havana Club restaurant and bar upstairs, where shoppers select expensive cigars. **Puerto Maya** (⊠ Carretera Sur at the southern cruise dock) is a mall geared toward cruise-ship passengers. It's close to the ships at the end of a huge parking lot. **Punta Langosta** (⊠ Av. Rafael E. Melgar 551, at Calle 7), a fancy multilevel shopping mall, is across the street from the cruise-ship dock. An enclosed pedestrian walkway leads over the street from the ships to the center, which houses several jewelry and sportswear stores. The center is designed to lure cruise-ship passengers into shopping in air-conditioned comfort and has decreased traffic for local businesses.

Specialty Stores

Clothing

Several trendy sportswear stores line Avenida Rafael E. Melgar between Calles 2 and 6. **Exotica** (⊠ Av. Juárez at the plaza ☎ 987/872–5880) has high-quality sportswear and shirts with nature-theme designs. **Island Outfitters** (⊠ Av. Rafael E. Melgar, at the plaza ☎ 987/872–0132) has high-quality sportswear, beach towels, and sarongs. If you need a dressy outfit for some unexpected reason (there's not much demand for evening gowns on Cozumel), **L'Chic** (⊠ Av. 5 at Calle 3 ☎ 987/872–4898) lives up to its name with long formal dresses as well as classy sundresses. **Mr. Buho** (⊠ Av. Rafael E. Melgar between Calles 6 and 8 ☎ 987/869–1601) specializes in white and black clothes and has well-made guayabera shirts and cotton dresses.

Crafts

The showrooms at **Anji** (⊠ Av. 5 between Calles Adolfo Rosado Salas and 1 Sur ☎ 987/869–2623) are filled with imported lamps, carved animals, and clothing from Bali. At **Balam Mayan Feather** (⊠ Av. 5 and Calle 2 Norte ☎ 987/869–0548) artists create intricate paintings on feathers from local birds. **Bugambilias** (⊠ Av. 10 Sur between Calles Adolfo Rosado Salas and 1 Sur ☎987/872–6282) sells handmade Mexican linens.

★ **Los Cinco Soles** (⊠ Av. Rafael E. Melgar and Calle 8 Norte ☎ 987/872–0132) is the best one-stop shop for crafts from around Mexico. Several display rooms, covering almost an entire block, are filled with clothing, furnishings, home decor items, and jewelry. Latin music CDs and English-language novels are displayed at **Fama** (⊠ Av. 5 between Calle 2 and the plaza ☎ 987/872–2050), which also has sandals, swimsuits, and souvenirs.

At Cozumel's best art gallery, **Galeria Azul** (⊠ Calle 10 Sur between Av. Salas and Calle 1 ☎ 987/869–0963), artist Greg Deitrich displays his engraved blown glass along with paintings, jewelry, and other works by local artists. The **Hammock House** (⊠ Av. 5 and Calle 4 ☎ No phone) has long been a local curiosity thanks to its bright-blue exterior and the inventory that hangs out front. Manuel Azueta Vivas has been selling hammocks here for more than four decades. **Indigo** (⊠ Av. Rafael E. Melgar 221 ☎ 987/872–1076) carries a large selection of purses, belts, vests, and shirts from bright blue, purple, and green Guatemalan fabrics. They also have wooden masks.

Librería del Parque (⊠ Av. 5 at the plaza ☎ 987/872–0031) is Cozumel's best bookstore; it carries the *Miami Herald, USA Today,* and English and Spanish magazines and books. **El Porton** (⊠ Av. 5 Sur and Calle 1 Sur ☎ 987/872–5606) has a collection of masks and unusual crafts. Antiques and high-quality silver jewelry are the draws at **Shalom** (⊠ Av. 10, No. 25 ☎ 987/872–3783).

Viva Mexico (⊠ Av. Rafael E. Melgar and Calle Adolfo Rosada Salas ☎ 987/872–0791) sells souvenirs and handicrafts from all over Mexico; it's a great place to find T-shirts, blankets, and trinkets.

Grocery Stores
The main grocery store, **Chedraui** (⊠ Carretera Chankanaab, Km 1.5 and Calle 15 Sur ☎ 987/872–3655), is open daily 8 AM–10 PM and also carries clothing, kitchenware, appliances, and furniture.

Jewelry
Diamond Creations (⊠ Av. Rafael E. Melgar Sur 131 ☎ 987/872–5330) lets you custom-design pieces of jewelry from a collection of loose diamonds, emeralds, rubies, sapphires, or tanzanite. The shop and its affiliates, Tanzanite International, Diamond Creations, and Silver International, have multiple locations along the waterfront and in the shopping malls—in fact, you can't avoid them.

Look for silver, gold, and coral jewelry—especially bracelets and earrings—at **Joyería Palancar** (⊠ Av. Rafael E. Melgar Norte 15 ☎ 987/872–1468). **Luxury Avenue (Ultrafemme)** (⊠ Av. Rafael E. Melgar 341 ☎ 987/872–1217) sells high-end goods including watches and perfume. **Pama** (⊠ Av. Rafael E. Melgar Sur 9 ☎ 987/872–0090), near the pier, carries imported jewelry, perfumes, and glassware. Innovative designs and top-quality stones are available at **Van Cleef & Arpels** (⊠ Av. Rafael E. Melgar Norte across from the ferry ☎ 987/872–6540).

COZUMEL ESSENTIALS

Transportation

BY AIR
The Aeropuerto Internacional de Cozumel, Cozumel's only airport, is 3 km (2 mi) north of San Miguel. Flight schedules and frequencies vary with the season, with the largest selection available in winter. Continental flies twice daily and three times on Saturday non-stop from Houston, and nonstop of Saturday from Newark. Delta flies nonstop from Atlanta on Saturday and Sunday. United Airlines flies from Chicago on Monday, Wednesday, and Saturday. US Airways flies nonstop daily from Charlotte, North Carolina, and nonstop from Philadelphia on Saturday. American Airlines has nonstop flights daily from Dallas. Aerocaribe flies between Cozumel and Cancún six times daily and twice daily from Mexico City.

At the airport, the *colectivo,* a van that seats up to eight, takes arriving passengers to their hotels; the fare is about $7–$20. If you want to avoid waiting for the van to fill or for other passengers to be dropped off, you can hire an *especial*—an individual van. A trip in one of these to hotel zones costs about $20–$25; to the city it's about $10; and to the all-inclusives at the far south it's about to $30. Taxis to the airport cost between $10 and $30 from the hotel zones and approximately $5 from downtown.

🚗 **Aeropuerto Internacional de Cozumel** ☎ 987/872-1995 or 987/872-0485. **Aerocaribe** ☎ 987/872-0877.

BY BOAT & FERRY

Passenger-only ferries to Playa del Carmen leave Cozumel's main pier approximately every hour on the hour from 5 AM to 10 PM (no ferries at 11 AM, 1, 7, and 9 PM). They also leave Playa del Carmen's dock about every hour on the hour, from 6 AM to 11 PM (no service at 7 AM, noon, 2 PM, and 9 PM). The trip takes 45 minutes. Call, or better yet, stop by the ferry pier, to verify the times. Bad weather sometimes prompts cancellations.

The traditional car ferry leaves from Puerto Morelos. The trip takes three to five hours. The fare starts at about $60 for small cars (more for larger vehicles) and $6 per passenger. Another car ferry travels between Calica south of Playa del Carmen and Cozumel three times daily. The fare starts at about $55 for small cars (more for larger vehicles) and $5 per passenger.

🚗 **Passenger-only ferry from Playa del Carmen** ☎ 987/872-1508 or 987/872-1588 ⊕ www.crucerosmaritimos.com.mx. **Car ferry from Puerto Morelos** ☎ 987/872-0950. **Car ferry from Calica** ☎ 987/872-7688.

BY CAR

As well as major rental agencies like Avis and Hertz, Cozumel also has several locally run agencies; among them, Aguila Rentals, Fiesta, and CP Rentals. The national and international companies have desks in the airport and San Miguel; most will deliver cars to your hotel. Rates are similar between all the companies. You can often get better deals when making advance reservations; make sure the quoted price includes all taxes and insurance. Some companies charge less if you're willing to pay cash.

🚗 **Aguila Rentals** ⊠ Av. Rafael E. Melgar 685 ☎ 987/872-0729. **Fiesta** ⊠ Calle 11, No. 598 ☎ 987/872-4311. **CP Rentals** ⊠ Av. 5 Norte between Calles 2 and 4 ☎ 987/878-4055.

BY MOPED

⚠ Mopeds are popular here, but also extremely dangerous because of heavy traffic, potholes, and hidden stop signs; accidents happen all too frequently. Mexican law requires all riders to wear helmets (it's a $25 fine if you don't). If you do decide to rent a moped, drive slowly, check for oncoming traffic, and don't ride when it's raining or if you've had any alcoholic beverages. Mopeds rent for about $25 per day; insurance is included.

🚗 Moped Rentals **Ernesto's Scooter Rental** ⊠ Carretera Costera Sur, Km 4 ☎ 987/872-3152. **Rentadora Cozumel** ⊠ Calle Adolfo Rosado Salas 3B ☎ 987/872-1503

✉ Av. 10 Sur and Calle 1 ☎ 987/872-1120. **Rentadora Marlin** ✉ Av. 5 and Calle 1 Sur ☎ 987/872-5501.

BY TAXI

Cabs wait at all the major hotels, and you can hail them on the street. The fixed rates run about $2 within town; $8–$20 between town and either hotel zone; $10–$30 from most hotels to the airport; and about $20–$40 from the northern hotels or town to Parque Chankanaab or Playa San Francisco. The cost from the Puerto Maya cruise-ship terminal by La Ceiba to San Miguel is about $10.

Drivers quote prices in pesos or dollars—the peso rate may be cheaper. Tipping isn't necessary. Despite the established taxi fares, many cab drivers have begun charging double or even triple these rates. Be firm on a price before getting into the car. Drivers carry a rather complicated rate sheet with them that lists destinations by zone. Ask to see the sheet if the price seems unreasonably high.

Contacts & Resources

BANKS & EXCHANGE SERVICES

Most of Cozumel's banks are in the main square and are open weekdays between 9 and 4 or 5. Many change currency all day. Most have ATMs that dispense pesos, although dollars are available at some ATMs near the cruise ship piers. The American Express exchange office is open weekdays 9–5. After hours, you can change money at Promotora Cambiaria del Centro, which is open Monday–Saturday 8 AM–9 PM.

🏦 Banks **Bancomer** ✉ Av. 5 Norte at the plaza ☎ 987/872-0550. **Banco Serfin** ✉ Calle 3 Sur and Av. 10 Sur ☎ 987/872-2853. **Bital** ✉ Av. 5 and Calle 1 ☎ 987/872-0142.

🏦 Exchange Services **American Express** ✉ Punta Langosta, Av. Rafael E. Melgar 599 ☎ 987/869-1389. **Promotora Cambiaria del Centro** ✉ Av. 5 Sur between Calles 1 Sur and Adolfo Rosado Salas ☎ No phone.

EMERGENCIES

For general emergencies throughout Cozumel, dial 060.

🏥 Emergency Contacts **Air Ambulance** ☎ 987/872-4070. **Police** ✉ Anexo del Palacio Municipal ☎ 987/872-0092.

🏥 Hospitals & Clinics **Centro Médico de Cozumel** (Cozumel Medical Center) ✉ Calle 1 Sur 101 and Av. 50 ☎ 987/872-0103 or 987/872-3545. **Médica San Miguel** ✉ Calle 6 Norte 135, betwen Avs. 5 and 10 ☎ 987/872-0103. **Medical Specialties Center** ✉ Av. 20 Norte 425 ☎ 987/872-1419 or 987/872-2919. **Red Cross** ✉ Calle Adolfo Rosada Salas and Av. 20 Sur ☎ 987/872-1058, 065 for emergencies.

🏥 Late-Night Pharmacies **Farmacia Canto** ✉ Av. 20 at Calle Adolfo Rosado Salas ☎ 987/872-5377. **Farmacia Dori** ✉ Calle Adolfo Rosado Salas between Avs. 15 and 20 Sur ☎ 987/872-0559. **Farmacia Joaquin** ✉ Av. 5 at North side of plaza ☎ 987/872-2520.

🏥 Recompression Chambers **Buceo Médico Mexicano** ✉ Calle 5 Sur 21B ☎ 987/872-1430 24-hr hotline. **Cozumel Recompression Chamber** ✉ San Miguel Clinic, Calle 6 between Avs. 5 and 10 ☎ 987/872-3070.

INTERNET, MAIL & SHIPPING

The local *correos* (post office), six blocks south of the plaza, is open weekdays 8–8, Saturday 9–5, and Sunday 9–1. For packages and important letters, you're better off using DHL. The Calling Station offers long-distance phone service, fax, Internet access, video and DVD rental, and shipping services. The ATM in front of the building is one of the few on the island that dispenses dollars. Laptop connections and computers for Internet access are available at CreWorld Internet. The Crew Office is air-conditioned and has a pleasant staff, and also offers international phone service and CD burning.

🖪 Cybercafés **Calling Station** ✉ Av. Rafael E. Melgar 27, at Calle 3 Sur ☎ 987/872-1417.**The Crew Office** ✉ Av. 5, No. 201, between Calle 3 Sur and Av. Rosada Salas ☎ 987/869-1485. **CreWorld Internet** ✉ Av. Rafael E. Melgar and Calle 11 Sur ☎ 987/872-6509. 🖪 Mail & Shipping **Correos** ✉ Calle 7 Sur and Av. Rafael E. Melgar ☎ 987/872-0106. **DHL** ✉ Av. Rafael E. Melgar and Av. 5 Sur ☎ 987/872-3110.

MEDIA
Most shops and hotels around town offer the *Blue Guide to Cozumel,* a free publication with good information and maps of the island and downtown.

TRAVEL AGENCIES
Fiesta Holidays works with individuals and groups and has a car rental department. Turismo Aviomar is conveniently located in San Miguel and can help with airline reservations as well as tours.

🖪 **Fiesta Holidays** ✉ Calle 11 Sur 598, between Avs. 25 and 30 ☎ 987/872-0923 works with individuals and groups and has a car rental department. **Turismo Aviomar** ✉ Av. 5 Norte 8, between Calles 2 and 4 ☎ 987/872-0407 is conveniently located in San Miguel and can help with airline reservations as well as tours.

VISITOR INFORMATION
The government tourism office, Fidecomiso, and the Cozumel Island Hotel Association have shared offices. The offices are open weekdays 9–2 and 5–8 and Saturdays 9–1, and offer information on affiliated hotels and tour operators.

🖪 **Fidecomiso and the Cozumel Island Hotel Association** ✉ Calle 2 Norte and Av. 15 ☎ 987/872-3132 ⊕ www.islacozumel.com.mx.

The Caribbean Coast

Xcaret

WORD OF MOUTH

"If driving in the area, stop by the ruins of Xel-Ha . . . across from the Xel-Ha park. It's a very small site, but the murals there are some of the most spectacularly preserved I have seen in this region. A walk down a *sacbe* to a beautiful *cenote* and small temple should not be missed."

—Belle

AROUND THE CARIBBEAN COAST

Boats in Quintana Roo

Getting Oriented

The Caribbean coast is in the state of Quintana Roo, bordered on the northwest by the state of Yucatán, on the west by Campeche, and on the south by Belize. Above all else, beaches are what define this region—powdery white sands that curve to embrace clear turquoise lagoons, and the vibrant marine life beneath. Inland landscapes, which range from scrub to jungle, are punctuated with Maya ruin sites.

TOP 5
Reasons to Go

1. Visiting the stunning ruins at Tulum—the only Maya site that overlooks the Caribbean.

2. Casting for bonefish off the Chinchorro Reef near the Reserva de la Biosfera Sian Ka'an.

3. Indulging in a decadent massage or body treatment at one of the Riviera Maya's luxurious spa resorts.

4. Diving or snorkeling at Puerto Morelos's Natural Reef Park, a preserve filled with parrot fish, spotted eagle rays, and other sealife.

5. Exploring the inland jungle south of Rio Bec, where you might glimpse howler monkeys, coatimundi, and Yucatán parrots.

The Río Bec Route In far-southern Quintana Roo, digs at Kohunlich have unearthed Río Bec-style temples, palaces, and pyramids. At the Belizean border, the seaside capital city of Chetumal is modern, but sprinkled with brightly painted wooden houses left over from an earlier era.

184
Polyu

Caobas

Rio Bec

Kohunlich

CAMPECHE

Ruins at Tulum

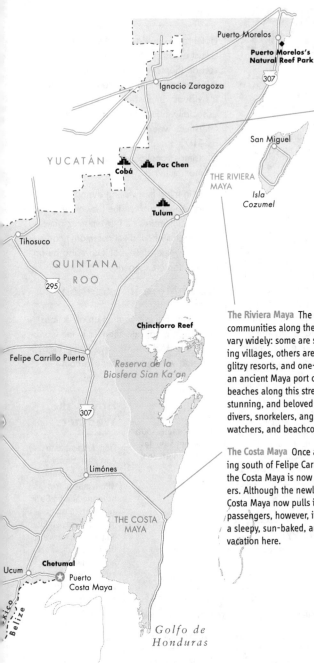

The Inland Jungle The pyramids at Coba are surrounded by jungle, where birds and monkeys call overhead. At the traditional Maya settlement of Pac Chen, residents live as they have for thousands of years. The 1.6 million acres of the Reserva de la Biosfera Sian Ka'an protect thousands of wildlife species.

The Riviera Maya The coastal communities along the Caribbean vary widely: some are sleepy fishing villages, others are filled with glitzy resorts, and one—Tulum—is an ancient Maya port city. The beaches along this stretch are stunning, and beloved by scuba divers, snorkelers, anglers, bird-watchers, and beachcombers.

The Costa Maya Once a no-man's-land stretching south of Felipe Carrillo Puerto to Chetumal, the Costa Maya is now being eyed by developers. Although the newly built port of Puerto Costa Maya now pulls in droves of cruise-ship passengers, however, it's still possible to find a sleepy, sun-baked, and inexpensive Mexican vacation here.

THE CARIBBEAN COAST PLANNER

A Sample Itinerary

Five days will give you enough time to explore many of the best parts of the Caribbean Coast. If you use Playa del Carmen as a base, you can try the following itinerary:

Start with a day-long visit to the Xcaret eco-park. Spend the morning of Day 2 at the gorgeous cliff-side ruins of Tulum; in the afternoon cool off at Xel-Há or at one of the numerous cenotes along Carretera 307. On Day 3, explore the beaches at Paamul and Xpu-há and continue on to Akumal and Yalkú. Spend Day 4 at the Maya village of Pac Chen in the morning and, after lunch, head for the ruins at Cobá. On Day 5, take a tour of the Reserva de la Biosfera Sian Ka'an.

When to Go

Hotel rates can drop on the Caribbean Coast by as much as 50% in the low season (September to approximately mid-December). In high season, however, it's virtually impossible to find low rates, especially in Playa del Carmen. During Christmas week, prices can rise as much as $100 a night—so if you're planning a Christmas vacation, you'd do well to book six months in advance.

Keep in mind that visiting during a traditional festival such as the Day of the Dead (which culminates on November 2 after three nights of candlelit ceremony) can be more expensive—but it can also be an unforgettable experience.

Need More Information?

For additional information on attractions, lodging, dining, and services in the Caribbean Coast, check out www.locogringo.com and www.playamayaews.com.

Tour Options

■ **Maya Sites Travel Services** (☎ 719/256-5186 or 877/620-8715 ⊕ www.mayasites.com) offers inexpensive personalized tours.

■ **Hilario Hiller** (✉ La Jolla, Casa Nai Na, 3rd floor ☎ 984/875-9066) is known for his custom tours of Maya villages, ruins, and the jungle. Tours cost about $100 day, plus transportation.

Dining & Lodging Prices

WHAT IT COSTS in Dollars

	$$$$	$$$	$$	$	¢
Restaurants	over $25	$15–$25	$10–$15	$5–$10	under $5
Hotels	over $250	$150–$250	$75–$150	$50–$75	under $50

Restaurant prices are per person, for a main course at dinner, excluding tax and tip. Hotel prices are for a standard double room in high season, based on the European Plan (EP) and excluding service and 12% tax (which includes 10% Value Added Tax plus 2% hospitality tax).

How's the Weather?

From November to April, the coastal weather is heavenly, with temperatures hovering around 80°F and near-constant ocean breezes. In July and August, however, the breezes disappear and humidity soars, especially inland where temperatures often reach the mid-90s. September and October bring the worst weather: there are often rain, mosquitoes, and the risk of hurricanes.

Exploring the Caribbean Coast

The coast is divided into two major areas. The stretch from Punta Tanchacté to Punta Allen is called the Riviera Maya; it has the most sites and places to lodge, and includes some of the Yucatán's most beautiful ruin sites. The more southern stretch, from Punta Allen to Chetumal, has been dubbed the Costa Maya. This is where civilization thins out and you can find the most alluring landscapes, including the pristine jungle wilderness of the Reserva de la Bisofera Sian Ka'an. The Río Bec Route starts west of Chetumal and continues into Campeche.

About the Restaurants

Restaurants here vary from quirky beachside affairs with outdoor tables and *palapas* (thatch roofs) to more elaborate and sophisticated establishments. Dress is casual at most places. Smaller cafés and fish eateries may not accept credit cards or travelers checks, especially in remote beach villages. Bigger establishments and those in hotels normally accept plastic. In general, it's best to order fresh local fish—grouper, dorado, red snapper, and sea bass—rather than shellfish like shrimp, lobster, and oysters, since the latter are often flown in frozen from the Gulf.

About the Hotels

Many resorts are in remote areas; if you haven't rented a car and want to visit local sights or restaurants, you may find yourself at the mercy of the hotel shuttle service (if there is one) or waiting for long stretches of time for the bus or spending large sums on taxis. Smaller hotels and inns are often family-run; a stay in one of them will give you the chance to mix with the locals.

THE RIVIERA MAYA

It takes patience to discover the treasures on this part of the coast. Beaches and towns aren't easily visible from the main highway—the road from Cancún to Tulum is 1–2 km (½–1 mi) from the coast. Thus there's little to see but dense vegetation, lots of billboards, many roadside markets, and signs marking entrances to various hotels and attractions.

Still, the treasures—which include spectacular white-sand beaches, and some of the peninsula's most beautiful Maya ruins—are here, and they haven't been lost on resort developers. In fact, the Riviera Maya, which stretches from Punta Tanchacté in the north down to Punta Allen in the south, currently houses about 23,512 hotel rooms. This frenzy of building has affected many beachside Maya communities, which have had to relocate to the inland jungle. The residents of these settlements, who mainly work in the hotels, have managed to keep Yucatecan traditions—including food, music, and holiday celebrations—alive in the area.

Wildlife has also been affected by the development of coastal resorts. Thanks to the federal government's foresight, however, 1.6 million acres of coastline and jungle have been set aside for protection as the Reserva de la Biosfera Sian Ka'an. Whatever may happen elsewhere along the coast, this preserve gives the wildlife, and the travelers who seek the Yucatán of old, someplace to go.

Caribbean Coastal History

THE MAYA CULTURE is the enduring backdrop for Mexico's Caribbean coast. Archaeologists have divided this civilization, which lasted some 3,000 years, into three main periods: Preclassic and Late Preclassic (2000 BC–AD 100, together), Classic (AD 100–AD 1000), and Postclassic (AD 1000–AD 1521). Considered the most advanced civilization in the ancient Americas, the Maya are credited with several major breakthroughs: a highly accurate calendar based on astronomical study; the mathematical concept of zero; hieroglyphic writing; and extraordinary ceremonial architecture. Although the Maya's early days were centered around the lowlands in the south-central region of Guatemala, the Maya culture spread north to the Yucatán Peninsula sometime around AD 987. Tulum, which was built during this period, is the only ancient Maya city that was built right on the water.

Until the 1960s, Quintana Roo was considered the most savage coast in Central America, a Mexican territory, not a state. The Caste Wars of the Yucatán, which began in 1847 and ended with a half-hearted truce in 1935, herded hardy Maya to this remote region. With the exception of *chicleros*, men who tapped *zapote* or chicle trees for the Wrigley Chewing Gum Corporation, few non-Maya roamed here. Whites and *mestizos* were not welcome; it was not safe.

By the 1950s the Mexican government began giving tracts of land to the *chicleros* in hopes of colonizing Quintana Roo. At that time, no roads existed. A few *cocals*, or coconut plantations, were scattered throughout the peninsula, headed by a handful of Maya families.

In 1967, the Mexican government sought a location for an international tourist destination with the finest beaches, the most beautiful water, and the fewest hurricanes. A stretch of unpopulated sand at the northeast tip of the Yucatán Peninsula fit the bill. Soon after identifying Cancún as the fortunate winner, that locale, Quintana Roo became Mexico's 31st state.

The 1980s saw an initial surge in tourism. And with the advent of the Riviera Maya in 2000, this 60-mile region stretching south from Puerto Morelos to Tulum developed into one of the world's most popular beach destinations, with Playa del Carmen the fastest growing city in Latin America.

Punta Tanchacté

 28 km (17 mi) south of Cancún.

The Riviera Maya experience starts at Punta Tanchacté (pronounced tan-chak-*te*), also known as Peten Pich (pronounced like "peach"), with small hotels on long stretches of beach caressed by turquoise waters. It's quieter here than in Cancún, and you can walk for miles with only the birds for company.

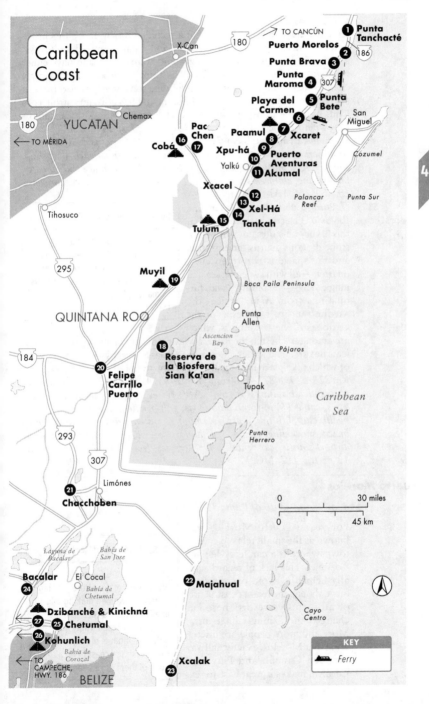

Where to Stay

$$$$ 🏨 **Azul Hotel and Beach Resort.** On a secluded beach, this all-inclusive hotel has ocean views, lush grounds, and palapa-covered walkways. Rooms are filled with Maya designs and colorful art, and have either two twin beds or one double as well as a tiny bathroom. The property changed hands in 2004 and has undergone some lovely renovations; it also now caters to families with children, and has cribs and strollers to lend. A shuttle transports you to nearby Puerto Morelos, Cancún, or Playa del Carmen. ⌧ *Carretera 307, Km 27.5* ☎ *998/872–8088* ⊕ *www.karismahotels.com/azul/fact.html* 🛏 *98 rooms* ⚐ *Restaurant, room service, in-room safes, 3 pools, outdoor hot tub, beach, dive shop, snorkeling, windsurfing, boating, volleyball, 3 bars, dance club, theater, babysitting, children's programs (ages 4–12), laundry service, concierge* ▤ *MC, V* ⏇ *AI.*

$$$$ 🏨 **Paraiso de la Bonita Resort and**
Fodor'sChoice **Thalasso.** Eclectic is the byword at
★ this luxury all-suites hotel. A pair of stone dragons guards the entrance, and the spacious two-room guest quarters—all with sweeping sea and jungle views—are outfitted with furnishings from Asia, Africa, the Mediterranean, Indonesia, or the Caribbean. The restaurants, which

> **WORD OF MOUTH**
>
> "Paraiso de la Bonita is a truly magical resort. The attention to detail is beyond words. The most beautiful place we've been. A transformative place and a transformative experience."   –TA

are among the best in the Riviera Maya, adroitly blend Asian and Mexican flavors. The knockout spa has thalassotherapy treatments, some of which take place in specially built saltwater pools. ⌧ *Carretera 307, Km 328* ☎ *998/872–8300 or 998/872–8314* ▤ *998/872–8301* ⊕ *www. paraisodelabonitaresort.com* 🛏 *90 suites* ⚐ *2 restaurants, in-room safes, cable TV, in-room data ports, golf privileges, tennis court, pool, health club, hot tub, massage, sauna, spa, steam room, saltwater pool, beach, snorkeling, fishing, bar, laundry service, Internet, meeting room, airport shuttle, car rental, travel services, free parking; no kids under 13* ▤ *AE, DC, MC, V.*

Puerto Morelos

❷ *8 km (5 mi) south of Punta Tanchacté.*

For years, Puerto Morelos was known as the small, relaxed coastal town where the car ferry left for Cozumel. This lack of regard actually helped it avoid overdevelopment, though the recent construction of all-inclusive resorts here has changed the fishing-village aura. More and more people are discovering that Morelos, exactly halfway between Cancún and Playa del Carmen, makes a great base for ex-

> **A SACRED JOURNEY**
>
> In ancient times Puerto Morelos was a point of departure for pregnant Maya women making pilgrimages by canoe to Cozumel, the sacred isle of the fertility goddess, Ixchel. Remnants of Maya ruins exist along the coast here, although none of them have been restored.

ploring the region. The town itself is small but colorful, with a central plaza surrounded by shops and restaurants; its trademark is a leaning lighthouse.

Puerto Morelos's greatest appeal lies out at sea: a superb coral reef only 1,800 feet offshore is an excellent place to snorkel and scuba dive. Its proximity to shore means that the waters here are calm and safe, though the beach isn't as attractive as others because it isn't regularly cleared of seaweed and turtle grass. Still, you can walk for miles here and see only a few people. In addition, the mangroves in back of town are home to 36 species of birds, making it a great place for bird-watchers.

The biologists running the **Croco-Cun** (⊠ Carretera 307, Km 30 ☎ 998/850–3719) crocodile farm and zoo just north of Puerto Morelos have collected specimens of many of the reptiles and some of the mammals indigenous to the area. They offer immensely informative tours—you may even get to handle a baby crocodile or feed the deer. Be sure to wave hello to the 500-pound crocodile secure in his deep pit. The farm is open daily 8:30–5:30; admission is $15.

South of Puerto Morelos, the 150-acre **Jardin Botanico del Dr. Alfredo Barrera Marín** (Dr. Alfredo Barrera Marín Botanical Garden; ⊠ Carretera 307, Km 36 ☎ No phone), named for a local botanist, exhibits the peninsula's plants and flowers, which are labeled in English, Spanish, and Latin. There's also a tree nursery, a remarkable orchid and epiphyte garden, a reproduction of a *chiclero* (gum arabic collector), an authentic Maya house, and an archaeological site. A nature walk goes directly through the mangroves for some great bird-watching; more than 220 species have been identified here (be sure to bring the bug spray, though). Spider monkeys can usually be spotted in the afternoons, and a tree-house lookout offers a spectacular view—but the climb isn't for those afraid of heights. The garden is open daily 8–4, and admission is $7.

Located in 500 acres of virgin jungle, **Land of the Motmot Jungle Resort (Le Lu'um Toh)** is a bird-watcher's paradise. You can spend the day wandering the paths and identifying some of the 300 species of birds that live in and migrate through the area, or spend the night in one of the private bungalows constructed from native limestone rock complete with fireplace. Bungalows run $50 per night; group rates are available. ⊠ Camino Central Vallarta, Km 13 ☎ 998/871–0683 or 998/871–0014, 651/565–2566 in U.S. ⊕ www.cancunjungleresort.com ⊙ Open year round, by reservation only; call to make arrangements.

Where to Stay & Eat

★ $$–$$$$ ✕ **John Gray's Kitchen.** The new digs for this former Ritz-Carlton chef are set right against the jungle, and his cooking attracts a regular crowd of locals from Cancún and Playa del Carmen. Using only the freshest ingredients—from local herbs and vegetables to seafood right off the pier—Gray works his magic in a comfortable and contemporary setting that feels more Soho than Maya. Don't miss the *boquineta*, a local white fish grilled to perfection and served with mango salsa. ⊠ Av. Ninos Heroes, Lote 6 ☎ 998/871–0666 or 998/871–0665 ▭ No credit cards ⊙ No lunch; closed Sun.

★ **$–$$$**   ✕ **Posada Amor.** This restaurant, the oldest in Puerto Morelos, has retained a loyal clientele for nearly three decades. In the palapa-covered dining room with its picnic-style wooden tables and benches, the gracious staff serves up terrific Mexican and seafood dishes, including a memorable whole fish dinner and a wonderfully creamy seafood bisque. Sunday brunches are also to die for. If Rogelio, the founder's congenial son, isn't calling you "friend" by the time you leave, you're probably having an off day. ⊠ *Avs. Javier Rojo Gomez and Tulum* ☎☎ *998/ 871–0033* ▭ *No credit cards.*

¢**–$$**   ✕ **El Pirata.** A popular spot for breakfast, lunch or dinner, this open-air restaurant seats you at the center of the action on Puerto Morelos's town square. If you're jonesing for American food, you can get a good hamburger with fries here; there are also also great daily specials. If you're lucky, they might include *pozole,* a broth made from cracked corn, pork, chilies, and bay leaves and served with tostada shells. ⊠ *Av. Jose Maria Morelos, Lote 4* ☎ *998/871–0489* ▭ *No credit cards.*

¢**–$**   ✕ **Cafe del Puerto** This Italian-owned outdoor café, smack in the middle of *el centro* (downtown), is the perfect spot to grab a cappuccino or tasty Greek salad and watch passersby. If you're coming for dinner, be sure to arrive early—this place is popular. A live saxophonist serenades here several evenings a week. ⊠ *Avs. Rafael E. Melgar and Tulum* ☎ *No phone* ▭ *No credit cards.*

¢   ✕ **Loncheria El Tio.** More like a hole in the wall than a restaurant, this short-order eatery is never empty and almost never closed. Yucatecan specialties such as *salbutes* (flour tortillas with shredded turkey, cabbage, tomatoes, and pickled onions) or *panuchos* (beans, chicken, avocado, and pickled onions on flour tortillas) will leave you satisfied, and you'll still have pesos left in your pocket. ⊠ *Av. Rafael E. Melgar, Lote 2, across from main dock* ☎ *No phone* ▭ *No credit cards.*

$$$$ ▥ **Ceiba del Mar Hotel & Spa.** In this secluded beach resort north of town, rooms are in six thatch-roofed buildings, all of which have ocean-view terraces. Painted tiles, wrought-ironwork, and bamboo details in the rooms complement the hardwood furnishings from Guadalajara; the on-site spa offers massage and beauty treatments. There's also butler service, and your Continental breakfast is discreetly delivered to your room through a hidden closet chamber. Although the property is ordinarily pretty tranquil, occasional large wedding groups converge here for ceremonies and fiestas, which can be disruptive if you've come for peace and quiet. ⊠ *Av. Niños Heroes s/n* ☎ *998/872–8060 or 877/545–6221* 🖷 *998/872– 8061* ⊕ *www.ceibadelmar.com* ➽ *120 rooms, 6 suites* △ *2 restaurants, in-room safes, cable TV with movies, tennis court, pool, hot tub, spa, beach, dive shop, bar, shop, laundry service, concierge, meeting room, car rental, travel services; no kids under 15* ▭ *AE, MC, V* ❑ *CP.*

$$$$
FodorsChoice
★   ▥ **Secrets Excellence Riviera Cancun.** This resort's sweeping driveway and grand entrance lead to a gorgeous Spanish marble lobby, where bellmen in pith helmets await you. The guest rooms are similarly opulent: all have Jacuzzi tubs, marble bathrooms, ornate Italianate furnishings, and private balconies. The property, which includes six swimming pools and more than a dozen restaurants and bars, is centered around a luxurious spa, where you can get a decadent Maya massage or facial. Af-

terward, you can sip margaritas under a beachside palapa, or take a sailing tour on the hotel's private yacht. ⊠ *Carretera Federal 307, Manzana 7, Lote 1* ☎ *998/872–8500* 🖷 *998/872–8501* ⊕ *www.secretsresorts. com* 🗩 *442 rooms* ⭘ *9 restaurants, room service, in-room hot tubs, in-room safes, cable TV with DVDs, in-room data ports, 2 tennis courts, 6 swimming pools, fitness classes, health club, spa, massage, beach, dive shop, snorkeling, windsurfing, boating, fishing, billiards, racquetball, 9 bars, concerige, Internet, meeting rooms, business center; no kids* ☰ *AE, D, MC, V* ⍟◎⍟ *AI.*

$–$$ ⊞ **Casita del Mar.** Although the rooms at this hotel are average-sized and simply furnished, the entire property is immaculate, and the beach and swimming pool are truly stunning. Ask for one of the ocean-facing units, which are slightly more expensive, but perfect for watching the sunrise. ⊠ *Calle Heriberto Frias 6, 4 blocks north of town* ☎🖷 *998/ 871–0301* ⊕ *www.hotelcasitadelmar.com* 🗩 *19 rooms* ⭘ *Restaurant, cable TV, in-room safes, pool, beach, dive shop, snorkeling, fishing, laundry service, airport shuttle, car rental, free parking; no room phones* ☰ *AE, MC, V* ⍟◎⍟ *BP.*

$ ⊞ **Cabanas Le Lu'um Toh.** Located 15 mi from Puerto Morelos in the inland jungle, this small lodge, also called Land of the Motmot Jungle Resort, is a bird-watcher's paradise. Two private circular bungalows sit amid more than 500 acres of property, which are crisscrossed by jungle paths. Each bungalow is made from native limestone rock, and has its own fireplace, double bed, and sleeping loft. There's also a restaurant serving breakfast, lunch, and dinner; at night, it's magical to wander to the bar atop the restaurant and listen to jungle sounds while sipping a cold *cerveza.* ⊠ *Central Vallarta Rd., Km 13* ☎ *998/871–0683, 998/871–0013 reservations, 651/565–2566 in the U.S.* ⊕ *www.cancunjungleresort.com/* 🗩 *2 bungalows* ⭘ *Restaurant, refrigerators, hiking, bar; no a/c, no room TVs, no room phones* ☰ *No credit cards* ⍟◎⍟ *MAP, BP.*

$ ⊞ **Casa Caribe.** Just a few blocks from the town center, this small hotel is also only five minutes from the beach. Breezy rooms have king-size beds, coffeemakers, and large tile baths. Terraces have hammocks and views of the ocean or the mangroves. You have use of a large kitchen (where the Continental breakfast is served each day), huge terrace, and the lounge area, as well as grounds that include a walled courtyard and a fragrant tropical garden. ⊠ *Avs. Javier Rojo Gómez and Ejercito Mexicano, 3 blocks north of town* ☎ *998/871–0049, 450/227–5864 in Canada* ⊕ *www.uswebmasters.com/casa-caribe* 🗩 *6 rooms* ⭘ *Fans, kitchen, refrigerators, bar; no a/c, no room phones, no room TVs* ☰ *No credit cards* ⍟◎⍟ *CP.*

$ ⊞ **Hotel Ojo de Agua.** This peaceful, family-run beachfront hotel is a great bargain. Half the rooms have kitchenettes; all are decorated in cheerful colors and have ceiling fans. Third-floor units have their own private balconies, with views of the sea or the courtyard gardens. An open-air restaurant serves good regional Mexican and American dishes; the beach offers superb snorkeling directly out front, including the Ojo de Agua, an underwater cenote shaped like an eye. ⊠ *Av. Javier Rojo Gómez, Sm 2, Lote 16* ☎ *998/871–0027* 🖷 *998/871–0202* ⊕ *www. ojo-de-agua.com* 🗩 *36 rooms* ⭘ *Restaurant, cable TV, in-room safes, some kitchenettes, pool, beach, snorkeling, free parking* ☰ *AE, MC, V.*

¢ 🏠 **Posada Amor.** In the early '70s, the founder of this small, cozy down-town hotel dedicated it to the virtues of peace and love *(amor)*. Although he's since passed away, the philosophy of peacefulness has been upheld by his wife and children, who now run the property. Rooms are clean, small and simple; all but two have private baths. The on-site restaurant serves delicious meals, the specialty being fresh fish, and on Sundays the breakfast buffet is not to be missed. The helpful staff makes you feel right at home. ⊠ *Avs. Javier Rojo Gomez and Tulum* ☎ *998/871–0033* 🖷 *998/871–0033* ✎ *pos_amor@hotmail.com* ⬅ *18 rooms* ♨ *Restaurant, fans, bar; no a/c some rooms, no room phones, no room TVs* ▭ *MC, V.*

¢–$ 🏕 **Acamaya Reef Cabanas and RV Park.** Just north of Puerto Morelos, this RV park and campground sits right on the beach. There are seven cabanas here, four of which have private baths, and two of which have air-conditioning. There are also 10 RV sites, plenty of tent sites, and a small restaurant. A 10-minute walk along the beach brings you right into town. ⊠ *Carretera 307, Km 27 (Turn at Crocun Crocodile Farm and drive east; turn right where the road ends and Acamaya is one block up on the beach)* ☎ *998/871–0131* 🖷 *998/871–0032* ⊕ *www.acamayareef.com* ⬅ *50 tent sites, $9 per day; 10 RV sites with full-hookups, $25 per day* ♨ *Flush toilets, full hookups, dump station, showers, grills, picnic tables, electricity, public telephone, play area, swimming (ocean), general store, food service (restaurant)* ▭ *No credit cards.*

Sports & the Outdoors

Mystic Diving and Adventure Tours (☎998/871–0634 ⊕www.mysticdiving.com), in Puerto Morelos's main square, can set up snorkeling and diving trips. Prices start at $34 for one-tank dives and $50 for two-tank dives. **Brecko's** (⊠ Calle Heriberto Frias 6, Casita del Mar ☎ 998/871–0301) offers snorkeling and deep-sea fishing in a 25-foot boat. Snorkeling trips start at $22 and fishing trips at $250. **Diving Dog Tours** (☎ 998/820–1886) runs snorkeling trips at various sites on the Great Mesoamerican Reef (which stretches some 600 km [373 mi], all the way down to Belize) for $25 per person. If you want to fish beyond the reef, a four-hour trip (for up to four people) costs $250. And yes, the company really does have a diving dog! Bertram, the French owner of **Original Snorkeling Adventure** (☎ 998/887–2792 or 800/717–1322) has run snorkeling excursions in the area for 17 years. For $49, he'll pick you up, take you for a two-hour snorkel trip on the reef, and provide a box lunch; $75 gets you a buffet lunch with shrimp, fresh fish, and *pollo pibíl* (chicken baked Yucatecan-style, in banana leaves), and then a trip back to Bertram's beach for lounging in a hammock under a palapa.

Shopping

Alma Libre Libros (⊠Av. Tulum on main plaza ☎998/871–0713) has more than 20,000 titles in stock. You can trade in your own books for 25% of their cover prices here, and replenish your holiday reading list. It's open October–April, Tuesday–Saturday 10–3 and 6–9; and on Sunday 4–9.

★ The **Collectivo de Artesanos de Puerto Morelos** (Puerto Morelos Artists' Cooperative; ⊠ Avs. Javier Rojo Gómez and Isla Mujeres ☎ No phone) is a series of palapa-style buildings where local artisans sell their jewelry, hand-embroidered clothes, hammocks, and other items. You might find some real bargains here. It's open daily from 8 AM until dusk.

Rosario & Marco's Art Shoppe (⊠ Av. Javier Rojo Gómez 14 ☎ No phone), close to the ferry docks, is run by the eponymous couple from their living room. They paint regional scenes such as markets, colonial homes, and flora and fauna as well as portraits. Marco also creates replicas of Spanish galleons.

Punta Brava

❸ *7 km (4½ mi) south of Puerto Morelos on Carretera 307.*

Punta Brava is also known as South Beach in Puerto Morelos. It's a long, winding beach strewn with seashells. On windy days, its shallow waters are whipped up into waves large enough for bodysurfing.

Where to Stay

\$\$\$\$ 🏨 **El Dorado Royale.** This resort has been eclipsed lately by newer, more luxurious resorts, but the staff is friendly and the location—amid 500 acres of jungle and on a long, unspoiled beach—is great. Junior suites have Mexican furnishings, small sitting rooms, king-size beds, hot tubs, coffeemakers, and ocean-facing terraces. Casitas have domed roofs, king-size beds, DVD players, and oceanfront palapa terraces. Five restaurants serve à la carte menus filled with exceptional dishes. There's free shuttle service to Cancún and Playa del Carmen. ⊠ *Carretera 307, Km 45, Punta Brava* ☎ *998/872–8030 or 800/290–6679* 🖷 *998/872–8031* ⊕ *www.eldorado-resort.com* ⇆ *359 junior suites, 34 casitas* ♿ *5 restaurants, room service, some in-room hot tubs, 2 tennis courts, 8 pools, spa, beach, snorkeling, boating, bicycles, 6 bars, shop, laundry service, Internet, car rental, travel services; no kids* ⊟ *AE, DC, MC, V* ⏐O⏐ *AI.*

Punta Maroma

❹ *2 km (1 mi) south of Punta Brava.*

On a bay where the winds don't reach the waters, this gorgeous beach remains calm even on blustery days. To the north you can see the land curve out to another beach, Playa del Secreto; to the south the curve that leads eventually to Punta Bete is visible.

Where to Stay & Eat

\$\$\$\$
FodorsChoice
★

⏐×🏨 **Maroma.** At this elegant, extravagant hotel, peacocks wander jungle walkways and the scent of flowers fills the air. Rooms, which have small sitting areas, are filled with whimsical decorative items and original artwork. The king-size beds are draped in mosquito nets. A full breakfast is served on each room's private terrace; the restaurant excels at such dishes as lobster bisque and honeyed rack of lamb. A cutting-

> **WORD OF MOUTH**
>
> "What was really extraordinary at Maroma was the attention to detail—candlelit paths, flower-strewn ponds and aromatherapy candles lit in your room as part of the turn-down service . . . Oh, did I mention beachside massages?"
> –Shelley

edge "flotarium" (a tank of water where you float deprived of light or sound) was recently added to the already luxurious spa. Eight new deluxe suites were also added in 2005. ⊠ *Carretera 307, Km 51* ☎ *998/872–8200 or 866/454–9351* 🖶 *998/872–8221* ⊕ *www.orient-expresshotels.com* 🛏 *52 rooms, 14 suites, 1 villa* ♻ *2 restaurants, room service, Internet, cable TV, golf privileges, pool, gym, hot tub, spa, beach, marina, snorkeling, windsurfing, boating, fishing, horseback riding, bar, library, theater, laundry service, airport shuttle; no kids* 🖃 *AE, D, MC, V* ⎁ *BP.*

Punta Bete

❺ *13 km (8 mi) south of Punta Maroma on Carretera 307, then about 2 km (1 mi) off main road.*

The one concession to progress here has been a slight improvement in the road. If you take this bumpy 2-km (1-mi) ride through the jungle, you'll arrive at a 7-km-long (4½-mi-long) isolated beach dotted with bargain bungalow-style hotels and thatch-roofed restaurants. A few more-comfortable accommodations are also available if you want to avoid getting sand in your suitcases.

Where to Stay

$$$$ 🏨 **Ikal del Mar.** The name, which means "poetry of the sea" is apt: this

FodorsChoice   romantic jungle lodge on Punta Bete's beach epitomizes understated lux-

★   ury and sophistication. Guests have included European heads of state, who surely cherish the privacy and serenity. Villas are named after poets and have thatched ceilings with intricate woodwork, sumptuous Egyptian-cotton sheets, Swiss piqué robes, and tony Molton Brown soaps and shampoos. Beside the sea near temple ruins, the spa delicately fuses Maya healing lore and ancient techniques into its treatments. The restaurant serves excellent Mediterranean–Yucatecan cuisine and has an outstanding wine cellar. ⊠ *Playa Xcalacoco, 9 km (5½ mi) north of Playa del Carmen* ☎ *984/877–3000 or 888/230–7330* 🖶 *984/877–3009, 713/528–3697 in U.S.* ⊕ *www.ikaldelmar.com* 🛏 *29 villas, 1 suite* ♻ *Restaurant, cable TV and DVD, in-room data ports, pool, fitness classes, gym, spa, massage, beach, dive shop, bar, shop, laundry service, concierge, car rental, travel services, free parking; no kids under 16* 🖃 *AE, D, MC, V.*

$$$ 🏨 **Posada del Capitán Lafitte.** This warm, family-friendly resort is named after a pirate known to have frequented local waters. Guest quarters are in duplexes and three- or four-unit cabanas—if you like quiet, opt for a newer cabana on the beach's tranquil north end. All units have balconies and hammocks, and some are practically flush with the ocean for wonderful views. One of the first resorts on the Riviera Maya, this hotel has aged gracefully; just try to disregard the tacky cement fortresslike structure that marks the highway turnoff. ⊠ *Carretera 307, Km 62* ✑ *reservations: Turquoise Reef Group, Box 2664, Evergreen, CO 80439* ☎ *303/674–9615 or 800/538–6802* 🖶 *984/873–0212* 🖶 *303/674–8735 in U.S.* ⊕ *www.mexicoholiday.com* 🛏 *62 rooms* ♻ *Restaurant, fans, minibars, pool, beach, dive shop, snorkeling, boating, fishing, horseback riding, bar, Internet, car rental; no TV in some rooms* 🖃 *AE, MC, V* ⎁ *MAP.*

¢–$ 🏠 **Cocos Cabañas.** Tranquillity and seclusion are the name of the game in these cozy palapa bungalows, just 30 yards from the beach. Although small, the bungalows are colorful and bright; each has a bath, a netting-draped queen- or king-size bed, hammocks, and a terrace that leads to a garden. Breakfast, lunch, and dinner are served at the Grill Bar, whose menu includes fresh fish dishes and Mexican and international fare. ⊠ *Playa Xcalacoco, follow signs and take dirt road off Carretera 307, Km 42, for about 3 km (2 mi)* ☎ *998/874–7056* 🖷 *998/887–9964* ⇆ *5 bungalows, 1 room* ⚴ *Restaurant, fans, pool, beach, snorkeling, fishing; no a/c in some rooms, no room phones, no room TVs* ▭ *No credit cards.*

Playa del Carmen

❻ *10 km (6 mi) south of Punta Bete, 68 km (42 mi) south of Cancún.*

Once upon a time, Playa del Carmen was a fishing village with a ravishing deserted beach. The villagers fished and raised coconut palms to produce copra, and the only foreigners who ventured here were beach bums.

That was a long time ago, however. These days, although the beach is still delightful—alabaster-white sand, turquoise-blue waters—it's far from deserted. In fact, Playa has become one of Latin America's fastest-growing communities, with a population of more than 135,000 and a pace almost as hectic as Cancún's. Hotels, restaurants, and shops multiply here faster than you can say "Kukulcán." Some are branches of Cancún establishments whose owners have taken up permanent residence in Playa, or commute daily between the two places; others are owned by American and European expats who came here years ago, as early adopters. It makes for a varied, international community.

Avenida 5, the first street in town parallel to the beach, is a colorfully tiled pedestrian walkway with shops, cafés, and street performers; small hotels and stores stretch north from this avenue. Avenida Juárez, running east–west from the highway to the beach, is the main commercial zone for the Riviera Maya corridor. Here, locals visit the food shops, pharmacies, auto-parts and hardware stores, and banks that line the curbs. People traveling the coast by car usually stop here to stock up on supplies—its banks, grocery stores, and gas stations are the last ones until Tulum.

The ferry pier, where the hourly boats arrive from and depart for Cozumel, is another busy part of town. The streets leading from the dock have shops, restaurants, cafés, a hotel, a basketball court, and food stands. If you take a stroll north from the pier along the beach, you'll find the serious sun worshippers. On the pier's south side is the edge of the sprawling Playacar complex. The development is a labyrinth of residences and all-inclusive resorts bordered by an 18-hole championship golf course. The excellent 32-acre **Xaman Ha Aviary** (⊠ Paseo Xaman-Ha, Playacar ☎ 984/873–0318), in the middle of the Playacar development, is home to more than 30 species of native birds. It's open daily 9–5, and admission is $8.

Where to Eat

$$–$$$$ ✕ **Alux Restaurant and Lounge.** The locale of this restaurant—it's in an ac-
Fodor'sChoice   tual underground cavern—is the real showstopper here. A rock stairway
★   lit by candles leads you down into a setting that's part Carlsbad Caverns,
part Fred Flintstone. Some of the "cavernous" rooms are for lounging,
some for drinking, some for eating, some for dancing; creative lighting
casts the stalactites and stalagmites in pale shades of violet, blue, and pink.
Although the food is mediocre compared to the atmosphere, you should-
n't miss this place. It's truly one of a kind. ⊠ *Av. Juarez, 3 blocks west
of Highway 307, Colonia Ejidal (on the south side of the street)* ☎ *984/
803–0713* ⊕ *www.alux-restaurantlounge.com* ⊟ *MC, V* ☾ *No lunch.*

$$$ ✕ **Espada's Brazilian Steakhouse.** Brazilian food in Mexico? If you're a car-
nivore, this expansive, candlelit eatery is for you. A dozen types of meat—
from prime rib to pork ribs to smoked turkey—are slow-cooked on
rotation skewers over charcoal here. Waiters come to your table with slabs
of meat. You point and pick, they carve. A full salad bar comes with the
meal. The waiters are personable and chatty. Espalda's adjoins another
restaurant where live music is played nightly. It's a pleasant combination
of food and fun. ⊠ *Av. 5 at Calle 14* ☎ *984/803–1006* ⊟ *AE, MC, V.*

★ **$$–$$$** ✕ **Blue Lobster.** You can chose your dinner live from a tank here, and if
it's grilled, you pay by the weight—a small lobster costs $15, while a
monster will set you back $50. At night, the candlelit dining room
draws a good crowd. People come not only for the lobster but also for
the ceviche, mussels, jumbo shrimp, or imported T-bone steak. Ask for
a table on the terrace overlooking the street. ⊠ *Calle 12 and Av. 5* ☎ *984/
873–1360* ⊟ *AE, MC, V.*

$–$$$ ✕ **Media Luna.** You can dine alfresco on the second-floor balcony at this
stylish restaurant, or people-watch from the street-level dining room.
A steady crowd flocks here for the vegetarian, fish, and chicken dishes,
including curried root-vegetable puree with cilantro cream, and black
pepper-crusted fish with sesame rice and mango salsa. ⊠ *Av. 5 between
Calles 12 and 14* ☎ *984/873–0526* ⊟ *No credit cards.*

$–$$$ ✕ **Palapa Hemingway.** A mural of Che Guevara sporting a knife and fork
looms larger than life in this palapa seafood restaurant focused on Cuba
and its revolution. The grilled shrimp, fish, and steaks are good choices,
as are the fresh salads, pastas, and chicken dishes. ⊠ *Av. 5 between Calles
12 and 14* ☎ *984/873–0004* ⊕ *www.palapahemingway.com* ⊟ *MC, V.*

$–$$$ ✕ **La Parrilla.** Reliably tasty Mexican fare is the draw at this boisterous,
touristy restaurant. The smell of sizzling *parrilla mixta* (a grilled, mar-
inated mixture of lobster, shrimp, chicken, and steak) can make it dif-
ficult to resist grabbing one of the few available tables. Also tempting
are the strong margaritas, the friendly service, and the live music. ⊠ *Av.
5 and Calle 8* ☎ *984/873–0687* ⊟ *AE, D, MC, V.*

$–$$$ ✕ **Sur.** This two-story enclave of food from the Pampas region of Ar-
gentina is a trendy spot. Sky-blue tablecloths and plants complement
hardwood floors in the intimate upstairs dining room. Entrées come with
four sauces, dominant among them *chimichurri,* made with oil, vine-

gar, and finely chopped herbs. You can start off with meat or spinach empanadas or Argentine sausage, followed by a sizzling half-pound *churrasco* (top sirloin steak), and finish your meal with warm caramel crepes. ⊠ *Av. 5 between Calles 12 and 14* ☎ *984/803–2995* ▤ *D, MC, V* ☾ *No lunch; closed Sun.*

★ $–$$$ ✕ **Yaxche.** One of Playa's best restaurants has reproductions of stelae (stone slabs with carved inscriptions) from famous ruins, and murals of Maya gods and kings. Maya dishes such as *halach winic* (chicken in a spicy four-pepper sauce) are superb, and you can finish your meal with a Café Maya (made from Kahlúa, brandy, vanilla, and Xtabentun, the local liqueur flavored with anise and honey). Watching the waiter light it and pour it from its silver demitasse is almost as seductive as the drink itself. ⊠ *Calle 8 and Av. 5* ☎ *984/ 873–2502* ⊕ *www.mayacuisine.com* ▤ *MC, V.*

> **WORD OF MOUTH**
>
> "Yaxche is my favorite place in Playa. Be sure to sit in the court-yard where it is tranquil and magi-cal—and order the Chaya soup!"
> –Elizabeth

$–$$ ✕ **Casa Tucan.** This sidewalk restaurant may be small—it has only 10 tables—but its refined Italian, Swiss, and Greek dishes are top-notch. Everything on the menu is fresh; even the herbs are homegrown. The spanakopita and the grilled salmon with brandy sauce are especially good. ⊠ *Calle 4 between Avs. 10 and 15* ☎ *984/873–0283* ⊕ *www. traveleasymexico.com* ▤ *AE, MC, V.*

★ ¢–$ ✕ **Babe's Noodles & Bar.** Paintings of 1940s Hollywood bathing beau-ties decorate the walls of this Asian–Indonesian restaurant, which is known for its fresh and interesting fare. Everything is cooked to order, no prefab here. Try the spring rolls with veggies and peanut sauce, or the sesame noodles, made with chicken or pork, veggies, lime, green curry, and ginger. In the Buddha Garden, you can sip a *mojito* (a drink made from rum, lime, fresh mint, and sugar), or snuggle in at the bar and watch the crowds on nearby Fifth Avenue. ⊠ *Calle 10 between Avs. 5 and 10* ☎ *984/804–1998* ⊕ *www.babesnoodlesandbar.com* ▤ *No credit cards.*

¢–$ ✕ **Hot.** If this place were a still-life painting, it would be titled *Two Side-walk Tables and a Grill.* It opens at 6 AM and whips up great egg dishes (the chili-and-cheese omelet is particularly good), baked goods, and hot coffee. Salads and sandwiches are lunch options. ⊠ *Calle 10 between Avs. 5 and 10* ☎ *984/876–4370* ▤ *No credit cards* ☾ *No dinner.*

¢–$ ✕ **Java Joe's.** This is one of Playa's favorite coffee spots, where you can buy your joe by the cup or by the kilo. You can also indulge in Joe's "hangover special"—an English muffin, Canadian bacon, and a fried egg—if you've had a Playa kind of night. There are also 16 types of bagels to choose from, along with other pastries and baked goodies. A dinner menu has recently been added. ⊠ *Calle 10 between Av. 5 and 10* ☎ *984/ 876–2694* ⊕ *www.javajoes.net* ▤ *No credit cards.*

144 <

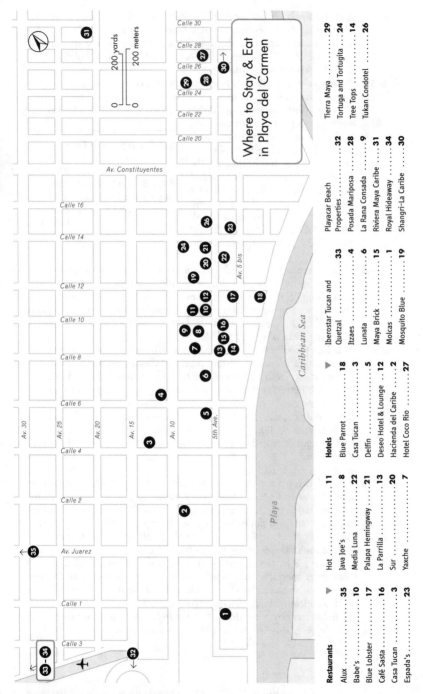

Where to Stay & Eat
in Playa del Carmen

Calle 30
Calle 28
Calle 26
Calle 24
Calle 22
Calle 20

Av. Constituyentes

Calle 16
Calle 14
Calle 12
Calle 10
Calle 8
Calle 6
Calle 4
Calle 2

Av. Juarez

Calle 1
Calle 3

Av. 30
Av. 25
Av. 20
Av. 15
Av. 10
5th Ave.
Av. 5 bis

Caribbean Sea
Playa

200 yards
200 meters

Restaurants
Alux **35**
Babe's **10**
Blue Lobster **17**
Café Sasta **16**
Casa Tucan **3**
Espada's **23**
Hot **11**
Java Joe's **8**
Media Luna **22**
Palapa Hemingway ... **21**
La Parrilla **13**
Sur **20**
Yaxche **7**

Hotels
Blue Parrot **18**
Casa Tucan **3**
Delfin **5**
Deseo Hotel & Lounge . **12**
Hacienda del Caribe ... **2**
Hotel Coco Rio **27**
Iberostar Tucan and
Quetzal **33**
Itzaes **4**
Lunata **6**
Maya Brick **15**
Molcas **1**
Mosquito Blue **19**
Playacar Beach
Properties **32**
Posada Mariposa **28**
La Rana Consada **9**
Riviera Maya Caribe ... **31**
Royal Hideaway **34**
Shangri-La Caribe **30**
Tierra Maya **29**
Tortuga and Tortugita . **24**
Tree Tops **14**
Tukan Condotel **26**

¢ ✕ **Café Sasta.** This sweet little café serves fantastic coffee drinks (cappuccino, espresso, mocha blends), teas, light sandwiches, and baked goods. The staff is very pleasant—something that's becoming rare in Playa. ⊠ *Av. 5 between Calles 8 and 10* ☎*984/873–3030* ▭*No credit cards.*

WORD OF MOUTH

"Café Sasta has to have the best coffee and desserts on the Mayan coast. Que rico!"
                              –Eric

Where to Stay

IN TOWN
$$$ 🏨 **Mosquito Blue Hotel and Spa.** Simultaneously casual, exotic, and elegant, the interiors at this hotel have Indonesian decor, mahogany furniture, and soft lighting. Most rooms have king-size beds and great views. The courtyard open-air bar is a soothing spot—it's sheltered by a thatched roof and pastel walls, near one of the swimming pools. The restaurant serves Mexican and Italian cuisine, and the new spa offers services like Maya healing baths, massage therapy, and facials. ⊠ *Calle 12 between Avs. 5 and 10* ☎ *984/873–1335* 🖷 *984/873–1337* ⊕ *www.mosquitoblue.com* ↪ *45 rooms, 1 suite* ⚭ *Restaurant, cable TV, 2 pools, massage, spa, in-room safes, dive shop, bar, laundry service, car rental, travel services; no kids under 16* ▭ *AE, MC, V.*

$$$ 🏨 **Shangri-La Caribe.** Although this resort's location used to be considered the outskirts of Playa, it's now simply the northern end of downtown. Still, the property is relatively tranquil, with attractive whitewashed bungalows and plenty of European guests. Rooms have comfortable beds, tile floors, baths, and balconies or patios with hammocks that look out over the sea. The restaurants serve Mexican and international fare. ⊠ *Calle 38 between Av. 5 and Zona Playa* ⚏ *reservations: Turquoise Reef Group, Box 2664, Evergreen, CO 80439* ☎ *984/873–0611 or 800/538–6802* 🖷 *984/873–0500* ⊕ *www.shangrilacaribe.net* ↪ *92 rooms, 15 suites* ⚭ *3 restaurants, 2 pools, beach, dive shop, snorkeling, fishing, laundry service, fans, cable TV, airport shuttle, car rental; no a/c some rooms* ▭ *AE, MC, V* ⦿ *MAP.*

$$–$$$ 🏨 **Blue Parrot Hotel and Suites.** One of Playa's first hotels, this property underwent a complete remodeling in 2004. The spacious rooms now sport luxurious details like mahogany-and-glass sliding doors and Tommy Bahama decor. The hotel complex includes a restaurant and a bar, adjoined by a common room beneath a towering beachfront palapa, where amber-colored sconces sit atop *zapote* beams for a romantic effect. You can happily kick off your shoes here—the floor is made of sand. ⊠ *Calle 12 Norte, 10 blocks north of the ferry dock* ☎ *984/873–0083, 888/854–4498 in the U.S.* 🖷*984/873–0049* ⊕*www.blueparrot.com* ↪*52 rooms* ⚭*Restaurant, in-room safes, beach, bar, meeting room* ▭ *AE, MC, V.*

$$–$$$ 🏨 **Deseo Hotel & Lounge.** The Deseo is somewhere between cutting-edge and corny. A Maya-pyramid-style stairway cuts through the stark modern main building here; the steps lead to a minimalist, white-on-white, open-air lobby, with huge daybeds for sunning, a trendy bar, and the pool, which is lit with purple lights at night. Each of the austere guest rooms has a bed, a lamp, and clothesline hung with flip-flops, earplugs (the bar has its own DJ), bananas, and a beach bag. Suites are large and

have claw-foot tubs. ⊠ *Av. 5 and Calle 12* ☎ *984/879–3620* 🖷 *984/879–3621* ⊕ *www.hoteldeseo.com* ↩ *15 rooms, 3 suites* �609 *Room service, in-room safes, minibars, pool, bar, lounge, car rental, travel services; no phones in some rooms, no TV in some rooms, no kids, no pets* ▤ *AE, MC, V.*

★ **$$–$$$** ⊞ **Lunata.** An elegant entrance, Spanish-tile floors, and hand-tooled furniture from Guadalajara greet you at this classy inn. Guest rooms have sitting areas, dark hardwood furnishings, high-quality crafts, orthopedic mattresses, and terraces—some with hammocks. Service is personal and gracious. Breakfast is laid out in the garden each day. ⊠ *Av. 5 between Calles 6 and 8* ☎ *984/873–0884* 🖷 *984/873–1240* ⊕ *www.lunata.com* ↩ *10 rooms* �609 *Refrigerators, cable TV, laundry service, car rental* ▤ *AE, MC, V* ❙◯❙ *CP.*

$$ ⊞ **Itzaes.** Although this modern hotel in a colonial-style building has amenities geared toward business travelers, divers also like to stay here as it's two blocks from the beach. The lobby, which opens onto a marble, vine-draped atrium, is a bit hard to see from the street; as you enter, though, you'll notice several homey sitting areas and a tapas bar. The extra-spacious guest rooms have tile floors, two double beds each, desks, and hair dryers. The staff is warm and efficient. ⊠ *Av. 10 and Calle 6* ☎ *984/873–2397* 🖷 *984/873–2373* ⊕ *www.itzaes.com* ↩ *16 rooms* �609 *Minibars, refrigerators, cable TV, in-room data ports, pool, hot tub, concierge, car rental* ▤ *AE, MC, V* ❙◯❙ *CP.*

$$ ⊞ **Riviera Maya Caribe.** It may not have the bells and whistles of other Playa hotels, but this small property is very pleasant. It's in a quiet neighborhood and just two blocks from the beach. Rooms have tile floors, cedar furnishings, and spacious baths; suites also have hot tubs. Amenities include a coffee shop and a beach club. ⊠ *Av. 10 and Calle 30* ☎ *984/873–1193 or 800/822–3274* 🖷 *984/873–2311* ⊕ *www.hotelrivieramaya.com* ↩ *17 rooms, 5 suites* �609 *Coffee shop, room service, fans, in-room safes, minibars, cable TV, pool, massage, hot tubs, dive shop, bicycles, shop, laundry service, Internet, car rental, airport shuttle (fee)* ▤ *MC, V.*

$$ ⊞ **Tierra Maya.** The Spanish owners have transformed this small inn just three blocks from the beach into a little work of art, with burnt-orange and ocher color schemes, stucco Maya masks, batik wall hangings, and rustic wood-frame beds. All guest rooms have balconies overlooking the garden and pool area, which also has a thatch-roofed restaurant, a reading pavilion, and a *temazcal* (sweat lodge). A temazcal ceremony led by a shaman costs $70 and includes purification rituals, massage, and fruit juices. The apartment and the suite have kitchenettes. ⊠ *Calle 24 between Avs. 5 and 10* ☎🖷 *984/873–3958* ⊕ *www.hoteltierramaya.com* ↩ *21 rooms, 1 suite, 1 apartment* �609 *Restaurant, fans, in-room safes, some kitchenettes, refrigerators, cable TV, pool, massage, bar, concierge, Internet, free parking* ▤ *MC, V.*

$$ ⊞ **La Tortuga and Tortugita.** European couples often choose this inn on one of Playa's quiet side streets. Mosaic stone pathways wind through the

> **WORD OF MOUTH**
>
> "The beautiful grounds at La Tortuga and Tortugita were kept meticulously clean. After a busy day we felt like we were in a quiet oasis of green and blue."   –barb

gardens here, and colonial-style hardwood furnishings gleam throughout. Rooms are small but have balconies and are well equipped; junior suites have hot tubs. The restaurant specializes in seafood. ☒ *Calle 14 and Av. 10* ☎*984/873–1484 or 800/822–3274* 🖷*984/873–0798* ⊕*www. hotellatortuga.com* ⋧*34 rooms, 11 junior suites* ⟃ *Restaurant, room service, fans, in-room safes, cable TV, pool, beach, hot tub, billiards, car rental, travel services; no kids under 15* ▤ *AE, MC, V.*

$$ ⊡ **Tukan Condotel Villas and Beach Club.** The immense jungle garden at the entrance to this hotel leads to a lobby and sitting area. The small, simple rooms and suites are well separated from one another and have private terraces, tiny kitchenettes, tile floors, and painted wood furniture. (Make sure you choose a newly painted room as mold settles in fast in the tropics.) The garden has a pool and a natural cenote for swimming. The included buffet breakfast is served at the Tucan Maya restaurant next door. ☒*Av. 5 between Calles 14 and 16* ☎*984/873–0417* 🖷*984/873–0668* ⊕ *www.eltukanconotel.com* ⋧*56 rooms, 39 suites* ⟃ *Kitchenettes, cable TV, pool, bar; no a/c in some rooms* ▤ *MC, V* ⎢⊘⎢ *BP.*

$–$$ ⊡ **Hacienda del Caribe.** This hotel evokes an old Yucatecan hacienda— albeit a colorful one—with wrought-iron balconies, stained-glass windows, and Talavera tile work. Guest rooms have such unique details as headboards with calla lily motifs and painted tile sinks. The pool is right off the lobby and adjoined by a small restaurant. The beach is a half block away. ☒ *Calle 2 between Avs. 5 and 10* ☎ *984/873–3130* 🖷*984/ 873–1149* ⊕ *www.haciendadelcaribe.com* ⋧*29 rooms, 5 suites* ⟃ *Restaurant, fans, in-room safes, cable TV, pool, car rental, travel services, free parking* ▤ *AE, D, MC, V.*

★ $–$$ ⊡ **Hotel Coco Rio.** A tropical garden beckons near the entry to this small hotel, located on a tree-lined street in Playa's north end. Spacious, sunny rooms with king- or queen-size beds are painted in soft pastels.; the generously large bathrooms sport bidets and arty mosaic tile work. It's the details, along with a super price, that make this hotel a real deal. If you want to splurge a bit, get a junior suite on the third floor, and look out over the Caribbean from your own private balcony. ☒ *Calle 26 between Avs. 5 and 10* ☎ *984/879–3361* 🖷 *984/879–3362* ⊕*www.hotelcocorio.com* ⋧*7 rooms, 8 suites* ⟃ *In-room safes, refrigerators, cable TV* ▤ *MC, V.*

$–$$ ⊡ **La Rana Consada.** Close to the downtown action yet far enough away to feel peaceful, this little hotel has all the creature comforts: a full kitchen that you can share with other guests, a lending library and reading room, and a bar right on the premises. Guests gather nightly under the large palapa, where the reception desk and sitting area are. The rooms, though small, have high ceilings, and are immaculately clean and newly painted. If partying isn't your thing, ask for an upstairs room or the suite, which are away from the bar. ☒ *Calle 10 between Avs. 5 and 10* ☎ *984/873– 0389* 🖷 *984/803–0586* ⊕ *www.laranacansada.com* ⋧*4 rooms, 1 suite* ⟃ *Kitchen, bar, library; no TV in some rooms, no room phones* ▤ *No credit cards.*

$ ⊡ **Delfín.** One of the area's longer-lived hotels, the Delfín evokes the laid-back charm of old Playa. It's covered with ivy and looks fresh and smart. Sea breezes cool the bright rooms, where mosaics lend touches of color. Some rooms also have wonderful ocean views. Restaurants and shops are close by. The management is exceptionally helpful. ⊠ *Av. 5 and Calle 6* ☎ *984/873–0176* ⊕ *www.hoteldelfin.com* ⇦ *14 rooms* ♧ *In-room safes, refrigerators, travel services; no room phones* ☰ *MC, V.*

$ ⊡ **Molcas.** Steps from the ferry docks, this colonial-style hotel has been in business since the early 1980s and has aged gracefully. Rooms have dark-wood furniture and face the pool, the sea, or the street. The second-floor pool area is glamorous, with white umbrellas. Although it's in the heart of town, the hotel is well insulated from noise, and the price is right. ⊠ *Av. 5 and Calle 1 Sur* ☎ *984/873–0070* ☎ *984/873–0135* ⊕ *www.molcas.com* ⇦ *25 rooms* ♧ *Refrigerators, pool, beach, bar* ☰ *AE, MC, V.*

$ ⊡ **Posada Mariposa.** Not only is this Italian-style property in the quiet north end of town impeccable and comfortable, but it's also a great value. Rooms center on a garden with a small fountain; all have ocean views, queen-size beds, wall murals, luxurious bathrooms, and shared patios. Suites have full kitchens. Sunset from the rooftop is spectacular, and the beach is five minutes away. ⊠ *Av. 5 No. 314, between Calles 24 and 26* ☎ *984/873–3886* ⊕ *www.posada-mariposa.com* ⇦ *18 rooms, 6 suites* ♧ *Cable TV; no room phones* ☰ *No credit cards.*

¢–$ ⊡ **Tree Tops.** Although the rooms are tiny and a bit cramped, this hotel has location, location, location going for it. It's tucked into a jungle setting, complete with cenote, right in the heart of Playa's shopping and dining area; the beach is nearby, too. Rooms have double beds and spacious tubs. Small terraces have hammocks. There are also simple, less-expensive palapa rooms without air-conditioning, TV, or phones. ⊠ *Calle 8 between Av. 5 and the beach* ☎ *984/873–1495* ☎ *984/873–0351* ⊕ *www.treetopshotel.com* ⇦ *15 rooms, 2 suites, 1 bungalow* ♧ *Some refrigerators, some cable TV, pool; no a/c in some rooms, no phones in some rooms, no TV in some rooms* ☰ *MC, V.*

★ ¢ ⊡ **Casa Tucan.** For the price, it's hard to beat this warm, eclectic, German-managed hotel a few blocks from the beach. Mexican fabrics decorate the cheerful rooms and apartments, and the property has a yoga palapa, a TV bar, a language school, a book exchange, and a specially designed 4.8-meter-deep pool that's used for instruction at the on-site dive center. Cabanas with a shared bathroom are also available for diving students. ⊠ *Calle 4 between Avs. 10 and 15* ☎ *984/873–0283* ⊕ *www.traveleasymexico.com* ⇦ *24 rooms, 4 apartments, 5 cabanas* ♧ *Restaurant, pool, dive shop, bar, recreation room, shops; no a/c in some rooms, no room phones, no room TVs* ☰ *MC, V.*

¢ ⊡ **Maya Brick & Tank-Ha Dive Center.** Though it's in the middle of Avenida 5, this hotel is surprisingly quiet. Rooms are small, with double beds and private baths, and open onto the garden and small pool. Since it adjoins a dive school, it's a natural favorite for scuba divers. Your room rate includes a free diving lesson in the pool. ⊠ *Av. 5 between Calles 8 and 10* ☎ *984/873–0011* ☎ *984/873–2041* ⊕ *www.mayabric.com* ⇦ *29 rooms* ♧ *Restaurant, fans, pool, airport shuttle; no a/c in some rooms, no room phones, no room TVs* ☰ *MC, V.*

PLAYACAR ⊡ **Iberostar Tucan and Quetzal.** This unique all-inclusive resort has preserved
$$$$ its natural surroundings—among the resident animals are flamingos, ducks, hens, turtles, toucans, and monkeys. Landscaped pool areas and

fountains surround the open-air restaurant and reception area. Spacious rooms have cheerful Caribbean color schemes and patios overlooking dense vegetation. The five restaurants serve decent Mexican and international fare. ⊠ *Fracc. Playacar, Playacar* ☎ *984/873–0200 or 888/923–2722* 🖷 *984/873–0424* ⊕ *www.iberostar.com* ⤴ *700 rooms* ♻ *5 restaurants, room service, fans, in-room safes, minibars, cable TV, 2 tennis courts, 4 pools, health club, spa, beach, dive shop, snorkeling, windsurfing, boating, basketball, 2 bars, lounge, library, nightclub, recreation room, shops, babysitting, children's programs (ages 4–12), laundry service, concierge, Internet, meeting rooms, free parking* ⊟ *AE, D, MC, V* ⊺⊙⊺ *AI.*

★ $$$$ **Royal Hideaway.** On a breathtaking stretch of beach, this 13-acre resort has exceptional amenities and superior service. Art and artifacts from around the world fill the lobby, and streams, waterfalls, and fountains dot the grounds. Rooms are in two- and three-story colonial-style villas, each with its own concierge, who will make reservations for you at the five on-site restaurants. Gorgeous rooms have two queen-size beds, sitting areas, and ocean-view terraces. The resort is wheelchair accessible. ⊠ *Fracc. Playacar, Lote 6, Playacar* ☎ *984/873–4500 or 800/858–2258* 🖷 *984/873–4506* ⊕ *www.allegroresorts.com* ⤴ *192 rooms, 8 suites* ♻ *5 restaurants, cable TV, in-room data ports, 2 tennis courts, 2 pools, exercise equipment, hot tub, spa, beach, snorkeling, windsurfing, bicycles, 3 bars, library, recreation room, theater, shops, laundry service, concierge, Internet, meeting rooms, travel services, free parking; no kids* ⊟ *AE, MC, V* ⊺⊙⊺ *AI.*

$$$ **Playacar Beach Properties.** You can rent a furnished condo or house on the beach at this upscale resort area. Units have from one to four bedrooms as well as air-conditioning and maid service; they start at $168 a night (for a one-bedroom). There's a five-night minimum stay during high season, and reservations must be made at least six months in advance. The rest of the year, the minimum stay is only three nights. A 50% deposit is required. ⊠ *Av. 10 Sur at entrance to Playacar* ☎ *984/873–0418* 🖷 *984/873–0539* ⊕ *www.playacarbeachproperties.com* ♻ *Kitchens, some swimming pools, concierge* ⊟ *No credit cards.*

Nightlife

★ **Alux** (⊠ Av. Juárez, Mz. 12, Lote 13A, Colonial Eijidal ☎ 984/803–0713) has a bar, disco, and restaurant and is built into a cavern. Live DJs spin discs—everything from smooth jazz to electronica—until 4 AM. **Apasionado** (⊠ Av. 5 ☎ 984/803–1100) has live jazz Thursday through Saturday nights. **Bar Ranita** (⊠ Calle 10 between Avs. 5 and 10 ☎ 984/873–0389), a cozy alcove, is a favorite with local business owners; it's run by a Swedish couple that really knows how to party. At the **Blue Parrot** (⊠ Calle 12 and Av. 1 ☎ 984/873–0083) there's live music every night until midnight; the bar is on the beach and sometimes stays open until 3 AM.

Capitán Tutix (⊠ Calle 4 Norte, near Av. 5 ☎ 984/803–1595) is a beach bar designed to resemble a ship. Good drink prices and live raggae, salsa, and rock music keep things humming until dawn. **Coco Bongo** (⊠ Calle 6 between Avs. 5 and 10 ☎ 984/973–3189) plays the latest Cuban

★ sounds for dancing. DJs spin disco nightly at the **Deseo Lounge** (⊠ Av. 5 at Calle 12 ☎ 984/879–3620), a rooftop bar and local hot spot. At **Mambo**

Cafe (✉ Calle 6 between Avs. 5 and 10 ☎ 984/879–2304), a dance review begins at 9:30 every night, and the salsa music begins an hour later. A younger crowd of locals and tourists typically fills the dance floor.

Sports & the Outdoors

GOLF   Playa's golf course is an 18-hole, par-72 championship course designed by Robert Von Hagge. The greens fee is $180; there's also a special twilight fee of $120. Information is available from the **Casa Club de Golf** (☎ 984/873–0624 or 998/881–6088). The **Golf Club at Playacar** (✉ Paseo Xaman-Ha and Mz. 26, Playacar ☎ 998/881–6088) has an 18-hole course; the greens fee is $180 and the twilight fee $120.

HORSEBACK   Two-hour rides along beaches and jungle trails are run by **Rancho Loma**
RIDING   **Bonita** (☎ 984/887–5465). The $66 fee includes lunch, drinks, and the
☼   use of the property's swimming pool and grounds (which has a children's playground).

SCUBA DIVING   The PADI-affiliated **Abyss** (✉ Calle 12 ☎ 984/873–2164) offers training ($80 for an introductory course) in addition to dive trips ($36 for one tank, $58 for two tanks) and packages. The oldest shop in town, **Tank-Ha Dive Shop** (✉ Av. 5 between Calles 8 and 10 ☎☎ 984/873–5037 ⊕ www.tankha.com), has PADI-certified teachers and runs diving and snorkeling trips to the reefs and caverns. A one-tank dive costs $35; for a two-tank trip it's $55; and for a cenote two-tank trip it's $90. Dive
★   packages are also available. **Yucatek Divers** (✉ Av. 15 Norte between Calles 2 and 4 ☎ 984/873–1363 or 984/877–6026 ⊕ www.yucatek-divers.com), which is affiliated with PADI, specializes in cenote dives, dive packages, and dives for those with disabilities. Introductory courses start at $80 for a one-tank dive and go as high as $350 for a four-day beginner course in open water.

SKYDIVING   Thrill seekers can take the plunge high above Playa in a tandem sky dive (where you're hooked up to the instructor the whole time). **SkyDive** (✉ Plaza Marina 32 ☎ 984/873–0192 ⊕ www.skydive.com) even videotapes your trip so you have proof that you did it. Jumps take place every hour, and cost $200.

Shopping

Avenida 5 between Calles 4 and 10 is the best place to shop along the coast. Boutiques sell folk art and textiles from around Mexico, and clothing stores carry lots of sarongs and beachwear made from Indonesian batiks. A shopping area called Calle Corazon, between Calles 12 and 14, has a pedestrian street, art galleries, restaurants, and boutiques.

Ambar Mexicano (✉ Av. 5 between Calles 4 and 6 ☎☎ 984/873–2357) has amber jewelry crafted by a local designer who imports the amber
★   from Chiapas. The retro '70s-style fashions at **Blue Planet** (✉ Av. 5 between Calles 10 and 12 ☎ 984/803–1504) are great for a day at the
★   beach. **La Calaca** (✉ Av. 5 between Calles 12 and 14 ☎ 984/873–0174) has an eclectic collection of wooden masks, whimsically carved angels and devils, and other crafts. **Caracol** (✉ Av. 5 between Calles 6 and 8 ☎ 984/803–1504) carries a nice assortment of clothes from every state in Mexico. **Crunch** (✉ Av. 5 between Calles 6 and 8 ☎ 984/873–1240)

sells high-style evening wear, swimsuits, and sportswear for women. **Etenoha Amber Gallery** (⊠ Av. 5 between Calles 8 and 10 📠 984/879–3716), run by a Swiss-Italian couple, has rustic-looking amber jewelry from Chiapas. Some of the stones have insects inside them, a characteristic that's highly prized by collectors.

At **La Hierbabuena Artesania** (☎ 984/873–1741) owner and former Californian Melinda Burns offers a collection of fine Mexican clothing and crafts. **Maya Arts Gallery** (⊠ Av. 5 between Calles 6 and 8 ☎ 984/879–3389) has an extensive collection of hand-carved Maya masks and *huipiles* (the traditional, white, embroidered cotton dresses worn by Maya women) from Mexico and Guatemala.

★ **Mundo Libreria–Bookstore** (⊠ 1 Sur No. 189 between Avs. 20 and 25 ☎ 984/879–3004 ⊕ www.pequemundo.com.mx) has an extensive selection of books on Maya culture, along with used English-language books. Profits from all English-language books here are donated to Mexico schools to buy texts. The **Opals Mine** (⊠ Av. 5 between Calles 4 and 6 ☎984/879–5041 ⊠ Av. 5 and Calle 12 ☎984/803–3658) has fire, white, pink, and orange opals from the Jalisco State as well as turquoise. You can buy loose stones or commission pieces of custom jewelry. **Santa Prisca** (⊠ Av. 5 between Calles 2 and 4 ☎ 984/873–0960) has silver jewelry, flatware, trays, and decorative items from the town of Taxco. Some pieces are set with semiprecious stones. **Xbal** (⊠ Av. 5 and Calle 14 ☎ 984/803–3352) is filled with attractive men's and women's cotton shirts, skirts, blouses, and shorts.

Xcaret

★ 🗻 🕓 ❼ *11 km (6½ mi) south of Playa del Carmen.*

Once a sacred Maya city and port, Xcaret (pronounced *ish*-car-et) is now a 250-acre ecological theme park on a gorgeous stretch of coastline. It's the coast's most heavily advertised attraction, billed as "nature's sacred paradise," with its own network of buses, its own published magazines, and a whole collection of stores.

A Mexican version of Epcot Center, the park has done a fabulous job to showcase, celebrate, and help preserve the natural environment of the Caribbean coast. ■ TIP→ → You can easily spend at least a full day here; there's tons to see and do. Among the most popular attractions are the Paradise River raft tour, that takes you on a winding, watery journey through the jungle; The Butterfly Pavillion, where thousands of butterflies float dreamily through a botanical garden while New Age music plays in the background; and an ocean-fed aquarium where you can see local sea life drifting through coral heads and sea fans without getting wet.

There are also a Wild Bird Breeding Aviary; nurseries for both abandoned flamingo eggs and sea turtles; and a series of underwater caverns that you can explore by snorkeling or "snuba" (a hybrid of snorkeling and scuba). Riding stables, which have been built to resemble a Mexican hacienda, offer trail rides through the jungle to see Maya ruins. A replica Maya village includes a colorful cemetery with catacomb-like caverns underneath; traditional music and dance ceremonies (including performances by the famed *Voladores de Papantla*—the Flying Birdmen of Papantla) are performed here at night.

The list of Xcaret's attractions goes on and on: you can visit a dolphinarium, a bee farm, a manatee lagoon, a bat cave, an orchid and bromeliad greenhouse, an edible mushroom farm, a small zoo. You can also visit a scenic tower that takes you 240 feet up in the air for a spectacular view of the park.

■ TIP→→ Although Xcaret has nine restaurants, many visitors bring their own lunches and take advantage of assorted picnic tables and palapa-shaded chairs scattered throughout the property. The entrance fee covers only access to the grounds and the exhibits; all other activities and equipment—from horseback riding to lockers to snorkel and swim gear—are extra. You can buy tickets from any travel agency or major hotel along the coast. ☎ 998/881–2451 in Cancún ⊕ www.xcaret.net ⊠ $49 (including show) ⊙ Daily 8:30 AM–9 PM.

Paamul

❽ *10 km (6 mi) south of Xcaret.*

Beachcombers and snorkelers are fond of Paamul (pronounced paul-*mool*), a crescent-shape lagoon with clear, placid waters sheltered by a coral reef. Shells, sand dollars, and even glass beads—some from the sunken, 18th-century pirate ship *Mantanceros,* which lies off nearby Akumal—wash onto the sandy parts of the beach. In June and July you can see one of Paamul's chief attractions: sea-turtle hatchlings.

Where to Stay

$$ ⊞ **Cabañas Paamul.** This rustic, secluded hostelry sits on a perfect white-sand beach. Ten bungalows have two double beds each, ceiling fans, and hammocks; farther along the beach are ten even more private cabanas. Much of the property has recently been renovated, and a new swimming pool has been added. The property includes 220 RV sites (gas and water hookups are $25 a day), as well as tent sites ($10 a day) with hot showers. A full-service dive shop with PADI and NAUI certification courses is also on-site. ⊠ *Carretera 307, Km 85* ☎ *984/875–1051* ⊟ *984/875–1053* ⊕ *www.paamulcabanas.com* ⤴ *20 cabanas, 220 RV sites; 30 campsites* ⟁ *Restaurant, fans, pool, beach, dive shop, bar, laundry service; no room phones, no room TVs* ⊟ *No credit cards.*

Puerto Aventuras

❾ *5 km (3 mi) south of Paamul.*

While the rest of the coast has been caught up in development fever, Puerto Aventuras has been quietly doing its own thing. It's become a popular vacation spot, particularly for families—although it's certainly not the place to experience authentic Yucatecan culture. The 900-acre self-contained resort is built around a 95-ship marina. It has a beach club, an 18-hole golf course, restaurants, shops, a great dive center, tennis courts, doctors, and a school. The **Museo CEDAM** displays coins, sewing needles, nautical devices, clay dishes, and other artifacts from 18th-century sunken ships. All recoveries were by members of the Mexican Underwater Expeditions Club (CEDAM), founded in 1959 by Pablo Bush Romero. ⊠ *North end of the marina* 🕾 *984/873–5000* 🎫 *Donation* ☉ *Daily 10–1 and 3:30–5:30.*

Where to Stay & Eat

$–$$$ ✕ **Café Olé International.** The laid-back hub of Puerto Aventuras is a terrace café with a varied menu. Chicken chimichurri and coconut shrimp are good lunch or dinner choices; steaks are also popular, and the baked goods are all freshly made. If you're lucky, the nightly specials might include locally caught fish in garlic sauce. In high season, musicians from around the world play until the wee hours on Sunday. ⊠ *Across from Omni Puerto Aventuras hotel* 🕾 *984/873–5125* 🗖 *MC, V.*

$$$$ 🏨 **Omni Puerto Aventuras.** Simultaneously low-key and elegant, this resort is a great place for some serious pampering. Each room has a king-size bed, a sitting area, an ocean-view balcony or terrace, and a hot tub. The beach is steps away, and the pool seems to flow right into the sea. A golf course and the marina are within walking distance. Breakfast and a newspaper arrive at your room every morning by way of a cubbyhole to avoid disturbing your slumber. Ask about the all-inclusive plan. ⊠ *Carretera 307, Km 269.5 (on beach near marina)* 🕾 *984/873–5101 or 800/843–6664* 🗖 *984/873–5102* ⊕ *www.omnihotels.com* 🛏 *30 rooms* ♺ *Restaurant, room service, cable TV, pool, gym, massage, beach, dive shop, 2 bars, shop, babysitting, laundry service, meeting room, free parking* 🗖 *AE, MC, V* ⊠️ *AI, CP.*

$$$ 🏨 **Casa del Agua.** This small, discreet, romantic hotel, lovingly designed
Fodor'sChoice by Mexican architect Manuel Oreanámos, has one of the coast's most
★ sumptuous beaches. Each of the four large suites is strikingly different from the next. The Arroyo suite has a stream of water running above a round king-size bed; the Caleta has a double shower in a secluded garden; the Cenote promotes relaxation with its meditation room and to-die-for ocean view; and the Cascada commands a stunning vista of Puerto Aventuras from its L-shape balcony. ⊠ *East of marina* 🕾 *984/873–5184* ⊕ *www.casadelagua.com* 🛏 *4*

> **WORD OF MOUTH**
>
> "[Casa del Agua has] wonderful views. Great huge showers. Terrific breakfast and massages. Charming marina village with restaurants, and yachts. Lots to do or nothin' to do. Your choice." –jim

suites ♺ *Room service, fans, minibars, massage, spa, beach, laundry service, Internet, airport shuttle; no room TVs, no kids* 🗖 *MC, V* ⊠️ *BP.*

Sports & the Outdoors

Aquanuts (⊠ *Center Complex, by marina* 🕾 *984/873–5041*) is a full-service dive shop that specializes in open-water dives, multi-tank dives, and certification courses. Dives start at $37 and courses at $385.

en route The Maya-owned and -operated eco-park of **Cenotes Kantún Chi** has cenotes and underground caverns that are great for snorkeling and diving, as well as some small Maya ruins and a botanical garden.

The place is not at all slick, so it's a nice break from the rather commercial feel of Puerto Aventuras. ⊠ *Carretera 307, 3 km (2 mi) south of Puerto Aventuras* ☏☏ *984/873–0021* 🎫 *$5* ⊙ *Daily 8:30–5.*

Xpu-há

❿ *3 km (2 mi) south of Puerto Aventuras.*

Xpu-há used to be a tranquil little beach community, but in recent years two megaresorts have taken over the area. (One of these hijacked a popular cenote that happened to lie on its property, and is no longer open to the public.) Despite the high-end developments, however, there are still a few enclaves here that offer funky, low-budget accommodations.

Where to Stay

$$$ 🏨 **Copacabana.** This lavish all-inclusive resort was designed around the surrounding jungle, cenotes, and beach. The lobby has bamboo furniture and a central waterfall underneath a giant palapa roof. Rooms have beautiful wood furniture, king-size beds, and private terraces with jungle views. Three large pools, separated from the outdoor hot tubs by an island of palm trees, look out onto the spectacular beach. The food is exceptional and served à la carte in two of the restaurants. ⊠ *Carretera 307, Km 264.5* ☏ *984/875–1800 or 866/321–6880* 🖷 *984/875–1818* ⊕ *www.hotelcopacabana.com* ⇝ *228 rooms* ⌂ *4 restaurants, room service, fans, in-room safes, cable TV, 3 pools, gym, hot tubs, massage, beach, snorkeling, windsurfing, boating, volleyball, 4 bars, dance club, shops, children's programs (ages 4–12), laundry service, meeting rooms, travel services* ⊟ *AE, D, MC, V* ⦿ *AI.*

$ 🏨 **Hotel Villas del Caribe.** Manager Leon Shlecter makes sure you're well looked after at this relaxed property—a throwback to simpler days. Rooms are basic, with double beds, simple furniture, and hot water. There's good, inexpensive food (especially the fish) at Café del Mar on the beach morning, noon, and night. Yoga classes are offered beneath a palapa. ⊠ *Carretera 307, Xpu-há X-4 (look for sun sign)* ☏ *984/876–9945 or 984/873–2194* ⊕ *www.xpuhahotel.com* ⇝ *16 rooms, 4 cabanas* ⌂ *Restaurant, massage, beach, bar; no a/c, no room phones, no room TVs* ⊟ *No credit cards.*

Akumal

⓫ *37 km (23 mi) south of Playa del Carmen.*

In Maya, Akumal (pronounced ah-koo-*maal*) means "place of the turtle," and for hundreds of years this beach has been a nesting ground for turtles (the season is June–August and the best place to see them is on Half Moon Bay). The place first attracted international attention in 1926, when explorers discovered the *Mantanceros,* a Spanish galleon that sank in 1741. In 1958, Pablo Bush Romero, a wealthy businessman who loved diving these pristine waters, created the first resort, which became the headquarters for the club he formed—the Mexican Underwater Expeditions Club (CEDAM). Akumal soon attracted wealthy underwater adventurers who flew in on private planes and searched for sunken treasures.

These days Akumal is probably the most Americanized community on the coast. It consists of three areas: Half Moon Bay, with its pretty beaches, terrific snorkeling, and large number of rentals; Akumal Proper, a large resort with a market, grocery stores, laundry facilities, a pharmacy; and Akumal Aventuras, to the south, with more condos and homes. The original Maya community has been moved to a planned town across the highway.

★ Devoted snorkelers may want to walk the unmarked dirt road to **Yalkú,** a couple of miles north of Akumal in Half Moon Bay. A series of small lagoons that gradually reach the ocean, Yalkú is an eco-park that's home to schools of parrot fish in superbly clear water with visibility to 160 feet. It has restrooms and an entrance fee of about $8.

Where to Stay & Eat

$–$$$ ╳ **Que Onda.** A Swiss-Italian couple created this northern Italian restaurant at the end of Half Moon Bay. Dishes are served under a palapa and include great homemade pastas, shrimp flambéed in cognac with a touch of saffron, and vegetarian lasagna. Que Onda also has a neighboring six-room hotel that's creatively furnished with Mexican and Guatemalan handicrafts. ⊠ *Caleta Yalkú, Lotes 97–99; enter through Club Akumal Caribe, turn left, and go north to very end of road at Half Moon Bay* ☎ *984/875–9101* ▤ *MC, V* ⊗ *Closed Tues.*

¢–$ ╳ **Turtle Bay Café & Bakery.** This funky café has delicious (and healthful) breakfasts, lunches, and dinners; the smoothies and fresh baked goods are especially yummy. It has a garden to sit and drink coffee in, and its location by the ecological center makes it the closest thing to a downtown Akumal has. ⊠ *Plaza Ukana I, Loc. 15 (beginning of Half Moon Bay road)* ☎ *No phone* ▤ *No credit cards.*

$$$ ▥ **Villas Akumal.** These white-stucco, thatch-roofed condos in a beachside residential development offer all the comforts of home and are perfect for extended stays (there are special rates if you book for a week). Units vary in size and configuration but most have cool tile floors, fabrics in tropical colors and prints, wicker furniture, and well-equipped kitchens. Many also have terraces with dynamite sea views—especially beautiful on evenings when the moon is full. On summer nights you can

watch nesting sea turtles. ✉ *Carretera Cancún–Tulum, Km 104, Fracc. Akumal C, Playa Jade* ☎ *984/875–7050 Ext. 307* 🖷 *984/875–7050* ⊕ *www.lasvillasakumal.com* 🛏 *18 suites, 8 studios* ⌂ *Kitchen, cable TV, pool, beach, snorkeling, airport shuttle, car rental, travel services, free parking* ▤ *AE, MC, V.*

$$–$$$ 🏨 **Club Akumal Caribe & Villas Maya.** Pablo Bush Romero established this resort in the 1960s to house his diving buddies, and it still has pleasant accommodations and a congenial staff—not to mention some of the best rates along the Riviera Maya. Rooms have rattan furniture, large beds, tile work, and ocean views. The bungalows are surrounded by gardens and have lots of beautiful Mexican tile. Although they do not have an ocean view, they are often preferred by guests due to the surrounding gardens. The secluded one-, two-, and three-bedroom villas, called Villas Flamingo, are on Half Moon Bay and have kitchenettes as well as a separate beach and pools. Dive and meal-plan packages available. ✉ *Carretera 307, Km 104* ☎ *984/875–9012, 800/351–1622 in U.S. and Canada, 800/343–1440 in Canada* 🖷 *915/581–6709* ⊕ *www. hotelakumalcaribe.com* 🛏 *22 rooms, 40 bungalows, 4 villas, 1 condo* ⌂ *2 restaurants, grocery, ice-cream parlor, pizzeria, snack bar, fans, some kitchenettes, refrigerators, pool, beach, dive shop, bar, babysitting; no room phones, no TV in some rooms* ▤ *AE, MC, V.*

$$ 🏨 **Vista Del Mar.** Each small room in the main building here has an ocean view, a terrace, a king-size bed, and colorful Guatemalan-Mexican accents. Next door are more expensive condos with Spanish-colonial touches. The spacious one-, two-, and three-bedroom units have full kitchens, living and dining rooms, and oceanfront balconies. ✉ *Carretera 307, Km 104, at the south end of Half Moon Bay* ☎ *984/875–9060 or 877/425–8625* 🖷 *984/875–9058* ⊕ *www.akumalinfo.com* 🛏 *16 rooms, 14 condos* ⌂ *Restaurant, grocery, some kitchenettes, minibars, refrigerators, cable TV with movies, pool, beach, dive shop; no room phones* ▤ *MC, V.*

Sports & the Outdoors

★   The **Akumal Dive Center** (✉ About 10 minutes north of Club Akumal Caribe ☎ 984/875–9025 ⊕ www.akumal.center.com) is the area's oldest and most experienced dive operation, offering reef or cenote diving, fishing, and snorkeling. Dives cost from $36 (one tank) to $120 (four tanks); a two-hour fishing trip for up to four people runs $110. Take a sharp right at the Akumal arches, and you'll see the dive shop on the beach.

TSA Travel Agency and Bike Rental (✉ Carretera 307, Km 104, next to the Ecology Center ☎ 984/875–9030 or 984/875–9031 ⊕ tours@akumaltravel.com) rents bikes for a 3½ hour jungle biking adventure. The cost is $35 per person.

en route   **Aktun-Chen** is Maya for "the cave with cenote inside." These amazing underground caves, estimated to be about 5 million years old, are the area's largest. You walk through the underground passages, past stalactites and stalagmites, until you reach the cenote

Fodor'sChoice   with its various shades of deep green. You don't want to miss this ★   one. ✉ *Carretera 307, Km 107* ☎ *984/884–0444* ⊕ *www. aktunchen.com* 🎟 *$18 (including 1-hr tour)* ⊙ *Daily 8:30–4.*

Xcacel

⑫ *7 km (4½ mi) south of Akumal.*

Xcacel (pronounced *ish*-ka-shell) is one of the few remaining nesting grounds for the endangered Atlantic green and loggerhead turtles. For years it was a federally protected zone, until it was sold—illegally—in 1998 to a Spanish conglomerate. The group immediately tried to push through an elaborate development plan that would have destroyed the nesting grounds. This prompted Greenpeace, in cooperation with biologists, scientists, and other locals, to fight an international campaign, which they won, to save the turtles. You can visit the turtle center or offer to volunteer. The Friends of Xcacel Web site (⊕ www.turtles.org/xcacel.htm) has more information.

Xel-Há

⑬ *3 km (2 mi) south of Laguna de Xcacel.*

Brought to you by the people who manage Xcaret, Xel-Há (pronounced shel-*hah*) is a natural aquarium made from coves, inlets, and lagoons cut from the limestone shoreline. The name means "where the water is born," and a natural spring here flows out to meet the saltwater, creating a perfect habitat for tropical marine life. Although there seem to be fewer fish each year, and the mixture of fresh- and saltwater can cloud visibility, there is still enough here to impress novice snorkelers.

The place gets overwhelmingly crowded, so come early. The grounds are well equipped with bathrooms, restaurants, and a shop. At the entrance you will receive specially prepared sunscreen that won't kill the fish; other sunscreens are prohibited. For an extra charge, you can "interact" (not swim) with dolphins. There's also an all-inclusive package with a meal, a towel, a locker, and snorkel equipment for $65. ☎ *984/875–6000* 🖷 *984/875–6003* ⊕ *www.xelha.com.mx* ✉ *$35 includes life vest and inner tube* ⊙ *Daily 8–6.*

The squat structures of the compact, little-visited **Xel-Há Archaeological Site** are thought to have been inhabited from about 300 BC–AD 100, until about 1200–1521. The most interesting sights are on the north end of the ruins, where remains of a Maya *sacbé* (road) and mural paintings in the **Jaguar House** sit near a tranquil, deep cenote. The site takes about 45 minutes to visit. ☎ *No phone* ✉ *$3; free Sun.* ⊙ *Daily 8–5.*

> ### EXPLORING XEL-HÁ
>
> Scattered throughout the park are small Maya ruins, including Na Balaam, known for a yellow jaguar painted on one of its walls. Low wooden bridges over the lagoons allow for leisurely walks around the park, and there are spots to rest or swim.

en route

FodorsChoice ★

Hidden Worlds Cenotes Park was made semi-famous when it was featured in a 2002 IMAX film, "Journey into Amazing Caves," that was shown at theaters across North America. The park, which was founded by Florida native Buddy Quattlebaum in 1998, contains some of the Yucatán's most spectacular cenotes. You can explore these startlingly clear freshwater sinkholes, which are full of fantastic stalactites, stalagmites, and rock formations, on guided diving or snorkeling tours. Hidden Worlds added a new feather in its cap in 2004 when a new, particularly gorgeous cenote, Dream Gate, was discovered on the property; the underwater topography of this cenote is so dazzling it's otherworldly. To get to the cenotes, you ride in a jungle buggy through dense tropical forest from the main park entrance. Prices start at $40 for snorkeling tours ($30 for children) and go up to $100 for diving tours. Be sure to bring your bug spray. ⊠ *7 km (4½ mi) south of Xel-Há on Carretera 307* ☎ *984/877–8535* ⊕ *www.hiddenworlds.com.mx* ☉ *Open daily 9 to 5; with snorkeling tours at 9, 11, 1, 2, and 3, and diving tours at 9, 11, and 1.*

Tankah

🕙 *9½ km (6 mi) south of Xel-Há on the dirt road off Carretera 307.*

Although in ancient times Tankah (which is between Xel-Há and Tulum) was an important Maya trading city, over the past few centuries it has lain mostly dormant. That's beginning to change, though; a number of small, reasonably priced hotels have cropped up here over the past few years, and several expats who own villas in the area rent them out year-round.

★ The **Gorgonian Gardens,** an underwater environment that lies just off-shore here, have made Tankah a particular destination for divers and snorkelers. From southern Tankah to Bahía de Punta Soliman, the sand-free ocean floor has allowed for the proliferation of Gorgonians, or soft corals—sea fans, candelabras, fingers that can reach 5 feet in height—as well as a variety of colorful sponges. Fish love to feed here, and so many of them swarm the gardens that some divers have compared the experience to being surrounded by clouds of butterflies. Although this underwater habitat goes on for miles, Tankah is the best place to view it. The **Lucky Fish Dive Center,** located at the Tankah Inn (☎ 984/875–9367 or 984/804–5051 ⊕ www.luckyfishdiving.com), runs dive trips to the Gorgonian Gardens, among other sites. Costs start at $40 for a one-tank dive.

Where to Stay & Eat

$$–$$$$ ✕ **Restaurante Oscar y Lalo.** A couple of miles outside Tulum, at Bahía de Punta Soliman, is this wonderful palapa restaurant run by two friends. The seafood is excellent here, although a bit pricey; Lalo's Special, a dish made with local lobster, shrimp, conch, fish, barracuda, and chicken fajitas, prepared for 2 to 10 people, is a standout. The beachfront here is so perfect looking that Corona chose it for one of their "escape to paradise" beer commercials. If you're inspired to sleep on the beach, there are campsites. RVs are also welcome, though there aren't any hookups. ⊠ *Carretera 307, north of Tankah (look for faded white sign)* ☎ 984/871–2209 ▭ No credit cards.

★ $$–$$$ 🏠 **Blue Sky.** Guest quarters here have eclectic and one-of-a-kind touches, such as Cuban oil paintings, Guatemalan bedspreads, handblown vases, inlaid-silver mirrors, and chairs hand-tooled of native *chichén* wood. A couple of suites have sofa beds. The open-air dining room is kept clear of mosquitoes by a special carbon-dioxide machine developed by the U.S. military. A swimming pool has recently been added to the property. ⊠ *Bahía Tankah, past Casa Cenote* ☎ 984/801–4004 or 877/ 792–9237 ⊕ *www.blueskymexico.com* ➷ *6 rooms, 2 suites* ♿ *Restaurant, refrigerators, pool, beach, snorkeling, boating, bicycles, library, shop, Internet; no room phones, no room TVs* ▭ *MC, V* ⊙ *CP, AI.*

$$ 🏠 **Casa Tropical.** This grand two-story villa has been divided into two units, one upstairs, one down. The cozy casita downstairs is less expensive and right on the beach; the larger upstairs unit has a rooftop patio with sweeping ocean views. Both are decorated in bright tropical prints, and have queen-size beds and twice-weekly maid service. There are beachside hammocks where you can sip a margarita and watch for exotic birds (you might see a roseate spoonbill fly past). The beach here has excellent snorkeling, with many small inlets. ⊠ *Tankah 3, Lote 3* ☎ 570/247–7065 🖷 570/247–7381 ⊕ *www.casatropical.com* ➷ *2 units* ♿ *Kitchens, beach, snorkeling; no room phones, no room TVs* ▭ *No credit cards.*

$$ 🏠 **Tankah Inn.** A friendly former Texan cowboy runs this guesthouse, which is popular with divers. Rooms are large, bright, and comfortable though not luxurious, and front a windswept beach. The Lucky Fish Dive Center is located right on the first floor and offers open-water diving and resort courses. ⊠ *Bahía Tankah 16* ☎ 998/804–9006 or 918/ 582–3743 ⊕ *www.tankah.com* ➷ *5 rooms* ♿ *Beach, dive shop, snorkeling; no a/c, no room phones, no room TVs* ▭ *No credit cards* ⊙ *CP.*

Tulum

🔺 ⑮ *2 km (1 mi) south of Tankah, 130 km (81 mi) south of Cancún.*

Fodor'sChoice
★

Tulum (pronounced tool-*lum*) is the Yucatán Peninsula's most-visited Maya ruin, attracting more than 2 million people annually. This means you have to share the site with roughly half of the tourist population of Quintana Roo on any given day, even if you arrive early. Though most of the architecture is of unremarkable Postclassic (1000–1521) style, the amount of attention that Tulum receives is not entirely undeserved. Its location by the blue-green Caribbean is breathtaking.

■ TIP→→ At the entrance you can hire a guide, but keep in mind that some of their information is more entertaining than historically accurate. (Disregard that stuff about virgin sacrifices atop the altars.) Because you aren't allowed to climb or enter the fragile structures—only three really merit close inspection

> **WORD OF MOUTH**
>
> The ruins at Tulum are a "don't miss" experience if you are anywhere in the area. Take water, a camera, an umbrella (for sun or rain), comfortable shoes, and a bathing suit. It opens at 7 am so if you are there early, you will beat the crowds.   –Jim Kutsko

Continued on page 164

ANCIENT ARCHITECTS: THE MAYA

As well as developing a highly accurate calendar (based on their careful study of astronomy), hieroglyphic writing, and the mathematical concept of zero, the Maya were also superb architects. Looking at the remains of their ancient cities today, it's hard to believe that Maya builders erected their immense palaces and temples without the aid of metal tools, the wheel, or beasts of burden—and in terrible heat and difficult terrain. Centuries later, these feats of ceremonial architecture still have the power to dazzle.

Calakmul

Preclassic Period: PETEN ARCHITECTURE

Between approximately 2000 BC and AD 100, the Maya were centered around the lowlands in the south-central region of Guatemala. Their communities were family-based, and governed by hereditary chiefs; their worship of agricultural gods (such as Chaac, the rain god), who they believed controlled the seasons, led them to chart the movement of heavenly bodies. Their religious beliefs also led them to build enormous temples and pyramids—such as El Mirador, in the Guatemalan lowlands—where sacrifices were made and ceremonies performed to please the gods.

The structures at El Mirador, as well as at the neighboring ruin site of Tikal, were built in what is known today as the Peten style; pyramids were steeply pitched, built on stepped terraces, and decorated with large stucco masks and ornamental (but sometimes "false" or unclimbable) stairways. Peten-style structures were also often roofed with corbeled archways. The Maya began to move northward into the Yucatán during the late part of this period, which is why Peten-style buildings can also be found at Calakmul, just north of the Guatemalan border.

4

Early Classic Period: RIO USUMACINTA ARCHITECTURE

The Classic Period, often referred to as the "golden age" of the Maya, spanned the years between about AD 100 and AD 1000. During this period, Maya civilization expanded northward and became much more complex. A distinct ruling class emerged, and hereditary kings began to rule over the communities—which had grown into densely populated jungle cities, filled with towering, increasingly impressive-looking palaces and temples.

During the early part of the Classic period, Maya architecture began to take on some distinctive characteristics, representative of what is now called the Rio Usumacinta style. Builders placed their structures on hillsides or crests, and the principal buildings were covered with bas-reliefs carved in stone. The pyramid-top temples had vestibules and rooms with vaulted ceilings, and many chamber walls were carved with scenes recounting important events during the reign of the ruler who built the pyramid. Some of the most stunning examples of Rio Usumacinta architecture that can be seen today are at the ruins of Palenque, near Chiapas.

Chicanná

Mid-Classic Period: RIO BEC AND CHENES ARCHITECTURE

It was during the middle part of the Classic Period (roughly between AD 600 and AD 800) that the Maya presence exploded into the Yucatán Peninsula. Several Maya settlements were established in what is now Campeche state, including Chicanna and Xpujil, near the southwest corner of the state. The architecture at these sites was built in what is now known as the Rio Bec style. As in the earlier Peten style, Rio Bec pyramids had steeply pitched sides and ornately decorated foundations. Other Rio Bec-style buildings, however, were long, one-story affairs incorporating two or sometimes three tall towers. These towers were typically capped by large roof combs that resembled mini-temples.

During the same part of the Classic Period, a different architectural style, known as Chenes, developed in some of the more northerly Maya cities, such as Hochob. While some Chenes-style structures share the same long, single-story construction as Rio Bec buildings, others have strikingly different characteristics—like doorways carved in the shape of huge Chaac faces with gaping open mouths.

Late Classic Period: PUUC AND NORTHEAST YUCATÁN ARCHITECTURE

Chichén Itzá

Some of the Yucatán's most spectacular Maya architecture was built between about AD 800 and AD 1000. By this time, the Maya had spread into territory that is now Yucatán state, and established lavish cities at Labná, Kabah, Sayil, and Uxmal—all fine examples of the Puuc architectural style. Puuc buildings were beautifully proportioned, often designed in a low-slung quadrangle shape that allowed for many rooms inside. Exterior walls were kept plain to show off the friezes above—which were embellished with stone-mosaic gods, geometric designs, and serpentine motifs. Corners were edged with gargoyle-like, curved-nose Chaac figures.

The fusion of two distinct Maya groups— the Chichén Maya and the Itzás—pro-

duced another striking architectural style. This style, known as Northeast Yucatán, is exemplified by the ruins at Chichén Itzá. Here, columns and grand colonnades were introduced. Palaces with row upon row of columns carved in the shape of serpents looked over grand patios, platforms were dedicated to the planet Venus, and pyramids were raised to honor Kukulcán (the plumed serpent god borrowed from the Toltecs, who called him Quetzalcoátl). Northeast Yucatán structures also incorporated carved stone Chacmool figures—reclining statues with offering trays carved in their midsections for sacrificial offerings.

Uxmal

▼
Between 2000 BC and AD 100, the Maya are based in lowlands of south-central Guatemala, and governed by hereditary chiefs.

2000 BC　　　　　　　　　　　　**1000**

PETEN

PRE CLASSIC

Postclassic Period: QUINTANA ROO COAST ARCHITECTURE

Although Maya culture continued to flourish between AD 1000 and the early 1500s, signs of decline also began to take form. Wars broke out between neighboring city-states, leaving the region vulnerable when the Spaniards began invading in 1521. By 1600, the Spanish had dominated the Maya empire.

Maya architecture enjoyed its last hurrah during this period, mostly in the region along the Yucatán's Caribbean coast. Known as Quintana Roo Coast architecture, this style can be seen today at the ruins of Tulum. Although the structures

here aren't as visually arresting as those at earlier, inland sites, Tulum's location is breathtaking: it's the only major Maya city overlooking the sea.

Tulum

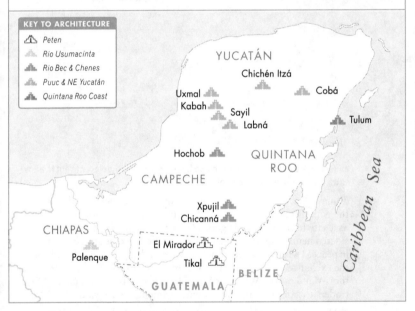

KEY TO ARCHITECTURE

- Peten
- Rio Usumacinta
- Rio Bec & Chenes
- Puuc & NE Yucatán
- Quintana Roo Coast

YUCATÁN

Chichén Itzá

Uxmal · Cobá
Kabah
Sayil
Labná · Tulum

Hochob · QUINTANA ROO

CAMPECHE

Xpujil
Chicanná

CHIAPAS El Mirador

Palenque Tikal

BELIZE

GUATEMALA

Caribbean Sea

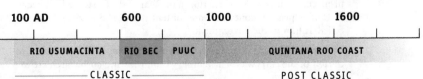

Maya civilization expands northward. Distinct ruling class emerges, and hereditary kings take charge.

Maya settlements established on Yucatán Peninsula, including what is now Campeche State.

Conflicts between city-states leave region weak when Spaniards invade. By 1600, the Spanish dominate the Maya.

100 AD | **600** | **1000** | **1600**

RIO USUMACINTA | RIO BEC | PUUC | QUINTANA ROO COAST

CLASSIC | POST CLASSIC

4

ANCIENT ARCHITECTS: THE MAYA

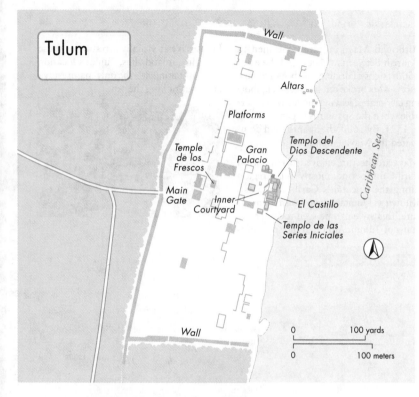

Tulum

Wall

Altars

Platforms

Temple
de los
Frescos

Gran
Palacio

Templo del
Dios Descendente

Caribbean Sea

Main
Gate

Inner
Courtyard

El Castillo

Templo de las
Series Iniciales

Wall

| 0 | 100 yards |
| 0 | 100 meters |

anyway—you can see the ruins in two hours. You might, however, want to allow extra time for a swim or a stroll on the beach.

Tulum is one of the few Maya cities known to have been inhabited when the conquistadores arrived in 1518. In the 16th century, it functioned as a safe harbor for trade goods from rival Maya factions; it was considered neutral territory where merchandise could be stored and traded in peace. The city reached its height when traders, made wealthy through the exchange of goods, for the first time outranked Maya priests in authority and power. When the Spaniards arrived, they forbade the Maya traders to sail the seas, and commerce among the Maya died.

Tulum has long held special significance for the Maya. A key city in the League of Mayapán (AD 987–1194), it was never conquered by the Spaniards, although it was abandoned about 75 years after the conquest. For 300 years thereafter, it symbolized the defiance of an otherwise subjugated people; it was one of the last outposts of the Maya during their insurrection against Mexican rule in the War of the Castes, which began in 1846. Uprisings continued intermittently until 1935, when the Maya ceded Tulum to the government.

The first significant structure is the two-story **Templo de los Frescos**, to the left of the entryway. The temple's vault roof and corbel arch are examples of classic Maya architecture. Faint traces of blue-green frescoes outlined in black on the inner and outer walls refer to ancient Maya beliefs (the clearest frescoes are hidden from sight now that you can't walk into the temple). Reminiscent of the Mixtec style, the frescoes depict the three worlds of the Maya and their major deities and are decorated with stellar and serpentine patterns, rosettes, and ears of maize and other offerings to the gods. One scene portrays the rain god seated on a four-legged animal—probably a reference to the Spaniards on their horses.

The largest and most famous building, the **Castillo** (Castle), looms at the edge of a 40-foot limestone cliff just past the Temple of the Frescoes. Atop it, at the end of a broad stairway, is a temple with stucco ornamentation on the outside and traces of fine frescoes inside the two chambers. (The stairway has been roped off, so the top temple is inaccessible.) The front wall of the Castillo has faint carvings of the Descending God and columns depicting the plumed serpent god, Kukulcán, who was introduced to the Maya by the Toltecs. To the left of the Castillo is the **Templo del Dios Descendente**—so called for the carving of a winged god plummeting to earth over the doorway.

■ **TIP→→** The tiny cove to the left of the Castillo and Temple of the Descending God is a good spot for a cooling swim, but there are no changing rooms. A few small altars sit atop a hill at the north side of the cove and have a good view of the Castillo and the sea. On the highway about 4 km (2½ mi) south of the ruins is the present-day village of Tulum. As Tulum's importance as a commercial center increases, markets, restaurants, shops, services, and auto-repair shops continue to spring up along the road. Growth hasn't been kind to the pueblo, however: it's rather unsightly, with a wide four-lane highway running down the middle. Despite this blight, it has a few good restaurants.

🎫 *$9; use of video camera extra* ☉ *Daily 8–5.*

Where to Stay & Eat

★ **$–$$$** ✕ **Il Giardino Ristorante Italiano.** This small, cozy café is like an outpost of Italy on the Caribbean Coast. A few tables are nestled under a palapa with a tile floor; there's also outdoor seating in a garden. Many of the Italian dishes contain fresh fish; the grilled calamari in a lemon-and-white wine sauce is wonderful as is the spaghetti marinara with mixed seafood. For a Maya twist, try the risotto with *chaya* (a Yucatecan type of spinach) and cheese. Be sure to leave room for dessert, too: the tiramisu is divine. ⊠ *Avs. Satelite and Sagitario (first road to the west as you enter Tulum)* ☎ *984/806–3601* ▭ *No credit cards.*

$–$$$ ✕ **El Pequeno Buenos Aires.** Owner and chef Sergio Patrone serves delicious *parrilladas* (a mixed, marinated grill made with chicken, beef, and pork) at this Argentine-inspired restaurant. There are Italian dishes, too, as well as a nice selection of wines. White tablecloths add a sophisticated touch, even though you're eating under a palapa roof. ⊠ *Av. Tulum, No. 42, at the corner of Veta Sur* ☎ *984/871–2708* ▭ *MC, V.*

$–$$$ ✕ **Vita e Bella.** Italian tourists travel miles out of their way to eat at this utterly rustic, authentically Italian place, where plastic tables and chairs are set beside the sea. The menu features 15 pasta dishes, and pizza prepared in a wood-burning oven with such toppings as squid, lobster, and Italian sausage. There are wine, beer, and margaritas to sip with your supper, too. ⊠ *Carretera Tulum Ruinas, Km 1.5* ☎ *984/877–8145* ⊟ *No credit cards.*

★ $-$$ ✕ **Charlie's.** This eatery, which is quite old in Tulum years (it's been here since 1997) is a happening spot where local artists display their talents. Wall murals are made from empty wine bottles, and painted chili peppers adorn the dining tables. There's a charming garden in back with a stage for live music, and on Sunday, flamenco guitarists entertain during tourist season. The chicken tacos and black bean soup are especially good here. ⊠ *Avs. Tulum and Jupiter, across from bus station* ☎ *984/ 871–2136* ⊟ *MC, V* ⊙ *Closed Mon.*

$ ✕ **Taqueria el Mariachi.** For traditional Mexican food, this eatery fits the bill. Try the fajitas with chicken or pork; the specialty, *arracheras* (grilled beef or pork with onions, bell peppers, and tomatoes) is also a winner. ⊠ *Avs. Tulum and Orion* ☎ *984/106–2032* ⊟ *No credit cards.*

¢ ✕ **Yum Bo'otic Cafe.** Fruit smoothies with a choice of 19 fresh fruits, great coffee, and homemade pastries (don't miss the key lime pie) are the draws at this lovely, efficient café. There are also sandwiches, among them the delicious Mozzarella Baguette. Prices are rock bottom all year round. ⊠ *Avs. Tulum and Orion* ☎ *No phone* ⊟ *No credit cards.*

★ $$$-$$$$ ✕▥ **Las Ranitas.** Stylish and ecologically correct Las Ranitas (The Little Frogs) creates its own power through wind-generated electricity, solar energy, and recycled water. Each chic room has gorgeous tile and fabric from Oaxaca, terraces overlook gardens and the ocean, and jungle walkways lead to the breathtaking beach. The pièce de résistance is the on-site restaurant's French chef, who whips up incredible French and Mexican cuisine ($$-$$$). ⊠ *Carretera Tulum–Boca Paila, Km 9 (last hotel before the Reserva de la Biosfera Sian Ka'an)* ☎🖶 *984/877–8554* ⊕ *www.lasranitas.com* ⇌ *15 rooms, 2 suites* ⚐ *Restaurant, pool, beach, snorkeling, paddle tennis; no a/c, no room phones, no room TVs* ⊟ *No credit cards* ⦾ CP ⊙ *Closed mid-Sept.–mid-Nov.*

$-$$ ✕▥ **Zamas.** On the wild, isolated Punta Piedra (Rock Point), where the ocean stretches as far as the eye can see, this kick-back hotel is a favorite with Americans. The romantically rustic cabanas—with mosquito nets over comfortable beds, spacious tiled bathrooms, and bright Mexican colors—are nicely distanced from one another. The restaurant ($-$$$) is considered one of the best in the area with an eclectic Italian-Mexican-Yucatecan menu. Try the pizza made in a wood-burning oven; it's delicious. ⊠ *Carretera Tulum–Boca Paila, Km 5* ☎ *984/871–2067, 415/387–9806 in U.S.* 🖶 *984/877–8523* ⊕ *www.zamas.com* ⇌ *15 cabanas* ⚐ *Restaurant, beach, snorkeling, bar, car rental; no a/c, no room phones* ⊟ *No credit cards.*

$$$ ▥ **Azulik Resort.** Billed as a high-end barefoot luxury resort, Azulik will soothe your senses. The charming hardwood villas here are perched right at the ocean's edge; each has a private deck on the ocean side, and floor-to-ceiling windows on the jungle side (with bamboo curtains when privacy is needed). Hand-carved soaking tubs made from hollowed out tree trunks add a natural feeling to this tropical paradise. ⊠ *Carretera Tulum Ruinas, Km 5.5* ☎ *877/532–6737 in the U.S.* 🖶 *604/608–9560*

⊕ *http://azulik.com* ⮐ *15 villas* ⚹ *Hot tub, massage, spa, beach; no a/c, no room phones, no room TVs, no kids* ⊟ *AE, MC, V.*

¢–$$$ 🏨 **Cabañas Copal.** At this eco-hotel on a rugged cliff, you can choose to rough it or stay in relative luxury. Dirt- or cement-floored cabanas are sheltered from the jungle elements by mosquito nets and thatched roofs; some have shared baths, and some have no electricity. Rooms, however, are bigger and more elegant, with hardwood floors, hand-carved furniture, and a kind of primitive whirlpool bath. At night thousands of candles light the walkways and grounds. Wellness programs, exercise classes, and spa treatments include yoga, dream classes, and Maya massages; there are also a flotation chamber and a temazcal (sweat lodge). ⊠ *Carretera Tulum Ruinas, Km 5 (turn right at fork in highway; hotel is less than 1 km [½ mi] on right)* ☎ *984/806–4406 or 984/806–8247* ⊕ *http://cabanascopal.com* ⮐ *45 rooms, 7 cabanas* ⚹ *Restaurant, fitness classes, massage, beach, snorkeling, fishing, bar, Internet; no a/c, no room phones, no room TVs* ⊟ *No credit cards.*

★ **¢–$$$** 🏨 **La Vita e Bella Beachfront Bungalows.** Perched on sand dunes above the sea, this small Italian resort has lodgings that are rustic but also supremely comfortable. The 10 roomy bungalows have wooden floors, palapa roofs, balconies with hammocks, and wide ocean views; most have queen-size beds. Smaller, less expensive cement-floored cabanas are also available; they're set further away from the beach, but are right near the on-site, sandy-floored restaurant. Like the bungalows, they're also immaculately clean. ⊠ *Carretera Tulum Ruinas, Km 1.5* ☎ *984/877–8145 or 984/806–0052* ⊕ *www.lavitaebella-tulum.com* ⮐ *10 bungalows, 10 cabanas* ⚹ *Restaurant, fans, snorkeling, massage, bar; no a/c, no room phones* ⊟ *No credit cards* ⎹⊙⎸ *BP.*

¢ 🏨 **Weary Traveler Hostel, Cafe and Bar.** Tulum is backpacker central, and if you're roughing it, this is one of the cheapest, most convenient area spots to hang your hat. Most rooms are shared, with either bunk or twin beds and a private bath. Furnishings are basic but neat and clean. You have use of a communal kitchen, and there are picnic tables in a central area for eating and meeting. John, the tireless owner, makes a great cup of java—and it's only 10 pesos for your morning fix. There's also a cheap Internet café on-site, and the bus station is across the street. ⊠ *Av. Tulum, between Avs. Jupiter and Acuario* ☎ *984/871–2386* ⊕ *www.weary.intulum.com* ⮐ *10 rooms* ⚹ *Kitchen, café, fans, bar, Internet; no a/c, no toom phones, no room TVs* ⊟ *No credit cards.*

Cobá

🏔 **⑯** *49 km (30 mi) northwest of Tulum.*

Fodor'sChoice
★

Cobá (pronounced ko-*bah*), Maya for "water stirred by the wind," flourished from AD 800 to 1100, with a population of as many as 55,000. Now it stands in solitude, and the jungle has overgrown many of its buildings. ■ TIP➔➔ Cobá is often overlooked by visitors who opt, instead, to visit better-known Tulum. But this site is much grander and less crowded, giving you a chance to really immerse yourself in ancient culture. Cobá exudes stillness, the silence broken by the occasional shriek of a spider monkey or the call of a bird. Processions of huge army ants cross the footpaths as the sun slips through openings between the tall hardwood trees, ferns, and giant palms.

Near five lakes and between coastal watchtowers and inland cities, Cobá exercised economic control over the region through a network of at least 16 *sacbéob* (white stone roads), one of which measures 100 km (62 mi) and is the longest in the Maya world. The city once covered 70 square km (27 square mi), making it a noteworthy sister state to Tikal in northern Guatemala, with which it had close cultural and commercial ties. It's noted for its massive temple-pyramids, one of which is 138 feet tall, the largest and highest in northern Yucatán. The main groupings of ruins are separated by several miles of dense vegetation, so the best way to get a sense of the immensity of the city is to scale one of the pyramids. ⚠ It's easy to get lost here, so stay on the main road; *don't* be tempted by the narrow paths that lead into the jungle unless you have a qualified guide with you.

The first major cluster of structures, to your right as you enter the ruins, is the **Cobá Group,** whose pyramids are around a sunken patio. At the near end of the group, facing a large plaza, is the 79-foot-high temple, which was dedicated to the rain god, Chaac; some Maya people still place offerings and light candles here in hopes of improving their harvests. Around the rear to the left is a restored ball court, where a sacred game was once played to petition the gods for rain, fertility, and other boons.

Farther along the main path to your left is the **Chumuc Mul Group,** little of which has been excavated. The principal pyramid here is covered with the remains of vibrantly painted stucco motifs (*chumuc mul* means "stucco pyramid"). A kilometer (½ mi) past this site is the **Nohoch Mul Group** (Large Hill Group), the highlight of which is the pyramid of the same name, the tallest at Cobá. It has 120 steps—equivalent to 12 stories—and shares a plaza with Temple 10. The Descending God (also seen at Tulum) is depicted on a facade of the temple atop Nohoch Mul, from which the view is excellent.

Beyond the Nohoch Mul Group is the **Castillo,** with nine chambers that are reached by a stairway. To the south are the remains of a ball court, including the stone ring through which the ball was hurled. From the main route follow the sign to **Las Pinturas Group,** named for the still-discernible polychrome friezes on the inner and outer walls of its large, patioed pyramid. An enormous stela here depicts a man standing with his feet on two prone captives. Take the minor path for 1 km (½ mi) to the Macanxoc Group, not far from the lake of the same name. The main pyramid at Macanxoc is accessible by a stairway.

Cobá is a 35-minute drive northwest of Tulum along a pothole-filled road that leads straight through the jungle. ■ TIP→→ You can comfortably make your way around Cobá in a half day, but spending the night in town is highly advised, as doing so will allow you to visit the ruins in solitude when they open at 8 AM. Even on a day trip, consider taking time out for lunch to escape the intense heat and mosquito-heavy humidity of the ruins. Buses depart to and from Cobá for Playa del Carmen and Tulum at least twice daily.

Taxis to Tulum are still reasonable (about $16). ✉ *$4; use of video camera $6; $2 fee for parking* ☉ *Daily 8–5.*

Where to Stay & Eat

¢–$ ✕ **El Bocadito.** The restaurant closest to the ruins is owned and run by a gracious Maya family, which serves simple, traditional cuisine. A three-course fixed-price lunch costs $6. Look for such classic dishes as *pollo pibíl* (chicken baked in banana leaves) and *cochinita pibíl* (pork baked in banana leaves). ✉ *On road to Cobá ruins, 1/2 km from the ruin site entrance* ☎ *987/874–2087* 🗖 *No credit cards* ☉ *No dinner.*

$ 🏠 **Uolis Nah.** This small thatch-roofed complex has extra-large, quiet rooms with high ceilings, two beds, hammocks, and tile floors. You're less than 2 km (1 mi) from the Tulum highway but away from the noise, and there's lots of privacy. An extra person in a double room costs $11 more. ✉ *On road to Cobá ruins, 28 km (18 mi) from ruin site entrance* ☎ *984/879–5685* ⊕ *www.uolisnah.com* ↪ *7 rooms* ⚘ *Fans, kitchenettes, car rental; no a/c, no room phones, no room TVs* 🗖 *No credit cards.*

Pac Chen

🏭 ⑰ *20 km (13 mi) southeast of Cobá.*

Fodor'sChoice
★

■ TIP→→ You can only visit Pac Chen (pronounced *pak chin*) on trips organized by Alltournative, an ecotour company based in Playa del Carmen. The unusual, soft-adventure experience is definitely worth your while. Pac Chen is a Maya jungle settlement of 125 people who still live in round thatch huts; there's no electricity or indoor plumbing, and the roads aren't paved. The inhabitants, who primarily make their living farming pineapple, beans, and plantains, still pray to the gods for good crops. Alltournative also pays them by the number of tourists it brings in, though no more than 80 people are allowed to visit on any given day. This money has made the village self-sustaining and has given the people an alternative to logging and hunting, which were their main means of livelihood before.

The half-day tour starts with a trek through the jungle to a cenote where you grab on to a harness and Z-line to the other side. Next is the Jaguar

> **WORD OF MOUTH**
>
> "Hard to believe it's the 21st century while visiting Pac Chen. The residents there let us into their homes!"   –jim

cenote, set deeper into the forest, where you must rappel down the cave-like sides into a cool underground lagoon. You'll eat lunch under an open-air palapa overlooking another lagoon, where canoes await. The food includes such Maya dishes as grilled achiote (annatto seed) chicken, fresh tortillas, beans, and watermelon.

THE COSTA MAYA

The coastal area south of Punta Allen is more purely Maya than the stretch between Cancún and Punta Allen. Fishing collectives and close-knit communities carry on ancient traditions here, and the proximity to Belize lends a Caribbean flavor, particularly in Chetumal, where you'll hear both Spanish and a Caribbean patois. The Costa Maya also encompasses the extraordinary Reserva de la Biosfera Sian Ka'an. A multimillion-dollar government initiative is attempting to support ecotourism and sustainable development projects here, which will perhaps prevent resorts from taking over much of the wild land.

The first of these government projects was the development of Puerto Costa Maya, a glitzy cruise-ship port at Majahual, which was completed in 2000. By building it, the government hoped to siphon off some of the tourism in the Cancún area and introduce visitors to some of the lesser-known Maya sites in the southern part of Quintana Roo. Since the port received its millionth visitor in 2005, it appears to be accomplishing this goal, but so far the development here has stayed relatively contained. The nearby fishing village of Majahual, a stone's throw from the newly constructed port, remains virtually untouched. Other ongoing projects for the region include the excavation and opening of more archeological sites that extend from the Rio Bec region to nearby Calakmul, Xpujil, Chicána, and Becán.

Reserva de la Biosfera Sian Ka'an

★ ♺ ⓲ *15 km (9 mi) south of Tulum to the Punta Allen turnoff and within Sian Ka'an.*

The Sian Ka'an ("where the sky is born," pronounced see-*an* caan) region was first settled by the Maya in the 5th century AD. In 1986 the Mexican government established the 1.3-million-acre Reserva de la Biosfera Sian Ka'an as an internationally protected area. The next year, it was named a World Heritage Site by the United Nations Educational, Scientific, and Cultural Organization (UNESCO); later, it was extended by 200,000 acres. The Riviera Maya and Costa Maya split the biosphere reserve; Punta Allen and north belong to the Riviera Maya, and everything south of Punta Allen is part of the Costa Maya.

The Sian Ka'an reserve constitutes 10% of the land in Quintana Roo and covers 100 km (62 mi) of coast. Hundreds of species of local and migratory birds, fish, other animals and plants, and fewer than 1,000 residents (primarily Maya) share this area of freshwater and coastal lagoons, mangrove swamps, cays, savannas, tropical forests, and a barrier reef. There are approximately 27 ruins (none excavated) linked by a unique canal system—one of the few of its kind in the Maya world in Mexico. This is one of the last undeveloped stretches of North American coast. ■ TIP➜➜ To see Sian Ka'an's sites you must take a guided tour.

Several kinds of tours, including bird-watching by boat, and night kayaking to observe crocodiles, are offered on-site through the **Sian Ka'an Visitor Center** (☎ 998/884–3667, 998/884–9580, or 998/871–0709 ⊕ www.ecotravelmexico.com), which also offers five rooms with shared bath and one private suite for overnight stays. Prices range from $65 to $85 and meals are separate. The visitor center's observation tower offers the best view of the Sian Ka'an Biosphere from high atop their deck and wood bridge.

Other, privately run tours of the reserve and surrounding area are also available. **Tres Palmas** (☎ 998/871–0709, 044–998/845–4083 cell ⊕ www.trespalmasweb.com) runs a day tour that includes a visit to a typical Maya family living in the biosphere, a tamale breakfast, a visit to the Maya ruins at Muyil, a jungle trek to a lookout point for bird-watching, a boat trip through the lagoon and mangrove-laden channels (where you can jump into one of the channels and float downstream), lunch on the beach beside the Maya ruins at Tulum, and a visit to nearby cenotes for a swim and snorkeling. The staff picks you up at your hotel; the fee of $129 per person includes a bilingual guide.

Many species of the once-flourishing wildlife have fallen into the endangered category, but the waters here still teem with rooster fish, bonefish, mojarra, snapper, shad, permit, sea bass, and crocodiles. Fishing the flats for wily bonefish is popular, and the peninsula's few lodges also run deep-sea fishing trips.

To explore on your own, follow the road past Boca Paila to the secluded 35-km (22-mi) coastal strip of land that's part of the reserve. You'll be limited to swimming, snorkeling, and camping on the beaches, as there are no trails into the surrounding jungle. The narrow, extremely rough dirt road down the peninsula is filled with monstrous potholes and after a rainfall is completely impassable. Don't attempt it unless you have four-wheel drive. Most fishing lodges along the way close for the rainy season in August and September, and accommodations are hard to come by. The road ends at Punta Allen, a fishing village whose main catch is spiny lobster, which was becoming scarce until ecologists taught the local fishing cooperative how to build and lay special traps to conserve the species. There are several small, expensive guesthouses. If you haven't booked ahead, start out early in the morning so you can get back to civilization before dark.

Where to Stay

$$$$ 🏨 **Boca Paila Fishing Lodge.** Home of the "grand slam" (fishing lingo for catching three different kinds of fish in one trip), this charming lodge has nine cottages, each with two double beds, couches, bathrooms, and screened-in sitting areas. Boats and guides for fly-fishing and bonefishing are provided; you can rent tackle at the lodge. Meals consist of fresh fish dishes and Maya specialties, among other things. From January through June and October through December a 50% deposit is required, and the minimum stay is one week (there's no required deposit and only a three-night minimum stay the rest of the year). ⊠ *Boca Paila Peninsula* ⚓ *reservations: Frontiers, Box 959, Wexford, PA 15090* ☎ *724/935–1577 or 800/245–1950* ⊕ *www.frontierstravel.com* ➪ *9 cottages* ⚒ *Restaurant, beach, boats, snorkeling, fishing, bar, laundry service, airport shuttle; no a/c in some rooms, no room phones, no room TVs* ⊟ No *credit cards unless arranged with Frontiers* ⦿ *AI.*

★ **$$$$** 🏨 **Casa Blanca Lodge.** This American-managed lodge is on a rocky outcrop on remote Punta Pájaros Island—reputed to be one of the best places in the world for light-tackle saltwater fishing. Modern guest rooms have tile-and-mahogany bathrooms. An open-air thatch-roofed bar welcomes anglers with drinks, fresh fish dishes, fruit, and vegetables at the start and end of the day. Only weeklong packages can be booked March through July. Rates include a charter flight from Cancún, all meals, a boat, and a guide; nonfishing packages are cheaper. A 50% prepayment fee is required. ⊠ *Punta Pájaros* ✆ *reservations: Frontiers, Box 959, Wexford, PA 15090* ☎ *724/935–1577, 800/245–1950 for Frontiers* ⊕ *www.frontierstravel. com* ⇨ *9 rooms* ♿ *Restaurant, beach, snorkeling, fishing, bar, laundry service; no room phones, no room TVs* ☰ *MC, V* ⏀ *AI.*

Muyil

⑲ *24 km (15 mi) south of Tulum.*

This photogenic archaeological site at the northern end of the Reserva de la Biosfera Sian Ka'an is underrated. Once known as Chunyaxché, it's now called by its ancient name, Muyil (pronounced mool-*hill*). It dates from the Late Preclassic era, when it was connected by road to the sea and served as a port between Cobá and the Maya centers in Belize and Guatemala. A 15-foot-wide sacbé, built during the Postclassic period, extended from the city to the mangrove swamp and was still in use when the Spaniards arrived.

Structures were erected at 400-foot intervals along the white limestone road, almost all of them facing west, but there are only three still standing. At the beginning of the 20th century, the ancient stones were used to build a chicle (gum arabic) plantation, which was managed by one of the leaders of the War of the Castes. The most notable site at Muyil today is the remains of the 56-foot **Castillo**—one of the tallest on the Quintana Roo coast—at the center of a large acropolis. During excavations of the Castillo, jade figurines representing the moon and fertility goddess Ixchel were found. Recent excavations at Muyil have uncovered some smaller structures.

The ruins stand near the edge of a deep-blue lagoon and are surrounded by nearly impenetrable jungle—so be sure to bring bug repellent. You can drive down a dirt road on the side of the ruins to swim or fish in the lagoon. The bird-watching is also exceptional here. ⊞ *$4; free Sun.* ⊙ *Daily 8–5.*

Felipe Carrillo Puerto

⑳ *60 km (37 mi) south of Muyil.*

Formerly known as Chan Santa Cruz, Felipe Carrillo Puerto—the Costa Maya's first major town—is named for the man who became governor of Yucatán in 1920, and who was hailed as a hero after instituting a series of reforms to help the impoverished *campesinos* (farmers or peasants). Assassinated by the alleged henchman of the presidential candidate of an opposing party in 1923, he remained a popular figure long after his death.

The town was a political, military, and religious asylum during the 1846 War of the Castes; rebels fled here after being defeated at Mérida. It was

Caste Wars

CLOSE UP

WHEN MEXICO ACHIEVED INDEPENDENCE FROM SPAIN IN 1821, the Maya didn't celebrate. The new government didn't return their lost land, and it didn't treat them with respect. In 1847, a Maya rebellion began in Valladolid. A year later, they had killed hundreds and the battle raged on. (The Indians were rising up against centuries of being relegated to the status of "lower caste" people. Hence the conflict was called the Guerra de las Castas, or War of the Castes.)

Help for the embattled Mexicans arrived with a vengeance from Mexico City, Cuba, and the United States. By 1850, the Maya had been mercilessly slaughtered, their population plummeting from 500,000 to 300,000. Survivors fled to the jungles and held out against the government until its troops withdrew in 1915. The Maya controlled Quintana Roo from Tulum, their headquarters, and finally accepted Mexican rule in 1935.

also in this town that the famous cult of the Talking Cross took hold. The Talking Cross was a sacred symbol of the Maya; it was believed that a holy voice emanated from it, offering guidance and instruction. In this case the cross appeared emblazoned on the trunk of a cedar tree, and the voice urged the Indians to keep fighting. (The voice was actually an Indian priest and ventriloquist, Manual Nahuat, prompted by the Maya rebel José Maria Barrera.) Symbolic crosses were subsequently placed in neighboring villages, including Tulum, and they inspired the Maya to continue fighting until 1915, when the Mexican army finally gave up. The Cruzob Indians then ruled Quintana Roo as an independent state, much to the embarrassment of the Mexican government, until 1935, when the Cruzob handed Tulum over and agreed to Mexican rule.

Felipe Carrillo remains very much a Maya city, with even a few old-timers who cling to the belief that one day the Maya will once again rule the region. It exists primarily as the hub of three highways, and the only vestige of the momentous events of the 19th century is the small uncompleted temple—on the edge of town in an inconspicuous, poorly marked park—begun by the Indians in the 1860s and now a monument to the War of the Castes. The church where the Talking Cross was originally housed also stands. Several humble hotels, some good restaurants, and a gas station may be incentives for stopping here on your southbound trek.

Where to Stay & Eat

¢ ✕🍽 **El Faisán y El Venado.** The price is right at this clean and comfortable hotel. The restaurant (¢–$) does a brisk business with the locals because it's centrally located and has good Yucatecan specialties such as *poc chuc* (pork marinated in sour-orange sauce), *bistec a la yucateca* (Yucatecan-style steak), and pollo pibíl. ☒ *Av. Benito Juárez, Lote 781* 🖀 *983/834–0702* 🛏 *35 rooms* ♨ *Restaurant, refrigerators, cable TV* ▭ *No credit cards.*

Chacchoben

㉑ *33 km (21 mi) southwest of Felipe Carrillo Puerto.*

Chacchoben (pronounced *cha*-cho-ben) is one of the more recent archaeological sites to undergo excavation. An ancient city that was a contemporary of Kohunlich and the most important trading partner with Guatemala north of the Bacalar Lagoon area, the site contains several newly unearthed buildings that are still in good condition. The lofty **Templo Mayor**, the site's main temple, was dedicated to the Maya sun god Itzamná and once held a royal tomb. (When archaeologists found it, though, it had already been looted.) Most buildings were constructed in the early Classic period around AD 200 in the Peten style, although the city could have been inhabited as early as 200 BC. The inhabitants made a living growing cotton and extracting gum arabic and copal resin from the trees. ⊠ *Carretera 307, take Calle Lazaro Cardenas Exit south of Cafetal, turn right on Carretera 293, continue 9 km (5½ mi)* ☎ *No phone* ☜ *$3* ☉ *Daily 8–5.*

Majahual

㉒ *71 km (44 mi) southeast of Felipe Carrillo Puerto on Carretera 307 to the Majahual Exit south of Limones; turn left and continue 56 km (35 mi).*

The road to Majahual (pronounced ma-ha-*wal*) is long. But if you follow it, you'll get a chance to see one of the coast's last authentic fishing villages. Majahual is very laid-back, with inexpensive accommodations, dirt roads, backpackers, and lots of small restaurants serving fresh fish. It's what Playa del Carmen must have been 30 years ago. Activities include lounging, fishing, snorkeling, and diving. An airport has been built here (though it's currently lying abandoned), as well as the huge cruiseship port and passengers-only shopping plaza of Puerto Costa Maya—so it may not be long before this place turns into the next Cozumel. Come and enjoy it while it remains a quaint village.

Where to Stay

$$$ ☒ **Maya Palms Resort.** New owners are now breathing life into this dive resort, whose buildings have been modeled on the architecture of Maya sites. In the restaurant-pool area a giant pyramid is decorated with reproductions of stelae found at famous ruins; the top offers a spectacular view of the Caribbean. The rooms all have double beds and refrigerators. There's a dive shop on-site, as well as a temazcal to help you to work out the kinks after a day of scuba. ⊠ *Follow dirt road, Carretera Antigua a Xcalak, from Majahual about 10 km (6 mi) or turn off at checkpoint and follow paved coastal road, Carretera Nueva a Xcalak, 15 km (9 mi); at junction, turn left onto dirt road and drive about 2 km (less than 1 mi)* ☎ *983/831–0065, 888/843–3483 in the U.S.* ☏ *314/291–1938* ⊕ *www.mayapalms.com* ☜ *14 rooms* ♨ *Restaurant, refrigerators, pool, massage, dive shop, boating, bar, laundry service, Internet, airport shuttle; no room phones, no room TVs* ⊟ *AE, MC, V* ◯ *MAP, EP.*

★ $ ▦ **La Posada de los 40 Canones.** This beachfront resort, built in 2004, is without a doubt the nicest place to stay in Majahual. Outside, it sparkles with new paint and new construction; inside, the spacious rooms are decorated with bright colors, and handmade mahogany furniture. The bathrooms are roomy and bright with Mexican tiles surrounding the mirrors. There's a second-floor suite with a huge private terrace that's great for watching the sunrise or late-night stargazing. A spiffy little restaurant adjoins the front office. ⊠ *Av. Majahual s/n* ☎ *983/834–5692* ⊕ *www.los40canones.com* 🛏 *8 rooms, 2 suites* ⚖ *Restaurant, fans; no a/c in some rooms, no room phones, no room TVs* ▭ *MC, V.*

¢ ▦ **Cabañas de Tio Phil.** Solar energy and wind power drive things at this small complex, whose heart is the main building's big, inviting front porch. The rustic cabanas have thatched roofs, wooden floors, two beds each with mosquito netting, and tile bathrooms with wall murals and plenty of hot water. The staff is friendly; one of them might even offer to cook your catch of the day. The kitchen serves breakfast; its big oven is used to cook pizza in the evenings. ⊠ *Carretera Antigua a Xcalak, Km 2* ☎ *983/835–7166* ✉ *tiophilhome@hotmail.com* 🛏 *7 cabanas* ⚖ *Restaurant, snorkeling, fishing; no a/c, no room phones, no room TVs* ▭ *No credit cards.*

Xcalak

❷❸ *Carretera 307 to the Majahual exit south of Limones; turn left, go 56 km (35 mi) to the checkpoint, and turn south (left) onto highway for 60 km (37 mi).*

It's quite a journey to get to Xcalak (pronounced *ish*-ka-lack), but it's worth the effort. This national reserve is on the tip of a peninsula that divides Chetumal Bay from the Caribbean. Flowers, birds, and butterflies are abundant here, and the terrain is marked by savannas, marshes, streams, and lagoons dotted with islands. There are also fabulously deserted beaches. Visitor amenities are few; the hotels cater mostly to rugged types who come to bird-watch on Bird Island or to dive at Banco Chinchorro, a coral atoll and national park some two hours northeast by boat.

Where to Stay

$$ ▦ **Costa de Cocos.** Wind generates the electricity at this small collection of cabanas, 2 km (1 mi) north of Xcalak. Each unit has a double bed and a bathroom; a family unit has two bathrooms. Owners Dave and Ilana Randall are knowledgeable about the peninsula and the offshore reef, and they can help you plan fishing trips, sea-kayak outings, bird-watching excursions, or diving courses with PADI instructors. Rates include two delicious meals per day. Reserve well in advance for stays here. ⊠ *Xcalak Peninsula, follow Carretera 307 to sign for Majahual, turn right at paved coast road to Xcalak* ☎ *983/831–0110* ⊕ *www. costadecocos.com* 🛏 *14 cabanas* ⚖ *Restaurant, fans, beach, dive shop, dock, snorkeling, boating, Internet; no a/c, no room phones, no room TVs* ▭ *No credit cards* ❙⊙❙ *MAP.*

$$ ▦ **Playa Sonrisa.** This American-owned property has beachfront and garden-view cabanas, suites and rooms—all with wood furniture, tile floors,

and blue color schemes. You can snorkel off the dock, and the staff can arrange fishing and scuba diving trips. Breakfast is served overlooking the beach, where clothing is optional. ⊠ *Xcalak Peninsula, 54 km (33 mi) south of Majahual, 5 km (3 mi) north of Costa de Cocos* 🕾🕾 *983/ 838–1872* ⊕ *www.playasonrisa.com* 🔊 *2 rooms, 2 cabanas, 2 suites* ♨ *Restaurant, fans, some refrigerators, beach, dock, snorkeling; no a/c in some rooms, no room phones, no room TVs* ⊟ *MC, V* ⌁ *CP.*

★ **$$** 🏨 **Sin Duda.** Located on a beach that's both wild and lovely, these rooms have single or double beds, trundle beds, and plenty of closet space. You and other guests have access to a fully equipped kitchen as well as to a dining area and a balcony. For more privacy, opt for Studio 6, which is in a separate building, or Apartment 7 or 8, which have their own kitchens and living rooms. There's also an "adult tree house"—an upper-floor studio set among trees. All guest quarters are adorned with Mexican pottery and other collectibles. ⊠ *Xcalak Peninsula, 54 km (33 mi) south of Majahual, 15 km (9 mi) north of Costa de Cocos* 🕾🕾 *983/ 831–0006* ⊕ *www.sindudavillas.com* 🔊 *5 rooms, 1 studio, 2 apartments* ♨ *Some kitchens, beach, snorkeling, fishing; no a/c, no room phones, no room TVs* ⊟ *No credit cards* ⌁ *CP.*

Bacalar

㉔ *112 km (69 mi) south of Felipe Carrillo Puerto, 40 km (25 mi) north- west of Chetumal.*

Founded in AD 435, Bacalar (pronounced *baa*-ka-lar) is one of Quin- tana Roo's oldest settlements. **Fuerte de San Felipe** (San Felipe Fort) is an 18th-century stone fort built by the Spaniards using stones from the nearby Maya pyramids. It was constructed as a haven against pirates and marauding Indians, though during the War of the Castes it was a Maya stronghold. Today the monolithic structure, which overlooks the enormous Laguna de Bacalar, houses government offices and a museum with exhibits on local history (ask for someone to bring a key if mu- seum doors are locked). 🕾 *No phone* 🎫 *$2* 🕙 *Tues.–Sun. 10–6.*

Seawater and freshwater mix in the 56-km-long (35-mi-long) **Laguna de Bacalar,** intensifying the aquamarine hues that have earned it the nick- name of Lago de los Siete Colores (Lake of the Seven Colors). Drive along the lake's southern shores to enter the affluent section of the town of Bacalar, with elegant waterfront homes. Also in the vicinity are a few hotels and campgrounds.

★ Just beyond Bacalar is Mexico's largest sinkhole, **Cenote Azul,** 607 feet in diameter, with clear blue waters that afford unusual visibility even at 200 feet below the surface. With all its underwater caves, the cenote (open daily 8–8) attracts divers who specialize in this somewhat tricky type of dive. At **Restaurant Cenote Azul** you can linger over fresh fish and a beer while gazing out over the deep blue waters or enjoy a swim off its docks. A giant all-inclusive

> **WORD OF MOUTH**
>
> "If you are going to Bacalar, don't miss Cenote Azul. The drive down there is very, very difficult after a rain. Go in dry season only. WONDERFUL."   –jim

resort keeps threatening to open here; try to visit before the tranquillity disappears.

Where to Stay

★ $$$ 🏨 **Rancho Encantado.** On the shores of Laguna Bacalar, 30 minutes north of Chetumal, the enchanting Rancho consists of Maya-themed *casitas* (cottages). Each one has Oaxacan furnishings, a patio, a hammock, a refrigerator, a sitting area, and a bathroom. Breakfast and dinner are included in the room rate (no red meat is served). You can swim and snorkel off the private dock leading into the lagoon or tour the ruins in southern Yucatán, Campeche, and Belize. Pick a room close to the water or your nights will be marred by the sound of trucks zooming by. ✉ *Off Carretera 307 at Km 3 (look for turnoff sign)* ✆ *reservations: 470 East Riverside Dr., Truth or Consequences, NM 87901* ☎ *983/831– 0037 or 800/505–6292* 🖷 *505/894–7074* ⊕ *www.encantado.com* 🛏 *12 casitas, 1 laguna suite* ♻ *Restaurant, refrigerators, hot tub, massage, bar, travel services, fans; no a/c, no room phones, no room TVs* ▤ *AE, MC, V* ⊚ *MAP.*

¢–$$ 🏨 **Laguna.** This brightly colored, eclectic hotel outside Bacalar is reminiscent of a lakeside summer camp. The main building resembles a lodge; cabins are on a hill overlooking the water. The spartan rooms are simple, clean, and comfortable with no frills. A garden path leads down to a dock-restaurant area where you can swim or use the canoes. The place is well manicured and maintained by a friendly, knowledgeable staff. ✉ *Carretera 307, Km 40* ☎☎ *983/834–2206* ⊕ *www.mexcom.com* 🛏 *3 cabins, 29 rooms* ♻ *Restaurant, fans, pool, boating; no a/c in some rooms, no room phones, no room TVs* ▤ *No credit cards.*

Chetumal

❷⑤ *58 km (36 mi) south of Bacalar.*

Chetumal (pronounced *chet*-too-maal) is the final-stop town on the Costa Maya. Originally called Payo Obis, it was founded by the Mexican government in 1898 in a partially successful attempt to gain control of the lucrative trade of precious hardwoods, arms, and ammunition and as a military base against rebellious Indians. The city, which overlooks the Bay of Chetumal at the mouth of the Río Hondo, was devastated by a hurricane in 1955 and rebuilt as the capital of Quintana Roo and the state's major port. Though Chetumal remains the state capital, it attracts few visitors other than those en route to Central America or those traveling to the city on government business.

At times, Chetumal feels more Caribbean than Mexican; this isn't surprising, given its proximity to Belize. Many cultural events between the two countries are staged. Further, a population that includes Afro-Caribbean and Middle Eastern immigrants has resulted in a mix of music (reggae, salsa, calypso) and cuisines (Yucatecan, Mexican, and Lebanese). Although Chetumal's provisions are modest, the town has a number of parks on a waterfront that's as pleasant as it is long: the Bay of Chetumal surrounds the city on three sides. The downtown area has been spruced up, and mid-range hotels and visitor-friendly restaurants have popped up along Boulevard Bahía and on nearby Avenida Héroes. Tours are run to the fascinating nearby ruins of Kohunlich, Dzibanché, and Kinichná, a trio dubbed the "Valley of the Masks."

Paseo Bahía, Chetumal's main thoroughfare, runs along the water for several miles. A walkway runs parallel to this road and is a popular gathering spot at night. If you follow the road it turns into the Carretera Chetumal–Calderitas and, after 16 km (11 mi), leads to the small ruins of **Oxtankah**. Archaeologists believe this city's prosperity peaked between AD 300 and 600. It's open daily 8–5; admission is $3.

★ ☾ The **Museo de la Cultura Maya**, a sophisticated, interactive museum dedicated to the complex world of the Maya, is outstanding. Displays, which have explanations in Spanish and English, trace Maya architecture, social classes, politics, and customs. The most impressive display is the three-story Sacred Ceiba Tree. The Maya use this symbol to explain the relationship between the cosmos and the earth. The first floor represents the roots of the tree and the Maya underworld, called Xibalba. The middle floor is the tree trunk, known as Middle World, home to humans and all their trappings. The top floor is the leaves and branches and the 13 heavens of the cosmic otherworld. ⊠ *Av. Héroes and Calle Mahatma Gandhi* ☎ *983/832–6838* ⊕ *www.iqc.gob.mx* ⌑ *$5* ☾ *Tues.–Sun. 9–7.*

Where to Stay & Eat

★ **$–$$$** ✕ **Sergio's Restaurant & Pizzas.** Locals rave about this restaurant's grilled steaks, barbecued chicken (made with the owner's own sauce), and garlic shrimp, along with smoked-oyster and seafood pizzas. The restaurant has a bit of a fancy feel, and the staff is extra-gracious; when you order the delicious Caesar salad for two, a waiter prepares it at your table. ⊠ *Av. Alvaro Obregón 182, at Av. 5 de Mayo* ☎ *983/832–0882* ▭ *D, MC, V.*

¢–$ ✕ **Expresso Cafe.** At this bright, modern café, you can look out over the placid Bay of Chetumal while you enjoy fresh salads, sandwiches, and chicken dishes, and your choice of 15 kinds of coffee. ⊠ *Blvd. Bahía 12* ☎ *983/832–2654* ▭ *No credit cards.*

$$–$$$ ▦ **Los Cocos.** The jungle theme of this hotel's popular outdoor restaurant and lobby ends when you enter the rooms, which are modern and spacious, and painted in subdued pastels. Some have balconies or outside sitting areas. There's a pool in a large pleasant garden, the waterfront is within easy walking distance, and in 2004 a group of junior suites was added to the property. There are also villas available; they're decorated much like the junior suites, but on a larger scale. ⊠ *Av. Héroes 134, at Calle Chapultepec* ☎ *983/832–0544* 🖷 *983/832–0920* ⊕ *www. hotelloscocos.com* ⇌ *80 rooms, 43 junior suites, 14 villas* ⌕ *Restaurant, some refrigerators, some in-room safes, minibars, cable TV, bar, pool, Internet, shops, meeting rooms, car rental* ▭ *AE, D, MC, V.*

$$ ▦ **Holiday Inn Puerta Maya.** Though it's small, the staff at this hotel works extra-hard to make it feel luxurious. The clublike lobby has dark-green leather furniture and lots of plants. In the light-filled guest rooms wood accents complement soft sunset colors; each room has a small terrace that overlooks the pool, which is itself surrounded by a garden with Maya sculptures. The hotel's location, directly across from the Maya museum, is another perk. ⊠ *Av. Héroes 171* ☎ *983/835–0400* 🖷 *983/832–1676* ⊕ *www.holidayinn.com* 🏷 *85 rooms, 9 suites* ♧ *Restaurant, in-room safes, cable TV, pool, bar, travel services, free parking, no-smoking rooms* ▤ *MC, V.*

¢ 🏨 **Hotel Marlon.** This clean, comfortable hotel, done in pastel colors, is one of the best deals in town. There's plenty of cool air and lots of hot water. The pool is good, the restaurant is great, and the bar is small but sweet. The staff demonstrates what traditional Mexican hospitality is all about. ⊠ *Av. Juárez 87* ☎ *983/832–9411 or 983/832–9522* 🖷 *983/832–6555* ⊕ *www.hotelmarlon.com* 🏷 *50 rooms* ♧ *Restaurant, cable TV, pool, bar, car rental* ▤ *AE, MC, V.*

THE RÍO BEC ROUTE

The area known as the Río Bec Route enjoyed little attention for years until the last decade, when the Mexican government opened it up by building a highway, preserving previously excavated sites, and uncovering more ruins. Visiting this region might still make you feel like something of a pioneer, though; historical discoveries are still being made here, and conditions are decidedly rustic.

The Río Bec Route continues beyond Quintana Roo's Valley of the Masks into Campeche. Xpujil, the first major site in Campeche, is 115 km (71 mi) west of Chetumal. Hotels and restaurants in the area are scarce, so it's a good idea to make Chetumal your base for exploring.

RIÓ BEC PYRAMIDS

Río Bec refers to a particular architectural style that is predominant among Maya sites along this route. Although most pyramids in Quintana Roo are built in the Peten style—an import from Guatemala whose chief characteristics are sloped sides and twin upper chambers—Río Bec pyramids are steep and have narrow staircases that lead up to cone-shape tops. Temples built in this style often have doorways carved like open mouths and stone roof combs reminiscent of latticework.

Kohunlich

★ ⛰ ㉖ *42 km (26 mi) west of Chetumal on Carretera 186, 75 km (47 mi) east of Xpujil.*

Kohunlich (pronounced *ko*-hoon-lich) is renowned for the giant stucco masks on its principal pyramid, the **Edificio de los Mascarones** (Mask Building). It also has one of Quintana Roo's oldest ball courts and the remains of a great drainage system at the **Plaza de las Estelas** (Plaza of the Stelae). Masks that are about 6 feet tall are set vertically into the wide staircases at the main pyramid, called **Edificio de las Estelas** (Building of the Stelae). First thought to represent the Maya sun god, they are now considered to be composites of the rulers and important warriors of Kohunlich. Another giant mask was discovered in 2001 in the building's upper staircase.

In 1902 loggers came upon Kohunlich, which was built and occupied during the Classic period by various Maya groups. This explains the eclectic architecture, which includes the Peten and Río Bec styles. Although there are 14 buildings to visit, it's thought that there are at least 500 mounds on the site waiting to be excavated. Digs have turned up 29 individual and multiple burial sites inside a residence building called **Temple de Los Viente-Siete Escalones** (Temple of the Twenty-Seven Steps). This site doesn't have a great deal of tourist traffic, so it's surrounded by thriving flora and fauna. ☎ *No phone* 🎫 *$4* ⊙ *Daily 8–5.*

Where to Stay

$$$$ ⊡ **Explorean Kohunlich.** At the edge of the Kohunlich ceremonial grounds,
Fodor'sChoice   this ecological resort gives you the chance to have an adventure with-
★   out giving up life's comforts. Daily excursions include trips to nearby ruins, lagoons, and forests for bird-watching, mountain biking, kayaking, rock climbing, and hiking. You return in the evening to luxurious, Mexican-style suites filled with natural textiles and woods. All guest quarters are strung along a serpentine jungle path; they're very private and have showers that open onto small back gardens. The pool and outdoor hot tub have views of the distant ruins. ✉ *Carretera Chetumal–Escarega, Km 5.65 (same road as the ruins)* ☎ *55/5201–8350 in Mexico City, 877/397–5672 in U.S.* ⊕ *www.theexplorean.com* ⇗ *40 suites* ⚏ *Restaurant, fans, pool, outdoor hot tub, massage, sauna, boating, kayaking, bicycles, hiking, bar, meeting room; no room TVs, no kids* ⊟ *AE, DC, MC, V* ⟉ *AI.*

Dzibanché & Kinichná

🏔 **㉗** *1 km (½ mi) east of turnoff for Kohunlich on Carretera 186; follow signs for 24 km (15 mi) north to fork for Dzibanché (1½ km [1 mi] from fork) and Kinichná (3 km [2 mi] from fork).*

The alliance between the sister cities Dzibanché (place where they write on wood, pronounced zee-ban-*che*) and Kinichná (House of the Sun, pronounced kin-itch-*na*) was thought to have made them the most powerful cities in southern Quintana Roo during the Maya Classic period (AD 100–AD 1000). The fertile farmlands surrounding the ruins are still used today as they were hundreds of years ago, and the winding drive deep into the fields makes you feel as if you're coming upon something undiscovered.

Archaeologists have been making progress in excavating more and more ruins, albeit slowly. At **Dzibanché,** several carved wooden lintels have been discovered; the most perfectly preserved sample is in a supporting arch at the **Plaza de Xibalba** (Plaza of Xibalba). Also at the plaza is the **Templo del Búho** (Temple of the Owl), atop which a recessed tomb was found, the second discovery of its kind in Mexico (the first was at Palenque in Chiapas). In the tomb were magnificent clay vessels painted with white owls—messengers of the underworld gods. More buildings and three plazas have been restored as excavation continues. Several other plazas are surrounded by temples, palaces, and pyramids, all in the Peten style. The carved stone steps at **Edificio 13** and **Edificio 2** (Buildings 13 and 2) still bear traces of stone masks. A copy of the famed lintel of **Templo IV** (Temple IV), with eight glyphs dating from AD 618, is housed in the Museo de la Cultura Maya in Chetumal. (The original was replaced in 2003 because of deterioration.) Four more tombs were discovered at **Templo I** (Temple I). ☎ *No phone* 🎟 *$4* ☉ *Daily 8–5.*

After you see Dzibanché, make your way back to the fork in the road and head to **Kinichná**. At the fork, you'll see the restored **Complejo Lamai** (Lamai Complex), administrative buildings of Dzibanché. Kinichná consists of a two-level pyramidal mound split into Acropolis B and Acropolis C, apparently dedicated to the sun god. Two mounds at the foot of the pyramid suggest that the temple was a ceremonial site. Here a giant Olmec-style jade figure was found. At its summit, Kinichná affords one of the finest views of any archaeological site in the area. ☎ *No phone* 🎟 *$4* ☉ *Daily 8–5.*

CARIBBEAN COAST ESSENTIALS

Transportation

BY AIR

Almost everyone who arrives by air into this region flies into Cancún, at the Aeropuerto Internacional Cancún. Chetumal, however, has an airport, Aeropuerto de Chetumal, on its southwestern edge, along Avenida Alvaro Obregón where it turns into Carretera 186.

Mexicana Airlines flies from Mexico City to Chetumal five times a week. Aerosaab, a charter company with four- and five-seat Cessnas, flies from a small airstrip in Playa del Carmen to Chichén Itzá and Isla Holbox. The five-hour Chichén Itzá tours costs $260. The three- to four-hour Isla Holbox tours cost $285. Aerosaab can be chartered for flights throughout the Riviera Maya and Costa Maya.

🏬 **Aeropuerto de Chetumal** ☎ 983/832-3525. **Aeropuerto Internacional Cancún** ✉ Carretera Cancún–Puerto Morelos/Carretera 307, Km 9.5 ☎ 998/848-7241. **Aerosaab** ☎ 984/873-0804 🖷 984/873-0501 ⊕ www.aerosaab.com. **Mexicana Airlines** ☎ 800/531-7921 in U.S., 01800/502-2000 in Mexico ⊕ www.mexicana.com.mx.

BY BOAT & FERRY

Passenger-only ferries and speedboats depart from the dock at Playa del Carmen for the 45-minute trip to the main pier in Cozumel. They leave daily, approximately every hour on the hour between 6 AM and 11 PM, with no ferries at 7 AM or 2 PM. Return service to Playa runs every hour on the hour between 5 AM and 10 PM, with no ferries at 6 or 11 AM and 2 PM. Call ahead, as the schedule changes often.

🏬 **Passenger-only ferries** ☎ 984/879-3112 in Playa, 984/872-1588 in Cozumel.

BY BUS

The bus station in Chetumal (Avenida Salvador Novo 179) is served mainly by ADO—Autobuses del Oriente. Caribe Express also runs buses regularly from Chetumal to Villahermosa, Mexico City, Mérida, Campeche City, and Veracruz, as well as Guatemala and Belize.

Buses traveling to all points except Cancún stop at the terminal Avenida 20 and Calle 12. Buses headed to and from Cancún use the main bus terminal downtown (Avenida Juárez and Avenida 5). ADO runs express, first-class, and second-class buses to major destinations.

🚍 **ADO–Autobuses del Oriente** ☎ 983/832-5110. **Caribe Express** ☎ 983/832-7889.

BY CAR

The entire 382-km (237-mi) coast from Punta Sam near Cancún to the main border crossing to Belize at Chetumal is traversable on Carretera 307—a straight, paved highway. A few years ago, only a handful of gas stations serviced the entire state of Quintana Roo, but now—with the exception of the lonely stretch from Felipe Carrillo Puerto south to Chetumal—they are plentiful.

Good roads that run into Carretera 307 from the west are Carretera 180 (from Mérida and Valladolid), Carretera 295 (from Valladolid), Carretera 184 (from central Yucatán), and Carretera 186 (from Villahermosa and, via Carretera 261, from Mérida and Campeche). There's an entrance to the *autopista* toll highway between Cancún and Mérida off Carretera 307 just south of Cancún. Approximate driving times are as follows: Cancún to Felipe Carrillo Puerto, 4 hours; Cancún to Mérida, 4½ hours (3½ hours on the autopista toll road, $27); Puerto Felipe Carrillo to Chetumal, 2 hours; Puerto Felipe Carrillo to Mérida, about 4½ hours; Chetumal to Campeche, 6½ hours.

⚠ **Defensive driving is a must. Follow proper road etiquette—vehicles in front of you that have their left turn signal on are saying "pass me," not "I'm going to turn." Also, south of Tulum, keep an eye out for military and immigration checkpoints. Have your passport handy, be friendly and cooperative, and don't carry any items, such as firearms or drugs, that might land you in jail.**

CAR RENTAL Several major car rental companies service Cancún and have branch offices at the Cancún airport (*see the* Smart Travel Tips A to Z *section at the front of this book for details*). Renting a car from one of these airport branches will get you the cheapest rates. Most first-class hotels in Puerto Aventuras, Akumal, and Chetumal also rent cars. If you're planning to stay in Puerto Morelos, though, it's better to rent a car in Cancún, as there aren't many bargains in town. In Playa del Carmen, stick with the bigger rental agencies: Hertz, Budget, and Thrifty. If you want air-conditioning or an automatic transmission, reserve your car at least one day in advance. Always include a full insurance package with your rental.

BY TAXI

You can hire taxis in Cancún to go as far as Playa del Carmen, Tulum, or Akumal, but the price is steep unless you have many passengers. Fares run about $65 or more to Playa alone; between Playa and Tulum or Akumal, expect to pay at least another $25–$35. It's much cheaper from Playa to Cancún, with taxi fare running about $40; negotiate before you hop into the cab. Getting a taxi along Carretera 307 can take a while. Ask your hotel to call one for you. You can walk to just about everything in Playa. If you need to travel along the highway or farther north than Calle 20, a reliable taxi service is Sitios Taxis.

🚕 **Sitios Taxis** ✉ Playa del Carmen ☎ 984/873-0032.

Contacts & Resources

BANKS & EXCHANGE SERVICES

Banamex ✉ Av. Juárez between Avs. 20 and 25, Playa del Carmen ☎ 984/873-0825. **Bancomer** ✉ Av. Juárez between Calles 25 and 30, Playa del Carmen ☎ 984/873-0356 ✉ Av. Alvaro Obregón 222, at Av. Juárez, Chetumal ☎ 984/832-5300. **Bancrecer** ✉ Av. 5 by the bus station, Playa del Carmen ☎ 984/873-1561. **Bital** ✉ Av. Juárez between Avs. 10 and 15, Playa del Carmen ☎ 984/873-0272 ✉ Av. 30 between Avs. 4 and 6, Playa del Carmen ☎ 984/873-0238. **HSBC Bank** ✉ Avs. Tulum and Alfa, Tulum ☎ 984/877-3044. **Scotiabank Inverlat** ✉ Av. 5 between Avs. Juárez and 2, Playa del Carmen ☎ 984/873-1488.

EMERGENCIES

For general emergencies throughout the Caribbean Coast dial 060. In Puerto Morelos, there are two drugstores in town on either side of the gas station on Carretera 307. In Playa del Carmen, the Health Center (Centro de Salud) is right near two pharmacies—both of them are on Avenida Juárez between Avenidas 20 and 25.

Ambulance ✉ Playa del Carmen ☎ 984/873-0493. **Centro de Salud** ✉ Av. Juárez and Av. 15, Playa del Carmen ☎ 984/873-1230 Ext. 147 **Police** ✉ Av. Juárez between Avs. 15 and 20, Playa del Carmen ☎ 984/873-4000. **Red Cross** ✉ Av. Juárez and Av. 25, Playa del Carmen ☎ 984/873-1233.

MEDIA

Morgan's Tobacco Shop and Tequila Collection, both in Playa del Carmen, sell English-language magazines and newspapers, and Mundo Libreria-Bookstore has a good collection of English-language books. Look for **Sac-Be,** an English and Spanish language newspaper published every other month and available all up and down the coast in stores, restaurants and hotels. This 40-page freebie is full of facts, fun things to do, and best of all, there's a special feature titled Beach of the Month, that tells where the locals go for fun in the sun.

Morgan's Tobacco Shop ✉ Av. 5 and Calle 6, Playa del Carmen ☎ 984/873-2166. **Tequila Collection** ✉ Av. 5 between Calles 4 and 6, Playa del Carmen ☎ 984/873-0876. **Mundo Libreria-Bookstore** ✉ Calle 1 Sur No.189, between Avs. 20 and 25 Playa del Carmen ☎ 984/879-3004

INTERNET, MAIL & SHIPPING

Many of the more remote places on the Caribbean coast rely on e-mail and the Internet as their major forms of communication. In Playa del Carmen, Internet service is cheap and readily available. The best places charge $3 per half hour and include Cyberia Internet Café and Atomic Internet Café. In Puerto Morelos, Computer Tips is open 9 to 9 daily. In Tulum, the Weary Traveler, across from the bus station, and Savanas, next to the Chilam Balam Hotel, have complete business services, including Internet and fax.

The Playa del Carmen *correos* (post office) is open weekdays 8–7. If you need to ship packages or important letters, go through the shipping company Estafeta.

Cybercafés Atomic Internet Café ✉ Av. 5 and Calle 8, Playa del Carmen. **Computer Tips** ✉ Av. Javier Rojo Gomez, on the main Sq., Puerto Morelos ☎ 998/871-0155. Cyberia Internet Café ⊠ Calle 4 and Av. 15, Playa del Carmen. **Internet Club** ⊠ Av. Oriente 89, Tulum.

🖪 Mail & Shipping Correos ⊠ Av. Juárez, next to the police station, Playa del Carmen ☎ 983/873-0300. **Estafeta** ⊠ Calle 20, Playa del Carmen ☎ 984/873-1008. **Savanas** ⊠ Av. Tulum between Avs. Orion and Beta Sur, Tulum ☎ 984/871-2091. **Weary Traveler** ⊠ Av. Tulum, across from bus station Tulum ☎ 984/871-2386.

TOUR OPTIONS

You can visit the ruins of Cobá and the Maya villages of Pac-Chen and Chi Much—deep in the jungle—with Alltournative Expeditions. The group offers other ecotours as well. ATV Explorer offers two-hour rides through the jungle in all-terrain vehicles; you can explore caves, see ruins, and snorkel in a cenote. Tours start at $38.50. Based in Playa del Carmen, Tierra Maya Tours runs trips to the ruins of Chichén Itzá, Uxmal, and Palenque (between Chiapas and Tabasco). The company can also help you with transfers, tickets, and hotel reservations.

Puerto Costa Maya offers a wide variety of tours exclusively for their cruise clients, including catamaran sailing tours, Chinchorro Reef excursions, Maya ruin tours at Kohunlich and Chacchoben, and tropical safari jeep tours.

🖪 Alltournative Expeditions ⊠ Av. 10 No. 1, Plaza Antigua, Playa del Carmen ☎ 984/873-2036 ⊕ www.alltournative.com. **ATV Explorer** ⊠ Carretera 307, 1 km (½ mi) north of Xcaret ☎ 984/873-1626. **Maya Sites Travel Services** ☎ 719/256-5186 or 877/620-8715 ⊕ www.mayasites.com. **Tierra Maya Tours** ⊠ Av. 5 and Calle 6 ☎ 984/873-1385. **Puerto Costa Maya** ⊠ the dock at Majahual ⊕ www.puertocostamaya.com.

VISITOR INFORMATION

The tourist information booths in Chetumal are open weekdays 9–4. In Playa del Carmen the booth is open Monday–Saturday 8 AM–9 PM.
🖪 Chetumal tourist information booths ⊠ Calles Cinco de Mayo and Carmen Ochoa ☎ No phone ⊠ Calle 22 de Enero and Av. Reforma ☎ 983/832-6647. **Playa del Carmen tourist information booth** ⊠ Av. Juárez by the police station, between Calles 15 and 20 ☎ 984/873-2804 in Playa del Carmen, 888/955-7155 in the U.S., 604/990-6506 in Canada.

Mérida, Chichén Itzá & Yucatán State

Chac-Mool, Temple of the Warriors, Chichén Itzá

WORD OF MOUTH

"Chichén Itzá is amazing. My fiancé proposed at the top of a pyramid there, so I'm a little biased, but it truly is a great place to get a feel for the ancient cities. One note: hire an English-speaking guide. We had one, but I saw people just walking around, and there's no way they could have learned all the little things that make the place so interesting. It was a great experience!"

—nhawkservices

AROUND MÉRIDA, CHICHÉN ITZÁ & YUCATÁN STATE

Flamingos in Celestún

TOP 5
Reasons to Go

① **Visiting the spectacular Maya ruins** at Chichén Itzá, and climbing the literally breathtaking El Castillo pyramid.

② **Living like a wealthy** *hacendado* at a restored *henequen* (sisal) plantation-turned-hotel.

③ **Browsing at markets** throughout the region for handmade *hamacas* (hammocks), piñatas, and other locally made crafts.

④ **Swimming in the secluded, pristine freshwater cenotes** (sinkholes) scattered throughout the inland landscape.

⑤ **Dining out in one of Mérida's 50-odd restaurants,** and tasting the diverse flavors of Yucatecan food.

Progreso & the Northern Coast Outside the unpretentious town of Progreso, empty beaches stretch for miles in either direction—punctuated only by fishing villages, estuaries, and salt flats. Bird-watchers and nature lovers gravitate to rustic Celestún and Río Lagartos, home to one of the hemisphere's largest colonies of pink flamingos.

A *calesa* in Mérida

Mérida Fully urban, and bustling with foot and car traffic, Mérida was once the main stronghold of Spanish colonialism in the peninsula. Tucked among the restaurants, museums and markets are grand, old, beautifully ornamented mansions and buildings that recall the city's heyday as the wealthiest capital in Mexico.

Getting Oriented

Yucatán State's topography has more in common with Florida and Cuba—with which it was probably once connected—than with central Mexico. Exotic plants like wild ginger and spider lilies grow in the jungles; vast flamingo colonies nest at coastal estuaries. Human history is evident everywhere here—in looming Franciscan missions, thatch-roofed adobe huts, and majestic ruins of ancient Maya cities.

Uxmal

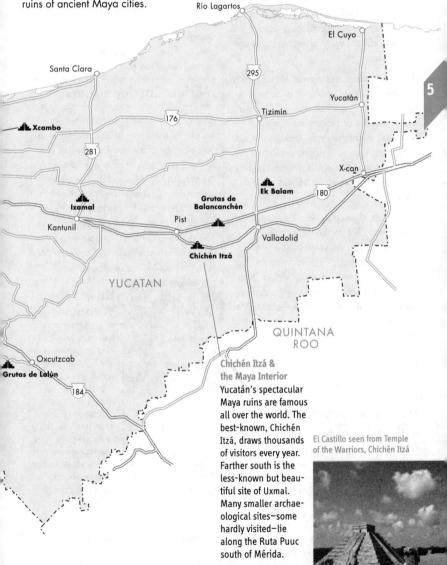

5

Chichén Itzá & the Maya Interior

Yucatán's spectacular Maya ruins are famous all over the world. The best-known, Chichén Itzá, draws thousands of visitors every year. Farther south is the less-known but beautiful site of Uxmal. Many smaller archaeological sites—some hardly visited—lie along the Ruta Puuc south of Mérida.

El Castillo seen from Temple of the Warriors, Chichén Itzá

MÉRIDA, CHICHÉN ITZÁ & YUCATÁN

When To Go

As with many other places in Mexico, the weeks around Christmas and Easter are peak times for visiting Yucatán state. Making reservations up to a year in advance is common.

If you like music and dance, Mérida hosts its *Otoño Cultural,* or Autumn Cultural Festival, during the last week of October and first week of November. During this two-week event, free and inexpensive classical-music concerts, dance performances, and art exhibits take place almost nightly at theaters and open-air venues around the city.

Thousands of people, from international sightseers to Maya shamans, swarm Chichén Itzá on the vernal equinox (the first day of spring). On this particular day, the sun creates a shadow that looks like a snake—meant to evoke the ancient Maya serpent god, Kukulcán—that moves slowly down the side of the main pyramid. If you're planning to witness it, make your travel arrangements many months in advance.

How Long To Stay

You should plan to spend at least five days in Yucatán. It's best to start your trip with a few days in Mérida; the weekends, when streets are closed to traffic and there are lots of free outdoor performances, are great times to visit. You should also budget enough time to day-trip to the sites of Chichén Itzá and Uxmal; visiting Mérida without traveling to at least one of these sites is like going to the beach and not getting out of the car.

Mérida Carriage Tours

One of the best ways to get a feel for the city of Mérida is to hire a *calesa*—a horse-drawn carriage. You can hail one of these at the main square or, during the day, at Palacio Cantón, site of the archaeology museum on Paseo de Montejo. Some of the horses look dispirited, but others are fairly well cared for. Drivers charge about $13 for an hour-long circuit around downtown and up Paseo de Montejo, and $22 for an extended tour.

How's the Weather?

Rainfall is heaviest in Yucatán between June and October, bringing with it an uncomfortable humidity. The coolest months are December–February, when it can get chilly in the evenings; April and May are usually the hottest. Afternoon showers are the norm June through September; hurricane season is late September through early November.

Dining & Lodging Prices

	$$$$	$$$	$$	$	¢
WHAT IT COSTS in Dollars					
Restaurants	over $25	$15–$25	$10–$15	$5–$10	under $5
Hotels	over $250	$150–$250	$75–$150	$50–$75	under $50

Restaurant prices are per person, for a main course at dinner, excluding tax and tip. Hotel prices are for a standard double room in high season, based on the European Plan (EP) and excluding service and 17% tax (15% Value Added Tax plus 2% hospitality tax).

CLOSE UP

Yucatán's History

FRANCISCO DE MONTEJO'S conquest of Yucatán took three gruesome wars over a total of 24 years. "Nowhere in all America was resistance to Spanish conquest more obstinate or more nearly successful," wrote the historian Henry Parkes. In fact the irresolute Maya, their ancestors long incorrectly portrayed by archaeologists as docile and peace-loving, provided the Spaniards and the mainland Mexicans with one of their greatest challenges. Rebellious pockets of Maya communities held out against the *dzulo'obs* (dzoo-loh-*obs*)—the upper class, or outsiders—as late as the 1920s and '30s.

If Yucatecans are proud of their heritage and culture, it's with good reason. Although in a state of decline when the conquistadores clanked into their world with iron swords and fire-belching cannons, the Maya were one of the world's greatest ancient cultures. As mathematicians and astromoners they were perhaps without equal among their contemporaries; their architecture in places like Uxmal was as graceful as that of the ancient Greeks.

To "facilitate" Catholic conversion among the conquered, the Spaniards superimposed Christian rituals on existing beliefs whenever possible, creating the ethnic Catholicism that's alive and well today. (Those defiant Maya who resisted the new ideology were burned at the stake, drowned, and hanged.) Having procured a huge workforce of free indigenous labor, Spanish agricultural estates prospered like mad. Mérida soon became a thriving administrative and military center, the gateway to Cuba and to Spain. By the 18th century, huge maize and cattle plantations were making the *hacendados* incredibly rich.

Insurrection came during the War of the Castes in the mid-1800s, when the enslaved indigenous people rose up with long-repressed furor and massacred thousands of non-Indians. The United States, Cuba, and Mexico City finally came to the aid of the ruling elite, and between 1846 and 1850 the Indian population of Yucatán was effectively halved. Those Maya who did not escape into the remote jungles of neighboring Quintana Roo or Chiapas or get sold into slavery in Cuba found themselves, if possible, worse off than before under the dictatorship of Porfirio Díaz.

The hopeless status of the indigenous people—both Yucatán natives and those kidnapped and lured with the promise of work from elsewhere in Mexico—changed little as the economic base segued from one industry to the next. After the thin limestone soil failed to produce fat cattle or impressive corn, entrepeneurs turned to dyewood and then to henequen (sisal), a natural fiber used to make rope. After the widespread acceptance of synthetic fibers, the entrepreneurs used the sweat of local labor to convert gum arabic from the peninsula's prevelant *zapote* tree into European vacations and Miami bank accounts. The fruits of their labor can be seen today in the imposing French-style mansions that stretch along Mérida's Paseo Montejo.

5

Exploring Yucatán State

Mérida is the hub of Yucatán and a good base for exploring the rest of the state. From there, highways radiate in every direction. To the east, Carreteras 180 *cuota* and 180 *libre* are, respectively, the toll and free roads to Cancún. The toll road (which costs about $25) has exits for the famous Chichén Itzá ruins and the low-key colonial city of Valladolid; the free road passes these and many smaller towns. Heading south from Mérida on Carretera 261 (Carretera 180 until the town of Umán), you come to Uxmal and the Ruta Puuc, a series of small ruins (most have at least one outstanding building) of relatively uniform style. Carretera 261 north from Mérida takes you to the port and beach resort of Progreso. To the west, the laid-back fishing village of Celestún—which borders on protected wetland—can be accessed by a separate highway from Mérida.

With the exception of the Mérida–Cancún toll highway, most roads in the state are narrow, paved, two-lane affairs that pass through small towns and villages. Rarely is traffic heavy on them, and they are in reasonably good shape, although potholes get worse as the rainy season progresses. The coastal highway between Progreso and Dzilám de Bravo was severely damaged in Hurricane Isidore in September 2002. The road itself has been repaired, although many of the small tourist-related ventures have yet to reinvent themselves.

Getting around the state is fairly easy, either by public bus or car. There are many bus lines, and most have several round-trip runs daily to the main archaeological sites and colonial cities. If you're visiting for the first time, a guided tour booked through one of the many Mérida tour operators provides a good introduction to the state. ■ TIP→→ **If you're independent and adventurous, hiring a rental car is a great way to explore Yucatán on your own. But be sure to check the lights and spare tire before taking off, carry plenty of bottled water, and fill up the gas tank whenever you see a station. It's also best not to drive at night.**

About the Restaurants

Dining out is a pleasure in Mérida. The city's 50-odd restaurants dish out a superb variety of cuisines—primarily Yucatecan, of course, but also Lebanese, Italian, French, Chinese, vegetarian, and Mexican—at very reasonable prices. Reservations are advised for $$$ restaurants, but only on weekends and in the high season. Beach towns north of Mérida, such as Progreso, Río Lagartos, and Celestún, tend to serve fresh-caught and simply prepared seafood.

Mexicans generally eat lunch at around 3, 4, or even 5 PM—and certainly not before 2. If you want to eat out at noon, call ahead to make sure the restaurant will be open. Casual but neat dress is acceptable at all Mérida restaurants. Avoid wearing shorts in the more expensive places, and anywhere at all—especially in the evening—if you don't want to look like a tourist. Local men and women don't wear shorts, period.

About the Hotels

Yucatán State has 7,000 hotel rooms—about a third of what Cancún has. Since in many cases, a hotel's façade won't reveal its true character, try to check out the interior before booking a room. In general the public spaces in Mérida's hotels are prettier than the sleeping rooms. Most hotels have air-conditioning, and even many budget hotels have installed it in at least some rooms—but it's best to ask.

■ TIP→→ Location is very important: if you plan to spend most of your time enjoying downtown Mérida, stay near the main square or along Calle 60. If you're a light sleeper, however, you may be better off staying in one of the high-rises along or near Paseo Montejo, about a 20-minute stroll (but an easy cab ride) from the main square. Pretty much all of the budget and inexpensive hotels are downtown. Inland towns such as Valladolid and Ticul are a good option if you're more interested in getting a slow-paced taste of the countryside.

There are several charming and comfortable hotels near the major archaeological sites Chichén Itzá and Uxmal, and a couple of foreign-run bed-and-breakfasts in Progreso, which previously had only desultory digs. Elsewhere, expect modest to very basic accommodation.

MÉRIDA

Travelers to Mérida are a loyal bunch, who return again and again to their favorite restaurants, neighborhoods, and museums. The hubbub of the city can seem frustrating—especially if you've just spent a peaceful few days on the coast or visiting Maya sites—but as the cultural and intellectual hub of the peninsula, Mérida is rich in art, history, and tradition.

Most streets in Mérida are numbered, not named, and most run one-way. North–south streets have even numbers, which descend from west to east; east–west streets have odd numbers, which ascend from north to south. Street addresses are confusing because they don't progress in even increments by blocks; for example, the 600s may occupy two or more blocks. A particular location is therefore usually identified by indicating the street number and the nearest cross street, as in "Calle 64 and Calle 61," or "Calle 64 between Calles 61 and 63," which is written "Calle 64 x 61 y 63." Although it looks confusing at first glance, this system is actually extremely helpful.

Zócalo & Surroundings

The *zócalo*, or main square, is in the oldest part of town—the Centro Histórico. Saturday nights and Sundays are special in downtown Mérida; this is when practically the entire population of the city gathers in the parks and plazas surrounding the zocalo to socialize and watch live entertainment. Cafés along this route are perfect places from which to watch the parade of people as

WORD OF MOUTH

"The best part of Mérida was just getting out and walking downtown and seeing what you can discover. We met some wonderful people, had great food, and found some really interesting and eclectic shops. All in all, a great little mini-vacation."   –CozAnnie

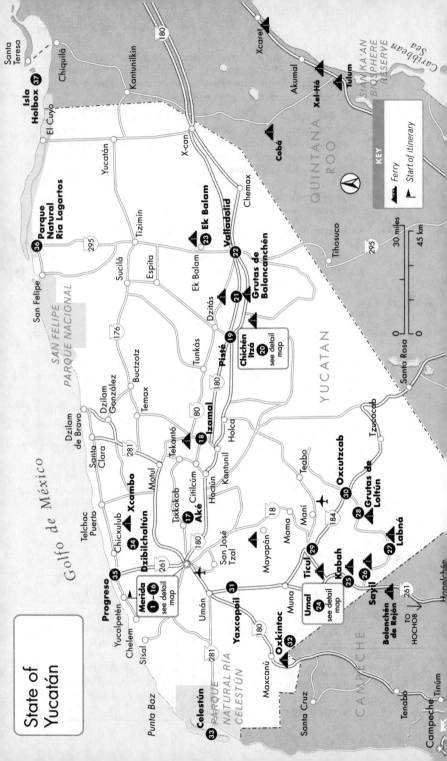

State of Yucatán

KEY

⬛ Ferry
▲ Start of itinerary

30 miles
45 km

Golfo de México

Caribbean Sea

QUINTANA ROO

YUCATAN

CAMPECHE

Santa Teresa

Isla Holbox **37**

Chiquilá

El Cuyo

Kantunilkin

Santa Rosa

Tihosuco

Xcaret

Akumal

Xel-Há **Xel-Há**

Tulum **Tulum**

SIAN KA'AN BIOSPHERE RESERVE

Cobá **Cobá**

X-can

Yucatán

Chemax

Valladolid **22**

Ek Balam **23**

Ek Balam

Grutas de Balancanchén **21**

Pisté **19**

Chichén Itzá **20** *see detail map*

Tizimín

Parque Natural Ría Lagartos **36**

San Felipe

SAN FELIPE PARQUE NACIONAL

295

Sucilá

Espita

Dzitós

Tunkás

180

Dzitás

295

Holca

Kaatunil

Hoctún

Citilcúm

Izamal **18**

80

Temax

Buctzotz

Dzilam González

Santa Clara

281

Dzilam de Bravo

Telchac Puerto

Chicxulub

Xcambo **Xcambo**

Dzibilchaltún **34**

Progreso **35**

Chelem

Sisal

Yucalpetén

Punta Baz

Motul

Tixkokob

Aké **17**

San José Tzal

Tekantó

176

Mérida **1–16** *see detail map*

261

180

Umán

Yaxcopoil **Yaxcopoil**

Oxkintoc **32**

Maxcanú

281

Santa Cruz

CAMPECHE

PARQUE NATURAL RÍA CELESTÚN

Celestún **33**

Chelem

Mayapán

Mama

Maní

Teabo

18

Muna

Umal **24** *see detail map*

Ticul **29**

Oxcutzcab **30**

Tzucacab

Grutas de Loltún **28**

Labná **27**

Sayil **26**

Kabah **25**

Bolonchén de Rejón

TO HOCHOB

261

Hopelchén

Tinúm

Tenabo

Campeche

184

Santa Rosa

0   0

well as folk dancers and singers. Calle 60 between Parque Santa Lucía and the main square gets especially lively; restaurants here set out tables in the streets, which quickly fill with patrons enjoying the free hip-hop, tango, salsa, or jazz performances.

A Good Walk

Start at the **zócalo** ❶ ⌐ : see the **Casa de Montejo** ❷ (now a Banamex bank), on the south side; the **Palacio Municipal** ❹ and the **Centro Cultural de Mérida Olimpo** ❸, on the west side; the **Palacio del Gobierno** ❺, on the northeast corner, and, catercorner, the **Catedral de San Ildefonso** ❻; and the **Museo de Arte Contemporáneo** ❼ on the east side. Step out on Calle 60 from the cathedral and walk north to **Parque Hidalgo** ❽ and the **Iglesia de la Tercera Orden de Jesús** ❾, which is across Calle 59. Continue north along Calle 60 for a short block to the **Teatro Peón Contreras** ❿, which lies on the east side of the street; the entrance to the **Universidad Autónoma de Yucatán** ⓫ is on the west side of Calle 60 at Calle 57. A block farther north on the west side of Calle 60 is the **Parque Santa Lucía** ⓬. From the park, walk north four blocks and turn right on Calle 47 for two blocks to **Paseo Montejo** ⓭. Once on this street, continue north for two long blocks to the **Palacio Cantón** ⓮. From here look either for a *calesa* (horse-drawn carriage) or cabs parked outside the museum to take you back past the zócalo to the **Mercado de Artesanías García Rejón** ⓯ and the **Mercado Municipal** ⓰—or walk if you're up to it.

What to See

❷ **Casa de Montejo.** This stately palace sits on the south side of the plaza, on Calle 63. Francisco de Montejo—father and son—conquered the peninsula and founded Mérida in 1542; they built their "casa" 10 years later. In the late 1970s, it was restored by banker Agustín Legorreta and converted to a bank. Built in the French style, it represents the city's finest—and oldest—example of colonial plateresque architecture, which typically has elaborate ornamentation. A bas-relief on the doorway—the facade is all that remains of the original house—depicts Francisco de Montejo the younger, his wife, and daughter as well as Spanish soldiers standing on the heads of the vanquished Maya. Even if you have no banking to do, step into the building weekdays between 9 and 5, Saturday 9 to 1, to glimpse the leafy inner patio.

❻ **Catedral de San Ildefonso.** Begun in 1561, St. Ildefonso is the oldest cathedral on the continent. It took several hundred Maya laborers, working with stones from the pyramids of the ravaged Maya city, 36 years to complete it. Designed in the somber Renaissance style by an architect who had worked on the Escorial in Madrid, its facade is stark and unadorned, with gunnery slits instead of windows, and faintly Moorish spires. Inside, the black Cristo de las Ampollas (Christ of the Blisters)—at 7 meters tall, perhaps the tallest Christ in Mexico—occupies a side chapel to the left of the main altar. The statue is a replica of the original, which was destroyed during the Revolution; this is also when the gold that typically decorated Mexican cathedrals was carried off. According to one of many legends, the Christ figure burned all night yet appeared the next morning unscathed—except that it was covered with the blisters for which it is named. You can hear the pipe organ play at 11 AM Sunday mass. ⊠ *Calles 60 and 61, Centro* ☎ *No phone* ⊙ *Daily 7–11:30 and 4:30–8.*

❸ Centro Cultural de Mérida Olimpo. Referred to as simply Olimpo, this is the best venue in town for free cultural events. The beautiful porticoed cultural center was built adjacent to City Hall in late 1999, occupying what used to be a parking lot. The marble interior is a showcase for top international art exhibits, classical-music concerts, conferences, and theater and dance performances. The adjoining 1950s-style movie house shows classic art films by directors like Buñuel, Fellini, and Kazan. There's also a planetarium with 90-minute shows explaining the solar system ($3; Tuesday–Saturday 10, noon, 5, and 7; Sunday 11 and noon), a bookstore, and a wonderful cybercafé-restaurant. ⊠ *Calle 62 between Calles 61 and 63, Centro* ☎ *999/942–0000* ☞ *Free* ⊙ *Tues.–Sun. 10–10.*

Ermita de Santa Isabel. At the southern end of the city stands the restored and beautiful Hermitage of St. Isabel. Built circa-1748 as part of a Jesuit monastery also known as the Hermitage of the Good Trip, it served as a resting place for colonial-era travelers heading to Campeche. One of the most peaceful places in the city, the chapel's gardens and interesting, inlaid-stone facade make it an interesting site to visit (although the church itself is almost always closed); this is perhaps a good destination for a ride in a calesa. Behind it, the huge and lush tropical garden, with its waterfall and footpaths, is usually unlocked during daylight hours. ⊠ *Calles 66 and 77, La Ermita* ☎ *No phone* ☞ *Free* ⊙ *Church open only during Mass.*

❾ Iglesia de la Tercera Orden de Jesús. Just north of Parque Hidalgo is one of Mérida's oldest buildings and the first Jesuit church in the Yucatán. It was built in 1618 from the limestone blocks of a dismantled Maya temple, and faint outlines of ancient carvings are still visible on the west wall. Although a favorite place for society weddings because of its antiquity, the church interior is not very ornate.

The former convent rooms in the rear of the building now host the **Pinoteca Juan Gamboa Guzmán,** a small but intereresting art collection. The most engaging pieces here are the striking bronze sculptures of indigenous Maya by celebrated 20th-century sculptor Enrique Gottdiener. On the second floor are about 20 forgettable oil paintings—mostly of past civic officials of the area. ⊠ *Calle 59 between Calles 58 and 60, Centro* ☎ *No phone* ☞ *$3* ⊙ *Tues.–Sat. 8–8, Sun. 8–2.*

⓯ Mercado de Artesanías García Rejón. Although many deal in the same wares, the shops or stalls of the García Rejón Crafts Market sell some quality items, and the shopping experience here can be less of a hassle than at the municipal market. You'll find reasonable prices on palm-fiber hats, hammocks, leather sandals, jewelry, and locally made liqueurs; persistent but polite bargaining may get you even better deals. ⊠ *Calles 60 and 65, Centro* ☎ *No phone* ⊙ *Weekdays 9–6, Sat. 9–4, Sun. 9–1.*

⓰ Mercado Municipal. Sellers of chilies, herbs, crafts, trinkets, and fruit fill this pungent and labyrinthine municipal market. In the early morning the first floor is jammed with housewives and restaurateurs shopping

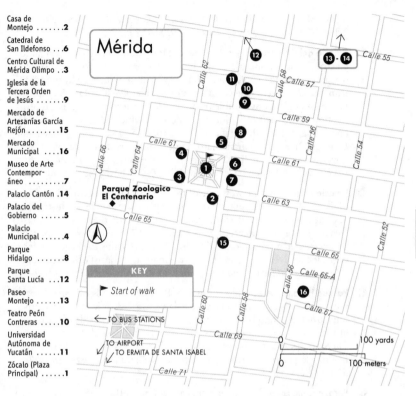

for the freshest seafood and produce. The stairs at Calles 56 and 57 lead
to the second-floor Bazar de Artesanías Municipales, on either side, where
you'll find local pottery, embroidered clothes, men's guayabera dress shirts,
hammocks, and straw bags. ⊠ *Calles 56 and 67, Centro* ☎ *No phone*
☉ *Mon.–Sat. dawn–dusk, Sun. 8–3.*

❼ Museo de Arte Contemporáneo. Originally designed as an art school and
used until 1915 as a seminary, this enormous, light-filled building now
showcases the works of contemporary Yucatecan artists such as Gabriel
Ramírez Aznar and Fernando García Ponce. ⊠ *Pasaje de la Revolución
1907, between Calles 58 and 60 on the main square, Centro* ☎ *999/
928–3236 or 999/928–3258* 🖼 *$2* ☉ *Wed.–Mon. 10–5:30.*

❶❹ Palacio Cantón. The most compelling of the mansions on **Paseo Montejo,** the stately palacio was built as the residence for a general between
1909 and 1911. Designed by Enrique Deserti, who also did the blue-
prints for the Teatro Peón Contreras, the building has a grandiose air
that seems more characteristic of a mausoleum than a home: there's marble everywhere, as well as Doric and Ionic columns and other Italianate
Beaux Arts flourishes. The building also houses the air-conditioned
Museo de Antropología e Historia, which gives a good introduction to
ancient Maya culture. Temporary exhibits sometimes brighten the stan-

dard collection. ⊠ *Paseo Montejo 485 at Calle 43, Paseo Montejo* ☎ *999/923–0469* 🖃 *$3* ⊙ *Tues.–Sat. 8–8, Sun. 8–2.*

❺ Palacio del Gobierno. Visit the seat of state government to see Fernando Castro Pacheco's murals of the bloody history of the conquest of the Yucatán, painted in bold colors in the 1970s and influenced by the Mexican mural painters José Clemente Orozco and David Alfaro Siquieros. On the main balcony (visible from outside on the plaza) stands a reproduction of the Bell of Dolores Hidalgo, on which Mexican independence rang out on the night of September 15, 1810, in the town of Dolores Hidalgo in Guanajuato. On the anniversary of the event, the governor rings the bell to commemorate the occasion. ⊠ *Calle 61 between Calles 60 and 62, Centro* ☎ *999/930–3101* 🖃 *Free* ⊙ *Daily 9–9.*

❹ Palacio Municipal. The west side of the main square is occupied by City Hall, a 17th-century building trimmed with white arcades, balustrades, and the national coat of arms. Originally erected on the ruins of the last surviving Maya structure, it was rebuilt in 1735 and then completely reconstructed along colonial lines in 1928. It remains the headquarters of the local government, and houses the municipal tourist office. ⊠ *Calle 62 between Calles 61 and 63, Centro* ☎ *999/928–2020* ⊙ *Daily 9–8.*

❽ Parque Hidalgo. A half block north of the main plaza is this small cozy park, officially known as Plaza Cepeda Peraza. Historic mansions, now reincarnated as hotels and sidewalk cafés, line the south side of the park; at night, the area comes alive with marimba bands and street vendors. On Sundays the streets are closed to vehicular traffic, and there's free live music performed throughout the day. ⊠ *Calle 60 between Calles 59 and 61, Centro.*

⓬ Parque Santa Lucía. The rather plain park at Calles 60 and 55 draws crowds with its Thursday-night music and dance performances (shows start at 9); on Sundays, couples also come to dance to a live band, and enjoy food from carts set up in the plaza. The small church opposite the park dates from 1575 and was built as a place of worship for the Maya, who weren't allowed to worship at just any Mérida temple.

☉ Parque Zoológico El Centenario. Mérida's greatest children's attraction, this large amusement complex features playgrounds, rides (including ponies and a small train), a roller-blading rink, snack bars, and cages with more than 300 native animals as well as exotics such as lions, tigers, and bears. It also has picnic areas, pleasant wooded paths, and a small lake where you can rent rowboats. The French Renaissance–style arch (1921) commemorates the 100th anniversary of Mexican independence. ⊠ *Av. Itzaes between Calles 59 and 65 (entrances on Calles 59 and 65), Centro* ☎ *No phone* 🖃 *Free* ⊙ *Zoo, daily 8–6.*

⓭ Paseo Montejo. North of downtown, this 10-block-long street was *the* place to reside in the late 19th century, when wealthy plantation owners sought to outdo each other with the opulence of their elegant mansions. Inside, the owners typically displayed imported Carrara marble and antiques, opting for the decorative styles popular in New Orleans, Cuba, and Paris rather than the style in Mexico City. (At the time there was more traffic by sea via the Gulf of Mexico and the Caribbean than there was overland across the lawless interior.) The broad boulevard, lined with tamarind and laurel trees, has lost much of its former panache; some of the once-stunning mansions have fallen into disrepair. Others, however, are being restored as part of a citywide, privately funded beautification program, and it's still a great place to wander, or to see by horse-drawn carriage.

⑩ Teatro Peón Contreras. This 1908 Italianate theater was built along the same lines as grand turn-of-the-20th-century European theaters and opera houses. In the early 1980s the marble staircase, dome, and frescoes were restored. Today, in addition to performing arts, the theater also houses the **Centro de Información Turística** (Tourist Information Center), which provides maps, brochures, and details about attractions in the city and state. The theater's most popular attraction, however, is the café/bar spilling out into the street facing Parque de la Madre. It's crowded every night with people enjoying the balladeers singing romantic and politically inspired songs. ⊠ *Calle 60 between Calles 57 and 59, Centro* ☎ *999/924–9290 Tourist Information Center* ☉ *Theater daily 7* AM–*1* AM; *Tourist Information Center daily 8* AM–*8* PM.

⑪ Universidad Autónoma de Yucatán. Pop in to the university's main building—which plays a major role in the city's cultural and intellectual life—to check the bulletin boards just inside the entrance for upcoming cultural events. The folkloric ballet performs on the patio of the main building most Fridays between 9 and 10 PM ($3). The Moorish-inspired building, which dates from 1711, has crenellated ramparts and arabesque archways. ⊠ *Calle 60 between Calles 57 and 59, Centro* ☎ *999/924–8000.*

▶ ❶ Zócalo. Meridians traditionally refer to this main square as the Plaza de la Independencia, or the Plaza Principal. Whichever name you prefer, it's a good spot from which to begin a tour of the city, to watch music or dance performances, or to chill in the shade of a laurel tree when the day gets too hot. The plaza was laid out in 1542 on the ruins of T'hó, the Maya city demolished to make way for Mérida, and is still the focal point around which the most important public buildings cluster. *Confidenciales* (S-shape benches) invite intimate tête-à-têtes; lampposts keep the park beautifully illuminated at night. ⊠ *Bordered by Calles 60, 62, 61, and 63, Centro.*

Where to Eat

$$–$$$ ✕ **Alberto's Continental Patio.** Though locals say this eatery has lost some of its star power, it's still a dependable place for good shish kebab, fried *kibi* (meatballs of ground beef, wheat germ, and spices), hummus, tabbouleh, and other Lebanese dishes. The strikingly handsome dining spot dates from 1727 and is adorned with some of the original stones from the Maya temple it replaced, as well as mosaic floors from Cuba. Even if you choose to have dinner elsewhere, stop in for almond pie and Turkish coffee on the romantic, candlelit courtyard. ⊠ *Calle 64 No. 482, at Calle 57, Centro* ☎ *999/928–5367* ▭ *AE, MC, V.*

★ **$–$$$** ✕ **Hacienda Teya.** This beautiful hacienda just outside the city serves some of the best regional food in the area. Most patrons are well-to-do Meridians enjoying a leisurely lunch, so you'll want to dress up a bit. Hours are noon–6 daily (though most Mexicans don't show up after 3), and a guitarist serenades the tables between 2 and 5 on weekends. After a fabulous lunch of *cochinita pibíl* (pork baked in banana leaves), you can stroll through the surrounding orchards and botanical gardens. If you find yourself wanting to stay longer, the hacienda also has six handsome suites for overnighters. ✉ *13 km (8 mi) east of Mérida on Carretera 180, Kanasín* ☎ *999/988–0800 (in Mérida)* ⌂ *Reservations essential* ▭ *AE, MC, V* ✆ *No dinner.*

★ **$–$$$** ✕ **Pancho's.** In the evenings, this patio restaurant (which frames a small, popular bar) is bathed in candlelight and the glow from tiny white lights decorating the tropical shrubs. Tasty tacos, fajitas, and other dishes will be pleasantly recognizable to those familiar with Mexican food served north of the border. Waiters—dressed in white muslin shirts and pants of the Revolution era—recommend the shrimp flambéed in tequila, and the tequila in general. Happy hour is 6 PM to 8 PM; afterwards there's live music on the tiny dance floor Wednesday–Saturday. ✉ *Calle 59 No. 509, between Calles 60 and 62, Centro* ☎ *999/923–0942* ▭ *AE, DC, MC, V* ✆ *No lunch.*

$$ ✕ **Santa Lucía.** Opera music floats above black-and-white tile floors in the dining room of this century-old restaurant near the main plaza. Pizzas and calzones are the linchpins of the Italian menu; luscious pecan pies, cakes, and cookies beckon from behind the glass dessert case. The original art on the walls, much of which was done by the late Rudolfo Morales of Oaxaca, is for sale. ✉ *Calle 60 No. 474A, Centro* ☎ *999/928–0704* ▭ *AE, MC, V.*

$–$$ ✕ **La Bella Epoca.** The coveted, tiny private balconies at this elegantly restored mansion overlook Parque Hidalgo. (You'll need to call in advance to reserve one for a 7 PM or 10 PM seating.) On weekends, when the street below is closed to traffic, it's especially pleasant to survey the park while feasting on Maya dishes like *sikil-pak* (a dip with ground pumpkin seeds, charbroiled tomatoes, and onions), or succulent *pollo pibíl* (chicken baked in banana leaves). ✉ *Calle 60 No. 497, between Calles 57 and 59, Centro* ☎ *999/928–1928* ▭ *AE, MC, V* ✆ *No lunch.*

$–$$
Fodor'sChoice
★
✕ **La Casa de Frida.** Chef-owner Gabriela Praget puts a healthful, cosmopolitan spin on Mexican and Yucatecan fare at her restaurant. Traditional dishes like duck in a dark, rich mole sauce (made with chocolate and chilies) share the menu with gourmet vegetarian cuisine: potato and cheese tacos, ratatouille in puff pastry, and crepes made with *cuitlachoche* (a delicious truffle-like corn fungus). The flavors here are so divine that diners have been known to hug Praget after finishing a meal. The dining room, which is open to the stars, is decorated with plants and self-portraits by Frida Kahlo. ✉ *Calle 61 No. 526 at Calle 66, Centro* ☎ *999/928–2311* ▭ *No credit cards* ✆ *Closed Sun. and Mon. No lunch.*

$–$$ ✕ **Nao de China.** If you're tired of tortillas, try heading to this bustling eatery for some authentic Chinese food. There are only a few vegetarian choices on the à la carte menu, but lots of chicken and shrimp dishes; the wontons and egg rolls are served hot and crispy. On weekends the

Yucatecan Cuisine

CLOSE UP

YUCATECAN FOOD IS SURPRISINGLY DIVERSE, and milder than you might expect. Anything that's too mild, however, can be spiced up in a jiffy with one of many varieties of chili sauce. The sour orange—large, green, and only slightly sour—is native to the region, and is also used to give many soups and sauces a unique flavor.

Typical snacks like *panuchos* (small, thick, fried rounds of cornmeal stuffed or topped with beans and sprinkled with shredded meat and cabbage), empanadas (turnovers of meat, fish, potatoes, or, occasionally, cheese or beans), and *salbutes* (fried tortillas smothered with diced turkey, pickled onion, and sliced avocado) are ubiquitous. You'll find them at lunch counters (*loncherías*), in the market, and on the menu of restaurants specializing in local food.

Some recipes made famous in certain Yucatecan towns have made their way to mainstream menus. *Huevos motuleños,* presumably a recipe from the town of Motul, are so yummy they're found on breakfast menus

throughout the region, and even elsewhere in Mexico. The recipe is similar to huevos rancheros (fried eggs on soft corn tortillas smothered in a mild red sauce) with the addition of sliced ham, melted cheese, and peas. Likewise, *pollo ticuleño*, which originated in Ticul, is served throughout the Yucatán. It's a tasty casserole of layered tomato sauce, mashed potatoes or cornmeal, crispy tortillas, chicken, cheese, and peas.

Tixin-Xic (pronounced teak-en-*sheek*) is fun to say and even better to eat. This coastal delicacy consists of butterflied snapper rubbed with salt and achiote (an aromatic paste made from the ground seeds of the annatto plant, and used to color food red as well as to subtly season it), grilled over a wood fire, and garnished with tomatoes and onions. As throughout Mexico, *aguas frescas*—fruit-flavored waters—are refreshing on a typically hot day, as are the dark beers Montejo and Leon Negro. Xtabentún is a sweet, thick, locally made liqueur made of anise and honey.

place is jammed, as it is Monday through Thursday during the 1–6 PM "executive special buffet," when a choice of three main dishes is offered along with unlimited egg rolls, rice, and other goodies, for less than $7. There's also an inexpensive, all-you-can-eat daily breakfast buffet between 7:30–11 AM. ⊠ *Calle 31 Circuito Colonias No. 113, between Calles 22 and 24, Col. México* ☎ *999/926–1441* ⊟ *AE, D, MC, V.*

$-$$ ✕ **El Pórtico del Peregrino.** Although still popular with travelers, the "Pilgrim's Porch," a Mérida institution for 30 years, has begun to rest heavily on its laurels. The setting is excellent, the location central, and the food good, if a little on the mild side, but the service has started to go downhill: waiters seem bored and sometimes downright unfriendly. In the antique-stuffed dining room and fern-draped interior patio, you can dine on traditional lime soup, *zarzuela de mariscos*—a casserole of squid, octopus, fish, and shrimp baked with white wine and garlic—or eggplant layered with marinara sauce, chicken, and grated cheese. ✉ *Calle 57 No. 501, between Calles 60 and 62, Centro* ☎ *999/928–6163* ▤ *AE, MC, V.*

$ ✗ **Los Almendros.** This large, two-salon Mérida institution, divided by a covered parking lot, provides a great introduction to Yucatecan cuisine. The English-language menu has pictures and descriptions of each dish. Especially good choices include the pork sausage; the cochinita pibíl and the *papadzules,* a concoction of tortillas, green sauce, ground pumpkin seeds, and hard-cooked eggs. The house sangria is tasty with or without alcohol. A musical trio plays romantic traditional ballads daily between 2 and 5. ✉ *Calle 50 No. 493, between Calles 57 and 59, La Mejorada* ☎ *999/928–5459* ✉ *Hotel Fiesta Americana, Av. Colón 451, at Prol. Montejo, Paseo Montejo* ☎ *999/942–1111* ▤ *AE, MC, V.*

$ ✗ **Café La Habana.** A gleaming wood bar, white-jacketed waiters, and the scent of cigarettes contribute to the European feel at this overwhelmingly popular café. Overhead, brass-studded ceiling fans swirl the air-conditioned air. Sixteen specialty coffees are offered (some spiked with spirits like Kahlúa or cognac), and the menu has light snacks as well as some entrées, including tamales, fajitas, and enchiladas. The waiters are friendly, and there are plenty of them, although service is not always brisk. Both the café and upstairs Internet joint are open 24 hours a day. ✉ *Calle 59 No. 511A, at Calle 62, Centro* ☎ *999/928–6502* ▤ *MC, V.*

$ ✗ **Ristorante & Pizzería Bologna.** You can dine alfresco or inside at this beautifully restored old mansion, a few blocks off Paseo Montejo. Tables have fresh flowers and cloth napkins; walls are adorned with pictures of Italy; and there are plants everywhere. Most menu items are ordered à la carte; among the favorites are the shrimp pizza and pizza *diabola,* topped with salami, tomato, and chilies. The beef fillet—served solo or covered in cheese or mushrooms—is served with baked potato and a medley of mixed sautéed vegetables. ✉ *Calle 21 No. 117A, near Calle 24, Col. Izimná* ☎ *999/926–2505* ▤ *AE, MC, V.*

$ ✗ **La Vía Olimpo.** Lingering over coffee and a book is a pleasure at this smart Internet café; the outdoor tables are a great place to watch the nonstop parade—or the free Sunday performances—on the main square. In the air-conditioned dining room, you can feast on *poc chuc* (slices of pork marinated in sour-orange juice and spices), turkey sandwiches, or burgers and fries. Crepes are also popular, and there are lots of salads and juices if you're in the mood for something lighter. Crowds keep this place hopping from 7 AM to 2 AM daily. Spirits are served, and you'll get an appetizer, like a basket of chips with freshly made guacamole, with most drink orders. ✉ *Calle 62 between Calles 63 and 61, Centro* ☎ *999/923–5843* ▤ *AE, MC, V.*

¢–$ ✗ **Alameda.** The waiters are brusque, the building is old, and the decor couldn't be plainer. But you'll find good, hearty, and cheap fare at this always-popular spot. The most expensive main dish here costs about $4—but side dishes are extra. Middle Eastern and standard Yucatecan fare share the menu with vegetarian specialties: meat-free dishes include tabbouleh and spongy, lemon-flavor spinach turnovers. Shopkeepers linger over grilled beef shish kebab, pita bread, and coffee; some old couples have been coming in once a week for decades. An English-language menu, which has explanations as well as translations, is essential even for Spanish speakers. Alameda closes at 5 PM. ⊠ *Calle 58 No. 474, near Calle 57, Centro* ☎ *999/928–3635* ⊟ *No credit cards* ⊘ *No dinner.*

¢–$ ✗ **Amaro.** The open patio of this historic home glows with candlelight in the evenings; during the day things look a lot more casual. Meat, fish, and shellfish are served here in moderation, but the emphasis is on vegetarian dishes like eggplant curry and chaya soup (made from a green plant similar to spinach), and healthful juices. If you're missing your favorite comfort foods, you can get your fix with a side-order of mashed potatoes or french fries. Live music is played Wednesday–Saturday evenings between 9 PM and midnight. ⊠ *Calle 59 No. 507, between Calles 60 and 62, Centro* ☎ *999/928–2451* ⊟ *MC, V.*

¢–$ ✗ **Dante's.** Couples, groups of students, and lots of families crowd this bustling coffeehouse on the second floor of one of Mérida's largest bookshops. The house specialty is crepes: there are 18 varieties with either sweet or savory fillings. Light entrées such as sandwiches, burgers, pizzas, and *molletes*—large open-faced rolls smeared with beans and cheese and then broiled—are also served, along with cappuccino, specialty coffees, beer, and wine. A small theater puts on evening comic sketches and live music from time to time, and free children's programs on Sunday mornings. ⊠ *Prolongación Paseo Montejo 138B, Paseo Montejo* ☎ *999/927–7441* ⊟ *No credit cards.*

¢–$ ✗ **Wayan'e.** Friendly owner Mauricio Loría presides over this oasis of carnivorous delights (mostly sandwiches) at the crossroads of several busy streets. In addition to ham and cheese and pork loin in smoky chipotle chili sauce, there are chorizo sausage, turkey strips sautéed with onions and peppers, and several delicious combos guaranteed to go straight to your arteries. Non-meat-eaters can try some unusual combos, like chopped cactus pads sautéed with mushrooms, or scrambled eggs with chaya or string beans. The storefront, which is almost always busy but still quick and efficient, closes at 3 PM on weekdays and 2 PM on Saturday. ⊠ *Calle 20 No. 92E, at Calle 15, Col. Itzimná* ☎ *999/938–0676* ⚠ *Reservations not accepted* ⊟ *No credit cards* ⊘ *Closed Sun. No dinner.*

Where to Stay

$$ ✗▦ **Villa María.** This spacious colonial home was converted to a hotel in 2004. Most rooms are airy and spacious, with second-loft bedrooms hovering near the 20-foot ceilings. But it's the large patio restaurant ($–$$) that really shines. Stone columns and lacy-looking Moorish arches frame the tables here, along with a lightly spraying central fountain; it's a lovely place to enjoy such European/Mediterranean fare as squash-blossom ravioli garnished with crispy spring potatoes, roast pork loin, or savory French onion soup. For dessert there's crème brûlée, ice cream, or warm apple–almond tart. Breakfast is fine, but less impressive than lunch or dinner. ⊠ *Calle 59 No. 553, at Calle 68, Centro* ☎ *999/923–3357* 🖷 *999/928–4098* ⊕ *www.hotelvillamariamerida.com* ⇆ *10 rooms, 2 suites* ⚒ *Restaurant, room service, fans, Internet, bar, meeting room, free parking* ⊟ *AE, MC, V.*

★ **$$$–$$$$**   Hacienda Xcanatun. The furnishings at this beautifully restored henequen hacienda include African and Indonesian antiques, locally made lamps, and oversize comfortable couches and chairs from Puebla. The rooms come with cozy sleigh beds, fine sheets, and fluffy comforters, and are impeccably decorated with art from Mexico, Cuzco, Peru, and other places the owners have traveled. Bathrooms are luxuriously large. Chef Alex Alcantara, trained in Lyon, France, and New York, produces "Yucatán fusion" dishes in the restaurant; the hacienda's spa cooks up innovative treatments such as cacao-and-honey massages. ⊠ *Carretera 261, Km 12, 8 mi north of Mérida* ☎ *999/941–0213 or 888/883–3633* ⊟ *999/941–0319* ⊕ *www.xcanatun.com* ⌂ *18 suites* ⚘ *Restaurant, room service, fans, some in-room hot tubs, minibars, 2 pools, spa, steam room, 2 bars, laundry service, meeting room, airport shuttle, free parking; no room TVs* ⊟ *AE, MC, V.*

> **WORD OF MOUTH**
>
> "The Hacienda Xcanatun is a wonderful place with a great restaurant and I cannot recommend it too highly! It's about 25 minutes by taxi from downtown and the fare is 100 pesos."
>
> –laverendrye

★ **$$**   Casa del Balam. This pleasant hotel has an excellent location two blocks from the zócalo in downtown's best shopping area. The rooms here include colonial touches, like carved cedar doors and rocking chairs on the wide verandas; but they also have such modern-day conveniences as double-pane windows to keep out the noise. The rich decor and thoughtful details, like the hand-painted plates, make this place seem more like a home than a hotel; the open central patio is a lovely spot for a meal or a drink. Guests have access to a golf and tennis club about 15 minutes away by car. ⊠ *Calle 60 No. 488, Centro* ☎ *999/924–8844 or 800/624–8451* ⊟ *999/924–5011* ⊕ *www.yucatanadventure.com.mx* ⌂ *44 rooms, 7 suites* ⚘ *Restaurant, room service, minibars, cable TV, golf privileges, pool, bar, free parking, no-smoking rooms* ⊟ *AE, D, DC, MC, V.*

> **WORD OF MOUTH**
>
> "The lobby of Casa del Balam is very atmospheric . . . in fact, the whole older part of the hotel is great, especially the balconies. Our room had plenty of nice touches, pretty tiles, handwoven bedspreads and drapes. All were a little worn, but still pleasant."
>
> –Michele

$$ Fiesta Americana Mérida. The facade of this posh hotel echoes the grandeur of the mansions on Paseo Montejo. The spacious lobby—with groupings of plush armchairs that guests actually use—is filled with colonial accents and gleaming marble; above is a 300-foot-high stained-glass roof. The tasteful and subdued guest rooms, which are inspired by late-19th-century design, have such extras as balconies, bathtubs, hair dryers, and coffeemakers. Downstairs are a department store, a Yucatecan restaurant, and myriad other shops and services. ⊠ *Av. Colón 451, Paseo Montejo* ☎ *999/942–1111 or 800/343–7821* ⊟ *999/942–1122* ⊕ *www.fiestaamericana.com* ⌂ *323 rooms, 27 suites* ⚘ *Restaurant, coffee shop, room service, minibars, cable TV with movies, in-room data* *ports, in-room safes, golf privileges, tennis court, pool, gym, massage, spa, steam room, bar, lounge, shops, babysitting, dry cleaning, laundry service, concierge, concierge floor, business services, car rental, travel services, free parking, no-smoking rooms* ▭ *AE, DC, MC, V.*

$$ 🏨 **Holiday Inn.** The most light-filled hotel in Mérida, the Holiday Inn has floor-to-ceiling windows throughout the colorful lobby and tiled dining room. Rooms and suites face an open courtyard and have comfy furnishings and marble bathrooms. Amenities include ironing boards, hair dryers, coffeemakers, alarm clocks, and more; be sure to ask about special rates, which can save you quite a bit. ⊠ *Av. Colón 468, at Calle 60, Paseo Montejo, 97000* ☎ *999/942–8800 or 800/465–4329* 🖷 *999/ 942–8811* ⊕ *www.basshotels.com* 🛏 *197 rooms, 15 suites* ♨ *Restaurant, café, room service, minibars, cable TV, tennis court, pool, bar, shop, babysitting, laundry service, concierge floor, Internet, business services, meeting rooms, airport shuttle, car rental, travel services, free parking, no-smoking rooms* ▭ *AE, D, DC, MC, V.*

★ **$$** 🏨 **Hyatt Regency Mérida.** The city's first deluxe hotel is still among its most elegant. Rooms are regally decorated, with russet-hue quilts and rugs set off by blond-wood furniture and cream-color walls. There is a top-notch business center, and a beautiful marble lobby. Upper-crust Meridians recommend Spasso Italian restaurant as a fine place to have a drink in the evening; for an amazing seafood extravaganza, don't miss the $20 seafood buffet at Peregrina bistro. ⊠ *Calle 60 No. 344, at Av. Colón, Paseo Montejo* ☎ *999/942–0202, 999/942–1234, or 800/233– 1234* 🖷 *999/925–7002* ⊕ *www.hyatt.com* 🛏 *296 rooms, 4 suites* ♨ *2 restaurants, patisserie, room service, minibars, cable TV with movies, in-room data ports, 2 tennis courts, pool, gym, hot tub, massage, steam room, 2 bars, shops, babysitting, laundry service, concierge, concierge floor, Internet, business services, convention center, car rental, travel services, free parking, no-smoking rooms* ▭ *AE, DC, MC, V* ▯◎ *EP, BP.*

★ **$$** 🏨 **Villa Mercedes.** More intimate than most of the hotels on Paseo Montejo, this converted Art Nouveau home is elegant yet welcoming. Common areas have gleaming marble floors, period furnishings, and sepia photos of old Mérida; guest rooms have wrought-iron beds, and each has a bidet and a tiny balcony. Buffet dinner is served on weekend nights out by the garden surrounding the swimming pool; the restaurant, dominated by Italian dishes, is formidably formal-looking. Extensive renovations in 2005 added 46 rooms on two executive floors, a ballroom, larger gym, and a state-of-the-art business center. ⊠ *Av. Colón 500, between Calles 60 and 62, Paseo Montejo* ☎ *999/942–9000* 🖷 *999/942–9001* ⊕ *www.hotelvillamercedes.com.mx* 🛏 *127 rooms, 3 suites* ♨ *Restaurant, room service, fans, some in-room data ports, some in-room hot tubs, in-room safes, minibars, cable TV, pool, exercise equipment, bar, laundry service, concierge, Internet, business services, meeting rooms, free parking, no-smoking floor* ▭ *AE, MC, V.*

¢–$$ 🏨 **Casa Mexilio.** Four blocks from the main square is this eclectic B&B. Middle Eastern wall hangings, French tapestries, and colorful tile floors crowd the public spaces; individually decorated rooms have tile sinks and folk-art furniture. Some find this inn private and romantic, although others may find it a bit too intimate for their liking. The grotto-like pool is surrounded by ferns, and the light-filled penthouse, up four dozen steps, has an excellent city view from its oversize balcony. A two-night minimum stay is required. ⊠ *Calle 68 No. 495, between Calles 57 and 59, Centro* ☎ *800/538–6802 in U.S. and Canada* 🖷 *999/928–2505* ⊕ *www.mexicoholiday.com* 🖙 *8 rooms, 1 penthouse* ☼ *Dining room, pool; no a/c in some rooms, no room phones, no room TVs* ▤ *MC, V* ⏐◉⏐ *CP.*

$ ⊡ **Maison LaFitte.** Jazz and tropical music float quietly above this hotel's two charming patios, where you can sip a drink near the fountain or swim in the small swimming pool. Rooms are simple here and the bathrooms a bit cramped, but the staff is friendly and the location, a few blocks from the central plaza and surrounded by shops and restaurants, is ideal. Thursday through Saturday evenings a trio entertains on the pretty outdoor patio. ⊠ *Calle 60 No. 472, between Calles 53 and 55, Centro, 97000* ☎ *999/923–9159* 🖷 *800/538–6802 in U.S. and Canada* ⊕ *www.maisonlafitte.com.mx* 🖙 *30 rooms* ☼ *Restaurant, café, room service, some fans, in-room safes, minibars, cable TV, pool, laundry service, Internet, travel services, free parking* ▤ *AE, MC, V* ⏐◉⏐ *BP.*

★ $ ⊡ **Marionetas.** Proprietors Daniel and Sofija Bosco, who are originally from Argentina and Macedonia, have created this lovely B&B on a quiet street seven blocks from the main plaza. From the Macedonian lace dust ruffles and fine cotton sheets and bedspreads to the quiet, remote-controlled air-conditioning and pressurized shower heads (there are no tubs), every detail and fixture here is of the highest quality. You'll need to book your reservation well in advance. ⊠ *Calle 49 No. 516, between Calles 62 and 64, Centro* 🖷 *999/ 928–3377 or 999/923–2790* ⊕ *www.hotelmarionetas.com* 🖙 *8 rooms* ☼ *Café, fans, Internet; no room TVs* ▤ *MC, V* ⏐◉⏐ *BP.*

> **WORD OF MOUTH**
>
> "Hotel Marionetas is wonderful! Daniel and Sofi are friendly, knowledgeable hosts who personally provide you with breakfast under an outdoor canopy every morning!"   –SerenaG

$ ⊡ **Medio Mundo.** A Lebanese-Uruguayan couple runs this hotel in a residential area downtown. The house has Mediterranean accents and spacious rooms off a long passageway. The original thick walls and tile floors are well preserved; rooms have custom-made hardwood furniture. A large patio in the back holds the breakfast nook, a small kidney-shaped swimming pool, and an old mango tree. There's also a pond with a delightful waterfall and fountain surrounded by fruit and flowering trees. ⊠ *Calle 55 No. 533, between Calles 64 and 66, Centro* 🖷 *999/924–5472* ⊕ *www.hotelmediomundo.com* 🖙 *12 rooms* ☼ *Dining room, fans, pool, laundry service, parking (fee); no a/c in some rooms, no room phones, no room TVs* ▤ *D, MC, V.*

$ ⊡ **Residencial.** A butter-yellow replica of a 19th-century French colonial mansion, the Residencial is a bit of a hike from the main plaza but right next to the Santiago church and public square, where a live big band attracts whirling couples on Tuesdays at 9 PM. Rooms have powerful showers, comfortable beds, remote-control cable TV, blow dryers, and spacious closets. The small swimming pool in the central courtyard is pleasant for reconnoitering, but far from private. ⊠ *Calle 59 No. 589, at Calle 76, Barrio Santiago* ☎ *999/924–3899 or 999/924–3099* 🖷 *999/ 924–0266* ⊕ *www.hotelresidencial.com.mx* 🖘 *64 rooms, 2 suites* ⬧ *Restaurant, room service, cable TV, pool, bar, meeting rooms, laundry service, free parking* ⊟ *MC, V.*

¢–$ 🏨 **Gran Hotel.** Cozily situated on Parque Hidalgo, this legendary 1901 hotel does look its age, with extremely high ceilings, wrought-iron balcony and stair rails, and ornately patterned tile floors. The period decor is so classic that you expect a mantilla-wearing Spanish señorita to appear, fluttering her fan, at any moment. The old-fashioned sitting room has formal seating areas and lots of antiques and plants. A renovation in 2004 enlarged some guest rooms and replaced tiny twin beds with doubles. Wide interior verandas on the second and third floors provide pretty outside seating. Porfirio Díaz stayed in one of the corner suites, which have small living and dining areas. ⊠ *Calle 60 No. 496, Centro* ☎ *999/923–6963* 🖷 *999/924–7622* 🖘 *25 rooms, 7 suites* ⬧ *Pizzeria, room service, fans, some in-room hot tubs, laundry service, free parking, some pets allowed* ⊟ *DC, MC, V.*

★ ¢ 🏨 **Dolores Alba.** The newer wing of this comfortable, cheerful hotel has spiffy rooms with quiet yet strong air-conditioning, comfortable beds, and many amenities; rooms in this section have large TVs, balconies, and telephones. Although even the older and cheaper rooms have air-conditioning, they also have fans, which newer rooms do not. The pool is surrounded by lounge chairs and shaded by giant trees, and there's a comfortable restaurant and bar at the front of the property. ⊠ *Calle 63 No. 464, between Calles 52 and 54, Centro, 97000* ☎🖷 *999/928– 5650* ⊕ *www.doloresalba.com* 🖘 *100 rooms* ⬧ *Restaurant, some fans, in-room safes, pool, Internet, bar, meeting room, travel services, free parking* ⊟ *No credit cards.*

¢ 🏨 **Hostal del Peregrino.** This recently restored old home is now part upscale hostel, part inexpensive hotel. Private rooms downstairs have few amenities but wonderfully restored *piso de pasta*—tile floors with intricate designs. Upstairs are shared co-ed dorm rooms with separate showers and toilets, and an open-air bar and TV lounge for hanging out in the evening with fellow guests. ⊠ *Calle 51 No. 488, between Calles 54 and 56, Centro* ☎ *999/924–5491* ⊕ *www.hostaldelperegrino.com* 🖘 *7 private rooms, 3 dorm rooms* ⬧ *Dining room, bar, bicycles* ⊟ *No credit cards* ⦿l *CP.*

Nightlife & the Arts

Mérida has an active and diverse cultural life, which features free government-sponsored music and dance performances many evenings, as well as sidewalk art shows in local parks. Thursday at 9 PM Meridians enjoy an evening of outdoor entertainment at the **Serenata Yucateca.** At Parque Santa Lucía (Calles 60 and 55), you'll see trios, the local orchestra, and soloists performing compositions by Yucatecan composers. On Saturday evenings after 7 PM, the **Noche Mexicana** (corner of Paseo Montejo and Calle 47) hosts different musical and cultural events; more free music, dance, comedy, and regional handicrafts can be found at the

Corazón de Mérida, on Calle 60 between the main plaza and Calle 55. Between 8 PM and 1 AM, multiple bandstands throughout this area, which is closed to traffic, entertain locals and visitors with an ever-changing playbill, from grunge to classical.

On Sunday, six blocks around the zócalo are closed off to traffic, and you can see performances—often mariachi and marimba bands or folkloric dancers—at Plaza Santa Lucía, Parque Hidalgo, and the main plaza. For a schedule of current performances, consult the tourist offices, the local newspapers, or the billboards and posters at the Teatro Peón Contreras or the Centro Cultural Olimpo.

Nightlife

BARS & AND DANCE CLUBS Meridians love to dance, but since they also have to work, many discos are open only on weekend nights, or Thursday through Sunday. ⚠ Be aware that it's becoming more and more common for discos geared toward young people to invite female customers onstage for some rather shocking "audience participation" acts. Since these are otherwise fine establishments, we can only suggest that you let your sense of outrage be your guide. Locals don't seem to mind.

If dancing to the likes of Los Panchos and other romanic trios of the 1940s is more your style, don't miss this Tuesday night ritual at **Parque de Santiago** (⊠ Calles 59 and 72, Centro ☎ No phone), where old folks and the occasional young lovers gather for dancing under the stars at 8:30 PM.

Popular with the local *niños fresa* (which translates as "strawberry children," meaning upper-class youths) as well as some middle-aged professionals, the indoor-outdoor lounge **El Cielo** (⊠Prol. Montejo between Calles 15 and 17 Col. México ☎ 999/944–5127) is one of the latest minimalist hot spots where you can drink and dance to party or lounge music videos. It's open Wednesday–Saturday nights after 9:30 PM. Their first-floor restaurant, Sky, opens at 1 (closed Monday) for sushi. Part bar, restaurant, and stage show, **Eladios** (⊠Calle 24 No. 100, at Calle 59, Col. Itzimná ☎ 999/927–2126), with its peaked palm-thatch room and ample dance floor, is a lively place often crammed with local families and couples. You get free appetizers with your suds (there's a full menu of Yucatecan food), which makes it a good afternoon pit stop, and there's live salsa, cumbia, and other Latino tunes between 2 and 6:30 PM. In the evening you can enjoy stage shows, or dance. **El Nuevo Tucho** (⊠ Calle 60 No. 482, between Calles 55 and 57, Centro ☎ 999/924–2323) has cheesy cabaret-style entertainment beginning at 4 PM, with no drink minimum and no cover. There's music for dancing in this cavernous—sometimes full, sometimes empty—venue. Drink orders come with free appetizers.

Mambo Café (⊠ Calle 21 between Calles 50 and 52, Plaza las Américas, Fracc. Miguel Hidalgo ☎ 999/987–7533) is the best place in town for dancing to DJ-spun salsa, merengue, cumbia, and disco tunes. You might want to hit the john during their raunchy audience-participation acts between sets. It's open from 9 PM Wednesday, Friday, and Saturday. **Pancho's** (⊠ Calle 59 No. 509, between Calles 60 and 62, Centro

☎ 999/923–0942), open daily 6 PM–2:30 AM, has a lively bar and a restaurant. It also has a small dance floor that attracts locals and visitors for a mix of live salsa and English-language pop music. Enormously popular and rightly so, the red-walled **Slavia** (⊠ Calle 29 No. 490, at Calle 58 ☎ 999/926–6587) is an exotic Middle Eastern beauty. There are all sorts of nooks where you can be alone yet together with upscale Meridians, most of whom simply call this "the Buddha Bar." Arabian music in the background, low lighting, beaded curtains, embroidered tablecloth, and sumptuous pillows and settees surrounding low tables produce a fabulous Arabian-nights vibe. It's open daily 7 PM–2 AM.

FodorsChoice
★

Tequila Rock (⊠ Prolongación Montejo at Av. Campestre ☎ 999/944–1828) is a disco where salsa, Mexican and American pop are played Wednesday through Saturday. It's popular mainly with those between 18 and 25. At dark, smoky, and intimate **La Trova** (⊠ Calles 60 and 57 at the Hotel Misión Mérida Centro ☎ 999/923–9500 Ext. 406 or 421), you can listen to sexy and romantic traditional ballads, performed by live trios between 9:30 PM and 2 AM. It's closed Sunday.

The Arts

FILM   **Cine Colón** (⊠ Av. Reforma 363A, Colón ☎ 999/925–4500) shows English action films with Spanish subtitles. Box-office hits are shown at **Cine Fantasio** (⊠ Calle 59 No. 492, at Calle 60, Centro ☎ 999/923–5431 or 999/925–4500), which has just one screen, but is the city's nicest theater. **Cine Hollywood** (⊠ Calle 50 Diagonal 460, Fracc. Gonzalo Guerrero ☎ 999/920–1089) is located within the popular Gran Plaza mall. International art films are shown most days at noon, 5, and 8 PM at **Teatro Mérida** (⊠ Calle 60 between Calles 59 and 61, Centro ☎ 999/924–7687 or 999/924–9990).

FOLKLORIC   Paseo Montejo hotels such as the Fiesta Americana, Hyatt Regency, and SHOWS   Holiday Inn stage dinner shows with folkloric dances; check with ★   concierges for schedules. The **Ballet Folklórico de Yucatán** (⊠ Calles 57 and 60, Centro ☎999/924–7260) presents a combination of music, dance, and theater every Friday at 9 PM at the university; tickets are $3. (Performances are every other Friday in the off-season, and there are no shows from August 1 to September 22 and the last two weeks of December.)

Sports & the Outdoors

Baseball

Baseball is played with enthusiasm between February and July at the **Centro Deportivo Kukulcán** (⊠ Calle 14 No. 17, Col. Granjas, across the street from the Pemex gas station and next to the Santa Clara brewery ☎ 999/940–0676). It's most common to buy your ticket at the on-site ticket booth the day of the game. A-league volleyball and basketball games and tennis tournaments are also held here.

Bullfights

Bullfights are held sporadically late November–February and around holidays at the **Plaza de Toros** (⊠ Av. Reforma near Calle 25, Col. García Ginerés ☎ 999/925–7996). Seats in the shade go for between $15 and

$30, depending on the fame of the bullfighter. You can buy tickets at the bullring or in advance at OXXO convenience stores. Check with the tourism office for the current schedule, or look for posters around town.

Golf

The 18-hole championship golf course at **Club de Golf de Yucatán** (✉ Carretera Mérida–Progreso, Km 14.5 ☎ 999/922–0053) is open to the public. It is about 16 km (10 mi) north of Mérida on the road to Progreso; greens fees are about $71, carts are an additional $32, and clubs can be rented. The pro shop is closed Monday.

Tennis

There are two cement public courts at **Estadio Salvador Alvarado** (✉ Calle 11 between Calles 23 and 60, Paseo Montejo ☎ 999/925–4856). Cost is $2 per hour during the day and $2.50 at night, when the courts are lighted. At the **Fiesta Americana Mérida** (✉ Av. Colón 451, Paseo Montejo ☎ 999/920–2194), guests have access to one unlit cement court. The one cement tennis court at **Holiday Inn** (✉ Av. Colón 498, at Calle 60, Colón ☎ 999/942–8800) is lighted at night. The **Hyatt Regency Mérida** (✉ Calle 60 No. 344, Colón ☎ 999/942–0202) has two lighted cement outdoor courts.

Shopping

Malls

Mérida has several shopping malls, but the largest and nicest, **Gran Plaza** (✉ Calle 50 Diagonal 460, Fracc. Gonzalo Guerrero ☎ 999/944–7657), has more than 90 shops and a multiplex theater. It's just outside town, on the highway to Progreso (called Carretera a Progreso beyond the Mérida city limits). **Plaza Américas** (✉ Calle 21 No. 331, Col. Miguel Hidalgo ☎ No phone) is a pleasant mall where you'll find the Cineopolis movie theater complex. Tiny **Pasaje Picheta** is conveniently located right on the north side of the town square. It has a bus ticket information booth and an upstairs art gallery, as well as souvenir shops and a food court.

Markets

The **Mercado Municipal** (✉ Calles 56 and 67, Centro) has lots of things you won't need, but which are fascinating to look at: songbirds in cane cages, mountains of mysterious fruits and vegetables, dippers made of hollow gourds (the same way they've been made here for a thousand years). There are also lots of crafts for sale, including hammocks, sturdy leather *huaraches,* and piñatas in every imaginable shape and color.
■ TIP→→ Guides often approach tourists near this market. They expect a tip and won't necessarily bring you to the best deals. You're better off visiting some specialty stores first to learn about the quality and types of hammocks, hats, and other crafts; then you'll have an idea of what you're buying—and what it's worth—if you want to bargain in the market. Another thing you should look out for around the market is pickpockets.

Sunday brings an array of wares into Mérida; starting at 9 AM, the Handicrafts Bazaar, or **Bazar de Artesanías** (✉ At the main square, Centro), sells lots of *huipiles* (traditional, white embroidered dresses) as well as hats and costume jewelry. As its name implies, popular art, or handicrafts, are sold at the **Bazar de Artes Populares** (⊠ Parque Santa Lucía, corner of Calles 60 and 55, Centro) beginning at 9 AM on Sunday. If you're interested in handicrafts, **Bazar García Rejón** (⊠ Calles 65 and 62, Centro) has rows of indoor stalls that sell items like leather goods, palm hats, and handmade guitars.

Specialty Stores

BOOKS ★ In addition to having a branch at all major shopping centers, **Librería Dante** (⊠ Calle 62 No. 502, at Calle 61, Parque Principal, Centro ☎ 999/928–2611 ⊠ Calle 17 No. 138B, at Prolongación Paseo Montejo, Col. Itzimná ☎ 999/927–7676) has several others downtown and on Paseo Montejo. The stores carry lots of art and travel books, with at least a small selection of English-language books. The Paseo Montejo store doubles as a popular creperie and coffeehouse (*see* Where to Eat).

CLOTHING You might not wear a guayabera to a business meeting as some men in Mexico do, but the shirts are cool, comfortable, and attractive; for a good selection, try **Camisería Canul** (⊠ Calle 62 No. 484, between Calles 57 and 59, Centro ☎ 999/923–0158). Custom shirts take a week to construct, in sizes 4, for the tiny gentleman in your life, to 52.

Guayaberas Jack (⊠ Calle 59 No. 507A, between Calles 60 and 62, Centro ☎ 999/928–6002) has an excellent selection of guayaberas (18 delicious colors to choose from!) and typical women's cotton *filipinas* (house dresses), blouses, dresses, classy straw handbags, and lovely rayon *rebozos* (shawls) from San Luis Potosí. These can be made to order, allegedly in less than a day, to fit anyone from a year-old to a 240-pound man. The shop has a sophisticated Web site, www.guayberasjack.com.mx, that allows online purchasing and browsing. **Mexicanísimo** (⊠ Calle 60 No. 496, at Parque Hidalgo, Centro ☎ 999/923–8132) sells sleek, clean-lined clothing made from natural fibers for both women and men.

LOCAL GOODS & CRAFTS Visit the government-run **Casa de las Artesanías Ki-Huic** (⊠ Calle 63 No. 503A, between Calles 64 and 66, Centro ☎ 999/928–6676) for folk art from throughout Yucatán. There's a showcase of hard-to-find traditional filigree jewelry in silver, gold, and gold-dipped versions. **Casa de los Artesanos** (⊠ Calle 62 No. 492, between Calles 59 and 61, Centro ☎ 999/923–4523), just half a block from the main plaza, sells mainly small ceramic pieces, including more modern, stylized takes on traditional designs. The **Casa de Cera** (⊠ Calle 74A No. 430E, between Calles 41 and 43, Centro ☎ 999/920–0219) is a small shop selling signed collectible indigenous beeswax figurines. Closed Sunday and afternoons after 3 PM.

A great place to purchase hammocks is **El Aguacate** (⊠ Calle 58 No. 604, at Calle 73, Centro ☎ 999/928–6429), a family-run outfit with many sizes and designs. Closed Sunday. **El Hamaquero** (⊠ Calle 58 No. 572, between Calles 69 and 71, Centro ☎ 999/923–2117) has knowledgeable personnel who let you try out the hammocks before you buy. Closed Sunday. **El Mayab** (⊠ Calle 58 No. 553-A, at Calle 71, Centro ☎ 999/924–0853) has a multitude of hammocks and is open on Sundays until 2 PM. **El Sombrero Popular** (⊠ Calle 65, between Calles 54 and 56, Centro ☎ 999/923–9501) has a good assortment of men's hats—

Hamacas: A Primer

CLOSE UP

YUCATECAN ARTISANS are known for creating some of the finest *hamacas*, or hammocks, in the country. For the most part, the shops of Mérida are the best places in Yucatán to buy these beautiful, practical items—although if you travel to some of the outlying small towns, like Tixkokob, Izamal, and Ek Balam, you may find cheaper prices—and enjoy the experience as well.

One of the first decisions you'll have to make when buying a hamaca is whether to choose one made from cotton or nylon; nylon dries more quickly and is therefore well-suited to humid climates, but cotton is softer and more comfortable (though its colors tend to fade faster). You'll also see that hamacas come in both double-threaded and single-threaded weaves; the double-threaded ones are sturdiest because they're more densely woven.

Hamacas come in a variety of sizes, too. A *sencillo* (cen-*see*-oh) hammock is meant for just one person (although most people find it's a rather tight fit); a *doble* (*doh*-blay), on the other hand, is very comfortable for one but crowded for two. *Matrimonial* or king-size hammocks accommodate two; and *familiares* or *matrimoniales especiales* can theoretically sleep an entire family. (Yucatecans tend to be smaller than Anglos are, and also lie diagonally in hammocks rather than end-to-end.)

For a good-quality king-size nylon or cotton hamaca, expect to pay about $35; sencillos go for about $22. Unless you're an expert, it's best to buy a hammock at a specialty shop, where you can climb in to try the size. The proprietors will also give you tips on washing, storing, and hanging your hammock. There are lots of hammock stores near Mérida's municipal market on Calle 58, between Calles 69 and 73.

---

especially *jipis,* better known as Panama hats, which cost between $12 and $65. The elder of this father-and-son team has been in the business for 40 years. Closed Sunday. You can get hammocks made to order—choose from standard nylon and cotton, super-soft processed sisal, Brazilian-style (six stringed), or crocheted—at **El Xiric** (⊠ Calle 57-A No. 15, Pasaje Congreso, Centro ☎ 999/924–9906). You can also get *Xtabentún*—a locally made liqueur flavored with anise and honey—as well as jewelry, black pottery, woven goods from Oaxaca, and T-shirts and souvenirs. **Miniaturas** (⊠ Calle 59 No. 507A, Centro ☎ 999/928–6503) sells a delightful and diverse assortment of different crafts, but specializes in miniatures. **Tequilería Ajua** (⊠ Calle 59 No. 506, at Calle 62, Centro ☎ 999/924–1453) sells tequila, brandy, and mezcal as well as Xtabentún and thick liqueurs made of local fruit.

JEWELRY Shop for malachite, turquoise, and other semiprecious stones set in silver at **Joyería Kema** (⊠ Calle 60 No. 502-B, between Calle 61 and 63, at the main plaza, Centro ☎ 999/923–5838). Beaders and other creative types flock to **Papagayo's Paradise** (⊠ Calle 62 No. 488, between Calles 57 and 59 Centro ☎ 999/993–0383), where you'll find loose beads and semiprecious stones, lovely necklaces and earrings, and Brussels-lace-trimmed, hand-embroidered, tatted, and crocheted blouses. This small but exceptional store also sells men's handkerchiefs and place mats. **Tane** (⊠Hyatt Regency, Calle 60 No. 344, at Av. Colón, Paseo Montejo ☎999/942–0202) is an outlet for exquisite (and expensive) silver earrings, necklaces, and bracelets, some incorporating ancient Maya designs.

CHICHÉN ITZÁ & THE MAYA INTERIOR

Although you can get to Chichén Itzá (120 km [74 mi] east of Mérida) along the shorter Carretera 180, there's a more scenic and interesting alternative. Head east on Carretera 281 through Tixkokob, a Maya community famous for its hammock weavers. Just 12 km (7 mi) from Tixkokob, on a signed road, the ruins of Aké can be visited briefly before returning to the highway and continuing through Citilcúm and Izamal; the latter is worthy of exploration, or at least a pit stop to see its amazing cathedral. From there, continue on through the small, untouristy towns of Dzudzal and Xanaba en route to Kantunil. There you can hop on the toll road or continue on the free road that parallels it through Holca and Libre Unión, both of which have very swimmable cenotes.

5

Aké

⑰ *35 km (22 mi) southeast of Mérida, 5 km (3 mi) southeast of Tixkokob.*

This compact archaeological site offers the unique opportunity to see architecture spanning two millennia in one sweeping vista. Standing atop a ruined Maya temple built more than a thousand years ago, you can see the incongruous nearby sight of workers processing sisal in a rusty-looking factory, which was built in the early 20th century. To the right of this dilapidated building are the ruins of the old Hacienda and Iglesia de San Lorenzo Aké, both constructed of stones taken from the Maya temples.

Experts estimate that Aké was populated between around 200 BC and AD 900; today many people in the area have Aké as a surname. The city seems to have been related to the very important and powerful one at present-day Izamal; in fact, the two cities were once connected by a sacbé (white road) 13 meters (43 feet) wide and 33 km (20 mi) long. All that's excavated so far are two pyramids, one with rows of columns (35 total) at the top, very reminiscent of the Toltec columns at Tula, north of Mexico City. ⊠ *$2.20* ⊙ *Daily 9–5.*

Izamal

⑱ *68 km (42 mi) southeast of Mérida.*

Although unsophisticated, Izamal is a charming and neighborly alternative to the sometimes frenetic tourism of Mérida. Hotels are humble, restaurants are few and offer basic fare. But for those who enjoy a quieter, slower-paced vacation, Izamal is worth considering as a base.

One of the best examples of a Spanish colonial town in the Yucatán, Izamal is nicknamed *Ciudad Amarillo* (Yellow City) because its most important buildings are painted a golden ocher color. It's also sometimes called "the city of three cultures," because of its combined pre-Hispanic, colonial, and contemporary influences. Calesas (horse-drawn carriages) are stationed at the town's large main square, fronting the lovely cathedral, day and night. The drivers charge about $5 an hour for sightseeing; many will also take you on a shopping tour for whichever items you're interested in buying (for instance, hammocks or jewelry). Pick up a brochure at the Visitor Center for details.

The drive to Izamal from Mérida takes less than an hour; take the Tixkokob road and follow the signs.

★ Facing the main plaza, the enormous 16th-century **Ex-Convento y Iglesia de San Antonio de Padua** (former monastery and church of St. Anthony of Padua) is perched on—and built from—the remains of a Maya pyramid devoted to Itzamná, god of the heavens. The monastery's ocher-painted church, where Pope John Paul II led prayers in 1993, has a gigantic atrium (supposedly second in size only to the Vatican's) facing a colonnaded facade and rows of 75 white-trimmed arches. The Virgin of the Immaculate Conception, to whom the church is dedicated, is the patron saint of the Yucatán. A statue of Nuestra Señora de Izamal, or Our Lady of Izamal, was brought here from Guatemala in 1562 by Bishop Diego de Landa. Miracles are ascribed to her, and a yearly pilgrimage takes place in her honor. Frescoes of saints at the front of the church, once plastered over, were rediscovered and refurbished in 1996.

The monastery and church are now illuminated in a light-and-sound show of the type usually shown at the archaeological sites. You can catch a Spanish-only narration and the play of lights on the nearly 500-year-old structure at 8:30 PM (buy tickets on-site at 8) Tuesday, Thursday, and Saturday.

Diagonally across from the massive cathedral, the small municipal market is worth a wander. It's a lot less frenetic than markets at major cities like Mérida. On the other side of the square, **Hecho a Mano** (⊠ Calle 31 No. 308, Centro ☎ 988/954–0344), run by an American couple, sells a nice collection of framed photographs and handicrafts.

Kinich Kakmó pyramid is all that remains of the royal Maya city that flourished here between AD 250 and 600. Dedicated to Zamná, Maya god of the dew, the enormous structure is the largest of its kind in the state, covering about 10 acres. More remarkable for its size than for any remaining decoration, it's nonetheless an impressive monument, and you can scale it from stairs on the south face for a view of the cathedral and the surrounding countryside.

Where to Stay & Eat

¢ ✕ **Los Mestizos.** This humble restaurant has brightly painted walls, and even the ceiling fans are painted a bright orange. The short menu includes regional fare such as *salbutes* and *panuchos*—both typical appetizers of fried cornmeal, the latter stuffed with beans—as well as chicken and turkey dishes. There's a bit of a view of the church beyond the marketplace from the outdoor terrace. ✉ *Calle 33 s/n, behind the market, Centro* ☏ *No phone* ▤ *No credit cards.*

¢ 🏨 **Green River Inn.** Individual block units are sprinkled around this landscaped property. Rooms have a dollhouse look and are decorated with lots of pinks, blues, and purples. Small TVs are mounted on the walls. Each ground-floor room has a whimsical-looking but clean bath, and a small terrace with a metal folding table and chairs. Things proceed slowly at this family-owned property; a swimming pool has been in the works for some time, and should be finished *mañana* (any day now). ✉ *Calle 39 No. 342, between Calles 38 and 40* ☏☏ *988/954–0337* ⌕ *18 rooms* ⌂ *Fans, minibars, cable TV, free parking; no room phones* ▤ *No credit cards.*

¢ 🏨 **Macanché.** Each freestanding guest room here has its own themed decor: the Asian room has a Chinese checkers board and origami decorations; the safari room has artifacts from Mexico and Africa. All have screened windows and are surrounded by exhuberant gardens of bamboo, bird of paradise, and bougainvillea. Some have skylights, or hammock chairs on a front porch. The restaurant offers salads and other health-conscious fare. ✉ *Calle 22 No. 305, between Calles 33 and 35* ☏ *988/954–0287* ⌕ *13 bungalows* ⌂ *Restaurant, fans, some refrigerators, pool, bar, billiards, bicycles, laundry service, free parking; no room phones, no room TVs, no a/c in some rooms* ▤ *No credit cards* ⎊ *BP.*

Pisté

⑲ *116 km (72 mi) southeast of Mérida.*

The town of Pisté serves as a base camp for travelers to Chichén Itzá. Hotels, campgrounds, restaurants, and handicrafts shops tend to be less expensive here than those at the ruins; they are strewn along the main street through town and impossible to miss.

Across from the Dolores Alba hotel is the **Parque Ik Kil** (place of the winds). A $6 entrance fee is required if you want to swim in the lovely cenote here, open daily between 8 AM and 6 PM. If you're going to eat in the adjacent restaurant, a sprawling place serving an international buffet ($10) to many bus tour groups, or sleep overnight, you don't need to pay the entrance fee. The site also has a swimming pool, lovely oval-shaped bungalows with private Jacuzzi tubs ($100 per night, no credit cards) inspired by Maya dwellings, and a few small stands selling souvenirs and crafts. ✉ *Carretera Mérida–Puerto Juárez, Km 122* ☏ *985/858–1525.*

Where to Stay

★ ¢ 🏨 **Dolores Alba.** The best low-budget choice near the ruins is this family-run hotel, a longtime favorite of international travelers. Spartan-ish rooms have hard beds and chunky, colonial-style furniture; but there are also two pools (one with palapas with hammocks), and a family-style restaurant where breakfast, lunch, and dinner are served. The convivial vibe, along with cheap prices, is the big draw here. Free transportation to Chichén Itzá is provided daily. ✉ *Carretera 180, Km 122, 3 km (2 mi) east of Chichén Itzá, 99751* ☏ *985/858–1555* ⊕ *www.*

Continued on page 222

The towering **El Castillo** pyramid, nearly 80 feet high, is the most striking structure at Chichén Itzá. Each side of the pyramid has 91 steps—which, with the addition of the topmost platform, equal 365, one for each day of the calendar year. At the vernal and autumnal equinoxes, thousands of people gather to watch as the shadow of the serpent god Kukulcán seems to slither down the side of the pyramid.

CHICHÉN ITZÁ

Carvings of ball players adorn the walls of the juego de pelota.

One of the most dramatically beautiful of the ancient Maya cities, Chichén Itzá draws some 3,000 visitors a day from all over the world. Since the remains of this once-thriving kingdom were discovered by Europeans in the mid-1800s, many of the travelers who make the pilgrimage here have been archaeologists and scholars, who study the structures and glyphs and try to piece together the mysteries surrounding them. While the artifacts here give fascinating insight into the Maya civilization, however, they also raise many, many unanswered questions.

The name of this ancient city, which means "the mouth of the well of the Itzás," is a mystery in itself. Although it likely refers to the valuable water sources at the site (there are several sinkholes here), and also to the Itzás, a group that occupied the city starting around the late 8th and early 9th centuries, experts have little information about who might have actually founded the city—some structures, which seem to have been built in the 5th century, pre-date the arrival of the Itzás. The reason why the Itzás eventually abandoned the city, around 1224, is also unknown.

Of course, most of the visitors that converge on Chichén Itzá come to marvel at its beauty, not ponder its significance. Even among laypeople, this ancient metropolis, which encompasses 6 square km (2½ square mi), is known around the world as one of the most stunning and well-preserved Maya sites in existence.

The sight of the immense ❶ **El Castillo** pyramid, rising imposingly yet gracefully from the surrounding plain, has been known to produce goose pimples on sight. El Castillo (The Castle) dominates the site both in size and in the sym-

CHICHÉN ITZÁ

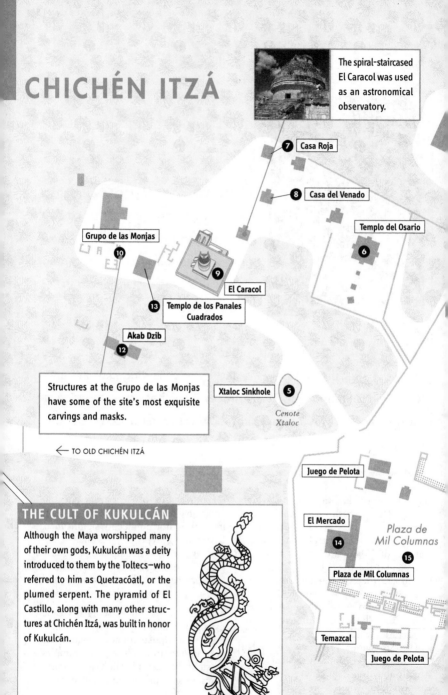

The spiral-staircased El Caracol was used as an astronomical observatory.

7 Casa Roja

8 Casa del Venado

Templo del Osario

6

Grupo de las Monjas

10

9 El Caracol

13 Templo de los Panales Cuadrados

Akab Dzib

12

Structures at the Grupo de las Monjas have some of the site's most exquisite carvings and masks.

Xtaloc Sinkhole **5**

Cenote Xtaloc

← TO OLD CHICHÉN ITZÁ

Juego de Pelota

THE CULT OF KUKULCÁN

Although the Maya worshipped many of their own gods, Kukulcán was a deity introduced to them by the Toltecs—who referred to him as Quetzacóatl, or the plumed serpent. The pyramid of El Castillo, along with many other structures at Chichén Itzá, was built in honor of Kukulcán.

El Mercado

14

Plaza de Mil Columnas

15

Plaza de Mil Columnas

Temazcal

Juego de Pelota

If you stand at one end of the juego de pelota and whisper something to a friend at the opposite end, incredibly, you will be heard.

Tourist Module

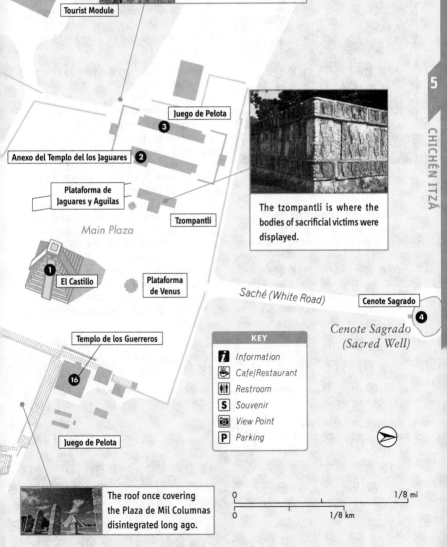

Juego de Pelota ③

Anexo del Templo del los Jaguares ②

Plataforma de Jaguares y Aguilas

Tzompantli

The tzompantli is where the bodies of sacrificial victims were displayed.

Main Plaza

El Castillo ①

Plataforma de Venus

Saché (White Road)

Cenote Sagrado ④

Cenote Sagrado (Sacred Well)

Templo de los Guerreros ⑯

KEY	
🛈	*Information*
☕	*Cafe/Restaurant*
🚻	*Restroom*
S	*Souvenir*
📷	*View Point*
P	*Parking*

Juego de Pelota

The roof once covering the Plaza de Mil Columnas disintegrated long ago.

0   1/8 mi

0   1/8 km

MAJOR SITES AND ATTRACTIONS

Rows of freestanding columns at the site have a strangely Greek look.

On the ❷ **Anexo del Templo de los Jaguares** (Annex to the Temple of the Jaguars), just west of El Castillo, bas-relief carvings represent more important deities. On the bottom of the columns is the rain god Tlaloc. It's no surprise that his tears represent rain—but why is the Toltec god Tlaloc honored here, instead of the Maya rain god, Chaac?

That's one of many questions that archaeologists and epigraphers have been trying to answer, ever since John Lloyd Stephens and Frederick Catherwood, the first English-speaking explorers to discover the site, first hacked their way through the surrounding forest in 1840. Scholars once thought that the symbols of foreign gods and differing architectural styles at Chichén Itzá proved it was conquered by the Toltecs of central Mexico. (As well as representations of Tlaloc, the site also has a *tzompantli*—a stone platform decorated with row upon row of sculpted human skulls, which is a distinctively Toltec-style structure.) Most experts now agree, however, that Chichén Itzá was only influenced—not conquered—by Toltec trading partners from the north.

metry of its perfect proportions. Open-jawed serpent statues adorn the corners of each of the pyramid's four stairways, honoring the legendary priest-king Kukulcán (also known as Quetzalcóatl), an incarnation of the feathered serpent god. More serpents appear at the top of the building as sculpted columns. At the spring and fall equinoxes, the afternoon light strikes the trapezoidal structure so that the shadow of the snake-god appears to undulate down the side of the pyramid to bless the fertile earth. Thousands of people travel to the site each year to see this phenomenon.

At the base of the temple on the north side, an interior staircase leads to two marvelous statues deep within: a stone jaguar, and the intermediate god Chacmool. As usual, Chacmool is in a reclining position, with a flat spot on the belly for receiving sacrifices.

Just west of the Anexo del Templo de los Jaguares is

The flat part of a reclining Chacmool statue is where sacrificial offerings were laid.

Although the rules of the game that were played on the ball court aren't known, it's thought that players had to pass some sort of ball through high stone loops.

The walls of the ball field are intricately carved.

another puzzle: the auditory marvel of Chichén Itzá's main ball court. At 490 feet, this ❸ **juego de pelota** is the largest in Mesoamerica. Yet if you stand at one end of the playing field and whisper something to a friend at the other end, incredibly, you will be heard. The game played on this ball court was apparently something like soccer (no hands were used), but it likely had some sort of ritualistic significance. Carvings on the low walls surrounding the field show a decapitation, blood spurting from the victim's neck to fertilize the earth. Whether this is a historical depiction (perhaps the losers or winners of the game were sacrificed?) or a symbolic scene, we can only guess.

On the other side of El Castillo, just before a small temple dedicated to the planet Venus, a ruined *sacbe,* or white road, leads to the ❹ **Cenote Sagrado** (Holy Well, or Sinkhole), also probably used for ritualistic purposes. Jacques Cousteau and his companions recovered about 80 skeletons from this deep, straight-sided, subsurface pond, as well as thousands of pieces of jewelry and figures of jade, obsidian, wood, bone, and turquoise. In direct alignment with this cloudy green cenote, on the other side of El Castillo, the ❺ **Xtaloc sinkhole** was kept pristine, undoubtedly for bathing

TIPS

To get more in-depth information about the ruins, hire a multilingual guide at the ticket booth. Guides charge about $35 for a group of up to 7 people. Tours generally last about two hours. 🖃 *$3.50* ⊙ Ruins daily 8–5, museum Tues.–Sun. 9–4.

and drinking. Adjacent to this water source is a steam bath, its interior lined with benches along the wall like those you'd see in any steam room today. Outside, a tiny pool was used for cooling down during the ritual.

The older Maya structures at Chichén Itzá are south and west of Cenote Xtaloc. Archaeologists have been restoring several buildings in this area, including the ❻ **Templo del Osario** (Ossuary Temple), which, as its name implies, concealed several tombs with skeletons and offerings. Behind the smaller ❼ **Casa Roja** (Red House) and ❽ **Casa del Venado** (House of the Deer) are the site's oldest structures, including ❾ **El Caracol** (The Snail), one of the few round buildings built by the Maya, with a spiral staircase within. Clearly built as a celestial observatory, it has eight tiny windows precisely aligned with the points of the compass rose. Scholars now know that Maya priests studied the planets and the stars; in fact, they were able to accurately predict the orbits of Venus and the moon, and the appearance of comets and eclipses. To modern astronomers, this is nothing short of amazing.

The Maya of Chichén Itzá were not just scholars, however. They were skilled artisans and architects as well. South of El Caracol, the ❿ **Grupo de las Monjas** (The

The doorway of the Anexo de las Monjas represents an entrance to the underworld.

Nunnery complex) has some of the site's most exquisite facades. A combination of Puuc and Chenes styles dominates here, with playful latticework, masks, and gargoylelike serpents. On the east side of the ⓫ **Anexo de las Monjas,** (Nunnery Annex), the Chenes facade celebrates the rain god Chaac. In typical style, the doorway represents an entrance into the underworld; figures of Chaac decorate the ornate facade above.

South of the Nunnery Complex is an area where field archaeologists are still excavating (fewer than a quarter of the structures at Chichén Itzá have been fully restored). If you have more than a superficial interest in the site—and can convince the authorities ahead of time of your importance, or at least your interest in archaeology—you can explore this area, which is generally not open to the public. Otherwise, head back toward El Castillo past the ruins of a housing compound called ⓬ **Akab Dzib** and the ⓭ **Templo de los Panales Cuadrados** (Temple of the Square Panels). The latter of these buildings shows more evidence of Toltec influence: instead of weight-bearing Maya arches—or "false arches"—that traditionally supported stone roofs, this structure has stone columns but no roof. This means that the building was once roofed, Toltec-style, with perishable materials (most likely palm thatch or wood) that have long since disintegrated.

Beyond El Caracol, Casa Roja, and El Osario, the right-hand path follows an ancient sacbé ("white road"), now collapsed. A mud-and-straw hut, which the Maya called a **na,** has been reproduced here to show the simple implements used before and after the Spanish conquest. On one side of the room are a typical pre-Hispanic table, seat, fire pit, and reed baskets; on the other, the Christian cross and colonial-style table of the post-conquest Maya.

Behind the tiny oval house, several un-excavated mounds still guard their secrets. The path meanders through a small grove of oak and slender bean trees to the building known today as ⓮ **El Mercado.** This market was likely one end of a huge outdoor market whose counterpart structure, on the other side of the grove, is the ⓯ **Plaza de Mil Columnas.** (Plaza of the Thousand Columns). In typical Toltec-Maya style, the roof once covering the parallel rows of round stone columns in this long arcade has disappeared, giving the place a strangely Greek—and distinctly non-Maya—look. But the curvy-nosed Chaacs on the corners of the adjacent ⓭ **Templo de los**

Guerreros are pure Maya. Why their noses are pointing down, like an upside-down "U, " instead of up, as usual, is just another mystery to be solved

The Templo de los Guerreros shows the influence of Toltec architecture.

5

CHICHÉN ITZÁ

WHERE TO STAY AT CHICHÉN ITZÁ

★ **$$$** ▥ **Mayaland.** This charming property is in a large garden, and close enough to the ruins to have its own entrance (you can even see some of the older structures from the windows). The large number of tour groups that come here, however, will make it less appealing if you're looking for privacy. Colonial-style guest rooms have decorative tiles; ask for one with a balcony, which doesn't cost extra. Bungalows have thatched roofs as well as wide verandas with hammocks. The simple Maya-inspired "huts" near the front of the property, built in the 1930s, are the cheapest option, but are for groups only. ✉ *Carretera 180, Km 120* ☎ *985/851–0100 or 800/235–4079* 🖷 *985/851–0128* 🖳 *985/851–0129* ⊕ *www.mayaland.com* 🛏 *60 bungalows, 30 rooms, 10 suites* ⚘ *4 restaurants, room service, fans, minibars, cable TV, tennis court, 3 pools, volleyball, 2 bars, shop, laundry service, free parking* ▭ *AE, D, MC, V.*

★ Fodor's Choice **$$–$$$** ▥ **Hacienda Chichén.** A converted 16th-century hacienda with its own entrance to the ruins, this hotel once served as the headquarters for the Carnegie expedition to Chichén Itzá. Rustic-chic, soap-scented cotes are simply but beautifully furnished in colonial Yucatecan style, with bedspreads and dehumidifiers; all of the ground-floor rooms have verandas, but only master suites have hammocks. There's a satellite TV in the library. An enormous (and deep) old pool graces the gardens. Meals are served on the patio overlooking the grounds, or in the air-conditioned restaurant. A big plus is the hotel's intimate size; it's a place for honeymoons and silver anniversaries, not tour groups. ✉ *Carretera 180, Km 120* ☎ *985/851–0045, 999/924–2150 reservations, 800/624–8451* 🖳 *999/924–5011* ⊕ *www.haciendachichen.com.mx* 🛏 *24 rooms, 4 suites* ⚘ *2 restaurants, fans, some minibars, pool, bar, laundry service, shop, free parking; no room phones, no room TVs* ▭ *AE, DC, MC, V.*

doloresalba.com ➡ *40 rooms* ☾ *Restaurant, fans, 2 pools, Internet, free parking; no room phones, no room TVs* 🖃 *MC, V* ⦿ *EP, MAP.*

Grutas de Balancanchén

🜲 ☾ ㉑ *6 km (4 mi) east of Chichén Itzá.*

How often do you get the chance to wander around below the earth? The caves translated as both "throne of the jaguar caves" or "caves of the hidden throne" are dank and sometimes slippery slopes to an amazing, rocky underworld. The caverns are lighted to best show off their lumpy limestone stalactites and niche-like side caves. It's a privilege also to view in situ vases, jars, and incense burners once used in sacred rituals, left right as they were. An arrangement of tiny *metates* (stone mortars for grinding corn) is particularly moving. At the end of the line is the underground cenote where Maya priests worshipped Chaac, the god of rain and water. Wear comfortable, nonslip walking shoes and be prepared to walk about one kilometer (round-trip). Also at the site is a sound-and-light show that recounts Maya history. The caves are just 6 km (4 mi) from Chichén Itzá; you can catch a bus or taxi or arrange a tour at the Mayaland hotel. Although there's a 6-person minimum, the ticket vendor will often allow even a pair of visitors to tour. 🖃 *$4.50 (including tour); sound-and-light show $5; parking $2 extra* ☉ *Daily 9–5; tours leave daily at 11, 1, and 3 (English); 9, noon, 2, and 4 (Spanish); and 10 (French).*

Valladolid

㉒ *44½ km (28 mi) east of Chichén Itzá.*

The second-largest city in Yucatán state, Valladolid (vay-ah-do-*lid*), is a picturesque provincial town that's been growing popular among travelers en route to or from Chichén Itzá (or Río Lagartos, to the north). Francisco de Montejo founded Valladolid in 1543 on the site of the Maya town of Sisal. The city suffered during the War of the Castes—when the Maya in revolt killed nearly all Spanish residents—and again during the Mexican Revolution.

Despite its turbulent history, Valladolid's downtown has many colonial and 19th-century structures. On Sunday evenings at 8 PM, the city's orchestra plays elegant, stylized *danzón*—waltz-like dance music to which unsmiling couples (think tango: no smiling allowed) swirl around the bandstand of the main square. On the west side of the plaza is the large **Iglesia de San Servacio,** which was pillaged during the War of the Castes.

★ Three long blocks away is the 16th-century, terra-cotta-colored **Ex-Convento y Iglesia San Bernadino,** a Franciscan church and former monastery. ■ TIP➜➜ If the priest is around, ask him to show you the 16th-century frescoes, protected behind curtains near the altarpiece. The lack of proportion in the human figures shows the initial clumsiness of indigenous artisans in reproducing the Christian saints.

CLOSE UP

Sacred Cenotes

TO THE ANCIENT (and tradition-bound modern) Maya, holes in the ground—be they sinkholes (*cenotes*) or caves—are considered conduits to the world of the spirits. A source of water in a land of no surface rivers, sinkholes are of special importance. The domain of Chaac, god of rain and water, cenotes like Balancanchén, near Chichén Itzá, were used as prayer sites and shrines. Sacred objects and sacrificial victims were thrown in the sacred cenote at Chichén Itzá, and in others near large ceremonial centers in ancient times.

There are at least 2,800 known cenotes in the Yucatán. Rainwater sinks through the peninsula's thin soil and porous limestone to create underground rivers, while leaving the dry surface river-free.

Some pondlike sinkholes are found near ground level; most require a bit more effort to access, however. Near

downtown Valladolid, Cenote Zací is named for the Maya town conquered by the Spanish. It's a relatively simple saunter down a series of cement steps to reach the cool green water.

Lesser-known sinkholes are yours to discover, especially in the area labeled "zona de cenotes." To explore this area southeast of Mérida, you can hire a guide through the tourism office. Another option is to head directly for the ex-hacienda of Chunkanan, outside the village of the same name, about 30 minutes southeast of Mérida. There, former henequen workers will hitch their horses to tiny open railway carts to take you along the unused train tracks. The reward for this bumpy, sometimes dusty ride is a swim in several incredible cenotes.

Almost every local has a "secret" cenote; ask around, and perhaps you'll find a favorite of your own.

A large, round, and beautiful sinkhole at the edge of town, **Cenote Zací** (⌂ Calles 36 and 37 ☎ 985/856–2107), is sometimes crowded with tourists and local boys clowning it up; at other times, it's deserted. Leaves from the tall old trees surrounding the sinkhole float on the surface, but the water itself is quite clean. If you're not up for a dip, visit the adjacent handicraft shop or have a bite or a drink at the well-loved, thatch-roofed restaurant overlooking the water. Five kilometers (3 mi) west of the main square and on the old highway to Chichén Itzá, you can swim ★ ☾ with the catfish in lovely, mysterious **Cenote X-Keken** (popularly called Cenote Dzitnup), which is in a cave lit by a small natural skylight; admission is $3.

Valladolid is renowned for its **longaniza en escabeche**—a sausage dish, served in many of the restaurants facing the central square. In the shops and market you can also find good buys on sandals, baskets, and Xtabentún liqueur.

Where to Stay & Eat

¢–$ ✕🏨 **El Mesón del Marqués.** On the north side of the main square, this well-preserved, very old hacienda house was built around a lovely, colonnaded, open patio. The rooms are less impressive, although comfortable; numbers 407, 408, and 409 are the newest, and have views of the cathedral. The charming restaurant ($–$$), in a courtyard with an old stone fountain and surrounded by porticoes, serves Yucatecan specialties. Again, the ambience is more impressive than the food itself, although the soups are pretty good. ✉ *Calle 39 No. 203* ☎ *985/856–2073 or 985/856–3042* 🖷 *985/856–2280* ⊕ *www.mesondelmarques.com* 🛏 *88 rooms, 2 suites* ♿ *Restaurant, room service, fans, cable TV, pool, bar, Internet, laundry service, free parking* ⦿ *EP, CP* ▤ *AE.*

¢ ✕🏨 **Ecotel Quinta Real.** This salmon-colored hotel is a mix of colonial and modern Mexico. Each whitewashed room is accented with one brightly colored wall; wrought-iron ceiling and wall fixtures; and substantial, hand-carved furniture. Junior suites each have a balcony (overlooking the parking area), a wet bar and living/dining area, king bed, and spa bath. Of the standard rooms, the nicest have terraces overlooking the orchard. There's a game room, arboretum with local flora, and an uninspiring, fenced-in area for ducks. You can borrow racquets and and tennis balls to use on the recently resurfaced cement court. The main restaurant ($–$$) has a substantial menu ranging from nachos and pizza to filet mignon and lobster. ✉ *Calle 40 No. 160A, at Calle 27* ☎🖷 *985/856–6372* 🖷 *985/856–3479* 🛏 *106 rooms, 8 suites* ♿ *2 restaurants, room service, some in-room hot tubs, some minibars, cable TV, tennis court, pool, billiards, Ping-Pong, bar, laundry service, meeting room, free parking* ▤ *AE, MC, V.*

¢ 🏨 **María de la Luz.** A worn but still somehow engaging budget hotel, Mary of the Light is conveniently situated on the main plaza. Motel-style buildings are centered around a swimming pool, where there are banana trees and tables for drinking or dining. The plain rooms are nothing to write home about, but consistently attract a diverse and bohemian clientele. The restaurant, where guests tend to gather, serves predictable but tasty Mexican dishes; pollo pibíl is a house specialty. You may be tempted to upgrade to the hotel's single suite—but it has the same uneventful decor, with a whirlpool tub and more beds of various sizes jammed in. ✉ *Calle 42 No. 193C* ☎🖷 *985/856–2071 or 985/856–1181* ⊕ *www.mariadelaluz.com.mx* 🛏 *68 rooms, 1 suite* ♿ *Restaurant, cable TV, pool, bar, free parking* ▤ *MC, V.*

Ek Balam

★ 🏔 ❷❸ *30 km (18 mi) north of Valladolid, off Carretera 295.*

What's most stunning about the Ek Balam ("black jaguar") site are the elaborately carved and amazingly well-preserved stucco panels of one of the temples, **Templo de los Frisos.** A giant monster mask crowns its summit, and its friezes contain wonderful carvings of figures often referred to as "angels" (because of their wings)—but which more likely represented nobles in ceremonial dress.

As is common with ancient Maya structures, this Chenes-style temple is superimposed upon earlier ones. The temple was a mausoleum for ruler Ukit Kan Lek Tok, who was buried with priceless funerary objects, including pearls, countless perforated seashells, jade, mother-of-pearl pendants, and small bone masks with moveable jaws. At the bases at either end, the name of the leader is inscribed on the forked tongue of a carved serpent, which obviously hadn't the negative Bibical connotation ascribed to the snake in Western culture today. A contemporary of Uxmal and Cobá, the city may have been a satellite city to Chichén Itzá, which rose to power as Ek Balam waned.

Another unusual feature of Ek Balam are the two concentric walls—a rare configuration in Maya sites—that surround the 45 structures in the main part of the site. They may have provided defense, or perhaps they symbolized more than provided safety for the ruling elite that lived within.

Ek Balam also has a ball court and quite a few free-standing stelae (stone pillars carved with glyphs or images for commemorative purposes). New-Age groups sometimes converge on the site for prayers and seminars, but it's usually quite sparsely visited, which adds to the mystery and allure. ▨ $3 ☉ Daily 8–5.

Where to Stay

¢ 🏨 **Genesis Retreat.** Close to the Ek Balam site, this simple retreat is modeled on dwellings of the region. Cabins of stucco, wood, and thatch surround a casually maintained open area with a ritual temezcal steam hut and a small swimming pool. You can "adopt" a family of local residents for cultural exchange, language-learning, or hammock- or tortilla-making classes; you can also rent a bike to tour nearby ruins and sinkholes. ✉ *Domicilio Conocido* ☎ *985/852–7980 or 985/858–9375* ⊕ *www.genesisretreat.com* ⌁ *7 cabins, 3 tent-cabins* ⚭ *Restaurant, bicycles; no a/c, no room phones, no room TVs* ▭ *No credit cards.*

¢ 🏨 **U-Najil Ek Balam.** Wooden, thatch-roofed guest houses at this eco-hotel simulate traditional homes in the area (although, with private bathrooms, they're a step above the average rural dwelling). Local boys or men will guide you on bike or walking tours, to area sinkholes for swimming, or to see community events. ✉ *U-Najil, Hacienda Ek Balam* ☎ *999/994–7488* ⌁ *11 cabins* ⚭ *Restaurant, fans, pool, bicycles; no a/c, no room phones, no room TVs* ▭ *No credit cards* ⊚ *EP, MAP.*

UXMAL & THE RUTA PUUC

Passing through the large Maya town of Umán on Mérida's southern outskirts, you enter one of the Yucatán's least populated areas. The highway to Uxmal (ush-*mal)* and Kabah is relatively free of traffic and runs through uncultivated low jungle. The forest seems to become more dense beyond Uxmal, which was connected to a number of smaller ceremonial centers in ancient times by sacbé (white roads). Several of these satellite sites—including Kabah, with its 250 masks; Sayil, with its majestic, three-story palace; and Labná, with its iconic, vaulted *puerta* (gateway)—are open to the public along a route known as the Ruta Puuc, which winds its way eastward through the countryside.

The last archeological site on the Ruta Puuc is the Grutas de Loltún, Yucatán's most mysterious and extensive cave system. You can make a loop to all these sites, ending in the little town of Oxcutzcab, or in somewhat larger Ticul, which produces much of the pottery (and the women's shoes) you'll see around the peninsula. There's daily transportation on the ATS bus line (*see* Bus Travel, *below*) to Uxmal, Labná, Xlapak, Sayil, Kabah, and Uxmal. For about $10, you can get transportation to each of these places, with 20–30 minutes to explore the lesser sites and nearly two hours to see Uxmal. A great value and convenience, this unguided tour leaves the second-class bus station (ATS line, platform 69) daily at 8 AM and gets back to Mérida by about 4.

Uxmal

24 *78 km (48 mi) south of Mérida on Carretera 261.*

FodorśChoice
★

If Chichén Itzá is the most expansive Maya ruin in Yucatán, Uxmal is arguably the most elegant. The architecture here reflects the Late Classical renaissance of the 7th to the 9th century and is contemporary with that of Palenque and Tikal, among other great Maya cities of the southern highlands.

The site is considered the finest and most extensively excavated example of Puuc architecture, which embraces such details as ornate stone mosaics and friezes on the upper walls, intricate cornices, rows of columns, and soaring vaulted arches. Although much of Uxmal hasn't been restored, the following buildings in particular merit attention:

At 125 feet high, the **Pirámide del Adivino** is the tallest and most prominent structure at the site. Unlike most other Maya pyramids, which are stepped and angular, the Temple of the Magician has a softer and more refined round-corner design. This structure was rebuilt five times over hundreds of years, each time on the same foundation, so artifacts found here represent several different kingdoms. The pyramid has a stairway on its western side that leads through a giant open-mouthed mask to two temples at the summit. During restoration work in 2002, the grave of a high-ranking Maya official, a ceramic mask, and a jade necklace were discovered within the pyramid. Continuing excavations have revealed exciting new finds that are still being studied.

West of the pyramid lies the **Cuadrángulo de las Monjas,** considered by some to be the finest part of Uxmal. The name was given to it by the conquistadores because it reminded them of a convent building in Old Spain. You may enter the four buildings; each comprises a series of low, gracefully repetitive chambers that look onto a central patio. Elaborate and symbolic decorations—masks, geometric patterns, coiling snakes, and some phallic figures—blanket the upper facades.

Heading south from the Nunnery, you'll pass a small ball court before reaching the **Palacio del Gobernador,** which archaeologist Victor von Hagen considered the most magnificent building ever erected in the Americas. Interestingly, the palace faces east, while the rest of Uxmal faces west. Archaeologists believe this is because the palace was built to allow observation of the planet Venus. Covering 5 acres and rising over an immense acropolis, it lies at the heart of what may have been Uxmal's administrative center.

Apparently the house of an important person, the recently excavated **Cuadrángalo de los Pájaros** (Quadrangle of the Birds), located between the above-mentioned buildings, is composed of a series of small chambers. In one of these chambers, archaeologists found a statue of the royal who apparently dwelt there, by the name of Chac (as opposed to Chaac, the rain god). The building was named for the repeated pattern of birds decorating the upper part of the building's frieze.

Today, you can watch a sound-and-light show at the site that recounts Maya legends. The colored light brings out details of carvings and mosaics that are easy to miss when the sun is shining. The show is performed nightly in Spanish; earphones ($2.50) provide an English translation. 🎫 *Site, museum, and sound-and-light show $8.50; parking $1; use of video camera $3 (keep this receipt if visiting other archaeological sites along the Ruta Puuc on the same day)* ⊙ *Daily 8–5; sound-and-light show just after dusk.*

Where to Stay & Eat

$ ✕ **Cana Nah.** Although they mainly cater to the groups visiting Uxmal, the friendly folks at this large roadside venue are happy to serve small parties. The basic menu includes local dishes like lime soup and pollo pibíl, and such universals as fried chicken and vegetable soup. After your meal you can laze in one of the hammocks out back under the trees, or dive into the property's large rectangular swimming pool. There's a small shop as well, selling figurines of *los aluxes,* the mischievous "lords of the jungle" that Maya legend says protect farmers' fields. ✉ *Carr.*

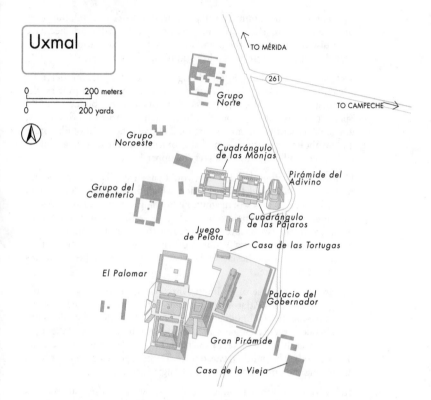

Uxmal

0   200 meters
0   200 yards

Grupo
Norte

TO MÉRIDA

(261)

TO CAMPECHE →

Grupo
Noroeste

Cuadrángulo
de las Monjas

Pirámide del
Adivino

Grupo del
Cementerio

Cuadrángulo
de las Pájaros

Juego
de Pelota

Casa de las Tortugas

El Palomar

Palacio del
Gobernador

Gran Pirámide

Casa de la Vieja

Muna–Uxmal, 4 km (2¹/₂ mi) north of Uxmal ☎ *999/991–7978 or 999/
910–3829* ▭ *No credit cards.*

$ ×🏠 **Villas Arqueológicas Uxmal.** Rooms in this pretty two-story Club Med
FodorśChoice property are small but functional, with wooden furniture and cozy twin
 ★ beds that fit nicely into alcoves. Half of the bright, hobbit-hole rooms
have garden views. Since rooms are small, guests tend to hang out in
the comfy library with giant-screen TV and lots of reading material, or
at thatch-shaded tables next to the pool. The indoor restaurant ($$–$$$)—
classy or old-Europe fussy, depending on your tastes—serves both regional fare and international dishes. With museum-quality reproductions
of Maya statues throughout (even in the pool), it's several times less expensive than, and equally charming as, the other options at the ruins.
✉ *Carretera 261, Km 76* ☎ *997/974–6020 or 800/258–2633* 🖨 *997/
976–2040* ⊕ *www.clubmedvillas.com* ⇆ *40 rooms, 3 suites* ⚭ *Restaurant, in-room safes, tennis court, pool, billiards, bar, library, shop, laundry service, free parking; no room TVs* ▭ *AE, MC, V.*

$$$–$$$$ 🏠 **Lodge at Uxmal.** The outwardly rustic, thatch-roofed buildings here
have red-tile floors, carved and polished hardwood doors and rocking
chairs, and local weavings. The effect is comfortable yet luxuriant; the

property feels sort of like a peaceful ranch. All rooms have bathtubs
and screened windows; suites have
king-size beds and spa baths. ☒ *Carretera Uxmal, Km 78* ☎ *997/976–
2030 or 800/235–4079* 🖷 *997/976–
2127* ⊕ *www.mayaland.com* 🛏 *40
suites* ⚓ *2 restaurants, fans, some in-
room hot tubs, minibars, cable TV,
2 pools, bar, laundry service, free
parking* ⊟ *AE, MC, V.*

WORD OF MOUTH

"We stayed over at the main
Uxmal lodge . . . after sharing one
bottle of wine and a very exciting
day of walking around and exploring the ruins in the sun, we were
ready to go to sleep in our beautiful thatched roof hotel room."
           –SandraHasWings

$$ 🏨 **Hacienda Uxmal.** The first hotel
built in Uxmal, this pleasant colonial-style building was looking posi-
tively haggard before a recent facelift, when sheets, towels, and furnish-
ings were finally replaced. Still in good shape are the lovely floor tiles,
ceramics, and iron grillwork. The rooms are fronted with wide, furnished
verandas; the courtyard has two pools surrounded by gardens. Each room
has an ample bathroom with tub, comfortable beds, and coffeemaker.
Ask about packages that include free or low-cost car rentals, or com-
fortable minivans traveling to Mérida, Chichén, or Cancún. ☒ *Carretera
261, Km 78* ☎ *997/976–2012 or 800/235–4079* 🖷 *997/976–2011,
998/884–4510 in Cancún* ⊕ *www.mayaland.com* 🛏 *80 rooms, 7 suites*
⚓ *Restaurant, room service, some in-room hot tubs, cable TV, 2 pools,
billiards, bar, shop, laundry service, free parking* ⊟ *AE, MC, V.*

Kabah

🏔 ㉕ *23 km (14 mi) south of Uxmal on Carretera 261.*

The most important buildings at Kabah, which means "lord of the
powerful hand" in Maya, were built between AD 600 and 900, during
the later part of the Classic era. A ceremonial center of almost Grecian
beauty, it was once linked to Uxmal by a sacbé, at the end of which looms
a great independent arch—now across the highway from the main ruins.
The 151-foot-long **Palacio de los Mascarones,** or Palace of the Masks,
boasts a three-dimensional mosaic of 250 masks of inlaid stones. On
the central plaza, you can see ground-level wells called *chultunes,* which
were used to store precious rainwater. 🎟 *$3* ⊙ *Daily 8–5.*

Sayil

🏔 ㉖ *9 km (5½ mi) south of Kabah on Carretera 31 E.*

Experts believe that Sayil, or "place of the red ants," flourished between
AD 800 and 1000. It is renowned primarily for its majestic **Gran Pala-
cio.** Built on a hill, the three-story structure is adorned with decorations
of animals and other figures, and contains more than 80 rooms. The
structure recalls Palenque in its use of multiple planes, columned por-

ticoes, and sober cornices. Also on the grounds is a stela in the shape of a phallus—an obvious symbol of fertility. 🎟 *$3* ⊙ *Daily 8–5.*

Labná

🏔 ❷❼ *9 km (5½ mi) south of Sayil on Carretera 31 E.*

The striking monumental structure at Labná (which means "old house" or "abandoned house") is a fanciful corbeled arch (also called the Maya arch, or false arch), with elaborate latticework and a small chamber on each side. One theory says the arch was the entrance to an area where religious ceremonies were staged. The site was used mainly by the military elite and royalty. 🎟 *$3* ⊙ *Daily 8–5.*

Grutas de Loltún

★ ☾ 🏔 ❷❽ *19 km (12 mi) northeast of Labná.*

The Loltún ("stone flower" in Maya) is one of the largest and most fascinating cave systems in the Yucatán peninsula. Long ago, Maya ceremonies were routinely held inside these mysterious caves; artifacts found inside date as far back as 800 BC. The topography of the caves themselves is fascinating: there are stalactities, stalagmites, and limestone formations known by such names as Ear of Corn and Cathedral. Illuminated pathways meander a little over a kilometer (½ mi) through the caverns, most of which are quite airy (claustrophobics needn't worry). Nine different openings allow air and some (but not much) light to filter in. ■ TIP→→ You can enter only with a guide. Although these guides were once paid a small salary, they are now forced to work for tips only—so be generous. Scheduled tours are at 9:30, 12:30, and 3:30 (in Spanish), and 11 and 2 (in English). 🎟 *$4.50* ⊙ *Daily 9–5.*

Ticul

❷❾ *27 km (17½ mi) northwest of the Loltún Caves, 28 km (17 mi) east of Uxmal, 100 km (62 mi) south of Mérida.*

One of the larger towns in Yucatán, Ticul has a handsome 17th-century church. This busy market town is a good base for exploring the Puuc region—if you don't mind rudimentary hotels and a limited choice of simple restaurants. Many descendants of the Xiu dynasty, which ruled Uxmal until the conquest, still live here. Industries include fabrication of huipiles and shoes, as well as much of the pottery you see around the Yucatán. **Arte Maya** (✉ Calle 23 No. 301 ☎ 997/972–1669) is a ceramics workshop that produces museum-quality replicas of archaeological pieces found throughout Mexico. The workshop also creates souvenir-quality pieces that are both more affordable and more easily transported.

off the
beaten
path

MAYAPÁN – Those who are enamored of Yucatán and the ancient Maya may want to take a 42-km (26-mi) detour east of Ticul (or 43 km [27 mi] from Mérida) to Mayapán, the last of the major city-states on the peninsula, which flourished during the Postclassic era. It was demolished in AD 1450, presumably by war. It is thought that the city, with an architectural style reminiscent of Uxmal, was as big as Chichén Itzá, and there are more than 4,000 mounds to bear this out. At its height, the population could have been well over 12,000. A half dozen mounds have been excavated, including the palaces of Maya royalty and the temple of the benign god Kukulcán, where murals in vivid reds and oranges, plus stucco sculptures, have been uncovered. The ceremonial structures that were faithfully described in Bishop Diego de Landa's writings will look like they have jumped right out of his book when the work is completed. ⊠ *Off road to left before Telchaquillo; follow signs* ⌁ *$2* ☉ *Daily 8–5.*

Where to Stay & Eat

$ ✕ **Pizzería La Góndola.** The wonderful smells of fresh-baked bread and pizza waft from this small corner establishment between the market and the main square. Scenes of Old Italy and the Yucatán adorn bright yellow walls; clients pull their padded folding chairs up to yellow-tile tables, or take their orders to go. Pizza is the name of the game here, although tortas and pastas are also for sale. To drink, you can choose from beer, wine, and soft drinks. ⊠ *Calle 23 No. 208, at Calle 26A* ☎ *997/972–0112* ▤ *No credit cards* ☉ *Closed daily 1–5* PM.

★ **$** ✕ **El Príncipe Tutul-Xiu.** About 15 km from Ticul in the little town of Maní, this large open restaurant under a giant palapa roof is a great place for lunch or an early dinner (it closes at 7 PM). Though you'll find the same Yucatecan dishes here as elsewhere—pollo pibíl, lime soup—the preparation is excellent and portions are generous. Best of all is the poc chuc—little bites of pork marinated in sour orange, garlic, and chili and grilled over charcoal. ⊠ *Calle 26 No. 208, between Calles 25 and 27* ☎ *997/978–4086* ▤ *No credit cards.*

¢–$ ✕ **Los Almendros.** One of the few places in town open until 9 PM, "the Almonds" is a good place to sample regional fare, including handmade tortillas, although the food can be greasy. The *combinado yucateco* gives you a chance to try poc chuc and cochinita pibíl (two pork dishes) as well as *pavo relleno* (stuffed turkey) and sausage. The newish building at the edge of town is often full of tour groups, or completely empty. There's a pool out back where you can swim—but do like mama says and wait at least a half hour after eating. ⊠ *Calle 22 s/n, at Carretera Ticul–Chetumal* ☎ *997/972–0021* ▤ *V.*

¢ 🏨 **Plaza.** There's not much to recommend the Plaza except that it's about a block from the main plaza. It has clean bathrooms and firm mattresses, hammock hooks, telephones, fans, and TV. Choose a room with air-conditioning; it will only cost you $4 extra. A café serves breakfast, which at least gets you out of your extremely plain room. ⊠ *Calle 23 No. 202, between Calles 26 and 26A, 97860* ☎ *997/972–0484* 🖷 *997/972–0077* ⊕ *www.hotelplayayucatan.com* ⇆ *25 rooms, 5 suites* ⌂ *Café, cable TV, free parking; no a/c in some rooms* ▤ *AE, MC, V (with 6% surcharge).*

Oxcutzcab

㉚ *22 km (14 mi) southeast of Ticul; 122 km (76 mi) south of Mérida.*

This market town, hungry for tourism, is a good alternative to Ticul for those who want to spend the night in the Puuc area. Strangers will greet you as you walk the streets. Even the teenagers here are friendly and polite. Oxcutzcab (osh-coots-*cob*) supplies much of the state with produce: avocado, mango, mamey, papaya, watermelon, peanuts, and citrus fruits are all grown in the surrounding region and sold daily at the cheerful municipal market, directly in front of the town's picturesque Franciscan church. Pedicabs line up on the opposite side of the market, ready for just a few pesos to take you on a three-wheeled tour of town. The town's coat of arms tells the etymology of the name Oxcutzcab. In Mayan, Ox means "ramon" (twigs cut for cattle fodder); "kutz" is tobacco, also grown in the area; and "cab" is honey. It's a sweet little town.

Where to Stay & Eat

¢ ✕▦ **Hotel Puuc.** This two-story, motel-style property opened in 2004. Rooms are plain but clean, with comfy beds, decoupage scenes of Puuc area ruins, and blond-wood furniture. Each has a shower and toilet crammed into a tiny room around the corner from a sink. Noise from the street, the front desk, and other rooms creeps in through thin walls. The international food at Peregrino Restaurant ($) is as plain and simple as the guest rooms, but portions are generous and the waitstaff, like most of the town, is friendly. ✉ *Calle 55 No. 80, at Calle 44,* ☎ *997/975–0103* ☞ *24 rooms* ⚐ *Restaurant, cable TV, laundry service, free parking; no room phones* ▭ *No credit cards.*

Yaxcopoil

③ *50 km (31 mi) north of Uxmal on Carretera 261.*

Yaxcopoil (yash-co-po-*il*), a restored 17th-century hacienda, makes for a nice change of pace from the ruins. The main building, with its distinctive Moorish double arch at the entrance, has been used as a film set and is the best-known henequen plantation in the region. The great house's rooms—including library, kitchen, dining room, drawing room, and salons—are fitted with late-19th-century European furnishings. You can tour these, along with the chapel, and the storerooms and machine room used in the processing of henequen. In the museum you'll see pottery and other artifacts recovered from the still-unexplored, Classic-era Maya site for which the hacienda is named. The hacienda has restored a one-room guesthouse ($) for overnighters, and will serve a Continental breakfast and simple dinner of traditional tamales and *horchata* (rice-flavored drink) by prior arrangement. You can reserve the guest cottage by visiting the property's Web site. ✉ *Carretera 261, Km 186* ☎ *999/927–2606 or 999/950–1001* ⊕ *www.yaxcopoil.com* ☞ *$4* ⊙ *Mon.–Sat. 8–6, Sun. 9–1.*

Where to Stay

$$$$ ▦ **Hacienda Temozón.** These luxurious accommodations may seem far from any town or city, but they're actually quite close to the ruins of Uxmal, the Ruta Puuc, and even Mérida. The converted henequen estate exudes luxury and grace, with mahogany furnishings, carved wooden doors, intricate mosaic floors in tile and stone, and a general air of genteel sophistication. Rooms have ceilings that are more than 20 feet high, with multiple ceiling fans, comfortable high beds with piles of pil-

lows, armoires, and twin hammocks. Modern lighting and quiet, remote-controlled air-conditioning units add creature comforts to the rustic-style rooms. ⊠ *Carretera 261, Km 182, Temozón Sur, 97825* ☎ *999/923–8089 or 888/625–5144* 🖷 *999/923–7963* ⊕ *www.luxurycollection. com* 🛏 *26 rooms, 1 suite* ⟂ *Restaurant, room service, fans, in-room safes, minibars, tennis court, pool, exercise equipment, bar, laundry service, concierge, meeting rooms, car rental, travel services, free parking; no room TVs* ⊟ *AE, MC, V.*

Oxkintoc

⛏ ㉜ *50 km (31 mi) south of Mérida on Carretera 180.*

The archaeological site of Oxkintoc (osh-kin-*tok*) is 5 km (3 mi) east of Maxcanú, off Carretera 180, and contains the ruins of an important Maya capital that dominated the region from about AD 300 to 1100. Little was known about Oxkintoc until excavations began here in 1987. Structures that have been excavated so far include two tall pyramids and a palace with stone statues of several ancient rulers. ⊠ *Off Carretera 184, 1½ km (1 mi) west of Carretera 180* 🕬 *$3* ⊙ *Daily 8–5.*

PROGRESO & THE NORTH COAST

Various routes lead from Mérida to towns along the coast, which are spread across a distance of 380 km (236 mi). Separate roads connect Mérida with the laid-back fishing village of Celestún, gateway to an ecological marine reserve that extends south to just beyond the Campeche border. Carretera 261 leads due north from Mérida to the relatively modern but humble shipping port of Progreso, where Meridians spend hot summer days and holiday weekends. To get to some of the small beach towns east of Progreso, head east on Carretera 176 out of Mérida and then cut north on one of the many access roads. Wide, white, and generally shadeless beaches here are peppered with bathers from Mérida during Holy Week and in summer—but are nearly vacant the rest of the year.

The terrain in this part of the peninsula is absolutely flat. Tall trees are scarce, because the region was almost entirely cleared for coconut palms in the early 19th century and again for henequen in the early 20th century. Local people still tend some of the old fields of henequen, even though there is little profit to be made from the rope fiber it produces. Other former plantation fields are wildly overgrown with scrub, and are only identifiable by the low, white, stone walls that used to mark their boundaries. Many bird species make their home in this area, and butterflies swarm in profusion throughout the dry season.

Celestún

㉝ *90 km (56 mi) west of Mérida.*

This tranquil and humble fishing village sits at the end of a spit of land separating the Celestún estuary from the Gulf of Mexico. Celestún is the point of entry to the **Reserva Ecológica de los Petenes,** a 100,000-acre wildlife reserve with extensive mangrove forests and one of the largest colonies of flamingos in North America. Clouds of the pink birds soar above the estuary all year, but the best months for seeing them in abundance are April through July. This is also the fourth-largest wintering ground for ducks of the Gulf-coast region, and more than 300 other species of birds, as well as a large sea-turtle population, make their home here. Conservation programs sponsored by the United States and Mexico protect the birds, as well as the endangered hawksbill and loggerhead marine tortoises, and other species such as the blue crab and crocodile.

The park is set among rocks, islets, and white-sand beaches. There's good fishing here, too, and several cenotes that are wonderful for swimming. Most Mérida travel agencies run boat tours of the *ría* (estuary) in the early morning or late afternoon, but it's not usually necessary to make a reservation in advance.

■ TIP→→ To see the birds, hire a fishing boat at the entrance to town (the boats hang out under the bridge leading into Celestún). A 75-minute tour for up to six people costs about $50, a two-hour tour around $75. Popular with Mexican vacationers, the park's sandy beach is pleasant during the morning but tends to get windy in the afternoon.

Where to Stay & Eat

$–$$$ ✕ **La Palapa.** Celestún's most popular seafood place has a conch-shell facade and is known for its *camarones a la palapa* (fried shrimp smothered in a garlic and cream sauce). Unless it's windy or rainy, most guests dine on the beachfront terrace. The menu has lots of fresh fish (including sea bass and red snapper), as well as crab, squid, and lobster. Although the restaurant's hours are 11 AM–6 PM, it sometimes closes early during the low season. ⊠ *Calle 12 No. 105, between Calles 11 and 13* ☎ *988/916–2063* ☰ *MC, V.*

$$$ ▦ **Hotel Eco Paraíso Xixim.** On an old coconut plantation outside town, this hotel offers classy comfort in thatched-roof bungalows along a shell-strewn beach. Each unit has two comfortable queen beds, tile floors, and attractive wicker, cedar, and pine furniture. The extra-large porch has twin hammocks and comfortable chairs. Biking and bird-watching tours as well as those to old haciendas or archaeological sites can be arranged; kayaks are available for rent. Vegetarian food is available for breakfast and dinner, included in the room price. ⊠ *Camino Viejo a Sisal, Km 10* ☎ *988/916–2100 or 800/400–3333 in the U.S. and Canada* ▤ *988/916–2111* ⊕ *www.ecoparaiso.com* ➷ *15 cabanas* ⚘ *Restaurant, fans, in-room safes, pool, beach, billiards, Ping-Pong, bar, library, Internet, no-smoking rooms; no a/c, no room phones, no room TVs* ☰ *AE, MC, V* ⦿| *MAP.*

¢ ▦ **Hotel Sol y Mar.** Gerardo Vasquez, the friendly owner of this small hotel across from the town beach, also owns the local paint store—so it's no accident that the walls here are a lovely cool shade of green. The spacious rooms are sparsely furnished; each has two double beds, a table, chairs, and a tile bathroom. The more expensive rooms downstairs also have air-conditioning, TV, and tiny refrigerators. Prices go down by about $5 in low season, which is everything except Easter,

Christmas, and August. There's no restaurant, but La Palapa is across the street. ⊠ *Calle 12 No. 104, at Calle 10* ☏ *988/916–2166* 🖋 *15 rooms* ⚬ *Fans, some refrigerators; no a/c in some rooms, no TV in some rooms* ▤ *No credit cards.*

Dzibilchaltún

🏔 ❸ *16 km (10 mi) north of Mérida.*

Dzibilchaltún (dzi-bil-chal-*tun*), which means "the place with writing on flat stones," is not somewhere you'd travel miles out of your way to see. But since it's located not far off the road, about halfway between Progreso and Mérida, it's convenient and, in its own small way, interesting. Although more than 16 square km (6 square mi) of land here are cluttered with mounds, platforms, piles of rubble, plazas, and stelae, only a few buildings have been excavated.

Scientists find Dzibilchaltún fascinating because of the sculpture and ceramics from all periods of Maya civilization that have been unearthed. Save what's in the museum, though, what you'll see is tiny **Templo de las Siete Muñecas** ("temple of the seven dolls," circa AD 500), one of a half dozen structures excavated to date. It's a long stroll down a flat dirt track sided by flowering bushes and trees to get to the low, trapezoidal temple exemplifying the Late Preclassic style. During the spring and fall equinoxes, sunbeams fall at the exact center of two windows opposite each other inside one of the temple rooms, an example of the highly precise mathematical calculations for which the Maya are known. Studies have found that a similar phenomenon occurs at the full moon between March 20 and April 20.

Dzibilchaltún's other main attraction is the ruined open chapel built by the Spaniards for the Indians. Actually, to be accurate, the Spanish forced Indian laborers to build it as a place of worship for themselves: a sort of pre-Hispanic "separate but equal" scenario.

☾ One of the best reasons to visit Dzibilchaltún is **Xlacah Cenote,** the site's smoked-green-glass sinkhole, whose crystalline water is ideal for cooling off after walking around the ruins. The second reason to visit is the **Museo Pueblo Maya**: small, but attractive and impressive. The site museum (closed Monday) has the seven crude dolls that gave the Temple of the Seven Dolls its name, and outside in the garden, several huge sculptures found on the site. It also traces the area's Hispanic history and highlights contemporary crafts from the region.

The easiest way to get to Dzibilchaltún is to get a *colectivo* taxi from Mérida's **Parque San Juan** (⊠ Calles 69 and 62, just a few blocks south of the Plaza Principal). The taxis depart whenever they fill up with passengers. Returns are a bit more dicey. If a colectivo taxi doesn't show up, you can take a regular taxi back to Mérida (it will cost you about $12–$15). You can also ask the taxi driver to drop you at the Mérida–Progreso highway, where you can catch a Mérida-bound bus for less than $2. 🎟 *$5.50 (including museum)* ◷ *Daily 8–5.*

Progreso

35 *16 km (10 mi) north of Dzibilchaltún, 32 km (20 mi) north of Mérida.*

The waterfront town closest to Mérida, Progreso is not particularly historic. It's also not terribly picturesque; still, it provokes a certain sentimental fondness for those who know it well. On weekdays during most of the year the beaches are deserted, but when school is out (Easter week, July, and August) and on summer weekends it's bustling with families from Mérida. Low prices are luring more retired Canadians, many of whom rent apartments here between December and April. It's also started attracting cruise ships, and twice weekly arrivals also bring tourist traffic to town.

Progreso's charm—or lack of charm—seems to hinge on the weather. When the sun is shining, the water looks translucent green and feels bathtub-warm, and the fine sand makes for lovely long walks. When the wind blows during one of Yucatán's winter *nortes,* the water churns with whitecaps and looks gray and unappealing, and the sand blows in your face. Whether the weather is good or bad, however, everyone ends up eventually at one of the restaurants lining the main street, Calle 19. Across the street from the oceanfront malecón, these all serve up cold beer, seafood cocktails, and freshly grilled fish.

Although Progreso's close enough to Mérida to make it an easy day trip, several B&Bs that have cropped up over the past few years make this a pleasant place to stay, and a great base for exploring the untouristy coast. Just west of Progreso, the fishing villages of Chelem and Chuburna are beginning to offer walking, kayaking, and cycling tours ending with a boat trip through the mangroves and a freshly prepared ceviche and beer or soft drink for about $33. This is ecotourism in its infancy, and it's best to set this up ahead of time through the Progreso tourism office (*see* Visitor Information *below*). Experienced divers can explore sunken ships at the Alacranes Reef, about 120 km (74 mi) offshore, although infrastructure is limited. Pérez Island, part of the reef, supports a large population of sea turtles and seabirds. Arrangements for the boat trip can be made through individuals at the private marina at neighboring Yucaltepén, 6 km (4 mi) from Progreso.

Where to Stay & Eat

$ ✕ **Flamingos.** This restaurant facing Progreso's long cement promenade is a cut above its neighbors. Service is professional and attentive, and soon after arriving you'll get at least one free appetizer—maybe black beans with corn tortillas, or a plate of shredded shark meat stewed with tomatoes. The creamy cilantro soup is a little too cheesy (literally, not figuratively), but the large fish fillets are perfectly breaded and lightly fried. Breakfast is served after 7:30 AM. There's a full bar, and although there's no a/c, large, glassless windows let in the ocean breeze. ✉ *Calle 19 No. 144-D, at Calle 72* ☎ *969/935–2122* ▭ *MC, V.*

$ ▦ **Casa Isidora.** A couple of Canadian English teachers have restored this grand, 100-year-old house a few blocks from the beach. Each guest room is individually decorated, but all have beautiful tile floors and a cozy, beachy style; some have small private patios. Breakfast is served in the dining room or out back, where the small swimming pool is surrounded by cushioned chaise longues. Mexican and American bar food and lots of tequilas are served in the cozy, popular, street-side bar. Spanish lessons and Internet use are free for hotel guests. ⊠ *Calle 21 No. 116* 🏠 *969/934–4595* ⊕ *www.casaisidora.com* 🛏 *6 rooms* ⚐ *Restaurant, fans, pool, bar, laundry service, Internet, free parking; no room TVs* ☰ *AE, MC, V* ⦿ *BP.*

Parque Natural Ría Lagartos

★ ☼ ㊱ *115 km (71 mi) north Valladolid.*

This park, which encompasses a long estuary, was developed with ecotourism in mind—although most of the alligators for which it and the village were named have long since been hunted into extinction. The real spectacle these days is the birds; more than 350 species nest and feed in the area, including flocks of flamingos, snowy and red egrets, white ibis, great white herons, cormorants, pelicans, and peregrine falcons. Fishing is good, too, and the protected hawksbill and green turtles lay their eggs on the beach at night.

You can make the 90-km (56-mi) trip from Valladolid (1½ hours by car or 2 hours by bus) as a day trip (add another hour if you're coming from Mérida; it's 3 hours from Cancún). There's a small information center at the entrance to town where Carretera 295 joins the coast road to San Felipe. Unless you're interested exclusively in the birds, it's nice to spend the night in Río Lagartos (the town is called *Río* Lagartos, the park *Ría* Lagartos) or nearby San Felipe, but this is not the place for Type AA personalities. There's little to do except take a walk through town or on the beach, and have a seafood meal. Buses leave Mérida and Valladolid regularly from the second-class terminals to either Río Lagartos or, 10 km (6 mi) west of the park, San Felipe.

The easiest way to book a trip is through the Núñez family at the Isla Contoy restaurant where you can also eat a delicious meal of fresh seafood. Call ahead to reserve an English- or Italian-speaking guide through their organization, Ría Lagartos Expeditions (⊕ www.riolagartosecotours.com). This boat trip will take you through the mangrove forests to the flamingo feeding grounds (where, as an added bonus, you can paint your face or body with supposedly therapeutic green mud). A 2½-hour tour, which accommodates five or six people, costs $60; the 3½-hour tour costs $75 (both per boat, not per person). You can take a shorter boat trip for slightly less money, or a 2-hour, guided walking-and-boat tour ($35 for 1–6 passengers), or a night tour in search of crocs (2½ hours, 1–4 passengers, $70). You can also hire a boat ($20 for 1–10 passengers) to take you to an area beach and pick you up at a designated time.

Where to Stay & Eat

★ $ ✕ **Isla Contoy.** Run by the amicable family that guides lagoon tours, this open-sided seafood shanty at the dock serves generous helpings of fish soup, fried fish fillets, shrimp, squid, and crab. If you've come with a group, order the combo for four (it can easily feed six, especially if you order a huge ceviche or other appetizer). The delicious platter comes with four shrimp crepes, fish stuffed with seafood, a seafood skewer, and one each of grilled, breaded, garlic-chili, and battered fish fillets (usually grouper or sea trout, whatever is freshest). There are also a few regional specialties and red-meat dishes. It's open for breakfast, too, and breakfast is included in the inexpensive (¢) rate charged for their four simple rooms on the beach. ⊠ *Calle 19 No. 134, at Calle 14* ☎ *986/862–0000* ▤ *No credit cards.*

¢ ▦ **Hotel San Felipe.** This three-story white hotel in the beach town of San Felipe, 10 km (6 mi) west of Parque Natural Ría Lagartos, is basic (for example, toilets have no seats), but adequate. Each room has two twin beds or a double—some are mushy, some hard—and walls are decorated with regional scenes painted by the owner. The two most expensive rooms have private terraces with a marina view (ask for a hammock) and are worth the small splurge. The owner can arrange fly-fishing expeditions for tarpon. ⊠ *Calle 9 No. 13, between Calles 14 and 16, San Felipe* ☎ *986/862–2027* 🖨 *986/862–2036* ⬅ *18 rooms* ♿ *Restaurant, fans, free parking; no a/c in some rooms, no room TVs* ▤ *No credit cards.*

Side Trip to Isla Holbox

㊲ *141 km (87 mi) northeast of Valladolid.*

Tiny Isla Holbox (25 km [16 mi] long) sits at the eastern end of the Ría Lagartos estuary and just across the Quintana Roo state line. A fishing fan's heaven because of the plentiful pompano, bass, barracuda, and shark just offshore, the island also pleases bird-watchers and seekers of tranquillity. Birds fill the air and the hunt in the mangrove estuaries on the island's leeward side; whale sharks cruise offshore April through September. Sandy beaches are strewn with seashells. And although the water is often murky—this is where the Gulf of Mexico and the Caribbean collide—the water is shallow and warm and there are some nice places to swim. Sandy streets lead to simple seafood restaurants where the fish fillets, conch, octopus, and other delicacies are always fresh.

Isla's lucky population numbers some 1,500 souls, and in the summer it seems there are that many biting bugs per person. Bring plenty of mosquito repellent. The Internet has arrived, and there's one Web café, but there are no ATMs, and most—if not all—businesses accept cash only, so visit an ATM before you get here. To get here from Río Lagartos, take Carretera 176 to Kantunilkin and then head north on the unnumbered road for 44 km (27 mi) to Chiquilá. Continue by ferry to the island; schedules vary, but there are normally five crossings a day. The fare is $3 and the trip takes about 35 minutes. A car ferry makes

> **WORD OF MOUTH**
>
> "We went to Isla Holbox our last time in Mexico and really enjoyed it. Remember, though, Isla Holbox is very laid back. Ferries do not always run (depending on weather) and staff is not really there to watch out for you. (So check to make sure your sea kayak is not leaking before you set out)."
>
> –GeordieFoley

CLOSE UP

Bird-Watching in Yucatán

RISE BEFORE THE SUN and head for shallow water to see flamingos dance an intricate mating dance. From late winter into spring, thousands of bright pink and black flamingos crowd the estuaries of Ría Lagartos, coming from their "summer homes" in nearby Celestún as well as from northern latitudes, to mate and raise their chicks. The largest flocks of both flamingos and bird-watching enthusiasts can be found during these months, when thousands of the birds—90% of the entire flamingo population of the Western Hemisphere—come to Ría Lagartos to nest.

Although the long-legged creatures are the most famous and best-appreciated birds found in these two nature reserves, red, white, black, and buttonwood mangrove swamps are home to hundreds of other species. Of Ría Lagartos's estimated 350 different species, one-third are winter-only residents—the avian counterparts of Canadian and northern-U.S. "snowbirds." Twelve of the region's resident species are endemic: found nowhere else on earth. Ría Lagartos Expeditions now leads walks through the low deciduous tropical forest in addition to boat trips through the mangroves.

More than 400 bird species have been sighted in the Yucatán, inland as well as on the coast. Bird-watching expeditions can be organized in Mérida as well as Ría Lagartos and Celestún. November brings hundreds of professional ornithologists and bird-watching aficionados to the Yucatán for a weeklong conference and symposium with films, lectures, and field trips.

the trip at 11 AM daily, returning at 5 PM. (You can also pay to leave your car in a lot in Chicquilá, in Quintana Roo.)

There are less expensive lodgings for those who eschew conventional beds in favor of fresh air and a hammock. Since it's a small island, it's easy to check several lodgings and make your choice. Hotel owners can help you set up bird-watching, fishing, and whale shark-viewing expeditions.

Where to Stay & Eat

$$ ×▦ **Villas Delfines.** Somewhat expensive by island standards, this fisherman's lodge consists of pleasant cabins on the beach. Deluxe bungalows have wood floors (rather than cement), larger balconies, and a few more creature comforts, such as hair dryers and safes. All are on stilts with rounded palapa roofs, and have waterless, "eco-friendly" toilets. You can get your catch grilled in the restaurant ($–$$), and if you're not into fishing, rent a kayak or arrange for a bird-watching trip. It's a 15-minute walk to the village's small main square. ✉ *Domicilio Conocido* ☎ *998/884–8606 reservations* 🖷🖷 *984/875–2196 or 984/875–2197* ⊕ *www.holbox.com* ⇆ *20 cabins* ⚹ *Restaurant, fans, some in-room safes, some minibars, beach, bicycles, volleyball, bar, airport shuttle; no room phones, no room TVs* ▭ *AE, D, MC, V* ⭍ *EP, BP, MAP.*

$$ 🏨 **Xaloc.** Each of these rustic bungalows has a tall, pointy, thatch roof, wood plank floors, and shuttered windows. Some are pushed right up next to the two swimming pools, which are lined with white limestone to recreate the look of the sand through the sea. Other bungalows face the garden; all have mosquito netting over the canopy beds to keep away biting bugs. The Maja'che restaurant serves mainly fish, with lots of fresh seasonal fruits. Rent a bike or golf course to explore the 12-square-mi island, or a kayak to check out the marine life in incredibly shallow seas. ☒ *Calle Chacchi s/n, at Calle Playa Norte* 🏨 *984/875–2160* 🏨 *800/ 728–9098 in the U.S. and Canada* ⊕ *www.mexicoboutiquehotels.com/ xaloc* ⌫ *18 bungalows* ♙ *Restaurant, fans, pool, beach, fishing, snorkeling, library, airport shuttle; no a/c, no room phones, no room TVs* ▤ *AE, MC, V* 🍽 *BP, MAP, FAP.*

MÉRIDA, CHICHÉN ITZÁ & YUCATÁN STATE ESSENTIALS

Tranportation

BY AIR

Mérida's airport, Aeropuerto Manuel Crescencio Rejón, is 7 km (4½ mi) west of the city on Avenida Itzaes. Getting there from the downtown area usually takes 20 to 30 minutes by taxi.

Aerocaribe, a subsidiary of Mexicana, has flights from Cancún, Cozumel, Mexico City, Oaxaca City, Tuxtla Gutiérrez, and Villahermosa, with additional service to Central America. Aeroméxico flies direct to Mérida from Miami with a stop in Cancún. Aviacsa flies from Mérida to Mexico City, Villahermosa, and Monterrey with connections to Los Angeles, Las Vegas, Chicago, Miami, Ciudad Juárez, Houston, and Tijuana, among other destinations. Continental flies daily nonstop from Houston. Mexicana has direct flights to Cancún from Los Angeles and Miami, and a number of connecting flights from Chicago and other U.S. cities via Mexico City.

🛈 **Aeropuerto Manuel Crescencio Rejón** 🏨 999/946–1340. **Aerocaribe** 🏨 999/942– 1862 or 999/942–1860 ⊕ www.aerocaribe.com. **Aeroméxico** 🏨 999/923–1790, 01800/ 021–4000 toll-free in Mexico ⊕ www.aeromexico.com. **Aviacsa** 🏨 999/925–6890, 01800/006–2200 toll-free in Mexico ⊕ www.aviacsa.com.mx. **Continental** 🏨 999/ 926–3100, 800/523–3273 in the U.S. ⊕ www.continental.com. **Mexicana** 🏨 999/946– 1332 ⊕ www.mexicana.com.mx.

BY BUS

Mérida's municipal buses run daily 5 AM–midnight. In the downtown area buses go east on Calle 59 and west on Calle 61, north on Calle 60 and south on Calle 62. You can catch a bus heading north to Progreso on Calle 56. Bus 79 goes from the airport to downtown and vice versa, departing from Calle 67 between Calles 60 and 62 about every 25 minutes; the ride takes about 45 minutes and is a hassle if you've got more than a day pack or small suitcase. City buses charge about 40¢ (4 pesos); having the correct change is helpful but not required.

For travel outside the city, there are several bus lines offering deluxe buses with powerful (sometimes too powerful) air-conditioning and comfortable seats. ADO and UNO have direct buses to Cancún, Chichén Itzá, Playa del Carmen, Tulum, Uxmal, Valladolid, and other Mexican cities, with intermediate service to Izamal. They depart from the first-class CAME bus station. ADO and UNO also have direct buses to Cancún from their terminal at the Fiesta Americana hotel, on Paseo Montejo. Regional bus lines to intermediate or more out-of-the-way destinations leave from the second-class terminal. The most frequent destination of tourists using Autotransportes del Sureste (ATS), which departs from the Terminal de Autobuses de 2da Clase, is Uxmal. Buses to Celestún depart from the Autobuses del Occidente station; those to Progreso are found at the Terminal de Autobuses a Progreso.

🚌 **ADO/UNO at Fiesta Americana** ✉ Av. Colón 451, at Calle 60, Paseo Montejo, Mérida ☎ 999/920-4444. **Autobuses de Occidente** ✉ Calles 50 and 67, Centro, Mérida ☎ 999/924-8391 or 999/924-9741. **CAME** ✉ Calle 70 No. 555, at Calle 71, Centro, Mérida ☎ 999/924-8391 or 999/924-9130. **Terminal de Autobuses a Progreso** ✉ Calle 62 No. 524, between Calles 65 and 67, San Juan, Mérida ☎ 999/928-3965. **Terminal de Autobuses de 2da clase** ✉ Calle 69 No. 544, between Calles 68 and 70, Centro, Mérida ☎ 999/923-2287.

BY CAR

Driving in Mérida can be frustrating because of the narrow one-way streets and dense traffic. Having your own wheels is the best way to take excursions from the city if you like to stop en route; otherwise, first- and second-class buses are ubiquitous, and even the latter are reasonably comfortable for short hauls. For more relaxed sightseeing, consider hiring a cab (most charge approximately $11 per hour). Carretera 180, the main road along the Gulf coast from the Texas border, passes through Mérida en route to Cancún. Mexico City is 1,550 km (961 mi) west, Cancún 320 km (198 mi) due east.

The autopista is a four-lane toll highway between Mérida and Cancún. Beginning at the town of Kantuníl, 55 km (34 mi) southeast of Mérida, it runs somewhat parallel to Carretera 180. The toll road cuts driving time between Mérida and Cancún—around 4½ hours on Carretera 180—by about an hour and bypasses about four dozen villages. Access to the toll highway is off old Carretera 180 and is clearly marked. The highway has exits for Valladolid and Pisté (Chichén Itzá), as well as rest stops and gas stations. Tolls between Mérida and Cancún total about $25.

CAR RENTAL   The major international chains are represented in Mérida, with desks at the airport and either downtown (many clumped together on Calle 60 between Calles 57 and 55) or on Paseo Montejo in the large chain hotels.

🚗 **Avis** ✉ Calle 60 No. 319-C, near Av. Colón, Centro, Mérida ☎ 999/925-2525. **Budget** ✉ Holiday Inn, Av. Colón No. 498, at Calle 60, Centro, Mérida ☎ 999/924-9985 or 999/925-6877 Ext. 516 ✉ Airport ☎ 999/946-1323. **Hertz** ✉ Fiesta Americana, Av. Colón 451, Paseo Montejo, Mérida ☎ 999/925-7595 ✉ Airport ☎ 999/946-1355. **Thrifty** ✉ Calle 55 No. 508, at Calle 60, Centro, Mérida ☎ 999/923-2040.

BY TAXI

Regular taxis in Mérida charge beach-resort prices, and so are a bit expensive for this region of Mexico. They cruise the streets for passengers and are available at 13 taxi stands (*sitios*) around the city, or in front of major hotels like the Hyatt Regency, Holiday Inn, and Fiesta Americana. The minimum fare is $3, which should get you from one downtown location to another. A ride between the downtown area and the airport costs about $8.

A newer fleet of metered taxis has recently started running in Mérida; their prices are usually cheaper than the ones charged by regular cabs. You can flag one of these down—look for the "Taximetro" signs on top of the cars—or call for a pickup.

🚖 Metered Taxis ☎ 999/928-5427. Sitio 14 (Regular Taxis) ☎ 999/924-5918.

BY TRAIN

The Expreso Maya is a private train that offers itineraries throughout the Maya world. Different tours visit a combination of one or more archaeological sites (Chichén Itzá, Uxmal, Edzná, Palenque) and major cities (Villahermosa, Mérida, Campeche) as well as laid-back Izamal, home of the beautiful St. Anthony of Padua Monastery and Church, and the lovely, little-visited Cenote Azul in Campeche state. Four- to six-night tours are available. Cost varies depending on tour selected and the level of accommodation, but expect to pay at least $1400 per person, double occupancy. The train has four air-conditioned passenger cars with swivel seats, and dining, bar, snack, and luggage cars. Individual passengers are welcome, but a minimum number of passengers must be booked through tour operators for the train to depart as scheduled. Groups and conventions may book their own train cars.

🚂 Expreso Maya ✉ Calle 1F No. 310, Fracc. Campestre, Mérida ☎ 999/944-9393 ⊕ www.expresomaya.com.

Contacts & Resources

BANKS & EXCHANGE SERVICES

Most banks throughout Mérida are open weekdays 9–4. Banamex has its main offices, open weekdays 9–4 and Saturday 9–1:30, in the handsome Casa de Montejo, on the south side of the main square, with branches at the airport and the Fiesta Americana hotel. All have ATMs. Several other banks, including Bital, can be found on Calle 65 between Calles 62 and 60, and on Paseo Montejo.

🏦 Banamex ✉ Calle 59 No. 485, Mérida ☎ 01800/226-2639 toll-free in Mexico ✉ Calle 26 No. 199D, Ticul ✉ Calle 41 No. 206, Valladolid. Banortel ✉ Calle 28 No. 31B, Izamal ☎ 988/954-0425 ✉ Calle 58 No. 524, between Calles 63 and 65, Centro, Mérida ☎ 999/923-4572. Bital ✉ Paseo Montejo 467A, Centro, Mérida ☎ 999/942-2378 ✉ Calle 58 No. 524, between Calles 63 and 65, Centro, Mérida ☎ 999/923-4572. Serfin ✉ Paseo Montejo 467A, Centro, Mérida ☎ 999/942-2378 ✉ Calle 30 No. 150, at Calle 80, Progreso ☎ 969/935-0855.

EMERGENCIES

For general emergencies throughout Yucatán state, dial **060**.

One of the largest and most complete medical facilities in Mérida is Centro Médico de las Américas. Clínica Santa Helena is less convenient to downtown Mérida, but the services—especially of Doctor Adolfo Baqueiro Solis, who specializes in emergency surgery and speaks excellent English—are highly recommended. Clínica San Juan is conveniently located near the main plaza.

Farmacia Arco Iris, open 24 hours, offers free delivery before 9 PM. Farmacia Yza delivers and has 24-hour service, but at press time, no English-speakers.

🔋 Doctors & Hospitals **Centro Médico de las Américas** ✉ Calle 54 No. 365, between Calle 33A and Av. Pérez Ponce, Centro, Mérida ☎ 999/927-3199. **Clínica San Juan** ✉ Calle 40 No. 238, Valladolid ☎ 985/856-2174. **Clínica Santa Helena** ✉ Calle 14 No. 81, between Calles 5 and 7, Col. Díz Ordaz, Mérida ☎ 999/943-1333.

🔋 Pharmacies **Farmacia Arco Iris** ✉ Calle 42 No. 207C, between Calles 43 and 45, Valladolid ☎ 985/856-2188. **Farmacia Yza** ☎ 999/926-6666 information and delivery. **Nova Farmacias** ✉ Calle 33-A No. 506, Local 1, across from Villa Mercedes, Paseo Montejo, Mérida ☎ 999/920-6660.

INTERNET, MAIL & SHIPPING

Mérida's post office is open weekdays 8–3 and Saturday 9–1. You can, however, buy postage stamps at some handicrafts shops and newspaper and magazine kiosks. The Mex Post service can speed delivery, even internationally, though it costs more than regular mail. Cybercafés are ubiquitous, though particularly prevalent along Mérida's main square and Calles 61 and 63. Most charge $1–$3 per hour.

🔋 Cybercafés **Café La Habana** ✉ Calle 59 No. 511-A, at Calle 62, Centro, Mérida ☎ 999/928-6502. **Phonet** ✉ Calle 42 between Calles 39 and 41, main plaza, Valladolid ☎ No phone. **Vía Olimpo Café** ✉ Calles 62 and 61, Centro, Mérida ☎ 999/923-5843.

🔋 Mail Service **Correo** ✉ Calles 65 and 56, Centro, Mérida ☎ 999/928-5404 or 999/924-3590.

MEDIA

Librería Dante has a great selection of colorful books on Maya culture, although only a few are in English. There are many locations throughout town, including most of the malls, and there's also a large, happening shop–café–performance venue on Paseo Montejo. The Mérida English Library has novels and nonfiction in English; you can read in the library for five days without having to pay the $18 annual membership fee. The giveaway "Yucatán Today," in English and Spanish, has good maps of the state and city and lots of useful information for travelers.

🔋 **Librería Dante** ✉ Calle 62 No. 502, at Calle 61 on the main plaza, Centro, Mérida ☎ 999/928-2611 ✉ Calle 17 No. 138B, at Prolongación Paseo de Montejo, Centro, Mérida ☎ 999/927-7676. **Mérida English Library** ✉ Calle 53 No. 524, between Calles 66 and 68, Centro, Mérida ☎ 999/924-8401.

TELEPHONES

Towns and cities throughout Mexico now have standardized three-digit area codes (LADAs) and seven-digit phone numbers. However, many of the numbers in brochures and other literature—even business cards—are still written in the old style, with six digits. To convert an older, 6-

digit number to a current one for local dialing, add a 9 at the beginning. Mérida's area code is 999. To dial another city within Mexico, dial 01, the area code, and the seven-digit number.

Coin-operated phones are few and far between—most take only Ladatel cards, electronic phone cards you can buy at newsstands, small grocieries, and pharmacies. Ladatel phone booths are at the airport and bus stations, in the main plaza, at Avenidas Reforma and Colón, and throughout the city. You can make both local and international direct calls at these public phones. To call the U.S. or Canada from Mexico, dial 001 and then the area code and phone number.

TOUR OPTIONS

Mérida has more than 50 tour operators, who generally go to the same places. Since there are many reputable and reasonably priced operators, there's no reason to opt for the less-predictable *piratas* ("pirates") who sometimes stand outside tour offices offering to sell you a cheaper trip.

A two- to three-hour group tour of the city, including museums, parks, public buildings, and monuments, costs $20 to $35 per person. Free guided tours are offered daily by the Municipal Tourim Department. These depart from City Hall, on the main plaza at 9:30 AM. The tourism department also runs open-air bus tours, which leave from Parque Santa Lucía and cost $7.50 (departures are Monday–Saturday at 10, 1, 4, and 7 and Sunday at 10 and 1).

An even more intriguing idea, however, is to take a tour on the Turibus, one of the city's new double-decker buses. This can be used as a standard, hour-long city tour ($10), or use it like a combo of transportation and guided tour. Buses pass the following sites, and you can stay on the bus or get off and jump on the next one (or any one; they stop on the half hour) after you're done sightseeing in the area. Buses run between 8:30 AM and 10 PM and stop at the Holiday Inn, Fiesta Americana, and Hyatt hotels, clustered near one another on Paseo Montejo; the plaza principal, downtown; Palacio Cantón; the old barrio of Izimná, east of Prolongación Paseo Montejo; the Gran Plaza shopping center (with multiplex theater); and the Monument to the Flag, near the Paseo Montejo hotels.

The Mérida English-Language Library (*see* Media, *above*) conducts home and garden tours (2½ hours costs $18) every Wednesday morning. Meet at the library at 9:30 AM.

Amigo Travel is a reliable operator offering group and private tours to the major archaeological sites and Celestún. They have transfer/accommodation packages, and well-crafted tours, like their Campeche and Yucatán combo, at a pace that allows one to actually enjoy the sites visited, and have some free time as well.

If you don't have your own wheels, a great option for seeing the ruins of the Ruta Puuc is the unguided ATS tour that leaves Mérida at 8 AM from the second-class bus station (Terminal 69, ATS line). The tour stops for half an hour each at the ruins of Labná, Xlapak, Sayil, and Kabah, giving you just enough time to scan the plaques, poke your nose into a crevice or two, and pose before a pyramid for your holiday card picture. You get almost two hours at Uxmal before heading back to Mérida at 2:30 PM. The trip costs $10 per person (entrance to the ruins isn't included) and is worth every penny.

Ecoturismo Yucatán also has a good mix of day and overnight tours. Their Calakmul tour includes several nights camping in the biosphere reserve for nature spotting, as well as visits to Calakmul, Chicanná, and other area ruins. The one-day biking adventure packs in biking as well as brief visits to two archaeological sites, a cave, and two cenotes for swimming or snorkeling.

Mayaland Tours specializes in tours to the archaeological sites and is owned by the Barbachano clan, members of which own the Mayaland hotel at Chichén Itzá and several lodgings at Uxmal. In addition to standard tours they offer "self-guided tours" which are basically a road map and itinerary, rental car, and lodgings at the archaeological sites. When you consider the price of lodgings and rental car, this is a pretty sweet deal.

Amigo Travel ✉ Av. Colón 508C, Col. García Ginerés, Mérida ☎ 999/920-0101 or 999/920-0107. **ATS** ✉ Calle 69 No. 544, between Calles 68 and 70, Centro, Mérida ☎ 999/923-2287. **Ecoturismo Yucatán** ✉ Calle 3 No. 235, between Calles 32A and 34, Col. Pensiones, Mérida ☎ 999/920-2772 ⊕ www.ecoyuc.com. **Mayaland Tours** ✉ Calle Robalo 30, Sm 3, Cancún ☎ 998/887-2495 in Cancún, 01800/719-5465 toll-free from elsewhere in Mexico, 800/235-4079. **Municipal Tourism Department Tours** ☎ 999/928-2020 Ext. 833. **Turibus** ☎ No phone ⊕ www.turibus.com.mx

TRAVEL AGENCIES

English-speaking agents at Carmen Travel Service sell airline tickets, make hotel reservations throughout the Yucatán peninsula, and book cruises. Viajes Valladolid offers services typical of any travel agency, including hotel reservations and airline bookings. They also arrange tours throughout the Yucatán and to Cuba and Central America, and will change your traveler's checks, too.

Carmen Travel Service ✉ Hotel María del Carmen, Calle 63 No. 550, at Calle 68, Centro, Mérida ☎ 999/924-1212. **Viajes Valladolid** ✉ Calle 42 No. 206, Valladolid ☎ 985/856-1881.

VISITOR INFORMATION

The Mérida city, municipal, and state tourism departments are open daily 8–8. The Progreso municipal tourism office is open Monday–Friday 8–2 and Saturday 9–1. The Izamal tourism office is open Monday–Saturday 9–6.

The Municipal Tourist Information Center offers brochures of area hotels and attractions, and maps of the city. The Municipal Tourism Department, in the State Government palace, is mainly recommended because of its location right on the main plaza. The young staffers and usually more experienced supervisor of the State Secretary of Tourism Office speak good English and are knowledgeable about what's going on in both the city and the state. They have the most complete information of all the city's tourism info booths.

🎬 **Izamal Tourism Department** ✉ Calle 30 No. 323, between 31 and 31-A, Centro, Izamal ☎ 988/954-0692 or 988/954-0009. **Municipal Tourism Department** ✉ Calles 61 and 60, Centro, Mérida ☎ 999/930-3101. **Municipal Tourist Information Center** ✉ Calle 62, ground floor of the Palacio Municipal, Centro, Mérida ☎ 999/928-2020 Ext. 133. **Progreso Municipal Tourism Office** ✉ Casa de la Cultura, Calles 80 and 25, Centro, Progreso ☎ 969/935-0104. **State Secretary of Tourism Office** ✉ Teatro Peón Contreras, Calle 60 between Calles 57 and 59, Centro, Mérida ☎ 999/924-9290 or 999/924-9389.

Campeche

Edzná

WORD OF MOUTH

"Very few Americans go to Campeche. It isn't about the sea or the sunshine (although there's plenty of that). The capital is truly a colonial gem, clean and beautiful and absolutely historic in its old downtown section. And out in the countryside are some of the best Maya archaeological sites you'll find anywhere."

—Jane O.

AROUND CAMPECHE

Campeche City

Getting Oriented

Campeche, the Yucatán's least-visited corner, is the perfect place for adventure. The state's colonial communities have retained an air of innocence, and its protected biospheres, farmland, and jungles are relatively unspoiled. More than 60% of the state is covered by tropical forests containing precious mahogany and cedar trees.

TOP 5
Reasons to Go

1. **Seeing the Yucatan at its most un-spoiled:** the beaches and Maya ruins of this state are rarely visited by tourists.

2. **Marveling at the 18th-century forts** and bastions of Campeche City, which once protected the port from pirate attacks.

3. **Wandering through the Reserva de la Biosfera Calakmul,** a preserve whose wildlife includes 350 species of butterfly.

4. **Getting to know the locals,** whose friendliness is so legendary that, all over Mexico, a good-natured, open-minded attitude is often described as *campechano*.

5. **Sampling fabulous Yucatecan dishes** like *camarones al coco* (shrimp with crispy coconut) and *pan de cazon* (baby shark with black beans and tortillas).

The Gulf Coast The hub of Ciudad del Carmen has little to lure tourists, but small towns and usually empty beaches lie to the north. Off the beaten path—but surprisingly, on the route of the Expreso Maya train tour—are the beautiful, largely undiscovered sinkholes of Cenote Azul and Cenote de los Patos.

Gulf of México

Sabancuy

Laguna de Términos

180

Ciudad del Carmen

186

TOBASCO

Paula Toro Theater, Campeché

Reserva de la Biosfera Calakmul

Campeche City Campeche City, population 196,000, has a lovely time-weathered air. The historic district has forts, walls, and stone arches that guarded against pirates more than two centuries ago. The narrow cobblestone streets, lined with renovated historic buildings and cafés, are a pleasure to explore on foot.

Becal

180

261

YUCATÀN

Campeche ☆

Cayal

Hopelchen

180

QUINTANA ROO

6

Dzibilnocac

Hochob

Champotón

80

261

CAMPECHE

Canote Azul & Canote de los Patos

Escàrcega

186

→

The Maya Interior
The small towns and villages, ruined haciendas, and forlorn-looking churches of northern Campeche are the outposts and protectors of traditional life in this state. In the small towns around Hocob and Dzibilnocac, visitors are still rare enough to elicit gales of unsolicited giggles from schoolkids, and shy smiles from parents.

Candelaria El Tigre

Reserva de la Biosfera Calakmul

Nueva Coahuila

Mexico
Guatemala

The Jungle Borderland The vast nature preserve of the Reserva de la Biosfera Calakmul is the major draw for explorers in this region. Candalaria, still untamed by tourism, is a jumping-off point for exploring the Maya ruins at El Tigre; along Carretera 186 are myriad other ruin sites, some right off the highway.

Reserva de la Biosfera Calakmul

Stonework in Calakmul.

CAMPECHE PLANNER

A Sample Itinerary

Three or four days will give you enough time to explore both Campeche City and some of the state's archaeological sites. Spend the first day wandering around the city's historical district, visiting the various *baluartes* (bastions), the Parque Principal, and Fuerte San Miguel. On Day 2, head to the Maya site of Edzná, stopping on the way back for a late-afternoon lunch (by prior reservation) at the glamorous restored hacienda Uayamón. On Day 3, set out early for the Hopelchén region, where you can explore some little-known Maya temples: Hochob, Santa Rosa Xtampak, and Dzibilnocac. You can also try visiting Las Grutas de Xtacumbilxunaan, one of the larger ceremonial cave systems on the peninsula.

When to Go

Make reservations well in advance for visits during the Christmas and Easter seasons; six months' lead time isn't out of line. December through February is a good time to come if you're bothered by high humidity and heat (though the water can be chilly, and most swimming pools here aren't heated). Campeche City celebrates Mardi Gras, or *carnaval,* with a week of activities leading up to Fat Tuesday in early to mid-February. Day of the Dead celebrations (Oct. 31 to Nov. 2) are private, but you can see some colorful graves in small towns north of Campeche City.

Speaking the Language

You'll need at least rudimentary Spanish; few people outside the capital and Ciudad del Carmen speak English. If you plan to venture off the beaten path, pack a Spanish–English dictionary.

Touring Options

■ **Voyager** (✉ Calle 59 No. 4C, Centro ☎ 981/816-7272 ⊕ www.voyager.com.mx) offers tours and/or transportation to Calakmul, Edzná, and other ruins, and also arranges tours of Campeche City. If guide service is not included, ask the tour operator to arrange for an English-speaking guide at the ruins.

■ **Intermar** (✉ Hotel Baluartes, Av. 16 de Septiembre 128, Campeche City ☎ 981/816-9006 or 981/811-3447) is recommended by the state's tourism department; it, too, has tours and/or transportation to Calakmul, Edzná, and other ruins, as well as tours of Campeche City.

How's the Weather?

Campeche's strongest rains fall July–September, but by November, the hurricane threat has passed. The weather cools between December and February, but then gets hot again (so much so that by March even the locals break a sweat). Summer brings heavy afternoon cloudbursts, usually by mid-June, although these bring little relief from the sweltering heat.

Dining & Lodging Prices

WHAT IT COSTS in Dollars					
	$$$$	$$$	$$	$	¢
Restaurants	over $25	$15–$25	$10–$15	$5–$10	under $5
Hotels	over $250	$150–$250	$75–$150	$50–$75	under $50

Restaurants: per person, for main course at dinner, excluding tax & tip. Hotels: standard double room on European Plan, excluding service and 17% tax.

Exploring Campeche

Campeche City, the state's most accessible spot, makes a good hub for exploring other areas, many of which have only basic restaurants and primitive lodgings.

Once you get outside the city, however, you'll see why Campeche's economy is largely supported by agriculture. The countryside here is covered with fields of tobacco, sugarcane, rice, indigo, maize, and cocoa as well as citrus groves; these stretch between the small villages and Maya sites that make this state an outpost of traditional culture.

North of Campeche City, Carretera 180 passes a handful of artisan villages and ancient Franciscan cathedrals that you can visit while traveling on the short route, called El Camino Real, to Mérida. Edzná archaeological site is a short detour south of Carreteras 180 and 188. The longer route to Mérida, Carretera 261 takes you through the agricultural town of Hopelchén and close to the Xtacumbilxunaan caves. The ruins in this area require a detour off Carretera 261.

South of the city, Carretera 180 hugs the coast, passing several small towns and fishing villages that have been all but eclipsed by the oil industry. From Champotón, the largest of these communities, Carretera 261 continues due south to the rowdy, truck-stop city of Escárcega, where it connects with Carretera 186. This east-bound highway links Campeche with Chetumal, the Caribbean capital of Quintana Roo. En route are numerous Maya ruins, some a half mile or less off the highway, others deep in the biosphere and all but unreachable in rainy season. A two-lane highway links these ruins with Hopelchén, in the northeast part of the state.

About the Restaurants

There's nothing fancy about Campeche's restaurants, but the regional cuisine is renowned throughout Mexico. Specialties include fish and shellfish stews, cream soups, shrimp cocktails, squid and octopus, crab legs, *panuchos* (chubby rounds of fried cornmeal covered with refried beans and topped with chopped onion and shredded turkey or chicken). Because regional produce is plentiful (and foreign visitors scarce), most restaurants fall into the $ to $$ price categories. Casual attire—with the occasional exception of shorts—is fine in restaurants throughout Campeche, and reservations are not required. Despite such informality, service is usually quite attentive.

About the Hotels

Campeche City's hotels tend to be either moderately priced waterfront accommodations with basic amenities—air-conditioning, restaurants, bars, and swimming pools—or small downtown lodgings with thin mattresses, no-credit-card policies, and, for a small additional charge, ancient air-conditioning to supplement the ceiling fans. The best in the latter category are pleasant little hotels in refurbished early-20th-century buildings. Note that most of the less expensive hotels *include* the value-added tax in their quoted prices. That amount has been subtracted to provide a fair comparison with other hotels, so the quoted price may be slightly higher than that given here.

CAMPECHE CITY

Within Mexico's most tranquil capital city are block upon block of lovely building facades, all painted in colors that might have been dreamed up by an artist: sea-foam green, banana-squash yellow, Venetian red. Tiny balconies overlook clean, geometrically paved streets; ancient wooden doors are embellished with ornate hardware. Charming old street lamps illuminate the scene at night.

In colonial days, the city center was completely enclosed within a 3-meter-thick wall. Two stone archways (originally there were four)—one facing the sea, the other the land—provided the only access. The defensive walls also served as a de facto class demarcation. Within them lived the ruling elite. Outside were the barrios of blacks and mulattoes brought as slaves from Cuba, and just about everyone else.

On strategic corners, seven *baluartes,* or bastions, gave militiamen a platform from which to fight off pirates and the other ruffians that continually plagued this beautiful city on the bay. But it wasn't until 1771, when Fuerte de San Miguel was built on a hilltop outside town, that pirates finally stopped attacking the city.

■ TIP→→ Campeche's historic center is easily navigable, in fact, it's a walker's paradise. Narrow roads and lack of parking spaces can make driving a bit frustrating, although drivers here are polite and mellow. Streets running roughly north–south are even-numbered, and those running east–west are odd-numbered.

A Good Walk

The old city center—where the colonial architecture comes in an edible array of colors—is the obvious place for a walking tour. You might begin at **Baluarte de la Soledad** ❶ ►, which has a small Maya museum. Nearby, compact **Parque Principal** ❷, the city's central plaza, is as mellow as any place in town. It is surrounded by some good examples of Spanish colonial architecture, including the **Catedral de la Inmaculada Concepción** ❸ and, on the opposite side of the street, **Casa Seis** ❹. On Calle 10 between Calles 51 and 53 is the **Mansión Carvajal** ❺, now home to government offices but still worth a peek inside. **Baluarte de Santiago** ❻ is about one block north and one west, on Calle 8 at the corner of Calle 51. Head away from the bay on Calle 51 about six blocks to the small, well-restored **Baluarte de San Pedro** ❼ at Circuito Baluartes Norte and Avenida Gobernadores. Walk south along Calle 18 to **Puerta de Tierra** ❽ and the Baluarte San Francisco; then take **Calle 59** ❾ past the **Iglesia y Ex-Convento de San Roque** ❿. Continuing to Calle 8, turn south (left) and proceed to **Baluarte de San Carlos** ⓫, at Calle 65, the bastion that once was connected to the Puerta de Tierra. From there, head to the **Ex-Templo de San José** ⓬ and then the **Iglesia de San Román** ⓭. Both are fine examples of colonial religious architecture. Finish the walk along the beachfront **malecón** ⓮ or do as the locals do, jogging, blading, or walking in the cool of the evening or the early morning.

What to See

⑪ Baluarte de San Carlos. Named for Charles II, King of Spain, this bastion, where Calle 8 curves around and becomes Circuito Baluartes, houses the **Museo de la Ciudad.** The free museum contains a small collection of historical artifacts, including several Spanish suits of armor and a beautifully inscribed silver scepter. The massive walls keep the building cool, and fans swirl the air around—except in the stifling basement dungeon, where captured pirates were once jailed. The unshaded rooftop provides an ocean view that's lovely at sunset. ⊠ *Calle 8 between Calles 65 and 63, Circuito Baluartes, Centro* ☎ *No phone* ✉ *Free* ☉ *Tues.–Fri. 8–8, Sat. 8–2 and 4–8, Sun. 9–1.*

⑦ Baluarte de San Pedro. Built in 1686 to protect the city from pirate attacks, this bastion flanked by watchtowers now houses a handicrafts-and-souvenir shop. The collection is small but choice; quality is good and prices are reasonable. The city has few worthwhile handcraft shops, so if you see something you like here, go for it. On the roof are well-preserved corner watchtowers; you can also check out (but not use) the original 17th-century potty. ⊠ *Calles 18 and 51, Circuito Baluartes, Centro* ☎ *No phone* ✉ *Free* ☉ *Daily 9–9.*

⑥ Baluarte de Santiago. The last of the bastions to be built (1704) has been transformed into the **X'much Haltún Botanical Gardens.** It houses more than 200 plant species, including the enormous ceiba tree, which had spiritual importance to the Maya, symbolizing a link between heaven, earth, and the underworld. Although the original bastion was demolished at the turn of the 20th century, and then rebuilt in the 1950s, the fort still resembles others in Campeche; it's a stone fortress with thick walls, watchtowers, and gunnery slits. ⊠ *Calles 8 and 49, Circuito Baluartes, Centro* ☎ *No phone* ✉ *Free* ☉ *Tues.–Fri. 8–2 and 5–8, weekends 8–2.*

★ **① Baluarte de la Soledad.** Originally built to protect the **Puerta de Mar,** a sea gate that was one of four original entrances to the city, this bastion stands on the west side of the Parque Principal. Because it uses no supporting walls, it resembles a Roman triumphal arch. The largest of the bastions, it has comparatively complete parapets and embrasures that offer views of the cathedral, municipal buildings, and the old houses along Calle 8. Inside is the **Museo de las Estelas** with artifacts that include a well-preserved sculpture of a man wearing an owl mask, columns from Edzná and Isla de Jaina, and at least a dozen well-proportioned Maya stelae from ruins throughout Campeche. ⊠ *Calles 8 between Calles 55 and 57, Centro* ☎ *No phone* ✉ *$2.50* ☉ *Tues.–Sat. 8–8, Sun. 9–1.*

⑨ Calle 59. Some of Campeche's finest homes were built on this city street between Calles 8 and 18. Most were two stories high, with the ground floors serving as warehouses and the upper floors as residences. These days, behind the delicate grillwork and lace curtains, you can glimpse genteel scenes of Campeche life, with faded lithographs on the dun-color walls and plenty of antique furniture and gilded mirrors. The best-preserved houses are those between Calles 14 and 18; many closer to the sea have been remodeled or destroyed by fire. Campeche's INAH (In-

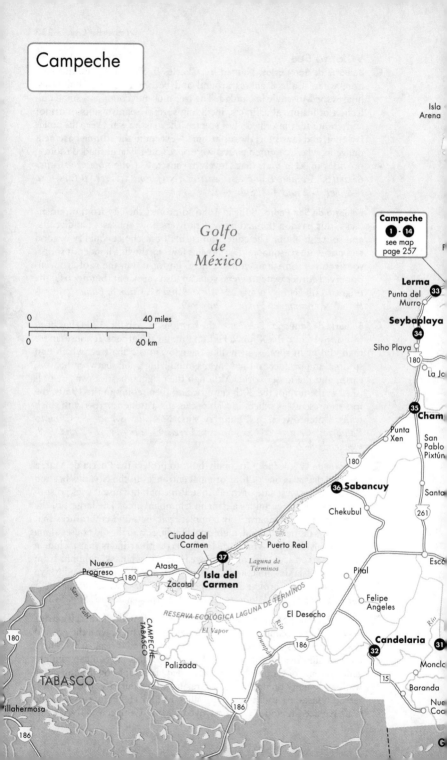

Campeche

Golfo de México

Isla Arena

Campeche
1 - 14
see map
page 257

0   40 miles
0   60 km

Lerma 33
Punta del Murro

Seybaplaya 34

Siho Playa
180

La Jo

35 **Cham**

Punta Xen

San Pablo Pixtún

180

36 **Sabancuy**

Chekubul

261

Santa

Ciudad del Carmen

Puerto Real

37
Isla del Carmen

Laguna de Términos

Nuevo Progreso

Atasta

Zacatal

180

Pital

Esco

Felipe Angeles

San Pablo

RESERVA ECOLÓGICA LAGUNA DE TÉRMINOS

El Vapor

El Desecho

Río Champotón

Candelaria 31

180

TABASCO

Palizada

186

32

15

Moncla

Baranda

illahermosa

186

Nue Coa

186

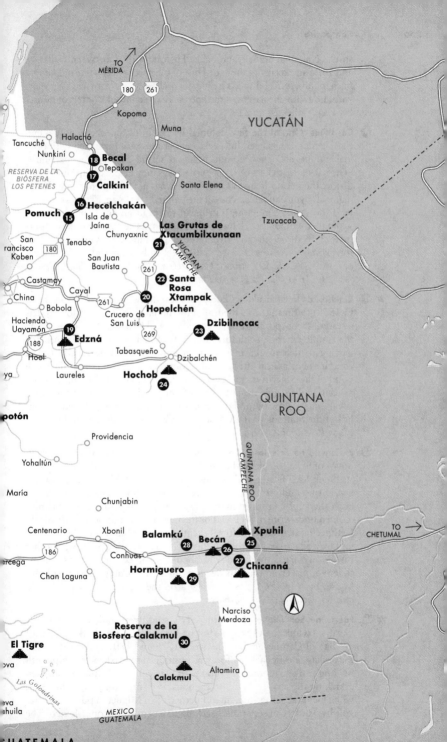

stituto Nacional de Antropología e Historia) office, between Calles 16 and 14, is an excellent example of one of Campeche City's fine old homes. Each month, INAH displays a different archaeological artifact in its courtyard. Look for the names of the apostles carved into the lintels of houses between Calles 16 and 18.

❹ Casa Seis. One of the first colonial homes in Campeche is now a cultural center. It has been fully restored—rooms are furnished with original antiques and a few reproductions, replicating a typical colonial house. (The bar-code stickers on some furnishings may help with inventory, but distort the period image.) Original frescoes at the tops of the walls remain, and you can see patches of the painted "wallpaper" that once covered the walls, simulating European tastes in an environment where wallpaper wouldn't stick due to the humidity. The courtyard has Moorish architecture with modern colored glass windows; it's used as an area for exhibits, lectures, and on some weekends theatrical performances at 7 PM. ⊠ *Calle 57 between Calles 10 and 8, Plaza Principal, Centro* ☎ *981/816–1782* ☎ *Free* ☉ *Daily 9–9.*

★ ❸ Catedral de la Inmaculada Concepción. It took two centuries (from 1650 to 1850) to finish the Cathedral of the Immaculate Conception, and as a result, it incorporates both neoclassical and Renaissance elements. On the simple exterior, sculptures of saints in niches are covered in black netting to discourage pigeons from unintentional desecration. The church's neoclassical interior is also somewhat plain and spare. The high point of the collection, now housed in the side chapel museum, is a magnificent Holy Sepulchre carved from ebony and decorated with stamped silver angels, flowers, and decorative curlicues; each angel holds a symbol of the Stations of the Cross. ⊠ *Calle 55 between Calles 8 and 10, Plaza Principal, Centro* ☎ *No phone* ☉ *Daily 6 AM–9 PM.*

⓬ Ex-Templo de San José. The Jesuits built this fine Baroque church in honor of Saint Joseph just before they were booted out of the New World. Its block-long facade and portal are covered with blue-and-yellow Talavera tiles and crowned with seven narrow stone finials—resembling both the roof combs on many Maya temples and the combs Spanish women once wore in their elaborate hairdos. Next door is the **Instituto Campechano,** used for cultural events and art exhibitions. These events and exhibits are regularly held here Tuesday evening at 7 PM; at other times you can ask the guard (who should be somewhere on the grounds) to let you in. From the outside, you can admire Campeche's first lighthouse, built in 1864, now perched atop the right tower. ⊠ *Calles 10 and 65, Centro* ☎ *No phone.*

★ ☙ Fuerte de San Miguel. Near the city's southwest end, Avenida Ruíz Cortínez winds its way to this hilltop fort with its breathtaking view of the Bay of Campeche. Built between 1779 and 1801 and dedicated to the archangel Michael, the fort was positioned to blast enemy ships with its long-range cannons. As soon as it was completed, pirates stopped attacking the city. In fact, the cannons were fired only once, in 1842, when General Santa Anna used Fuerte de San Miguel to put down a revolt by Yucatecan separatists seeking independence from Mexico. The

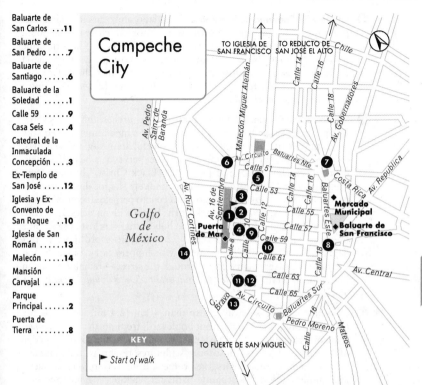

Campeche
City

TO IGLESIA DE   TO REDUCTO DE
SAN FRANCISCO   SAN JOSÉ EL ALTO

*Golfo
de
México*

Mercado
Municipal

Baluarte de
San Francisco

KEY

TO FUERTE DE SAN MIGUEL

► *Start of walk*

6

fort houses the **Museo de la Cultura Maya,** whose exhibits include the
skeletons of long-ago Maya royals, complete with jewelry and pottery,
which are arranged just as they were found in Calakmul tombs. Other
archaeological treasures are funeral vessels, masks, many wonderfully
expressive figurines and whistles from Isla de Jaina, stelae and stucco
masks from the Maya ruins, and an excellent pottery collection. Although
it's a shame that most information is in Spanish only, many of the pieces
speak for themselves. The gift shop sells replicas of artifacts. ⊠ *Av. Francisco Morazán s/n, west of town center, Cerro de Buenavista* ☎ *No phone*
💰 *$2.50* ☉ *Tues.–Sun. 9–7:30.*

Iglesia de San Francisco. With its flat, boldly painted facade and bells en-
sconced under small arches instead of bell towers, Church of Saint
Francis looks more like a Mexican city hall than a Catholic church. Outside the city center in a residential neighborhood, the beautifully restored
temple is Campeche's oldest. It marks the spot where, some say, the first
Mass on the North American continent was held in 1517—though the
same claim has been made for Veracruz and Cozumel. One of Cortés's
grandsons was baptized here, and the baptismal font still stands. ⊠ *Avs.
Miguel Alemán and Mariano Escobedo, San Francisco* ☉ *Daily 8–noon
and 5–7.*

⑩ Iglesia y Ex-Convento de San Roque. The elaborately carved main altarpiece and matching side altars here were restored inch by inch in 2005, and this long, narrow church now adds more than ever to historic Calle 59's old-fashioned beauty. Built in 1565, it was originally called Iglesia de San Francisco; in addition to a statue of Saint Francis, humbler-looking saints peer out from smaller niches. ⊠ *Calles 12 and 59, Centro* ⊙ *Daily 8:30–noon and 5–7.*

⑬ Iglesia de San Román. Like most Franciscan churches, this one is sober and plain; its single bell tower is the only ornamentation. The equally spare interior is brightened by some colorful stained-glass windows, though, and the carved and inlaid altarpiece serves as a beautiful backdrop for an ebony image of Jesus, the "Black Christ," brought from Italy in about 1575. Although understandably skeptical of Christianity, the Indians whom the Spaniards forced into perpetual servitude eventually came to associate this black Christ figure with miracles. As legend has it, a ship that refused to carry the holy statue was lost at sea, while the ship that accepted him reached Campeche in record time. To this day, the Feast of San Román—when worshippers carry a black-wood Christ and a silver filigree cross through the streets—remains a solemn but colorful affair. ⊠ *Calles 10 and Bravo, San Román* ⊙ *Daily 7–1 and 3–7.*

★ **⑭ Malecón.** A broad sidewalk more than 4 km (2.4 mi) long runs the length of Campeche's waterfront boulevard, from northeast of the Debliz hotel to the Justo Sierra Méndez monument at the southwest edge of downtown. With its landscaping, sculptures, rest areas, and fountains lit up at night in neon colors, the promenade attracts joggers, strollers, and families. (Note the separate paths for walking, jogging, and biking.) On weekend nights, students turn the malecón into a party zone.

⑤ Mansión Carvajal. Built in the early 20th century by one of the Yucatán's wealthiest plantation owners, this eclectic mansion logged time as the Hotel Señorial before becoming an office for the state-run Family Institute. The black-and-white tile floor and blue-and-white Moorish arcades are reminders of the city's heyday, when Campeche was the peninsula's only port. Local legend insists that the Art Nouveau staircase with Carrara marble steps and iron balustrade, built and delivered in one piece from Italy, was too big and had to be shipped back and redone. ⊠ *Calle 10 No. 584, between Calles 51 and 53, Centro* ☎ *981/816-7644* ⊠ *Free* ⊙ *Weekdays 9–3.*

Mercado Municipal. The city's heart is this municipal market, where locals shop for seafood, produce, and housewares in a newly refurbished setting. The clothing section has some nice, inexpensive embroidered and beaded pieces among the jeans and T-shirts. Beside the market is a small yellow bridge aptly named **Puente de los Perros**—where four white plaster dogs guard the area. ⊠ *Av. Baluartes Este and Calle 53, Centro* ⊙ *Daily dawn–dusk.*

② Parque Principal. Also known as the Plaza de la Independencia, this central park is small by Mexican standards, and while pleasant, fairly non-

CLOSE UP

Campeche's History

CAMPECHE CITY'S GULF LOCATION played a pivotal role in its history. Ah-Kim-Pech (Maya for "lord of the serpent tick," from which the name Campeche is derived) was the capital of an Indian chieftainship here, long before the Spaniards arrived in 1517. In 1540, the conquerors—led by Francisco de Montejo and later by his son—established a real foothold at Campeche (originally called San Francisco de Campeche), using it as a base to conquer the peninsula.

At the time, Campeche City was the Gulf's only port and shipyard. So Spanish ships, loaded with cargoes of treasure plundered from Maya, Aztec, and other indigenous civilizations, dropped anchor here en route from Veracruz to Cuba, New Orleans, and Spain. As news of the riches spread, Campeche's shores were soon overrun with pirates. From the mid-1500s to the early 1700s, such notorious corsairs as Diego the Mulatto, Lorenzillo, Peg Leg, Henry Morgan, and Barbillas swooped in repeatedly from Tris—or Isla de Términos, as Isla del Carmen was then known—pillaging and burning the city and massacring its people.

Finally, after years of appeals to the Spanish crown, Campeche received funds to build a protective wall, with four gates and eight bastions, around the town center. For a while afterward, the city thrived on its exports, especially *palo de tinte*—a valuable dyewood more precious than gold because of demand by the nascent European textile industry—but also hardwoods, chicle, salt, and *henequen* (sisal hemp). But when the port of Sisal opened on the northern Yucatán coast in 1811, Campeche's monopoly on Gulf traffic ended, and its economy quickly declined. During the 19th and 20th centuries, Campeche, like most of the Yucatán peninsula, had little to do with the rest of Mexico. Left to their own devices, *Campechanos* lived in relative isolation until the petroleum boom of the 1970s brought businessmen from Mexico City, Europe, and the United States to its provincial doorstep.

Campeche City's history still shapes the community today. Remnants of its gates and bastions split the city into two main districts: the historical center (where relatively few people live) and the newer residential areas. Because the city was long preoccupied with defense, the colonial architecture is less flamboyant here than elsewhere in Mexico. The narrow flagstone streets reflect the confines of the city's walls; homes here emphasize the practical over the decorative. Still, government decrees, and an on-and-off beautification program, have helped keep the city's colonial structures in good condition despite the damaging effects of humidity and salt air. An air of antiquity remains.

6

descript. In its center is an old-fashioned kiosk with a pleasant café-bar where you can sit and watch city residents out for an evening stroll and listen to the itinerant musicians that often show up to play traditional ballads in the evenings. ⊠ *Bounded by Calles 10, 8, 55, and 57, Centro.*

🕐 ❽ **Puerta de Tierra.** Old Campeche ends here; the Land Gate is the only one of the four city gates with its basic structure intact. The stone arch intercepts a stretch of the partially crenellated wall, 26 feet high and 10 feet thick, that once encircled the city. Walk the wall's full length to the **Baluarte San Juan** for excellent views of both the old and new cities. The staircase leads down to an old well, underground storage area, and dungeon. There is a two-hour light show ($2), accompanied by music and dance, at Puerta de Tierra; it's presented in Spanish with French and English subtitles. Shows are on Tuesday, Friday, and Saturday at 8:30 PM, and daily during spring, summer, and Christmas vacation periods. ✉ *Calles 18 and 59, Centro* ⊙ *Daily 8 AM–9 PM.*

🕐 **Reducto de San José el Alto.** This lofty redoubt, or stronghold, at the northwest end of town, is home to the **Museo de Armas y Barcos.** Displays focus on 18th-century weapons of siege and defense. Also look for ships in bottles, manuscripts, and religious art. The view is terrific from the top of the ramparts, which were once used to spot invading ships. The "El Guapo" tram ($7) makes the trip here daily at 9 AM and 5 PM, departing from the east side of the main plaza. Visitors get about 10 minutes to admire the view before returning to the main plaza. ✉ *Av. Escénica s/n, north of downtown, Cerro de Bellavista* ☎ No phone 🎟 *$2.20* ⊙ *Tues.–Sun. 8–8.*

Where to Eat

$–$$$ ✕ **Marganzo.** Campeche cuisine is served by a traditionally attired waitstaff at this colorful restaurant a half block south of the plaza. Tour groups and locals converge here to tuck into *pompano en escabeche* (fish marinated in sour orange juice and grilled with chilies) and fresh shrimp dishes. (The soups, which may or may not be made with leftover seafood, are less popular.) A trio strums romantic ballads in the evenings after 7:30 and Sundays 1–5. ✉ *Calle 8 No. 267, between Calles 57 and 59, Centro* ☎ 981/811–3898 ▭ MC, V ⊙ *Closed Mon.*

$–$$$ ✕ **La Pigua.** This spot is where local professionals go to linger over
Fodor'sChoice lunch, and it's the town's hands-down favorite. The seafood is delicious,
★ and the setting is unusual: glass walls replicate an oblong Maya house, incorporating the profusion of plants outside into a design element. A truly ambitious lunch might start with a seafood cocktail, a plate of stone crab claws, or *camarones al coco* (coconut-encrusted shrimp), followed by fresh local fish, pampano, prepared in one of many ways. For dessert, the classic choice is *ate*, slabs of super-condensed mango, sweet potato, or other fruit or vegetable jelly served with tangy Gouda cheese. It's open noon to 6. ✉ *Av. Miguel Alemán 179A, Col. San Martin* ☎ 981/811–3365 ▭ AE, D, MC, V ⊙ *No dinner.*

★ **$** ✕ **Casa Vieja.** Whether you're having a meal or an evening cocktail, try to snag a table on this eatery's outdoor balcony for a fabulous view over Campeche's main plaza. The interior is usually warm and humid, and the brightly painted walls are crammed with art. There's sometimes live Cuban music in the evening, and yes, that's your waiter dancing with the singer. (Service is not a strength.) On the menu is a rich mix of international dishes, including those from the owners' native lands: Cuba and Campeche. In addition to pastas, salads, and regional food, there's a good selection of aperitifs and digestifs. To get here look for the stairway on the plaza's east side. ✉ *Calle 10 No. 319 Altos, between Calles 57 and 55, Centro* ☎ *981/811–8016* 🗖 *No credit cards.*

$ ✕ **Hot Beach Pizza.** Can't face another unpronounceable local dish? Locals agree this is the best pizza in town. The two branches most convenient to historic Camepeche are at "restaurant row," southeast of downtown and under the portales de San Francisco near the popular dinner spot of the same name. The most popular pie is the *mexicana,* with ham and hot jalapeño peppers. For vegetarians, there's a veggie version with fresh tomato, onion, and mild peppers. Open 2 PM–11 PM, Hot Beach delivers to your hotel room, or you can dine on-site. ✉ *Av. Resurgimiento 57, Malecón* ☎ *981/811–1133* 🗖 *No credit cards* ✉ *Bajos Portales de San Francisco, San Francisco* ☎ *981/811–3131* 🗖 *No credit cards.*

$ ✕ **Restaurant Campeche.** This bustling restaurant on the central plaza serves hearty Mexican and regional dishes; the menu includes everything from burgers and fries to tacos and chicken mole (in a chocolate-chili sauce). It's open from 6:30 AM to midnight. Breakfast items like pancakes and eggs are served all day, although the numbered specials are available in the morning only. For lunch or dinner try the *camarones tropicales,* shrimp served with mango sauce, rice, and steamed veggies. ✉ *Calle 57 at the main plaza, Centro* ☎ *981/816–2128* 🗖 *MC, V.*

¢–$ ✕ **Beijing.** Whether you speak fluent Mandarin or just have an exaggerated sense of culinary adventure, visit this hole-in-the-wall for authentic Chinese food. The menu's in Spanish, and the friendly, recently immigrated owners barely speak the *lingua franca.* Still, a huge plate of perfectly steamed broccoli with oyster sauce, succulent sweet-and-sour chicken, or yummy *gong bao* (little pieces of pork with vegetables) help all but the crabbiest of customers overcome the language barrier. The all-you-can-eat buffets Friday–Sunday (when kids under 7 eat free) make choosing easier. ✉ *Calle 8 No. 445, San Román* ☎ *981/811–6188* 🗖 *No credit cards.*

★ ¢–$ ✕ **Cenaduría los Portales.** Campechano families come here to enjoy a light supper, perhaps a delicious sandwich *claveteado* of honey-and-clove-spiked ham, along with a typical drink such as *horchata* (rice water flavored with cinnamon). Although the place opens at 6 PM, most people come between 8 and midnight. Mark your choices on the paper menu: for tacos, "m" means "masa," or corn tortillas, while "h" stands for "harina," or flour. The dining area is a wide colonial veranda with tables decked out in checkered tablecloths. There's no booze, but a beer stall at one end of the colonnade is open until around 9 PM. ✉ *Calle 10 No. 86, at Portales San Francisco, 8 blocks northeast of Plaza Principal, San Francisco* ☎ *981/811–1491* 🗖 *No credit cards* ☉ *No lunch.*

¢–$ ✕ **La Parroquia.** The large open doorway of this restaurant, which faces Calle 55, is the best place in town for people-watching. Open 24 hours, this locals' den has recently gotten a makeover—as well as allegedly faster service, the place now sports fabric tablecloths, and an expanded bar. Daily specials are full meals with soup, soft drink, dessert, and tortillas, in addition to choice of three entrées—all for around four bucks! Some of the best choices are inexpensive seafood dishes, including coconut shrimp or *pan de cazón* (shredded shark layered with tortillas, tomato sauce, and black beans). ⊠ *Calle 55 No. 8, between Calles 10 and 12, Centro* ☎ *981/816–2530* ▭ *No credit cards.*

¢ ✗ **Las Puertas.** Popular with students, intellectuals, politicians, and java-lovers of all ages, this cheerful café occupies an airy house just outside the perimeter of the old city walls. In additional to American coffee, cappuccino, and espresso, you can get cake, pastries, soft drinks, and light fare such as burritos and salads. Breakfast is served 9–noon. It's also a lecture hall and gallery, and the artwork on the walls is usually for sale. Jazz and other good tunes in the background and the warm-and-fuzzy attitude of the owner himself encourage customers to linger and loaf. ⊠ *Calle 10 No. 415, between Calles Bravos and Allende, San Román* ☎ *981/816–4218* ▭ *No credit cards.*

Where to Stay

★ $$$ ▦ **Hacienda Puerta Campeche.** Finally, Campeche has a hotel worth bragging about. The 17th-century mansions on most of a city block were reconfigured to create this lovely Starwood property just across from *la Puerta de Tierra,* the old city's historic landmark. Many of the original walls and lovely old tile floors have been retained, and the unusual indoor-outdoor heated swimming pool is surrounded by half-tumbled walls with hints of original paint. Rooms are sumptuously painted and decorated in classic Starwood style. ⊠ *Calle 59 No. 71, Centro* ☎ *981/ 816–7508 or 888/625–5144 in the U.S. and Canada* 🖷 *999/923–7963 (in Mérida)* ⊕ *www.starwoodhotels.com* ➪ *12 rooms, 3 suites* ⟵ *Restaurant, room service, fans, in-room safes, some refrigerators, cable TV with movies, in-room DVD players, pool, bar, lounge, laundry service, concierge, business services, free parking* ▭ *AE, MC, V.*

$$ ▦ **Hotel Del Mar.** Functionality, rather than charm, is the draw at this hotel facing the seawalk. As it's just a five-minute walk from the main plaza, it's popular with business travelers and travelers who like to be where the action is. Rooms are plain, with understated furniture, tile floors, faux-rattan furniture, and tiny triangular balconies that overlook the pool or the bay across the street. The coffee shop, El Poquito, serves generous portions of standard but tasty fare, and Lafitte's pirate-themed bar-restaurant is the city's most enduring night spot. ⊠ *Av. Ruíz Cortínez 51, Centro* ☎ *981/811–9191* 🖷 *981/811–6118* ⊕ *www.delmarhotel.com. mx* ➪ *138 rooms, 11 suites* ⟵ *Restaurant, coffee shop, room service, in-room safes, some minibars, cable TV, pool, gym, sauna, bar, night-club, shop, laundry service, Internet, business services, meeting rooms, car rental, travel services, free parking* ▭ *AE, MC, V* ⦿ *EP, CP.*

$ ▦ **Baluartes.** Between the waterfront and the Puerta del Mar (gateway to the old city), this hotel has a stylish lounge with plump, ocean-blue sofas—and a bar that's mysteriously closed until 7 PM. Luckily, there's also a coffee shop that's open all night on Fridays and Saturdays. Renovations to this property in 2004 focused on the common areas; some of the guest rooms still have dinged doors and messy grout. Although the rooms don't have balconies, their windows open, and floors two through four have plain bay views. ⊠ *Av. 16 de Septiembre 128, Centro* ☎ *981/816–3911* 🖷 *981/816–2410* ⊕ *www.baluartes.com.mx* ⟿ *100 rooms* ⚭ *Restaurant, coffee shop, room service, in-room safes, cable TV, pool, bar, shop, laundry service, Internet, business services, meeting rooms, car rental, travel services, free parking* ▭ *AE, MC, V.*

$ 🎬 **Debliz.** Northeast of the town center, this large hotel caters to tour groups. Although the rather faded exterior and the lobby look like those of an office building, the pool and deck areas—surrounded by bright pink and purple walls and hibiscus and bamboo plants—are more attractive. Rooms have modern wood furnishings, light tile floors, and plush built-in headboards. Carpets, tile, lamps, and other aspects of room decor were remodeled in 2005. Each room includes a small table and two chairs, but their tiny balconies have no furniture. You have to take a cab to the historical center—it's a bit too far to walk. ⊠ *Av. Diá Ordaz 55, Col. La Ermita* ☎ *981/815–2222* 🖷 *981/815–2277* ⊕ *www.hoteldebliz.com.mx* ⟿ *137 rooms, 6 suites* ⚭ *Restaurant, snack bar, cable TV, in-room data ports, pool, bar, laundry service, meeting room, free parking* ▭ *AE, MC, V.*

$ 🎬 **Francis Drake.** This small spiffy hotel sits right in the center of town. Its rooms offer few amenities, but their yellow walls, ocean-blue drapes, and bright patterned curtains and spreads lend a cheerful air. The restaurant is formal, and a bit sterile, and there is no bar or other place for guests to mingle. Still, it's a good place to park if you're looking to stay inexpensively in the heart of the old city. ⊠ *Calle 12 No. 207, between Calles 63 and 65, Centro* ☎ *981/811–5626 or 981/811–5627* 🖷 *981/811–5628* ⊕ *www.hotelfrancisdrake.com* ⟿ *9 rooms, 15 suites* ⚭ *Restaurant, room service, some in-room safes, minibars, cable TV, some in-room data ports, shop, laundry service, business center, free parking* ▭ *AE, MC, V.*

$ 🎬 **Hotel Plaza Campeche.** Plush sofas, heavy floor-to-ceiling lobby drapes, and a rather fussy-looking restaurant give this hotel a formal and elegant feel. Rooms are pleasant and modern, with firm mattresses, digital air-conditioning units, and green tile work. All bathrooms have tubs most of the junior suites have a terrace or balcony. ⊠ *Calle 10 No. 126A, Centro* ☎☎ *981/811–9900* ⊕ *www.hotelplazacampeche.com* ⟿ *82 rooms, 1 suite* ⚭ *Restaurant, café, room service, fans, cable TV, in-room data ports, in-rooms safes, pool, bar, laundry service, Internet, business services, meeting room, free parking* ▭ *MC, V.*

¢–$ 🎬 **Hotel América.** A converted colonial home, the aged América has scuffed black-and-white-checked floors offsetting white Moorish arches. There's a small, formal sitting area near the front door and a plainer but quieter place to gather or play cards on the second floor's central interior balcony. Breakfast is served at the umbrella-shaded tables on the ground-floor patio. Rooms themselves are simple and plain with local television only, and bamboo or pressed-wood furniture. This is one of the few hotels in the town center with parking, and you can check your e-mail for free at the front desk. ⊠ *Calle 10 No. 252, between Calles 59 and 61, Centro* ☎ *981/816–4588 or 981/816–4576* 🖷 *981/811–0556* ⊕ *www.hotelamericacampeche.com* ⟿ *49 rooms* ⚭ *Fans, cable TV, meeting room, free parking; no a/c in some rooms* ▭ *MC, V* ¶◑ *CP.*

6

¢ 🏨 **Colonial.** This romantic building dates from 1812 but was converted into a hotel in the 1940s. Rooms here vary, but all have quirky, old-fashioned tile bathrooms with curtainless showers (the original plumbing still works quite well). Most also have high ceilings, window screens, and relatively new mattresses, box springs, and bedspreads. Rooms with air-conditioning cost a bit more, but even these are extremely inexpensive; the owners' refusal to modernize with fax, in-room phones or TVs, or Internet access allows for rock-bottom prices. Public areas include a small sunroof and a second-floor sitting room. ⊠ *Calle 14 No. 122, between Calles 55 and 57, Centro* ☎ *981/816–2222 or 981/816–2630* ⇨ *30 rooms* ⚭ *Fans; no a/c in some rooms, no room phones, no room TVs* ▭ *No credit cards.*

¢ 🏨 **Del Paseo.** A block from the ocean, this sweet if faded hotel lies in the quiet neighborhood of San Román, about a 10-minute walk from the main square. Rooms are neither modern nor fancy, but most are clean and bright, with painted rattan furniture and either one double bed or two twins. Some have balconies overlooking a tiny covered courtyard with a restaurant, beauty shop, and a few other businesses. ⊠ *Calle 8 No. 215, San Román* ☎ *981/811–0100* 🖷 *981/811–0097* ⊕ *www. hoteldelpaseo.com* ⇨ *48 rooms, 2 suites* ⚭ *Restaurant, room service, cable TV, in-room data ports, bar, shop, laundry service, car rental, free parking* ▭ *AE, MC, V.*

¢ 🏨 **Monkey Hostel.** Though it typically attracts a young international crowd, this friendly if slightly grubby-walled hostel overlooking the main plaza offers refuge for penny-pinching older travelers as well. It's got multilingual managers, a common kitchen and modern laundry facilities, a book-exchange library, and a busy Internet corner. If you're lucky enough to get them, the five private rooms are a super deal. Other accommodations include men's, women's, and coed dorm rooms, each with either six or eight beds. Linens and storage boxes are provided, and there are bikes for rent. ⊠ *Calles 57 and 10, Centro* ☎ *981/811–6500* ⊕ *www.hostalcampeche.com* ⇨ *2 private rooms without bath; 3 8-bed dorm rooms without bath* ⚭ *Dining room, fans, bicycles, laundry facilities, Internet, travel services; no a/c, no room phones, no room TVs* ▭ *No credit cards* ⦿ CP.

Nightlife & the Arts

Each Saturday between 3 and 10 PM, the streets around the main square are closed to traffic and filled with folk and popular dance performances, singers, comics, handicrafts, and food and drink stands. If you're in town on a Saturday, don't miss these weekly festivities, called *Un Centro Histórico para Disfrutar* ("A Historic Downtown to Enjoy")—the entertainment is often first-rate and always free. In December, concerts and other cultural events take place as part of the Festival del Centro Histórico.

Bars & Discos

Campeche residents generally aren't big dancers, so their discos are mainly open on weekends. **Iguana Azul** (⊠ Calle 55 No. 11, between Calles 10 and 12, Centro ☎ 981/811–1311 or 981/816–2248), open daily after

6 PM, is a tranquil, cozy, blue-lit watering hole where you can have a few regional appetizers with drinks. **KY8** (✉ Calle 8 between Calles 59 and 61, Centro ☎ No phone), open Friday and Saturday only, has disco music downstairs, with rock upstairs for the slightly older crowd. Probably the most popular place to dance and party is the pirate-themed **Lafitte's Boulevard Café** (✉ Av. Ruíz Cortínez 51, Centro ☎ 981/811–9191) at Hotel del Mar. The wood-floored dance floor, surrounded by ropes and riggings, gets packed on weekend nights with people of all ages.

Shooters (✉ Av. Resurgimiento at Calle Lazareto, Montecristo ☎ No phone) is a both a dance venue and a beer bar with billiards tables. It's popular with people who don't mind talking over the music, but it's closed Mondays.

Film

Cinema Hollywood (✉ Av. Miguel Alemán 612, Centro ☎ 981/816–1452) is close to the malecón and Plaza Comercial Ah-Kim-Pech and has six large screens showing the latest blockbuster movies. Most are in English with Spanish subtitles.

Sports & Outdoors

Fishing and bird-watching are popular throughout the state of Campeche. Contact **Fernando Sansores** (✉ Calle 30 No. 1, Centro ☎☎ 982/828–0018) at the Snook Inn to arrange area sportfishing or wildlife photo excursions. **Francisco Javier Hernandez Romero** (✉ La Pigua restaurant, Av. Miguel Alemán 179A, Centro ☎ 981/811–3365) can arrange boat or fishing trips to the Reserva Ecológica Petenes. To enjoy a tour of Campeche Bay and the surrounding area, contact the **Marina Yacht Club** (✉ Av. Resurgimiento 120, Carretera a Lerma ☎☎ 981/816–1990). Times and duration of tours are per customer requests. The club's informal restaurant ($–$$), open daily between noon and 7 PM, is quite decent and overlooks the water.

Shopping

Although Campeche's handicrafts have traditionally been limited to baskets, straw hats, embroidered cloth, and clay trinkets, a few stores provide stylish women's clothing and slightly more sophisticated souvenirs. Folk art is still rather limited, however, and most shops are dominated by ships in bottles, statues made of seashells, and mother-of-pearl and black-coral jewelry. ⚠ Be aware that buying black coral is environmentally incorrect, since coral reefs take thousands of years to grow.

Markets & Malls

At the **Mercado Público Pedro Sainz de Baranda** (✉ Av. Circuito Baluartes Este between Calles 51 and 55, Centro), don't be put off by the sight of a skinned pig's head or two; as well as a place for locals to buy freshly butchered meats, seafood, and produce, it's also got pretty women's cotton blouses and dresses for sale. There's rooftop parking with an elevator to the ground floor; the recently remodeled market stalls are clean and orderly. There are even exhaust fans to suck up any offensive smells.

LA HUACHITA

This bakery, founded in 1891 and located on the west side of the square, is duly famous for the aromatic breads it produces throughout the morning. Try a *pichón* (a huge ham-and-cheese loaf); *budín* (which is similar to bread pudding); *pan de elote, anis,* or *canela* (corn, anise, and cinnamon bread, respectively); or an *empanada de camote* (a sweet-potato turnover), among other artisan breads.

Campeche City's two large, fairly modern shopping malls are within walking distance of each other. **Plaza Comercial Ah-Kim-Pech** (⊠ Avs. Pedro Sainz de Baranda and Ruíz Cortínez, Centro), on the waterfront, has boutiques, clothing, and souvenir shops, as well as a grocery store. Not far from Plaza Comercial Ah-Kim-Pech, **Plaza del Mar** (⊠ Av. Ruíz Cortínez at Av. Pedro Sáinz de Baranda, Centro ☎ 981/811–3491) is closest to the center of town and home to a number of specialty stores. **Plaza Universidad** (⊠ Av. Agustín Melgar 45 between Calle 18 and Av. Universidad, Universidad ☎ 981/816–4922) has several good jewelry stores and boutiques.

Specialty Shops

CLOTHING **Códice** (⊠ Calle 10 No. 256, between Calles 59 and 61, Centro ☎ 981/
★ 811–4694) carries an organic-looking line of women's dresses, skirts, and blouses made with muslin, linen, and other natural fibers. They also have tasteful T-shirts and hats and bags made of dyed or natural palm fiber. Right on the main square, **Liz Minelli** (⊠ Calle 10 No. 319A, Los Portales, Centro ☎ 981/811–6814) offers an impressive selection of glad rags for women, including swingy dresses in clingy materials. There are also short, ruffled tops and skirts and dresses in mixed fibers, as well as suits, jackets, jean jackets, ball gowns, and a selection of sexy undies.

CRAFTS In an old mansion, the government-run **Casa de Artesanía Tukulná**
★ (⊠ Calle 10 No. 333, between Calles 59 and 61, Centro ☎ 981/816–9088) sells well-made embroidered dresses, blouses, pillow coverings, regional dress for men and women, hammocks, Campeche's famous Panama hats, posters, books on Campeche ecology in Spanish, jewelry, baskets, and stucco reproductions of Maya motifs. The colonial-era house is worth a visit if only to admire its arched doorways, black-and-white tile floors, and chandeliers. It's closed Sunday.

Tiny **Hecho en Mexico** (⊠ Calle 59 No. 3, between Calles 10 and 12, Centro ☎ 981/816–4405) has a nice collection of quality crafts and jewelry from elsewhere in Mexico. There are coconut masks from Guerrero, masks, small stamped tin mirrors, and silver jewelry. **Veleros** (⊠ Plaza Comercial Ah-Kim-Pech, Centro ☎ 981/811–2446), owned by craftsman David Pérez, stocks miniature scale-model ships, seashells, figures of carved mahogany and cedar, furniture with nautical motifs, and jewelry made from sanded and polished bull's horn—a material that somewhat resembles tortoiseshell. It's closed Sunday.

EL CAMINO REAL

The so-called short route to Mérida (192 km, or 119 mi) takes you past several traditional villages along the old King's Highway, as the stretch of road north of Campeche has traditionally been called. Artisans in these humble towns produce the state's best-known handicrafts. Many pieces are made for distribution elsewhere, so there isn't a large selection for sale here, but viewing the places where they're produced provides a glimpse of the local way of life. Also along the Camino Real are old Franciscan churches, both abandoned and refurbished haciendas, and small towns where life still revolves around the market and the central plaza. Don't count on finding many people who speak English, and note that villages mentioned offer little in the way of restaurants and accommodations.

Pomuch

⑮ *53 km (32 mi) north of Campeche, along Carretera 180 toward Mérida.*

This town of brightly painted buildings is known for its homemade bread, as well as preserves of mangoes, plums, and other fruits that you can buy from stands lining the highway.

Interestingly, Pomuch is also known for participating in a unique Day of the Dead ritual: on November 1, the townspeople unearth their dead, clean off their bones, and return them to their crypts wrapped in clean cloth. While the anthropologically minded find this fascinating, queasy sorts may wish to avoid the town for this particular festival.

Hecelchakán

⑯ *60 km (37 mi) north of Campeche, along Carretera 180 toward Mérida.*

A faded but still vital 15th-century town with an idiosyncratic Franciscan church and former monastery, Hecelchakán (pronounced e-sell-cha-*kan*) is a good spot to observe a small town in action and see some colonial facades. Kiosks in front of the church dispense *cochinita pibíl*, pit-baked pork, a traditional morning snack served with hot tortillas, but these days, kids fiddling with noisy video games can take away from the experience.

On the outskirts of town are several old haciendas, such as Chunkanán, as well as the village of Dzibalchén, where the Dzibalchén Verses (descriptions of Maya ceremonies and rituals) were written. The local church dates from 1768.

Hecelchakán's primary attraction is the **Museo Arqueológico del Camino Real.** In a 1660 house, this museum has an impressive collection of clay figurines from Isla de Jaina and stelae of the Puuc style. A diorama depicts the peninsula's first *mestizos,* children of the shipwrecked Spanish soldier Gonzalo Guerrero and his Indian wife. Stone axe heads, arrow points, and other primitive tools and bowls are also on display. ⊠ *Main plaza* ☎ *No phone* 💲 *$2.40* ⏰ *Tues.–Sun. 9–1 and 4–8.*

The rutted road to **Isla de Jaina,** part of the Reserva de la Biósfera Los Petenes, starts in Hecelchakán. Previously thought to have been only a giant Maya cemetery (more than a thousand grave sites have been discovered here), Isla de Jaina is currently under excavation, and recent finds include a pyramid some 60 feet tall and a double ball court. The site is off-limits without prior written permission from the Instituto Nacional de Antropología e Historia (INAH) in Campeche; the easiest way to tour the island is by boat with **Espacios Naúticos** (⇨ Tours), which will help you secure the necessary permit.

Where to Stay

$$ **Hacienda Blanca Flor.** Although it's often deserted, this hacienda has been tastefully if simply restored. For those who want something rustic, old-fashioned (think *Like Water for Chocolate*), and relatively remote, it's a good base for exploring northern Campeche. Surrounding the ancient open patio filled with bright bougainvillea, rooms have screened windows and loud air-conditioning. There's an outdoor pool (often dry), but no poolside furniture, and a small, unmanned outdoor bar by the vegetable garden. Groups (the bulk of the hacienda's clientele) dine in the a cavernous, rock-walled dining room; single parties eat in the more intimate front room amid old family photos. The ranch-style food is refreshingly simple and tasty. ⊠ *Carr. 261, Km 88, Hecelchakán* ☎ *999/925–8042 or 999/925–9655 (both in Mérida)* 🖷 *999/925–9111* ✉ *hblancaf@prodigy.net.mx* ➷ *20 rooms, 6 cottages* ♤ *Dining room, fans, pool, bar, horseback riding, free parking; no room phones* ▤ *No credit cards.*

Calkiní

🔞 *24 km (15 mi) north of Hecelchakán.*

After passing through the double Maya arch at the entrance to town (similar to those used in classic Maya civilization), you'll enter this sweet, simple town with very little claim to fame. Chocolate-and-cherry painted houses line the main street along with pizzerias, video stores, and pharmacies. Men pump their three-wheeled cycles, called *tricitaxis* (tree-see-*tack*-sees), transporting young kids or plump matrons en route to the market; entire families can be seen perched on two-wheeled bikes. Old men in well-pressed guayaberas accompany traditionally dressed women in crisp white huipiles, with shawls wrapped around the waist and hanging down off their shoulders as their mothers and grandmothers wore them.

Among the most important towns along the Camino Real, Calkiní dates from the pre-Columbian Maya Ah-Canul dynasty. The chieftainship was founded here in 1443 after the destruction of the Postclassic kingdom of Mayapán, in what is now Yucatán state. The site chosen was beneath an enormous ceiba, a tree sacred to the Maya as a conduit between heaven, earth, and the underworld.

Calkiní's major attraction is the **Parroquia de San Luis Obispo.** Franciscan friars built this church-fortress-convent beginning in 1561, and the

Clarisas have used it as a cloistered convent since 1980. You can enter the church (even if the front gate is padlocked) by asking at the office around the right side of the building, but the convent itself is off-limits. Inside the church is an exquisite carved cedar altarpiece in burnished gold, red, and black along with a handsome pulpit carved with the symbols of the four Evangelists. The shell motif above the doorway is typically Franciscan. ⊠ *Off the town Sq.* ☎ *No phone* 🎫 *Free* ☉ *Wed. and Fri.–Mon. 7–noon and 3–8, Thurs. 7 AM–9 PM.*

North of town is the village of Tepakán, home of **Cal-kin** (⊠ Carretera Calkiní–Tepakán, Km 1 ☎ 996/961–0232), the ceramics factory that produces the distinctive, hand-painted white, beige, and blue ceramics of Campeche. A four-piece place setting starts at $40. The factory's small store is typically open weekdays 8–5, Saturday 8–4.

> **off the beaten path**

NUNKINÍ – In this small, traditional Maya village 28 km (17 mi) west of Calkiní, women weave mats and rugs from the reeds of *huano* palm, incorporating traditional designs. The colorful church of San Diego Apóstol is here as well. Farther west are the villages of Santa Cruz and Tankuché, and El Remate, a wonderful water hole surrounded by mangroves and sapodilla trees. The road continues on to Reserva de la Biósfera Los Peténes, where flamingos, frigates, herons, and ibis thrive in the isolation of the mangroves. Fishermen at Isla Arena, a tiny fishing village at the end of the road, can be hired for a small fee for boat trips to see these birds.

Becal

18 *10 km (6 mi) north of Calkiní.*

The statue of three giant hats in the center of the town plaza isn't a joke: Becal is famous for its *jipis,* known to most of the world as Panama hats. Local residents weave reeds of the huano palm in "caves" belowground, where the humidity keeps the reeds flexible. As a result, the finest, most tightly woven of these hats are so pliable that they can be rolled up in a suitcase (for a short while) with no harm done. First produced in the 19th century by the García family, the hats have become a village tradition. Since most of the hats produced here are sold to wholesalers, you'll find good prices, but a limited selection. Still, buying jipis directly from the makers helps to sustain this craft and keep the tradition alive. Most vendors will send you to their competitors if they don't have what you want.

Artesanías Chari (⊠ Calle 30 No. 231 ☎ 996/431–4326) has a larger inventory of headbands, earrings, handbags, and other items as well as hats for men and women. Ask to see their subterranean weaving area in the backyard. The **Sociedad de Artesanas Becaleñas** (⊠ Calle 34 between Calles 33 and 35 ☎ 996/431–4275) produces and sells souvenirs, hammocks, and hats. Ask to see the "prensa" where hats are finished as well as the underground cave.

off the
beaten
path

HALACHÓ – Just 6 km (4 mi) north of Becal in the state of Yucatán, this village is worth a stop if you're looking for handcrafted baskets, rugs, and bags. Halachó, which means "reed rats," was so named because it was founded on the shores of a lake (long since dried up), where rats once lived in abundance in the tall grasses along the shore. This type of reed is still cultivated and used to make the baskets and other crafts that are for sale here.

THE CHENES ROUTE

This scenic route, leading through green forested hills and valleys covered by low scrub, cornfields, and citrus orchards, is the longer way to reach the Yucatán capital of Mérida. Its name refers to the Chenes ruins of eastern Campeche, which are along the way. Chenes-style temples are recognizable by their elaborate stucco facades decorated with geometric designs and giant earth-monster masks, with the open doorway representing the open mouth. It's a good idea to visit Edzná first; then, continue south on Carretera Bonfil–Dzibalchén through the town of Laureles, founded by Guatemalan refugees, and then on to Dzibalchén and Hochob before continuing northwest to Hopelchén.

Edzná

🏛 **⑲** *61 km (37 mi) southeast of Campeche City.*

Fodor'sChoice
★

A leaf-strewn nature trail winds slowly toward the ancient heart of Edzná. Although only 55 km (34 mi)—less than an hour's drive—southeast of Campeche City, the site receives few tour groups. The scarcity of camera-carrying humans intensifies the feeling of communion with nature, and with the Maya who built this once-flourishing commercial and ceremonial city.

Despite being refreshingly under-appreciated by 21st-century travelers, Edzná is considered by archaeologists to be one of the peninsula's most important ruins. A major metropolis in its day, it was situated at a crossroads of sorts between cities in modern-day Guatemala as well as Chiapas and Yucatán states, and this "out-of-state" influence can be appreciated in its melange of architectural elements. Roof combs and corbeled arches are reminiscent of those at Yaxchilán and Palenque, in Chiapas; giant stone masks are characteristic of the Peten-style architecture of southern Campeche and northern Guatemala.

Edzná began as a humble agricultural settlement around 300 BC, reaching its pinnacle in the Late Classic period, between AD 600 and 900, and gradually waning in importance until being all but abandoned in the early 15th century. Today, soft breezes blow through groves of slender trees where brilliant orange and black birds spring from branch to branch, gathering seeds. Clouds scuttle across a blue backdrop, perfectly framing the mossy, multi-stepped remains of once-great structures.

A guide can point out features often missed by the untrained eye, like the remains of arrow-straight sacbés. These raised roads in their day connected one important ceremonial building within the city to the next, and also connected Edzná to trading partners throughout the peninsula.

The best place to survey the site is 102-foot **Pirámide de los Cinco Pisos,** built on the raised platform of the **Gran Acrópolis** (Great Acropolis). The Five-Story Pyramid consists of five levels terminating in a tiny temple crowned by a roof comb. Hieroglyphs were carved into the vertical face of the 15 steps between each level; some were recemented in place by archaeologists, although not necessarily in the correct order. On these stones, as well as on stelae throughout the site, you can see faint depictions of the opulent attire once worn by the Maya ruling class—quetzal feathers, jade pectorals, and jaguar skin skirts.

In 1992, Campeche archaeologist Florentino Garcia Cruz discovered that the Pirámide de los Cinco Pisos was constructed so that on certain dates the setting sun would illuminate the mask of the creator-god, Itzamná, inside one of the pyramid's rooms. This happens annually on May 1, 2, and 3, the beginning of the planting season for the Maya—then and now. It also occurs on August 7, 8, and 9, the days of harvesting and giving thanks. On the pyramid's fifth level, the last to be built, are the ruins of three temples and a ritual steam bath.

West of the Great Acropolis, the Puuc-style **Plataforma de los Cuchillos** (Platform of the Knives) was so named by a 1970 archaeological exploration that found a number of flint knives inside. To the south, four buildings surround a smaller structure called the **Pequeña Acrópolis.** Twin sun-god masks with huge protruding eyes, sharply filed teeth, and oversize tongues flank the **Templo de los Mascarones** (Temple of the Masks, or Building 414), adjacent to the Small Acropolis. The mask at bottom left (east) represents the rising sun, while the one on the right represents the setting sun.

If you're not driving, consider taking one of the inexpensive day trips offered by tour operators in Campeche; this is far easier than trying to get to Edzná by municipal buses. ⊠ *Carretera 261 east from Campeche City for 44 km (27 mi) to Cayal, then Carretera 188 southeast for 18 km (11 mi)* ☎ *No phone* 🎟 *$3.30* ⊙ *Daily 8–5.*

Where to Stay

★ **$$$$** 🏨 **Hacienda Uayamón.** Abandoned in 1905, this former hacienda was resurrected nearly a century later and transformed into a luxury hotel with an elegant restaurant. The original architecture and decor have been carefully preserved: the library has exposed beam ceilings, cane chairs, sisal carpets, and wooden bookshelves at least 12 feet high. Each casita has its own private garden, hot tub, and bathroom as well as a cozy bedroom. The remaining two walls of the machine house shelter the outdoor pool, and candles are still lighted at the ruined chapel. ⊠ *9 km (5½ mi) north of Edzná* ☎ *981/ 829–7527, 888/625–5144 in U.S. or Canada* 🖶 *999/923–7963*

> **WORD OF MOUTH**
>
> "Hacienda Uayamón was incredibly luxurious with lovely tropical gardens, lotus flowers in the ponds, romantic ruins with pillars coming out of the swimming pool . . . it has to be seen to be believed."   –angela

⊕ *www.starwood.com* ⇨ *2 suites, 10 casitas* ⌂ *Restaurant, room service, fans, in-room safes, minibars, cable TV, pool, spa, massage, lounge, babysitting, laundry service, concierge, meeting room, travel services, free parking, some pets allowed* ⊟ *AE, MC, V.*

Hopelchén

㉑ *84 km (134 mi) east of Campeche on Carretera 261, 153 km (95 mi) north of Xpujil.*

Don't be surprised to see groups of sandy-haired, blue-eyed and oddly dressed folks in this town; the men in white *sombreros* and bib overalls, and the women in long flowered dresses and head scarves, are simply members of the colony of Mennonites who've lived here since 1985. These immigrant farmers, who came from northern Mexico, and who have settled in the farmlands around Hopelchén, still speak a Dutch-German dialect as well as Spanish. Many of them make and sell Mennonite cheese, which can be purchased in shops and restaurants throughout the state.

Otherwise, Hopelchén—the name means "place of the five wells"—is a traditional Maya and mestizo town noted for the Iglesia de San Francisco, built in honor of St. Antonio of Padua in 1667. (Later priests switched allegiance and now honor the Virgin of the Immaculate Conception.) Corn, beans, tobacco, fruit, squash, and henequen are cultivated in this rich agricultural region. If you want an ice-cream cone, a magazine, or an old-fashioned treadle sewing machine, check out the general store called Escalante Heredia Hermanas right on the town square—it's also the place to make long-distance phone calls.

Grutas de Xtacumbilxunaan

㉑ *34 km (21 mi) north of Hopelchén.*

Just short of the state line between Campeche and Yucatán and a few miles before Bolonchén de Rejón are the Grutas de Xtacumbilxunaan (pronounced shta-*cum*-bil-shu-nan), the "caverns of the hidden women" in Spanish and Maya—where legend says a Maya girl disappeared after going for water. In ancient times, cenotes (sinkholes) deep in the extensive cave system provided an emergency water source during droughts. Only a few chambers are open to the public, because the rock surfaces are dangerously slippery and the depth of the caverns is 240 feet. In the upper part of the caves, you can see delicate limestone formations that have been given whimsical names such as "Witch's Ball" and "Devil's Bridge." There are sometimes guides at the site who can show you around, but not always. 🎫 *$2* ⊗ *Tues.–Sun. 9–2.*

Santa Rosa Xtampak

⛰ **㉒** *107 km (64 mi) from Campeche City; entrance at Carretera 261, Km 79, travel 30 km (19 mi) down signed side road; 25 km (16 mi) east of Hopelchén.*

A fabulous example of the zoomorphic architectural element of Chenes architecture, Xtampak's **Casa de la Boca del Serpiente** (House of the

Serpent's Mouth) has a perfectly preserved and integrated zoomorphic entrance. Here, the mouth of the creator-god Itzamná stretches wide to reveal a perfectly proportioned inner chamber. The importance of this city during the Classic period is shown by the large number of public buildings and ceremonial plazas; archaeologists believe there are around 100 structures here, although only 12 have been cleared. The most exciting find was the colossal **Palacio** in the western plaza. Inside, two inner staircases run the length of the structure, leading to different levels and ending in subterranean chambers. This combination is extremely rare in Maya temples. ⊠ *East of Hopelchén on Dzibalchén–Chencho road, watch for sign* ☎ *No phone* 🎫 *$2.50* ☉ *Daily 8–5.*

Dzibilnocac

㉓ *18 km (11 mi) northeast of Dzibalchén, 69 km (43 mi) southeast of Hopelchén.*

Off the beaten path, Dzibilnocac is not the place for the casually curious. Although there are at least seven temple pyramids here, the only one that has been partially excavated is the **Palacio Principal,** a Late Classic (AD 600–800) palace. Only one of the three towers remains intact; it contains a square, one-room temple with beautifully executed carvings of Chaac on the outside walls. Under what remains of the middle tower, two small underground chambers can be accessed through a Maya arch. The farthest tower has a roof comb sticking up from a mound of grass, trees, and stones—an incongruous sight. Archaeologists can't agree on whether Dzibilnocac (pronounced dzi-bil-no-*cak*) translates as "painted ceiling" or "great painted turtle," but they do concur that is was a fair-size ceremonial center between AD 250 and 900. The Chenes architectural style is typified by zoomorphic masks; Río Bec elements include rounded lateral towers and false stairways.

To reach the rarely visited archaeological site of Dzibilnocac, you must first get to the village of Dzibalchén by traveling south on the road named for this destination. (From Edzná, continue south on the road to Pich and Laureles, and then on to Hochob and Dzibalchén.) From there, proceed north on a small side road to Vicente Guerrero, also known as Iturbide, a farming community 19 km (12 mi) north—literally at the end of the road. Each corner of the town square has a small stone guardhouse built in 1850 during the War of the Castes, and the road around them eventually turns into a dirt path that passes houses and ends at the ruins. ⊠ *South to Dzibalchén and then north to Vicente Guerrero* ☎ *No phone* 🎫 *Free* ☉ *Daily 8–5.*

Hochob

㉔ *55 km (34 mi) south of Hopelchén, 15 km (9 mi) west of Dzibilnocac.*

The small Maya ruin of Hochob is an excellent example of the Chenes architectural style, which flowered from about AD 100 to 1000. Most ruins in this area (central and southeastern Campeche) were built on the highest possible elevation to prevent flooding during the rainy season, and Hochob is no exception. It rests high on a hill overlooking the surrounding valleys. Another indication that these are Chenes ruins is the number of *chultunes,* or cisterns, in the area. Since work began at Hochob in the early 1980s, four temples and palaces have been excavated at the site, including two that have been fully restored. Intricate and perfectly preserved geometric designs cover the temple known as **Estructura II**; these are typical of the Chenes style.

The doorway represents the open mouth of Itzamná, the creator-god; above it the eyes bulge; fangs are bared on either side of the base. It takes a bit of imagination to see the structure as a mask; color no doubt enhanced the effects in the good old days. Squinting helps a bit: the figure's "eyes" are said to be squinting as well. But anyone can appreciate the intense geometric relief carvings decorating the facades, including long cascades of Chaac rain god masks along the sides. Evidence of roof combs can be seen at the top of the building. Ask the guard to show you the series of natural and man-made chultunes that extend back into the forest. ⊠ *Southwest of Hopelchén on Dzibalchén–Chencho Rd.* 📞 *No phone* 💲 *Free* ☉ *Daily 8–5.*

CARRETERA 186 TOWARD CHETUMAL

Xpujil, Chicanná, Calakmul . . . exotic, far-flung-sounding names dot the map along this stretch of jungly territory. These are places where the creatures of the forest outnumber the tourists: in Calakmul, four- and five-story ceiba trees sway as families of spider monkeys swing through the canopy; in Xpujil, brilliant blue motmots fly from tree to tree in long, swoopy arcs.

The vestiges of at least 10 little-known Maya cities lie hidden off Carretera 186 between Escárcega and Chetumal. You can see Xpujil, Becán, Hormiguero, and Chicanná in one rather rushed day by starting out early from Campeche City, or from Chetumal, Quintana Roo, and spending the night in Xpujil. If you plan to see Calakmul, spend the first night at Xpujil, arriving at Calakmul as soon as the site opens the next day. That provides the best chance to see armadillo, wild turkey, families of howler and spider monkeys, and other wildlife.

Until 1950, this part of Campeche was barely populated. After offering land to city-dwelling Campechanos without much success, the Mexican government began colonizing the area with settlers from Tabasco who'd lost their land to cattle barons. Later immigrants came from Veracruz and Chiapas. Their imported slash-and-burn technique of farming, for which precious forests are burned to make way for crops, is being replaced when possible by more environmentally friendly industries like beekeeping and pig farming.

A good way to explore this little-visited region is to hire one of the government-trained local guides—many of whom are versed in Maya culture as well as the local flora and fauna—to show you around. You can arrange this through the tourist office in Campeche City (ask for a guide who speaks basic English).

A two-lane highway runs north from Xpujil, connecting to Hopelchén, east of Campeche City. Travelers can continue north from Xpujil to visit several Chenes-style ruins, from there returning to Campeche City or continuing north toward Yucatán state.

| en route | If you're headed east from Champotón or Campeche toward the sites of Xpujil, Chicanná, or Becán, don't miss **La Teca,** a great truck stop and Mexican restaurant at the crossroads of Carreteras 186 and 261. Open 24 hours, the restaurant has an air-conditioned dining room and a large open-sided patio overlooking the highway. Both have TVs blaring nonstop and serve Yucatecan dishes such as smoked pork, breaded chicken, and spicy *pollo pibíl* (chicken baked in banana leaves). They're nicely presented—albeit on plastic plates—with refried beans, greasy french fries, pickled onions, and fresh salsa. ✉ *Carretera 186, Km 1, by the Pemex station* ☎ *982/824–0635* ▭ *No credit cards.*

Xpujil

🏛 ㉕ *Carretera 186, Km 150; 300 km (186 mi) southeast of Campeche, 130 km (81 mi) south of Dzibilnocac, 125 km (78 mi) west of Chetumal.*

Xpujil (meaning "cat's tail," and pronounced ish-*poo*-hil) gets its same from the reedy plant that grows in the area. Elaborately carved facades and doorways in the shape of monsters' mouths reflect the Chenes style, while adjacent pyramid-towers connected by a long platform show the influence of Río Bec architects. Some of the buildings have lost a lot of their stones, making them resemble "day after" sand castles. In **Edificio I,** all three towers were once crowned by false temples, and at the front of each are the remains of four vaulted rooms, each oriented toward one of the compass points and thought to have been used by priests and royalty. On the back side of the central tower is a huge mask of the rain god Chaac. Quite a few other building groups amid the forests of gum trees and *palo mulato* (so called for its bark with both dark and light patches) have yet to be excavated. 🎫 *$2.20* 🕐 *Daily 8–5.*

Where to Stay & Eat

¢ ✕🏨 **Hotel Calakmul.** Simple but pleasant rooms have brightly painted walls, tile floors, and bathrooms with hot water. Flowered curtains cover screened, wood-shuttered windows, and each unit has a ceiling fan. The original wooden cabins are cramped and rustic, with no TV or a/c, but have mosquito nets. With its peaked palapa roof and large windows overlooking tropical plants, the restaurant (¢–$) offers good food—the best in town—and generous portions. Try the *mole poblano* (turkey leg topped with rich, spicy chocolate and chili sauce) or the more straightforward fried chicken served with beans, rice, avocado, and tortillas. ✉ *Carretera 186, Km 153* ☎ *983/871–6029* ➾ *16 rooms, 9 cabanas with shared bath* ㊟ *Restaurant, fans; no room phones, no TV in some rooms* ▭ *No credit cards.*

★ $$ 🏨 **Chicanná Ecovillage Resort.** Rooms in this comfortable jungle lodge are in two-story stucco duplexes with thatch roofs. Each ample unit has a tile floor, an overhead fan, screened windows, a wide porch or balcony with a table and chairs, and one king or two double beds with bright

CLOSE UP

Ecotourism in Campeche

ECOTOURISM IN CAMPECHE IS IN ITS INFANCY; there's little infrastructure and few foreign tourists compared with those who visit Quintana Roo and Yucatán states. Nonetheless, state, federal, and private entities are working to preserve Campeche's wilderness.

Southern Campeche contains one of the last primary-growth rain forests in Mexico, legally protected under UNESCO's Man and the Biosphere program as the Reserva de la Biosfera Calakmul. It adjoins the much larger Reserva de la Biosfera Maya across the Guatemalan border, as well as a smaller reserve in Belize. This block of rainforest, along with the Montes Azules biosphere reserve in Chiapas, forms one of the most important rainforest "lungs"—great expanses of trees that help oxygenate our world—in the Americas. Most of the conservation area is inaccessible except to locals and dedicated adventurers, who, à la Indiana Jones,

are prepared to hire a local guide and begin bushwhacking. In the biosphere's most accessible sections, a few rutted roads lead to archaeological sites. Most impressive is Calakmul itself, home to orchids and jungle wildlife, including spider monkeys, peccaries, boa constrictors and several species of highly poisonous snakes, and hundreds of species of birds.

The petroleum industry has taken its toll on parts of Campeche; as a result, the state has evolved into one of Mexico's most environmentally aware regions. Because it's primarily an agricultural society, Campeche hasn't undergone urban sprawl or global commercialization—meaning it still has something left to preserve. For the most part, the people of Campeche, with their cultural traditions of respect for the land, support ecotourism. It promises to grow over the coming years.

cotton bedspreads. There's a library with a television and VCR, and a small pool filled with rainwater and surrounded by flowering plants. There is no phone or fax at the hotel; both are available in nearby Xpujil. For reservations, contact the Del Mar Hotel in Campeche City. ⊠ *Carretera 186, Km 144, 9 km (5½ mi) north of village of Xpujil* ☎ 981/811–9191 *for reservations* 🖷 981/811–9192 ⊕ *www.hotelmex.net* 🛏 *36 rooms* ⚪ *Restaurant, fans, pool, hot tub, bar, library, laundry service, meeting room, free parking; no a/c, no room phones, no room TVs* ▭ *AE, MC, V.*

Becán

★ ⛰ ❷ *7 km (4½ mi) west of Xpujil, Carretera 186, Km 145.*

An interesting feature of this once important city is its defensive moat—an unusual feature among ancient Maya cities but barely evident today. The seven ruined gateways—which once permitted the only entrance to the guarded city—may have clued archaeologists to its presence. Becán (usually translated as "canyon of water," referring to the moat) is thought to have been an important city within the Río Bec group, which once encompassed Xpujil, Chicanná, and Río Bec. Most of the site's many buildings date from between about AD 600 and 1000, but since there are no traditionally inscribed stelae listing details of royal births, deaths, battles, and ascendencies to the throne, archaeologists have had to do a lot of guessing about what transpired here.

You can climb several of the structures to get a view of the area, and even spot some of Xpuhil's towers above the treetops. Duck into **Estructura VIII,** where underground passages lead to small subterranean rooms and to a concealed staircase that reaches the top of the temple. One of several buildings surrounding a central plaza, Estructura VIII has lateral towers and a giant zoomorphic mask on its central facade. The building was used for religious rituals, including blood-letting rites during which the elite pierced earlobes and genitals, among other sensitive body parts, in order to present their blood to the gods. ☉ *Daily 8–5.*

Chicanná

🏔 ㉗ *Carretera 186, Km 141; 3 km (2 mi) east of Becán.*

6

Thought to have been a satellite community of the larger, more commercial city of Becán, Chicanná ("house of the serpent's mouth") was also in its prime during the Late Classic period. Of the four buildings surrounding the main plaza, **Estructura II,** on the east side, is the most impressive. On its intricate facade are well-preserved sculpted reliefs and faces with long twisted noses, symbols of Chaac. In typical Chenes style, the doorway represents the mouth of the creator-god Itzamná; surrounding the opening are large crossed eyes, fierce fangs, and earrings to complete the stone mask, which still bears traces of blue and red pigments. 🎟 *$3* ☉ *Daily 8–5.*

Balamkú

🏔 ㉘ *Carretera 186, Km 95; about 60 km (37 mi) west of Xpujil.*

Near the western boundary of the Reserva de la Biosfera Calakmul is the Templo del Jaguar, famous for the intricate molded stucco and polychrome frieze discovered here in 1995. Dated to AD 550–650 (in the Classic period), this dazzling work is nearly 56 feet long and 13 feet high. On the middle panel, the aquatic symbols—two frogs and two crocodiles—represent the fertility of the earth. Above this are representations of the god and below, figures relating to the *inframundo,* or underworld. Three subterranean chambers are symbolic entrances to the world of the dead. In places you can still see the original red and black paint. The fresco is enclosed to protect it from the elements, and flash cameras are prohibited. You can view other structures here, including remnants of residences up a path to the left as you enter the site, but they're anticlimactic in comparison to the impressive frieze. 🎟 *$2* ☉ *Daily 8–5.*

Hormiguero

🏛 ㉙ *14 km (9 mi) southeast of Xpujil.*

Bumping down the badly-potholed, 8-km (5-mi) road leading to this site may give you an appreciation for the explorers who first found and excavated it in 1933. Hidden throughout the forest are at least five magnificent temples, two of which have been excavated to reveal ornate facades covered with zoomorphic figures whose mouths are the doorways. The buildings here were constructed roughly between 400 BC and AD 1100 in the Río Bec style, with rounded lateral towers and ornamental stairways, the latter built to give an illusion of height, which they do wonderfully. The facade of **Estructura II,** the largest structure on the site, is beautiful: intricately carved and well-preserved. **Estructura V** has some admirable Chaac masks arranged in a cascade atop a pyramid. Nearby is a perfectly round chultun (water storage tank), and, seemingly emerging from the earth, the eerily-etched designs of a still-unexcavated structure.

Hormiguero is Spanish for "anthill," referring both to the looters' tunnels that honeycombed the ruins when archaeologists discovered them and to the number of large anthills in the area. Among the other fauna sharing the jungle here are several species of poisonous snakes. Although these mainly come out at night, you should always be careful of where you walk and, when climbing, where you put your hands. 🎟 *$2.50* ⊘ *Daily 8–5.*

Reserva de la Biosfera Calakmul

🏛 ㉚ *Entrance at Carretera 186, Km 65; 107 km (66 mi) southwest of*
FodorśChoice *Xpujil.*
★

Vast, lovely, green, and mysterious Calakmul may not stay a secret for much longer. You won't see any tour buses in the parking lot, and on an average day, site employees and laborers still outnumber the visitors that traipse along the moss-tinged dirt paths snaking through the jungle. But things are changing. The nearest town, Xpujil, already has Internet access. And the proposed building of a water retention aqueduct in the same area will, if it becomes a reality, almost surely bring increased tourism—maybe even chain hotels—to the area. So if you're looking for untrammeled Mexican wilderness, don't put it off any longer: the time to visit Calakmul is now.

Calakmul encompasses some 1.8 million acres of land along the Guatemalan border. It was declared a protected biosphere reserve in 1989, and is the second-largest reserve of its kind in Mexico after Sian Ka'an in Quintana Roo. All kinds of flora and fauna thrive here, including wildcats, spider and howler monkeys, and hundreds of exotic birds, orchid varieties, butterflies, and reptiles. (There's no shortage of insects, either, so don't forget the bug repellent.)

The centerpiece of the reserve, however, is the ruined Maya city that shares the name Calakmul (which translates as "two adjacent towers"). Although Carretera 186 runs right through the reserve, you'll need to drive about an hour and a half from the highway along a 50-km (31-mi) authorized entry road to get to the site. Although structures here are still being excavated, the dense surrounding jungle is being left in its natural state: as you walk among the ruined palaces and tumbled stelae, you'll hear the screams of howler monkeys, and see massive strangler figs enveloping equally massive trees.

This magnificent city, now in ruins, wasn't always so lonely. Anthropologists estimate that in its heyday (between AD 542 and 695), the region was inhabited by more than 50,000 Maya; archaeologists have mapped more than 6,250 structures, and found 180 stelae. Perhaps the most monumental discovery so far is the remains of royal ruler Garra del Jaguar (Jaguar Claw); his body was wrapped (but not embalmed) in a shroud of palm leaf, lime, and fine cloth, and locked away in a royal tomb in about AD 700. In an adjacent crypt, a young woman wearing fine jewelry and an elaborately painted wood-and-stucco headdress was entombed together with a child. Their identity is still a mystery. The artifacts and skeletal remains have been moved to the Maya Museum in Campeche City.

Unlike those at Chichén Itzá (which also peaked in importance during the Classic era) the pyramids and palaces throughout Calakmul can be climbed for soaring vistas. You can choose to explore the site along a short, medium, or long path, but all three eventually lead to magnificent **Templo II** and **Templo VII**—twin pyramids separated by an immense plaza. Templo II, at 175 feet, is the peninsula's tallest Maya building. Scientists are studying a huge, intact stucco frieze deep within this structure, but it's not currently open to visitors.

Arrangements for an English-speaking Calakmul tour guide should be made beforehand with the Campeche City tourist office, or through Chicanná Ecovillage near Xpujil. Camping is permitted near the entrance gate; be sure to tip the caretakers. Primitive camping is permitted near the second checkpoint. Even if day-tripping, though, you'll need bring your own food and water; there are no places to buy provisions here. ✉ *97 km (60 mi) east of Escárcega to the turnoff at Cohuas, then 50 km (31 mi) south to Calakmul* ☎ *No phone* 🖅 *$4 per car (more for larger vehicles), plus $4 per person* ☉ *Daily 8–5.*

Where to Stay

$ 🏨 **Puerta Calakmul.** Built with natural wood and stone from the area, these rustic cabins are tucked away in the forest on the edge of the Calakmul biosphere. The cabins combine earthiness and sophistication with their cement floors, rough cotton drapes, comfortable beds, pounded tree-bark lamp shades, blue tile showers, and screened-in porches. Small ponds and sitting areas complete the Garden of Eden setting, and nearby trails allow for hiking and bird-watching in the woods. You'll need to book your reservation through the hotel's Web site. ✉ *Carretera 186, Km 98.5, inside entrance to Calakmul biosphere* ☎ *998/109–0249* ⊕ *www.puertacalakmul.com.mx* 🍽 *15 cabanas* ⚍ *Restaurant, fans, pool; no a/c, no room phones, no room TVs* ⊟ *No credit cards.*

El Tigre

31 *46 km (28 mi) south of Candelaria.*

If you want to feel like a real explorer, try visiting this one-time port on the Río Candelaria the old-fashioned way: by taking a boat from the nearby town of Candelaria. During the 45-minute journey along the green and glassy waterway, you'll be able to spot turtles, storks, and other wildlife; and after landing at a small dock, you can climb a small rise to glimpse ruined temples through the trees.

By around 300 BC, El Tigre had become an important trading post connecting the Campeche coast with what is now northern Guatemala. The structures here are still being studied and restored. Beneath a man-made awning that protects them from the elements, oversized stucco masks glare at you with anthropomorphic eyes. The most impressive building at the site is the pyramid called **Edificio IV**, which has trees growing up from its sloping, stepped sides. Visible through the trees from the site's main plaza, the structure is much closer by than it looks, and is definitely worth checking out. According to history, it was here that Cuauhtémoc, the last Aztec emperor, was hanged for refusing to disclose the location of a wealth of royal treasure.

El Tigre is more than three hours from Campeche by car (and the round trip by boat takes all day), so most folks overnight in Candelaria. From there it's a 90-minute drive. If you want to come by water, arrange the trip ahead of time through the Autel Jardines hotel. It costs about $150 for a maximum of 5 passengers. ☎ *No phone* 🎫 *$2.50* ⏲ *Daily 8–5.*

Candelaria

32 *95 km (59 mi) west of Reserva de la Biosfera Calakmul.*

Bird-watching and fly-fishing in Lake Salsipuedes and Vieja Lagoon in the Candelaria River basin are what make this out-of-the-way and somewhat rough and rowdy spot an increasingly popular destination. Primarily an agricultural hub producing corn and sugarcane, Candelaria is also a good starting point for a visit to El Tigre. Or, if you're departing from Campeche City, you might spend the night in Candelaria after your visit to the ruins.

Where to Stay & Eat

¢–$ ✕ **Comedor los Reyes.** With a thatched roof, lilac walls, an ocher cement floor and matching oilcloths, this unassuming little place almost lives up to its name as the "diner of kings." You can order the delicious *pellizcadas* (thick rounds of lightly fried cornmeal topped with melted cheese, chopped onion, and black beans), or choose from more recognizable items like burritos and enchiladas. Mainly locals eat here, so don't expect English menus or explanations. Happily, almost anything you point to on the menu should be a winner. It's open from 7:30 AM to 9 PM, which is later than most places in provincial Candelaria. ✉ *Calle 27 s/n, Col. Acalán* ☎ *982/826–0574* 💳 *No credit cards.*

¢–$ 🏨 **Autel Jardines.** Offering the most comfortable accommodations in town, this motel-like lodging has a parking place outside each unit. Heavy curtains block the tropical sun, and air-conditioning units are effective, if somewhat noisy. Suites are no larger than standard rooms, but have cozy king-size beds with pillow-top mattresses, DVD players, and tiny refrigerators. With advance notice, owner Manuel Valladares Hernández can make arrangements for a river tour, fly-fishing, or a visit to El Tigre. ✉ *Calle 27 No. 1, Col. Acalán* ☎ *982/826–0515* 📠 *981/816–0075* ⊕ *www.auteljardines.com.mx* 🛏 *28 rooms, 2 suites* 🜚 *Some fans, some refrigerators, some in-room safes, some in-room TVs, some in-room hot tubs, pool, exercise equipment, bar, dance club, laundry service, free parking; no a/c in some rooms* ▭ *No credit cards.*

CARRETERA 180 TO VILLAHERMOSA

Heading southwest from Campeche, Carretera 180 hugs the coast, offering views of narrow beaches and the Gulf of Mexico. Most of the beaches are simply solitary stretches of narrow sand with no services and no bathers. Still, there's nothing to stop you from pulling off the road for a walk along the shore. The deep-green sea here is so shallow that the Continental Shelf is almost visible at low tide. Waves are rare and the current runs at a nearly imperceptible 0.3 knots.

6

Lerma

🔞 *13 km (8 mi) southwest of Campeche City.*

🜚 Playa Bonita, the most popular bathing spot southwest of Campeche City, is at the far end of this rural village. The sandy beach has lockers, changing rooms, showers, and several snack bars. It's lonely on weekdays but crowded on weekends and holidays, when the rocky coves fronting homes at the beach's north end fill up with families. During the winter, cooler temperatures and lots of dead seagrass at the shoreline make swimming less desirable than during the rest of the year. A basketball court and soccer field and children's play equipment are available for those who prefer nonaquatic exercise. Roving vendors sell mangoes and sweets, but most families bring picnics. You can rent tables, chairs, and palapas for shade. Public buses to Lerma depart daily 6 AM–11 PM from the market in Campeche City (Circuito Baluartes, between Calles 53 and 55). If you're driving yourself, turn toward the sea at the Lerma sign and again at the first traffic circle. The parking fee is 50¢.

Seybaplaya

🔞 *About 7 km (4½ mi) southwest of Lerma.*

Dozens of identical, turquoise-and-white fiberglass motor launches line the beach at the traditional fishing port of Seybaplaya. Its palm-fringed setting is among the prettiest seascapes on the Campeche coast. Snorkeling is good here, as a number of large coral heads are just offshore, along with an underwater cemetery for boats. For a challenge, climb the huge staircase that juts up the mountain, ending at a giant statue of Jesus with outstretched arms. The view is incredible, but be warned: it's quite a hike. A couple of miles north along the beach road is Payucán—a beach with fine white sand and lots of herons, sandpipers, pelicans, and other seabirds—and Punta del Morro, a huge seaside cavern created by centuries of erosion. The sound of crashing waves echoes off the cavern's walls, adding to its drama.

About 9 km (5½ mi) southwest is Siho Playa, a rocky beach and the old home of the pirate Henry Morgan. Here the sea is quite calm and stays shallow for about 10 yards. Three kilometers (2 mi) southwest is the Costa Blanca beach, with shells, birds, and calm surf.

Where to Stay

$$ ⊡ **Tucán Siho-Playa.** Just less than halfway between Seybaplaya and Champotón, the Tucán has a mainly Mexican and European clientele. Rooms are simply furnished and let in plenty of light—a contrast to the dark, low-ceilinged hallways. Each room has a tiled floor, a wall made of rock, and a small balcony (ask for chairs). There's a large rectangular pool; a sandy little beach is surrounded by rocks and has a few individual palapas for shade. This is a good spot for those with a car, or who just want to stay put and read by the pool. ⊠ *Carretera Libre Campeche–Champotón, Km 35* ☎ *982/823–1200 or 982/823–1202* 🖷 *982/823–1203* ⇆ *70 rooms, 4 suites* ⚍ *Restaurant, room service, some minibars, cable TV, pool, exercise equipment, beach, billiards, Ping-Pong, shop, playground, meeting room, free parking* ⊟ *MC, V.*

Champotón

㉟ *35 km (22 mi) southwest of Seybaplaya.*

Carretera 180 curves through a series of hills before reaching Champotón's immensely satisfying vista of open sea. This is an appealing, untouristy little town with palapas at the water's edge, and plenty of swimmers and boats. The Spaniards dubbed the outlying bay the Bahía de la Mala Pelea, or "bay of the evil battle," because it was here that the troops of the Spanish conqueror and explorer Hernández de Córdoba were first trounced, in 1517, by pugnacious Indians armed with arrows, slingshots, and darts. The famous battle is commemorated with a small reenactment each year on March 21.

The 17th-century church of Nuestra Señora de la Inmaculada Concepción is the site for a festival honoring the Virgin Mary (Our Lady of the Immaculate Conception). The festival culminates each year on December 8. On that day the local fishermen carry the saint from the church to their boats for a seafaring parade. In the middle of town are the ruins of the Fortín de San Antonio. The Champotón area is ideal for birdwatching and fishing. More than 35 kinds of fish, including shad, snook, and bass, live in Río Champotón. The mangroves and swamps are home to cranes and other waterfowl. The town is primarily an agricultural hub—its most important exports are lumber and honey, as well as coconut, sugarcane, bananas, avocados, corn, and beans.

★ About a dozen small seafood restaurants make up **Los Cockteleros,** an area 5 km (3 mi) north of the center of Champotón. This is where Campechanos head on weekends to munch fried fish and slurp down seafood cocktails. The open-air palapa eateries at the beach are open daily during daylight hours.

Approximately 15 km (9 mi) southwest of Champotón, Punta Xen is a beautiful beach popular for its calm, clean water. It's a long stretch of deserted sand interrupted only by birds and seashells. Across the highway are a few good, basic restaurants.

★ The Expreso Maya train makes one of its few stops at **Cenote Azul,** a sinkhole about 1½ hours from the town of Champotón. The train stops a few hundred yards from stairs to the sinkhole, which is just outside the small community of Miguel Colorado. Infrastructure for getting to and from this private, special spot is still not in place, but those interested in visiting and swimming at this isolated spot can contact the Champotón tourism office (☎ 982/828–0343, or 982/828–0067 Ext. 207) for help in arranging transportation or getting driving directions. A second sinkhole, Cenote de los Patos, is a short but rather rugged walk from the first. Both are gorgeous and isolated, though; most find the hike well worth it. The dirt road from Miguel Colorado may be impassable for two-wheel-drive vehicles during the rainy season.

Where to Stay & Eat

$ ✕ **Las Brisas.** A favorite with locals, this is the best place in town for fresh fish, shrimp, and octopus. Open until 6 PM, Las Brisas is on the main street by the water, overlooking the bay. ⊠ *Av. Eugenio Echeverría Castellot s/n between Calles 18 and 16* ☎ *982/828–0515* ▭ *No credit cards* ☺ *No dinner.*

¢ ⊞ **Geminis.** Not far from the town's main plaza, this modest hotel is about as fancy as Champotón gets. In other words, it's quite plain, as reflected in the modest room rates. Some mattresses are mushy, others are firm; all have orange chenille spreads. The louvered windows have no screens to keep the bugs out, and TVs are tiny. Rooms surround a largish pool with a few tables and chairs. There's karaoke in the adjoining bar on weekend nights. ⊠ *Calle 30 No. 10* ☎ *982/828–0008* 🖷 *982/828–0094* ⏎ *42 rooms* ♻ *Fans, cable TV, pool, bar, free parking; no a/c in some rooms, no room phones* ▭ *No credit cards.*

¢ ⊞ **Snook Inn.** Like its competition, Geminis, the Snook Inn is all business. Most clients are hunters or fishermen who have signed up for trips with the Sansore clan, the hotel's longtime owners and outdoor enthusiasts. The clean, kidney-shaped pool has both a slide and a diving board, and it's surrounded by the two-story, L-shaped, 1960s-era hotel. Simple rooms have remote-control TVs, tile floors, unadorned walls, and hammock hooks in the walls (bring your own hammock). The parking area is quite small. ⊠ *Calle 30 No. 1* 🖷🖷 *982/828–0018* ⏎ *19 rooms* ♻ *Cable TV, pool, laundry service, free parking* ▭ *No credit cards.*

Sabancuy

36 *47 km (29 mi) west of Champotón.*

A launching point for exploring the Laguna de Términos and its many estuaries and mangroves, Sabancuy (whose name translates as "Serpent That Bites the Ankle") is the final village before high-tension lines start to follow the coastal highway and oil country starts. Most travelers here are European or Mexican, the former sometimes on escorted tours. An unnamed secondary road (pitted with potholes, which makes for slow going at times) leads to the ruins of El Tigre.

Where to Stay & Eat

$ ✕ **Viaductoplaya Restaurant Bar Turístico.** Menus in Spanish and German give you a clue about who frequents this large seaside shanty. Mexican favorites like grilled chicken are on the menu, but the restaurant's strength is clearly seafood, including shrimp, squid, and fish. The *ensaladas,* which usually means salads, are really different varieties of ceviche (fish or seafood cured in lime, with chopped chili, cilantro, and onions). Waiters recommend the fresh fish fillet stuffed with seafood or with shrimp and cheese. Beer, wine, and liquor are available. ⊠ *Carretera Carmen–Champotón, Km 77.5* ☎ *982/825–0008* ▭ *No credit cards.*

¢ ▦ **Hotel Sabancuy Plaza.** Though unassuming, the Plaza offers the best accommodations in town. The better rooms, higher up in the four-story building, have tiny balconies overlooking the estuary and rusty rooftops—but no chairs where you can sit while taking in the so-so view. Tiled rooms have blue printed drapes and bedspreads, wood headboards, and reasonably strong air-conditioning units. If you want two double beds (instead of two twins) and a/c, ask for a "suite," which is about twice the price of a regular room. ⊠ *South side of plaza principal* ☎ *982/825–0081* ⇸ *35 rooms* ♦ *Restaurant, cable TV, free parking; no room phones, no TV in some rooms* ▭ No credit cards.

Isla del Carmen

37 *147 km (91 mi) south of Champotón.*

It was on this barrier island protecting the lagoon from the Gulf that pirates who raided Campeche regularly hid out from the mid-1500s to their expulsion in the early 18th century. Isla del Carmen has served as a depot for everything from dyewoods and textiles to hardwoods, chicle, and shrimp. Today, oil is the big export; the area produces about 75% of Mexico's petroleum.

■ TIP→→ A major hub and the second-largest city in Campeche, Ciudad del Carmen is, frankly, no place for tourists. But if you're headed toward Tabasco, Veracruz, Chiapas, or other points west or south of Campeche, you might decide to pass through. Most other out-of-towners are Mexican and foreign business travelers.

The city is short on sights and long on franchise restaurants like KFC, Pizza Hut, and Bennigan's. Parts of the bay are polluted, and the city is battling social problems such as prostitution, which is reflected in the cheap, ugly motels advertised as "men's clubs." Be prepared to pay higher prices for a safe hotel room than you would in Campeche City or other, more tourist-oriented, cities. Ciudad del Carmen is actually not on the island but on the adjoining peninsula's east end. The island is connected by two bridges to the mainland.

Locals recommend Puerto Real, 30 km (19 mi) north of town along the Campeche highway (just before the bridge connecting to Isla Aguado), as a good spot to find bathrooms, showers, and several restaurants that are lively only on holidays and warm-weather weekends.

Where to Stay & Eat

$$-$$$ ✕ **El Cactus.** Carnivores will be happy here, where meaty entrées are the best menu choices. Rib-eye steak and filet mignon are served with baked potato and sautéed vegetables; the bone-marrow soup and the cheese pie are also popular. The restaurant's exterior resembles an adobe house with—of course—cacti growing at the doorway. Inside, whitewashed stucco walls, wood furnishings, and quiet background music are conducive to closing business deals. There's a parking lot here, which is a plus. ⊠ *Calle 31 No. 132, at Calle 50, Col. Cuauhtémoc (next to Hotel Lino)* ☎ *938/382–4986* ⊟ *AE, MC, V.*

$$ ✕🏨 **Eurohotel.** Geared toward Mexican business travelers, this contemporary, upscale hotel is close to the center of town. The video bar, restaurant, and gambling salon are currently being remodeled, but the disco is open Thursday through Saturday nights. Modern rooms are done in pastels: "singles" have king-size beds, doubles have two double beds. Junior suites have a separate living area and bathtub; master suites have small kitchenettes. ⊠ *Calle 22 No. 208, Centro Ciudad del Carmen* ☎ *938/ 382–3044 or 888/562–0222 Ext. 257* 🖶 *938/382–3044* ⊕ *www. eurohotel.com.mx* 🛏 *80 rooms, 12 suites* ↺ *Restaurant, coffee shop, room service, in-room data ports, in-room safes, some kitchenettes, some refrigerators, cable TV with movies, pool, bar, dance club, laundry service, concierge, Internet, business services, meeting rooms, airport shuttle, free parking* ⊟ *AE, MC, V.*

$$ 🏨 **Holiday Inn.** This low-rise hotel offers all the amenities you'd expect from a Holiday Inn, including irons and ironing boards, alarm clocks, coffeemakers, and hair dryers. Most rooms have king-size beds and small patios or terraces. All have wireless Internet access, as does the business-oriented lobby, with couches here and there for conversing with colleagues. Off the lobby are the airy restaurant and the unremarkable lounge-style bar, with plush chairs. There's a golf course not far away. ⊠ *Calle 31 No. 274, between Av. Periférica and Calle 56, Col. Benito Juárez, 24170* ☎ *938/381–1500 or 800/465–4329* 🖶 *938/382–0520* ⊕ *www.holiday-inn.com* 🛏 *148 rooms, 10 suites* ↺ *Restaurant, room service, some in-room safes, some refrigerators, cable TV, pool, gym, bar, shop, babysitting, laundry facilities, laundry service, dry cleaning, concierge, business services, meeting rooms, airport shuttle, car rental, travel services, free parking, no-smoking rooms* ⊟ *AE, MC, V.*

¢ 🏨 **Lossandes.** Geared toward businesspeople who want something more intimate than a chain hotel, this friendly property has round tables under a thatch-roofed, poolside patio that provide an informal place to work or conduct meetings. Rooms are simple but comfortable; each has a tub. Rooms on the third floor at the back are the quietest. ⊠ *Av. Periférica Norte 67, Col. Lomas de Lolche, 24167* ☎ *938/382–2400* 🖷 *938/382–2388* ⊕ *www.lossandes.com.mx* 🛏 *95 rooms* ♿ *Restaurant, room service, cable TV, pool, gym, bar, laundry service, Internet, meeting rooms, airport shuttle, car rental, free parking* ⊟ *AE, MC, V.*

CAMPECHE ESSENTIALS

Transportation

BY AIR

Aeroméxico has several flights daily from Mexico City to Campeche City. Mexicana de Aviación also has several daily flights from Mexico City to Campeche City and from Mexico City to Ciudad del Carmen. Campeche's Aeropuerto Internacional Alberto Acuña Ongay is 16 km (10 mi) north of downtown. Aeropuerto Internacional de Ciudad del Carmen is in the eastern sector of Campeche City.

Taxis are the only means of transportation to and from Campeche's two airports. The fare to downtown Campeche from Aeropuerto Internacional Alberto Acuña Ongay is about $7. At the airport you pay your fare ahead of time at the ticket booth outside the terminal; a dispatcher then directs you to your cab. Cabs from Ciudad del Carmen's airport cost about $9.

🔢 **Aeroméxico** ☎ 981/816-6656, 981/816-5678 in Campeche City, 01800/021-4000 toll-free in Mexico, 800/237-6639. **Aeropuerto Internacional Alberto Acuña Ongay** ☎ 981/816-3109. **Aeropuerto Internacional de Ciudad del Carmen** ⊠ Prolongación Calle 31, 1 block from Plaza Comercial Aviación ☎938/382-8001 or 938/382-1510. **Mexicana de Aviación** ☎ 981/816-6656 in Campeche, 938/382-1171 in Ciudad del Carmen, 800/531-7921.

BY BUS

Within Campeche City, the route of interest to most visitors is along Avenida Ruíz Cortínez; the ride costs the equivalent of about 30¢.

Buses from Campeche City's main ADO bus station leave for Mérida, Villahermosa, and Ciudad del Carmen almost every hour, with less frequent departures for Cancún, Chetumal, Oaxaca, and other destinations. Unión de Camioneros provides service to intermediate points throughout the Yucatán Peninsula, as well as second-class (and less desirable) service to Chetumal, Ciudad del Carmen, Escárcega, Mérida, Palenque, Tuxtla Gutiérrez, and Villahermosa.

In Ciudad del Carmen, the ADO bus station has departures for Campeche City many times a day, with fewer departures to Villahermosa, Mérida, and other points in southern Mexico. In eastern Campeche near Calakmul, several buses leave the Xpujil ADO bus station each day for Escárcega and Campeche City; there is one night bus for Hopelchén.

■ TIP➔➔ For destinations to (and from) major destinations within the Yucatán peninsula, purchase tickets with a credit card by phone through Ticketbus; make sure to ask from which station the bus departs.

ADO ✉ Av. Patricio Trueba at Casa de Justicia 237, Campeche City ☎ 981/811-9910, ext. 2402 ✉ Periférica s/n and Av. Francisco Villa, Ciudad del Carmen ☎ 938/382-0680 ✉ Carretera 186 s/n, Xpujil ☎ 983/871-6027. **Ticketbus** ☎ 01800/702-8000 toll-free in Mexico. **Unión de Camioneros** ✉ Calle Chile and Av. Gobernadores, Campeche City ☎ 981/816-3445.

BY CAR

Highways in Campeche are two-lane, paved roadways that pose few problems beyond the need to pass slow-moving trucks. With the exception of the Champotón–Ciudad del Carmen segment, roads are generally narrow and have little shoulder. ⚠ Drive with extreme caution on Highway 186 between Escárcega and the Quintana Roo state border; the road is curvy and narrow in many spots, and it's often under repair. It's best to avoid driving at night, especially on this highway. Military checkpoints pop up here and there, but the machine gun-wielding soldiers are nothing to fear; they'll usually just wave you right on.

FROM MÉRIDA TO CAMPECHE CITY
Campeche City is about 2 to 2½ hours from Mérida along the 180-km (99-mi) *via corta* (short way), Carretera 180. The alternative route, the 250-km (155-mi) *via ruinas* (ruins route), Carretera 261, takes 3 to 4 hours, but passes the major Maya ruins of Uxmal, as well as those of Kabah and Sayil.

FROM CAMPECHE CITY TO CHAMPOTÓN
A toll road from Campeche City to Champotón costs $4.50 one way and shortens the drive from 65 km (40 mi) to 45 km (28 mi). Look for the Carretera 180 CUOTA sign when leaving the city. Carretera 180 continues to Ciudad del Carmen (90 minutes to 2 hours); the bridge toll entering or leaving Ciudad del Carmen is about $3.

CHAMPOTÓN TO THE SOUTH & SOUTHEAST
From Champotón, Carretera 261 heads inland to Escárcega (about 2 hours from Campeche City to Escárcega), where you pick up Carretera 186 east to Xpujil (about 157 km, or 97 mi—a drive of just under 2 hours). From Xpujil it's about 140 km (87 mi) to Chetumal, on the coast of Quintana Roo. All of these, including Carretera 261, which connects Xpujil and Hopelchén in northeastern Campeche, are two-lane highways in reasonably good condition. If you're headed to Mérida, you can continue north on Carretera 261 from Hopelchén.

CAR RENTAL
The only international car rental agencies you'll find in Campeche are in Ciudad del Carmen. Expect to pay $28–$50 per day for a manual economy car with air-conditioning. You can often save significantly by booking through an international company before you go; make sure to ask for confirmation in writing.

Budget ✉ Calle 31 No. 117, between Calles 42 and 42A, Col. Cuauhtémoc, Ciudad del Carmen ☎ 938/382-7844. **Hertz** ✉ Calle 31 No. 132, at Hotel Lino, Col. Cuauhtémoc, Ciudad del Carmen ☎ 938/382-7954. **Localiza** ✉ Hotel Baluartes, Av. 16 de Septiembre 128, Campeche City ☎ 981/811-3187. **Maya Rent-a-Car** ✉ Del Mar Hotel, Av. Ruíz Cortínez and Calle 59, Campeche City ☎ 981/816-4611 Ext. 352.

BY TAXI

You can hail taxis on the street in Campeche City or Ciudad del Carmen; there are also stands by the bus stations, the main plaza, and the municipal market. The minimum fare is $2; it's $2.50 from the center to the bus station and $4 to the airport (it's cheaper to go to the airport than from it). After 11 PM, prices may be slightly higher. There's a small fee, less than 50¢, to call for a cab through Radio Taxis; you can also call Taxis Plus any time, day or night.

Radio Taxis ⊠ Campeche City ☎ 981/815-5555, 981/813-1333, or 981/813-3540. **Taxis Plus** ⊠ Ciudad del Carmen ☎ 983/382-1151.

Contacts & Resources

BANKS & EXCHANGE SERVICES

Campeche City banks will change traveler's checks and currency weekdays 9–4. Almost without exception, banks in towns and cities have long lines; it's easier to cash traveler's checks at your hotel despite the slightly lower rate, or use the banks' ATM, most of which are open 24 hours. You get a great exchange rate using the ATM, but don't forget there's an international transaction fee, usually $2–$4.

Banamex ⊠ Calle 29 No. 103, Champotón ☎ 01800/021-2345 toll-free in Mexico. **Bancomer** ⊠ Av. 16 de Septiembre 120, Campeche City ☎ 981/816-6622. **Banorte** ⊠ Calle 8 No. 237, between Calles 53 and 55, Campeche City ☎ 981/811-4250. **Scotiabank Inverlat** ⊠ Calle 31 No. 10, near main plaza, Ciudad del Carmen ☎ 938/382-4115.

EMERGENCIES

For general emergencies throughout Campeche, dial **060**.

The Hospital Manuel Campos and Clínicia Campeche both have 24-hour pharmacies on site.

Doctors & Hospitals Clínica Campeche ⊠ Av. Central No. 72, Centro Campeche City ☎ 981/816-5612. **Hospital Manuel Campos** ⊠ Av. Boulevard s/n, Campeche City ☎ 981/811-1709 (dial Ext. 138 for pharmacy) or 981/816-0957.

INTERNET, MAIL & SHIPPING

Cybercafés have popped up all over Campeche City; try Ciber Club downtown. Some Campeche City lodgings and most of Ciudad del Carmen's business hotels have Internet access. Average cost is $1–$2 per hour. The *correo* in Campeche City is open weekdays 8:30–3:30. For important letters or packages, it's best to use the DHL courier service.

Cybercafés Ciber Club ⊠ Calle 67 No. 1B Altos, Campeche City ☎ 981/811-3577. **Compuniverso** ⊠ Centro Comercial Plaza Real Norte, Avs. Periférica Norte and Concordia, Ciudad del Carmen ☎ 938/384-3677.

Mail & Shipping Correo ⊠ Av. 16 de Septiembre between Calles 53 and 55, Campeche City ☎ 981/816-2134. **DHL** ⊠ Av. Miguel Alemán 140, Campeche City ☎ 981/816-0382.

TOUR OPTIONS

Guided trolley tours of historic Campeche City leave from Calle 10 on the Plaza Principal on the hour 9–noon and 5–8. You can buy tickets ahead of time at the adjacent kiosk, or once aboard the trolley. (Trips run less frequently in the off-season, and it's always best to double-check schedules at the kiosk.) The one-hour tour costs $7; if English-speakers request it, guides will do their best to speak the language. For the same price, the green "El Guapo" trolley makes unguided trips to Reducto de San José at 9 AM and 5 PM (also at 10, 11, and noon during vacation periods such as Christmas and Easter). You'll only have about 10 minutes to admire the view, though.

You can take the Super Guapo tram hourly 9–12 or 5–8 in the evening to visit Fuerte de San Miguel. The tour doesn't allow enough time to visit the museum, but you can linger to see the worthwhile exhibits before calling a taxi or walking downhill to catch a downtown bus en route from Lerma.

Rappelling, spelunking, or mountain-bike tours are occasionally offered through Expediciones Ecoturísticos de Campeche. For tours of Isla de Jaina—where archaeologists are working and where you'll need special permission to visit—contact Hector Solis of Espacios Naúticos. If you like, you can augment the island tour with breakfast, lunch, or swimming at the beach. Espacios Naúticos also offers waterskiing, bay tours, snorkeling, and sportfishing.

🚏 El Guapo and Super Guapo trams ☎ 981/811-3989 **Espacios Naúticos** ✉ Av. Resurgimiento 120, Campeche City ☎ 981/816-8082. **Expediciones Ecoturísticos de Campeche** ✉ Calle 12 No. 168A, Centro, Campeche City ☎ 981/816-6373 or 981/816-1310.

TRAVEL AGENCIES

American Express/VIPs will replace lost traveler's checks and book hotel and airplane reservations. Intermar Campeche can arrange transfers to Mérida or Mexico City as well as the tours mentioned above.

🚏 American Express/VIPs ✉ Prolongación Calle 59, Edificio Belmar, Depto. 5, Centro, Campeche City ☎ 981/811-1010 or 981/811-1000. **Intermar Campeche** ✉ Av. 16 de Septiembre 128, Campeche City ☎ 981/811-3447.

VISITOR INFORMATION

Campeche's State Tourism Office is open daily 8 AM–9 PM. The Municipal Tourist Office is open 9–9 every day.

🚏 Municipal Tourist Office ✉ Calle 55 between Calles 8 and 10, Campeche City ☎ 981/811-3989 or 981/811-3990. **State Tourism Office** ✉ Av. Ruíz Cortínez s/n, Plaza Moch Couoh, across from Gobierno, Campeche City Centro ☎ 981/811-9229 🖷 981/816-6767.

UNDERSTANDING CANCÚN, COZUMEL & THE YUCATÁN

A PLACE APART

THE YUCATÁN PENINSULA has captivated travelers since the early Spanish explorations. "A place of white towers, whose glint could be seen from the ships—temples rising tier on tier," is how the expeditions' chroniclers described the peninsula, then thought to be an island. Rumors of a mainland 10 days west of Cuba were known to Columbus, who obstinately hoped to find "a very populated land," and one that was richer than any he had yet discovered. Subsequent explorers and conquistadores met with more resistance there than in almost any other part of the New World, and this rebelliousness continued for centuries.

Largely because of their geographic isolation, Yucatecans tend to preserve ancient traditions more than many other indigenous groups in the country. This can be seen in such areas as housing (the use of the ancient Maya thatched hut, or *na*); dress (*huipiles* have been made and worn by Maya women for centuries); and occupation (most modern-day Maya are farmers, just as their ancestors were). Maya culture is also evident in today's Yucatecan language (although it has evolved, it is still very similar to what was spoken in the area 500 years ago); and religion. Ancient deities persist, particularly in the form of gods associated with agriculture, such as the *chacs,* or rain gods, and festivals to honor the seasons and benefactor spirits maintain the traditions of old.

This vast peninsula encompasses 113,000 square km (43,630 square mi) of a flat limestone table covered with sparse topsoil and scrubby jungle growth. Geographically, it comprises the states of Yucatán, Campeche, and Quintana Roo, as well as Belize and a part of Guatemala (these two countries are not discussed in this book). Still one of the least-Hispanicized (or Mexicanized) regions of the country, Yucatán catapulted into the tourist's vocabulary with the creation of its most precious man-made asset, Cancún.

Mexico's most popular resort destination owes its success to its location on the superb eastern coastline of the Yucatán Peninsula, which is washed by the exquisitely colored and translucent waters of the Caribbean. The area is also endowed with a semitropical climate, unbroken stretches of beach, and the world's second-longest barrier reef, which separates the mainland from Cozumel. Cancún and, to a lesser extent, Cozumel incarnate the success formula for sun-and-sand tourism: luxury hotels, sandy beaches, water sports, nightlife, and restaurants that specialize in international fare.

Cancún's popularity has allowed the peninsula's Maya ruins—long a mecca for archaeology enthusiasts—to become satellite destinations of their own. The proximity of such compelling sites as Chichén Itzá, Uxmal, and Tulum allows Cancún's visitors to explore the vestiges of one of the most brilliant civilizations in the ancient world without having to journey too far from their base.

Yucatán offers a diversity of other charms, too. The waters of the Mexican Caribbean are clearer and bluer than those of the Pacific; many of the beaches are unrivaled. Scuba diving (in natural sinkholes, caves, and along the impressive barrier reef), snorkeling, deep-sea fishing, and other water sports attract growing numbers of tourists—who can also bird-watch, camp, spelunk, and shop for Yucatán's splendid handicrafts. There is a broad spectrum of settings and accommodations to choose from: the pricey strip of hotels along Cancún's Boulevard Kukulcán; the less showy properties on Cozumel, beloved of scuba divers; and the relaxed ambience of Isla Mujeres, where most lodgings consist of rustic bungalows with ceiling fans and hammocks.

There are also the cities of Yucatán. Foremost is Mérida, wonderfully unaltered by time, where Moorish-inspired, colonnaded colonial architecture blends handsomely with turn-of-the-19th-century pomposity. In Mérida, café life remains an art, and the Maya still live proudly as Maya. Campeche, one of the few walled cities in North America, possesses an eccentric charm; it is slightly out of step with the rest of the country and not the least bothered by the fact. Down on the border with Belize stands Chetumal, a modest commercial center that is pervaded by the hybrid culture of coastal Central America and the pungent smell of the sea. Progreso, at the other end of the peninsula on the Gulf of Mexico, is Chetumal's northern counterpart, an overgrown fishing village–turned–commercial port. Hotels in these towns, although for the most part not as luxurious as the beach resort properties, range from the respectable if plain 1970s buildings to the undated fleabags so popular with filmmakers and writers exploring the darker side of Mexico (for example, *Under the Volcano,* by Malcolm Lowry). As a counterpoint to this, the Yucatán countryside now shines with magnificently restored haciendas turned into luxury lodgings.

The peninsula is also rich in wildlife. Iguanas, lizards, tapirs, deer, armadillos, and wild boars thrive on this alternately parched and densely foliated plain. Flamingos and herons, manatees and sea turtles, their once-dwindling numbers now rising in response to Mexico's newly awakened ecological consciousness, find idyllic watery habitats in and above the coastline's mangrove swamps, lagoons, and sandbars, acres of which have been made into national parks. Both Ría Lagartos and the coast's Reserva de la Biosfera Sian Ka'an sparkle with Yucatán's natural beauty. Orchids, bougainvillea, and poinciana are ubiquitous, and the region's edible tropical flora—coconuts, limes, papaya, bananas, and oranges—supplements the celebrated Yucatecan cuisine.

But it may be the colors of Yucatán that are most remarkable. From the stark-white sun-bleached sand, the sea stretches out like some immense canvas painted in bands of celadon green, pale aqua, and deep dusty blue. At dusk the sea and the horizon meld in the sumptuous glow of lavender sunsets, the sky just barely tinged with periwinkle and violet. Inland, the beige, gray, and amber stones of ruined temples are set off by riotous greenery. The colors of newer structures are equally intoxicating: the tawny, gray-brown thatched roofs of traditional huts; the creamy pastels and white arches, balustrades, and porticoes of colonial mansions. Cascades of dazzling red, pink, orange, and white flowers spill into courtyards and climb up the sides of buildings.

The Yucatán is historically colorful, too. From the conquistadores' first landfall off Cape Catoche in 1517, to the bloody skirmishes that wiped out most of the Indians, to the razing of Maya temples and burning of their sacred books, the peninsula was a battlefield. Pirates wreaked havoc off the coast of Campeche for centuries. Half the Indian population was killed during the 19th-century uprising known as the War of the Castes, when the enslaved indigenous population rose up and massacred thousands of Mexicans; Yucatán was attempting to secede from Mexico, and dictator Porfirio Díaz sent in his troops. These events, like the towering Maya civilization, have left their mark throughout the peninsula: in its archaeological museums, its colonial monuments, and the opulent mansions of the hacienda owners who enslaved the natives to cultivate their henequen.

But despite the violent conflicts of the past, the people of Yucatán treat today's visitors with hospitality and friendliness, especially outside the beach resorts. If you learn a few words of Spanish, you will be rewarded with an even warmer welcome.

CANCÚN AT A GLANCE

Cancún

Origin: "Cancún" is Maya for "pit of snakes."

State: Quintana Roo is the most easterly state in Mexico. Until 1974, it was a territory where dissidents were sent to be eaten alive by mosquitoes and die of malaria; only after Cancún was built and became a successful tourist destination did it become a recognized state. It covers 50,212 square km (19,382 square mi), and represents 2.6% of Mexico's landmass.

Common traffic signs: *Obedezca las señales* (Obey the signs); *No maltrate las señales* (Do not mistreat the signs); *No deje piedras sobre el pavimento* (Do not leave rocks on the road).

What's nearby: Cancún is 847 km (526 mi) away from Miami; that's closer than Mexico City, which is 1,300 km (808 mi) away. Closest of all, however, is Cuba, which is just 90 km (48 mi) away.

Flag: The Mexican flag was formed in 1821 by the Ejército Trigarante (Army of the Three Guarantees), after the Mexicans won their independence from Spain. Each color stands for one part of the agreement. Green is for independence; white is for religion; red is for union. The flag of Quintana Roo symbolizes the ocean and forests of the state.

Mayor: The first municipal president took charge when the seat of the Municipality Government was established on April 10, 1975.

Legal system: There are three judicial levels: the Lower Court, the High Court, and the Supreme Court. As the interpreter of civil law, the Supreme Court is the highest court, and has 11 judges.

And you thought American politics were complicated: There are 11 main political parties: CDPPN (Democratic Convergence National Political Party); PAN (National Action Party); PARM (Authentic Revolutionary Mexican Party); PAS (Social Alliance Party); PCD (Democratic Center Party); PDS (Social Democracy Party); PRD (Party of the Democratic Revolution); PRI (Institutional Revolutionary Party); PSN (Nationalist Society Party); PT (Labor Party); PVEM (Green Ecological Mexican Party). At present, the PRI is the party in power.

Population: 450,000; expected to grow to 475,000 by the end of 2006. Prior to 1974 there were only 117 people living in the area.

Density: 296 inhabitants per square kilometer.

Language: Spanish and Maya. English is used in the tourist areas.

Sunshine: Cancún has 285 days of sunshine per year.

Ethnic groups: 60% of the inhabitants of Cancún come from Yucatán, Campeche, and Quintana Roo; 24% of the population comes from Guerrero, Tabasco, Veracruz, and Mexico City; and the remaining 16% are natives of Cancún or foreigners.

Visitors: In 2004, 3,616,450 tourists arrived at Cancún's international airport.

Contribution to Western cuisine: Gum was first invented using the sap from the chicle tree found in Quintana Roo.

Contribution to romance: Cancún is the sixth most popular place in the world to get married or have a honeymoon. Four witnesses are required for each ceremony, though.

Religion: There are over 29 gods in the Maya religion. Among the most important are Itzamná, the creator-god, the feathered serpent called Kukulcán, and Chaac, the god of rain.

CHRONOLOGY

11,000 BC	Hunters and gatherers settle in Yucatán.

Preclassic Period: 2000 BC–AD 100

2,000 BC	Maya ancestors in Guatemala begin to cultivate corn and build permanent dwellings.
1500–900 BC	The powerful and sophisticated Olmec civilization develops along the Gulf of Mexico in the present-day states of Veracruz and Tabasco.
	Primitive farming communities develop in Yucatán.
900–300 BC	Olmec iconography and social institutions strongly influence the Maya populations in neighboring areas. The Maya adopt the Olmecs' concepts of tribal confederacies and small kingships as they move across the lowlands.
600 BC	Edzná is settled. It will be inhabited for nearly 900 years before the construction of the large temples and palaces found there today.
400 BC–AD 100	Dzibilchaltún develops as an important center in Komchen, an ancient state north of present-day Mérida. Becán, in southern Campeche, is also settled.
300 BC	Major construction begins in the Maya lowlands as the civilization begins to flourish.
300 BC–AD 200	New architectural elements, including the corbeled arch and roof comb, develop in neighboring Guatemala and gradually spread into the Yucatán.
300 BC–AD 900	Edzná becomes a city; increasingly large temple-pyramids are built.

Classic Period: AD 100–AD 1000

	The calendar and the written word are among the achievements that mark the beginning of the Classic period. The architectural highlight of the period is large, stepped pyramids with frontal stairways topped by limestone and masonry temples, arranged around plazas and decorated with stelae (stone monuments), bas-reliefs, and frescoes. Each Maya city is painted a single bright color, often red or yellow.
200–600	Economy and trade flourish. Maya culture achieves new levels of scientific sophistication and some groups become warlike.
250–300	A defensive fortification ditch and earthworks are built at Becán.
300	The first structures are built at San Gervasio on Cozumel.
300–600	Kohunlich rises to dominate the forests of southern Quintana Roo.
400–1100	Cobá grows to be the largest city in the eastern Yucatán.
432	The first settlement is established at Chichén Itzá.

6th Century — Influenced by the Toltec civilization of Teotihuacán in Central Mexico, larger and more elaborate palaces, temples, ball courts, roads, and fortifications are built in southern Maya cities, including Becán, Xpujil, and Chicanná in Campeche.

600–900 — Northern Yucatán ceremonial centers become increasingly important as centers farther south reach and pass developmental climax; the influence of Teotihuacán wanes. Three new Maya architectural styles develop: Puuc (exemplified by Chichén Itzá and Edzná) is the dominant style; Chenes (in northern Campeche) is characterized by ornamental facades with serpent masks; and Río Bec features small palaces with high towers exuberantly decorated with serpent masks.

850–950 — The largest pyramids and palaces of Uxmal are built. By 975, however, Uxmal and most other Puuc sites are abandoned.

Postclassic Period: AD 1000–AD 1521

900–1050 — The great Classic Maya centers of Guatemala, Honduras, and southern Yucatán are abandoned. The reason for their fall remains one of archaeology's greatest mysteries.

circa 920 — The Itzá, a Maya tribe from the Petén rain forest in Guatemala, establish themselves at Champotón and then at Chichén Itzá.

987–1007 — The Xiu, a Maya clan from the southwest, settle near the ruins of Uxmal.

1224 — An Itzá dynasty known as Cocomes emerges as a dominant group in northern Yucatán, building its capital at Mayapán.

1263–1440 — Mayapán, under the rule of Cocomes aided by Canul mercenaries from Tabasco, becomes the most powerful city-state in Yucatán. The league of Mayapán—including the key cities of Uxmal, Chichén Itzá, and Mayapán—is formed in northern Yucatán. Peace reigns for almost two centuries. To guarantee the peace, the rulers of Mayapán hold members of other Maya royal families as lifelong hostages.

1441 — Maya cities under Xiu rulers sack Mayapán, ending centralized rule of the peninsula. Yucatán henceforth is governed as 18 petty provinces, with constant internecine strife. The Itzá return to Lake Petén Itzá in Guatemala and establish their capital at Tayasal (modern-day Flores), one of the last un-Christianized Maya capitals, which will not be conquered by the Spanish until 1692.

15th Century — The last ceremonial center on Cancún island is abandoned. Other Maya communities are developing along the Caribbean coast.

1502 — A Maya canoe is spotted during Columbus's fourth voyage.

1511 — Spanish sailors Jerónimo de Aguilar and Gonzalo Guerrero are shipwrecked off Yucatán's Caribbean coast and taken to a Maya village on Cozumel.

1517 — Fernández de Córdoba discovers Isla Mujeres.

Trying to sail around Yucatán, which he believes to be an island, Córdoba lands at Campeche, marking the first Spanish landfall on the mainland. He is defeated by the Maya at Champotón.

1518 Juan de Grijalva sights the island of Cozumel but does not land there.

1519 Hernán Cortés lands at Cozumel, where he rescues Aguilar. Guerrero chooses to remain on the island with his Maya family.

Colonial Period: 1521–1821

1527, 1531 The Spanish make unsuccessful attempts to conquer Yucatán.

1540 Francisco de Montejo founds Campeche, the first Spanish settlement in Yucatán.

1541 Another takeover is attempted—unsuccessfully—by the Spanish.

1542 Maya chieftains surrender to Montejo at T'ho; 500,000 Indians are killed during the conquest of Yucatán. Indians are forced into labor under the *encomienda* system, by which conquistadores are charged with their subjugation and Christianization. The Franciscans contribute to this process.

Mérida is founded on the ruins of T'ho.

1543 Valladolid is founded on the ruins of Zací.

1546 A Maya group attacks Mérida, resulting in a five-month-long rebellion.

1562 Bishop Diego de Landa burns Maya codices at Maní.

1600 Cozumel is abandoned after smallpox decimates the population.

1686 Campeche's city walls are built for defense against pirates.

1700 182,500 Indians account for 98% of Yucatán's population.

1736 The Indian population of Yucatán declines to 127,000.

1761 The Cocomes uprising near Sotuta leads to the death of 600 Maya.

1771 The Fuerte (fort) de San Miguel is completed on a hill above Campeche, ending the pirates' reign of terror.

1810 The Port of Sisal opens, ending Campeche's ancient monopoly on peninsular trade and its economic prosperity.

Postcolonial/Modern Period: 1821–Present

1821 Mexico wins independence from Spain by diplomatic means. Various juntas vie for control of the new nation, resulting in frequent military coups.

1823 Yucatán becomes a Mexican state encompassing the entire peninsula.

1839–42 American explorer John Lloyd Stephens visits Yucatán's Maya ruins and describes them in two best-selling books.

1840–42   Yucatecan separatists revolt in an attempt to secede from Mexico. The Mexican government quells the rebellion, reduces the state of Yucatán to one-third its previous size, creates the federal territories of Quintana Roo and Campeche, and recruits Maya soldiers into a militia to prevent further disturbance.

1846   Following years of oppression, violent clashes between Maya militiamen and residents of Valladolid launch the War of the Castes. The entire non-Indian population of Valladolid is massacred.

1848   Rebels from the Caste War settle in the forests of Quintana Roo, creating a secret city named Chan Santa Cruz. An additional 20 refugee families settle in Cozumel, which has been almost uninhabited for centuries. By 1890 Cozumel's population numbers 500, Santa Cruz's 10,000.

1850   Following the end of the Mexican War with the United States in 1849, the Mexican army moves into the Yucatán to end the Indian uprising. The Maya flee into the unexplored forests of Quintana Roo. Military attacks, disease, and starvation reduce the Maya population of the Yucatán Peninsula to fewer than 10,000.

1863   Campeche achieves statehood.

1872   The city of Progreso is founded.

1880–1914   Yucatán's monopoly on henequen, enhanced by plantation owners' exploitation of Maya peasants, leads to its golden age as one of the wealthiest states in Mexico. Prosperity will last until the beginning of World War II.

Waves of Middle Eastern immigrants arrive in Yucatán and become successful in commerce, restaurants, cattle ranching, and tourism.

Payo Obispo (present-day Chetumal) is founded on the site of a long-abandoned Spanish colonial outpost.

1901   The Cult of the Talking Cross reaches the height of its popularity in Chan Santa Cruz (later renamed Felipe Carrillo Puerto). The Cruzob Indians continue to resist the Mexican army.

U.S. consul Edward Thompson buys Chichén Itzá for $500 and spends the next three years dredging the Sacred Cenote for artifacts.

1902   Mexican president Porfirio Díaz asserts federal jurisdiction over the Territory of Quintana Roo to isolate rebellious pockets of Indians and increase his hold on regional resources.

1915   The War of the Castes reaches an uneasy truce after the Mexican Army leaves the Cruzob Indians to rule Quintana Roo as an independent territory.

1915–24   Felipe Carrillo Puerto, Socialist governor of Yucatán, institutes major reforms in land distribution, labor, women's rights, and education during Mexican Revolution.

1923–48   A Carnegie Institute team led by archaeologist Sylvanus Moreley restores the ruins of Chichén Itzá.

1934–40   President Lázaro Cárdenas implements significant agrarian reforms in Yucatán.

1935   Chan Santa Cruz rebels in Quintana Roo relinquish Tulum and sign a peace treaty.

1940–70   With the collapse of the world henequen markets, Yucatán gradually becomes one of the poorest states in Mexico.

1968   The Mexican government selects Cancún as the site of the country's largest tourist resort.

1974   Quintana Roo achieves statehood. The first resort hotels at Cancún open for business.

1988   Hurricane Gilbert shuts down Cancún hotels and devastates the north coast of the Yucatán. The reconstruction is immediate. Within three years, the number of hotels on Cancún triples.

1993   Under the guise of an environmentalist platform, Quintana Roo's newly elected governor Mario Villanueva begins systematically selling off state parks and federally owned land to developers.

1994   Mexico joins the United States and Canada in NAFTA (North American Free Trade Association), which will phase out tariffs over a 15-year period.

Institutional Revolutionary Party (PRI) presidential candidate Luis Donaldo Colosio is assassinated while campaigning in Tijuana. Ernesto Zedillo, generally thought to be more of a technocrat and "old boy"–style PRI politician, replaces him and wins the election.

Zedillo, blaming the economic policies of his predecessor, devalues the peso in December.

1995   Recession sets in as a result of the peso devaluation. The former administration is rocked by scandals surrounding the assassinations of Colosio and another high-ranking government official; ex-president Carlos Salinas de Gortari moves to the United States.

Quintana Roo governor Mario Villanueva is suspected of using his office to smuggle drugs into the state.

1996   Mexico's economy, bolstered by a $28 billion bailout led by the United States, turns around, but the recovery is fragile. The opposition National Action Party (PAN), which is committed to conservative economic policies, gains strength. New details emerge of scandals within the former administration.

1997   Mexico's top antidrug official is arrested on bribery charges. Nonetheless, the United States recertifies Mexico as a partner in the war on drugs. Party elections are scheduled for midyear. When Mexican environmentalists discover that Villanueva has sold the turtle sanctuary on Xcacel beach to a Spanish hotel chain, they begin an international campaign to save the site; Greenpeace stages a protest on the beach.

1998   Mexican author Octavio Paz dies.

U.S. Congress demands an investigation into the office of Mario Villanueva. Villanueva is refused entry into the United States when the DEA reveals that it has an open file on his activities.

1999   Raúl Salinas, brother of former Mexican president Carlos Salinas di Gortari (in exile in Ireland), is sentenced for the murder of a PRI leader.

Joaquin Hendricks, a retired military officer, is elected the new governor of Quintana Roo. Although he is thought to be an enemy of Mario Villanueva, the ex-governor sanctions Hendricks's rise to power. The Mexican government decides to arrest Villanueva on drug charges; Villanueva disappears.

2000   Spurning the long-ruling PRI, Mexicans elect opposition candidate Vicente Fox president.

Fox government implements the "Financial Strengthening Program 2000–2001" as part of an economic reform and vows to clean up corruption. Fox also appeals to the United Nation for help in reducing the country's long-standing human rights problems—mostly associated with political corruption—and promises to launch an investigation.

2001   Ex-governor Mario Villanueva is captured, aided by DEA agents. A bitter dispute erupts over the election of PAN candidates. The old guard, led by the PRI, demands a reelection. The PAN wins for a second time.

Fox's Human Rights Commission presents a 3,000-page report concluding that federal, state, and municipal authorities have been guilty of abducting and torturing citizens over the past three decades, beginning with a massacre of student protesters in 1968. The report sets off a backlash against political activists.

2002   Fox continues to clean house, charging 25 prominent public officials after uncovering a network that aided and abetted drug traffickers and organized-crime groups.

Fox urges President Bush to legalize the millions of Mexicans who work in the United States illegally. He reveals that money sent home to Mexico by workers in the United States is Mexico's second-largest source of income. Bush promises to begin work on a new immigration policy.

The presidency of the Gulf of Mexico States Accord was transferred from Jeb Bush, Governor of Florida, to Joaquin Hendricks, Governor of Quintana Roo. It is primarily a figurehead role.

Pope John Paul II comes to Mexico to beatify two Mexican Indian martyrs, Juan Bautista and Jacinto de los Angeles, after declaring Juan Diego the first Indian saint in the Americas.

Hurricane Isidore hits Mérida and dozens of smaller coastal communities, destroying buildings, tearing down power lines, and uprooting thousands of trees. More than 300,000 people are left homeless; many towns are still recovering today.

2003   Mexico's foreign minister closes the country's first high-level human rights office on the same day Amnesty International releases a report criticizing the government's role in the killings and disappearances of more than 300 women in Ciudad Juárez. Another independent inquiry investigating the massacre of student protesters before the 1968 Mexico City Olympics is closed and the Zapatista (Indian rights revolutionaries) from Chiapas begin protesting over human rights violations.

In July, voters held Fox to account, cutting back by 51 the number of seats the PAN holds in the lower house of Mexico's Congress.

Quintana Roo registers 8% growth, and 3,013,708 foreign tourists come through its borders.

2004   Scandal hits Cancún when Mayor "Chacho" (Juan Ignacio Garcia Zalvidea) is accused of mismanaging city funds and jailed; during his incarceration, a citizens' group begins running the city. After an investigation, the Supreme Court of Mexico orders Chacho reinstated as mayor declaring his prosecution as unconstitutional.

The discovery of several murdered federal agents sparks concern about the possible resurgence of a drug cartel that made the Cancún area infamous during the 1990s. An investigation results in the arrest and firing of several high-ranking officers who may have collaborated with the cartel; authorities continue to monitor the situation.

The Cozumel thrasher, a bird indigenous to Cozumel and thought to have been extinct since 1995, was spotted several times by scientists on the island. Thrashers (cousins to the mockingbird) were plentiful on Cozumel before the 1970s—and seem to be making a comeback.

2005   The newly developed cruise-ship port of Puerto Costa Maya, built by private developers and the Mexican government outside the Caribbean coastal town of Majahual, receives its millionth visitor.

VOCABULARY

	English	Spanish	Pronunciation
Basics			
	Yes/no	Sí/no	see/no
	OK	De acuerdo	de a-**kwer**-doe
	Please	Por favor	pore fah-**vore**
	May I?	¿Me permite?	may pair-**mee**-tay
	Thank you (very much)	(Muchas) gracias	(**moo**-chas) **grah**-see-as
	You're welcome	Con mucho gusto	con **moo**-cho **goose**-toe
	Excuse me	Con permiso	con pair-**mee**-so
	Pardon me	¿Perdón?	pair-**dohn**
	Could you tell me?	¿Podría decirme?	po-dree-ah deh-**seer**-meh
	I'm sorry	Disculpe	Dee-**skool**-peh
	Good morning!	¡Buenos días!	**bway**-nohs **dee**-ahs
	Good afternoon!	¡Buenas tardes!	**bway**-nahs **tar**-dess
	Good evening!	¡Buenas noches!	**bway**-nahs **no**-chess
	Goodbye!	¡Adiós!/¡Hasta luego!	ah-dee-**ohss/ah** -stah-**lwe**-go
	Mr./Mrs.	Señor/Señora	sen-**yor**/sen-**yohr**-ah
	Miss	Señorita	sen-yo-**ree**-tah
	Pleased to meet you	Mucho gusto	**moo**-cho **goose**-toe
	How are you?	¿Cómo está usted?	**ko**-mo es-**tah** oo-**sted**
	Very well, thank you.	Muy bien, gracias.	**moo**-ee bee-**en**, **grah**-see-as
	And you?	¿Y usted?	ee oos-**ted**
Days of the Week			
	Sunday	domingo	doe-**meen**-goh
	Monday	lunes	**loo**-ness
	Tuesday	martes	**mahr**-tess
	Wednesday	miércoles	me-**air**-koh-less
	Thursday	jueves	hoo-**ev**-ess
	Friday	viernes	vee-**air**-ness
	Saturday	sábado	**sah**-bah-doh

Months

January	enero	eh-**neh**-roh
February	febrero	feh-**breh**-roh
March	marzo	**mahr**-soh
April	abril	ah-**breel**
May	mayo	**my**-oh
June	junio	**hoo**-nee-oh
July	julio	**hoo**-lee-yoh
August	agosto	ah-**ghost**-toh
September	septiembre	sep-tee-**em**-breh
October	octubre	oak-**too**-breh
November	noviembre	no-vee-**em**-breh
December	diciembre	dee-see-**em**-breh

Useful Phrases

Do you speak English?	¿Habla usted inglés?	**ah**-blah oos-**ted** in-**glehs**
I don't speak Spanish	No hablo español	no **ah**-bloh es-pahn-**yol**
I don't understand (you)	No entiendo	no en-tee-**en**-doh
I understand (you)	Entiendo	en-tee-**en**-doh
I don't know	No sé	no seh
I am American/ British	Soy americano (americana)/ inglés(a)	soy ah-meh-ree-**kah**-no (ah-meh-ree-**kah**-nah)/ in-**glehs** (**ah**)
What's your name?	¿Cómo se llama usted?	koh-mo seh **yah**-mah oos-**ted**
My name is . . .	Me llamo . . .	may **yah**-moh
What time is it?	¿Qué hora es?	keh **o**-rah es
It is one, two, three . . . o'clock.	Es la una. . . . Son las dos, tres	es la **oo**-nah/sohn lahs dohs, tress
How?	¿Cómo?	**koh**-mo
When?	¿Cuándo?	**kwahn**-doh
This/Next week	Esta semana/ la semana que entra	**es**-teh seh-**mah**-nah/lah seh-**mah**-nah keh **en**-trah
This/Next month	Este mes/el próximo mes	**es**-teh mehs/el **proke**-see-mo mehs

English	Spanish	Pronunciation
This/Next year	Este año/el año que viene	**es**-teh **ahn**-yo/el **ahn**-yo keh vee-**yen**-ay
Yesterday/today/ tomorrow	Ayer/hoy/mañana	ah-**yehr**/oy/mahn-**yah**-nah
This morning/ afternoon	Esta mañana/ tarde	**es**-tah mahn-**yah**-nah/**tar**-deh
Tonight	Esta noche	**es**-tah **no**-cheh
What?	¿Qué?	keh
What is it?	¿Qué es esto?	keh es **es**-toh
Why?	¿Por qué?	pore **keh**
Who?	¿Quién?	kee-**yen**
Where is . . . ?	¿Dónde está . . . ?	**dohn**-deh es-**tah**
the bus stop?	la parada del autobus?	la pah-**rah**-dah del oh-toh-**boos**
the post office?	la oficina de correos?	la oh-fee-**see**-nah deh koh-**reh**-os
the museum?	el museo?	el moo-**seh**-oh
the hospital?	el hospital?	el ohss-pee-**tal**
the bathroom?	el baño?	el **bahn**-yoh
Here/there	Aquí/allá	ah-**key**/ah-**yah**
Open/closed	Abierto/cerrado	ah-bee-**er**-toh/ ser-**ah**-doh
Left/right	Izquierda/derecha	iss-key-**er**-dah/ dare-**eh**-chah
Straight ahead	Derecho	dare-**eh**-choh
Is it near/far?	¿Está cerca/lejos?	es-**tah sehr**-kah/ **leh**-hoss
I'd like . . .	Quisiera . . .	kee-see-ehr-ah
a room	un cuarto/una habitación	oon **kwahr**-toh/ **oo**-nah ah-bee-tah-see-**on**
the key	la llave	lah **yah**-veh
a newspaper	un periódico	oon pehr-ee-**oh**-dee-koh
a stamp	la estampilla	lah es-stahm-**pee**-yah
I'd like to buy . . .	Quisiera comprar . . .	kee-see-**ehr**-ah kohm-**prahr**
a dictionary	un diccionario	oon deek-see-oh-**nah**-ree-oh
soap	jabón	hah-**bohn**
suntan lotion	loción bronceadora	loh-see-**ohn** brohn-seh-ah-**do**-rah
a map	un mapa	oon **mah**-pah

a magazine	una revista	**oon**-ah reh-**veess**-tah
a postcard	una tarjeta postal	**oon**-ah tar-**het**-ah post-**ahl**
How much is it?	¿Cuánto cuesta?	**kwahn**-toh **kwes**-tah
Telephone	Teléfono	tel-**ef**-oh-no
Help!	¡Auxilio! ¡Ayuda! ¡Socorro!	owk-**see**-lee-oh/ ah-**yoo**-dah/ soh-**kohr**-roh
Fire!	¡Incendio!	en-**sen**-dee-oo
Caution!/Look out!	¡Cuidado!	kwee-**dah**-doh

Salud (Health)

I am ill	Estoy enfermo(a)	es-**toy** en-**fehr**-moh(mah)
Please call a doctor	Por favor llame a un médico	pohr fah-**vor ya**-meh ah oon **med**-ee-koh
acetaminophen	acetaminofen	a-say-ta-**mee**-no-fen
ambulance	ambulancia	ahm-boo-**lahn**-see-a
antibiotic	antibiótico	ahn-tee-bee-**oh**-tee-co
aspirin	aspirina	ah-spi-**ree**-na
capsule	cápsula	**cahp**-soo-la
clinic	clínica	**clee**-nee-ca
cold	resfriado	rays-free-**ah**-do
cough	tos	toess
diarrhea	diarrea	dee-ah-**ray**-a
fever	fiebre	fee-**ay**-bray
flu	Gripe	**gree**-pay
headache	dolor de cabeza	doh-**lor** day cah-**bay**-sa
hospital	hospital	oh-spee-**tahl**
medication	medicamento	meh-dee-cah-**men**-to
pain	dolor	doh-**lor**
pharmacy	farmacia	fahr-**mah**-see-a
physician	médico	**meh**-dee-co
prescription	receta	ray-**say**-ta
stomach ache	dolor de estómago	doh-**lor** day eh-**sto**-mah-go

INDEX

S

Sabancuy, *284*
Safety, *F47–F48*
Sailing. *See* Boating and sailing
Salt mines, *62*
San Gervasio (Maya site), *91, 96*
San Miguel, *91, 97, 109–111*
Santa Rosa Xtampak, *272–273*
Santuario Maya a la Diosa Ixchel, *58*
Sayil (Maya site), *229–230*
Scuba diving and snorkeling, *F12*
Cancún, *40–42*
Caribbean coast, *150, 153, 156*
Cozumel, *93, 95, 114–120*
Isla Mujeres, *76–78*
Secrets Excellence Riviera Cancun ⊡ , *136–137*
Semana Santa, *F17*
Senior-citizen travel, *F48*
Sergio's Restaurant & Pizzas ✕ , *178*
Seybaplaya, *281–282*
Ship travel. ⇨ *See* Cruises
Shipping. ⇨ *See* Mail and shipping
Shopping, *F22, F48–F49*
business hours, *F24*
Campeche, *265–266*
Cancún, *42–45*
Caribbean coast, *138–139, 150–151*
Cozumel, *121–123*
Isla Mujeres, *78–79*
Mérida and Yucatán State, *208–211*
Sightseeing guides, *F49*
Sin Duda ⊡ , *176*
Skydiving, *150*
Slavia (club), *207*
Snorkeling. ⇨ *See* Scuba diving and snorkeling
Sociedad de Artesanas Becaleñas, *269*
Sol a Sol International Regatta, *F17*
Spas, *F12*
Sports
Campeche, *265*
Cancún, *32, 40–42*
Caribbean coast, *138, 150, 153*
Cozumel, *113–121*

Isla Mujeres, *76–78*
Mérida and Yucatán State, *207–208*
Student travel, *F49–F50*
Submarine tours, *50, 113*
Symbols, *F11*

T

Tankah, *158*
Taxes, *F50*
Taxis
Campeche, *287–288*
Cancún, *48*
Caribbean coast, *182*
Cozumel, *125*
Isla Mujeres, *83*
Mérida, *241–242*
Teatro Peón Contreras, *193, 197*
Telephones, *F50–F51*
Mérida, *243–244*
Temple de Los Viente-Siete Escalones (Maya site), *180*
Templo de las Siete Muñecas (Maya site), *235*
Templo de los Frescos (Maya site), *164*
Templo de los Frisos (Maya site), *225*
Templo de los Guerreros (Maya site), *221*
Templo de los Mascarones (Temple of the Masks), *271*
Templo de los Panales Cuadrados, *220*
Templo del Búho (Maya site), *180*
Templo del Dios Descendente (Maya site), *165*
Templo del Osario (Maya site), *220*
Templo Mayor (Maya site), *174*
Tennis, *208*
Theme parks, *152–153*
Theme trips, *F52*
Ticul, *230–231*
Time zones, *F51*
Timing the visit, *F10*
Tipping, *F51*
Tortugranja (Turtle Farm), *62*
Tours and packages, *F51–F52*
Campeche, *288–289*
Cancún, *4, 50*
Caribbean coast, *184*
Cozumel, *88*

Isla Contoy, *80*
Isla Mujeres, *84*
Mérida and Yucatán State, *244–245*
Train travel, *242*
Travel agencies, *F52*
Campeche, *289*
Caribbean coast, *130*
Cozumel, *126*
Isla Mujeres, *84*
Mérida and Yucatán State, *245*
Traveler's checks, *F45*
Trolley tours, *288–289*
Tulum (Maya site), *159, 164–167*

U

Universidad Autónoma de Yucatán, *193, 197*
Uxmal (Maya site), *226–229*

V

Valladolid, *222–224*
Vaquerías (cattle-branding feasts), *F18*
Ventanas al Mar ⊡ , *111*
Villa Mercedes ⊡ , *203*
Villa rentals, *F40–F41*
Villas Arqueológicas Uxmal ⊡ , *228*
Visas, *F46–F47*
Visitor information, *F53*
Campeche, *289*
Caribbean coast, *184*
Cozumel, *126*
Mérida and Yucatán State, *245–246*

W

Water sports
Campeche, *265*
Cancún, *32, 40–42*
Caribbean coast, *138, 150, 153*
Cozumel, *113, 114–120, 121*
Isla Mujeres, *76–78*
Weather, *5, 57, 89, 130, 188*
Web sites, *F53*
Wildlife preserves
Campeche, *269, 278–279*
Caribbean coast, *170–172*
Cozumel, *91, 95*
Isla Contoy, *79–80*
Yucatán State, *233–234*
Women and safety, *F48*

PHOTO CREDITS

Cover Photo *(Coastline at Tulum, Yucatan Peninsula): Robin Hill/Index Stock Imagery.* F6, *Karamba Bar, Cancún.* F7 (left), *Georgie Holland/age fotostock.* F7 (right), *Guillermo Aldana/Mexico Tourism Board* F10, *Mark Newman/age fotostock.* F12, *cancuncd.com.* F13 (left), *Bruce Herman/Mexico Tourism Board.* F13 (right), *Doug Scott/age fotostock.* F14, *Stefano Morini/Cancún Convention and Visitors Bureau.* F15 (left), *Bruce Herman/Mexico Tourism Board.* F15 (right), *Jon Arnold/Agency Jon Arnold Images/age fotostock.* F16, *Angelo Cavalli/age fotostock.* F17, *Stefano Morini/Cancún Convention and Visitors Bureau.* F18, *Alvaro Leiva/age fotostock.* **Chapter 1: Cancún** 1, *Angelo Cavalli/age fotostock* 2 (top), *Mary Magruder/www.viestiphoto.com.* 2 (center), *Jimmy Buffett's Margaritaville.* 2 (bottom left, bottom right), *Corbis.* 4, *Walter Bibikow/www.viestiphoto.com.* 5, *Bruce Herman/Mexico Tourism Board* 33, *Señor Frog's, Cancún.* 34, 35, *La Boom Club Cancún.* 36, *Worldscapes/age fotostock.* 37, *Dady Rock Cancún.* 38, *Karamba Bar, Cancún.* 39, *Philip Coblentz/Brand X Pictures.* **Chapter 2: Isla Mujeres:** 51, *Bruce Herman/Mexico Tourism Board.* 52 (top), *Bruce Herman/Mexico Tourism Board.* 52 (center), *Stefano Morini/Cancún Convention and Visitors Bureau.* 52 (bottom left), *Jack Milchanowski/age fotostock.* 52 (bottom right), *Walter Bibikow/www.viestiphoto.com.* 53, *Stefano Morini/Cancún Convention and Visitors Bureau.* 54, *Miguel A. Núñez/Cancún Convention and Visitors Bureau.* 55 (left), *Bruce Herman/Mexico Tourism Board.* 55 (right), *Stefano Morini/Cancún Convention and Visitors Bureau.* **Chapter 3: Cozumel:** 85, *Miguel A. Núñez/Cancún Convention and Visitors Bureau* 86 (top), *cancuncd.com.* 86 (center), *Bruce Herman/Mexico Tourism Board.* 86 (bottom left), *Robert Winslow/www.viestiphoto.com.* 86 (bottom right), *Richard Cummins/www.viestiphoto.com.* 89 (left), *cancuncd.com.* 89 (right), *Mark Newman/age fotostock.* 114, *cancuncd.com.* 115, *cancuncd.com.* 117 (top), *Georgie Holland/age fotostock.* 117 (bottom), *Georgie Holland/age fotostock.* 118, *cancuncd.com.* 119, *Georgie Holland/age fotostock.* **Chapter 4: The Caribbean Coast:** 127, *Stefano Morini/Cancún Convention and Visitors Bureau.* 128 (top, bottom), *Bruce Herman/Mexico Tourism Board.* 129 (top), *Philip Coblentz/Brand X Pictures.* 129 (bottom), *Bruce Herman/Mexico Tourism Board.* 160, *Campeche Tourism.* 161, *Philip Baird/www.anthroarcheart.org.* 162 (top), *Ken Welsh/age fotostock.* 162 (bottom), *SuperStock/age fotostock.* 163, *Philip Coblentz/Brand X Pictures* **Chapter 5: Mérida & Yucatán State:** 185, *Bruno Perousse/age fotostock.* 186 (top, bottom center, bottom right), *Guillermo Aldana/Mexico Tourism Board.* 186 (bottom left), *Stefano Morini/Cancún Convention and Visitors Bureau.* 187 (top), *J. D. Heaton/Picture Finders.* 187 (bottom), *Corbis.* 188, *Luis Castañeda/age fotostock.* 214, *Larry Williams/Masterfile.* 215, *Corbis.* 216 (top), *José A. Granados/Cancún Convention and Visitors Bureau.* 216 (bottom), *William Wu.* 217 (top), *Gonzalo Azumendi/age fotostock.* 217 (center), *Philip Baird/www.anthroarcheart.org.* 217 (bottom), *Mexico Tourism Board.* 218 (top), *Corbis.* 218 (bottom), *Bruno Perousse/age fotostock.* 219 (top inset), *Luis Castañeda/age fotostock.* 219 (top), *José A. Granados/Cancún Convention and Visitors Bureau.* 219 (bottom), *Joe Viesti/www.viestiphoto.com.* 220, *Marco/www.viestiphoto.com.* 221, *Joe Viesti/www.viestiphoto.com.* **Chapter 6: Campeche:** 247, *Martin Siepmann/age fotostock.* 248 (top, bottom right), *Campeche Tourism.* 248 (bottom left), *S. Murphy-Larronde/age fotostock.* 249 (left, right), *Campeche Tourism.*

FODOR'S KEY TO THE GUIDES

Caribbean

AMERICA'S **GUIDEBOOK LEADER** PUBLISHES GUIDES FOR **EVERY KIND OF TRAVELER**. CHECK OUT OUR MANY SERIES AND FIND YOUR **PERFECT MATCH**.

FODOR'S GOLD GUIDES
America's favorite travel-guide series offers the most detailed insider reviews of hotels, restaurants, and attractions in all price ranges, plus great background information, smart tips, and useful maps.

COMPASS AMERICAN GUIDES
Stunning guides from top local writers and photographers, with gorgeous photos, literary excerpts, and colorful anecdotes. A must-have for culture mavens, history buffs, and new residents.

FODOR'S 25 BEST / CITYPACKS
Concise city coverage in a guide plus a foldout map. The right choice for urban travelers who want everything under one cover.

FODOR'S AROUND THE CITY WITH KIDS
Up to 68 great ideas for family days, recommended by resident parents. Perfect for exploring in your own backyard or on the road.

SEE IT GUIDES
Illustrated guidebooks that include the practical information travelers need, in gorgeous full color. Perfect for travelers who want the best value packed in a fresh, easy-to-use, colorful layout.

FODOR'S FLASHMAPS
Every resident's map guide, with 60 easy-to-follow maps of public transit, parks, museums, zip codes, and more.

FODOR'S LANGUAGES FOR TRAVELERS
Practice the local language before you hit the road. Available in phrase books, cassette sets, and CD sets.

THE COLLECTED TRAVELER
These collections of the best published essays and articles on various European destinations will give you a feel for the culture, cuisine, and way of life.

At bookstores everywhere.   www.fodors.com/books

ABOUT OUR WRITERS

When author Jeanine Kitchel first embarked on a vacation to Quintana Roo in 1985, little did she realize she'd be living there a decade later, in the Caribbean Coast village of Puerto Morelos. In 1997 she founded an English language bookstore in the town, and in 2003, she wrote a nonfiction book about her Mexican experiences, *Where the Sky Is Born: Living in the Land of the Maya.* She has also recounted her adventures in her *Tales from the Yucatán* travel series on Planeta.com, as well as in writings for *Sac-Be,* the *Miami Herald, Mexico File,* and *Mexico Connect.* She updated the Caribbean Coast chapter for this book.

Journalist–turned–travel writer Shelagh McNally has lived part-time on the Yucatán Peninsula since 1997, when she left her native Canada for a four-month Mexican vacation with her young daughter and decided to stay on and learn more about the Maya history and culture. She has covered Cancún, Cozumel, Campeche, Isla Mujeres, and elsewhere on the Caribbean coast for Fodor's, and is the author of *The Adventure Guide to Guatemala.* She has also written for the *Miami Herald, Montréal Gazette, Mundo Maya Magazine,* and other publications and Web sites in Mexico, Canada, the United Kingdom, and the United States. She updated the Cancún and Isla Mujeres chapters of this book.

Recipient of the prestigious Pluma de Plata award for writing on Mexico and the Golondrina award for her coverage of Cozumel, Maribeth Mellin has spent nearly three decades exploring Mexico. Her home in California is filled with folk art and photos from Latin America; books she has authored on Mexico, Peru, Argentina and Costa Rica line her office shelves. She writes a monthly column, Report from Mexico, for the *San Diego Union Tribune* and her recent articles and photos have appeared in *Cooking Light, Alaska Airlines* magazine, *NWA World Traveler, TravelAge West* and other publications and Web sites. Maribeth authored the Cozumel chapter for this book.

Since earning a B.A. in Spanish language and literature, Jane Onstott has lived and traveled extensively in Latin America. She worked as director of communications and information for the Darwin Research Station in the Galapagos Islands, and studied painting (and loafing) for three years in Oaxaca. She has authored books about Mexico and about her hometown, including *Insider's Guide to San Diego,* a detailed description of her primary residence. Since 1986, Jane has contributed to Fodor's guides to Mexico and South America; this year, she updated the chapters on Campeche, and Mérida, Chichén Itzá & Yucatán.